# The Ypres Salient

## A Guide to the Cemeteries and Memorials of the Ypres Salient

## 1914-18

*by*
Michael Scott

The Naval & Military Press Ltd

*Published by*

**The Naval & Military Press Ltd**
Unit 5 Riverside, Brambleside,
Bellbrook Industrial Estate,
Uckfield, East Sussex,
TN22 1QQ England

Tel: +44 (0) 1825 749494
Fax: +44 (0) 1825 765701

www.naval-military-press.com
www.nmarchive.com

# CONTENTS

| | |
|---|---|
| Introduction | 2 |
| Cemeteries | 3 |
| Commonwealth War Graves Commission | 236 |
| Ieper – Ypres | 237 |
| The Battles of the Ypes Salient | 239 |
| Orders of Battle | 243 |
| Cemetery Dead | 267 |
| Victoria Cross Winners | 273 |
| Terms and Abbreviations | 275 |
| Bibliography | 277 |
| Index | 279 |

# INTRODUCTION

A war that ended in 1918 and in which most of the men who fought are now dead is even today of great historical interest for many British people. The Centenary Celebrations have brought a renewed level of interest in a conflict that is still 'touchable' in that almost all of us know someone at one or two, or even three, generations distance from us. We feel they are our family though time has brought separation. When we make our journeys to the battlefields, we take part in a pilgrimage of sorts, one that remembers those who took part in the battles, the day to day trudge of existence, the familial brotherhood of survival, the occasional laughter and pleasure of simple things, but also honours those who will not get to do what we do, which is return to our families and live our lives to a hopefully old and fulfilled age.

The Ypres Salient was an area of particularly intense fighting throughout that 'Great War'. Everyone who visits the cemeteries and memorials to the men who died defending Ypres will be affected in some way, and many of today's pilgrims return to the battlefields of Flanders again and again.

Each year I take groups to the battlefields of World War One. In trying to provide these groups with as much information about the area as possible I found that there was no straight forward guide available. The books that did exist did not answer the questions that my parties most frequently asked such as 'Why is this cemetery here?' and 'What happened?' or often 'What did he do?' when pointing at a grave. It was important to me to be able to have answers that showed that every cemetery, and every headstone, (or name on a memorial) has a story.

Therefore, in 1992, I decided to create a simple but informative guide to the cemeteries of the Ypres Salient which would also include information on other features such as the fighting near each cemetery, the towns and the memorials. This book was driven by my interest in understanding the history through the tangible remains, the cemeteries and memorials. It took some criticism for not being a weighty analysis of the battles of substantial piece of research. Both criticisms were valid, but the book was never intended to be either analytic or in-depth research. I did not claim it to be either and did not represent the book as anything other than it was. Nonetheless, I have valued that criticism and kept it in mind as I worked on this second version. While there is research into the stories, it is limited and I only want to create something that opens doors. I intend to, as I have said earlier, show that every cemetery is made up of burials that are real people with stories to tell.

Twenty-five years on, and having completed a sister volume on 'The Somme' to my original work, I feel this does improve upon the first attempt. You would hope that after twenty-five years I could improve upon the work I had done in the previous century. Over time, our interests and focus change, and my interest now is in the people buried in the cemeteries, and their stories. Whether the famous such as those who have been awarded medals or the sportsmen, to the less fortunate, or the 'ordinary' men and women buried and commemorated by the CWGC, if any can be considered 'ordinary'. It is the people that have become the focus of the book. So, the update has led to a different book.

Defining the Ypres Salient was an arbitrary decision with which some readers may disagree but I had to set some markers and mine serve the purpose that I need. It is a slightly different boundary from the first edition of this book. Hence, the southern boundary is the A25 autoroute from Junction 13 to Junction 9 and then an arbitrary line following a road around the west of Armentieres until it picks up the French-Belgian border north of Armentieres and follows this to the east where it becomes the River Lys. The boundary follows the river to the bridge in Comines. For here a straight line to the eastern edge of Passendale and a line from there to the centre of Staden. The northern boundary is a straight line from Staden to the French border just south-west of Leisele. Then the eastern boundary is the French border to the D948 or N38 Poperinge-Steenvoorde road. A slight kink west following this road to Junction 13 of the A25 and we have completed the boundary.

All the graveyards are accessible though it is not possible to get a car right up to the entrance of each one and sometimes great care will have to be taken when using/driving larger vehicles.

I have included each British cemetery alphabetically using the names as spelt by the Commonwealth War Graves Commission. In a separate section are the 'small' cemeteries containing less than ten CWGC burials from WW1. There may be more than ten CWGC burials from WW2. This is followed by the Belgian, French and German cemeteries containing graves dating from the Great War.

I have used the Flemish spellings where appropriate and historical or French spellings where I feel appropriate. Hence, Messines is sometimes Mesen, Ieper is sometimes Ypres and so on. However, I have kept to the original spelling for the titles of the battles such as the Battle of the Menin Road and for CWGC spellings of the names of cemeteries which may differ from the way the village name is now spelt. There is a consistency of approach that underpins why I have chosen a spelling at a particular point. I hope it comes through, but if you disagree with my choice, we will have to agree to disagree. I do not believe that this will cause confusion.

To use a phrase I use often – 'it is what it is'. I hope you find the book useful and have as much enjoyment reading it as I did in writing it.

# ABEELE AERODROME MILITARY CEMETERY

## HISTORY

The cemetery was opened in April 1918 by the French. It was then used by the British in the summer of 1918 and remained in use until the end of the war. Some burials were made after the war when bodies were concentrated here.

## INFORMATION

Located at the site of a Royal Flying Corps Aerodrome opened in April 1915, the men who landed planes in the fields near this cemetery must have been taking their lives in their hands with each landing on such rough ground. However, the cemetery does not contain any members of the Royal Flying Corps or Royal Air Force.

The aerodrome was in use until evacuated in March 1918. Many Squadrons flew from here but one that was located at the aerodrome almost throughout the war was No. 6 Squadron. One of the Squadron's most famous fliers was the first British 'Ace', Major Lanoe Hawker, DSO, VC, killed in action while commanding No. 24 Squadron whenshot through the head on 23 November 1916 above Bapaume aged 25 years. He was awarded the Distinguished Service Order on 22 April 1915 for attacking a German zeppelin shed at Gontrode using hand grenades thrown from his BE2c. He was awarded the Victoria Cross for an act on 25 July 1915. The citation reads 'When flying alone he attacked three German aeroplanes in succession. The first managed eventually to escape, the second was driven to ground damaged, and the third, which he attacked at a height of about 10,000 feet, was driven to earth in our lines, the pilot and observer being killed. The personal bravery shown by this Officer was of the very highest order, as the enemy's aircraft were armed with machine guns, and all carried a passenger as well as the pilot.' Also here with No. 6 Squadron for a period was Louis Arbon Strange, DSO, OBE, MC, DFC & Bar. He won the Military Cross in 1915 by carrying out one of the first tactical bombing missions. The Distinguished Flying Cross was awarded in 1918 and the Distinguished Service Order in October 1918. The Bar to his DFC was for service in 1940 when he had returned to the RAF as a Reserve Officer.

The cemetery was begun by the French during the Battles of the Lys in 1918 when they buried 99 men with four British officers interred on the south-east side of the cemetery. The British subsequently laid 75 men to rest during July and August of 1918. At this time 84 American soldiers were also buried here though the French and American dead were removed after the war.

Among those here is Captain Kingsmill Williams Jones, DSO, Royal Army Medical Corps attached 1st Buffs (East Kents), killed in action on 2 August 1918 aged 43 years. Before the war he was a Doctor in Ireland, Wales and Manchester where he was elected to the City Council and joined the 3rd (East Lancashire) Field Ambulance in February 1912 as a Lieutenant. He was sent to France in September 1914 with the 16th (Special Reserve) Field Ambulance. He was wounded at Hooge Crater in August 1915 during an early morning attack by the 16th and 18th Brigades, for which he received the Distinguished Service Order. The citation for his DSO reads 'For conspicuous gallantry and devotion to duty at Hooge. During the entire night of 9-10 Aug 1915, and the whole of the following day and night, he was attending to and evacuating wounded from the front trenches, time after time exposing himself to shell and rifle fire. He was twice slightly wounded, but stuck to his work with unflagging energy. It was entirely owing to Capt Jones that the crater was successfully evacuated of wounded.' He was again wounded in September 1916 and was gassed in May 1918. He was killed while attending to the wounded in the front line.

Also here is Major Reginald Walter Barnett, MC & Bar, MiD, King's Royal Rifle Corps, GSOII (General Staff Officer (Grade 2)), 6th Division (formerly Brigade Major, 189th Royal Naval Brigade), killed in action on 12 August 1918 aged 26 years. He had just received his BA from Cambridge in Mechanical Sciences when the war began. He immediately volunteered and was made an officer going to France with the 11th King's Royal Rifle Corps in July 1915. He was soon promoted becoming Adjutant and then being appointed Brigade Major to the 189th Brigade. In March 1918 he went home having been gassed returning a few weeks later when he received another promotion. He was awarded the Military Cross on 1 January 1917 and a Bar to the Military Cross on 26 March 1917. He was killed in the morning by a sniper while escorting a Sergeant of the US 27th Division on a visit to the front line at an advanced post near Hooge.

Concentrated here:

Boeschepe Churchyard – located about 3km south-east of here, it contained the graves of twenty-five British soldiers killed from April to August 1918.

UK - 104         Area – 864 sq mts

## LOCATION

Abeele Aerodrome Cemetery is situated south of L'Abeele village east of the D948 or N38 Poperinge-Steenvoorde road. This is reached most easily from the Poperinge southern by-pass towards the French border leaving the road about 200m on the Belgian side of the border.

# AEROPLANE CEMETERY

**HISTORY**
The cemetery was opened as the 'New Cemetery, Frezenberg' on 1 August 1917 by the 15th and 16th (Irish) Divisions. It was used until March 1918, when this area was occupied by the Germans, and used again in September 1918. After the war, Plots II to VIII, and part of Plot I, were formed when nearly 1000 graves were concentrated here from small burial grounds and the surrounding battlefields.

**INFORMATION**
From 8 to 11 May 1915 the front-line had been withdrawn from the Zonnebeke side of Frezenberg and formed here 800m east of Potijze Chateau. On 12 May the 1st Cavalry Brigade took over this section of line with the 2nd (Queen's Bays) Dragoon Guards north of the road. South of the road to Hooge the 6th and 7th Cavalry Brigades held the line. On 13 May the Germans launched a heavy bombardment followed by an infantry attack which inflicted severe casualties on the Queen's Bays, especially 'B' Squadron.

The 8th Cavalry Brigade was the divisional reserve from a point in Wieltje to the Menin Road. The 10th (Prince of Wales's Own Royal) Hussars, north of the road, and Essex Yeomanry on the road, were sent up as reinforcements but could not successfully take the front-line. The limited section of line that they managed to occupy was exposed and their hold tenuous, In addition their rifles soon began to jam. South of the road the Royal Horse Guards were ordered to counter-attack. Although the regiment on the Queen's Bays' left flank withdrew, the German artillery's accurate fire on these trenches meant that the German infantry could not occupy them. This, combined with counter-attacks by the 8th Cavalry Brigade, saw the German advance falter. The Queen's Bays suffered 60 casualties out of 250 men who had gone into the line. The 10th Hussars were reduced to four officers and 98 men. The Royal Horse Guards lost eleven officers (including Viscount Lieutenant Albert Wendover who died of his wounds on 19 May and is buried at home near Milton Keynes) and 112 men out of 277 ranks. With them a detachment thirteen men of the 19th London Sanitary Section, Royal Army Medical Corps, had gone into action. All were killed.

On 15 July 1915 a line from here south to Railway Wood was held by the 1st North Staffordshires when the Germans launched a surprise attack after a period of quiet.

No help could come from either flank as the Germans were also attacking there. Hence, the North Staffordshires counter-attacked on their own surprising the Germans. As a result the line was held.

Until 31 July 1917 this site was in no man's land but during the first day of Third Ypres, the 15th (Scottish) and 55th (West Lancashire) Divisions took Verlorenhoek and Frezenberg.

The cemetery gained its present name after the wreck of a British aeroplane near the site of the Cross of Sacrifice by October 1917.

Among those buried here is Lieutenant The Honourable Albert Edward George Arnold Keppel, MiD, 2nd Rifle Brigade, killed in action on 31 July 1917 aged 19 years. He was son of the 8th Earl of Albemarle and was the nephew of Alice Keppel who was the mistress of King Edward VII.

Also here is Captain Ralph Ingram Moore, MC, DCM, MiD, 'C' Company, 3rd Australian Infantry, killed in action on 7 October 1917 aged 29 years. He enlisted as a 26 year old on 1 September 1914 in New South Wales from a job as a mining engineer. He was Mentioned in Despatches while serving at Gallipoli as a Corporal for acts from 25 April to 5 May 1915. He was also awarded the Military Cross for gallantry at Gallipoli on 3 June 1915 and the Distinguished Conduct Medal for 'From 25th until 29th April, 1915, during operations near Gaba Tepe. Commanded his section under heavy and continuous fire from snipers who were within 30 yards of his trench. He displayed exceptional courage in twice advancing alone about 20 yards, and on the second occasion he accounted for five of the enemy.' Moore received gunshot wounds to the head, chest and left arm and hand at Gallipoli on 7 August 1915. He was promoted to Sergeant on 4 October 1915.

Two cousins from Canada are buried together. They are Private Tom Manning and Frank Manning, 5th Canadian Infantry, both killed in action at St. Eloi on 6 April 1916. They have consecutive service numbers so joined up together on 17 April 1915 and died together.

Buried here are three men executed on 26 July 1915 when five men were executed on a wet, windy morning at 4.00am on the ramparts of Ypres in what became the largest single execution by the British Army during the war. They were all men of the 3rd Worcestershires who had deserted in late 1914 or early 1915. They were originally buried on the ramparts and their graves were moved after the war. The three below were concentrated here while Corporal Ives and Private Fellows were moved to Perth Cemetery (China Wall).

Private John Robinson, aged 31 years, was a 'Regular' since 1902 had been in France since August 1914. Private Alfred D. Thompson, aged 25 years was a 'Regular' who had joined the Battalion in November 1914. On 27 June 1915, Robinson and Thompson absconded together after they were told that they were to be on night duty in trenches near Hooge. The Battalion had been in action since 16 June. On 5 July 1915 both were arrested at Abancourt on a train bound for Rouen. At their court martial in a statement it said that both men were good soldiers, but that it appeared they were suffering from nervous strain at the time they went absent.

Private Bert Hartells arrived in France in August 1914 as a 'Regular' who had been in the army since 1914, and, at 32 years, was the oldest of the men to be executed. On 25 November 1914 he went absent without permission for 71 days. On 24 February 1915 he was sentenced to one year's imprisonment with hard labour, but this was commuted to three months in March 1915. Shortly after his release on 15 June 1915 he went absent again, but this time he was listed as a deserter. He was recaptured and executed.

Nearby is the Scottish Memorial on the road from Zonnebeke to St Jan. Upon it are words from the Declaration of Arbroath.

Concentrated here:

Bedford House Cemetery (Enclosure No. 5) – on the east side of the Ieper-Wijtschate Road about 3.5km south-west of here. The enclosure was separate from those now forming the Bedford House Cemetery. It contained fourteen men of the 1st Duke of Cornwall's Light Infantry and six men of the 1st Devonshires who died in April 1915.

Lock 8 Cemetery – located in a field about 200m north of Lock 8 on the Ypres-Comines canal. This was close to Bedford House Cemetery. It contained nineteen British, two Australian and two German soldiers who died during July to September 1917.

| | | |
|---|---|---|
| UK - 831 | Aust - 208 | NZ – 17 |
| Can - 47 | NF - 1 | S Afr - 1 |
| KUG - 1 | Unnamed - 637 | |

Area – 4159 sq mts

Special Memorials to four British and four Australian men buried among the unnamed.

### LOCATION

Aeroplane Cemetery is about 3km north-east of Ieper on the south side of the Potijze-Zonnebeke road. It is 1.2km from the roundabout in Potijze and 300m from the French cemetery.

# ARTILLERY WOOD CEMETERY

### HISTORY

The cemetery was begun in August 1917 by the Guards Division shortly after they had taken the wood that used to be just south of here between this cemetery and the former railway next to the Boezinge-Langemark road. It remained in use until March 1918, when it contained 141 graves. It was enlarged after the war by the concentration of over 1150 graves from the battlefields surrounding Boezinge.

### INFORMATION

This point marks the approximate northern limit of the British sector of the front. From here to the coast, the Belgians and French held the line for most of the time.

The Guards took an almost empty German front-line on the first day of the Third Battle of Ypres. The Royal Engineers had to cut through the canal banks to lay bridges over the canal for the attack on 31 July 1917. The Germans, learning from the experience of the Battle of Messines only a month before, thought that the noise was being made by tunnellers laying mines and, hence, evacuated the front-line moving back to a second line 200m to the east. As a result, only a skeleton force held the positions when the Guards attacked. However, it may be that this thinly held front-line was part of a new German tactic to have strength of defence deeper behind the front ready to counter-attack when required. A case can be made for both theories.

Private Ellis Humphrey Evans, 15th (London Welsh) Royal Welsh Fusiliers was killed in action on 31 July 1917, the first day of the Third Battles of Ypres, aged 30 years. His unit assembled east of the canal with objectives being Pilkem, the Pilkem Ridge and then to cross the Steenbeek near Langemark. The attack began at 3.50am. His Battalion came under heavy artillery fire and fell behind the British artillery barrage that was creeping ahead of them. They reached the Iron Cross Ridge but met strong resistance at Rudolphe Farm and blockhouses near Iron Cross. The Battalion lost every officer. Evans was wounded and taken back to the Regimental Aid Post where he died and was buried about 1km north-east of this cemetery. He is better known as the war poet 'Hedd Wyn', a well know Welsh poet who had featured at National Eisteddfods winning several awards for his poetry. His long poem called 'The Hero' or 'Yr Awr' was the winner of the Bardic Chair at the Eisteddfod on 6 September 1917. There is a memorial plaque to him on the Langemark-Boezinge road near the Welsh Memorial Park where a Last Post Ceremony takes place on the first Monday of each month at 7.00pm.

Another war poet buried here is Lance Corporal Francis Edward Ledwidge, 1st Royal Inniskilling Fusiliers, also killed in action on 31 July 1917 aged 29 years who was moved here from his original burial just east of the cemetery with those killed with him. His Battalion was not involved in the initial attacks but a group were road-laying, a vital task. While Ledwidge was drinking tea in a mud hole with his comrades, a shell exploded alongside, killing the poet and five others. There is a memorial to him near the spot at which he died about 150m south of the cemetery. Ledwidge had left school aged thirteen, and while he continued to educate himself, he took what work he could find, as a farm hand, shop assistant, road builder and supervisor of roads, and as a copper miner though he was sacked for organising a strike for better mining conditions. This was three years before the 1913 General Strike, and he had been a trade union activist since 1906. He was a keen poet, writing whereever he could. From the age of fourteen his works were published in his local newspaper and received the patronage of Lord Edward John Moreton Drax Plunkett, 18th Baron of Dunsany. Ledwidge was a keen patriot and nationalist. He was a founding member in 1914, with his brother Joseph, of the Slane Branch of the Irish Volunteers, a nationalist force created in response to the arming of the Ulster Volunteers. On the outbreak of the war the Irish Volunteers split into two factions, the National Volunteers who supported John Redmond's appeal to join Irish regiments, and those who did not, to whom Ledwidge was originally allied. However, he said he could not see others die to defend him and his country so he enlisted in October 1914 into the 5th Royal Inniskilling Fusiliers. Ledwidge was soon promoted to Lance Corporal serving in Gallipoli and the Salonika Campaign with the 10th Division while continuing to write his poetry though he lost much work, for example, in atrocious weather in Serbia. Ledwidge was demoted in May 1916 for overstaying his leave and being drunk in uniform and kept on home service. He received his Lance Corporal's stripe again in January 1917 when returning to the Western Front, joining the 1st Royal Inniskilling Fusiliers.

Lieutenant George Southerton Rigg, DSO, MiD, 3rd York and Lancasters attached 52nd Battalion, Machine Gun Corps (Infantry), killed in action on 31 July 1917 aged 40 years. Before the war he worked at the City Bank, Sydney. He was commissioned on 31 July 1915. He was awarded the Distinguished Service Order for actions near Arras in May 1917. The citation reads 'For conspicuous gallantry and devotion to duty. At an extremely critical moment, when the enemy had broken through on our flanks and were surrounding our line, he rallied the infantry and reorganised the line with such success that the enemy were repulsed on all sides and finally cut off in their attempt to retreat. His gallantry and initiative saved a very dangerous situation'. He was Mentioned in Despatches by Haig after the Battle of Arras in 1917 having arrived on the Western Front on 11 July 1916.

Also here is Lieutenant Kenneth O'Gorman Harvard, 2nd Grenadier Guards, killed in action on 1 August 1917 aged 20 years. He is a descendant of John Harvard who founded the University in Massachusetts in 1663. His brother Captain Lionel de Jersey Harvard, 1st Grenadier Guards, was killed in action on 30 March 1918 is buried in Boisleux-au-Mont Communal Cemetery.

2nd Lieutenant Henry Joseph Ignatius (Constable-) Maxwell-Stuart, 3rd Coldstream Guards was killed on 9 October 1917 aged 30 years one of four bothers killed in the war. Lieutenant Edmund Joseph (Constable-) Maxwell-Stuart, 175th Tunnelling Company, Royal Engineers was killed on 26 April 1916 aged 23 years and is buried in Poperinge New Military Cemetery. Lieutenant Alfred Joseph (Constable-) Maxwell-Stuart, 1st Coldstream Guards, was killed on 24 August 1918 aged 20 years and is buried in Bagneux British Cemetery, Gezaincourt. Lieutenant Joseph Joachim (Constable-) Maxwell-Stuart, 9th Duke of Wellington's, died on 2 March 1916 aged 19 years and is buried in Reninghelst New Military Cemetery. 2nd Lieutenant Logie Colin Leggatt, 2nd Coldstream Guards died on 31 July 1917 aged 22 years. He played first class cricket in one match for Cambridge University in a defeat against Yorkshire in 1914.

At the crossroads 250m south of the cemetery are a group of monuments. The 'Carrefour des Roses' are memorials to the 87th French Territorial Infantry Division (Les Peperes) and the 45th Infantry Division (Les Joyeux) who defended this area during the first gas attack in April 1915. An orientation table and map stand next to the Breton Calvary from Brittany.

Concentrated here:

Boezinge Chateau Grounds Cemetery – situated about 800m south-west of here on the south-west side of the road between the village and the former railway station, now the 'old' road through town. It contained nineteen British soldiers, mainly of the Guards Division, who died from June to August 1917. There were other British graves elsewhere in the chateau grounds as well as a French cemetery that have all been removed.

Brissein House Cemetery, Bikschote – situated about 4km north-east of here and 2km north of Langemark. This was a French cemetery in which 22 British soldiers were buried from December 1917 to March 1918.

Captain's Farm Cemetery – located about 3km west of Langemark and just north of this cemetery. It contained 63 soldiers, mainly of the Guards and 29th Divisions, who were buried from July 1917 to March 1918.

| UK - 1255 | Aust - 5 | NZ - 2 | Can – 30 |
| NF - 10 | S Afr – 1 | KUG – 4 | |
| Unnamed - 506 | | Area – 4442 sq mts | |

Special Memorials to twelve British men buried among the unnamed.

**LOCATION**

Artillery Wood Cemetery is on the east side of the canal near Boezinge about 4km north of Ieper town centre. It is about 250m north of the Boezinge-Langemark road and is reached most easily from the crossroads at the French Memorial. Turn left at the junction 200m north of the cemetery to return to the canal.

## BAILLEUL COMMUNAL CEMETERY

**HISTORY**

The Communal Cemetery was first used for British burials in October 1914. It was closed in April 1915 when the available space had been filled. A new area was set aside at the east end of the cemetery as the Extension.

**INFORMATION**

Bailleul was an ancient lace-making and linen centre and a military base for most of the war. The town fell to the Germans in early October 1914 but was taken by the 19th Brigade on 14 October 1914. It was an important railhead, air depot and rest centre for the British Army until the German advance in 1918. It was also a Corps headquarters until July 1917, when it was severely bombed and shelled. The Germans had a numerical advantage here of four to one in April 1918. The advantage was enhanced by the fact that most of the British troops in the area had just arrived for rest from the German onslaught on the Somme so they were battle-weary and depleted in strength. The Germans reached Bailleul by 11 April and the Battle of Bailleul, one of the Battles of the Lys, lasted from 13-15 April. Among the defenders were the 29th, 31st, 34th and 59th (North Midland) Divisions, with the 4th Guards and 147th (West Riding) Brigades who were forced to withdraw having suffered heavy casualties. For example, Lieutenant Chicken withdrew with the three survivors of his two Platoons of 'C' Company of the 1st Borders. The Germans took the ruins on the evening of 15 April and Bailleul remained in German hands until it was retaken by the 25th Division who found it empty on 30 August.

The 2nd, 3rd, 8th, 11th, 53rd, 1st Canadian and 1st Australian Casualty Clearing Stations were located here near to a well-known clinic and asylum. Dr J S Haldane and Professor H B Baker were sent by the British Government on 26 April 1915 to report on the effects of the German gas attack. Their report was highly publicised in Britain and caused revulsion towards the Germans.

The British graves in the cemetery are, in places, separated from a French military cemetery which contains 132 graves, though some of these are within the bounds of the British section. Many of the British headstones have two or three names inscribed upon them.

Among those buried here is Bandsman Joseph William McDivitt, 1st Royal Scots Fusiliers, who died of wounds on 13 January 1915 aged 24 years. He enlisted at Bristol in 1908 when he was 16 years of age. He served first in Ireland and was then in India, where he spent three years, before moving to South Africa. He played first solo cornet in the Regimental Band and acted as a stretcher-bearer in France arriving on 14 August 1914. He was wounded in action dying in a Casualty Clearing Station in the town.

Also here is Captain Clive Guise Moores, MiD, Royal Engineers, who died of wounds on 30 November 1914 aged 27 years. While his father had been a Lieutenant Colonel in the Devonshires, Clive had won the Pollock Medal for the best cadet at the Royal Military Academy Woolwich in 1906 and the Haynes Medal in 1909. The Pollock Medal is named after General Pollock and was struck to commemorate Pollock's victories in Afghanistan. It was awarded to the best cadet at several locations over the years and was replaced by the Queen's Medal at Sandhurst after WW2. The Haynes Medal was awarded to two men each year after 1902 – one for the 'best Sapper in his class in the Field Work Course at the School of Military Engineering' and one for 'an officer in each batch of young officers after going through the course of fieldworks, the nomination being made by the Commandant'. So, Moores was clearly a very capable engineer. He was promoted to Captain in October 1911. He was serving with 56th Field Company at Kemmel, when his brother officer, Captain Lionel John Neville, who had been with the unit for only a few hours, was shot and mortally wounded. The bullet continued through Neville hitting Moores in the heart.

Another man buried here is Captain Charles Paget O'Brien-Butler, Royal Army Medical Corps attached 5th (Royal Irish) Lancers, died on 31 October 1914 aged 33 years. He had a good reputation as a sportsman, and although having a strong record at rugby, before the war he was best known as an amateur jockey. In 1907 he was on top of the list of winning amateur jockeys. On 29 July 1907, he was commissioned as a Lieutenant in the Medical Services, served in India in 1909, was promoted to Captain in January 1911, and then returned to Ireland in 1913. In the following racing season he won thirteen of 25 races. He went to France in August 1914 as the Medical Officer of the 5th (Royal Irish) Lancers. On 12 October 1914 the 5th Lancers, as part of the 3rd Cavalry Brigade, were attacking the abbey on top of the Mont des Cats, held by the 3rd Bavarian Cavalry Division, taking it after heavy fighting. Amongst the German wounded was Oberleutnant Prince Maximilian von Hesse, a great-grandson of Queen Victoria, of the Leib-Dragoner-Regiment Nr 24. Paget O'Brien Butler treated him and the Prince gave his gold watch as thanks. His wounds were so severe that he died shortly afterwards and was originally buried within the abbey grounds. In 1926 his body was removed back to Germany. On 31 October Paget O'Brien Butler was shot down by machine gun fire or possibly shell-fire when going across an open space to help some wounded comrades. After the war the gold watch was returned by the O'Brien-Butler family to the House of Hesse. The family had already lost Lieutenant Pierce O'Brien Butler, Army Service Corps, who died on 15 January 1902 aged 24 in the South African Wars. The eldest of the three brothers he had become an international rugby player, playing for Ireland as a full back between 1897 and 1900. Following his last International on 10 February 1900 he set sail with the Royal Dublin Fusiliers for the South African Wars, transferring to the Army Service Corps and being promoted to Lieutenant in November 1901. However, he fell ill with dysentery and died on 15 January 1902. The youngest brother was Captain Capel O'Brien Butler, MC, 6th Royal Irish, who died on 7 June 1917 aged 27 years. He received the Military Cross for bravery in early 1917 and is buried in Kemmel Chateau Cemetery. Another member of the family to die was Captain Hugh O'Brien, 2nd Royal Munster Fusiliers, who died on 22 December 1914 aged 34 years. The son of Lieutenant Colonel H O'Brien, Royal Army Medical Corps,

Hugh was married to a sister of the O'Brien Butler brothers. He had already seen service in the South African Wars and on the North West Frontier of India and joined the Battalion on the outbreak of the war. He was killed in the Germans last offensive of 1914 when his Battalion had been sent from Bailleul to reinforce the Indian troops. They arrived and O'Brien was leading an attack which had been started by the 1st Manchesters though they were by now withdrawing. He was wounded but continued to rally his men though the Munsters losses were mounting from the German machine gun fire. Whilst he was being bandaged a shell exploded next to Captain O'Brien and he was killed. Although he was buried close to where he fell the grave was lost and he is now commemorated on the Le Touret Memorial to the Missing.

One of the commanding officers buried here is Lieutenant Colonel Reginald Alexander, twice MiD, 3rd Rifle Brigade, died of wounds on 29 December 1914 aged 48 years. His father had been an officer in the 1st Life Guards, so Alexander was commissioned as a 2nd Lieutenant in the Army from the West Kent Militia in January 1889 and then posted to the 1st Rifle Brigade in May. He became a Lieutenant in 1891, Captain in 1897 and served as Adjutant from 1894-1898. He served in the South African Wars with the 2nd Rifle Brigade twice being Mentioned in Despatches. He was promoted to Major in the 4th Rifle Brigade in 1905 serving in Egypt and India. In October 1913 he was made Lieutenant Colonel in 3rd Rifle Brigade. He went to France commanding his Battalion in September 1914, was wounded on 13 October and invalided to England. He returned to France a month later and rejoined the Battalion on 22 November before he was mortally wounded on 26 December 1914 dying here.

Lieutenant Colonel George Algernon Egerton, 19th (Queen Alexandra's Own Royal) Hussars, died of wounds on 13 May 1915 aged 44 years. He was grandson of the 1st Earl of Ellesmere and son of The Honourable Algernon Fulke Egerton, both politicians. He served with the 19th Hussars in South Africa and died of wounds received in action on 12 May while walking in reserve trenches at Potijze Wood. The unit War Diary shows him as a Major.

Lieutenant Colonel George Francis Reginald Forbes, MID, 1st Royal Irish, died of wounds on 17 March 1915 aged 48 years. He was a grandson of the 6th Earl of Granard, and joined the army as a 2nd Lieutenant in the Royal Irish (which was raised by the 1st Earl of Granard in 1684) in July 1889. He was promoted Lieutenant in 1891, Captain in 1895, Major in 1904 and Lieutenant Colonel in 1912 when he took command of 1st Royal Irish in India. He served in the Tirah Campaign, 1897-8, was adjutant of the Bombay-Baroda Railway Volunteers in India from 1899 to 1904, and was Staff Captain, No. 12 (South Down) District in Ireland from 1905 to 1909. He took the Battalion to France in December 1914 and died three days after being wounded at St. Eloi.

Another burial of note is Major Aeneas Charles Perkins, 40th Pathans, who died of wounds on 28 April 1915 aged 43 years. He was son of the late General Sir Aeneas Perkins, KCB, who had served at the Siege of Delhi in the Indian Mutiny. Major Perkins had joined the The Buffs (East Kents) in 1892 as a 2nd Lieutenant, became a Lieutenant in 1895 and joined the Indian Army in 1897. He was promoted to Captain in 1901 and Major in 1910 going to France with his unit in 1914.

A more junior officer buried here is 2nd Lieutenant Philip Maurice Ramsey Anderson, MiD, 3rd Royal Irish, who died of wounds on 24 February 1915 aged 26 years. At the outbreak of the war Ramsay was in Argentina. He came home immediately and joined the King Edward's Horse but on hearing of his brother's death he applied for a commission, which he received on 22 December 1914, with the Royal Irish to fill the role formerly held by his dead brother. He was soon in France and severely wounded in action on 14 February 1915, dying a few days later. He was one of 60 Catholic officers Mentioned in Despatches by Field Marshal French in June 1915. His brother was 2nd Lieutenant Alan James Ramsay Anderson, 3rd attached 2nd Royal Irish, killed in action on 20 October 1914 aged 21 years. He is commemorated on the Le Touret Memorial. As 3rd Royal Irish were only a Reserve and Training Battalion, I would assume Philip followed his brother's footsteps by being attached to the 2nd Battalion.

The 25th Division Memorial in the town can be reached by passing through the town square on the main road to Hazebrouck (D933). There is also a municipal War Memorial, a copy of a tower and belfry forming part of the Church of St. Armand, unveiled in 1925 by the Lord Mayor of Bradford, just off the square behind the Town Hall.

UK – 585          Can – 21          India – 4
Fr – 132          Bel Civilians – 2   Unnamed - 10
Ger - 8 (Concentrated here during 1939-45 War)
Area – 591 sq mts
Special Memorials to seventeen graves, including four Indian, destroyed by shell-fire.

**LOCATION**
Bailleul is about 15km south-west of Ieper in northern France. The Communal Cemetery is located on the north side of the town. Near the square in Bailleul is a CWGC sign, part of several local direction signs, pointing to a side street on the left. So, from the Grand Place, take the Ieper road and follow for 400m until you find the sign to the cemetery. A narrow road leads to the main entrance at a fork in the road, though the entrance you want is 150m down the left fork. When you enter the cemetery by the first side entrance the British graves are to your left.

# BAILLEUL COMMUNAL CEMETERY EXTENSION

## HISTORY

This cemetery was opened when the space in the Communal Cemetery was filled. Hence, burials started in the Extension in April 1915 and continued throughout the British occupation, halting only during the German offensive in 1918. It was enlarged after the war with the concentration of 300 graves from the neighbouring battlefields.

## INFORMATION

For general information please refer to Bailleul Communal Cemetery.

Buried here is Sergeant Thomas Mottershead, VC, DCM, No. 20 Squadron, Royal Flying Corps, who died of wounds on 12 January 1917. The citation for his Victoria Cross reads 'For most conspicuous bravery, endurance and skill, when attacked at an altitude of 9,000 feet; the petrol tank was pierced and the machine set on fire. Enveloped in flames, which his Observer, Lt. Gower was unable to subdue, this very gallant soldier succeeded in bringing his aeroplane back to our lines, and though he made a successful landing, the machine collapsed on touching the ground, pinning him beneath wreckage from which he was subsequently rescued. Though suffering extreme torture from burns, Serjt. Mottershead showed the most conspicuous presence of mind in the careful selection of a landing place, and his wonderful endurance and fortitude undoubtedly saved the life of his Observer. He has since succumbed to his injuries.' That for his Distinguished Conduct Medal reads 'For conspicuous gallantry when on a bombing raid. He dived down to 1,500 feet, blew up one ammunition train with bombs, and attacked another with machine gun fire. On rising he was attacked by a "Fokker" from behind, but by skilful and daring manoeuvring he enabled his observer to destroy it by fire.' Mottershead originally enlisted as an air mechanic in August 1914 He gained his aviator's certificate in June 1916 going to France with No. 25 Squadron in July. One of his first operations was on 22 September with 2nd Lieutenant C. Street as his observer. As well as receiving the DCM he was promoted to the rank of Flight Sergeant and transferred to No. 20 Squadron. Mottershead is unique in that he was the only non-commissioned flying officer in the Royal Flying Corps or Royal Air Force to be awarded the Victoria Cross in the war.

There are three men buried here who were executed. Private William W. Roberts, 4th Royal Fusiliers was injured at Hooge in June 1915 when his Battalion suffered 369 casualties. He returned to duty in September 1915 but deserted soon after during heavy fighting again at Hooge. He surrendered to the authorities on 4 May 1916 at Brandhoek and was tried at Loker on 20 May before his execution on 29 May 1916.

Lance-Corporal William A. Moon, 11th Cheshires deserted during the Battle of the Somme. He was executed near Bailleul on 21 November 1916 following a Court Martial ten days earlier. He had seen his friends head blown off just before he deserted, probably suffering from shell-shock.

Private John Rodgers, 2nd South Lancashires was executed on at 6.00am 9 March 1917 for desertion. His Battalion joined the 25th Division which was in action on the Somme from 5 July to 22 November 1916. On the 31 October 1916 Divisional Headquarters moved to Bailleul and the Division assumed responsibility for the Ploegsteert Sector. Rodgers was serving with his Battalion in the trenches in 1917 when he deserted. The Court Martial was on 5 March 1917.

Also here is Brigadier General Charles Henry Jeffries Brown, DSO, three times MiD, commanding 1st New Zealand Infantry Brigade, NZEF, who died on 8 June 1917 aged 45 years. His is one of three New Zealand Brigadier Generals killed in the war, two of whom are buried here. He joined the Denniston Rifle Volunteers in 1900, was promoted to Captain in 1904 and joined the New Zealand Staff Corps in 1911 reverting to Lieutenant. When the war began Brown was moved to the New Zealand Expeditionary Force and left for Egypt and Gallipoli where the NZEF became part of the ANZAC Division and Brown was promoted to Major. A few days after the 25 April landings at Gallipoli Brown was promoted to Lieutenant Colonel and given command of the Canterbury Battalion but he was severely wounded a month later during the Third Battle of Krithia. He went to England to recover, received the Distinguished Service Order and was Mentioned in Despatches. After recovering, Brown was appointed commandant of the New Zealand Base Depot for convalescing New Zealand soldiers at Hornchurch. In June 1916, he was given command of the 2nd Auckland Battalion. He was Mentioned in Despatches for the second time for his leadership during the Battle of Flers-Courcelette. In February 1917 Brown was promoted to Brigadier-General and given command of the 1st New Zealand Infantry Brigade. He led the Brigade during the Battle of Messines, for which he would be Mentioned in Despatches for a third time. While visiting the Le Moulin de l'Hospice on 8 June 1917, he was killed at about 11.40am during an artillery barrage as he stood talking with Major-General Andrew Russell, commanding the New Zealand Division. His two sons were at his funeral.

Brigadier General Francis Earl Johnston, CB, four times MiD, Cross of the Karageorge Third Class with swords (Serbia), commanding 3rd New Zealand (Rifle) Brigade, NZEF, late North Staffordshires, was killed in action on 7 August 1917 aged 45 years. He was a New Zealand born British Army officer, who was seconded to the New

Zealand Military Forces. He commanded both the 1st NZ Infantry Brigade, at Gallipoli, and 3rd NZ (Rifle) Brigade, on the Western Front, from July 1917. He was commissioned as 2nd Lieutenant into the North Staffordshires in 1891, promoted to Lieutenant in 1895, Captain in 1900, and Major in 1910, serving with them in the Sudan and South African Wars. He was twice Mentioned in Despatches. In 1914 Johnston was in New Zealand on leave, where he was seconded as a temporary Lieutenant Colonel from his regiment, then serving in India. He was soon promoted to Colonel in command of the New Zealand Infantry Brigade, subsequently 1st New Zealand Infantry Brigade from 1916. While missing the 25 April Gallipoli landings through illness, Johnston led the Brigade in several actions at Gallipoli. He was appointed a Companion of the Order of the Bath and the Serbian Cross of the Karageorge 3rd Class with swords, as well as being twice Mentioned in Despatches for his conduct at Gallipoli. The Brigade then went to France but in December 1916, Johnston went to England for medical treatment and was diagnosed with neurasthenia. He later took command of the 4th New Zealand Infantry Brigade Reserve Camp returning to the Western Front in late July 1917, this time as commander of the 3rd New Zealand (Rifle) Brigade. He was killed by sniper fire while visiting the front lines near Ploegsteert Wood. His grave is close to that of Brigadier-General Charles Henry Brown, Johnston's successor as commander of the 1st New Zealand Brigade, who had been killed just a few weeks previously.

Among other commanding officers buried here is Lieutenant Colonel Loftus De Vallentin Fitzgerald, Royal Irish Fusiliers attached 2nd Royal Inniskilling Fusiliers, who died on 16 September 1918. He had been promoted to command the Fusiliers on 17 August 1918, having previously served with the Rifle Brigade until 1907 when he went into the Territorial Royal Warwickshires as a Captain in reserve. He joined the Royal Irish Fusiliers in 1914 with whom he went to war as a Captain.

Lieutenant Colonel Laurence Godman, DSO, three times MiD, 46th Brigade, Royal Field Artillery, was killed in action on 30 September 1917 aged 37 years. He was commissioned to the Royal Field Artillery, but was soon transferred to the Royal Horse Artillery, and served with it in South Africa and India. He was an Instructor when the war started. He went to France as Captain in 15th Battery, Royal Field Artillery in August 1914 taking part in the Retreat from Mons, the Battles of the Marne, the Aisne and First Ypres. He was Brigade Major to the 9th Division at the Battle of Loos in September 1915, and commanded 'C' Battery, 47th Brigade, Royal Field Artillery in the Battle of the Somme. He was ordered home, against his wishes, in November 1916, to be an Instructor, but he returned to France in April 1917 to command the 46th Brigade, Royal Field Artillery in the Battle of Arras and Third Ypres. He was about to return to England on 7 October 1917, to again be an Instructor, but on 29 September, while looking for Observation Posts in front of the trenches at Messines, a shell struck him and two other officers. He refused to be taken in the first ambulance, as one of the others appeared to be more severely wounded than himself, but he died in hospital at Bailleul on the next day. He was Mentioned in Despatches in January 1915, November 1915, and April 1917, and was awarded the Distinguished Service Order in the New Year's Honours List of January 1916. His nephew, Captain Arthur Peter Godman, Oxfordshire and Bucks Light Infantry, was killed in action on 27 May 1940 and is buried in Comines Communal Cemetery about 8km east of here.

Lieutenant Colonel Harold Bowyer Roffey, DSO, MiD, Lancashire Fusiliers attached 2/5th Lincolnshires, was killed in action on 15 April 1918 aged 42 years. He had been with the 2/5th Lincolnshires since 10 January 1917 taking them to France in February 1917. He received his Distinguished Service Order in the New Year's Honours List in January 1918 when he was also Mentioned in Despatches. He took temporary command of the 177th Infantry Brigade in early 1918 before returning to his Battalion. They had such a hard time dealing with the German advance on the Somme in March 1918 that on 22 March the Battalion comprised Roffey, a Captain, five 2nd Lieutenants and 80 men. The Battalion moved north to rest just as the Germans moved their objectives to this sector for a new assault. The Battalion took further heavy casualties on 15 April just east of Bailleul, were in Loker on 16 and 17 April when they merged with 4th Lincolnshires and were then in a fighting retreat from east of Bailleul, where Roffey was originally buried before concentration here in December 1919, to north of Bailleul on 18 April in which Roffey was killed with three officers and 352 men also becoming casualties.

Lieutenant Colonel Herbert Gaussen Sargeaunt, twice MiD, 16th Heavy Artillery Group, Royal Garrison Artillery, killed in action on 15 June 1917 aged 44 years. He was commissioned into the army in 1893, promoted to Lieutenant in 1896, to Captain in 1900 and Major in April 1914. He served in Gibraltar, India, Aden and Singapore, returning home in 1902 due to illness. He then served in Ireland and England before moving to posts in Sri Lanka and Hong Kong. He went to France in March 1916 and was killed in action near Armentieres. His brother, Lieutenant Colonel Arthur Frederick Sargeaunt, Royal Engineers, twice MiD, was killed in action on 31 July 1915 aged 44 years and is buried in Brandhoek Military Cemetery.

Lieutenant Colonel George Frederick Steele, CMG, twice MiD, Prussian Order of the Red Eagle, 1st (Royal) Dragoons, died of wounds on 22 May 1915. Steele was commissioned as a 2nd Lieutenant in the Royal Dragoons in 1892, promoted to Lieutenant in 1893, was appointed Adjutant in 1898, before being promoted to Captain in 1899. Steele served in South Africa from 1899-1902 where he was twice Mentioned in Despatches. On return from South Africa, during an inspection by the Regiment's Colonel in Chief, Kaiser Wilhelm II, Emperor of Germany, Steele was awarded the Prussian Order of the Red Eagle. He then went to India in 1904, where he was promoted to Major, and South Africa in 1911 where he became a Lieutenant Colonel commanding the unit. Steele took them to Ostende in October 1914. He was made a Companion of the Order of St. Michael and St. George in February 1915 but was mortally wounded leading his men during the attack on the Frezenberg Ridge before he could return to England for the investiture.

You will find here Corporal William Carroll, 282nd Siege Battery, Royal Garrison Artillery, who died on 4 May 1917 aged 23 years. He was one of four brothers killed in the war. Private John Carroll, 7th/8th King's Own Scottish Borderers, was killed in action attacking Frezenberg on 31 July 1917 aged 27 years. He is commemorated on the Menin Gate. Private Joseph Carroll, MM, 2nd Duke of Wellington's was killed in action on 8 May 1918. He is buried in Lapugnoy Military Cemetery about 17km south of here. Battery Quartermaster Serjeant Michael Carroll, 253rd Siege Battery, Royal Garrison Artillery, died on 27 January 1918 aged 35 years. He had seen service in the South African Wars and was a regular soldier. The family came from Yorkshire but William and Michael had moved to the Isle of Wight where they started families. Michael is buried in Totland (St. Saviour) Roman Catholic Churchyard.

Buried here is Private Joseph Percy Long, 13th Cheshires attached 74th Trench Mortar Battery who died on 5 May 1917. He enlisted in late 1916 and probably died from natural causes. His brother, Private Leonard Long, 1/5th Northumberland Fusiliers, died as a prisoner of war on 20 November 1916 aged 26 years having been captured near Flers and is buried in Hermies Hill British Cemetery. Another brother, Private George Long, 1st Cheshires, was killed in action on 19 September 1916 and is commemorated on the Thiepval Memorial.

Serjeant Herbert McKay, 2nd Cheshires killed on 15 May 1915 aged 25 years is buried here. His brother, Lieutenant Ernest McKay, 1/7th Cheshires was killed on 19 September 1915 aged 21 years and is buried at Azmak Cemetery at Gallipoli. Another brother, Serjeant Charles McKay, 16th Cheshires, died of wounds on 11 May 1917 and is buried in Nesle Communal Cemetery. Their father, Lieutenant and Quartermaster Robert McKay, 4th Cheshires and another brother died during the South African Wars. A fifth brother, Major Arthur Alexander McKay, 10th Lancashire Fusiliers was killed on 27 December 1942 aged 46 years fighting the Japanese and is commemorated on the Rangoon Memorial. He fought in WW1 with the Cheshires.

Also here is 2nd Lieutenant Hastings Fortescue Boles, No. 1 Squadron, Royal Flying Corps and 17th (Duke of Cambridge's Own) Lancers, who died of wounds, received on 23 May over Bailleul, on 24 May 1915 aged 19 years. His father was Lieutenant Colonel of the 3rd Devonshires until 1917, a Conservative MP and later a Baronet. His younger brother, Captain Sir Gerald Fortescue Boles, was killed as the 2nd Baronet on 9 April 1945 aged 44 years while serving as a Captain in the Royal Armoured Corps. He is buried in Bari War Cemetery.

Also of note is Private James Alex Steenson Baird, 1st Otago Regiment, NZEF, who died 7 June 1917 aged 23 years who had represented his country at rugby union on one occasion. He was hit early in the attack being wounded in the hands, stomach and buttocks.

Captain John Wyndham Hamilton McCulloch, 8th Borders died on 21 October 1915 aged 20 years of a leg wound received on 20 October. He played cricket for Middlesex twice in 1914.

2nd Lieutenant George Eric Fairbairn, 10th Durham Light Infantry died on 20 June 1915 aged 26 years. He was a British rower who competed in the London 1908 Summer Olympics for Great Britain though born in Australia. He won his 'Blue' for Cambridge University in the victorious Boat Race of 1908. Most of the crew then formed the Great Britain eight who won a bronze medal at the 1908 London Olympics. But Fairburn formed part of the coxless pairs winning a silver medal. He also played rugby for Rosslyn Park. He was at the Front for a week before he was mortally wounded by a shrapnel grenade dying later in the day.

Captain Robert Balderston Burgess, Inland Water Transport Unit, Royal Engineers died on 9 December 1915 aged 24 years. He represented Ireland at Rugby Union for a single match, on 30 November 1912 against the touring South Africans, which the visitors won. From 1913 to 1914, Burgess was playing for Dublin University Football Club and was the club's honorary secretary. He was invited to play for the Barbarians against Newport RFC in December 1913, losing 14–0. Early in the war he volunteered for, and obtained, a commission in the Army Service Corps, and was promoted to Captain in the Royal Engineers in January 1915. He was hit by a shell while cycling in Armentières and died at a casualty clearing station. He was the fourth Irish international rugby player to be killed in action.

Another of note is Captain John Doran MacDonald, Special List (Directorate of Graves Registration and Enquiries) who died on 18 March 1916 aged 49 years. His epitaph says that he was 'Killed By Shellfire When Erecting Crosses On The Ypres-Menin Road'.

Concentrated here:

Pont de Nieppe German Cemetery – situated about 7km south-east of here, on the south side of the hamlet. It was used in summer 1918 and included two British graves.

Reninghelst Chinese Cemetery – the village is about 8km north of here and the cemetery was in a field a little south of the Poperinge Road. It contained thirty men of the Chinese Labour Corps who died from November 1917 to March 1918.

| | | |
|---|---|---|
| UK - 3453 | Aust - 398 | NZ – 252 |
| Can - 290 | NF – 1 | S Afr – 1 |
| BWI – 3 | Guernsey - 1 | India – 5 |
| Chinese Labour Corps - 31 | Fr – 2 | |
| WW2 – 17 | Ger – 154 (9 from WW2) | |
| Unnamed - 181 | | Area – 9467 sq mts |

Special Memorials to eleven British soldiers buried here in 1918 whose graves were destroyed by shell-fire.

**LOCATION**
See Bailleul Communal Cemetery. The Extension is at the east end of the cemetery.

# BARD COTTAGE CEMETERY

**HISTORY**
The cemetery was begun in June 1915 and used until October 1918. It was increased in size with the concentration of 46 graves after the war.

**INFORMATION**
Bard Cottage was a house that stood opposite the site of the present cemetery close to a bridge, now gone, over the canal called the Bard's Causeway. The house and the cemetery were protected from observation from the canal by a high bank.

Many graves here are of the 49th (West Riding) and 38th (Welsh) Divisions showing that those units were nearby during Third Ypres. Later, the artillery that moved into this area as the front-line moved forward to the east in 1917 buried their dead here.

The senior officer buried here is Lieutenant Colonel Alfred Garnett Horsfall, DSO, MiD, 2nd Duke of Wellington's, killed in action on 9 October 1917 aged 41 years. He joined the Duke of Wellington's in 1896 as a 2nd Lieutenant, was promoted to Captain in 1902, Major in December 1914 and acting Lieutenant Colonel in December 1916. He was in Burma at the start of the South African Wars but took part of the 2nd Duke of Wellington's to South Africa in 1901 before returning to India. He went to France in October 1916. He was awarded the Distinguished Service Order in July 1917. The citation reads 'He displayed the greatest courage and determination. It was largely due to his personal example that the operations of his Battalion were so successfully carried out.' He was shot through the heart by a sniper while leading his men in an attack at Landing Farm. He was posthumously Mentioned in Despatches.

Another recipient of the DSO is Major Charles Gamble Bishop, DSO, Royal Engineers, died on 30 October 1917 aged 39 years. His DSO was awarded posthumously in the New Year's Honours List of January 1918 for services in the field rather than for a single act. He was a pre-war Territorial who had become a Lieutenant in 1908.

One of three brothers to die on service is Gunner Christopher Fagan, V/38th Trench Mortar Battery, Royal Field Artillery who was killed in action on 30 May 1917 aged 24 years, a member of a Catholic family from Liverpool. His elder brother, Serjeant Michael Fagan, 4th King's (Liverpools) had served in South Africa before re-joining the army at the start of the war. He was killed in action on 10 March 1915 aged 32 years but his original burial location was lost so he is commemorated on the Le Touret Memorial. The third brother to die in service was Private James Fagan, 3rd King's (Liverpools) who died at home on 11 October 1918. He enlisted in August 1914 and was discharged exactly two years later suffering from tuberculosis so unfit for service. He is buried at Ford Roman Catholic Cemetery in Liverpool.

Among those here is Captain Francis Harold Lewin, MC, MiD, 7th Queen's Own (Royal West Kents), killed in action at Poelkapelle on 12 October 1917 aged 22 years. At the start of the war, he offered his services, but was rejected owing to poor eyesight. He had an operation for the problem and was subsequently accepted by the army becoming a 2nd Lieutenant in the Royal West Kents in November 1914 arriving in France in July 1915. He was promoted to Lieutenant in July 1916 and Captain in April 1917. He was twice wounded and awarded the Military Cross in October 1916 'For conspicuous gallantry in action. He laid telephone wires under heavy fire, and maintained communications both forward and backward throughout the day and during the night. He used the enemy's wire when his own was finished, and frequently repaired his wires under heavy shell fire.' He was Mentioned in Despatches in December 1917. His brother Lieutenant Edward Chaloner Lewin, 1st Queen's Own (Royal West Kents), was killed in action at Gouzeaucourt, France on 27 September 1918, age 25 years. He is buried at Gouzeaucourt New British Cemetery.

Buried here are Gunner Charles Thomas Catlett aged 23 years, and Gunner Thomas Catlett aged 21 years. They both served with 131st Heavy Battery, Royal Garrison Artillery, both died on 25 August 1917, have consecutive service numbers as they enlisted together on 7 December 1914, and are buried side by side.

Buried here is Lieutenant Dermot O'Brien, 'B' Battery, 291st (London) Brigade, Royal Field Artillery, who died on 26 September 1917 aged 20 years. Before the war he was training as an accountant but joined the Honourable Artillery Company as a Private. He was commissioned in the Royal Field Artillery in August 1915, promoted to Lieutenant in July 1916 and sent to the Front in January 1917. During the Battle of Polygon Wood he was controlling the fire of his Battery which was keeping up a heavy barrage to protect the infantry. A German shell landed next to him and he died of his wounds before reaching the nearest medical aid post. His brother, 2nd Lieutenant Robert Edward O'Brien, 2nd attached 1/8th Argyll and Sutherland Highlanders died of pneumonia on 20 February 1919 and is buried at Halle Communal Cemetery on the south-western outskirts of Brussels.

Pioneer James Knight, 6th Army Tramway Company, Royal Engineers, died on 5 June 1917 aged 47 years. He had been in the police for a period before the war but is also recorded as being a groundsman at a golf course. It was not unusual for older men with families to serve in Pioneer units. His son, Lance Corporal Robert Charles Knight, 14th Battalion, Machine Gun Corps (Infantry) was killed in action on 17 June 1918 aged 26 years. He is buried in Premont

British Cemetery which is about 15km north-east of St. Quentin and a similar distance south-east of Cambrai.

Gunner James Fraser, DCM, 'B' Battery, 291st Brigade Royal Field Artillery, died of wounds on 30 September 1917 aged 22 years at No. 33 Field Ambulance, No. 18 Corps Main Dressing Station. He was posthumously awarded the Distinguished Conduct Medal in 1918. The citation reads 'When his Battery was being heavily shelled, while in action, this man assisted the wounded and helped to dig out men who had been buried. He volunteered for dangerous duties of all kinds, and entered a gun pit while the camouflage was on fire and the ammunition exploding, to see if any wounded still remained.'

Private Harry Manders, 5th King's Shropshire Light Infantry, died of wounds on 21 January 1916 aged 16 years. He was mortally wounded by a shot in the back just as he was climbing back into the trenches having rescued a man from no-man's land and survived only a short time.

Gunner George Albert Hawkins, 254th Siege Battery, Royal Garrison Artillery, was killed in action on 20 September 1917 aged 33 years. He came fourth in the athletics 200m final at the 1908 London Olympics becoming the first British man to reach an Olympic sprint final. He was killed when a shell exploded in the doorway of a dugout.

Concentrated here:

Marengo Farm Cemetery – located nearly 200m to the south of this cemetery and from which most of the graves concentrated into Bard Cottage Cemetery came. It was used from June 1915 to August 1916 for the burial of 32 men and, like many farms in this area of the Salient, was originally named by the French Army who were stationed here first.

| UK – 1619 | Can – 9 | NF - 6 | S Afr – 2 |
| BWI – 3 | Ger - 4 | Unnamed – 39 | |

Area – 5464 sq mts

Special Memorials to three soldiers known/believed to be buried here in unnamed graves.

## LOCATION

Bard Cottage Cemetery can be found on the west side of the road to Boezinge about 2km north of Ieper.

# BEDFORD HOUSE CEMETERY

## HISTORY

The cemetery was begun in 1914 and used throughout the war. It was enlarged after the war with the concentration of graves from other smaller burial grounds.

## INFORMATION

The Chateau Rosendal was a country house in a wooded, moated park, and though the house and wood have gone the moats and some ruins can still be seen. It was in British hands throughout the war, though the front-line ran through what is now the cemetery after the German advance in 1918. The Chateau that stood on this site was used as the headquarters for many units and for Dressing Stations and Field Ambulances. As a consequence, the grounds of the chateau were used for burials. Bedford House and Woodcote House were the names given by the Army to the Chateau Rosendal.

By the end of the war the grounds had become covered by a series of burial sites which were combined into this one cemetery. Deceptively large, much of it cannot be seen from the road, the cemetery is, in effect, several 'enclosures' linked by a common name and boundary. This is a place that invites you to explore and it is possible to spend hours here.

Of the five enclosures that existed at the end of the war, No. 1 was removed to White House Cemetery and No. 5 to Aeroplane Cemetery.

Enclosure No. 2 was begun in December 1915 and used until October 1918. It was enlarged after the war with the concentration of 437 graves from the Ecole de Bienfaisance and Asylum Cemeteries in Ypres. There are two Special Memorials to men buried in Ypres but whose graves were destroyed by shell-fire.

Enclosure No. 3, the smallest, was used from February 1915 to December 1916. Of the graves, 22 are men of the 7th East Yorkshires. A Belgian soldier has been removed.

Enclosure No. 4, the largest, was used from June 1916 to February 1918, mainly by the 47th (London) Division, and, again, after the war for the concentration of 3,324 graves, almost 70% of whom are unidentified. There are Special Memorials to twenty men known or believed to be buried here among the unnamed. There are also 25 Special Memorials to men whose graves in cemeteries concentrated here were lost. This also contains the Indian Plot of graves, located near the Chatri style mausoleum.

Enclosure No. 6 was rediscovered after the war and laid out in the 1930's. Most of the graves are unidentified. Most of the burials are from men concentrated here when their remains were discovered in the Salient, though a small number are original burials. This enclosure also contains WW2 burials, soldiers who died in the defence of the Ypres-Comines canal and railway at the end of May 1940.

Among those buried here is Temporary 2nd Lieutenant Rupert Price Hallowes, VC, MC, MiD, 4th Middlesex, killed in action on 30 September 1915 aged 34 years. The citation for his Victoria Cross, won for actions at Sanctuary Wood, reads 'For most conspicuous bravery and devotion to duty during the fighting at Hooge between 25th September and 1st October, 1915. 2nd Lieutenant Hallowes displayed throughout these days the greatest bravery and untiring energy, and set a magnificent example to his men during four heavy and prolonged bombardments. On more than one occasion he climbed up on the parapet, utterly regardless of danger, in order to put fresh heart into his men. He made daring reconnaissance's of the German positions in our lines. When the supply of bombs was running short he went back under very heavy shell fire and brought up a fresh supply. Even after he was mortally wounded he continued to cheer those around him and to inspire them with fresh courage.' In 1900 Hallowes joined the 20th Middlesex (Artists) Volunteer Rifle Corps which became the 1/28th (Artists Rifles) Londons. Hallowes resigned his commission when he moved to Wales to work. He re-joined the Artists Rifles in August 1914, quickly being promoted to Corporal, Lance Sergeant and Sergeant by the end of September. Hallowes arrived in France in December 1914, and in February 1915 he reverted to the rank of Private at his own request in the hope of gaining a commission again. He joined 4th Middlesex as an officer in April 1915. On 19-20 July 1915, during the Battle of Hooge, he was awarded the Military Cross. The citation reads 'During an enemy attack down a communications trench there was a shortage of bombs. He climbed out of the trench exposing himself to fire at the enemy and hitting several of them. He also assisted in constructing a block, dug out a communications trench under heavy shell fire and rebuilt a parapet that had been blown in. Throughout the night he assisted in keeping touch and supplying bombs'.

Also here is Private Frederick Turner of the 1/6th Northumberland Fusiliers who had deserted from his unit in August 1917 while they were near Arras in France. After capture he escaped before recapture and trial. He was executed on 23 October 1917.

Buried here is Captain Loftus Edward Perceval Jones, 7th Yorkshires, killed in action on 3 August 1915 aged 39 years. Before the war he was a lawyer, qualifying in Australia winning the Supreme Court Prize and practicing in Shanghai. His Battalion arrived in France in July 1915 taking their place in the trenches on 2 August. Jones was in a support trench when an enemy shell scored a direct hit killing him and two Privates, wounding seventeen others. He had been in the front-line for a day.

Of those buried here who had relatives killed in the war Lieutenant Lionel Henry Salvin Bowlby, 2nd Dragoons (Royal Scots Greys), was killed in action near Bailluel on 4 June 1916 aged 24 years. His brother, Captain Geoffrey Vaux Salvin Bowlby, Royal Horse Guards, was killed in action near Nieuwkerke on 13 May 1915 and is commemorated on the Menin Gate. He has a private Memorial erected by his family, one of two to be found just north of RE Grave and the Ieper-Zonnebeke road.

Another buried here is Private John Carlyle McKellar, 8th Australian Infantry, who died of wounds on 26 October 1917 aged 29 years. He was a teacher before the war, enlisted in April 1916 and arrived in France in February 1917. He was wounded in action on 25 October and died at the 2nd Australian Field Ambulance. He was buried in Asylum Cemetery and moved here in 1924. His brother Private Duncan Mitchell McKellar, 46th Australian Infantry, died in German hands as a prisoner of war on 11 April 1917. His body was lost and he is commemorated on the Villers-Bretonneux Memorial. It was reported at the time that he was in Germany when he died or even that he had been killed while a prisoner. This shows the emotions felt at the time as neither claim is likely.

Brothers, Privates George Hamilton and Sydney Hamilton, both 21st Canadian Infantry and both killed near Mount Sorrel on 14 June 1916 are buried here in Plot I of Enclosure Four, though not side by side.

Among those with awards is Corporal Lewis George Eastman, DCM, 3rd Canadian Infantry, died 13 June 1916 aged 43 years. The citation for his Distinguished Conduct Medal reads 'For conspicuous gallantry at Wulverghem on 30 October 1915. When on sentry duty in the front line trenches he saw a German bomb coming into the trench. It would have fallen into a dugout in which were two of his comrades, but he dashed forward, caught the bomb and hurled it over the parapet, when it immediately exploded. Private Eastman's cool daring and presence of mind probably saved the lives of his two comrades.' While he served with the Canadians, he was from Michigan, USA. This is not unusual as many Americans crossed the border to join up, or those who were in Europe enlisted in local armies. However, not too many won such senior awards.

Similarly, Lance Sergeant Alfred Keddie Curry, DCM, 7th Canadian Infantry, died on 3 June 1916 aged 22 years. Though from the Bahamas he enlisted in the Canadian Forces in September 1914. The citation for his Distinguished Conduct Medal reads 'For conspicuous coolness and courage when in charge of the blocking party during a bombing attack near Messines on the night of 16/17 November 1915.'

Highly decorated Lance Corporal George Reading, DCM, MM & Bar, 23rd Division Signal Company, Royal Engineers was killed in action on 21 October 1917 aged 40 years. He was a telegraphist before the war and enlisted in May 1915. He was awarded the Military Medal in January 1916 and the Bar in June 1917. The Distinguished Conduct Medal was awarded in September 1917 just before his death. The citation reads 'For conspicuous gallantry and devotion to duty when in charge of a cable-laying detachment. He carried out his work with great success, working continuously under fire to keep the lines repaired. He did splendid work throughout the operations'.

Of the senior officers buried here Lieutenant Colonel Oswald Mosley Croshaw, DSO, MiD, Glasgow (Queen's Own Royal) Yeomanry attached 53rd Australian Infantry, was killed in action on 26 September 1917 aged 38 years. He was buried at the Ecole de Bienfaisance Cemetery and moved here in 1921. The citation for his Distinguished Service Order, awarded in September 1916 for his actions during the Battle of Fromelles in July 1916, reads 'For conspicuous gallantry in action. When attached to Brigade Headquarters, he twice voluntarily passed through a very heavy artillery and machine-gun barrage, and brought back accurate information of the situation.' He was Mentioned in Despatches in April 1917 for his work during the advance on Bapaume in early 1917. He joined the 19th (Alexandra, Princess of Wales's Own) Hussars and was promoted to Lieutenant in 1900, Captain in 1905 and was then seconded as Adjutant of Imperial Yeomanry in 1907 which led to a position with the 11th (Prince Albert's Own) Hussars and then the Lanarkshire (Queen's Own Royal Glasgow) Imperial Yeomanry a year later. In 1911 he returned to the 19th Hussars, but in 1912 he resigned his commission becoming part of the Reserve of Officers and was made a Major in 1913. He was seconded to the Australians in early 1916 at which point he was promoted to Lieutenant Colonel from the Reserve of Officers. He was killed in action at Polygon Wood which is described in the Official History as 'The 14th Bde had easily seized the main objective, together with some 200 prisoners and 34 machine guns. Its casualties were not heavy, but included one of the noblest British officers in the AIF, Lt Col Croshaw, who was mortally wounded by a German shell early in the attack, his adjutant being hit at the same time.' He is remembered as having said to his officers just before the attack in which he was killed 'God bless you lads, till we meet again.'

Lieutenant-Colonel Walter Herbert Paterson, twice MiD, 1st East Surreys, was killed in action on 21 April 1915 at Hill 60. He joined his regiment in 1890, became a Lieutenant in 1892, Captain in 1896 and Major in 1908. He served in the South African Wars. He was Mentioned in Despatches in January and May 1915 and promoted posthumously to Lieutenant-Colonel.

Lieutenant Colonel George Swinton Tulloh, MiD, commanding 2nd Gloucestershires, was killed in action on the Frezenberg Ridge on 9 May 1915 aged 48 years. He was hit three times by snipers whilst helping bring up ammunition which led to his death.

A burial of note is Private Harry Reidler, 1002nd Russian Company, Labour Corps, who died on 17 July 1919 aged 29 years. A Russian immigrant, his 'real' name seems to have been Isaac and he was one of a large number of Russian Jews who joined the 8th and 9th Labour Battalions of the Labour Corps together from London late in the war. Isaac enlisted in September 1917, but was not called for service until June 1918 when he was posted to the 8th Labour Battalion of the Labour Corps, which was formed in April 1918, and then in July to the 1002nd Russian Company. On 4 August 1918 the 1002nd Russian Company went to France. He returned from leave on 17 May 1919 and is recorded as having committed suicide between 16 and 22 July 1919 using a Mills Bomb. Isaac was found dead on 23 July 1919.

A final thought is with Private Thomas Samuel Henry Peaceful, 4th Royal Fusiliers, who died on 4 June 1915 aged 21 years having gone from south London to France in November 1914. He is considered to be the name that inspired the book by Michael Morpurgo, though there is also a Private Henry James Percy Peaceful, 1/2nd (Royal Fusiliers) Londons, killed in action 1 July 1916, aged 24 years, in the attack on Gommecourt and buried now in Gommecourt British Cemetery No. 2. He was also from south London and went to France in August 1915. My research now shows these to be brothers.

Concentrated here:

Asylum Cemetery – situated about 1km north-west of here in the grounds of the psychiatric hospital (Hospice du Sacre Coeur) on the Poperinge Road. It was used from February 1915 to November 1917 for the burial of 265 British, nine Canadian and seven Australian men and two men of the British West Indies Regiment.

Boezinge French Cemetery No. 2 – located a little south of Bard Cottage which is about 3km north of here. It contained one Canadian soldier.

Droogenbroodhoek German Cemetery, Moorslede – located about 8km north-east of here, it contained two British soldiers who died in October 1914.

Ecole de Bienfaisance, Ypres – located in the grounds of a school on the north side of the Poperinge Road near the Asylum. It was used from 1915 to 1917 for the burial of 133 British, three Canadian and three Australian men and one man of the British West Indies Regiment.

Kerkhove Churchyard – located about 30km east of here, it contained five British graves, with seven Germans, who died in October and November 1918.

Poelcapelle German Cemetery No. 4 - situated on the St. Juliaan Road between Langemark and Poelkapelle about 5km north of here. It held the remains of 52 British men who died from 1914 to 1916.

Zonnebeke British Cemeteries No.'s 1 & 3 – located about 5km north-east of here these (and two others) were made by the Germans on either side of the Zonnebeke-Broodseinde road on what was known as Devil's Hill. No. 1 contained 31 British men (mainly 2nd East Surreys) who died in April 1915, and No. 3 had 69 British men who died in April and May 1915.

| UK – 4422 | Can – 390 | Aust – 249 |
|---|---|---|
| NZ – 36 | SAfr – 21 | India – 21 |
| BWI – 6 | Ger – 2 | Other – 2 |
| RGLI – 3 | WW2 – 69 (3 unnamed) | |
| Unnamed – 3014 | | Area - 21541 sq mts |

Special Memorials to 24 British soldiers and one Australian known or believed to be buried among the unnamed.

Special Memorials to 25 British soldiers, buried in other cemeteries, whose graves could not be found at the time of concentration.

**LOCATION**

Bedford House Cemetery can be found about 1km south of Ieper on the road to St. Eloi and Lille (Rijsel). It is on the east hand side of the road.

# BELGIAN BATTERY CORNER CEMETERY

### HISTORY
This cemetery was begun by the 8th Division at the start of the Battle of Messines in June 1917 and was used until October 1918.

### INFORMATION
Belgian Battery Corner was the name given by the Army to the point where the Dikkebus Road bends sharply to the south and forks from a road to Brandhoek. It is believed that the Battery after which the corner was named was the 1st Groupe Regiment d'Artillerie Provisoire (97, 98 and 99 Batteries) that was posted nearby in 1915, though it is not certain. Artillery units account for 206 of the men buried here which reflects the type of activity in the area during the war. This area was behind the front-line but the artillery pieces were an obvious target for the German guns.

The cemetery was used mainly for burials from the nearby Dressing Station.

Serjeant Oliver Victor Poulton, DCM, 15th Field Company, Royal Engineers, died on 26 June 1917 aged 30 years. The citation for his award reads 'For conspicuous gallantry on 18 December 1914, when engaged with a party of men cutting the enemy's wires, he lay on the parapet of a German trench for one hour shooting at every head that appeared. Corporal Poulton subsequently assisted in rescuing a wounded comrade under fire.'

Also of note is Company Serjeant Major Daniel Patrick O'Hea, MM & Bar, 'D' Company, 12th Highland Light Infantry, who died on 30 September 1918 aged 26 years. Daniel was one of four brothers, all of whom fought in WW1. His brother Seaman Gunner Albert Henry O'Hea died aboard HMS Monmouth, part of the Fourth Cruiser Squadron (the West Indies Squadron), which suffered from poor armament and guns so low on the ship they could only be used in the best of weather. The Monmouth was sunk by the German ships Scharnhorst and Gneisenau at the Battle of Coronel fought off the coast of Chile on Sunday 1 November 1914. It took just forty minutes to reduce HMS Good Hope and HMS Monmouth to blazing wrecks that quickly sank with all 1600 crew. Another brother, Private John Francis O'Hea, of the 1/8th (Post Office Rifles) Londons, was captured at Vimy Ridge and spent the rest of the war as a prisoner of war. Collie O'Hea served with the Connaught Rangers.

Lieutenant Colonel Cecil Robert Arthur Pye, DSO, MiD, 19th Australian Infantry, was killed in action on 4 October 1917 aged 27 years. He was a qualified Doctor who travelled to China as ship's surgeon in 1902. He moved on to England before returning to Australia where he took a commission in 1909. By August 1915 he was a Major serving in Gallipoli with the 17th Australian Infantry before being evacuated to hospital in October suffering from dysentery. He went to Australia to train recruits and returned to France with replacements in December 1916 taking temporary command of the 17th Australian Infantry in February 1917. He was awarded the Distinguished Service Order for planning and leading an attack near Bapaume in March 1917. This led to command of the 19th Australian Infantry and action in the Second Battle of Bullecourt on 3 May for which he was Mentioned in Despatches. Pye was fatally wounded when visiting his forward companies at Broodseinde Ridge.

Lieutenant Colonel Alfred Joseph Elton Sunderland, three times MiD, 2nd Devonshires, was killed in action on 31 July 1917 aged 42 years. He joined his regiment in 1895 and served in the South African Wars where he became a Captain. He was appointed a Major in 1915 and a Lieutenant Colonel in 1916 commanding the Battalion from 14 January 1917. He was killed on the Bellewaerde Ridge on the first day of Third Ypres.

Notably here now is Company Serjeant Major Andrew Gale, 10th Queen's (Royal West Surreys), killed on 28 September 1918 aged 41 years. For many years Gale was commemorated on the Tyne Cot Memorial and the headstone read 'unknown Company Serjeant Major of the Great War'. The rededication service was held on 30 September 2016 with his great grandson in attendance because a member of the CWGC administrative staff was walking through the cemetery and came across the headstone with almost all the information needed to identify the 'unknown' soldier. They checked the records and Gale's name has been put where he belongs. Proof, if needed, that the CWGC does outstanding work in caring, in many ways, for the dead and their families.

| | | |
|---|---|---|
| UK - 430 | Aust - 125 | NZ – 8 |
| Can – 7 | India - 2 | Unnamed - 9 |

Area – 3350 sq mts

Special Memorials to two Australians whose graves have been lost.

### LOCATION
Belgian Battery Corner Cemetery lies in the southern suburbs of Ieper about 300m west of the point where the N375 bends sharply to the south. A road to Brandhoek leaves the N375 at this point, at the first cross-roads of which is a CWGC sign directing to the cemetery. Turn right and the cemetery is soon on your right. Don't try any track to the right at the south end of the cemetery as they lead to private property.

# BERKS CEMETERY EXTENSION

## HISTORY
The cemetery was opened in June 1916 at the start of the Battle of Messines and was used until September 1917.

## INFORMATION
This cemetery is directly opposite the much smaller Hyde Park Corner Cemetery, which is dominated by this because of the large Memorial to the Missing. At the end of the war, the extension was what we now see as Plot I. Plots II and III were added in 1930.

The two cemeteries are separated by a road on which a junction north of Ploegsteert Wood gave the location its name of Hyde Park Corner. Nearby Hill 63 was to the north-west and nearby were the 'Catacombs', deep shelters capable of holding two Battalions, used from November 1916 to the end of the war.

Among those buried here are Rifleman Leonard Crossley and Rifleman William Crossley, 21st (Yeoman Rifles) King's Royal Rifle Corps, killed in action on 30 June 1916 aged 31 years. They were twin brothers who had consecutive service numbers and are buried side by side. They had been in France and Belgium since 4 May 1916 and spent about three weeks in billets near Bailleul before going into the line at Ploegsteert. They were in reserve billets when they were killed by the same shell during a retaliatory bombardment.

Another buried here is Rifleman John Cleland Baird, 14th Royal Irish Rifles, died on 17 February 1917 aged 22 years. His brother Serjeant Samuel Baird, 'A' Company, 2nd Royal Irish Rifles, died on 24 November 1916 aged 20 years and is buried across the road in Hyde Park Corner (Royal Berks) Cemetery.

Concentrated here:

Rosenberg Chateau Military Cemetery and Extension – located about 1km north-west of here in the grounds of the chateau. The cemetery was used from November 1914 to August 1916. The Extension was begun in May 1916 and used until March 1918. Together, the cemetery and extension were sometimes referred to as 'Red Lodge Cemetery and Extension'. By 1930, the French owner of the chateau was unhappy with the burials remaining on his land as he planned to rebuild the destroyed chateau. Negotiations with the landowner took some time before a decision to move the bodies here was finalised. The Belgian Minister of the Interior tried to use his influence to avoid any interference with the dead, but the owner insisted on his right to the land and finally it was decided to remove the bodies. It contained 171 British, 146 Canadian, 128 Australian and 35 New Zealand men.

UK – 467    Aust – 180    NZ – 80
Can – 149   Ger – 4
Area – 3125 sq mts

**Ploegsteert Memorial**

The Memorial records the names of 11366 (plus 44 under an alias) British and South African missing, some from battles, but most killed in day-to-day trench warfare or in small scale engagements. They are often the forgotten men of the war. The original intention had been to erect the memorial in Lille.

The Memorial takes the form of a circular temple, 22m in diameter and 12m high, with the names on panels within the interior. At the entrance there are two huge stone lions, the most memorable feature for many people to whom I have spoken, notably as one of the lions is smiling. The Memorial was designed by Harold Charlton Bradshaw, sculptured by Sir Gilbert Ledward and unveiled by the Duke of Brabant on 7 June 1931.

There are three men commemorated on the Memorial who were executed but whose graves were lost. Private Archibald Browne of the 2nd Essex was the fourth British soldier to be executed in the war and the last in 1914. Having deserted from his Battalion in November 1914 he was quickly found by French Police in a house in Hazebrouck wearing civilian clothes. He claimed to have been captured by the Germans but was not believed. He was found guilty of desertion, plundering and escaping arrest before his execution on 19 December 1914.

Private A. Pitts of the 2nd Royal Warwickshires deserted near Zonnebeke on 24 October 1914 during a battle but was captured at Boulogne on 12 January 1915 where he was trying to get back to England using false papers. Pitts was executed on 8 February 1915.

Private Thomas Hope of the 2nd Leinsters deserted on 23 December 1914. Hope had only been with his unit for a couple of months when he disappeared while collecting rations. He was captured, disguised as a Military Policeman, on 9 February 1915 and was executed on 2 March 1915.

In addition, three men commemorated on the Memorial were awarded the Victoria Cross. Sapper William Hackett, VC, 254th Tunnelling Company, Corps of Royal Engineers died on 27 June 1916 aged 43 years. He won his Victoria Cross for actions at Givenchy on 22-23 June 1916. His citation reads 'For most conspicuous bravery when entombed with four others in a gallery owing to the explosion of an enemy mine. After working for 20 hours, a hole was made through fallen earth and broken timber, and the outside party was met. Sapper Hackett helped three of the men through the hole and could easily have followed, but refused to leave the fourth, who had been seriously injured, saying, "I am a tunneller, I must look after the others first." Meantime, the hole was getting smaller, yet he still refused to leave his injured comrade. Finally, the gallery collapsed, and though the rescue party worked desperately for four days the attempt to reach the two men failed. Sapper Hackett well knowing the nature of sliding earth, the chances against him, deliberately gave his life for his comrade.' A rescue party could have saved Hackett but not Collins and the Nottingham miner decided to stay with him. However, there was another explosion and both were buried alive. The four day difference between the date given for the act and his death is accounted for by the days taken to confirm him as dead, though Hackett possibly died some days earlier than his official date of death. Hackett enlisted in the Royal Engineers tunnelling companies in October 1915, after being rejected three times by the York and Lancaster Regiment for being over age. William Hackett was the only tunneller to receive the Victoria Cross. The man he was trying to save was Private Thomas Collins who is commemorated on the Thiepval Memorial. Both men lie where they were entombed at Givenchy lès la Bassée (near Béthune) where you will find the Tunnellers' Memorial.

Private James MacKenzie, VC, 2nd Scots Guards, was killed in action on 19 December 1914 aged 25 years. The citation reads 'For conspicuous bravery at Rouges Bancs on the 19th December 1914, in rescuing a severely wounded man from in front of the German trenches, under a very heavy fire and after a stretcher-bearer party had been compelled to abandon the attempt. Private Mackenzie was subsequently killed on that day whilst in the performance of a similar act of gallant conduct.'

Acting Captain Thomas Tannatt Pryce, VC, MC and Bar, 4th Grenadier Guards, died of wounds on 13 April 1918. The citation reads 'For most conspicuous bravery, devotion to duty, and self-sacrifice when in command of a flank on the left of the Grenadier Guards. Having been ordered to attack a village he personally led forward two Platoons, working from house to house, killing some thirty of the enemy, seven of whom he killed himself. The next day he was occupying a position with some thirty to forty men, the remainder of his Company having become casualties. As early as 8.15am, his left flank was surrounded and the enemy was enfilading him. He was attacked no less than four times during the day, and each time beat off the hostile attack, killing many of the enemy. Meanwhile the enemy brought three field guns to within 300 yards of his line, and were firing over open sights and knocking his trench in. At 6.15pm, the enemy had worked to within sixty yards of his trench. He then called on his men, telling them to cheer and charge the enemy and fight to the last. Led by Captain Pryce, they left their trench and drove back the enemy with the bayonet some 100 yards. Half an hour later the enemy had again approached in stronger force. By this time Captain Pryce had only seventeen men left, and every round of his ammunition had been fired. Determined that there should be no surrender, he once again led his men forward in a bayonet charge, and was last seen engaged in a fierce hand-to-hand struggle with overwhelming numbers of the enemy. With some forty men he had held back at least one enemy Battalion for over ten hours. His Company undoubtedly stopped the advance through the British line, and thus had great influence on the battle.' At the start of the war he enlisted in the Honourable Artillery Company and went to France with them in December 1914. He was commissioned into the 6th Gloucestershires in October 1915 and was wounded in a night raid at Gommecourt, where he gained the Military Cross. He returned to the Front in May 1916, and won a Bar to his Military Cross soon after. In September he transferred to the Grenadier Guards and went out again with a draft in February 1917.

Commemorated on the memorial is Brigadier General Norman Reginald McMahon, DSO, three times MiD, General Staff, HQ 10th Infantry Brigade, commanding 4th Royal Fusiliers, killed in action on 11 November 1914 aged 48 years. He joined his regiment as a Lieutenant in 1885, was promoted to Captain in 1896, Major in 1901 and Lieutenant Colonel commanding the 4th Royal Fusiliers in 1911. He served with the Burmese Expedition in 1886-7 and in the South African Wars where he was wounded, Mentioned in Despatches and awarded the Distinguished Service Order. He went on to command the School of Musketry from 1905 to 1909 where he set the high standard of firing rate for infantry soldiers. He was twice Mentioned in Despatches while he was in France and Flanders. He was promoted to Brigadier General but was killed in action before he could take up his post.

Also of note is Captain Jehu Fosbrooke Gerrard Aubin, DSO, MC & Bar, MiD, 6th Durham Light Infantry, who died on 9 April 1918 aged 26 years. The citation for his posthumous Distinguished Service Order, gazetted in September 1918, reads 'For conspicuous gallantry and devotion to duty. The Battalion was holding a village, covering the retirement of another unit, when it was attacked by the enemy, and withdrew, leaving one Company as rearguard under this officer. He remained with his rear Platoon under machine-gun fire and sniping, and beat off the attack while the rest withdrew. Later, three companies were ambushed in the marshes, and he collected almost all the men, organising a rear guard, so that each Company in turn could cross by a bridge, he himself being the last to cross. A few days later his Company was in support, when the three forward companies began to fall back. He went up under intense fire, rallied them, and re-established the front line. His grasp of the situation saved the Battalion.' He joined the Northumberland Fusiliers as a Private in September 1914 and was gazetted as 2nd Lieutenant in June 1915. His Military Cross was gazetted in January 1917, and a Bar gazetted in January 1918.

While there are many men on the memorial who lost brothers there are several commemorated who lost more than one brother. Lance Corporal John Gray, 5th Royal Scots, killed in action on 15 April 1918 aged 32 years, lost two brothers. Engine Room Artificer 4th Class Frederick Balfour Gray, HMS Laurentic, Royal Naval Volunteer Reserve, died on 25 January 1917 and is buried in Upper Fahan (St. Mura's) Church of Ireland Churchyard. The Laurentic was sunk within an hour when she struck two mines with the loss of 354 passengers and crew. Private George M Gray, 7th Cameronians (Scottish Rifles), was killed in action on 2 September 1918 and is buried in Queant Road Cemetery.

Another to lose two brothers is Private Edward Robert Saunders, 21st (Islington) Middlesex, killed in action on 9 April 1918 aged 18 years. His brother Corporal J W E Saunders, MM, 110th Brigade, Royal Field Artillery died on 18 September 1918 aged 23 years and is buried in Peronne Communal Cemetery Extension. His brother Rifleman W E Saunders, 16th (St. Pancras) Rifle Brigade, died on 23 December 1916 aged 20 years. He is buried in Essex Farm Cemetery about 10km north of here.

Similarly, Private Jack Auty Mills, 12th Suffolks, killed in action on 12 April 1918 aged 20 years. Private Michael Daniel Mills, 9th Essex, died on 21 October 1915 is buried in Vermelles British Cemetery. Acting Bombardier Fredrick William Mills, 14th Battery, 4th Brigade, Royal Field Artillery, died on 1 July 1916 aged 28 years. He is buried in Basra War Cemetery.

Private Frank Jarrett, 2nd East Lancashires, killed in action on 9 May 1915 aged 21 years. Gunner George Jarrett, Royal Garrison Artillery, died on 14 January 1917 and is buried in Combles Communal Cemetery Extension on the Somme. Private John Jarrett, 10th Royal Fusiliers attached 111th Trench Mortar Battery, died on 27 April 1917 aged 20 years and is buried in Etaples Military Cemetery.

Private Edwin Dugan, 2nd Hampshires died on 19 April 1918 is commemorated here. Private James Dugan, 2nd Hampshires died on 21 August 1917 aged 43 years is commemorated on the Tyne Cot Memorial. His brother, Private Wesley Dugan, 15th Hampshires died on 15 September 1916 and is commemorated on the Thiepval Memorial. Here we have a family to lose several members and that have no grave to visit.

Private John William Duxbury, 12th King's Own Yorkshire Light Infantry, killed in action on 13 April 1918 aged 29 years. Private Fred Duxbury, 8th King's Own Yorkshire Light Infantry was killed on the first day of the Battle of the Somme, 1 July 1916 at Authuille Wood and is commemorated on the Thiepval Memorial. Private Arthur Duxbury, 12th King's Own Yorkshire Light Infantry, died as a prisoner of war on 28 April 1918 aged 41 years and is buried in Hamburg Cemetery in Germany.

Private John Murchie MacMillan, 1st King's Own Scottish Borderers, was killed in action on 11 April 1918. His brother Private Gavin MacMillan, 1/9th Argyll and Sutherland Highlanders was killed in action on 10 May 1915 and is commemorated on the Menin Gate. Another brother Private James MacMillan, 'C' Company, 13th Royal Scots, was killed in action on 28 March 1918 aged 32 years, and is buried at Feuchy Chapel British Cemetery.

One of four brothers killed in the war is Private Frederick Stooke, 3rd Coldstream Guards, killed in action on 13 April 1918 aged 20 years. Air Mechanic 1st Class Arthur Augustus Stooke, No. 4 Kite Balloon Section, Royal Flying Corps, died on 3 January 1917 aged 27 years and is commemorated on the Arras Flying Services Memorial. Sapper Frank Stooke, 59th Company, Royal Engineers, died of wounds on 16 May 1915 aged 35 years and is buried in Boulogne Eastern Cemetery. Private Edgar Stooke, 2nd Sherwood Foresters (Notts and Derby Regiment), died of wounds on 26 April 1918 aged 18 years and is buried in Brandhoek New Military Cemetery No. 3 which is about 11km north of here.

One of five brothers to die in the war is Serjeant Bernard Reeve Beechey, 2nd Lincolnshires, killed in action on 25 September 1915 aged 38 years. He was the first of the brothers to die and was killed charging to his death in the Battle of Loos. Private Charles Reeve Beechey, 25th (Frontiersmen) Royal Fusiliers, was killed in action by machine-gun fire on 20 October 1917 while defending Lukeledi Mission in East Africa against a German assault aged 39 years. He is now buried in Dar es Salaam War Cemetery in Tanzania. 2nd Lieutenant Frank Collett Reeve Beechey, 13th East Yorkshires, died of wounds at Serre in some of the last acts of the Battles of the Somme on 14 November 1916 aged 30 years. A shell took Frank's legs off during the attack on 13 November and he lay in no-man's land under fire from dawn until dusk before an army doctor risked his life to crawl out and administer morphine. He is buried in Warlincourt Halte British Cemetery. Lance Corporal Harold Reeve Beechey, 48th Australian Infantry, was killed on 10 April 1917 aged 26 years. He is commemorated on the Villers-Bretonneux Memorial. He had emigrated to be a farmer in Western Australia but enlisted at the start of the war. He fought at Gallipoli and Pozieres being wounded and invalided with disease. He was killed by a shell at Bullecourt but his body was not identified. Rifleman Leonard Reeve Beechey, 18th (London Irish Rifles) Londons, died of wounds on 29 December 1917 aged 36 years. He was gassed and wounded at Bourlon Wood. He is buried in St. Sever Cemetery Extension, Rouen. Another brother, who had emigrated to Australia with Harold, Christopher William Reeve Beechey, was wounded at Gallipoli serving as a stretcher bearer with the 4th Field Ambulance. He was unable to walk for any great distance for the rest of his life. Two other brothers, Samuel St. Vincent Reeve Beechey and Eric Reeve Beechey served and survived the war.

Similarly, Private Alfred Stewart, 13th York and Lancasters who died on 13 April 1918 aged 29 years. He had enlisted in 1909 and served as a drummer. Private William Arthur Stewart, 8th Duke of Wellington's, died on 24 October 1915 aged 29 years and is commemorated on the Helles Memorial. He was killed by a sniper at Gallipoli. 2nd Lieutenant Charles Edward Stewart, MM, MiD, 20th Manchesters, died of wounds on 10 September 1916 aged 32 years and is buried in Abbeville Communal Cemetery. He was shot in the head while leading his men and died later in hospital. His mother was able to travel to France to see him on his deathbed. Private Leonard Stewart, 2nd West Yorkshires died on 26 June 1917 aged 21 years and is buried in Leeds (Lawnswood) Cemetery. He was badly wounded and had been sent home to recuperate but then returned to the trenches. There he contracted pleurisy, was again returned to England where he died in a Manchester hospital. Leonard is the only Stewart brother actually buried in the family grave in Lawnswood Cemetery. A fifth brother died, though he is not officially recognised as a casualty of war. Private Walter Stewart was a mechanic with the Army Service Corps and serving in East Africa. He did not survive the journey home and was buried at sea on 10 March 1919. The eldest son, James Frederick Patrick Stewart, also served in the war. It is believed that he was injured and suffered from shell shock. He lived until 1944. Robert Henry Stewart served in the Merchant Marine and survived the war. He died on 25 October 1928 aged 35 years. The youngest brother, George Mears Stewart, appears to have served in the Royal Army Ordnance Corps during the WW2. Even though he would have been 41 years old in 1939, he was a 2nd Lieutenant and was promoted to Captain by the time he left the military in 1947. He lived until 1957.

There are five sets of brothers who died on the same day in the Battle of Aubers Ridge, Sunday 9 May 1915, commemorated on the memorial. They are Privates Walter Sidney Belsten, aged 24 years, and Corporal William Henry Belsten, aged 23 years, both 1/13th (Kensington) Londons; Private William Robert Felce and Private Herbert Felce, both 2nd Northamptonshires; Rifleman George Wimble, aged 24 years, and Rifleman Herbert Wimble, aged 24 years, both 2nd Rifle Brigade; Lance Corporal Alfred Tame and Corporal William George Tame, both 2nd Royal Berkshires; and Private Arthur Gordon Millington, aged 30 years, and Private Dudley Graham Millington, aged 19 years, both 1/13th (Kensington) Londons. The Millingtons had a third brother die on service. He was Corporal Victor Charles Millington, Army Pay Corps, who died on 15 October 1918 and is buried in Chingford Mount Cemetery. The Tames also had a third brother die on service. He is Private John Tame, 2nd Royal Berkshires killed in action on 19 August 1917 and commemorated at Tyne Cot.

Private Walter Southgate, 2nd Northamptonshires was killed on 9 May 1915. His brother, Private Frederick Southgate, 1st Northamptonshires had enlisted on the same day but after training they were drafted to different Battalions. Both Battalions were involved in the Battle of Aubers Ridge in which both men were killed. However, Frederick is commemorated on the Le Touret Memorial while Walter is here.

Private Charles Edward George King aged 20 years and Private John King aged 18 years, both 'C' Company, 2nd Royal Berkshires and both killed on 25 September 1915 are commemorated here. They were killed in the German counter-attack during the Battle of Loos, their first battle. Another pair of brothers commemorated here are Privates John and Joseph Newell, both 'A' Company, 2nd Royal Inniskilling Fusiliers. John was killed in action on 7 November 1914 and Joseph on 21 October 1914.

Lieutenant The Honourable Felix Charles Hubert Hanbury-Tracy, 2nd Scots Guards, died of wounds on 19 December 1914 aged 30 years. He was son of the 4th Baron Sudeley and died in a German Field Hospital at Destage le Ventre near Armentières. His brother Brevet Major The Honourable Algernon Henry Charles Hanbury-Tracy, CMG, three times MiD, Royal Horse Guards, died of a heart attack on 3 December 1915 aged 44 years. He had seen service in Uganda (1897-8), Abyssinia (1901), and the South African Wars. He is buried at Petersham (St. Peter) Churchyard. His son, Major Richard Algernon Frederick Hanbury-Tracy, 6th Baron Sudeley, Royal Horse Guards and No. 8 Commando, was killed in action on 26 August 1941 aged 30 years but his body was lost so he is commemorated on the Brookwood 1939-1945 Memorial. His nephew, Captain Michael David Charles Hanbury-Tracy, 1st Scots Guards, died of wounds, received at Dunkirk, on 22 August 1940 aged 31 years and is buried in Toddington (St. Andrew) Churchyard.

2nd Lieutenant Geoffrey Vincent Pearce, 2nd Royal Warwickshires died on 19 December 1914 aged 24 years. He was the son of Sir William Pearce, Liberal MP for Tower Hamlets. He first joined the 1/28th (Artist Rifles) Londons and went to France with them in September 1914. He was commissioned on 15 December 1914 moving to the Royal Warwickshires and was killed when he went into his first attack four days later.

Captain Geoffrey Percy Robert Toynbee, 1st Rifle Brigade died on 15 November 1914. He made three first class cricket appearances, once for the MCC and twice for Hampshire in 1912.

2nd Lieutenant Ernest James Keeley, 4th South African Infantry died on 23 July 1918 aged 28 years. He represented South Africa in shooting at the 1912 Stockholm Olympics. He enlisted at the start of the war, was wounded at Delville Wood and Arras before being commissioned.

Also commemorated here is Private Henry Mills Goldsmith, Devonshire Regiment attached 2nd Lincolnshires, killed on 9 May 1915 aged 29 years. He won the Bronze Medal in the Coxed Eights Rowing Team at the 1908 London Olympics.

A commemoration of note is 2nd Lieutenant Edward Mason, 3rd attached 2nd Northamptonshires, killed in action on 9 May 1915 aged 36 years. Before the war he spent seventeen years on the Music Staff at Eton College. He was Principal Cellist in the Royal Albert Hall Orchestra and was founder and Conductor of the Edward Mason Choir.

Another of note is Major William Worsley Ashcroft, MiD, 25th Company, Machine Gun Corps (Infantry), killed in action on 11 April 1918 aged 39 years. He was the father of the actress, Dame Peggy Ashcroft.

An actor who appeared at His Majesty's Theatre, the Prince of Wales and the Garrick in London between 1908 and 1914 commemorated on the Memorial is Private Sidney William Sherwood, 1/13th (Kensington) Londons who died on 9 May 1915 aged 23 years. He was killed in the attack by his Battalion on the Aubers Ridge.

Of interest is Private Arthur Holdsworth, 1st East Yorkshires, was killed on 28 October 1914. He was an archaeologist and father of wildlife documentary filmmaker Michaela Holdsworth Denis.

Also of note is 2nd Lieutenant Leonard James Brown, 1st East Surreys attached 2nd Royal Fusiliers, killed in action on 19 August 1918. His real name is Pope. He ran away from home in 1912, made his way to Ireland and enlisted with the Royal Irish claiming to be eighteen years of age, two years older than his real age. He fought with the 2nd Royal Irish throughout 1914 and 1915 until wounded at Festubert. He was back with his Battalion on the Somme in 1916. He then transferred to the 2nd Leinsters and by 1917 had been wounded three more times. His next move was to become an officer gaining a commission in the 1st East Surreys, seeing action with them in Italy and France. In July he moved again, this time to the 2nd Royal Fusiliers with whom he was killed. Unusually, he is still recorded by the CWGC under his false name.

Private Sidney Alfred Wyllie, 1/1st (Royal Fusiliers) Londons, was killed on 9 May 1915 in the Battle of Aubers Ridge, aged 15 years. He enlisted on 9 January 1915 from his job as a clerk and arrived in France a few days before he was killed in his first attack.

Finally, I draw your attention to a man, probably not alone, whose name should not be commemorated here. 2nd Lieutenant Thomas Henry Bowley, 1st Leicestershires, was killed in action at Kruiseek Hill on 26 October 1914. He had been an enlisted soldier since 1893, serving with the 1st and 2nd Borders. At the start of the war, as a Company Sergeant Major, he applied for a commission, which he gained with the Leicestershires, rather than the Borders where all the officer posts were considered filled. However, he never had time to complete his transfer and was still with the Borders when killed. When the Memorials were being constructed, the records showed Bowley to be an officer with the 1st Leicestershires, who were south of Armentieres on the day he died. Hence, his name is here though it should be on the Menin Gate.

UK - 11366           SAfr - 13

**LOCATION**

Royal Berkshire Corner Cemetery lies on the east side of the Armentieres road, about 1km north of Ploegsteert, and at the foot of Hill 63, which is approximately 13km south of Ieper.

# BERTENACRE MILITARY CEMETERY, FLETRE

**HISTORY**

The cemetery was begun by the French and was used by the British Army during the war only after the Battles of the Lys in July to September 1918. After the war over 40 British graves were concentrated here.

**INFORMATION**

The cemetery was begun by the French when it was named the 'Cemetiere du Calvaire de Bertenacre' after a crucifix on the road nearby. This is one of the most isolated cemeteries included in this book and one of the more difficult to reach. The views of the Monts des Flandres make the journey worthwhile but the noise from the motorway, by which this graveyard stands, can be intrusive.

Most of the burials here were made by the 36th (Ulster) Division. After the war 115 French and two German graves were removed. Most of the burials from the 1939-45 War were men of the 5th (Cinque Ports) Royal Sussex Regiment. Among those here is Major Robert Goodman Kerr, MC, 7th Royal Inniskilling Fusiliers, killed in action on 11 July 1918 aged 28 years. He was a pre-war Rugby Union player with Lansdowne having qualified from Trinity College, Dublin. He was commissioned into the 7th Royal Inniskilling Fusiliers early in the war, won his Military Cross in the 1917 New Year's Honours List and commanded the Battalion for a short period as Acting Lieutenant Colonel. In May 1918, Major Kerr was transferred to the 9th Royal Irish Fusiliers. At 1.00am on 11 July 1918 Kerr was with Colonel Lowe as they reconnoitered the front line when he was shot and killed. His wife also lost her brother, 2nd Lieutenant Henry Eyre Linde, 7th Royal Inniskilling Fusiliers killed on 24 June 1917 aged 23 years. He is buried in La Laiterie Military Cemetery.

Also here is Private Denis Eric Whitlock, 5th (Cinque Ports) Royal Sussex, killed in action on 22 May 1940 aged 21 years. His brother Private John Frederick Whitlock, 1st The Queen's Royal Regiment (West Surreys) was killed on 7 May 1944 aged 23 years and is commemorated on the Rangoon Memorial.

Concentrated here

Royal West Surrey Cemetery - situated about 500m to the south-east of this cemetery. It contained the graves of 42 men who were killed in an air raid on their camp on 18 August 1917, of whom 38 belonged to the 10th (Battersea) Queen's (Royal West Surreys), and one Canadian who died in June 1918.

UK - 109           Can – 2           WW2 - 32

Area – 717 sq mts

Special Memorial to one man whose grave was destroyed by shell-fire.

**LOCATION**

Bertenacre Cemetery lies 2km south of Godewaersvelde and south-west of Ieper. The easiest route is via the Poperinge by-pass and the road to Steenvoorde, leaving the latter at the crossroads with the D10, and following the directions for Bailleul and then Godewaersvelde. Pass through the village and you will soon come to a sharp left bend just after which the road forks, take the right fork to Hazebrouck. Just before the road crosses the motorway you find the old road at a CWGC sign. This ends at a farm track that leads to the path to the cemetery. The CWGC says on its website 'The rough track leading to the cemetery may be difficult under wet weather conditions, and is unsuitable for private cars during the winter months.'

# BETHLEEM FARM EAST

## HISTORY
The cemetery was begun when the farm was captured on 7 June 1917, the first day of the Battle of Messines, and remained in use with three burials on 3 July and one in September though most burials were made during June.

## INFORMATION
This is the smallest cemetery on the Messines Ridge. It was the location of a farm used as a German headquarters and strongpoint captured by the 3rd Australian Division on 7 June 1917. The Australian Field Ambulance set up a medical unit here and most of the burials are those who became casualties on 8 or 10 June 1917 and died in the Field Ambulance.

It is clear from this spot how the Messines Ridge dominates the countryside and, therefore, how important it was to hold the ridge. On 31 October 1914 the position was held by the 57th (Wilde's) Rifles of the Indian Army. They were being relieved by the 2nd Royal Inniskilling Fusiliers when the Germans attacked. The British were forced to withdraw into the village where a new line was held with the help of the 5th (Princess Charlotte of Wales's) Dragoon Guards.

As you pass through the square in Messines you can see the Town Hall within which is an excellent small museum founded in 1972 by the Mayor. It is possible to visit the museum and the church, rebuilt in 1928, in which Adolph Hitler spent some time at a German Dressing Station, and also made a painting of the Church which is now found in the museum. The crypt, the only one in the area, in Roman style, dates from the Eleventh Century and contains the grave of Countess Adela of France, mother-in-law of William the Conqueror, who died at the Abbey of Messines in 1079. The tower, from which you can get possibly one of the best views of the Salient, features a tough and daunting climb for those who have any fear of heights - it is made worse when the church bells start to play as you are climbing the open steps to the tower just above the bells. These are part of the Peace Carillon of which the largest bell, named Pax, was blessed by Pope John Paul II in 1985.

Among those here is Private Littleton Campbell Groom, 42nd Australian Infantry, killed in action on 10 June 1917 aged 28 years. He had enlisted in February 1916 from his job as a newspaper reporter and arrived in Europe in early 1917. However, he spent time in hospital before joining his unit at the Front April 1917 and was killed by German shelling. His brother, Private Colin Groom, 26th Australian Infantry, was killed in action near Lagnicourt, France on 26 March 1917 aged 22 years. His body was lost and he is commemorated on the Villers-Bretonneux Memorial. He had been wounded at Pozieres in 1916 and spent a month in hospital. He returned to the Front and was again wounded at Pozieres taking longer to recover. A third brother survived the war.

UK - 1          Aust - 43          Unnamed – 8
Area – 339 sq mts
Special Memorial to one Australian soldier known to be buried among the unnamed.

## LOCATION
Bethleem Farm East Cemetery is located 10km south of Ieper and 1 km south-east of Mesen/Messines. In the town square there are CWGC signs to the Bethleem Farm cemeteries directing you through the south-east corner of the square out of the village passing housing for 200m until you reach open space from which you can see the cemeteries in the fields below. The entrance to this cemetery is 100m from the road and 100m to the left of the farm track from the road. It is just possible to get cars to the path to the cemetery if you are adventurous, but it would be easier to park and walk the final 200m.

# BETHLEEM FARM WEST CEMETERY

## HISTORY
This cemetery was begun at the start of the Battle of Messines, when the area was captured by the 3rd Australian Division on 7 June 1917, and remained in use until December.

## INFORMATION
This cemetery was begun by the 3rd Australian Division who captured Bethleem Farm on 7 June 1917. They called it the '3rd Division General Cemetery'. The 14th (Light) Division used it until 1917. The cemetery also contains one unidentified burial made in WW2.

Outside the east wall of the cemetery ran Ungodly Trench, one of the German defences which protected the strongpoint at Bethleem Farm, previously known as Schnitzel Farm.

According to Peter Oldham in his 'Battleground Europe' series book on the Messines Ridge, Hitler was billetted at the German strongpoint here for a time when he served as a messenger in the winter of 1914/1915. In 1940 he revisited the farm, which had been rebuilt nearby, and presented the farmer's wife with a bouquet of flowers.

Among those here is Private Robert Munson, 33rd Australian Infantry, killed in action on 23 July 1917 aged 24 years. He enlisted in January 1916 and arrived in France in November. His cousin, Gunner Eric Robert Garriock, 4th Brigade, Australian Field Artillery, who died on 15

September 1917 aged 20 years is buried in Birr Crossroads Cemetery about 6km north of here. He joined up in late 1915 but spent most of 1916 in medical units. So, the cousins spent a similar amount of time at the Front before their deaths.

UK - 24       Aust - 114       NZ – 26
Unnamed - 2     WW2 – 1 (unnamed)
Area – 630 sq mts
Special Memorial to one New Zealander whose grave was destroyed by shell-fire.

**LOCATION**
Directions are as for Bethleem Farm East Cemetery except that the entrance is on the right 50m south of that for the East Cemetery. Then you have a walk of 200m to the path to the cemetery which is next to the farm. You can take a car down here but it is private land. The CWGC website says 'Visitors to this site should note a short grassed access path which is unsuitable for vehicles.'

## BEVEREN-IJZER CHURCHYARD

**HISTORY**
This churchyard was used by the British for the burial of men who died from April to October 1918.

**INFORMATION**
There was a Belgian Military Hospital in Beveren–IJzer at the crossroads of IJzerstraat-Lindestraat, 2km from the centre of Beveren. All of the French and 66 of 72 Belgians who died in the hospital were buried here, but have since been removed. The British buried here in WW1 also died of wounds in the hospital. Intriguingly, for some time they were recorded as having died as German prisoners of war which implied that they were moved here from German cemeteries. However, this has been proved to be untrue.

All of the Second World War burials date from May 1940 and the withdrawal to Dunkirk ahead of the German advance.

Buried here is 2nd Lieutenant Herbert Wilson Leitham, 5th attached 8th Black Watch (Royal Highlanders) who died on 17 October 1918 aged 19 years. Between the end of the war and 1926 there is a record of his body having been exhumed in 1921, at which time it was found to be buried in a coffin with no uniform but with no other evidence of identity, and a Special Memorial headstone being erected to him, and several others. Previously a student at St. Andrews University, he died in the Belgian Military Hospital of wounds that he received at Winkel St. Eloi which is about 35km east of here.

UK - 20         WW2 – 8 (2 unidentified)       Bel - 6
Area – 864 sq mts
Special Memorials for three men believed or known to be buried here but whose graves have been lost

**LOCATION**
This burial ground is located about 25km north-east of Ieper lying on the N364. The village is in one of the corners of the area covered by this book. The cemetery is located next to the church on the Sint Brigida-plein.

## BIRR CROSSROADS CEMETERY

**HISTORY**
The cemetery was begun in August 1917, next to a Dressing Station, and was used until the Germans took this point in the spring of 1918. It was enlarged after the war when over 650 graves were concentrated here.

**INFORMATION**
The area was within British lines for most of the war. At the end of the war the cemetery was what is now Plot I.
Birr Crossroads is at the eastern corner of the cemetery, and was named by the 1st Leinsters, after the name of their depot in Ireland, when they were stationed here in 1915. The line of the road changed after the war such that the northern part of the crossroads, Cambridge Road, is now about 100m to the east.

On 16 June 1915 an attack by the Honourable Artillery Company was made from trenches opposite this cemetery in the direction of 'Y' Wood and the Bellewaerde Spur near the site of RE Grave. 'Y' Wood was a small copse that used to exist between here and the Bellewaerde Spur which got its name from its shape in the form of the letter 'Y'. The trenches at the wood were undefended but the Honourable Artillery Company found Germans buried alive by the British artillery bombardment along with parts of bodies blown to pieces by the shelling.

The Germans reached the Hellfire Corner crossroads during their advance in April 1918, taking Birr Crossroads for the only time, the closest that they got to Ypres. This is signified by the demarcation stone at Hellfire Corner. The area was re-captured by the II Corps on 8 September 1918. The 'crossroads' is now a roundabout.

The large roundabout, about 200m west of the cemetery, known as Hellfire Corner is one of the most well-referred to locations of the war. The point at which the Zillebeke-St. Jan Road crossed the Menin Road as did the Railway to Zonnebeke, the junction was one of the most important crossroads as vast amounts of munitions, men and equipment passed through it. The junction was exposed to almost constant German artillery fire as the enemy knew the exact distance to its position.

Commemorated here is Captain Harold Ackroyd, VC, MC, Royal Army Medical Corps, attached 6th Royal Berkshires, died on 11 August 1917. He is believed to be buried here, the record of this decision being taken in 1922. The citation for his Victoria Cross won at Hooge from 31 July 1917 to 1 August 1917, reads 'For most conspicuous bravery. During recent operations Capt. Ackroyd displayed the greatest gallantry and devotion to duty. Utterly regardless of danger, he worked continuously for many hours up and down and in front of the line tending the wounded and saving the lives of officers and men. In so doing he had to move across the open under heavy machine-gun, rifle and shell fire. He carried a wounded officer to a place of safety under very heavy fire. On another occasion he went some way in front of our advanced line and brought in a wounded man under continuous sniping and machine-gun fire. His heroism was the means of saving many lives, and provided a magnificent example of courage, cheerfulness, and determination to the fighting men in whose midst he was carrying out his splendid work. This gallant officer has since been killed in action.' There were 23 separate recommendations made that he should receive the Victoria Cross. He was awarded the Military Cross for his actions on 19 July 1916 at Delville Wood on the Somme when he was recommended eleven times for the award of the Victoria Cross. The citation reads 'For conspicuous gallantry and devotion to duty during operations. He attended the wounded under heavy fire, and finally, when he had seen that all our wounded from behind the line had been got in, he went out beyond the front line and brought in both our own and enemy wounded, although continually sniped at.' He was killed during the period between the first attack in the Third Battles of Ypres and the next phase of the campaign. He was looking for wounded going from one shell-hole to another, when he was shot through the head by a sniper.

Buried here is Private James Balmer, 9th Northumberland Fusiliers, who died 20 November 1915 aged 24 years. He was originally buried in Gordon House Cemetery No. 1 which was next to the Union Street Graveyards. His brother, Lance Corporal George H Balmer, MM, 149th Company, Machine Gun Corps (Infantry) died on 30 July 1917 and is buried in Achiet-Le-Grand Communal Cemetery Extension on the Somme. Another brother, Private John Balmer, 2nd Yorkshires died on 2 April 1917 and is commemorated on the Arras Memorial.

Gunner George Butterfield, 230th Siege Battery, Royal Garrison Artillery, died on 24 September 1917. He represented Great Britain at the 1908 London Olympics in athletics middle distance events.

A final name of note is Sergeant Camille Jean Edouard De Wattine, Belgian Army, who was an interpreter with the British. He died on 30 September 1918 aged 22 years. His body is lost so he is commemorated by a Special Memorial. He was honored as a Knight in the Order of Leopold II and also held the French Croix de Guerre.

Concentrated here:

Bellewaarde Ridge Military Cemetery – it was located a little north-east of the Bellewaerde lake on the spur north of the Menin Road and about 500m east of here. It contained eleven British men and seventeen Australians who died in September and October 1917.

Birr Crossroads Cemetery No. 2 – located about 75m south of here. It contained eighteen British men who died in July and August 1917.

Union Street Graveyards No.'s 1 & 2 - located about 500m west of here north of the village in a trench formation south of Hellfire Corner. They contained nineteen British men who died in August and September 1915.

| | | |
|---|---|---|
| UK – 660 | Aust – 143 | NZ – 12 |
| Can – 15 | NF – 1 | S Afr – 1 |
| BWI – 1 | Bel – 1 | Unnamed – 333 |

Area – 2712 sq mts

Special Memorials to five British men and three Australians known/believed buried among the unnamed.

Special Memorials to eighteen British men buried in Birr Crossroads No. 2 Cemetery and Union Street Graveyards whose graves were destroyed by shell-fire.

Special Memorial to a Belgian interpreter whose grave is also lost.

**LOCATION**

Birr Crossroads Cemetery is on the south side of the Menin Road, east of Ieper, 900m east of Hellfire Corner. The CWGC website says 'This cemetery contains graves in which more than one soldier is buried and on which more than one headstone is erected. As each of these graves has a single grave number it follows that the numbering of a grave given in the register will in some cases not correspond with the number of the headstone as determined by counting from the beginning of the row. Visitors should therefore examine the whole row if they do not at once find the grave in which they are interested.'

# BLAUWEPOORT FARM CEMETERY

## HISTORY
The French began the cemetery in November 1914. The British Army did not begin to make burials until they moved here in February 1915 and it then remained in use for a year until February 1916.

## INFORMATION
The majority of the men buried here served in the Staffordshire, Norfolk or Scottish Highland Regiments, though the Cheshires were the first British unit to occupy the trenches nearby. Only one burial was made in March 1915, one in December 1915 and two in February 1916. The other 78 were made between April and October 1915, mostly for men killed fighting on Hill 60. There are no officers buried here.

This cemetery was begun by a French Regiment of Chasseurs Alpins (Mountain Hunters) though the French graves have been removed from the northern corner around the grave of Lance Corporal J Todd, 2nd King's Own Scottish Borderers, killed in action on 9 April 1915 aged 21 years.

Among those buried here is Gunner Thomas James Evans, DCM, 'C' Battery, 52nd Brigade, Royal Field Artillery, died on 20 December 1915. The citation for his Distinguished Conduct Medal, awarded in March 1916, reads 'For conspicuous bravery and resource. Gunner Evans accompanied Lieutenant Hollwey with the infantry attack, laying telephone wires. When the officer was wounded he assisted to carry him back under very heavy fire, and then returned and finished laying a wire to a trench. This wire was so badly cut it proved impossible to mend it, so he returned and laid a new wire to another point under a heavy and continuous fire. Finally, when this wire was cut, and he had used up all his spare wire, he carried back messages to our lines.' He had gone to France in May 1915. Also here is Private William Randell England, 1st Norfolks who died on 27 May 1915 aged 19 years leaving four sisters. He attested on 1 August 1914 and had been with the battalion since December. He had receieved a gunshot wound to the face in April before rejoining his unit. He is one of the men who fulfilled Brooke's poem by making a corner of a foreign field truly 'forever England'. There are 84 men called 'England' buried on or near the Western Front killed in action or died of wounds in medical units, 23 of whom are buried in cemeteries covered by this book. Others called England are on Memorials, died on other battlefields in the war or at home.

UK - 82        KUG - 7        Area – 1097 sq mts

## LOCATION
Blauwepoort Farm Cemetery is near the road to Comines, south of Ieper, 350m beyond the railway crossing and the entrance to Zillebeke Lake. It lies 200m to the west of the road at the end of a track which has a CWGC sign at the road. The cemetery, entered by a very stiff gate, is in a small valley next to a private house, Blauwepoort Farm.

# BLEUET FARM CEMETERY

## HISTORY
The cemetery was begun in preparation for the Third Battles of Ypres in 1917. It was used from June to December 1917 serving the Dressing Station in the farm. The cemetery was enlarged after the war with the addition of two isolated graves from the surrounding battlefields.

## INFORMATION
The village had become a major centre during the war for railways, hospitals, stores and camps. Elverdinge chateau was used as a headquarters for several units until it was accidentally burnt down by British cooks. A light railway ran along the road from Elverdinge to the front-line.

Many of the graves, 148, are men of the Guards Regiments. A French grave was removed after the war. A further nine graves were made during World War II.

Buried here is Serjeant James McCheyne, 'D' Company, 1st King's Own Scottish Borderers, who died of wounds on 3 October 1917 aged 26 years. He was aged 15 years when he joined the army in November 1906 lying about his age. He served in India before being medically discharged in 1909. When the war began James was called up as he was a reserve. While he was away at war his daughter died aged three years. James was sadly one of four brothers who died in the war. Ordinary Seaman Francis Wallace McCheyne, HMS Narborough, Royal Navy, was lost on 12 January 1918 aged 19 years. The destroyer Narborough and her sister ship sank in a snowstorm off the coast of Orkney when they hit rocks while returning to Scapa Flow from patrol. One man survived from the 180 crew. McCheyne is commemorated on the Plymouth Naval Memorial. Lance-Corporal David McCheyne, 7th Queen's Own Cameron Highlanders, died of wounds on 13 March 1917 aged 22 years. He had enlisted in September 1914 and was wounded on 12 March. He is buried in Aubigny Communal Cemetery Extension. Private Alexander Joseph McCheyne, 7th Queen's Own Cameron Highlanders was killed in action on 28 April 1916 aged 19 years. He was the youngest of six brothers serving in the war and had been at the Front since December 1915. He was killed while on guard at headquarters. He had gone to call for help for a wounded comrade when he was struck in the back with a splinter from a shell and was killed instantaneously. He is commemorated on the Loos Memorial. A sister Mary McCheyne, died at Lot-et-Garonne aged 36 years during the German occupation in 1916 while two brothers, John and Frederick, survived the war

There are three men buried in this cemetery who were executed as they had committed offences during Third Ypres and were tried afterwards when their Battalions were in camps near here at the rear of the Salient. Private Thomas Hawkins, 7th Queen's (Royal West Surreys) was already under a suspended sentence of death when he deserted again. He had enlisted in September 1914, aged 16 years and was only 19 when he was executed at 6.53am on 22 November 1917.

Private Arthur Westwood, 8th East Surreys deserted during the Battle of Poelkapalle. He was executed on 23 November 1917.

Private Frederick W. Slade, 2/6th (2nd City of London Rifles) Londons was a stretcher bearer and had refused to go into action during the Battle of Passchendaele on 26 October 1917. He claimed to be suffering from stress but the Medical Officer denied the claim. Hence, he was executed for disobedience on 14 December 1917.

Another man buried here is Serjeant Harry Colley, DCM, 253rd Tunnelling Company, Royal Engineers who was killed by shellfire on 25 November 1917. Colley was originally with the Leicestershires, and enlisted soon after the outbreak of war. The citation for his Distinguished Conduct Medal, won for an act in November 1916, reads 'For conspicuous gallantry in action. He worked at rescue operations under heavy fire in full view of the enemy, thereby saving the lives of three men who were buried.'

Another to win the DCM buried here is Serjeant Harold Fredrick Mayo, 84th Battery, 11th Brigade, Royal Field Artillery, who died on 11 August 1917 aged 27 years. He arrived in France as an acting Bombardier in January 1915 and was awarded the DCM for his gallantry especially for an act on 14 March 1915 when 'after being blown over by a shell, he finished the repairing work on which he was engaged before leaving the spot.'

Another man of note is 2nd Lieutenant Ernest Walter Winton, 2nd Siege Battery, Royal Garrison Artillery, killed in action on 15 December 1917 aged 19 years. He left Cambridge University after two terms to join the army. He joined his Battery on 27 November 1917, and was killed while taking ammunition up to the firing positions when going into action with his Battery for the first time. He had been with his unit for barely two weeks.

| | | |
|---|---|---|
| UK - 437 | Can - 1 | NF – 1 |
| S Afr - 3 | Ger - 1 | WWII - 9 |

Area – 2119 sq mts

**LOCATION**
Bleuet Farm Cemetery is found west of Elverdinge, north of Ieper, on the Elverdinge-Boezinge road. The cemetery is in the fields next to the farm 150m from the road.

# BRANDHOEK MILITARY CEMETERY

**HISTORY**
This cemetery was begun in May 1915 next to a Dressing Station and used until the field was full in July 1917. It was replaced by the New Military Cemetery.

**INFORMATION**
Brandhoek was considered to be within a safe area, out of range of German artillery, during much of the war. It also had the railway to bring wounded troops to sidings nearby.

As a result it became a centre for supplies, camps, Field Ambulances, and naturally, burial grounds. This is, therefore, one of three cemeteries in this small hamlet.

Buried here is Brigadier General Frederick James Heyworth, CB, DSO, MiD, General Staff commanding 3rd Guards Brigade formerly Scots Guards, died on 9 May 1916 aged 53 years. He joined the Scots Guards in December 1883, was promoted to Captain in 1896, and Major in 1900. He served in the South African Wars for which he was awarded the Distinguished Service Order and Mentioned in Despatches. He was made Lieutenant Colonel in 1906 and was commanding the Scots Guards from 1913 until given command of 20th Brigade in November 1914. He had gone up to the front line to inspect a new mine crater blown by the Germans during the night and was killed at 7.00am by a German sniper in 'Muddy Lane' just north of Birr Crossroads east of Ypres. His inscription contains the words 'Djenan', an Arabic name chosen by his wife, which links to his service, early in his career, in 1885 in the Sudan. He was made a Commander of the Order of the Bath posthumously in June 1915.

Lieutenant Colonel James Clark, CB, 9th Argyll and Sutherland Highlanders was killed in action on 10 May 1915 aged 56 years. He received an MA from Glasgow University and graduated in law from Edinburgh University. He was a Deputy Lieutenant of the City of Edinburgh and a chairman of the Edinburgh School Board. In 1911 he was made Companion of the Order of the Bath. He was Colonel of the 9th Royal Scots from its creation in 1904 until 1912. In 1914 he went to France and was killed in action at Hooge leading a counter-attack from Zouave Wood.

Lieutenant Colonel Charles Conyers, 2nd Royal Irish Fusiliers attached 2nd Leinsters, was killed in action on 12 May 1915 aged 46 years. He had just returned to the trenches after an operation for a previous wound when he was killed. His wife was a novelist, writing romantic novels featuring horses and hunting. She describes his death as leading a charge but it was in fact a chaos of attacks and counter attacks that caused heavy casualties amongst the Leinsters that day.

Lieutenant Colonel Arthur Frederick Sargeaunt, Royal Engineers, twice MiD, was killed in action on 31 July 1915 aged 44 years. He joined the army in February 1890, was promoted to Lieutenant in 1893, Captain in 1901 and Major in 1910. He served in the South African Wars and was twice Mentioned in Despatches in 1915. He went to France commanding 12th Field Company, was promoted to Lieutenant Colonel when he was appointed as Commanding Royal Engineer with 14th Division on 12 July 1915. He was killed by shellfire near Zillebeke. His brother, Lieutenant Colonel Herbert Gaussen Sargeaunt, twice MiD, 16th Heavy Artillery Group, Royal Garrison Artillery, was killed in action on 15 June 1917 aged 44 years and is buried in Bailleul Communal Cemetery Extension.

Captain Thomas Barrie Erskine, MC, MiD, 4th Argyll and Sutherland Highlanders attached 1st Gordon Highlanders, was killed in action on 20 July 1915 aged 25 years. He left his studies training to be a Doctor at Glasgow University when the war began. In July 1915 he was awarded the Military Cross for 'gallantry during active operations against the enemy'. Only eight days after this was awarded, his Battalion supported the 4th Middlesex in an assault at Hooge when he was killed. He was posthumously awarded a MA (Hons) degree by the University of Glasgow. His brother, Captain Ralph Erskine, MiD, No. 66 Squadron, Royal Flying Corps and General List, was killed in action aged 25 years when his Sopwith Camel was shot down on 1 January 1918. He was the first British airman to be killed in Italy and is buried in Tezze British Cemetery in Italy. Ralph had won the Scottish, European and World Amateur Featherweight Boxing titles by 1912 among his many sporting skills. His father served in the 7th Gordon Highlanders and Royal Air Force.

Buried here is Captain Henry Evelyn Arthur Platt, MiD, 2nd Company, 1st Coldstream Guards, died on 15 May 1916 aged 32 years. He joined the 19th Hussars in 1903 and was promoted to Captain in 1912. He went to war in 1914 fighting in almost every campaign of 1914 while commanding 'C' Squadron who acted as divisional cavalry for 6th Division. He was gassed in May 1915. Soon after, in October 1915, though the dispute has begun in August, as a consequence of a disagreement with his Major about how good he was at leading and training cavalry men, he transferred to the Coldstream Guards, becoming one of the first cavalry officers to transfer to the infantry. He was Mentioned in Despatches in November 1915. He was killed while part of a night wiring party at Railway Wood. He was trying to help a wounded officer in the party, Lieutenant G B F Ramsden, when he was killed.

Lieutenant Ronald Philip Ochs, 5th attached 4th Middlesex, was killed in action on 26 September 1915 aged 18 years. He was killed in a 2km wide diversionary attack at Hooge to take attention away from the Battle of Loos. Towards midnight on 26-27 September the Middlesex saw a party of Germans in front of them, engaged the enemy and drove them back to their own lines, but this started a 45 minute artillery duel in which Ochs, the Medical Officer, Captain Arthur Ernest Bullock, who is also buried here, and several men were killed.

Lieutenant Arthur Norman Victor Harcourt Ommundsen, Honourable Artillery Company, died on 19 September 1915 aged 37 years. The son of a Norwegian shipping agent and his Scottish wife, Ommundsen worked as a law clerk before joining the British army. He won the King's Prize at the Bisley from which he became a member of the British Shooting team as a Sergeant, exclusively made up of soldiers, who were runners-up to the USA in the military rifle competition at the 1908 London Olympics. At Stockholm in 1912, he earned another silver medal in the same event. He co-authored the book 'Rifles and ammunition and rifle shooting' which was considered the book of its day on marksmanship. His holds a number of patents including one for an 'improved support for use whilst playing cards'.

Captain John Hugh Gunner, 15th Hampshires died on 9 August 1918 aged 34 years. He represented Hampshire in six first class cricket matches in 1906-07. He was mortally wounded in a trench raid and died while being carried back to the British lines. His father also played cricket for Hampshire, though only once.

Buried side by side are Lieutenant Thomas Farquhar Lucas aged 30 years and Captain Edward Arthur Wickson aged 33 years, both 20th Balloon Company, Royal Flying Corps killed on 16 June 1917 when their observation balloon fell to earth. They are buried next to each other.

Among those buried here is 2nd Corporal Jack Whibley, 61st Field Company, Royal Engineers, died 9 August 1915 aged 22 years. His brother Private Alfred Whibley, 22nd (Kensington) Royal Fusiliers, died on 17 February 1917. He is buried at Serre Road Cemetery No. 1 on the Somme. Another brother Carpenter Leo Whibley, died on the SS Orama with the Merchant Navy on 8 June 1940 aged 40 years and is commemorated on the Tower Hill Memorial.

Another to take note of is Gunner Charles William Jenkins, 6th Battery, 40th Brigade, Royal Field Artillery who died on 7 June 1916 aged 15 years.

| | | |
|---|---|---|
| UK - 600 | Aust - 4 | Can – 63 |
| BWI - 2 | Ger – 2 | Unnamed – 4 |
| Area – 3010 sq mts | | |

**LOCATION**

The three Brandhoek cemeteries, about 3km west of Ieper, lie west of Vlamertinge and just south of the road to Poperinge. They are visible from the road and easily accessed from a junction with traffic lights. This is the closest of the three cemeteries to the main road.

# BRANDHOEK NEW MILITARY CEMETERY

## HISTORY

This was begun in July 1917 as the Military Cemetery became full and because the number of casualties from Third Ypres was expected to be high. It was used until closed in August 1917 as the space available was filled and another cemetery opened close by.

## INFORMATION

The cemetery was used for the burial of men who died in the 32nd, 44th and 3rd Australian Casualty Clearing Stations.

Among those buried here is the only man to win the Victoria Cross and Bar in WW1, one of only three men to win a Bar to their VC. Captain Noel Godfrey Chavasse, VC & Bar, DSO, MC, Royal Army Medical Corps, attached 1/10th (Liverpool Scottish) King's (Liverpools) died of wounds on 4 August 1917 aged 32 years. He won the Victoria Cross at Guillemont on the Somme on 9 August 1916. The citation reads 'For most conspicuous bravery and devotion to duty. During an attack he tended the wounded in the open all day, under heavy fire, frequently in view of the enemy. During the following night he searched for wounded on the ground in front of the enemy's lines for four hours. Next day he took one stretcher-bearer to the advanced trenches, and under heavy shell fire carried an urgent case for 500 yards into safety, being wounded in the side by a shell splinter during the journey. The same night he took up a party of twenty volunteers, rescued three wounded men from a shell hole twenty-five yards from the enemy's trench, buried the bodies of two Officers, and collected many identity discs, although fired on by bombs and machine guns. Altogether he saved the lives of some twenty badly wounded men, besides the ordinary cases which passed through his hands. His courage and self-sacrifice were beyond praise.' The Bar was won at the start of the Third Battle of Ypres and awarded posthumously. The citation reads 'For most conspicuous bravery and devotion to duty, when in action. Though severely wounded early in the action whilst carrying a wounded soldier to the Dressing Station, Capt. Chavasse refused to leave his post, and for two days not only continued to perform his duties, but in addition went out repeatedly under heavy fire to search for and attend to the wounded who were lying out. During these searches, although practically without food during this period, worn with fatigue and faint with his wound, he assisted to carry in a number of badly wounded men, over heavy and difficult ground. By his extraordinary energy and inspiring example, he was instrumental in rescuing many wounded who would have otherwise undoubtedly succumbed under the bad weather conditions. This devoted and gallant officer, subsequently died of his wounds.' He was wounded on a number of occasions between the start of the battle on 31 July and receiving the mortal wound on 2 August near Potijze. Before being moved to Brandhoek he was treated by Lieutenant Colonel Arthur Martin-Leake, VC and Bar, the only other man at that time to have a Bar to his VC. He had won the VC in the Boer War in 1902 while serving as a Surgeon Captain in the South African Constabulary attached to the 5th Field Ambulance, and the Bar whilst serving with the Royal Army Medical Corps near Zonnebeke in 1914. This was the only time the two men were at the same place and time. Chavasse died of wounds in No. 32 Casualty Clearing Station, a special hospital for abdominal cases, in Brandhoek. He was awarded the Military Cross as a Lieutenant for actions on 17 June 1915 near Hooge when he went to the front line to tend to the wounded despite orders to stay behind the line. At dusk he got out of the trench and covered all the ground over which the Battalion had advanced and examined every shell-hole until satisfied everyone was accounted for. In August 1915 he was promoted to Captain. He was son of the Bishop of Liverpool who was also founder of St. Peter's College, Oxford. He was identical twin to Christopher Maude Chavasse OBE, MC, Croix de Guerre, Army Chaplain's Department who volunteered early in August 1914 rising to Lieutenant Colonel by 1918. He became Bishop of Rochester in 1940. In 1908, both twins had represented Great Britain in the Olympic Games in the 400m in London. His younger brother Francis Bernard Chavasse was the Medical Officer of the 17th King's (Liverpools) and was awarded a MC. His youngest brother Aidan served with the 11th King's (Liverpools) before transferring also to the 17th Battalion. He was mortally wounded on 3 July 1917 dying a day later but his body was never identified so has no known grave and he is commemorated on the Menin Gate. A cousin Captain Arthur Ryland Chavasse, No. 2 General Hospital, Royal Army Medical Corps died of pneumonia on 12 March 1916 aged 28 years and is buried in Ste. Marie Cemetery, Le Havre. Another cousin, Captain Francis Chavasse Squires, Adjutant 1st Battalion, 23rd Sikh Pioneers died of wounds on 7 July 1915 in Aden and is buried in Maala Cemetery, Aden. A final thought is about the headstone on his grave. Ann Clayton's book on Chavasse tells us that 'When the New Military Cemetery at Brandhoek was laid out by the Imperial War Graves Commission, Noel's headstone was inscribed with the representation of a single Victoria Cross. However, in 1959 the Commonwealth War Graves Commission received information from its Belgian office that a Distinguished Service Order should be credited to Captain Chavasse. When the headstone was replaced in 1975, the DSO was included, but the mistake was soon challenged by visitors to the grave. In 1979 the letters DSO were blotted out by a stone-filling technique, and a complete re-design of the stone was begun. A design with two small VC emblems was approved and was erected over the grave on 28 April 1981.' Not far from the cemetery, near the village church, is a memorial to Captain Chavasse.

Also of note is Private Charles Arundel Rudd, 1/10th King's (Liverpools), who died of wounds on 10 August 1917 aged 20 years. He was Chavasses's batman.

Another here is Captain Frank Rhodes Armitage, DSO, Royal Army Medical Corps attached 232nd Brigade, Royal Field Artillery who was killed in action on 30 July 1917 aged 34 years. He was in a dugout along with Captain C E Hickman, who received serious injuries to the head, when it was hit by a shell. He received the Distinguished Service Order in the New Year's Honours List of January 1917. His younger brother, 2nd Lieutenant Douglas William Armitage, 9th Royal Sussex went missing during the Battle of Loos on 25 September 1915 and is commemorated on the Loos Memorial.

Lieutenant Colonel Thomas Henry Boardman, DSO, 8th Royal Inniskilling Fusiliers who died on 5 August 1917 aged 40 years is buried here. A graduate of Cambridge he became a teacher before the war. In 1908 he became a Lieutenant in the Territorials and in October 1914 was made a Major in the Royal Fusiliers. In late 1915 he was posted with the Regiment to France and saw heavy and continued fighting until September 1916 when he was promoted and transferred to command the 8th Royal Inniskilling Fusiliers. He was awarded the Distinguished Service Order in the 1917 New Year's Honours List for 'distinguished service in the field'. During the Battle of Pilckem Ridge he was seriously wounded late on 4 August, dying of his wounds early the following day.

Lieutenant Colonel James Cosmo Russell, DSO, 9th Hodson's Horse, attached and commanding 6th Cameron Highlanders was killed in action just east of Potijze on 31 July 1917 aged 38 years. He served with the Indian Army from 1902 until he was given command of the Highlanders in March 1916. He was awarded his Distinguished Service Order in the New Year's Honours List in January 1917.

Buried here is Major Gawain Murdoch Bell, DSO, 'A' Company, 11th Hampshires, killed in action on 31 July 1917 aged 40 years. He had been a master at Winchester before the war and left to train this Battalion which became the pioneer Battalion for the 16th (Irish) Division. He became second-in-command of the Battalion and was awarded the Distinguished Service Order in the New Year's Honours List of 1917. He was recommended for the command of a Battalion shortly before his death, but was fatally wounded by German shelling on the Ypres-Menin Road early in the morning whilst overseeing repair work on the road.

UK - 512   Aust - 11   Can – 6
Ger - 28   India – 1   Area – 1254 sq mts

**LOCATION**

Directions are as for the Military Cemetery except that as soon as you leave the Poperinge road turn right to this cemetery which is behind the houses on the right and is reached by a path from the road.

## BRANDHOEK NEW MILITARY CEMETERY No. 3

**HISTORY**

Opened as the New Military Cemetery became full in August 1917, this cemetery was used until May 1918 and was linked to the many local medical units.

**INFORMATION**

See Brandhoek Military Cemetery and Brandhoek New Military Cemetery for further information.

Of the graves here, 286 (25%), are those of artillerymen due to the large number of gun positions that were nearby. Four French graves have been removed.

Among those buried here is Corporal William Bathgate, 113th Field Ambulance, Royal Army Medical Corps who died of wounds on 15 August 1917 aged 31 years and was laid to rest by his brother Sergeant Robert Bathgate, 112th Field Ambulance, Royal Army Medical Corps. Both Field Ambulances were part of the 16th (Irish) Division.

Also here is Lieutenant Colonel Thomas Craik Irving, DSO, MiD, Canadian Engineers Commanding HQ 4th Division who was killed in action on 29 October 1917 aged 38 years. He joined up in September 1914 and had served as Captain and Major with 2nd Field Company in 1st Canadian Division. He was awarded his Distinguished Service Order for his role in the Canadian action at Mount Sorrel in June 1916 and was promoted to Lieutenant Colonel in time for the Third Battles of Ypres. He was apparently writing a letter to his wife when hit in the chest by shrapnel from a bomb dropped from a plane. They attempted to save his life, but their efforts failed and he died at 9:10pm. He was posthumously Mentioned in Despatches.

Lieutenant Colonel Stafford James Somerville, 1st Royal Inniskilling Fusiliers attached 9th Royal Irish Fusiliers, died of wounds on 16 August 1917 aged 46 years. He joined the army in 1890 serving in the Tirah Campaign on the North West Frontier in 1897-8. He became a Captain in 1898 and a Major in 1910. He was at Gallipoli where he briefly took command of his Battalion and was then wounded. He took command of the 9th Royal Irish Fusiliers in March 1917 and was mortally wounded on Hill 35 near Langemark. The eldest of his two sons, Captain Stafford Dudley Somerville, 5th King's Own Yorkshire Light Infantry, was killed in action at Hamel on 5 July 1916, fighting in the trenches recently vacated by the 9th Royal Irish Fusiliers. He is buried in Authuille Military Cemetery.

2nd Lieutenant Richard Douglas Miles, MC, 9th Royal Irish Fusiliers, died of wounds on 17 August 1917 aged 27 years. He was the eldest son of The Honourable Alfred Henry Miles, CMG, DSO, ISO, formerly Collector General of Jamaica. At the outbreak of war, he joined the 31st (Alberta) Canadian Infantry and went to Europe becoming a Company Sergeant-Major in his Battalion. He was then given a commission in the 4th Royal Irish Fusiliers and served in Dublin during the Easter riots in 1916. He was awarded the Military Cross for a special service in the winter campaign of 1916-17. He was mortally wounded on 16 August 1917 with his commanding officer, Lieutenant Colonel Somerville, and three other officers from the Battalion, at Hill 35.

Another buried here is Major Fred Leslie Biddle, DSO, MiD, 4th Battery, 2nd Brigade, Australian Field Artillery who died of wounds on 17 August 1917 aged 31 years. He was Mentioned in Despatches in January 1917 and received his Distinguished Service Award for his calmness under fire at Pozieres from 22-24 July 1916 while acting as liaison officer with the HQ of the Australian 1st Brigade before he was wounded on 24 August. He joined the Citizen's Militia Force artillery as a Gunner and had 10 years' service before being commissioned in October 1910 and promoted to Captain in September 1913. He was promoted to Major in March 1916.

One of four brothers killed in the war is Private Edgar Stooke, 2nd Sherwood Foresters (Notts and Derbys), who died of wounds on 26 April 1918 aged 18 years. Private Frederick Stooke, 3rd Coldstream Guards, was killed in action on 13 April 1918 aged 20 years is commemorated on the Ploegsteert Memorial. Air Mechanic 1st Class Arthur Augustus Stooke, No. 4 Kite Balloon Section, Royal Flying Corps, died on 3 January 1917 aged 27 years and is commemorated on the Arras Flying Services Memorial. Sapper Frank Stooke, 59th Company, Royal Engineers, died of wounds on 16 May 1915 aged 35 years and is buried in Boulogne Eastern Cemetery.

The gates were presented by Mr. G. H. Strutt. His son, Lieutenant Anthony Harold Strutt, 16th (Chatsworth Rifles) Sherwood Foresters, who died of wounds on 27 April 1918, is buried here.

| UK - 851 | Aust - 46 | NZ – 18 |
| --- | --- | --- |
| Can - 54 | S Afr - 5 | BWI - 1 |
| Chinese Labour Corps - 1 | | Unnamed – 1 |
| Area – 2926 sq mts | | |

**LOCATION**

Directions to this cemetery are exactly as for the New Military Cemetery, except this is on the other side of the road, further from the junction. It is not behind any houses.

# BRIDGE HOUSE CEMETERY

**HISTORY**

The cemetery was begun and closed at the end of September 1917, after this area was taken by the British.

**INFORMATION**

All except five graves are men of the 59th (2nd North Midland) Division and almost all died in the Battle of Polygon Wood in the few days from 25-29 September 1917 while attacking St. Juliaan. Bridge House was the name given to the farmhouse close by.

On 8 May 1915 the 84th Brigade held the line which passed through here. South of the road the line ran to Frezenberg and north of the road to Mousetrap Farm. In the German attack the 2nd Cheshires were wiped out losing all three front-line companies and their Battalion headquarters; the 1st Suffolks lost their commanding officer, eleven officers and 432 men. The 1st Monmouthshires, mainly miners, could only muster 120 men that night. The 1/12th (Rangers) Londons were sent up to reinforce the line but only a few men reached the Monmouthshires and only 53 out of 200 men were left by nightfall. The Territorial Battalion had effectively ceased to exist.

Among those buried here is 2nd Lieutenant John George Roe, 3rd attached 2/8th Sherwood Foresters (Notts and Derbys), killed in action on 26 September 1917 aged 21 years. He was the Battalion's intelligence officer and was one of fourteen officers who became casualties in the attack in St. Juliaan.

The single monument to the 1/1st Monmouthshires, and to 2nd Lieutenant Henry Anthony Birrell-Anthony of that Regiment who was killed in action on 8 May 1915, is 700m to the east of Bridge House Cemetery on the south side of a road that leads to the junction where the St. Jan road (N313) joins the St. Juliaan road.

UK - 45        Unnamed - 4        Area – 186 sq mts

### LOCATION

Bridge House Cemetery lies about 4km north-east of Ieper and 1km south of St. Juliaan. It is reached from St. Juliaan by following the road with CWGC signs on the corner. This passes St. Julien D.S. Cemetery immediately and comes to a junction, in about 1km, from which you can see the cemetery almost directly opposite. Alternatively, the old road from Wieltje will bring you to the cemetery.

## BUFFS ROAD CEMETERY

### HISTORY

The cemetery was begun on 31 July 1917 just after this piece of no man's land had been captured, and remained in use until the German Spring Offensive of March 1918. Then it was enlarged after the war with the concentration of graves from the surrounding battlefields.

### INFORMATION

Buffs Road, now called Hoge Zeikenweg, was the name given to the road that runs parallel to, and north of, the new road in the valley. The road ran from the cemetery, through the crossroads 200m to the east where Admiral's Road (Mortelweg) passed through Admiral's Corner (both were named after a naval officer who experimented with bullet proof shields mounted on wheels like a small tank), to the next crossroads, with Boundary Road (Briekestraat), at the corner of New Irish Farm Cemetery.

The cemetery was mainly used by the 11th, 12th and 13th Royal Sussex (1st, 2nd and 3rd South Downs) during the Third Battles of Ypres. One Belgian soldier has been removed while one British officer was brought here from Brielen Churchyard when others were concentrated here.

On 29 April 1915 the 2nd Lancashire Fusiliers took over the line here at Mousetrap Farm which you can see on the ridge to the west and watched an attack by the Sirhind Brigade of the Lahore Division, Indian Army fail. On 2 May incendiary shells and gas, a green yellowish fog, were employed against the British here, causing the Lancashire Fusiliers to abandon the front-line and make their way towards Ypres. However, the trenches were not taken by the Germans due to the lingering gas. Hence, the British were the first to re-occupy the line. The Fusiliers began the day with 33 officers and 1,070 men, they ended it with eight officers and 80 men.

During the German attack Private John 'Jack' Lynn won the Victoria Cross by manning his machine-gun for several hours without a gas mask. Machine-gunners were not part of the chain of command so he would probably not have received the order to withdraw and gas masks were not standard issue at that time. He halted the German advance saving his comrades and was found, barely alive in the trenches, by the Battalion that was sent to re-occupy the line. He had been awarded the Distinguished Conduct Medal and Order of St. George (Russia) for his actions in December 1914. Jack Lynn died of the effects of gas and is buried at Grootebeek Cemetery.

By 24 May the 2nd Royal Dublin Fusiliers took over the line here. When the Germans attacked, again using gas, the Fusiliers, and the 1/9th (Dumbartonshire) Argyll and Sutherland Highlanders stood firm. At the end of the day the Dubliners were ordered to retire, which they did with just one officer and twenty men out of seventeen officers and 650 men.

Among those buried here is Gunner Augustus Dand, 'C' Battery, 290th Brigade, Royal Field Artillery, killed in action on 9 October 1917. His brother, Private Cecil Dand, 4th Essex died at home on 22 May 1916 aged 19 years and is commemorated in the City of London Cemetery and Crematorium, Manor Park, London. Another to lose a brother in the war is Sapper James Thomas Baker, 474th Field Survey Company, Royal Engineers who died on 28 September 1917 aged 28 years. His brother, Lance Serjeant Albert Charles Baker, 2nd Scots Guards was killed in action on 18 December 1914 aged 23 years and is commemorated on the Ploegsteert Memorial.

UK - 265        Aust - 13        Can - 10
S Afr - 1       Unnamed - 86     Area - 1275 sq mts
Special Memorials to ten men whose graves were destroyed by shellfire

### LOCATION

Buffs Road Cemetery lies north-east of Ieper just north of the end of the motorway (A19) and is easily reached from the northern by-pass. Turn off the N38 at the small crossroads just west of the motorway junction onto Mortelweg, reaching the crossroads from which you can see the cemetery to the east. This cemetery has good views of the Salient and would be a pretty, peaceful little cemetery but for the end of the motorway that intrudes upon the environment.

# BUS HOUSE CEMETERY

## HISTORY
This cemetery was begun at the start of the Battle of Messines in June 1917 and remained in use until the end of the Third Battle of Ypres in November 1917. Five men, a soldier who died in January 1915 and four more killed in April 1918, were brought here during the war.

## INFORMATION
The farm next to the cemetery was named after a local wartime estaminet in a farmhouse which was in turn named after a London Omnibus that had broken down here as it was taking troops to the nearby front-line during the frantic days of the First Battle of Ypres in October and November 1914. This was one of 300 London General Omnibus Company B-Type buses in use in France and Flanders in 1914, many still painted bright red as they had been while on service in London. By comparison the French sent troops to the battle-front in taxis from Paris during the Battle of the Marne in September 1914. The cost was as on the meter. It is thought that the bus was carrying the 1/14th (London Scottish) Londons to Wijtschate where they were to become the first full Battalion of Territorial troops in action in the war.

St. Eloi, 200m to the west, was bitterly fought over many times because of its strategic position in controlling the crossroads and the routes to the Messines Ridge and Lille. Mines were blown at 'The Mound' on several occasions.

In February 1915 the 3rd and 4th King's Royal Rifle Corps took part of the German trench system at St. Eloi but lost it soon after. On 14 March the 1st Leinsters briefly retook the trenches suffering heavy casualties of sixteen officers and 257 men. They were Mentioned in Despatches on St. Patrick's Day. Even so, on the next day the 4th Rifle Brigade and Princess Patricia's Canadian Light Infantry had to attack from positions at Bus House and Bedford House Cemeteries respectively. With support from the 2nd King's Shropshire Light Infantry they cleared the Germans from St. Eloi. By October the 1st North Staffordshires had to retake the trenches at 'The Mound' which they did with surprisingly slight losses.

From 27 March to 16 April 1916 the 12th West Yorkshires, 8th East Yorkshires, 4th Royal Fusiliers and 1st Northumberland Fusiliers had to take the craters again. For this attack six mines using 73,000lbs of explosive enabled the Battalions to capture parts of St. Eloi though they suffered heavy casualties. For example, the Royal Fusiliers lost 40 officers and 809 men in the action. Captain, the Reverend, Chaplain, Edward Noel Mellish tended the wounded and rescued men from 27 to 29 March for which he was awarded the Victoria Cross.

At the start of the Battle of Messines on 7 June 1917, the 4th Division attacked from Bus House towards their second objective of the 'Dammstrasse' which is east of the village. They were accompanied by two tanks, as were most of the Divisions during the attack. Put simply, the 'male' had a big naval 6 pounder gun for shells while the 'female' was armed with smaller weapons and machine guns.

In May 1940 the British army tried to defend Ypres as it had in 1914. However, the Germans took the area in just a few days. The men who were killed during the battle on the Ypres-Comines canal, and originally buried where they died, were brought in from the battlefield and isolated communal cemeteries in 1941 for reburial in this cemetery. Among those buried here is Driver Edward Leslie Wright, 594th Mechanical Transport Company attached X Corps Heavy Artillery, Army Service Corps, died of wounds on 3 July 1917 aged 35 years. He was an Associate of the Royal Institute of British Architects who worked in Cardiff and later in Mansfield. He had been at the Front since January 1917. His brother, Captain Henry Gordon Wright, 8th Sherwood Foresters, was killed in action while sniping the Germans on 6 June 1915 at Loker and is buried at Kemmel Chateau Military Cemetery. Also here is Fusilier Stanley Milner, 2nd Royal Scots Fusiliers killed in action 10 May 1940 aged 17 years.

| | | |
|---|---|---|
| UK - 192 | Aust - 10 | NZ – 1 |
| Can - 2 | BWI - 1 | Unnamed - 12 |
| WW2 – 79 (9 unnamed) | | Fr – 2 |

Area – 1558 sq mts

Special Memorials to two British men known to be buried among the unnamed.

## LOCATION
Bus House Cemetery is located on the south side of the St. Eloi-Voormezele road, 400m west of the roundabout in the centre of St. Eloi, which is about 2km south of Ieper.

# BUTTES NEW BRITISH CEMETERY

## HISTORY
This cemetery was created after the war when it was used for the concentration of graves from the battlefields of Zonnebeke and Polygon Wood.

## INFORMATION
Polygon Wood (the 'Polygone de Zonnebeke', or Polygoneveld) was, before 1914, the Belgian Army's firing range, the Buttes providing the cemetery with its name and one of its most distinctive features, the large mound that

dominates the cemetery. The wood was also the site for a riding school and a racecourse.

At the south-east corner of the wood, on the Reutal Ridge, on 24 October 1914, the 2nd Wiltshires were overwhelmed with only a Quarter Master Sergeant-Major and 170 men surviving. Once the Germans were in the wood the 2nd Royal Warwickshires counter-attacked with a Squadron of the Northumberland Hussars Yeomanry in support, the first men of a Territorial unit to see action in the Salient. These were followed by the 2nd Highland Light Infantry and the 2nd Worcestershires who fought north and east to the position of this cemetery clearing the wood of Germans. The Worcestershires were warned not to use bullets, as no trench line existed and they might kill British troops, so they mounted a bayonet charge instead.

By the end of October 1914 men of eleven Battalions and five Brigades had died to hold the wood. The 2nd Royal Warwickshires had lost their commanding officer, Lieutenant-Colonel Walter Latham Loring, killed in action on 23 October, one of three brothers killed in the early months of the war. By the end of the First Battle of Ypres the 2nd Royal Warwickshires numbered one officer, Lieutenant Richard Francis Richardson (who later died of wounds received at Loos in September 1915) and 100 men despite having received a draft of 200 men on 26 October.

On 11 November 1914 a British force of just under 8000 men held up an attack by 17000 German troops, including elite Prussian Guardsmen. The action by the 1st Black Watch, the Scots Guards, the Queen's Own Cameron Highlanders, 1st Northamptonshires, 2nd Oxford & Bucks Light Infantry, 2nd Worcestershires, British and French artillery halted the German attempt to break through the Allied line to capture Ypres.

On 12 November 1914 Brigadier-General Charles Fitzclarence, VC, known to his men as GOC (General Officer Commanding) Menin Road, was killed leading an attack by the 2nd Grenadier Guards and 1st Irish Guards on German trenches near Black Watch Corner. This is at the south-east corner of Polygon Wood marked by a Scottish Memorial to the Black Watch. He was at the time officially the commanding officer of the 1st Brigade which mustered 468 men and five officers out of a strength that should have been 4,000 men and 100 Officers. As his grave was lost Fitzclarence is commemorated on the Menin Gate.

In May 1915, the Battalions holding the wood withdrew as the British line was drawn back after the German gas attack in April. The 2nd King's Own (Royal Lancasters), 1st King's Own Yorkshire Light Infantry and 1/3rd Monmouthshires left the wood so quietly that the Germans were still shelling it the next day thinking they were still there.

The Battle of Polygon Wood, part of Third Ypres, in which this area fell to the 5th Australian Division, was given the dates 26 September to 3rd October 1917. On 26 September a major air battle took place over the wood in which 94 British and German aeroplanes fought for supremacy of the skies. This was repeated on the following day as the British lured the Germans into a trap downing approximately 30 German machines.

On 4 October 1917 fifteen tanks of the 1st Tank Battalion attacked in an easterly direction from Black Watch Corner. The route markers which had been laid out were destroyed, therefore, the unit leader, Captain Clement Robertson, led his tanks into battle on foot. He was killed, and is buried in Oxford Road Cemetery, but gained the first Victoria Cross for a member of the Tank Corps.

The wood was evacuated during the Battles of the Lys in the spring of 1918 but was retaken by the 9th (Scottish) Division on 28 September 1918. It had been completely destroyed and it is thought that many bodies still lie undiscovered within its boundaries.

Among those buried here is Lieutenant Colonel Alan Humphrey Scott, DSO, three times MiD, 56th Australian Infantry, killed in action on 1 October 1917 aged 27 years. He joined the 4th Australian Infantry as a Lieutenant in August 1914 serving in almost all of the major campaigns in which the Australians saw action before his death. He was Mentioned in Despatches in January, June and December 1917. The citation for his Distinguished Service Order reads 'For conspicuous gallantry in the attack on Lone Pine, Gallipoli Peninsula, on 6-7 August 1915. He held on to a very exposed position, till all the wounded had been removed. Later, after a heavy bombing attack in superior force had compelled him to retire, he led a bayonet charge which retook and held the position in face of the enemy's enfilading machine gun fire. This position was of great importance, as linking up the positions captured on either flank.' While standing on top of the Buttes, familiarising the commanding officer who was to take over from Scott's Battalion, he was killed by a bullet that reputedly hit a discarded British helmet on the ground killing Scott and the other officer, Lieutenant Colonel Dudley Turnbull, DSO, three times MiD, Gordon Highlanders commanding 20th Manchesters and also buried here. Turnbull won his DSO as a 2nd Lieutenant leading his Battalion's machine gun section in October 1914. He had been in temporary command of several Battalions as a Captain and Major before he was made Lieutenant Colonel commanding the Manchesters. He had played rugby for London Scottish before the war. There is a bunker in the wood, captured by Scott, that is named after him.

Another holder of the DSO buried here is Major Charles Matthew Kemp, DSO, 21st attached 20th Manchesters, killed in action on 9 October 1917 aged 39 years and originally buried on the south-east edge of the wood. He had lived in South Africa serving with the police before the war and reached the Front in August 1915 as a 2nd Lieutenant, commanding the 21st Manchesters as a Major for a month in May-June 1916. He had been commanding the 20th Manchesters for one day as a successor to Lieutenant-Colonel Turnbull.

Major Gother Robert Carlisle Clarke, MiD, 34th Australian Infantry died on 12 October 1917 aged 42 years. He played cricket seven times for New South Wales from 1899-1902. He enlisted in 1915 when he was made the Regimental Medical Officer having qualified as a Doctor in the 1880's. He arrived in France in 1916 and was killed by shellfire while attending to wounded men outside the Hamburg Pillbox at Tyne Cot. He was Mentioned in Despatches for the action in which he was killed.

Also buried here is Private Leslie Clegg McMurdo, 31st Australian Infantry, killed in action on 26 September 1917 aged 17 years. When he was 16 Leslie attempted to join the South African Army but was refused as he was still at school. He ran away from home and stowed away aboard a ship to Australia where he joined the Australian Imperial Force. He joined his Battalion at the Front on 24 August and just one month later was killed by a German sniper while carrying a wounded comrade back to his lines.

Buried in a separate row near the New Zealand Memorial are the bodies of five Australian soldiers who were discovered in 2006 during work to lay a new gas pipeline. A local well-known amateur archaeologist, Johan Vandewalle, stayed with the remains overnight until the authorities could make the area secure. Two men, Sergeant George Calder, 51st Australian Infantry, killed in action on 30 September 1917 aged 23 years and Private John Hunter, 49th Australian Infantry, killed in action on 26 September 1917 aged 28 years were identified in 2007 using DNA analysis. Calder was positively identified after his 77-year-old great-niece Faye Harris provided a sample. They were the first men, who had been lost and later found on the battlefields, to be identified in this way. A third man of the five, Private George Richard Storey, 51st Australian Infantry, killed in action on 30 September 1917 aged 22 years was identified using the DNA method in 2008. The men had been buried near a Regimental Aid Post when they died. The temporary cemetery, or a part of it, was probably missed by the Exhumation Companies at the end of the war, because a road next to the cemetery had been realigned across the graves. Faye Harris's daughters flew from Australia, along with relatives of Hunter, for the re-burial of the men which took place with full military honours. This DNA work paved the way for the later large scale exhumation and identification that took place at Fromelles.

The cemetery continues to be used for reburials. On 20 July 2016 an unidentified Australian soldier was buried here. His remains were discovered at a farm near Broodseinde in April 2013 and despite a three-year investigation, he was still unidentified. He was given a funeral with full military honours.

UK - 1297        Aust - 564        NZ – 162
Can - 50        KUG - 30
Unnamed - 1677 (over 80% of the total)
Area – 15075 sq mts
Special Memorials to 23 New Zealanders and twelve British men known or believed to be buried among the unnamed.

### New Zealand Memorial to the Missing

At the south-west end of the cemetery is a New Zealand Memorial to the Missing. The Memorial, which is located on the west end of the cemetery, commemorates 378 men of the New Zealand Division who died in the Polygon Wood sector between September 1917 and May 1918, and who have no known grave. Most were lost in 'holding the line', which means occupying the trenches and carrying the many tasks needed to hold the ground taken, while the Germans would be sniping and shelling the Allied troops. This is one of seven memorials in France and Belgium to the New Zealand soldiers whose graves are not known. The memorials are all in cemeteries chosen as appropriate and local to the fighting in which the men died.
NZ - 378

On the Butte is the 5th Australian Division Memorial. In nearby Glencorse Wood a Memorial has been erected to Captain Ewen James Brodie of the 1st Cameron Highlanders who died in the wood during the German attack on 11 November 1914. Glencorse Wood is on the north side of the road from the Menin Road to Black Watch Corner. At Black Watch Corner is the Black Watch Memorial, unveiled in 2014, which commemorates the actions by the 1st Black Watch (Royal Highlanders) and the part played by officers and men in battles in France and Belgium from August 1914 to November 1918.

### LOCATION

Buttes New British Cemetery is on the north-east edge of Polygon Wood which lies nearly 5km east of Ieper and north of the Menin Road and motorway. You can leave the Menin Road at the junction just east of the Bellewaerde Pleasure Park, known in the war as Clapham Junction, where a CWGC sign indicates to the Princess Patricia's Canadian Light Infantry Monument. Once off the Menin Road continue ahead rather than follow north to the PPCLI Monument. Once you cross the motorway turn left and then right at a local café keeping the wood on your right. Once past Polygon Wood Cemetery on the left you will find a large parking area with a safe path to the cemetery entrance. In a beautiful and peaceful location hidden in, and surrounded by, the wood, the cemetery is reached by a cool, dark, walled avenue leading to the contrasting bright island of sunlight. It is possible to walk through the wood, which is owned by the state and now called 'Dien Doel'. Naturally, this can be reached from other directions, notably almost direct from Zonnebeke.

# CABIN HILL CEMETERY

## HISTORY
The cemetery was opened by the 11th Division in June 1917 during the Battle of Messines and used as a front-line cemetery until the German Offensive in March 1918.

## INFORMATION
The 9th (Queen's Royal) Lancers held the line here in late October 1914, though at that point they numbered only 150 men, when the Germans attacked with a numerical advantage of six to one. The Lancers were pushed back, with the other units here, such as 'J' Battery, Royal Horse Artillery, suffering heavy casualties. It remained in German hands until the area was retaken on 7 June 1917. On 10 April 1918 the 10th Royal Warwickshires were in the front-line nearby when they were forced to withdraw by the German attack suffering casualties over the next few days of 450 men before the Germans captured the area on 16 April. The village was recovered for the last time on 28 September 1918.

Among those buried here is Corporal Frederick Ernest Leach, MM & Bar, 59th Australian Infantry, killed in action on 30 November 1917 aged 25 years. As a Private he was recommended for the Distinguished Conduct Medal for his work on 24 March 1917 at Beaumetz and as a Lance Corporal for actions on 26 September 1917 at Polygon Wood. The first was awarded as a Military Medal and the second posthumously as a Bar to his Military Medal. The recommendation that became the Military Medal reads 'Near BEAUMETZ on 24th March, 1917, Private LEACH displayed conspicuous bravery and coolness. During an attack made on the enemy position on the above date, Private LEACH, a Lewis Gunner of the 59th Battalion, pushed his gun forward under heavy shell fire, and established himself just in rear of the shell crater strongly held by the enemy. Although shells were landing practically everywhere except on the gun, Private LEACH continued to pour incessant fire on the crater. As the enemy retired along the SUNKEN ROAD he inflicted heavy casualties on them. His personal example of bravery and coolness was instrumental in enabling the crater to be occupied with few casualties and the fire he brought to bear afforded excellent covering for the waves that subsequently followed.'

UK - 42     Aust - 25     Area - 379 sq mts

## LOCATION
Cabin Hill Cemetery is about 2km south-east of Wijtschate and 1km north-west of Messines. The site is in a small valley near the source of the Blauwepoortebeek on the edge of the Messines Ridge. It is reached from the Messines Road in Wijtschate by taking the turn for Torreken Farm Cemetery and continuing for 1.2km to a cross-roads reached as you start to descend off the ridge. The cemetery is to the left past the farm and 75m from the road in a small hollow. There is a small grassed access path to this cemetery which is unsuitable for vehicles.

# CALVAIRE (ESSEX) MILITARY CEMETERY

## HISTORY
The cemetery was begun in November 1914 and remained in use until July 1916.

## INFORMATION
This area was in British hands for most of the war. It was in German hands from 10 April to 29 September 1918.

This is a good example of a number of cemeteries used in 1914 and 1915 by one or two regiments at a time. As such each Plot, or part of a Plot, is constituted almost entirely of burials from one or two Battalions. The order of burials also gives us an insight into the order in which units were posted to the area. Its dual name comes from the fact that the first burials made in the cemetery were the dead of the 2nd Essex. However, it can also be argued that the name comes from the fact that it is established beside a building known as Essex House.

The burials here are:
- Plot I, Rows A to M - 2nd Essex and 1/2nd Monmouthshires
- Plot I, Row O - 9th Royal Fusiliers and 11th Middlesex
- Plot II - 7th Suffolk and 9th Essex
- Plot III - 6th Buffs (East Kents)
- Plot IV, Rows A to C - 1/7th and 1/8th Worcestershires
- Plot IV, Rows D to M - 11th (Lambeth) Queen's (Royal West Surreys) and 10th Queen's Own (Kent County) (Royal West Kents).

Among those buried here is Captain Robert Laurence Pillman, 'D' Company, 10th Queen's Own (Royal West Kents), who died of wounds on 9 July 1916 aged 23 years. He was a trainee solicitor before the war but was much better known for his sporting skills. A scratch golfer, he won the Gold Medal of the London Solictors Golfing Society. More widely known is the one match in which he represented his country at Rugby Union before representing her on the battlefield. A regular for Blackheath, his only England cap came in the Grand Slam winning victory against France in 1914, a match missed by his brother, Charles, due to a broken leg suffered in the Calcutta Cup against Scotland. He enlisted in the 10th Royal Fusiliers on 1 September 1914, and was commissioned in July 1915; promoted Captain in January 1916 and arrived in France in May 1916. He had volunteered to be Brigade Bombing Officer. He was hit on the parapet, near Armentieres, whilst returning from a late night raid and died from his wounds a few hours later.

Also here is Lance Corporal John Beagin, DCM, 1/7th Worcestershires, who died of wounds on 2 June 1915 aged 23 years. He won his Distinguished Conduct Medal as leader of the Battalion's signals section on 19 April 1915 at Le Gheer less than 1km north-east of here. The citation reads 'The telephone wire having been cut at an isolated post that the enemy were shelling, Lance Corporal Beagin at once voluntarily proceeded 100 yards across an open space under shell and rifle fire, and connected up the post again with a spare instrument.' He risked his life again in June in which action he was mortally wounded.

Private George John Hance, 'C' Company, 9th Essex, was killed in action on 13 July 1915 aged 27 years. His Battalion arrived in France in May 1915 and he is believed to have been killed by a sniper while on sentry duty. Two of his brothers died during the war. Private Edward Elmer Hance, 9th Essex, killed in action on 3 July 1916 aged 26 years at Ovillers on the Somme. On 2 July the 9th Essex was brought in to the front line opposite Ovilliers. They were to attack on the morning of 3 July but as they prepared themselves in the early hours, they came under heavy machine gun fire, when Edward Hance became a casualty. He is buried in Gordon Dump Cemetery. Private Samuel Hance, 23rd (1st Sportsmen's) Royal Fusiliers, formerly Royal Sussex was killed in action on 3 May 1917 aged 30 years and is commemorated on the Arras Memorial.

UK - 218                    Area – 1547 sq mts

**LOCATION**
Calvaire Cemetery is about 1.5km south-east of Ploegsteert, and about 15km south of Ieper. Approximately 1.4km south of Ploegsteert square you will find, on the east side of the road, near a supermarket, a tree of CWGC signs. The road to the north-east, the Chemin de Blanche, leads to Calvaire Cemetery, which is on the south side of the road beyond Gunners Farm Cemetery.

# CANADA FARM CEMETERY

**HISTORY**
The cemetery was begun at the start of the Battle of Messines in June 1917 and mainly used until the end of the Third Battles of Ypres in November, though a few graves were added later.

**INFORMATION**
The farm after which this cemetery is named was used as a Dressing Station from June to October 1917. The cemetery was mostly for the burials of men who died at the Dressing Station in the farm. Most of the men buried here are either of the Royal Artillery (438), or from the Guards Division (144) who fell in the opening attack of Third Ypres.

Buried here is Corporal James Llewellyn Davies, VC, 'C' Company, 13th (1st North Wales Pals) Royal Welsh Fusiliers, killed in action on 31 July 1917 aged 31 years. The citation for his Victoria Cross reads 'For most conspicuous bravery during an attack on the enemy's line, this non-commissioned officer pushed through our own barrage and single-handed attacked a machine gun emplacement, after several men had been killed in attempting to take it. He bayoneted one of the machine gun crew and brought in another man, together with the captured gun. Cpl. Davies, although wounded, then led a bombing party to the assault of a defended house, and killed a sniper who was harassing his Platoon. This gallant non-commissioned officer has since died of wounds received during the attack.'

Also buried here is Lieutenant Colonel Eric Beresford Greer, MC, MiD, 2nd Irish Guards, killed in action on 31 July 1917. He was killed on the Pilkem Ridge near Boezinge. At about 5.30am, Greer, while standing outside his advanced Battalion Headquarters dug-out in the first objective line recently taken from the Germans, was killed instantly by shrapnel. At the time he was the youngest Battalion commander in the Guards. He was awarded the Military Cross for conspicuous gallantry and devotion to duty in the field and was also posthumously Mentioned in Despatches. His brother, Lieutenant Francis St. Leger Greer, MC, 2nd Irish Guards was killed in action on 1 February 1917 aged 23 years and is buried in Heilly Station Cemetery.

Another senior officer buried here is Lieutenant Colonel Edward Byng George Gregge-Hopwood, DSO, twice MiD, 1st Coldstream Guards who died on 20 July 1917 aged 36 years. He joined the Militia in 1898 and served in the South African Wars. He went to France as a Captain in the 2nd Coldstream Guards in August 1914, and was present in the retreat from Mons and all of the Battalion's actions up until being wounded at Givenchy in March 1915. He was awarded the Distinguished Service Order in June 1915 for conspicuous valour and devotion to duty. Having then returned to the Front in July 1915, and again been wounded, he was promoted to Major in June 1916 and, as an Acting Lieutenant-Colonel, was appointed to the command of the 1st Coldstream Guards at the end of 1916. He was killed in the line near Boezinge.

Lieutenant Colonel Frank George Greir Morris, DSO, MiD, 1st Border attached 16th Middlesex, died on 16 August 1917 aged 48 years. He had been at the Western Front for a year arriving from Gallipoli with the 1st Borders and commanded the Middlesex for three days before his death. He was awarded the Distinguished Service Order 'For conspicuous gallantry and devotion to duty when commanding his Battalion in the attack. He personally supervised the consolidation of the position, which he extended beyond the line specified in order to obtain better observation, and inspired his companies with his own determination and bravery.'

Among those buried here is Bombardier Charles Samuel Handley, 136th Heavy Brigade, Royal Garrison Artillery, died on 19 June 1918 aged 30 years. Before the war he had been an Under Butler at Buckingham Palace. He had enlisted in November 1916.

One man buried here was one of four brothers to lose their lives in the war. Gunner Walter Ware, 136th Heavy Battery, Royal Garrison Artillery, died on 15 June 1918 aged 36 years. His brother, Serjeant Wynn Ware, 5th Royal Irish Fusiliers died on 17 September 1915 aged 29 years and is commemorated by a Special Memorial in Green Hill Cemetery in Gallipoli where he is believed to be buried but the exact location has been lost. Another brother Private George Ware, 1st Duke of Cornwall's Light Infantry was killed on 14 September 1914 aged 20 years and is commemorated on the La Ferte-Sous-Jouarre Memorial. A fourth brother, Corporal Jack Ware, 33rd Casualty Clearing Station, Royal Army Medical Corps, died on 20 December 1916 aged 21 years and is buried in Calais Southern Cemetery.

UK - 879     Can - 5     NF – 4
BWI - 19     Area – 3422 sq mts

**LOCATION**
Canada Farm Cemetery is about 2km west of Elverdinge, 3km north-east of Poperinge and 6km north-west of Ieper. It lies north of the Poperinge-Elverdinge road. The cemetery stands in open ground on a slight rise.

# CEMENT HOUSE CEMETERY

### HISTORY
Cement House Cemetery was begun in August 1917 once this area had been captured during the Third Battle of Ypres. It was used by front-line units and Field Ambulances until April 1918 when the Germans retook the area. It was greatly enlarged after the war when graves were brought in from the battlefields and small burial grounds around Langemark and Poelkapelle, mostly dating from the battles of 1917. It is still in use today for the occasional burial of remains found in the Salient.

### INFORMATION
Langemark has given its name to the Battles of 21-24 October 1914 and 16-18 August 1917. The village was in German hands from April 1915 to August 1917 and from April to September 1918. This site saw much fighting in the war particularly in August 1917. On 14 August the 10th and 11th Rifle Brigade attacked from either side of the road towards Langemark. They had to cross the Steenbeek, running almost north-south 400m east of here, a 'stream', swollen by rain and a wide marsh by this time. The Battalions suffered heavy casualties in reaching the mill 200m further on, but as they could not take this heavily defended position they withdrew. On 16 August another attempt was made by the Rifle Brigade with the support of men from the 83rd Field Company, Royal Engineers, who went to deal with the bunker. Through careful planning and preparation the bunker was taken by the 12th Rifle Brigade which enabled the rest of the 60th and 61st Brigades to attack Langemark though the attack was halted by machine-guns in blockhouses on the edge of the village. Cement House was the name used by the British Army for the fortified farm building at the east end of the present cemetery, a bunker that can still be seen. The original burial ground comprises Plot I of this large cemetery, mainly made by the 4th and 17th Divisions, while the rest was made soon after the war forming most of Plots II - XV. Plots XVI, XVII and XVIII originally contained about 500 French graves, but these were removed in 1922. The space has been used for burials made, and still being made, since 1922. For example, a group of eighteen graves were brought here from a graveyard in Maisieres near Mons in the early 1970's, to make way for a new road. Among them was the grave of Captain Jonathan Edward Knowles, 4th Middlesex, a veteran of the South African Wars and one of the earliest British officer casualties of the war. It has also been used to rebury remains from communal cemeteries where their continued care and maintenance could not be guaranteed. Others have been brought here to facilitate building projects. Hence, several plots have been extended to accommodate these graves. As such, I put a caveat on the statistics for those buried here in that they will change.

Among those buried here is Captain The Honourable Patrick Julian Harry Stanley Ogilvy, MC, 1st Irish Guards, died on 9 October 1917 aged 21 years. He was the youngest of the six children of the 6th Earl of Airlie. However, this has to be treated with caution as the different family claims of the Earldom, and the rebellious history of parts of the family, mean that the 6th Earl under some definitions is the 11th Earl by others, notably the Act of Parliament of 26 May 1826 reversing the Act of Attainder of 13 Nov 1715 against members of the family. His father was killed during the South African Wars. Ogilvy was killed in an attack on Houthulst Wood which achieved none of its objectives. Every Company commander was killed or wounded. He had been promoted to Captain on 22 July 1917, but when gazetted, he had been killed.

Captain Thomas Walter Nash, DFC & Bar, Croix de Guerre with Palms (France), No. 204 Squadron, Royal Air Force, was killed on 23 October 1918 aged 27 years and was originally buried in Meerendre Churchyard. He was commissioned as a Sub-Lieutenant in the Royal Naval Air Service in February 1918 which became No. 204 Squadron in the Royal Air Force a month later. He shot down eight German planes between 22 July and 9 October 1918 making him an 'ace'. He was one of five pilots shot down when attacked by a German Squadron of twelve planes. For his actions on 15 August, Nash was awarded the Distinguished Flying Cross, which was gazetted posthumously on 1 November 1918. The citation read 'After four months' excellent service as a pilot this officer was appointed Flight Commander. His brilliant leadership has fully justified his selection. On a recent patrol his formation accounted for six enemy 'planes, he himself destroying two. We suffered no casualties, mainly owing to the skill and judgment displayed by Lieutenant Nash.' A few days later, on 5 November, permission was granted to accept the Croix de Guerre with Palms, awarded by the French government for his services in Flanders. On 1 January 1919 Nash was awarded a posthumous Bar to his Distinguished Flying Cross.

Alongside him is Lieutenant Frederick Gordon Bayley, DFC, No. 204 Squadron, Royal Air Force killed in the same combat on 23 October 1918. His Distinguished Flying Cross was awarded posthumously in the New Year's Honours List of January 1919.

Lieutenant Burnet James, Royal Field Artillery attached No. 7 Squadron, Royal Flying Corps was killed on 26 September 1915 aged 28 years. He made three first class cricket appearances for Gloucestershire in the 1914 season. He joined the 240th (1st South Midland) Brigade, Royal Field Artillery in 1914, with whom he had previously served as a Territorial from 1907-12, but soon moved to the Royal Flying Corps. He was killed with his pilot, 2nd Lieutenant Louis William Yule who is buried beside him, when their plane developed engine trouble and crashed.

Lieutenant Sir Robert (Robin) George Vivian Duff, 2nd Life Guards, was killed in action on 16 October 1914 aged 37 years and was originally buried in Oostnieuwerke Churchyard. His father, who won the Grand National horse race three times, was made a Baronet but died in September 1914 making Robert the 2nd Baronet for a brief period. He was also one of the early pioneers of aviation, and obtained his Aviators Certificate, No. 709, from the Royal Aeronautical Club in 1913. He had been in the Life Guards since 1900 becoming a Lieutenant a year later before joining the Reserve of Officers. The War Diary records that he was killed, shot by a sniper on his first day back with the unit, as his Squadron scouted and approached a farm about 2.5km south-west of Oostnieuwerke that was strongly held by Germans. He was the first officer of his unit to be killed in the war.

Major John Boyd Orr, DSO, 1st Norfolk, died of wounds received in the Battle at Mons on 24 August 1914 aged 43 years, one of the first officers to be killed in the war. He was originally buried in Thulin New Communal Cemetery. He had served in the South African Wars, and was ADC to the Brigadier commanding the Mounted Infantry Brigade from November 1900 to October 1901. He remained in Africa until the start the war. He entered the Norfolk Regiment in October 1893, became Lieutenant in August 1896, Captain in October 1901 and Major in 1913. He was Mentioned in Despatches in September 1901 and received the Distinguished Service Order in 1901 'In recognition of services during the operations in South Africa'. He was awarded the Royal Humane Society's Medal in 1894 for saving from drowning a woman who had attempted suicide by throwing herself into the river in Norwich.

Private Arthur Arnold Crow, 2nd Essex, died on 10 October 1917 aged 25 years. He enlisted as a Private in the 1/28th (Artists Rifles) Londons in August 1914, was made an officer with 5th Loyal North Lancashires in November 1914, a Lieutenant in December and Captain in July 1915. He was appointed Adjutant of the Officers Instruction School, Tunbridge Wells, in the spring of 1915 where he remained until he resigned his Captaincy the Loyal North Lancashires due to ill-health in July 1916 and went to Messines to assist the Church Army in canteen work. The Review of Exemption Act in 1917 meant he could get back to active service. Although he passed the medical and was marked fit for active service, he was still not allowed to go to France as an officer. So, he enlisted as a Private again, this time in the 2nd Essex and went to France in September 1917. He was at the front for a month when he was killed north of Poelkapelle attacking the Passendale Ridge.

Private Victor Leo Hepworth, 50th Australian Infantry, was killed in action on 18 October 1917 aged 17 years and 9 months. He had enlisted in December 1916 arriving in Europe in early 1917. Originally buried on the south-western outskirts of Zonnebeke his body was moved here in 1939. He is the youngest known casualty buried here.

Captain Laurence William Ludovic Cadic, MC, 2nd Essex, died of wounds on 10 October 1917 aged 20 years. He was commissioned into the Essex Regiment in December 1914 joining the 2nd Battalion at the front in March 1915 fighting in the Second Battles of Ypres. He was just 19 years old when he was awarded the Military Cross whilst a Lieutenant for his actions on 1 July 1916, the first day of the Battle of the Somme, on the Serre Road attacking a position known as the Quadrilateral. The citation reads 'For Conspicuous Gallantry in Action. When his CO was wounded, he continued to reorganise the men in the second line of the enemies trench under heavy shell and machine-gun fire. His fine example did much to steady the men under trying circumstances.' He was wounded three times on the Somme. He was mortally wounded on 9 October in an attack north of Poelkapelle. His brother, Captain Bernard Francis Cadic, Royal Garrison Artillery (Transport) died of wounds in hospital at home on 20 August 1916 aged 21 years and is buried in Gravesend Cemetery. Their father, Lieutenant Colonel Louis Stephen Cadic served with the Royal Engineers during the war.

Approximately 400m to the east of this cemetery, on the road to Langemark, is the Memorial to the 20th (Light) Division who captured the village on 16 August 1917. It is 600m from the traffic lights in the centre of Langemark. Closer to this cemetery, on the bridge over the Steenbeek, is the small Memorial to the Belgian forces who captured the village in 1918.

About 300m south-east of this cemetery on the road to Boezinge is the Welsh Memorial Park unveiled in August 2014 with its magnificent red dragon. It is a memorial to all men and women of Welsh origin who served in the war as well as the non-Welsh soldiers serving in Welsh units. It is the first Welsh war memorial built in Belgian Flanders.

Concentrated here:

Asquillies Churchyard – situated about 5km south of Mons and 100km south-west of here, it contained the graves of eleven British soldiers who were killed in November 1918.

Audregnies Churchyard – situated about 10km south-west of Mons and 100km south-east of here, it contained the graves of eight British soldiers killed in August 1914 and one in November 1918.

Elverdinghe Churchyard – located about 4km south-west of here it contained the graves of nine British soldiers killed in October 1914.

Hensies Churchyard – located about 10km west of Mons and 100km south-east of here, it contained the graves of one Canadian and three British soldiers who died in November 1918 and one British soldier who died in August 1914.

Heule Churchyard – situated in what is now a suburb of Kortrijk, this is 30km east of here and contained the graves of six British soldiers and one unidentified airman buried in October 1918.

Maisieres Communal Cemetery – located on the northern edge of Mons which is about 110km south-east of here. It contained the graves of sixteen British soldiers buried in August 1914.

Meerendre Churchyard – located on the western edge of Ghent about 60km north-east of here, it contained the graves of four Royal Air Force officers buried in October 1918.

Oostnieuwerke Churchyard – situated about 10km north-east of here, it contained the graves of five Canadian and five British soldiers buried in April 1915 and one British officer buried in October 1914.

Pheasant Trench Cemetery, Langemark – located in the fields a little east of Langemark village and about 1.5km east of here. Pheasant Trench and Pheasant Farm were taken by the 51st (Highland) Division on 20 September 1917, but the cemetery was begun two months later. It contained the graves of fourteen British soldiers.

Proven Churchyard – located about 12km west of here, it contained the graves of one Canadian officer and three British soldiers.

Quaregnon Communal Cemetery - situated about 5km south-west of Mons 100km south-east of here, it contained the graves of eight British soldiers buried in 1914.

Rolleghem Churchyard – located on the southern edge of Kortrijk and 20km south-west of here, it contained the graves of one Royal Air Force officer and four British soldiers buried in 1918.

Thulin New Communal Cemetery - situated about 15km south-west of Mons and 100km south-east of here, it contained the graves of eight British soldiers buried in August 1914 and two Royal Air Force officers buried in October 1918.

Winkel St. Eloi Churchyard – located about 10km east of here, it contained the graves of 30 British soldiers and four men from Newfoundland buried in October 1918.

| | | |
|---|---|---|
| UK - 3472 | Aust - 19 | NZ - 10 |
| Can - 58 | NF – 14 | S Afr - 1 |
| Guernsey - 5 | Fr - 1 | Ger - 1 |
| Unnamed - 2425 | | KUG - 1 |

WWII - 22 (UK – 20, Aust – 1, Can-1, Unnamed – 5)

Area – 9705 sq mts

Special Memorials to five British men and three Newfoundlanders believed to be buried among the unnamed.

Special Memorials to three men of the 15th (Nottingham Pals) Sherwood Foresters buried in Pheasant Trench Cemetery but whose graves are lost.

**LOCATION**

The cemetery is on the south side of the Langemark-Boezinge road about 600m west of the centre of Langemark. This is about 5km north of Ieper.

## CHESTER FARM CEMETERY

**HISTORY**

This cemetery was begun in March 1915 and used as a front-line cemetery until November 1917.

**INFORMATION**

Most of those buried here are from fighting in the wooded area known as 'The Bluff' which is across the road on the hill next to the old Ypres-Comines Canal. It is now possible to take a pleasant walk along the old canal and 'The Bluff' through to Pallingbeek Park.

Chester Farm was the name given to a farm about 1km south of Blauwepoort Farm, on the road from Zillebeke to Voormezele. This is an example of the regimental cemeteries in use early in the war as men of the same regiment are buried in the same Plot even though they may have died months apart. For example, there are ninety-two men of the 2nd Manchesters in Plot I.

Rifleman Ernest Elgar Gordon Miles, 1/18th (London Irish Rifles) Londons died on 12 June 1917 aged 17 years. While the CWGC has him as 17, his baptism which took place in August 1900 and the Birth Registration Index, which has him recorded in the July to September 1900 quarter, indicate that Miles may have been 16 when he died just short of his 17th birthday. Another young soldier is Private Alfred Bootham, 2nd Manchesters who died on 9 June 1915 aged 16 years. He had been at the Front since December 1915.

Also of note is Lieutenant Ernest Stafford Carlos, 8th Buffs (East Kents) who died on 14 June 1917 aged 34 years. He was a painter and war artist who had exhibited at the Royal Academy and whose work was reproduced by the Independent Labour Party in some of their election material. He is best known for his works depicting the early days of the Scouting Movement. At the start of the war in 1914, Carlos volunteered for the Army, but was rejected on health grounds. He succeeded in his second application and became a Private in the 1/16th (Queen's Westminster Rifles) Londons but was commissioned into the 8th Buffs as a Lieutenant in 1916. He was killed in action during the Battle of Messines on 14 or 15 June 1917 while his unit was assaulting a German held position known as 'Buff's Bank'.

UK - 306    Aust - 21    Can – 87
Ger – 4    Unnamed - 7

Special Memorials to five British men and one Canadian known or believed to be buried here but whose graves were lost.

### LOCATION
Chester Farm Cemetery is located about 2.5km south of Ieper, west of the Comines road between Zillebeke and St. Eloi. The cemetery is on the right 1.3km from the Comines road or 500m from the Ieper-St. Eloi and Messines road, though the access here is by a smaller road.

# COLNE VALLEY CEMETERY

### HISTORY
The cemetery was begun in July 1915 and remained in use until February 1916.

### INFORMATION
The oldest of three graveyards in the vicinity, Colne Valley Cemetery was begun by Territorial Battalions of the 49th (West Riding) Division. Colne Valley, Skipton Road and Huddersfield Road were names given to trenches by the 49th Division when they held the line here, from which the cemetery gets its name, in July 1915.

The Germans reached the site of this cemetery by the evening of 22 April 1915 on the day of the first German gas attack as they exploited a gap of 5000m in the line from Colne Valley to St. Juliaan. At one point on the night of 22 April a Staff officer from the 1st Canadian Division's headquarters found a French machine-gun crew at Fusilier Farm, just south of here, who claimed that they were the front-line - this was probably close to being the truth.

A British attack on 23 April through the position of this cemetery failed to regain any ground but cost heavy casualties for the 1st York and Lancasters who lost their commanding officer and 425 men, while the 2nd East Yorkshires lost seven officers and 280 men.

By July 1917 this area was in no man's land until it was captured at the start of the Third Battle of Ypres.

Those buried here come from three regiments, the Duke of Wellington's who fell in July and August 1915, the Rifle Brigade who were killed in December 1915 and January 1916, and King's Royal Rifle Corps dead of January and February 1916. This gives a good reflection of the units holding the front-line here during that period.

An example of the fact that the Salient still has some surprises today was provided in February 1992. A farmer ploughing a field on his tractor just west of the cemetery fell into a World War I British communications centre eight metres below the surface. The telephone exchange had twelve rooms containing tables and chairs, bayonets and rifles, communications equipment and a tool machine room. This type of exciting find is becoming increasingly rare though smaller finds are not yet uncommon.

Among those buried here is Captain Maynard Percy Andrews, 'A' Company, 1/4th Duke of Wellington's, MiD, killed in action on 15 August 1915 aged 44 years. He was a teacher of modern languages in Germany and France, then at Leicester, Bolton and Lancing College but had also been a cowboy in the USA during the 1890's. In 1911 he became Headmaster of the Hipperholme Grammar School near Halifax. He had joined his Territorial Battalion on his arrival in Yorkshire having some previous experience so became a Lieutenant soon after taking up his post in Hipperholme. He was made a Captain in October 1914 arriving at the Front in April 1915. He was shot in the throat and killed while helping his Company's stretcher-bearers carry wounded men across no-man's land. He is buried with some of those he was trying to rescue. He was Mentioned in Despatches in January 1916.

UK - 47    Unnamed - 4    Area – 319 sq mts

**LOCATION**

Colne Valley Cemetery lies about 2km north of the centre of Ieper, south-east of Boezinge, and east of the canal and on the eastern edge of industrial developments. It is reached most easily by taking the road south from the French Memorial on the Boezinge-Langemark road. The cemetery is on the right below the level of the road.

# CROONAERT CHAPEL CEMETERY

**HISTORY**

The cemetery was begun by the 19th Division Burial Officer in June 1917, and used until the following November. Two further burials were made in April 1918 and January 1919.

**INFORMATION**

The cemetery was named after a nearby shrine that was was in no man's land before the Battle of Messines. It was begun by the 19th (Western/Butterfly) Division in June 1917 after this part of no man's land had been captured. There were 51 Germans buried here, who were killed in the Battle of Messines, but they were removed after the war.

On 31 October 1914 the French pushed back the Bavarians into the wood nearby. On 5 November 1914 Captain Hoffman of the 16th Bavarian Reserve Infantry Regiment lay in the open in front of the wood so a young Corporal crawled out of the wood to rescue him. The Captain died of his wounds but the Corporal developed a sense of his own infallibility, immortality and destiny. He received the Iron Cross from the Kaiser for his actions, the first of two he was to win in the war. He was Adolph Hitler who subsequently painted 'Painting from Croonaert'. He returned here on 1 June 1940 as Leader of the German Reich.

The wood was known to the Allies as Croonaert Wood and to the Germans as 'Bayernwald' because of the Bavarian troops stationed there.

Among those buried here is 2nd Lieutenant Frank Bannatyne Gadsdon, 9th Cheshires, killed in action on 7 June 1917 aged 22 years. He enlisted with his elder brother as a Private in the Honourable Artillery Company in November 1914 and went with them to France in April 1915. He was commissioned into the 9th Cheshires in January 1916. His death came as his Battalion attacked from approximately this position to Onraet Farm and Wood about 1km south-east of here.

Where the path to the cemetery leaves the road there is a Memorial to both Lieutenant Lasnier, as well as the eleven non-commissioned officers, 174 Corporals and the men of the 1st French Battalion of Light Infantry who died here between 3 and 15 November 1914.

About 100m to the south-east Hollandescheschur Farm had been turned into a German machine-gun redoubt under which a mine was exploded on the first day of the Battle of Messines. It was on a high point under which three mines had been dug by the 250th Tunnelling Company, Royal Engineers. A total of 67,600lbs of explosive was set off enabling a successful British advance. Nearby are the Bayernwald Trenches, a set of reconstructed German trenches which are built to show how some German trenches looked during the war. The location gives a good idea of the view the Germans had over the British as much as an insight in the archaeology of German trenches. The Passendale Museum in Zonnebeke also has re-constructed trenches designed to give a good understanding of contrasting trench design and construction, which also helps to give an insight into the political motivation of trench building. Tickets to enter the Bayernwald trenches are available from the Tourist Office in Kemmel.

UK – 74  Chinese Labour Corps – 1
Unnamed – 7  Area – 455 sq mts

**LOCATION**

Croonaert Chapel Cemetery is found 6km south of Ieper, about 2km north of Wijtschate on the road to Voormezele which leaves Wijtschate town square from the north-west corner. The CWGC website says 'Visitors to this site should note a 200m grassed access path which is unsuitable for vehicles.' The parking for the Bayernwald Trenches is a good place to park for this cemetery.

# DERRY HOUSE CEMETERY No. 2

**HISTORY**

This cemetery was begun in June 1917, during the Battle of Messines, after this area was captured from the Germans. It was used as a front-line cemetery until December 1917, and then again in October 1918.

**INFORMATION**

Wijtschate was in German hands from 1914 until it was captured on 7 June 1917 by men of the Catholic 16th (Irish) Division and Protestant 36th (Ulster) Division during the Battle of Messines. The 1st Wiltshires held the line nearby until forced to withdraw on 10 April 1918 when the Germans attacked. It fell into German hands on 16 April

1918. The village changed hands for the last time on 28 September.

The cemetery was begun by the 11th (Northern) Division among the ruins of a farm after which it was named by soldiers of the Royal Irish Rifles and was last used by the 2/14th (2nd London Scottish) Londons. This cemetery was the second of two created in the vicinity though Derry House No. 1 Cemetery no longer exists. It has two distinct sections separated by a neck of land in which stands the Cross of Sacrifice. Most of the Australians buried here were from the 47th Australian Infantry. Within the cemetery are the remains of a concrete command post built by engineers of the 37th Division in July 1917.

There is an excellent example of the nature of history and how 'facts' suffer as time passes. I give several examples of errors elsewhere of which I have been guilty, but this is not one of mine. There are two men buried here named Booth. One is Private George Booth, 'B' Company, 11th Royal Warwickshires, killed in action on 22 July 1917 aged 24 years. His CWGC entry says he was son of Ann Isabella Booth from Gateshead, and the late John Booth. Also here is Private Thomas Rodger Booth, 8th Duke of Wellington's, who was killed on 10 June 1917 aged 32 years. He was from West Yorkshire near Huddersfield and was married in 1910. You can find, as I did in doing this research, several sources talking of two Booth brothers being buried in this cemetery when referring to these men. However, they don't seem to be brothers as they have different recorded backgrounds. That intrigued me, so I endeavored to find if either had a brother killed in the war. I found Private Thomas Booth, 10th West Yorkshires, killed on 22 April 1918 aged 22 years and commemorated on the Pozieres Memorial on the Somme. His CWGC entry says he was the son of Ann Isabella Booth from Gateshead, and the late John Booth. As you can see he and George are brothers, though not buried together. Easy mistake to make as we have two Thomas Booth's involved, but a wonderful example of how errors, such as I have executed in the past and will no doubt continue to commit, can be made.

Also here is Captain Wilfrid Thomas Chaning-Pearce, MC, Royal Army Medical Corps attached 18th (2nd Liverpool Pals) King's (Liverpools), killed on 1 October 1917 aged 32 years. Before the war, after gaining his medical qualifications, he held the posts of obstetric resident and house anaesthetist at Guy's Hospital, and of house-surgeon to the West London Hospital and to the Croydon General Hospital. When the war began he joined the Royal Army Medical Corps in October 1914 as a Lieutenant arriving in France in May 1915 and becoming a Captain in October 1915. He was awarded the Military Cross for actions in September 1917 just before his death 'For conspicuous gallantry and devotion to duty in attending to wounded men belonging to nine different Battalions under heavy and continuous shell fire. His aid post was the only one in the vicinity in such a forward position, and he worked continuously and without rest until all the wounded had been attended to, displaying splendid devotion to duty.' This was gazetted in January 1918. Wilfred was shot by a German at close range while carrying out his duty.

UK - 126        Aust - 37        Area – 1673 sq mts

**LOCATION**

This cemetery is about 8km south of Ieper and 1km south-east of Wijtschate. It is reached from a crossroads on the Armentieres road in Wijtschate with CWGC signs on the corner. Turn east onto Houtemstraat and follow the signs at the next fork onto Krommestraat heading south for 400m. As you crest the ridge you can see the cemetery 100m to your left.

## DICKEBUSCH OLD MILITARY CEMETERY

**HISTORY**

Begun as a front-line cemetery and used from January to March 1915, it was closed once the space was filled. The New Cemetery and the Extension, which are situated close by, provided extra space for burials in the village.

**INFORMATION**

The village was used for a number of base camps, for example the 1/16th (Queen's Westminster Rifles) Londons were here in 1917 before moving to the Front during Third Ypres. As were the 19th and 248th Machine Gun Companies of the 33rd Division who moved from billets in Dikkebus and Watou to various front-line positions at the beginning of the Battle of the Menin Road on 20 September 1917. At the start of the attack two sections of the 248th were wiped out. Even so, the machine-gun companies helped in taking Inverness Copse, Dumbarton Lakes and Tower Hamlets on 20 and 21 September.

At first view, one wonders why it was considered that the available space in this cemetery was full, and why there was a need for new cemeteries as early as they were begun, but seventy-eight French graves have been removed which accounts for the space now visible. Some of this space was taken up by the burial of ten British men who died in the 1939-45 war. These burials all date from the retreat to Dunkirk in May 1940.

Dikkebus churchyard used to contain CWGC graves but most were removed shortly after the war. One Canadian and three British officers who died in 1915 were not removed until February 1962.

Lyn Macdonald in 'They Called it Passchendaele' tells us that Pastor van Walleghem, of Dikkebus church, visited a scale model of the Messines Ridge which had been made on the slopes of the Scherpenberg to train officers who were to be involved in the attack at the start of the Battle of Messines. He toured this model with the Dean of De Klijte church without any challenge by the British, so much for security!

Among those buried here is Captain Denzel Onslow Cochrane Newton, MVO, Order of the Rising Sun (Japan), Princess Patricia's Canadian Light Infantry (Eastern Ontario Regiment) who died on 9 January 1915 aged 35 years. He was originally buried in Dikkebus Churchyard and was one of those moved here in 1962. He had served with the Bedford and Middlesex regiments in the 1890's, saw service in the South African Wars and was made a Captain in 1910. He served as a staff Officer for Earl Grey, the Governor General of Canada for which he was made a Member of the Victorian Order in July 1908, and served the Duke of Connaught when he was Governor General of Canada before joining the PPCLI as one of the first in September 1914. He was the first PPCLI officer to be killed in the war when he became lost between two outposts and wandered into no man's land. On trying to return to his unit's trenches he was challenged by a sentry. He did not hear the challenge and was shot by the sentry who was following standard orders. As his target cried out in pain the appalled sentry recognised the voice of his officer and without hesitation climbed over the parapet and pulled Newton to safety, but Newton died of his wounds.

Commemorated by a Special Memorial is Captain Roger Charles Noel Bellingham, MiD, 37th Battery, Royal Field Artillery, who died on 4 March 1915 aged 30 years. He was also originally buried in Dikkibus Churchyard but the grave has been lost. He was commissioned in December 1903 and made a Lieutenant in 1906. His father was the fourth baronet, his brother the fifth and his son the sixth. He held the office of Aide-de-Camp to the Lord-Lieutenant of Ireland between 1912 and 1914 when he was on the Special Reserve of Officers. He was Mentioned in Despatches in June 1915 and was found dead in his bed after a weeks hard service.

UK - 43    Can - 3    Ger – 1
Unnamed – 2    WW2 – 10 (1 unnamed)
Area - 995 sq mts

**LOCATION**
The cemeteries in Dikkebus are on the eastern edge of the village which is about 3.5km south-west of Ieper. The Old Cemetery is located behind the church 100m east of the N375 to Loker.

## DICKEBUSCH NEW MILITARY CEMETERY

**HISTORY**
This cemetery was begun in February 1915, as the Old Cemetery was considered to be full, and used until May 1917 when the space here was also filled and the Extension begun. However, four more burials were made in March and April 1918.

**INFORMATION**
See Dickebusch Old Military Cemetery.
The New Cemetery contains the War Stone while the Extension opposite contains the Cross of Sacrifice. Of the men buried here 92 are from artillery units reflecting the nature of activity in the village for much of the war as Dikkebus was usually well behind the front-lines.

A senior officer buried here is Lieutenant Colonel James William Alston, 2nd Royal Irish Rifles who was killed in action on 15 April 1915 aged 41 years. He had commanded the Battalion since November 1914 though he had gone to France earlier that month as a Major in the 1st Royal Irish Rifles. He was killed by a bullet deflected through a sandbag while observing from a forward position in the front-line near this village.

Lance-Corporal Joseph Stanley Victor Fox of the 1st Wiltshires was executed on 20 April 1915 after being convicted of desertion. He joined the Reserve Battalion of the Wiltshires in 1911 and was called up in August 1914 landing in France on 14 August as a member of the 3rd Cyclist Company, 3rd Infantry Division. During the fighting in October 1914, elements of the 3rd Cyclist Company, including Fox, were moving along a canal when they were attacked by the Germans and forced to abandon their cycles in order to fight back. When they reached their Company HQ they were ordered to retrieve the bicycles. Fox's had been destroyed so he, the Lance-Corporal, sent the men with bikes back to their unit. He did not follow and was absent until February 1915 when he was challenged and then arrested by an officer. At his Court Martial Fox stated that he had been unable to find his unit that day and that when he had been away for a while he had become scared of returning because he had heard that men were being shot for absenteeism. After a fifteen minute hearing he was found guilty and sentenced to death. On hearing the news of his son's death his father immediately enlisted. His brother was already a prisoner of war. Both survived the war to learn the truth of Fox's death.

Among those buried here is Captain Percy William Norman Fraser, DSO, MiD, 2nd Cameron Highlanders who died on 22 February 1915 aged 36 years. He joined his regiment in April 1898, was promoted to Lieutenant one year later and to Captain in April 1902. He served on the Nile Expedition in 1898 and saw action in the South African Wars where he was ADC to Major-General Sir Bruce Hamilton, KCB and acted as Staff Lieutenant at Headquarters as well as being involved in several actions. For his service in South Africa he was awarded the Distinguished Service Order and Mentioned in Despatches. He went on to serve in East Africa where he became a Major before joining the Reserve of Officers. He reverted to Captain to get to the Front.

Another man buried here is Lance Corporal Kenneth Weir, DCM, MM, 7th (British Columbia) Canadian Infantry who died of wounds on 20 April 1916 aged 26 years. The citation for his Distinguished Conduct Medal reads 'For conspicuous gallantry and resource near Messines on the night of the 16th/17th November, 1915. Corporals Babcock, Odium and Weir and Lance-Corporal Berry worked for 4 hours on a bright moonlight night cutting wire close to a heavily manned German trench. They also assisted in placing a bridge over the Douve river about 16 yards from the German parapet, and guided bombing parties through the lanes they had cut. It was largely due to their coolness and resource that the attack was a success.' He had enlisted into the 47th Canadian Infantry in May 1915. The citation for his Military Medal reads 'For gallantry near la Petite Douve on the night of January 30th, 1916 when, although wounded, he voluntarily returned to the front trenches to rescue his leader Lieutenant Owen. His record has been that of consistent courage and devotion to duty extending over months.' It is reported in the Toronto Star that he was promoted to Lieutenant in the field at the same time as winning his Military Medal, but this is not what is recorded by the CWGC or Canadian Department of Veterans Affairs.

Also here is Gunner Alexander George Mackenzie, 20th Trench Mortar Battery, Trench Howitzer School, Royal Garrison Artillery who died of wounds on 4 April 1915 aged 16 years.

Notable are Private Cyril Charles Hill, 65448, aged 19 years and Private Horace E K Hill, 65449, aged 22 years, both 24th Canadian Infantry and both killed on 30 April 1916. The brothers had enlisted together, trained together and died together on the same day finally being buried side by side. They were killed, among twelve others, by German shelling of their positions nearby.

Another burial of note is Lieutenant Robert William Sterling, 1st Royal Scots Fusiliers killed in action on 23 April 1915 aged 21 years. He was a war poet who also wrote many poems praising his Oxford College, Pembroke. He was commissioned at the start of the war and, after training, arrived in Ypres in February 1915 where the Battalion spent their time in and out of trenches around St. Eloi. In early April Sterling was in hospital with influenza but returned to his unit on 18 April just as the Germans launched their campaign now known as Second Ypres. Sterling was killed at the end of a day holding a line of trench with just fifteen men against the Germans.

UK - 529   Aust - 11   Can - 84
Unnamed – 8
Area – Approx. 3000 sq mts, 4080 sq mts with the extension

**LOCATION**
Directions for this cemetery are the same as those for the Old Cemetery until you pass the church at which point continue on the road to Vierstraat. The New Military and New Military Extension cemeteries are on either side of the road 100m east of the church.

## DICKEBUSCH NEW MILITARY CEMETERY EXTENSION

**HISTORY**
The extension was used from May 1917 until January 1918 as the space in the Old and New Military Cemeteries had been filled.

**INFORMATION**
See Dickebusch Old Military Cemetery.

Dickebusch New Military Cemetery Extension lies opposite to the New Military Cemetery. The two are usually considered to be one, for example the Extension has the Cross of Sacrifice and the New Cemetery has the War Stone. They are only a short distance from the church and the Old Cemetery.

Of the men buried here 260 were from Artillery units. 'C' Battery, 2nd City of Edinburgh Brigade, Royal Artillery, were resting nearby in 1917 when a shell landed in the middle of their unit as they fed their horses. Nine men were killed, many wounded and the Battery ceased to exist.

A senior officer buried here is Lieutenant Colonel Harold Thomas Belcher, DSO, MiD, Order of St Anne 3rd Class (Russia), 52nd Brigade, Royal Field Artillery killed in action on 8 July 1917 aged 42 years. He joined the Royal Artillery from Woolwich in 1895 becoming a Lieutenant in 1898, Captain in 1901 and Major in 1912. He served in the South

African Wars being wounded, Mentioned in Despatches and awarded the Distinguished Service Order. He served in India and then worked at Woolwich from 1910-14. He went to France in September 1915 and was made Lieutenant-Colonel in January 1916. His brother, Captain Gordon Belcher, MC, 3rd attached 'B' Company, 1st Royal Berkshires was killed in action between 15 and 17 May 1915 and is buried in Rue-Des-Berceaux Military Cemetery. He played one first class cricket match for Hampshire, but was bowled in both innings for a duck. Another brother, Major Raymond Douglas Belcher, DSO, MC, 'C' Battery, 63rd Brigade, Royal Field Artillery, died of wounds on 7 December 1917 aged 34 years. He was awarded the DSO for his leadership in the Battle of Cambrai during which he was mortally wounded.

Another senior officer here is Lieutenant Colonel Wigram Clifford, DSO, MiD, 1st attached 10th Northumberland Fusiliers who died on 20 June 1917 aged 41 years. He joined the Loyal North Lancashires from Sandhurst in 1898 and was promoted to Lieutenant in April 1899. He served in the South African Wars being wounded, Mentioned in Despatches and awarded the Distinguished Service Order. He was then promoted to Captain and joined the Northumberland Fusiliers. He served in India and went with the Fusiliers to France in 1914 being promoted to Major in September 1915. He commanded the 2/7th Duke of Wellington's from 20 September 1916 to 21 March 1917 before returning to the Fusiliers.

Another here is Major Kenneth Mitchell Potter, DSO, MiD, 'D' Battery, 52nd Brigade, Royal Field Artillery, who died on 8 June 1917 aged 35 years. He was commissioned in July 1901, promoted to Lieutenant in 1904, Captain in July 1914 and Major in November 1915. His Distinguished Service Order was awarded for gallantry on the night of 1 June 1917 when he restored order during shelling and a gas attack. He had to remove his gas-mask but saved the lives of his men before he collapsed from the effects of gas and died.

| UK - 520 | Aust - 24 | Can - 2 |
| S Afr - 1 | Ger - 1 | Unnamed - 5 |

Area – approx. 1080 sq mts, 4080 sq mts with the New Military cemetery

**LOCATION**
Directions are as for Dickebusch New Military Cemetery.

# DIVISIONAL CEMETERY

**HISTORY**
The cemetery was used from April 1915 until May 1916. It was used again during Third Ypres in 1917 when mainly men of artillery units were buried here.

**INFORMATION**
The cemetery was created in 1914 by Belgian troops before the British began to use it. There are 23 men of the Duke of Wellington's (West Riding) Regiment, who died in the German gas attack at Hill 60 on 5 May 1915, buried in a collective grave at Row C, grave 18. Three Belgian graves have been removed.

Among those buried here is Driver Horace 'Pompey' Falconer Cobb, MiD, 4th (Howitzer) Battery, New Zealand Field Artillery who was killed in action on 11 October 1917 aged 28 years. While it was not unknown for 'other ranks' to be Mentioned in Despatches, it was unusual. So, this is a rare occurrence and great to see. The citation, dated 1 June 1917, reads 'Operations from 20th September 1916 to 26th February 1917. During the period that the New Zealand Artillery was at the Somme this N.C.O. displayed great courage under fire. On one occasion he guided ammunition wagons to the advanced position of the Battery in Devil's Valley, five hundred yards west of Delville Wood, when the roads were almost impassable owing to heavy shelling. Again on a later date he acted as guide and showed great courage and resource in guiding his wagons successfully through heavy barrage fire and in helping teams in distress. His gallantry and devotion to duty were an example to the other men.' In Egypt he transferred to the 4th Battery, New Zealand Field Artillery, thinking that he would have a better chance of reaching Gallipoli, but as he was in charge of horses he never landed. He was killed while leading a gun up to an exposed position in support of the infantry.

One buried here to lose brothers in the war is Gunner John Brennan, New Zealand Field Artillery, killed on 11 October 1917. He left New Zealand in April 1915 as a Trooper with the Wellington Mounted Rifles. His brother, Private William Brennan, 1st Otago Regiment, NZEF, was killed on 29 June 1916 aged 21 years and is buried in Cite Bonjean Military Cemetery about 10km south of here. Another brother, Lance Corporal Richard Mortimer Brennan, 1st Otago Regiment, NZEF, was killed on 8 October 1918 aged 21 years and is buried in Marcoing British Cemetery. A fourth brother, Private Adolphus Michael Brennan, died at Wellington Hospital from a hemorrhage on 23 March 1915 aged 19 years while in training with the New Zealand Training Unit and is buried in Wellington (Karori) Cemetery. Lieutenant Colonel The Honourable Percy Cecil Evans-Freke, Leicestershire Yeomanry, was killed in action on the Frezenberg Ridge on 13 May 1915 aged 44 years. He was son of 8th Baron Carbery. He was commissioned into the Yeomanry in December 1895, was promoted to Lieutenant in March 1899, Captain in May 1903, Major in February 1905, and took command of the regiment in 1913. He had served in the South African Wars and arrived at Ypres on 2 November 1914. He was killed when hit by bullets while crossing open land between the trenches to get to the position where his Battalion's Major had been hit. He was within 10m of reaching safety when he was killed.

Major Victor Rogers, DSO, MiD, 5th Battery, New Zealand Field Artillery, was killed on 8 February 1918 aged 29 years. At the start of the war he enlisted in the artillery and was soon commissioned. He served in Gallipoli and then on the Western Front being wounded twice. He was Mentioned in Despatches in November 1916 and was awarded the Distinguished Service Order in the New Year's Honours List in January 1917. The citation reads 'During operations in September 1916 this officer, though wounded, continued to carry on his duties in a most efficient manner. He has always displayed great coolness and has brought his Battery to a most satisfactory state of efficiency. During operations on the 15th September he re-organised and practically took over command of the 12th Battery when its O.C. became a casualty. This he again did in a most efficient manner on the 25th when its O.C. was again casualtied, and by his personal supervision and coolness, instilled confidence in the Battery personnel during heavy shellfire.' He was killed by a shell when returning to his Battery after attending a Court Martial.

Another of note buried here is Private Oswald Rees Keene, 2nd Duke of Wellington's, killed in action on 5 May 1915 aged 24 years. He was a 2nd Lieutenant in the 1/5th Borders before the war but resigned his commission, which he had received in 1911, due to ill health. He enlisted in the 3rd York and Lancasters in December 1914 before being transferred to the Duke of Wellington's. He went to the Front on 29 April 1915 lasting a week before he was killed by poison gas on Hill 60.

UK - 188   NZ - 65   Can – 26
Bermuda – 1   Unnamed – 5   KUG – 1
Area - 1436 sq mts

**LOCATION**
Divisional Cemetery lies in a housing/industrial area in the suburbs west of Ieper about 800m from the Market Square. There are clear CWGC signs directing you south from the old road to Poperinge (N308) to the cemetery which is about 100m from the N308.

## DIVISIONAL COLLECTING POST CEMETERY

**HISTORY**
The original cemetery was begun in August 1917 during the Third Battle of Ypres, and was closed in January 1918.

**INFORMATION**
The original burial ground and the Extension are bounded by the same wall and are considered to be one, certainly it is difficult to see any physical distinction between the original cemetery and the post-war additions. However, the original burials, now forming Plot 1, Rows B to E, are near the Cross of Sacrifice furthest from the road and facing the Cross. The concentrated burials that form the Extension face the War Stone and the road looking in the opposite direction to the wartime burials.

The burial grounds get their name from the Collecting Post for casualties that was here during Third Ypres situated on a trench to the rear called Coney Street. The cemetery was begun by the 48th (South Midland) and 58th (2/1st London) Divisions and was closed containing 86 graves.

Buried here is Gunner Charles Walter Whetstone, MM, 'B' Battery, 58th Brigade, Royal Field Artillery who died on 22 September 1917 aged 23 years. He was awarded the Military Medal for the action in which he was killed. A brother was at his funeral. One of his brothers, Private Walter George Whetstone, 1st Royal Irish Fusiliers was killed on 21 October 1918 aged 19 years and is buried in Harlebeke New British Cemetery about 25km east of here. Another brother Private Alfred Whetstone, 50th Company, Machine Gun Corps (Infantry) was killed on 26 March 1918 and is commemorated on the Pozieres Memorial.

UK – 86   Ger 1   Area – 502 sq mts
Special Memorials next to the Cross to two men buried in Westrozebeke Church whose graves have been lost.

**LOCATION**
The Divisional Collecting Post Cemetery lies north of Ieper and 300m north of the northern by-pass (N38) on a road that runs parallel to the by-pass from which it is reached easily. There are two other cemeteries nearby.

## DIVISIONAL COLLECTING POST CEMETERY EXTENSION

**HISTORY**
The cemetery was made after the war as a concentration cemetery, mainly from 1924-26, for men brought in from the battlefields and a few small cemeteries.

**INFORMATION**
See Divisional Collecting Post Cemetery.

The records of the original burials and concentrations were kept separately until they were combined in 2001.

Among those buried here is Chaplain 4th Class, The Reverend Geoffrey Maynard Evans, MC, Army Chaplains' Department who was killed in action on 11 August 1917 aged 35 years. He had been attached to the 3rd Worcestershires for two years when he was killed by a shell in the front line trenches at Westhoek Ridge. He had fought in the South African Wars and then served as an officer with the Welsh Regiment for ten years. He was ordained in 1913, went to France in 1915 and was awarded the Military Cross in June 1916.

Also here is Private Frederick James Goodwin, 45th Australian Infantry, killed on 13 October 1917 aged 33 years. He had enlisted in December 1916 arriving at the Front in July 1917. He had volunteered to be a stretcher bearer and was carrying the wounded off the field at night, when he and the other stretcher bearers became lost. He waited with the wounded whilst the other stretcher bearers went to find the Dressing Station. On their return they found that Private Goodwin had been hit by a shell and was unconscious. His friend stretchered him to the Dressing Station and stayed with him until he died. He was originally buried just north of Zonnebeke and brought here in 1925.

Concentrated here:

Deerlyck Churchyard – located about 25km east of here it contained twenty British men (mostly 31st Division) who were killed in October and November 1918.

De Voorstraat German Cemetery (No. 50) – situated about 800m south-east of Zandvoorde containing two British men who died in 1914-15.

Houthulst Forest Chateau West Cemetery – located about 10km north of here this German cemetery in the middle of the forest contained the graves of two British men who died in 1914.

Westrozebeke Churchyard – located about 8km north-east of here it contained nine British men buried by the Germans.

| UK - 493 | Aust - 102 | NZ – 5 |
| Can - 73 | NF - 2 | S Afr – 1 |
| Unnamed - 511 (80%) | | Area – 2192 sq mts |

**LOCATION**
See Divisional Collecting Post Cemetery.

# DOCHY FARM NEW BRITISH CEMETERY

**HISTORY**
This cemetery is a concentration cemetery created after the war to contain bodies found in isolated graves and small burial grounds in the area, the battlefields of Boezinge, St. Juliaan, Frezenberg and Passendale.

**INFORMATION**
On 19-21 October 1914 the Germans tried to break the flank of the British 7th Division but the 22nd Brigade held the line until forced to pull back on 22 October. The French reoccupied Zonnebeke on the following day before the British 2nd Division took over the line from here to Reutal in late October.

The town of Zonnebeke and this ridge were in British hands until Second Ypres in April 1915 when the British were forced to consolidate their line after the German use of gas. A line from Frezenberg to this cemetery was an objective of the first day of Third Ypres. The first target, the German front-line north and south of Verlorenhoek, along the line of the modern motorway, fell at 3.45am and Frezenberg was taken by the 9th Black Watch and 8/10th Gordon Highlanders by 6.00am. The Potsdam Redoubt, where the road to Zonnebeke crosses the Hannebeek, was captured next, under heavy fire, by the 7/8th King's Own Scottish Borderers. The final objective for that day was a line from Potsdam Redoubt to Kansas Cross near this cemetery, taken by the 6/7th Royal Scots Fusiliers and 6th Cameron Highlanders with the 11th Argyll and Sutherland Highlanders and 13th Royal Scots. However, the Battalions suffered severe casualties including the commanding officer of the Camerons. The 12th Highland Light Infantry were sent up to support and consolidate the line during the night. On the next morning the Germans attacked a gap in the line north of the road to Zonnebeke. The Royal Scots were forced back from the line during which there were many examples of heroism in holding the Germans long enough for the Battalion to withdraw under controlled conditions. Colonel Hanway, at his headquarters just north of Frezenberg, ordered his Staff and the 46th Company, Machine Gun Corps to counter-attack with the remaining 130 men of the Royal Scots Fusiliers and the Argyll and Sutherland Highlanders.

Zonnebeke was taken by the British on 26 September 1917 but lost in the German Spring Offensive in April 1918. The Belgians finally captured Zonnebeke on 28 September 1918 by which time there was very little of the town left.

The farm after which this cemetery is named, which had become a German strong-point, was captured by the 4th New Zealand Brigade on 4 October 1917 during the Battle of Broodseinde, part of Third Ypres, and was situated down the slope across the main road. The cemetery has a very formal layout which shows clearly that it was not here during the fighting.

There is a Memorial to the New Zealanders that you can see across the road and valley to north-east. An obelisk in a small copse, the Memorial can be reached from the nearby crossroads called Kansas Cross. This Memorial was unveiled by the New Zealand High Commissioner on 2 August 1924 and honours the New Zealand contribution at Passendale in 1917. On 12 October, in the space of two hours, over 2800 New Zealand soldiers were killed, wounded or listed as missing, the most disastrous day in New Zealand's military history. The memorials here and at Messines and Longueval on the Somme are obelisks of Nebrasina stone from Italy with the inscription 'From the Uttermost Ends of the Earth' on a plinth at their base as well as a badge incorporating a fern leaf superimposed on crossed taiaha with a frame of Maori carving. You can also see Tyne Cot Cemetery across the area known as the Abraham Heights that was fought over in October 1917 by the New Zealanders.

Also nearby (this is the closest cemetery) is the Scottish Memorial on the road from Zonnebeke to St Jan. Upon it are words from the Declaration of Arbroath.

There are now several places to visit in the town including the Passendale Museum, the church and the Bremen Redoubt. A plaque on the west outer wall of the church is a Memorial to D/21 Battery, Canadian Field Artillery who were stationed in the churchyard and almost the only defenders of the Frezenberg Ridge in April 1915.

Lieutenant Roland Belfield Glanville, MC, 8th Australian Infantry, who was killed in action on 4 October 1917 aged 25 years. A New Zealander he was killed by a shell on Broodseinde Ridge just after the Battalion had reached their objectives. He had enlisted as Private in August 1914 and was commissioned in January 1917 and joined the 8th Battalion in July. He was awarded the Military Cross for several actions including the one in which he was killed. He was originally buried on the southern edge of Zonnebeke and moved here in 1925.

Also here is Serjeant James H Speirs, MM, 7th Cameron Highlanders, killed in action on 20 August 1917 aged 31 years. He was an international footballer for Scotland playing one match in 1908 while at Glasgow Rangers, a victory over Wales. In his ten-year career as a professional footballer, he had played 256 games in all competitions and had scored 104 goals. He had an FA Cup Winners medal leading Bradford City to their sole FA Cup triumph in 1911 scoring the winning goal. He also played for Clyde and Leeds City. Having played his final game for Leeds City in a 2-0 home loss to Barnsley on 24 April 1915, Speirs returned home to Glasgow to enlist. He went to France in March 1916, was wounded soon after and was back in action during the Battle of Arras in April 1917 when he was awarded the Military Medal for bravery in the field and promoted to Serjeant. He was killed in an attack on Hill 35 near St. Juliaan when his Battalion suffered nearly 150 casualties of the 450 men who went into action. He was buried about 1km west of here and moved in 1921.

UK - 523        Aust - 304      NZ – 98
Can - 82        NF - 1          S Afr - 17
KUG - 412       Unnamed - 958 (60%)
Area – 4525 sq mts

Special Memorials to one British soldier and one Australian man believed to be among the unnamed.

### LOCATION
Dochy Farm Cemetery is located on the ridge north-west of Zonnebeke, about 1.5km from the village, on the west side of the road to Vancouver Corner and Langemark. The simplest route to Zonnebeke is by the road that follows the old railway line north-east from Hellfire Corner on the eastern edge of Ieper.

## DOZINGHEM MILITARY CEMETERY

### HISTORY
The cemetery was opened in July 1917 for the casualties of Third Ypres. It remained in use until March 1918. Some later burials in the war took place and three British graves were concentrated here from the former French cemeteries at Hoogstade-Linde, Hoogbrug and Krombeke after the war. The cemetery was later used in WW2.

### INFORMATION
In preparation for the British offensive in 1917 many Casualty Clearing Stations were put into position in the rear of the Salient at locations such as Brandhoek, Proven and the '-Vleterens'. Westvleteren was considered an area safe enough for hospitals and bases for rest from the fighting.

The cemeteries that grew up associated with some of them were named by the soldiers Bandaghem, Mendinghem and Dozinghem, which played ironically upon the Flemish language and spelling for their apt description of the function of the Casualty Clearing Stations near each cemetery. The 4th, 47th and 61st Casualty Clearing Stations were located here and the cemetery which grew up next to them remained in use until March 1918.

The burials made after March 1918 in WW1 are mainly in Plots XV and XVI. There were 118 Belgian graves near the entrance in a Belgian Cemetery used from June to October 1918 within the British cemetery but these have been removed. The space vacated has been used for the burial of seventy-three men who died during World War II.

Nearby is La Lovie Chateau, now a private school and hospital. King George V stayed there in July 1917 and it was used as a British headquarters from May 1915 for various Corps and Divisions. Also nearby is the St. Sixtus Abbey in which the monks produce a strong beer. It is sign-posted from the cemetery and can be visited as part of a tour.

Buried here is Commander Walter Sterndale-Bennett, DSO & Bar, MiD, Drake Battalion, Royal Naval Division, Royal Naval Volunteer Reserve, who died of wounds on 7 November 1917 aged 24 years. He became the youngest Battalion commander in the war when, aged 23 years, he took command of his Battalion during the storming of Gavrelle in March 1917 and youngest man in the Royal Navy to hold the rank of Commander. For this action he was awarded a Bar to the Distinguished Service Order that he had won for conspicuous gallantry during the assault on Beaucourt in the Battle of the Ancre Heights in 1916. On the same day the Royal Naval Division lost more than 1,700 men, around 100 of whom were officers, but took more prisoners than any Division had done in one day to that date. At the close of battle, Walter was one of only four officers to escape unscathed. The citation for his DSO reads 'For conspicuous gallantry in action. He assumed command of and handled his Battalion with marked courage and ability. He personally collected a party and bombed the enemy out of part of their second line, where they might have held up the attack.' The citation for his Bar reads 'On discovering the wire uncut, except in a few places, he went forward himself and led his Battalion through the partially cut gaps. He finally gained his objective and held on against very strong resistance. The success of the operation was almost entirely due to his personal example.' He was also recommended for the Victoria Cross. He had served at Gallipoli, and died from wounds received in action on 4 November 1917 while attacking Sourd Farm near Passendale. He was great-grandson of the famous English composer Sir William Sterndale-Bennett and had already sailed the world by 1912.

Chaplain 3rd Class The Reverend Father Simon (Francis) Stock Knapp, OCD, DSO, MC, MiD, Army Chaplains' Department attached 2nd Irish Guards, died on 1 August 1917 aged 59 years. He belonged to the Order of Discalced (barefeet) Carmelites (ODC) which he joined in 1878, an order in which monks take a saint's name and are often known by it as well as, or rather than, their own name. This can be confusing when conducting research but he has been identified as living in the Carmelite Priory in Kensington before the war. He served in the South African Wars with Major Allenby, later General Sir Edmund Allenby, in the 6th (Inniskilling) Dragoons. He joined the Chaplain's Department in October 1914 and was almost immediately sent across the Channel. At this time Roman Catholic Padres were allocated at one per Division, but we don't know who he was with. Once the 2nd Irish Guards arrived in France he was attached to them after a short period with 1st Irish Guards. He was awarded the Military Cross for his work during, and after, the Battle of Loos in late 1915. He was awarded the Distinguished Service Order in the June 1917 Birthday Honours List. He was mortally wounded at Canada Farm on 31 July.

Lieutenant Colonel Norman Randall Davidson, DSO & Bar, MiD, Royal Horse Artillery, died of wounds on 5 October 1917 aged 39 years. Davidson enlisted into the army in 1892 and was transferred to the Royal Artillery in 1898. He was promoted to Lieutenant in 1901 whilst serving in the South African wars where he was Mentioned in Despatches, Captain in 1906 and Major in 1914. He went to France on 17 July 1917 and served in the HQ of the 4th Division. He was awarded the Distinguished Service Order in the New Year's Honours List in January 1917 and a posthumous Bar in October 1917.

Lieutenant Colonel Brian Surtees Phillpotts, DSO, MiD, commanding the 38th Division Royal Engineers, died of wounds on 4 September 1917 aged 42 years. He was commissioned as a 2nd Lieutenant in the Royal Engineers in 1895, promoted to Lieutenant in 1898, Captain in 1904 and Major in 1914. He was made Commandant Royal Engineers (CRE) and Lieutenant-Colonel in 1916. He was Mentioned in Despatches in June 1916 and awarded the Distinguished Service Order in the New Year's Honours List in January 1917. He was mortally wounded in action on 2 September 1917.

Buried here is Captain Reuben Wright, DSO, 7th King's Own Yorkshire Light Infantry, who died of wounds on 17 August 1917. He was awarded the Distinguished Service Order in November 1916 for taking command of his Battalion while a Lieutenant and organising the position under heavy fire. He was made a Captain in April 1917.

Among the WW2 burials here is Captain Charles Talbot Orton, Royal Warwickshire Regiment, who died of wounds on 28 May 1940 aged 29 years. His father was Major-General Sir Ernest Frederick Orton, KCIE, CB, and his brother Captain John Ernest Orton, 5th Battalion, 13th Frontier Force Rifles who died on 27 September 1940 and is buried in Rawalpindi War Cemetery.

Buried here is Lance Corporal Harry Reeves Squires, MM, 2nd Hampshires, died of wounds on 24 August 1917 aged 29 years. He was wounded in action north of Langemark when his unit, part of the 29th Division, attacked on 16 August 1917. He received his Military Medal posthumously. His brother, Private Charles Edward Squires, 4th Worcestershires, also part of the 29th Division, was killed in action on 9 October 1917 while attacking along the line of the old railway north-east of Langemark. He is commemorated on the Tyne Cot Memorial. Another brother, Rifleman Albert Thomas Squires, 1/8th Hampshires was killed in action on 19 April 1917 and is commemorated on the Jerusalem Memorial.

Another to lose two brothers is Lieutenant Wilfred James Dashwood, 1st Grenadier Guards, who died of wounds, received on 31 July during the fighting at Pilkem Ridge, on 2 August 1917 aged 34 years. He was previously with the 18th (Public Schools) Royal Fusiliers. His brother Captain Ernest George Dashwood, 1/4th Oxford and Bucks Light Infantry died on 12 May 1915 aged 35 years and is buried in Rifle House Cemetery in Ploegsteert Wood about 15km south-east of here. Another brother, 2nd Lieutenant Lionel Albert Dashwood, 2nd Oxford and Bucks Light Infantry was killed in action at the Battle of Festubert on 16 May 1915 aged 27 years and is commemorated on the Le Touret Memorial. They were sons of the 6th Baronet Dashwood. Another brother, Edward John, was killed flying with the Royal Air Force on the North-West Frontier in 1925.

Buried here is Captain The Honourable Henry Simon Feilding, 2nd Coldstream Guards, who died of wounds on 11 October 1917 aged 23 years. He was son of the 9th Earl and Countess of Denbigh, 8th Earl of Desmond. He joined the Coldstream Guards in June 1916 having been in the cavalry since 1913. He was wounded north of Passendale on 9 October. His brother, Lieutenant-Commander The Honourable Hugh Cecil Robert Feilding, HMS Defence, Royal Navy, was killed in the Battle of Jutland on 31 May 1916 aged 29 years. His ship sunk, with no survivors, having been attacked by one German battlecruiser and four dreadnoughts. He is commemorated on the Plymouth Naval Memorial.

Lieutenant The Honourable Ernest Aloysius French, 2nd South Wales Borderers, died of wounds on 16 August 1917 aged 22 years. He was son of the 4th Baron De Freyne. His brothers Captain Arthur Reginald French, 5th Baron De Freyne, MiD, aged 35 years and Lieutenant The Honourable George Philip French, aged 25 years, both 3rd attached 1st South Wales Borderers were killed on 9 May 1915 in the Battle of Aubers Ridge fighting side by side and now lie together with one headstone. They are buried in Cabaret-Rouge British Cemetery. They were originally buried in Edward Road Cemetery No. 2, one of several named after a trench called Edward Road that was situated north of Richebourg l'Avoué, and concentrated in 1925. Another brother, 2nd Lieutenant The Honourable Edward Fulke French, 296th Brigade, Royal Field Artillery died as a prisoner of war on 13 November 1918 aged 32 years. He was originally buried in Mainz but was moved to Niederzwehren Cemetery in 1924.

Buried here is Private Francis Gerald Vane Smith de Heriz, 3rd Company, 2nd Coldstream Guards who died of wounds on 15 October 1917 aged 35 years. One brother, Private Walter Vane Smith de Heriz, 18th Australian Infantry, committed suicide on 23 May 1916 aged 37 years in Egypt and is buried in the Port Said War Memorial Cemetery. Another brother, Gunner Cyril Ralph Vane Smith de Heriz, 15th (Warwick) Brigade, Royal Horse Artillery, died on 9 April 1917 aged 31 years. He is buried in Beaurains Road Cemetery near Arras.

Buried here is Private Edward King, 2nd Essex, died of wounds 9 October 1917 aged 36 years. His brother Private Charles Walter King, 35th Royal Fusiliers, 104th Company, Labour Corps, died on 12 August 1917 aged 22 years. He is buried in Vlamertinghe New Military Cemetery about 4km east of here. His mother, Charlotte Bibby King, is reported to have pulled chunks of her hair out on receiving the news of his death. A third brother, Private Thomas Robert King, 7th Queen's (Royal West Surreys) died on 20 November 1916 aged 27 years and is buried in Albert Communal Cemetery Extension.

Buried here is 2nd Lieutenant Edward Revere Osler, 'A' Battery, 59th Brigade, Royal Field Artillery, who died on 30 August 1917 aged 21 years. He was the great grandson of Paul Revere, a Boston silversmith and engraver, who, dressed as a Native American, took part in the Boston Tea Party and gained everlasting fame in America as the patriot who rode all night to warn of the approach of the British in 1775 before the battles of Lexington and Concord. His father, Sir William Osler, was Regius Professor of Medicine at Oxford. When the war began he was unable to get a position in the British Army so pulled some strings to get into the Canadian Forces and in February 1915 was attached to the Canadian Red Cross, Duchess of Connaught Hospital, at Cliveden. They went to France but Osler wanted to be at the Front. For him, this meant returning to England to get a commission in the Royal Artillery, which was accomplished in October 1916. On 27 August 1917, his Battery was preparing to move the guns when a German shell landed. Osler was seriously wounded and sent, via Canada Farm and Essex Farm, to No. 47 Casualty Clearing Station here. Several expert surgeons and friends of Sir William Osler, mainly Americans, made their way to treat Osler, but, despite their efforts he died from his wounds.

Buried here is 2nd Lieutenant Ernest Denny, 15th (Prince of Wales' Own Civil Service Rifles) Londons attached 17th (British Empire League) King's Royal Rifle Corps, who died of wounds on 4 August 1917 aged 29 years. He was a Private in the 1/28th (Artists Rifles) Londons before receiving his commission. He was a war poet who had 'Triumphant Laughter Poems, 1914-1917' published after his death.

Lieutenant John Congreve Murray, 1/8th Royal Scots died on 23 September 1917 aged 35 years. He made three first class cricket appearances for Scotland one each in 1909, 1912 and 1913. He arrived at the Front just a few weeks before he was mortally wounded.

An Olympian here is the German, Oberleutnant Bernhard von Gaza, 185th Infantry Regiment who died on 25 September 1917 aged 36 years. He was considered one of Germany's finest rowers, winning German championships in more than one event, and writing several highly influential books on rowing. He represented Germany at the 1908 London Olympics winning a Bronze medal in the single sculls. He won another Bronze Medal at the European Championships of 1913. He was awarded the Iron Cross in 1916 having been wounded in 1915. He was mortally wounded in a British attack and taken prisoner before dying of his wounds.

| | | |
|---|---|---|
| UK - 3021 | Aust - 6 | NZ – 14 |
| Can - 61 | NF - 19 | S Afr - 15 |
| BWI - 34 | KUG - 1 | Chinese – 3 |
| Ger - 65 | WWII – 73 | Area – 12309 sq mts |

**LOCATION**

Dozinghem is about 12km west of Ieper. It is included in very few maps and it took me a morning to find it on the first occasion that I tried. It is possible to get here from Krombeke or Proven or most easily from Poperinge. The cemetery is in a wood on the east side of the Poperinge-Krombeke road about 4km from the centre of Poperinge. It is 250m from the main road on a dirt track. In very wet weather this track may not be passable and you are advised to park by the road and walk. The track is not suitable for vehicles bigger than a car.

# DRAGOON CAMP CEMETERY

**HISTORY**
This cemetery was opened by the 13th (1st North Wales Pals) Royal Welsh Fusiliers on 9 August 1917 and remained in use until October 1917.

**INFORMATION**
Dragoon Camp was a German camp until the start of Third Ypres when this area was taken on 31 July 1917. Captured by the 38th (Welsh) Division, Dragoon Camp was a name used by the soldiers, its official name being House 10, or Villa Gretchen Cemetery. Of the known graves only six are not of Royal Welsh Fusiliers or Royal Field Artillery.

This cemetery is one of three small cemeteries in the immediate area. The others are Welsh (Caesar's Nose) Cemetery and Colne Valley Cemetery.
Buried here is Major Evan Davies, MiD, 15th (London Welsh) Royal Welsh Fusiliers killed in action on 28 July 1917 on Pilkem Ridge. He had attended London University before the war. The war diary records that he was wounded and taken prisoner on 27 July. His Company was sent to reconnoiter the German positions having received information in error that the Germans were withdrawing.
UK - 66          Unnamed - 10     Area – 532 sq mts

**LOCATION**
Dragoon Camp Cemetery lies about 3km north of Ieper, east of the canal, about 1km east of Boezinge. Turn towards Ieper at the French Memorials on the Boezinge-Langemark road and in 400m you come to a CWGC sign directing along a track to the cemetery in the middle of fields. For the adventurous, you can drive a car almost to the cemetery, but you will have to walk the last 100m along a neat grass path that seems out of place in the middle of the fields. The CWGC website says 'Please note that this cemetery is accessed via very long unmade paths and these will prove problematic for wheelchair users at certain times of year.' The cemetery is very small with good views of this part of the Salient. It is peaceful because of its distance from the road which means a long walk for visitors.

# DRANOUTER CHURCHYARD

**HISTORY**
The churchyard was used from the start of fighting in this area in October 1914 until the Military Cemetery nearby was opened in July 1915.

**INFORMATION**
Dranouter was occupied by the 1st Cavalry Division on 14 October 1914. It was in Allied hands until captured by the Germans, from the 154th French Division, on 25 April 1918. It was recaptured by the 30th Division on 30 August 1918. Several small plots were made within the churchyard some of which still exist though nineteen graves were moved to the Military Cemetery in 1923 when the church was rebuilt.
Buried here are brothers, Captain Meaburn Staniland, 1/4th Lincolnshires, killed in action on 29 July 1915 aged 35 years and 2nd Lieutenant Geoffrey Staniland, 1/4th Lincolnshires, killed in action on 13 April 1915 aged 34 years. Meaburn, a Company commander, was shot by a sniper in the night near Hooge as he did his rounds of the trenches. Geoffrey was killed by enemy shelling at Lindenhoek as he tried to get his men to safety. They are buried close to each other.
Also here is their commanding officer, Lieutenant Colonel John William Jessop, 1/4th Lincolnshires, killed in action on 4 June 1915 aged 55 years. He was killed while near the HQ of the Battalion, the 1/5th Leicestershires, that the Lincolnshires were about to replace in the line near Kemmel. He had gone forward to discuss the handover when the Germans began shelling. He was standing with two horses, two orderlies, and the commander of the Leicestershires, Lieutenant Colonel Jones. All were killed by the shell except Jones who was wounded.
Buried here is Lieutenant Robert Bradford Flint, DSO, four times MiD, Legion d'Honneur, 59th Field Company, Royal Engineers, killed in action on 23 January 1915 aged 23 years. He was commissioned into the Royal Engineers in 1911. He received the Legion d'Honneur for his actions in August 1914 while the Distinguished Service Order was awarded for his actions a month later. The citation reads 'At Misy, on 14 September, under a heavy shellfire he assisted Captain W H Johnson in working all day until 7.00pm with their own hands (with) two rafts bringing back wounded and returning with ammunition, thus enabling

the advanced [14th] Brigade to maintain its position on the other side of the river.' During the retreat from Mons he blew up a river bridge alone. He was mortally wounded while working in the trenches near Wulvergem.

UK - 79   Unnamed - 2

**LOCATION**
Dranouter Churchyard is in the centre of the village which lies about 11km south-west of Ieper. It is difficult to miss the church from whichever direction you enter Dranouter as it lies in the heart of the village at a junction of several roads.

# DRANOUTRE MILITARY CEMETERY

**HISTORY**
Begun in July 1915, as burials in the churchyard were ended, the cemetery was used until the German advance in March 1918. The graves in Plot III were added in September and October 1918. In addition, nineteen graves were moved here from the churchyard in 1923 during rebuilding operations.

**INFORMATION**
See Dranouter Churchyard.
Many of the burials were made by the 72nd Brigade of the 24th Division from April to June 1916.

Among those buried here is Captain Robert Curwen Richmond Blair, DSO, EM, 'A' Company, 1/5th Borders killed in action on 21 July 1916 aged 36 years. He was involved in rescuing men from the Wellington Colliery Disaster in May 1910 for which he was awarded the Edward Medal, the equivalent of the Albert Medal or the George Cross. The Edward Medal was only awarded to miners and quarrymen, of which 66 were awarded for the Wellington Disaster, the highest for any single event. There were no survivors from the gas explosion and fire. Blair was commissioned into the 1/5th Borders in 1908, promoted to Lieutenant in 1909 and Captain in 1914. His first taste of fighting was in June 1915 at Hooge. Parts of the Battalion had already been in the front-line as the Borders had been split up during Second Ypres and attached to various units. After further action Blair was awarded the Distinguished Service Order. The citation reads 'For conspicuous gallantry on the night of 27th September 1915, at ARMENTIERES. He went out with a party of 10 to bomb the enemy's trenches. Finding conditions unfavourable, the party lay down and waited about 50 yards from the enemy's wire. Soon afterwards a party of 14 Germans were seen advancing towards them. Capt. BLAIR held his fire till they were 10 yards away when he shot four of them with his revolver. His party accounted for all the remainder except two and returned unscathed. Capt. BLAIR has constantly taken part in arduous and enterprising night work.' He was killed in no-man's land while identifying places in the British wire that needed to be repaired.

Chaplain The Reverend Thomas George Danks Trueman, Australian Young Men's Christian Association attached 5th Australian Infantry, died on 22 March 1918 aged 30 years. He was killed by shell fire during his sleep.

Lieutenant Colonel William Albert De Courcey King, DSO, Chief of Royal Engineers (CRE), 36th (Ulster) Division, Royal Engineers was killed in action on 27 May 1917 aged 42 years. King attended the Royal Military Academy, Woolwich, and then the School of Military Engineering, Chatham. He received his commission as a 2nd Lieutenant in the Royal Engineers in 1894, was promoted to Lieutenant in 1897, Captain in 1904, Major in 1913, acting Lieutenant-Colonel in 1916 and posthumously to Brevet Lieutenant Colonel. He had served in Saint Lucia in the 1890s and the South African Wars. He was Chief Instructor at the British Army School of Ballooning, Farnborough from 1906 until June 1910. While there, he, with Samuel Cody and Colonel Capper, participated in the Maiden Voyage of the first British Airship (British Dirigible No. 1) 'Nulli Secundus', on 10 September 1907. He was awarded the Distinguished Service Order in 1916 while a Major. He was killed by shellfire while taking up new positions at Ulster Camp, west of Dranouter. His son was an officer in the Royal Navy winning the DSO & Bar in 1940 and the Distinguished Service Cross. He was the only person to command a submarine on both the first and last day of the war. He was the oldest participant in the first solo non-stop around-the-world yacht race 1969-73.

Also here is Major George Richard Owen Edwards, DSO & Bar, MiD, 'C' Battery, 173rd Brigade, Royal Field Artillery, killed in action on 17 June 1917 aged 42 years. He served in the South African Wars with the Natal Mounted Rifles, the Natal Artillery, the Durban Garrison Artillery and the Royal Artillery. He fought in the German South West African Campaign for which he was Mentioned in Despatches in 1915. He then transferred to the Royal Field Artillery in France. Interestingly, for which I cannot find an explanation, the Bar to the Distinguished Service Order is dated as 1 January 1917 and the DSO is dated as 22 August 1918 which was awarded for service with the 12th Citizen Battery in German South West Africa.

Buried here is Private George Henry Rea, 2nd Wiltshires who died on 1 September 1917 aged 33 years. His brother Private Ernest Rea, 1/7th Worcestershires died on 25 April 19817 aged 21 years and is commemorated on the Thiepval Memorial. Another brother, Private William J. Rea, 8th Bedfordshires died on 14 September 1917 and is buried in Bethune Town Cemetery.

Private Frederick Broadrick of the 11th Royal Warwickshires deserted from billets at Loker on 1 July 1917 and was caught in Calais five days later. As this was his second offence he was executed in Dranouter on 1 August and is buried in this cemetery.

Private Other Beaumont Jeffreys Philpott, 25th Australian Infantry, who was killed on 17 June 1916 aged 27 years is buried here. He was returning from a scouting patrol in the Messines area when he was killed by gas and shellfire. He was with Private James Jackson Mollison of the same Battalion who is buried at La Plus Dove Farm Cemetery. They were the first Australians to die in Belgium during the war. Another 12747 would follow. His first name is 'Other' and I can only wonder at why he was given that name.

| | | |
|---|---|---|
| UK - 422 | Aust - 16 | NZ – 1 |
| Can - 19 | Ger - 1 | KUG – 3 |
| Other (Australian YMCA) – 1 | | Area - 3808 sq mts |

**LOCATION**

Dranoutre Military Cemetery lies on the southern edge of the village. The cemetery is reached from the Dranouter-Loker road, at the point at which a CWGC sign indicates off the main road, by means of a track that seems to be leading into a lumber yard. The cemetery can be seen on the left once you are past the buildings. There is a path to the cemetery next to a drainage ditch which can be fairly aromatic in the summer!

# DUHALLOW ADVANCED DRESSING STATION (A.D.S.) CEMETERY

**HISTORY**

The cemetery was begun on the first day of Third Ypres next to the Advanced Dressing Station, and remained in use until the end of the war in November 1918. After the war the cemetery was almost doubled in size with the concentration of many graves.

**INFORMATION**

The name of the cemetery is believed to have been taken from a Southern Irish hunt. The Dressing Station was located next to the canal, and was created by the 39th Division ready for the attack on 31 July. In the first day of use, when the battle began in 1917, the five Medical Officers of the 39th Division treated 2680 casualties. The 11th, 36th and 44th Casualty Clearing Stations were posted here in October and November 1918.

Of the original 875 burials, which make up Plots I to IV, 215 were artillerymen and 77 engineers. Many others were men of the 39th Division wounded in the attack at St. Juliaan and Kitchener's Wood on 31 July 1917. There are 41 men of the 13th Company, Labour Corps buried in Plot II, who were killed when a truck load of ammunition salvaged from the surrounding area was detonated by a bomb dropped from a German aircraft on 9 January 1918. One man who died in World War II is buried in Plot V, while six American and one Belgian graves have been removed.

Both cemeteries concentrated here were badly shelled in 1918 and many graves were destroyed. Hence, Duhallow A.D.S. cemetery contains Special Memorials which are located near the entrance while the French and Belgian graves are at the canal end of the cemetery.

Buried here is Private John Seymour of the 2nd Royal Inniskilling Fusiliers who was executed nearby for desertion on 24 January 1918 aged 21 years. He had joined the 1st Royal Inniskilling Fusiliers in April 1915 but did not have a good service record. He went absent in May 1915 and was sentenced to two years imprisonment but this was commuted and he was sent back to the Front. He went absent again in December 1915 for which he received a death sentence though this was again commuted to a prison sentence. In October 1917 he was released to fight in Third Ypres being sent to the 2nd Battalion of his regiment. He went absent once more on 27 November as his unit were being prepared for an attack. He claimed he went to collect rations, got drunk with men he did not know, woke up in a hut near Poperinge and could not then find his Battalion. But he stayed away until found by Military Police in Poperinge in late December. At his Court Martial he also claimed his nerves got the better of him. Unfortunately, his previous conduct was enough for the death sentence to be imposed and carried out. He was the only man executed in January 1918.

Captain Gordon Daubeney Gresley Elton, DSO, MC, four times MiD, Royal Irish Fusiliers attached Divisional Staff died on 5 November 1917 aged 29 years. He became a 2nd Lieutenant in 1909, Lieutenant in 1911 and Captain in 1914. When war broke out, he was in India, so resigned his post and returned to England to fight with the 82nd Brigade in France as a Captain in the Royal Irish Fusiliers. He was severely wounded in Second Ypres on 12 May 1915. Once recovered in November 1915 he briefly served as Brigade Major in Gallipoli, and was one of the last to leave Suvla Bay when the evacuation took place. In July 1916 he was in France and in June 1917 he was appointed General Staff Officer to the 58th (2/1st London) Division. He was killed in action walking, with his Divisional commander, through the trenches near Poelkapelle. He was Mentioned in Despatches four times from 1915–1917 and was awarded the Military Cross on 14 March 1915 'For conspicuous gallantry at St. Eloi from 14th to 16th March 1915, when he obtained valuable and very essential information relative to the enemy position on four separate occasions, whilst exposed to heavy close range rifle fire'. In the June 1917 Birthday Honours List he was awarded the Distinguished Service Order. His father and grandfather had both been Colonels.

Captain Charles Cadwaladr Trevor-Roper, 1/8th attached 14th (1st Portsmouth Pals) Hampshires, died of wounds on 3 August 1917 aged 33 years. He had been a Lieutenant in the Royal Welsh Fusiliers but gained a commission with the Hampshires before going to the Western Front in September 1916. He was mortally wounded near St. Juliaan on 31 July. His brother, Private Geoffrey Trevor-Roper, 32nd (East Ham) Royal Fusiliers, was killed in action when shot in the head during an attack east of Sanctuary Wood during the Battle of the Menin Road on 20 September 1917 and is commemorated on the Tyne Cot Memorial. His son Flight Lieutenant (Air Gunner) Richard Algernon Dacre Trevor-Roper, DFM, DFC, Royal Air Force Volunteer Reserve, was killed in action on 31 March 1944 aged 28 years. He joined the Royal Air Force in 1939 transferring from the Royal Artillery. He had been awarded the Distinguished Flying Medal in 1941 at the end of a year's service with No. 50 Squadron and commissioned at the same time. He was moved to No. 617 Squadron, the Dambusters, for the raids on the Ruhr Dams. He was awarded the Distinguished Flying Cross for his part in the raid in which he was the Rear Gunner in the aircraft flown by Wing Commander Guy Gibson. He was shot down in a raid on Nuremburg in which all the crew were killed and buried in Durnbach War Cemetery.

2nd Lieutenant Albert E. Taylor, MC & Bar, DCM, 1st Royal Newfoundland Regiment died on 17 October 1918 aged 24 years. He enlisted in May 1915 and was awarded the Distinguished Conduct Medal while a Sergeant Major in December 1917. The citation reads 'For conspicuous gallantry and devotion to duty. He has performed consistent good work and has always carried out his duties in a highly efficient manner.' His Military Cross was awarded in November 1917. The citation reads 'For conspicuous gallantry and devotion to duty. At Boesinghe Sector on 9th October 1917, his captain was killed beside him by a machine gun which was a short distance away. He at once attacked the machine gun with one other man and put it out of action. His personal example and courage throughout the day were the greatest possible asset to the Company. He personally killed with the bayonet a large number of the enemy.' The Bar was awarded posthumously in 1919. The citation reads 'For conspicuous bravery and devotion to duty during the attack on Keiberg Ridge on 29th September 1918. The right flank of the Belgian Army was held up by a six inch gun firing at them with open sights. This gun had a machine gun protecting it on either flank. The left of the Royal Newfoundland Regiment was also stopped. 2nd Lieut. Taylor, grasping the situation, at once led his Platoon forward by short rushes, and under covering fire the left flank Company captured the gun and also the two machine guns. This officer showed great coolness and dash and during this advance he continually exposed himself.'

Buried here is Corporal James George Washington Hagen, MM & Bar, 1st Royal Newfoundland Regiment died of wounds on 21 October 1918 aged 25 years. He enlisted in January 1914, the Attestation papers were signed by Captain Eyres one of the family of four cousins, two pairs of brothers, killed on 1 July 1916, three at Beaumont-Hamel. He served in Gallipoli where he contracted typhoid. He seems to have gone absent on more than one occasion in 1916, being called 'a deserter' in one letter home in September 1916 from the Paymaster. He returned in early 1917, undertaken a brief imprisonment until July before returning to his Battalion. He was demoted from Lance-Corporal in January 1918. However, he gained his stripes back becoming a Corporal in August 1918 and seems to have changed character. He was awarded the Military Medal in February 1918 for his actions on 20 November 1917 near Marcoing when he took messages under fire, helped the other signalers, got rations up to the men in the front-line and led by example when his officer was wounded. He was awarded a Bar to his Military Medal in June 1918. He was mortally wounded by a shell on 20 October near Harlebeke about 25km east of here and died at No. 44 Casualty Clearing Station. It is also recorded that he died of gunshot wounds to the neck.

Another man awarded the Military Medal is Private Harold Victor Atkinson, MM, 'C' Company, 15th (1st Salford Pals) Lancashire Fusiliers, who died on Christmas Day, 25 December 1917 aged 20 years. He was one of two 'runners' to be awarded the MM for their actions on 2-3 December 1917 near Westrosebeke north of Ypres. His was posthumous. Two brothers survived the war.

Buried here is Lieutenant Follett McNeill Drury, 1/1st Hertfordshires, who died on 7 January 1918 aged 24 years. Follett landed in France on 20 September 1914 as a Private in the Honourable Artillery Company and was wounded three times before being commissioned into the Hertfordshires. He was killed around 11.00pm when a German shell hit his Company HQ, killing him instantly.

Concentrated here:

Malakoff Farm Cemetery – located between Solferino Farm Cemetery and Dawson's Corner about 1.5km north-west of here, it contained 33 graves, including thirteen men of the 1/4th (Hallamshire) York and Lancasters who were killed from April 1915 to July 1917.

Fusilier Wood Cemetery – located about 5km south-east of here, it contained 66 British men and one Australian who were killed from September 1917 to January 1918.

| UK - 1442 | Aust - 13 | NZ – 6 |
|---|---|---|
| Can - 26 | NF - 12 | S Afr - 3 |
| BWI - 2 | Indian - 2 | Bel – 1 |
| Fr - 2 | Ger - 54 | WW2 - 1 |
| Unnamed – 231 | | Area – 5064 sq mts |

Special Memorials to ten soldiers buried in Malakoff Farm Cemetery and 29 buried at Fusilier Wood Cemetery whose graves have been destroyed.

Special Memorial to a man of the Loyal North Lancashire Regiment who is believed to be buried here.

**LOCATION**

Duhallow A.D.S. Cemetery is in the northern suburbs of Ieper about 1.5km from the town centre on the eastern side of the N369 to Boezinge between the road and the canal.

# ELZENWALLE BRASSERIE CEMETERY

**HISTORY**
This cemetery was opened in February 1915 and used until November 1917.

**INFORMATION**
The cemetery was named after a brewery, founded as 'Kemmel Brewery', and brasserie situated opposite the graveyard. However, Elzen is Dutch for 'Alder'. There were many Alder trees here so that may have had a role to play in the name of the Brasserie.

The cemetery is a series of regimental burial grounds that reflect the Battalions that held the front-line at the time the burials were made. For example, Plot III was made by the 22nd (Quebec) Canadian Infantry. As such, the cemetery lacks a formal pattern, which invites you to explore the graves.

Nearby is the Chateau Elsenwalle just north of, and visible from, the cemetery. This is a fascinating design in that the owner, Belgian architect Ernest Blérot, has incorporated the war damage in the rebuilding of the chateau, much of which was rebuilt with concrete rather than the original bricks. It lies in the remains of Scottish Wood and is, in my opinion, with the building painted white, one of the most beautiful of the chateaux on the Salient. The chateau was used as a Battalion Headquarters by a number of units in the war. For example, the writer and poet Edmund Blundon talks in one of his books, 'The Minds Eye', of the shelling of the château in 1918 whilst his Battalion, the 11th Royal Sussex were using it as their HQ.

Among those buried here is Corporal Charles Lawrence, DCM, 7th/8th Royal Irish Fusiliers who died on 8 May 1917 aged 20 years. He was awarded the Distinguished Conduct Medal in November 1916. The citation reads 'For conspicuous gallantry in action. During an enemy counter-attack he was the senior NCO left with his Platoon. He rallied his men, and by his courage and cool example he was able to drive off the enemy, and retake two machine guns.' He was killed by German shelling north of Wijtschate, one shell falling on the Battalion HQ killing six men.

UK - 106      Can - 41      BWI - 2
Unnamed - 5                  Area – 1825 sq mts

**LOCATION**
Elzenwalle Brasserie Cemetery lies about 3km south of Ieper on the west side of the road to Kemmel.

# ESSEX FARM CEMETERY

**HISTORY**
The cemetery was begun in April 1915, next to a Dressing Station, and remained in use until August 1917.

**INFORMATION**
This is one of the most visited sites on the Salient. For many, it has almost everything the tourist wants within a small area. It has the last resting place of one of the youngest to die in the war, the grave of a holder of the Victoria Cross, Memorials and a set of famous dug-outs. It is very convenient from the centre of town. Hence, almost every visitor to the Salient comes to Essex Farm. But, are these three stories, and am I as guilty of focussing on them when I guide and even in this section of this book, enough reason to come here? I feel we must challenge ourselves to remember the other 1000 men buried here, to consider the cemeteries that few visit and ask, 'why am I here at this location?' There are good enough reasons to come to Essex Farm - but are they good enough at the expense of other locations? Maybe it is the combination of those buried here that makes this one of the places that everyone wants to visit. I will now step down from my sturdy soapbox.

The area was in Allied hands for the duration of the war, though the Germans came close to the bank across the canal at times. The track by the side of the cemetery leads to the canal bank at a point where there was a bridge during the war. This is now a popular spot with the inhabitants of Ypres for their Sunday afternoon relaxation. The cemetery gets its name from the small farm building that was here in the war in which the Dressing Station was established in April 1915 and remained for a while, both in the farm and other wooden buildings and tents. As the 2nd Essex were one of the first Battalions to use the farm, it is probable that it gets its name from them. The concrete dug-outs we see today were established in 1917.

One of the Doctors who worked here, in the wooden huts shortly after the Dressing Station was established, was Captain (later Lieutenant-Colonel) John MacRae, Royal

Canadian Medical Corps. He had been a writer and poet before the war as well as serving in the military, notably in the South African Wars. He had been in Belgium since February 1915. On 2nd May 1915 one of Captain McCrae's friends, Lieutenant Alexis Helmer, was killed by a shell as he stepped from his tent. McCrae led the funeral as there was no padre at hand to conduct the service. Shortly after, and there are several conflicting stories of exactly what happened, McCrae wrote his poem 'In Flanders Fields' reflecting what he could see and hear as much as what he felt. Stories of MacRae emerging from surgery in the concrete dugouts are fanciful as he did not see the dugouts we see today as McRae was moved to Boulogne in June. The poem was published anonymously in Punch magazine on 6 December 1915 and has led to him being remembered. His poem has a role to play in the poppy becoming the symbol or remembrance for the war. MacRae died of pneumonia on 28 January 1918 aged 45 years and is buried in Wimereux Cemetery in France. There is a Memorial to him.

There is argument about how the poppy became the iconic symbol of remembrance, but certainly Field Marshal Earl Haig took up the idea of mass producing poppies and selling them for charity leading to the Royal British Legion's annual Poppy Day. Haig spent much of the last part of his life raising money for the men and families of those who suffered or lost their lives in the war, a task that can be argued to show he did appreciate some of what he had done and wished to make amends. Money raised today by the appeal continues to look after service personnel and their families who have suffered or lost their lives in serving their country, my own family included. Hence, I can justify visiting Essex Farm if only for being at the place where an iconic image of remembrance was born. Incidentally, the French symbol of remembrance is a blue Daisy.

Buried in the cemetery is one of the youngest known casualties of the war, Private Valentine Joseph Strudwick, 8th Rifle Brigade who died on 14 January 1916, aged 15 years and 11 months. He had enlisted in January 1915, aged just 14 and arrived at the Front a few weeks later. He was from Dorking in Surrey and had been a labourer for his uncle, a coal merchant, once he left school. He died not in any major battle but in the daily round of shellfire and gunshots, as his Battalion were shelled while 'holding the line'. It is quite right to visit the grave of one so young, especially when I bring so many school groups to this location. But, Strudwick is not the youngest to die on the Western Front, nor even in the Salient. On the other hand, as said above with the story of the poppy, there are other valuable stories to be learnt from a visit to Essex Farm.

Another interesting story is that of Private Thomas Barrett, VC, 7th South Staffordshires, killed in action on 27 July 1917 aged 22 years. The citation for his Victoria Cross reads 'For most conspicuous bravery when as Scout to a patrol he worked his way towards the enemy line with the greatest gallantry and determination, in spite of continuous fire from hostile snipers at close range. These snipers he stalked and killed. Later his patrol was similarly held up, and again he disposed of the snipers. When during the subsequent withdrawal of the patrol it was observed that a party of the enemy were endeavouring to outflank them, Pte. Barratt at once volunteered to cover the retirement, and this he succeeded in accomplishing. His accurate shooting caused many casualties to the enemy, and prevented their advance. Throughout the enterprise he was under heavy machine gun and rifle fire, and his splendid example of coolness and daring was beyond all praise. After safely regaining our lines, this very gallant soldier was killed by a shell.' He had seen action at Gallipoli before reaching the Western Front.

But as well as these three famous stories what of the others here? For example, Lieutenant Frederick Leopold Pusch, DSO, 1st Irish Guards, killed on 27 June 1916 aged 20 years. The son of Russian immigrants he was commissioned into the 1/19th (St. Pancras) Londons in 1913. He went with them to France in March 1915 where he was awarded the Distinguished Service Order for his actions at the Battle of Loos. The citation reads 'For conspicuous gallantry, marked ability and resource at Loos on 25th and 27th September, 1915. During the advance through Loos he led a party of bombers, and, going alone into a house, captured seven Germans, although badly shot in the face by one of them. Notwithstanding his serious injury this very gallant Officer continued clearing the enemy out of the cellars in the town. Lieutenant Pusch organized the bombing attack of Grenadiers on 27th September, operating from the Chalk Pit against the Copse, at great personal risk, and helped materially in its capture.' He transferred to the Irish Guards in November and was attached to the 1st Battalion a few days before his death. He was killed by a German sniper who had already wounded one of Pusch's men to whom he was attending and bandaging the wound. His brother, 2nd Lieutenant Ernst J Pusch, 11th Royal Warwickshires was killed in action a few weeks later aged 19 years on 8 August 1916 on the Somme and is buried at Flatiron Copse Cemetery, Mametz. While a holder of the Victoria Cross is buried here, also buried here is Lance Corporal Alfred Quick, DCM, 12th Rifle Brigade, who died on 15 April 1916 aged 19 years. The citation for his Distinguished Conduct Medal, a senior award for men from the ranks and non-commissioned officers, awarded in March 1916 reads 'For conspicuous gallantry when in charge of a grenadier section. During an enemy attack, when parties of enemy bombers had got into our trench, he bombed out two parties one after the other with great coolness and courage. Next day he was buried by a trench mortar, but stuck to his post.' He is one of four men who are buried here to hold this award.

And, as in many cemeteries, while there are men who lost a brother, there is one here who is one of three brothers killed in the war. Rifleman William E Saunders, 16th (St. Pancras) Rifle Brigade, died on 23 December 1916 aged 20 years. A brother Corporal John William E Saunders, MM, 110th Brigade, Royal Field Artillery died of wounds on 18 September 1918 aged 23 years and is buried in Peronne Communal Cemetery Extension. Another brother, Private Edward Robert Saunders, 21st Middlesex, died on 9 April 1918 aged 18 years and is commemorated on the Ploegsteert Memorial.

Also here is a man whose father was killed. Lieutenant Donald Campbell, 3rd Coldstream Guards, died on 19 July 1916 aged 20 years. His father, Captain The Honourable John Beresford Campbell, DSO, 1st Coldstream Guards was killed in action on 25 January 1915 at Givenchy aged 48 years and is commemorated on the Le Touret Memorial. He was killed when the Germans exploded a mine under his trench. His body was never found. He was the eldest son of the 3rd Baron Stratheden and 3rd Baron Campbell.

Buried here is Lieutenant C R Le Blanc-Smith, 8th Rifle Brigade died 27 November 1915. He was a keen rower who represented Cambridge University in the annual Boat Race in 1910, 1911 & 1912, though found himself on the losing side each year. He was also part of the victorious crew who won the Visitors Challenge Cup at Henley in 1910 and was President of Cambridge University Boat Club in 1913.

On the first day of Third Ypres, 31 July 1917, the 1/9th (Highlanders) Royal Scots were waiting beside the cemetery before attacking as part of the second wave. Two officers were stood on the canal bank watching the progress of the rest of the 51st (Highland) Division particularly the 1/4th Gordon Highlanders. They ignored the advice of other officers to come off the bank when a shell exploded next to them killing one officer and blowing an arm off the other who was then placed in an ambulance that was hit by a shell and destroyed.

As well as the Memorial to John McRae and the plaques with copies of 'In Flanders Fields' by the bunkers, another memorial, a tall obelisk on the canal bank, can be reached from Essex Farm Cemetery. It is a Monument to the 49th (West Riding) Division who have men buried in Plot I and who held the line nearby in 1915. The 38th (Welsh) Division have men buried in Plot III who fell during the autumn of 1916.

UK - 1107    Can - 9         Ger - 5
KUG - 83     Unnamed - 102   Area - 6059 sq mts
Special Memorials to nineteen British men who are believed/known to be buried here.

**LOCATION**
Essex Farm Cemetery lies on the northern edge of Ieper, about 1.5km from the centre, and just north of the by-pass on the N369 to Boezinge between the road and the canal.

## 1st D.C.L.I. CEMETERY, THE BLUFF

**HISTORY**
The cemetery dates from April to July 1915. There were 23 graves concentrated here after the war.

**INFORMATION**
1st D.C.L.I. Cemetery contains 51 men of the 1st Duke of Cornwall's Light Infantry who died in defending 'The Bluff' in early 1915 as well as men from other units who died in that action. The concentrated graves are in Row D.

'The Bluff' was at the edge of the Ypres-Comines canal on a ridge and was probably created out of spoil from the excavations from the canal. The 2nd Manchesters held 'The Bluff' for 87 consecutive days from 15 April to 25 July 1915 during which time Lieutenant Arthur Brooks Close-Brooks of the Manchester Regiment won the Military Cross for rescuing his Sergeant from no man's land after they had both been on patrol on 10 June. However, the Sergeant was found to be dead when they got to the British lines. Close-Brooks died of wounds on 10 January 1917, having been promoted to Captain, and is buried in Amara War Cemetery.

'The Bluff' was lost on 14-15 February 1916, when it was held by the 10th Lancashire Fusiliers, after the Germans had blown a mine. A counter-attack by 'A' Company, 7th York and Lancasters, failed to retake it though 'The Bluff' was recaptured on the night of 2-3 March by the 2nd Suffolks who attacked next to the canal through, and around, the crater. To their left the 8th King's Own (Royal Lancasters) and 1st Gordon Highlanders attacked the line between 'The Bluff' through the position of this cemetery and Woods Cemetery situated in what was known as 'The Ravine'. The attack was so successful that much of the original German line was taken with the old British trenches, but the Suffolks suffered 50% casualties. The Germans failed to over-run 'The Bluff' in July even after blowing a mine under the position.

It fell to the Germans in their Spring Offensive in 1918 but was finally recaptured by the 14th (Light) Division on 28 September 1918.

Buried here is Captain Charles Burnett Woodham, DSO, MiD, 1st Duke of Cornwall's Light Infantry, killed in action on 15 June 1915 aged 40 years. He was commissioned into the regiment in 1895, promoted to Lieutenant in 1898 and

Captain in 1901. He served in the South African Wars. He was Mentioned in Despatches in October 1914, and was awarded the Distinguished Service Order in February 1915 'for services in connection with operations in the field.'

The three cemeteries here are in Pallingbeke Park with benches, long grassed avenues and public artwork. They reflect the very social nature of the Belgian nation, where Saturdays and Sundays are still days for friends to gather and take part in a social activity organised by Trade Unions, the Church, Scouting movement or private groups, making the weekend 'special', which is something I admire.

UK - 76    Unnamed - 13    Area - 474 sq mts

**LOCATION**

1st D.C.L.I. Cemetery is about 5km south of Ieper lying in fields halfway between the Comines and Warneton roads south-west of Zillebeke near Hill 60. There is a road between the Ieper-Comines road and the Ieper-St. Eloi road upon which you will see CWGC signs pointing to the three cemeteries in this group. There is parking here and safe paths to the three cemeteries. Or you can drive closer to the cemeteries but there is less space for parking at the side of the road – though it is viable. From here the path leads to three cemeteries. The CWGC site says 'Visitors to this site should note the 100m grassed access path leading to this cemetery which is not accessible by vehicle.' The grass path splits within 100m. Straight on will bring you to Woods Cemetery. Taking the path to your right will bring you to the 1st DCLI Cemetery. Continuing along the front of that cemetery (passing its gate) and then turning right will bring you to Hedge Row Trench Cemetery. There is a long walk from the parking area to this cemetery. The two smaller graveyards are particularly tranquil.

# FERME-OLIVIER CEMETERY

**HISTORY**

This cemetery was used from 9 June 1915 to 5 August 1917 for burials from Dressing Stations located in the Chateau.

**INFORMATION**

The 62nd, 16th, 9th, 11th, 129th and 130th Field Ambulances were posted successively to the Dressing Stations that this cemetery served. The burials in Plots I and II are not grouped in order of date but those in Plot III are, reflecting the order of postings to the area and the occupation of the Chateau in Elverdinge by the 38th (Welsh) and Guards Divisions as well as the Royal Artillery. Plot II, Row E contains 41 men of the 1/3rd Monmouthshires killed while on parade in December 1915 by a single shell from a large German gun sited in Houthulst Forest. They were preparing a withdrawal from the area for a well earned six weeks of rest and had received orders to parade ready to move off at 2.30 pm.

In Elverdinge churchyard, which can be found in the centre of the nearby village, nine British soldiers were buried in late 1914 and early 1915. The church and churchyard were severely damaged by shell-fire, the village, though not Ferme Olivier Cemetery, being just inside the range of German guns until the British advance in Third Ypres. The graves were removed to Cement House Cemetery in 1973. Buried here is Colonel Ernest Octavius Wight, 49th (West Riding) Division Assistant Director of Medical Services, Royal Army Medical Corps killed in action on 19 December 1915 aged 57 years. He was commissioned as a Surgeon Captain, Royal Army Medical Services in 1892 and promoted to Lieutenant Colonel in 1902. He saw service in China and Burma. He held the Royal Humane Society's bronze medal for saving a private of the 4th Madras Pioneers from drowning on 7 May 1892 and had saved lives on two other occasions for which he received awards. He retired in 1907 joining the Territorials in 1908 as Assistant Director of Medical Services of the Home Counties Division. He joined 49th Division in April 1915 and was killed by a shell while trying to help ambulances get out of difficulties. Also here is Lieutenant Colonel George Trevor Gregor, VD, 1st (Welsh) Howitzer Brigade, 53rd (Welsh) Division, Royal Field Artillery who died on 1 July 1917 aged 47 years. He had served as a volunteer for many years before the war so was entitled to the Volunteer Officers Decoration (VD). He was killed by a shell that fell on the Officers Mess.

Another here is Lieutenant Colonel Frederick George Howard, DSO, MVO, MiD, 57th Field Company, Royal Engineers who died on 19 October 1915 aged 43 years. He was commissioned in 1892, promoted to Lieutenant in 1895, Captain in 1902 and Major in 1912. He served with the Chitral Operation in 1895, Tirah on the North-West Frontier 1897-8 and was Assistant Military Secretary and ADC to the Governor and Commander-in-Chief in Malta from 1911-12. His Distinguished Service Order was awarded in February 1915 'for services in connection with operations in the field' and he was Mentioned in Despatches in October 1914.

Two young men are buried here. Private Harry Price, 113th Company, Machine Gun Corps died on 14 October 1916 aged 16 years. Rifleman Leonard Charles Streatfield, 9th King's Royal Rifle Corps died 6 January 1916 aged 16 years. Also buried here are two men who were executed when their units were in camp in Elverdinge. Private George Watkins, 13th (2nd Rhondda Pals) Welsh deserted in the Salient in December 1916 and was caught in March 1917. He had joined the army in 1904 and was recalled as a reservist in 1914. He was in France within days and had served since the Retreat from Mons having a good record and being wounded twice. He was executed and buried here on 15 May 1917 aged 32 years.

Private Robert Hope, who enlisted and served as James Hepple which is the name on his headstone, 1st Royal Inniskilling Fusiliers deserted near Arras in January 1917 and was absent for eleven weeks until caught sleeping in an empty house in Albert. He had served briefly at Gallipoli from November 1915 before being sent to France where he was involved in the disastrous attack during the first day of the Battle of the Somme in which his Battalion suffered over 50 casualties. He was tried on 9 June 1917 on the Somme and was executed on 5 July 1917 aged 21 years after his Battalion had moved north to the Salient.

Buried here is Private Stephen Oliver Ferry, 11th Durham Light Infantry killed in action 16 March 1916 aged 32 years. In December 1914 the War Office decided upon the formation of pioneer Battalions as divisional troops. They were originally meant to be to be skilled labour for the Royal Engineers and to take the burden of working parties and general labour off the infantry. It was believed that these units would spend much of their time digging, so it was planned that at least 50% of the unit strength would be of men used to working with pick and shovel with the other 50% possessing a trade such as joiner or bricklayer. In addition to road making, demolition and entrenching the men were to be trained in technical work such as building railway embankments. However, the Battalions were also to be equipped and trained as infantry so that, on many occasions, the pioneers found themselves in battle fighting with the infantry. Early in January 1915 the 11th Durham Light Infantry, 95% of whom were colliery men, became the Pioneer Battalion of the 20th (Light) Division. On 17 August 1915 Private Stephen Ferry joined the Battalion. In February and March 1916 the Battalion was in the Salient digging and revetting trenches, putting out wire, making dugouts and machine gun emplacements, sinking wells, and repairing tramways. Snow came at the end of February followed by a thaw leaving the trenches in a bad condition. Stephen Ferry was killed in action whilst working in the British Lines by German shell fire.

Buried here is Major Brinley 'Brin' Richard Lewis, MiD, 'B' Battery, 122nd Brigade, Royal Field Artillery, died 2 April 1917 aged 26 years. He was a rugby union international for Wales gaining two caps, one victory against Ireland in 1913 and a defeat against the same country in 1912, as well as playing for Cambridge University where he gained three 'blues', Swansea, London Welsh and the Barbarians. He enlisted in 1914 but was soon commissioned. He was killed when the Germans shelled the rear of 'B' Battery, hitting the mess where Lewis was situated, killing him instantly. He was Mentioned in Despatches in April 1916.

One of the Germans here is Leutnant Hans von Keudell, Jasta 27, killed in action on 15 February 1917. He was an experienced pilot and had formed Jasta 27 ten days earlier. He was the unit's first commander and its first casualty.

Also of note is Gunner John Hogan, 299th Siege Battery, Royal Garrison Artillery, killed on 24 June 1917. He enlisted with the Lancashire Fusiliers in September 1914 but was wounded in January 1915 and sent home before being discharged in October 1915. He re-enlisted in May 1916. His son, also an artilleryman, Gunner Bernard Hogan, 51 Medium Regiment, Royal Artillery, was killed in action on 25 January 1944 aged 31 years and is buried in Minturno War Cemetery north of Naples in Italy.

UK - 409                    Ger - 3

**LOCATION**
Ferme Olivier Cemetery lies on the northern edge of Elverdinge about 5km north-west of Ieper. It is located on the south side of the N333 Poperinge road about 1km from its junction with the N8, which is just north of the traffic lights in Elverdinge.

## GODEWAERSVELDE BRITISH CEMETERY

**HISTORY**
The cemetery was begun in July 1917 during the lull in fighting between the Battle of Messines and Third Ypres. It remained in use until August 1918.

**INFORMATION**
Three Casualty Clearing Stations were posted here in July 1917 and the cemetery grew up servicing them. The 37th and 41st remained until November 1917 while the 11th stayed until the German advance in April 1918. Burials during the German Offensive were then carried out by fighting units and Field Ambulances.

The nurses at No. 11 Casualty Clearing Station suffered from the effects of a gas attack on 12 July 1917 as the substance was brought in on the clothes of the wounded soldiers. The nurses later in the month went on to the Mont des Cats to watch the bombardment that was the prelude to the Third Battle of Ypres.

The French made a large Plot at the 'higher' end of the cemetery in May and June 1918 but the graves were removed after the war. At that time five graves of men of the 110th Brigade Royal Field Artillery were brought from the slopes of the Mont des Cats and four graves, consisting of one British body, one Canadian soldier and two Indians, were concentrated from the churchyard in the village.

Buried here is Major George St. John Fancourt McDonald, DSO, 36th Australian Heavy Artillery, who died on 22 March 1918 aged 34 years. He was promoted to Major in June 1916 and was awarded the Distinguished Service Order in the New Year's Honours List in January 1917 and Mentioned in Despatches in November 1917. He died of wounds, caused by a shell landing on his hut while he was sleeping, at No. 11 Casualty Clearing Station.

Another buried here is Lieutenant Colin Gernon Palmer Campbell, MC, 94th Brigade, Royal Field Artillery who died of wounds on 10 October 1917 aged 22 years. He enlisted at Halifax, Canada in August 1914, and served with the 23rd Battery, 2nd Brigade, Canadian Field Artillery until wounded, as a Corporal, at La Bassee in June 1915. Once recovered he was commissioned as a Lieutenant into the British Army. He was one of six brothers who served in the war, one of which, Lieutenant Kenneth Archibald Campbell, 42nd Canadian Infantry was killed on 23 January 1917 when he insisted on looking over the edge of a forward position and was shot in the head by a sniper.

One Sister of the Territorial Nursing Force is also buried here, one of only two nurses killed in the war to be buried in Belgium. She is Sister Elise Margaret Kemp, 58th Casualty Clearing Station, Territorial Force Nursing Service, who died on 20 October 1917 aged 36 years killed in a German air raid. She was born in New Zealand and is the only nurse from that country to die in the war. Her father was a Doctor and the family had moved to London by 1901. She began nursing in 1908 and joined up in 1914 serving on the Western Front from 1916. Two of her brothers served with the Royal Army Medical Corps through the war.

Also buried here is Sapper Albert Edward Hancox, 101st Field Company, Royal Engineers, who died on 24 July 1917 aged 19 years. His brother Corporal William Rufus Hancox, 1/4th Oxford and Bucks Light Infantry was killed in action at The Nab near Authuille on the Somme when the Germans counter-attacked their position on the night of 13-14 August 1916 aged 20 years. He is commemorated on the Thiepval Memorial. Another brother Sapper Walter David Hancox, 154th Field Company, Royal Engineers died on 1 July 1916, the first day of the Battle of the Somme aged 30 years. He is buried in Bienvillers Military Cemetery. Also here is Private John Edmunds, 1st Duke of Cornwall's Light Infantry who died on 5 October 1917 aged 30 years. He was a farm labourer who enlisted in April 1915, saw action on the Somme and died of gunshot wounds received in action. His brother, Driver Melbourne Edmunds, 26th Horse Transport Company, Army Service Corps died of a fever on 2 June 1916 aged 22 years and is buried at Etaples Military Cemetery. Another brother, Lance Corporal William Edmunds, 2nd Oxford and Bucks Light Infantry died on 30 July 1916 aged 26 years and is commemorated on the Thiepval Memorial.

| UK - 988 | Aust - 65 | NZ – 2 |
|---|---|---|
| Can - 5 | S Afr - 2 | India – 3 |
| Ger – 19 | Area – 2645 sq mts | |

## LOCATION

Godewaersvelde Cemetery lies on the northern edge of the village about 15km south-west of Ieper and south of Poperinge. It is a very pleasant cemetery, situated on rising ground between the valley and the Mont des Cats just east of the road into the village on a dead-end side road. The easiest route is via Poperinge and the new road to Steenvoorde leaving this by taking the D10 towards Bailleul before turning to Godewaersvelde.

# GODEZONNE FARM CEMETERY

Among those buried here is Captain The Honourable Douglas Kinnaird, 2nd Scots Guards, killed in action on 24 October 1914 aged 35 years. He was Master of Kinnaird and eldest son of 11th Baron Kinnaird. He joined the 3rd Scots Guards in 1901 being promoted to Lieutenant in 1904 and Captain in 1912. It seems he was originally buried near the north-east corner of Polygon Wood at Zonnebeke Farm and moved here in 1925. His brother The Honourable Arthur Middleton Kinnaird, MC, 1st Scots Guards was killed during the Battle of Cambrai on 27 November 1917 aged 32 years and is buried at Ruyaulcourt Military Cemetery.

South of the cemetery is a Memorial to men of the French 32nd Infantry Division who died nearby in 1914 and 1918.

| UK - 74 | Aust - 1 | Can – 1 |
|---|---|---|
| S Afr - 3 | Unnamed - 44 | Area – 765 sq mts |

## HISTORY

The cemetery was used from February to May 1915 with three graves added in 1916. Then it was enlarged after the war by the concentration of 59 graves which were added to the twenty made during the war.

## INFORMATION

The cemetery was created in the garden of Godezonne Farm on the edge of a road known as 'Cheapside'. The seventeen original graves made in 1915 and making up Plot I, Rows A and B, were of men of the 4th Middlesex and the 2nd Royal Scots.

## LOCATION

Godezonne Farm Cemetery is located about 5km south of Ieper, and about 1km north of Kemmel. It is on a road that runs roughly north-south parallel to and just west of the Ieper-Kemmel road. From the crossroads in Vierstraat, distinguished by two extremely large warehouses, turn west to a small crossroads at a CWGC sign and left to the cemetery which is on the left after 500m. This little cemetery has good views of the Salient, especially of the Kemmelberg.

# GROOTEBEEK BRITISH CEMETERY

### HISTORY
This cemetery was begun in April 1918 during the Battles of the Lys and used at intervals until the end of September.

### INFORMATION
Burials in this area, which was under British occupation throughout the war, were mostly carried out in the cemeteries in Reningelst. But at the start of the Battles of the Lys the Field Ambulances stationed here created a new burial ground known as Ouderdom Military Cemetery which was later renamed after the stream which runs either side of it. Grootebeek absorbed a small Indian Cemetery that had been made in April 1915. The graves of three French soldiers have been removed and replaced by those of two men killed in May 1940 buried in Row G.

Commemorated here is Private John Walter Harrison Lynn VC, DCM, MiD, Cross of the Order of St. George, 4th Class (Russia), 2nd Lancashire Fusiliers, died 3 May 1915 aged 28 years. There is a Special Memorial to Lynn whose grave in Vlamertinge Churchyard was destroyed by shell-fire. The citation for his Victoria Cross, won for his actions near Mousetrap Farm, reads 'For most conspicuous bravery near Ypres on 2nd May 1915. When the Germans were advancing behind their wave of asphyxiating gas, Pte. Lynn, although almost overcome by the deadly fumes, handled his machine gun with very great effect against the enemy, and when he could not see them he moved his gun higher up on the parapet, which enabled him to bring even more effective fire to bear, and eventually checked any further advance. The great courage displayed by this soldier had a fine effect on his comrades in the very trying circumstances. He died from the effects of gas poisoning.' He was also Mentioned in Despatches for this act. He was awarded the Distinguished Conduct Medal for an act in December 1914. The citation reads 'For gallant conduct. Took charge of an isolated machine gun when his Serjeant was killed, brought it out of action when jammed and took it back again to the firing line when repaired.' He was posthumously awarded his Russian Order. He joined the 3rd Lancashire Fusiliers as a band boy in 1901 and served until 1913 being called up as a reservist in 1914.

Also here is Naik Lalak, IOM, 57th Wilde's Rifles (Frontier Force) who died on 27 April 1915. From Fort Lokhart on the North West Frontier he was awarded the Indian Order of Merit in February 1915 for service with the Indian Army.

| | | |
|---|---|---|
| UK - 99 | NZ - 1 | S Afr – 1 |
| Bermuda - 1 | India - 7 | WW2 - 2 |
| Unnamed - 1 | | Area – 1694 sq mts |

Special Memorials to two graves destroyed by shell-fire.

### LOCATION
Grootebeek Cemetery lies in the village of Ouderdom on its northern edge about 5km south-west of Ieper. The path to the cemetery is well marked though the CWGC website says 'Visitors to this site should note a 100m grassed access path which is not suitable for vehicles'. This is a beautiful little burial ground set away from the road behind a hop field and on the edge of open fields. The Grootebeek stream surrounds the cemetery making it an island reached by a small stone bridge which also contains the register.

# GUNNERS FARM MILITARY CEMETERY

### INFORMATION
The cemetery gets its name from the farm opposite. The area was in German hands from 10 April to 29 September 1918.

This is a good example of a number of cemeteries used in 1914 and 1915 by one or two regiments at a time. As such each Plot, or part of Plot, is constituted almost entirely of burials from one Battalion. The order of burials also gives us an insight into the order in which units were posted to the area.

The burials here are:
- Rows A to C - 9th Essex and 7th Suffolks
- Rows D to J - 9th Loyal North Lancashires and 11th Lancashire Fusiliers
- Rows J to Q - 9th (Scottish) Division
- Rows R to W - 11th (Lambeth) Queen's (Royal West Surreys) and 10th (Kent County) (Royal West Kents)

Among those buried here is Private William Liddell, DCM, 9th Divisional Company, Army Cyclist Corps who died of

### HISTORY
This cemetery was begun in July 1915 and remained in use until June 1916 except for three British and four German burials made later.

wounds on 25 February 1916 aged 33 years. He had enlisted with the Seaforth Highlanders in August 1914 before transferring to the Army Cyclist Corps in January 1915. He arrived in France in May 1915. The citation for his Distinguished Conduct Medal, awarded in March 1916, reads 'For conspicuous gallantry. Hearing a wounded man of another Battalion, who was lying out in the open, calling for assistance, he accompanied by Captain Campbell, jumped over the parapet and together they carried the wounded man to safety. Private Liddell's clothing was hit in several places by the enemy's bullets.'

UK - 163        Aust - 2        NZ - 1        S Afr - 9
Ger - 4        Area – 1421 sq mts

**LOCATION**
Gunners Farm Cemetery is about 1.5km south-east of Ploegsteert, and about 15km south of Ieper. Approximately 1.4km south of Ploegsteert square you will find, on the east side of the road, near a supermarket, a tree of CWGC signs. The road to the north-east, the Chemin de Blanche, leads to this cemetery, which is on the north side of the road beyond.

# GWALIA CEMETERY

**HISTORY**
Begun early in July 1917, in the period between the Battle of Messines and the Third Battle of Ypres, the cemetery remained in use until the end of fighting on the Salient in September 1918.

**INFORMATION**
Situated on a rise in fields, Gwalia Cemetery is a fitting resting place for those who gave their lives for their country. The graveyard gets its name from 'Gwalia Farm' by which you walk to reach the cemetery. The farm and burial ground were situated among the camps in the rear of the Salient. Gwalia is an old Welsh word meaning 'Wales' and was once popular as a poetic name for the country.

Of those buried here, 179 were from artillery units, 30 from the Royal Engineers and 30 from Labour Corps units of the (Royal) Army Service Corps. One American and two French graves have been removed.

In Plot I, Row H, fourteen men of the 9th Lancashire Fusiliers are buried. They were killed in an air raid over Dirty Bucket Camp, which was near to Hospital Farm Cemetery, in the early morning of 4 October 1917.

Among those buried here is Captain James Bliss, MC & Bar, 1/6th (Morayshire) Seaforth Highlanders, who died on 31 July 1917 aged 29 years. He worked for the railways before the war and enlisted as a Private in late 1914. The citation for his Military Cross, won during the capture of Beaumont-Hamel in November 1916, reads 'For conspicuous gallantry in action. He led his men to their objective with great courage and initiative. Later he rallied men of several units and led them forward setting a splendid example to his men.' He was awarded a Bar to his MC during fighting at Arras in April 1917. The citation reads 'For conspicuous gallantry and devotion to duty in continuing to command his Company, though wounded, at a critical moment when the enemy had broken through our front. With great skill and gallantry he first held up the enemy and then drove them back. He subsequently led a bombing attack, and whilst directing a counter attack was wounded for a second time.' He was mortally wounded on the first day of Third Ypres between Pilkem and St. Juliaan. His brother also died in the war. 2nd Lieutenant Thomas Bliss had served with the Seaforth Highlanders until 1912, joined the Army Service Corps as a Private in February 1915 and was commissioned into the same Battalion as his brother before dying of wounds on 23 December 1916. He is buried in Aveluy Communal Cemetery Extension on the Somme.

Lieutenant Colonel Percy William Beresford, DSO, twice MiD, 2/3rd Royal Fusiliers, died of wounds on 26 October 1917 aged 42 years. Before the war he was an assistant priest in Kent where, while serving with the Militia and Territorials, he founded one of the first Cadet Corps in the country in 1902 – the Westerham and Chipstead Cadet Corps attached to the 1st Volunteer Battalion, The Queen's Own (Royal West Kents). He joined the 3rd Royal Fusiliers in January 1915, was wounded in April and gassed in September 1915. He was promoted to Lieutenant Colonel in May 1916. The citation for his Distinguished Service Order, won at Bullecourt in March 1917, reads 'For conspicuous gallantry and ability in command of his Battalion during heavy enemy counter-attacks. The skill with which he handled his reserves was of the utmost assistance to the Division on his right, and his determination enabled us to hold on to an almost impossible position. He repulsed 3 counter-attacks, and lost heavily in doing so.'

A casualty who represents one of the truisms of the war, that the average life expectancy of a Subaltern on the Western Front was approximately 'eleven days' is 2nd Lieutenant Roper Henry Whitrod, 4th King's (Liverpools), killed on 28 May 1918 aged 28 years. He joined the Coldstream Guards as a boy soldier aged 14 years and served in Egypt. He was at the Front early in the war and was promoted to Sergeant in 1916. He was given a commission in 1918 and joined his Battalion on 14 May 1918. Between that date and his death, when killed by a shell while returning from a working party, he did not see action. So, his time 'at the Front' as a 2nd Lieutenant lasted for fourteen days, though he spent few of them in the line and only for working party.

Captain and Adjutant William St. Clair Grant, MC, Croix de Guerre (Belgium), 5th Cameron Highlanders died on 26 September 1918 aged 24 years mortally wounded by shellfire. He played four first class cricket matches for Gloucestershire in 1914. He was commissioned into the Gloucestershire regiment in September 1914 and was a Captain in October 1915 before transferring to the Highlanders. He was awarded the Military Cross in July 1918 for leading reconnaissance missions twice under fire.

UK - 435   Aust - 2   NZ – 5
Can – 5   S Afr – 1   BWI – 14
Chinese Labour Corps – 4   Ger – 3
Area – 1199 sq mts

### LOCATION
Gwalia Cemetery lies in open fields about 6km north-west of Ieper and about 2.5km north-east of Poperinge. It is approximately 250m north of the road from Poperinge to Elverdinge (N333) nearly halfway between the two towns. A CWGC path leads from a lay-by at the roads' edge past the farm to the cemetery which can be seen from the road. The CWGC website says 'Visitors to this site should note a 400m grassed access path which is unsuitable for vehicles.'

# HAGLE DUMP CEMETERY

### HISTORY
Begun next to the stores dump of the same name in April 1918 during the Battles of the Lys, the cemetery was in use until October and was then greatly enlarged after the war.

### INFORMATION
This cemetery was within British lines throughout the war and replaced Ferme Olivier and Hospital Farm cemeteries as they were filled. The concentrated graves are to be found in Plots III and IV. Most of the original graves in Plot I show the type of units you find behind the lines such as Siege Battery Gunners, Light Railway and Army Tramway companies, which makes this part of the cemetery very interesting. The graves of 26 Americans, who died from July to September 1918, and two French soldiers, have been removed.

Plot I, Rows C and D is partly made up of men from the 10th Queens Own (Royal West Kents) killed on 27 April 1918 in their camp in reserve. It had been, as was often the case, located next to an ammunition dump. The dump exploded at about 12.30pm when a German shell hit it.

There are two men buried here who deserted from their units during the German Spring Offensive in 1918. Private Walter Dossett of the 1/4th (Hallamshire) York and Lancasters was executed at a rifle range near Vlamertinge on 25 June 1918 aged 22 years following a Court Martial on 8 June. He had served in three different Machine Gun Companies from 1916, the 143rd, 118th and 63rd until moving to 1/4th Yorks and Lancasters.

Private George Ainley of the 1/4th King's Own Yorkshire Light Infantry was executed on 30 July 1918 aged 20 years. Ainley was Court Martialled on 28 January 1918 for a self-inflicted wound and subsequently deserted three times. He was tried for all three offences on 13 July.

Buried here is Captain Hugh Roger Partridge, MC & Bar, 1/1st West Riding Field Ambulance, 49th Division, Royal Army Medical Corps who died on 24 July 1918 aged 27 years. The citation for his Military Cross, awarded in October 1916, reads 'For conspicuous gallantry and devotion to duty during operations. During several weeks he was in charge of a collecting posts and repeatedly under heavy shellfire. He has shown the greatest coolness, and has worked incessantly evacuating the wounded. He has been hit more than once by debris, and has set a fine example to those around him.' The citation for the Bar to his MC, awarded in January 1918, reads 'For conspicuous gallantry and devotion to duty. During an intense bombardment of a town with high explosive and gas shells he led search parties into different parts of the town, collecting the wounded and placing them in a cellar, where he attended to them. Later, when the bombardment subsided he superintended their removal to the advanced dressing station. On his return to the dressing station he continued to perform his duties, although his eyes were so swollen by gas that he was obliged to keep them open with his fingers. He undoubtedly saved several lives by his splendid devotion and total disregard of personal danger. He was eventually evacuated to the casualty clearing station.'

Also here is Company Sergeant Major James William Dames, DCM, MSM, Princess Patricia's Canadian Light Infantry (Eastern Ontario Regiment) killed in action on 8 May 1915 aged 45 years. He enlisted in 1885, aged 14 years, into the Sherwood Foresters, served in Mashonaland in 1896 and on the North-West Frontier of India in the Tirah Campaign 1897-98 and in the South African Wars with the Malta Mounted Infantry but was invalided home when twice wounded. He was awarded the Distinguished Conduct Medal for his service. He was awarded the Meritorious Service Medal for his work in the War Office between his return from South Africa and emigrating to Canada in 1909. He subsequently joined the Canadian Forces in September 1914, arrived in France in December and was killed at Bellewaerde Lake during Second Ypres. He was originally buried alone east of Polygon Wood and north of the Menin Road near the lake.

His remains were concentrated into this cemetery in 1925, though still unidentfied even though his medal ribbons were noted. He lay in this cemetery as an unidentified soldier, also being commemorated on the Menin Gate, until finally recognised in 1992.

Another buried here is Major Vernon Holden, DSO, MC, MiD, 10th Queen's Own (Royal West Kents) attached 11th Queen's (Royal West Surreys), died of wounds on 2 October 1918 aged 25 years. He enlisted as a Lance Corporal in the Kings Royal Rifle Corps in August 1915 and was commissioned in November into the Royal West Kents. He was promoted to Lieutenant in November 1916, Captain in March 1917 and Major in May 1918. He served on the Western Front from May 1916, Italy in November 1917 and then was Commandant of a Brigade School and Commanding Officer of the 41st Divisional Reception Camp from May 1918. He rejoined his regiment in August 1918. The citation for his Military Cross reads 'Night of 31st July 1917 - 1st August 1917 - For conspicuous gallantry and devotion to duty. He organised the consolidation of his Battalion front under heavy machine gun and rifle fire, continually going to and fro to advanced battalion headquarters, through heavy fire, to report personally upon the situation. All the other officers were casualties, and his courage and splendid personal example, under trying circumstances, were of the utmost value.' That for his Distinguished Service Order awarded in September 1918 reads 'For conspicuous gallantry and devotion to duty during an enemy advance. When his Battalion was surrounded he withdrew his Company with marked skill through the enveloping enemy, and collected men near him and formed a new line of defence. Throughout his fine leadership and coolness under most difficult circumstances were of a high order.' He was mortally wounded on 1 October.

Concentrated here:
Brielen Military Cemetery - situated on the south side of the village about 3km east of here, and used from April 1915 to September 1917, it contained 31 French, sixteen British and four Canadian men.

UK - 397        Aust - 26        Can – 14
Ger – 2         Unnamed – 139    Area – 1818 sq mts

**LOCATION**
Hagle Dump Cemetery is found about 1km north of the old road to Poperinge (N308), 4km west of Ieper, and about 3km west of Vlamertinge.

# HARINGHE (BANDAGHEM) BRITISH CEMETERY

**HISTORY**
Haringhe was one of several cemeteries, set up in preparation for the Third Battles of Ypres in July 1917, and attached to Casualty Clearing Stations. It remained in use until October 1918.

**INFORMATION**
The cemetery acquired its ironic name, Bandaghem, with two other local cemeteries, Dozinghem and Mendinghem, from the soldiers, who were playing upon the Flemish language to describe the job of the Dressing Stations, though this cemetery has now been renamed after the town by which it is located. It carries the name spelt as in the war though the current Flemish spelling is without the last 'h'.

The Casualty Clearing Stations posted here in 1917 were the 62nd and 63rd with the 36th arriving in 1918. The 62nd was designated to receive all 'N. Y. D. N.' (Not Yet Diagnosed Nervous) cases, who we might today call 'battle fatigue', 'shell-shock' or 'post traumatic stress syndrome'. These were usually evacuated to base hospitals but for the Third Battle of Ypres the British commanders had decided that they would be held at Haringe for one month to sort out the genuine cases.

During the offensive, No. 62 Casualty Clearing Station dealt with 5000 cases. Only 16% were eventually evacuated to base hospitals in Rouen or Etaples; this breaks down as 4% who were not 'N.Y.D.N.' but had been sent to Haringe by mistake, 12% psycho-neurotic and 4% psycho-neurotic with physical complications. 55% were immediately returned to their units and 29% went to work for four weeks on farms away from the front-line before returning to their units.

Four French Plots were removed after the war as was a Plot of German graves, two American and two Belgian graves, whereas five British men were buried here during World War II.

Among those buried here are three men awarded the Albert Medal for their part in an incident at Krombeke about 5km north of Poperinge and 3km east of here on 30 April 1918 in which they lost their lives. They are Company Serjeant Major Alfred Henry Furlonger, AM, DCM, 29th Light Railway Operating Company, Royal Engineers aged 31 years; Sapper Joseph Collinton Farren, AM, 12th Light Railway Operating Company, Royal Engineers aged 23 years; and Sapper George Edward Johnson, AM, 21st Light Railway Operating Company, Royal Engineers aged 25 years. The citation reads 'In Flanders, on the 30th April, 1918, a train of ammunition had been placed at an ammunition refilling point, and after the engine had been detached, and was being run off the train, the second truck suddenly burst into flames. Furlonger immediately ordered Bigland, the driver, to move the engine back on to the train for the purpose of pulling away the two trucks nearest the engine. Bigland did so without hesitation, and the engine was coupled up by Furlonger, assisted by Farren, while the burning truck was uncoupled from the remainder of the train by Woodman. The two trucks were then drawn away clear of the ammunition dump, it being the intention to uncouple the burning wagon from the engine and the first wagon and so isolate it, with the object of localising the fire as far as possible. The uncoupling was about to be done when the ammunition exploded, completely wrecking the engine and both trucks, killing Furlonger, Farren and Johnson (a member of the train crew), and seriously wounding Bigland. Had it not been for the prompt and courageous action of these men, whereby three of them lost their lives and one was seriously injured, there is not the slightest doubt that the whole dump would have been destroyed and many lives lost.' In addition, Lance Corporal John Edward Bigland, 12th Light Railway Operating Company, Royal Engineers and Sapper Thomas Henry Woodman, 29th Light Railway Operating Company, Royal Engineers were awarded the Albert Medal. Warrant Officer Class 1 Stanley Corsellis Randall, 61st Broad Gauge Workshop Company, Royal Engineers was awarded the Military Medal for the same event. You will see that, among many other extraordinary men who served in the front lines, Furlonger, who served behind the lines, had been involved in two acts for which he received senior awards. The citation for his Distinguished Conduct Medal won during Third Ypres and gazetted in February 1918 reads 'For conspicuous gallantry and devotion to duty. He was in charge of trains evacuating the wounded from an aid post. The enemy shelled the line and cut it in seven places, preventing a train from reaching the aid post. He at once organised a party, and had the line repaired under heavy fire. When one of the trucks was hit by a shell he transferred the wounded on it to another truck, and got the train away to safety. He showed great courage and ability throughout the day.'

Buried here is Lieutenant Colonel Hubert Podmore, DSO, three times MiD, 12th Middlesex late 6th Northamptonshires, died on 31 December 1917 aged 30 years. He was a pupil at Rugby School and returned as a Master after studying at Oxford University. On the outbreak of the war he was commissioned into the Northamptonshires, was promoted to Lieutenant in October 1914 and Captain in November. The Battalion went to France in May 1915 and he was awarded the Distinguished Service Order in May 1916. The citation reads 'For conspicuous gallantry and ability during a night attack by the enemy. It was largely due to Captain Podmore that his Company held its own in spite of very heavy bombardment, and repelled every attack.' He was wounded at Trones Wood in July 1916 and promoted to Major in October. He was wounded again at Glencorse Wood in August 1917 and returned in December as the commanding officer of the 12th Middlesex. He was Mentioned in Despatches in June 1916, January 1917 and May 1917. He had only been in command of the 12th Middlesex for eight days when he was accidentally killed by an explosion of mortar ammunition, whilst watching a trench mortar practice at Proven. Six other soldiers were also killed in the same explosion.

Major Richard Fielding Morrison, MC & Bar, twice MiD, 51st Brigade, Royal Field Artillery died of wounds on 25 April 1918 aged 27 years. His father had been commanding officer of the 18th (Queen Mary's Own) Hussars. He was educated at Wellington College, where he captained the Shooting eight, and at Woolwich, where he passed out at the head of the gunners' list, receiving the Tombs Memorial Prize, in July 1910. He joined the 126th Howitzer Battery and went to war with it serving at Mons until he transferred to the Royal Horse Artillery in 1915. He was promoted to Captain in 1916 and took charge of a Battery and was promoted to Major in July 1916. He was Mentioned in Despatches in 1915 and again posthumously. He was awarded the Military Cross in the New Year Honours' List of 1917. A Bar was awarded in July 1918. The citation reads 'For conspicuous gallantry and devotion to duty. Whether in command of his Battery or of the Brigade, or acting as infantry liaison officer, he displayed coolness and resource of a very high order. Once, when his Battery came under heavy shell fire and direct hits on the teams caused some confusion, his fine example and complete command of the situation at once restored order. His courage and fine leadership were conspicuous throughout.'

| | | |
|---|---|---|
| UK - 732 | Aust - 2 | NZ – 11 |
| Can - 1 | NF - 5 | S Afr – 7 |
| BWI – 4 | Bermuda - 1 | KUG – 5 |
| Chinese Labour Corps - 4 | | Ger – 39 |
| Fr Civilian - 1 | WWII - 5 | Area – 2264 sq mts |

**LOCATION**
Haringhe Cemetery in is the village of Haringe about 20km north-west of Ieper and about 10km north-west of Poperinge. Lying 2km south-west of Roesbrugge on the southern edge of the village of Haringe, just east of the border with France, it is reached most easily via the Poperinge by-pass and the N308 through Proven and then the road south-east to Haringe from Roesbrugge. The cemetery is 200m south-east of Haringe.

# HEDGE ROW TRENCH CEMETERY

**HISTORY**
This was opened in March 1915 and used until August 1917.
**INFORMATION**
Further information about 'The Bluff' can be found by referring to 1st D.C.L.I. Cemetery.
This is the furthest from the road of the three cemeteries on 'The Bluff'. It stands high on the crest of the ridge and can only just be seen from the road. This was named after a nearby communication trench and was previously known as Ravine Wood Cemetery.

The cemetery suffered from the effects of very severe shell-fire later in the fighting so that after the war the individual graves could not be identified. The names of the dead, however, were known, and Special Memorial headstones were erected bearing the inscription 'Known to be buried in this cemetery'. Therefore, it is unusual in that every headstone here is actually a Special Memorial arranged symmetrically in a pattern around the Cross of Sacrifice.

Among those here is Captain Harold Walter Joel, 21st (First Surrey Rifles) Londons, killed in action on 7 June 1917 aged 20 years. He was involved with the Boy Scouts before the war being the second King's Scout in the country, but on his 18th birthday in March 1915 he enlisted as a Private in the London Rifle Brigade. He was soon made a Sergeant and commissioned into the Surrey Rifles in October. He arrived at the Front in May 1916, was wounded on the Somme and promoted to Captain in April 1917. On the first day of the Battle of Messines he was killed instantaneously in the enemy trenches having led his men to take their objectives in heavy fighting.

The three cemeteries here are in Pallingbeke Park with benches, long grassed avenues and public artwork. They reflect the very social nature of the Belgian nation, where Saturdays and Sundays are still days for friends to gather and take part in a social activity organised by Trade Unions, the Church, Scouting movement or private groups, making the weekend 'special', which is something I admire.

UK - 94        Can - 2        KUG – 2

Area - 679 sq mts

Special Memorials to 96 men known to be buried here.

**LOCATION**

Hedge Row Trench Cemetery is about 5km south of Ieper lying in fields halfway between the Comines and Warneton roads south-west of Zillebeke near Hill 60. There is road between the Ieper-Comines road and the Ieper-St. Eloi road upon which you will see CWGC signs pointing to the three cemeteries in this group. There is parking here and safe paths to the three cemeteries. Or you can drive closer to the cemeteries where there is less space for parking at the side of the road – though it is viable. From here the path leads to three cemeteries. The CWGC site says 'Visitors to this site should note the 100m grassed access path leading to this cemetery which is not accessible by vehicle.' The grass path splits within 100m. Straight on will bring you to Woods Cemetery. Taking the path to your right will bring you to the 1st DCLI Cemetery. Continuing along the front of that cemetery (passing its gate) and then turning right will bring you to Hedge Row Trench Cemetery. There is a long walk from the parking area to this cemetery. The two smaller graveyards are particularly tranquil.

# HOOGE CRATER CEMETERY

**HISTORY**

This cemetery was begun in October 1917 once the land had been secured by the British 8th Division during Third Ypres. It remained in use until April 1918 during the German Spring Offensive. The burial ground was significantly enlarged after the war with the concentration of 5,800 graves from the battlefields of Zillebeke, Zandvoorde and Geluveld.

**INFORMATION**

The cemetery, which has a formal layout with good views of Sanctuary Wood, is entered across the route of the former light railway that ran by the side of the Menin Road.

The circular depression at the entrance represents the crater blown in 1915.

Hooge Cemetery lies on the site which the German front-line occupied at the start of the Third Battle of Ypres. Opened by the Burial Officer of the 7th Division it held 76 graves, now Plot I, Rows A to D, until the German Spring Offensive in 1918 when the area was again lost to the Germans. The number of burials in Plot II, Row G is not known but it is assumed to be 23.

Hooge Chateau, opposite the site of this cemetery, was the headquarters for various units including at times Sir John French and Douglas Haig before French was removed and Haig promoted. On 31 October 1914, during the First Battle of Ypres, the Staffs of the 1st and 2nd Divisions were in conference at Hooge Chateau when a shell fell on the meeting. Only one officer was unhurt and most were killed. The dead have been buried in Ypres Town Cemetery. The Chateau was defended from 24 May to 3 June 1915 against German attacks but fell on 30 June. On 16 June the 3rd Division had suffered 3500 casualties. Among those who survived was the then Major Wavell who went on to become Commander-in-Chief in North Africa during World War II.

A huge mine was blown, after the 175th Tunnelling Company had dug a 60m tunnel to lay 3,500lbs of Amonal under the grounds of the Chateau, at 7.00pm on 19 July 1915 killing 145 Germans. The 3rd Division again attacked, with the objective of taking the ridge from Bellewaerde

Farm to Hooge, and the 4th Middlesex, of the 8th Brigade, attacked the mine crater though the mine explosion had already killed ten men of their Battalion. The fighting here to take the crater and trenches turned into a prolonged bombing fight, the Middlesex holding as much trench as they could with dwindling supplies of ammunition. They consolidated their position at the lip of the crater and in German trenches, repulsing all attacks, until handing over to the 1st Gordon Highlanders in the morning.

As a retaliation the Germans introduced flamethrowers (Flammenwerfen) to the war. These, in their earliest form, were a tank of fuel strapped to a soldier who became a walking bomb that pumped fuel up to 25m at the British. The Germans had been shelling the British front line at Hooge for days destroying the trench system. At 3.15am on 30 July 1915 the 8th Rifle Brigade became the first to suffer from an attack by flame throwers which pushed those who survived the initial onslaught back with the 7th King's Royal Rifle Corps into Sanctuary Wood where they held the German advance. It was not until 9 August that a planned counter-attack took place. The distance between the trenches was in places only 15m and this action saw the first use of tin hats by the British in the war. At 2.45am a short but heavy barrage was laid down on the German positions. At 3.15am it stopped and the 2nd Durham Light Infantry took the German trenches and the crater. The attack by the Durham Light Infantry had been particularly violent as this had been their first opportunity to gain revenge for the German attacks on the British town of Hartlepool where many of the Durhams had families as well as revenge for those who had died such a nasty death at the hands of the flame throwers.

The ground was littered with dead Germans killed in the blowing of the crater amongst whom were the dead of the 2nd Durham Light Infantry. The Germans counter-attacked on 12 August and, although the site of this cemetery was exposed to fire from north of the Menin Road, the line held. On 18 and 19 August the Leinsters buried the dead of the Durham Light Infantry in graves containing three and four men in each. The Germans retook the area in June 1916 during the Battle of Mount Sorrel.

On 31 July 1917 the plan here was for the 30th Division, led by the 90th Brigade, to capture Inverness Copse, Clapham Junction and Glencorse Wood having crossed the valley next to this cemetery. The 18th (Eastern) Division would capitalise on this by taking Polygon Wood and the 8th Division would attack north of the Menin Road through Hooge Chateau Wood. The 30th Division got lost and went straight through the position of what would become Hooge Cemetery into Hooge Chateau Wood, already captured by the 8th Division. They then reported that they had taken Glencorse Wood at which point the reserve of the 18th Division advanced along the valley here to take Polygon Wood believing that the first objectives had fallen, but instead they walked in to a storm of fire from the untouched German line on the Menin Road. Even so, they persevered into impossible conditions.

Lieutenant-Colonel Gerald Victor Wilmot Hill, DSO & two Bars, of the 8th Suffolks and Lieutenant-Colonel Bertie Gordon Clay, DSO, of the 6th Royal Berkshires urged their men forward with the 79th Company, Royal Engineers, helping on the flanks. The Menin Road was taken by the Suffolks at 9.00am at the same time as five tanks arrived only to become stuck in the valley. A link-up with the 8th Division was achieved, though not in Polygon Wood. During the desperate fighting on this day Captain Harold Ackroyd, Royal Army Medical Corps, Medical Officer of the 6th Royal Berkshires was awarded the Victoria Cross after 23 separate recommendations were made about his actions. He was killed in action on 11 August 1917 and is believed to be buried at Birr Crossroads Cemetery.

On 26 August 1917, just before the cemetery was created, the 280th Brigade, Royal Field Artillery were stationed at the southern edge of this location. When a shell fell on 'A' Battery, Gunner Harding was the only man left alive, but he continued to fire the gun in support of an infantry attack.

The position was lost for the last time in April 1918 as the Germans surged down the Menin Road towards Ypres reaching Hellfire Corner. It was retaken for the last time in an advance by 9th (Scottish) and 29th Divisions on 28 September 1918.

Buried here is Private Patrick J. Bugden, VC, 31st (Queensland and Victoria) Australian Infantry, killed in action on 28 September 1917. The Victoria Cross citation reads 'For most conspicuous bravery and devotion to duty when on two occasions our advance was temporarily held up by strongly defended "pill-boxes". Pte. Bugden, in the face of devastating fire from machine guns, gallantly led small parties to attack these strong points and, successfully silencing the machine guns with bombs, captured the garrison at the point of the bayonet. On another occasion, when a Corporal, who had become detached from his Company, had been captured and was being taken to the rear by the enemy, Pte. Bugden, single-handed, rushed to the rescue of his comrade, shot one enemy and bayoneted the remaining two, thus releasing the Corporal. On five occasions he rescued wounded men under intense shell and machine gun fire, showing an utter contempt and disregard for danger. Always foremost in volunteering for any dangerous mission, it was during the execution of one of these missions that this gallant soldier was killed.'

Also here is Lieutenant Francis Willie Goodwin, MC & Bar, twice MiD, 8th Australian Infantry, killed in action on 4 October 1917 aged 31 years. He was originally buried in Pill-box Cemetery. The citation for his Military Cross, awarded in September 1916, reads 'For gallant conduct during protracted operations. He led a patrol forward gaining valuable information and supervised supplies for the front line and worked without ceasing for three days and nights in the removal of the wounded under heavy fire.' The citation for the Bar, awarded in November 1916, reads 'For conspicuous gallantry during operations. While tending a wounded man, a shell burst near, killing the man. Though himself knocked out for half an hour, he brought in two other wounded men as soon as he had recovered consciousness. All this time the enemy kept up constant fire from machine guns and artillery. Next day he assisted another officer in rescuing a man from near the enemy trenches.' He enlisted in August 1914 and was wounded in the leg at Gallipoli in April 1915. He was Mentioned in Despatches in January and April 1916 and was killed by machine gun fire.

Lieutenant Colonel Henry Osbert Samuel 'Hal' Cadogan, twice MiD, 1st Royal Welsh Fusiliers was killed in action on 30 October 1914 aged 46 years. He was commissioned in 1888 rising to Lieutenant-Colonel in 1912. He served in China, India and Malta arriving in Belgium on 4 October 1914 and Ypres ten days later. He was killed at Zandvoorde in the morning while trying to save his Adjutant Captain Dooner. He was buried by the Germans and moved here after the war. He was twice posthumously Mentioned in Despatches. The German wooden cross found above his grave is now in Gayhurst Church, Buckinghamshire. Captain Alfred Edwin Claud Toke Dooner, MiD, 1st Royal Welsh Fusiliers died with Cadogan and is buried here next to him as is his Batman, Private Alan Davies, who tried to rescue them both.

Lieutenant Colonel James Andrew Jones, DSO, MC, 2nd Durham Light Infantry attached 17th Lancashire Fusiliers died of wounds on 14 October 1918. He had commanded the Fusiliers for a month since 12 September 1918. The citation for his Distinguished Service Order reads 'He commanded his Battalion with conspicuous success during a most difficult operation, involving the capture of Zandvoorde on 28 September 1918. By his behavior under heavy machine-gun fire at close range, he set a splendid example to the officers and men of his Battalion at a very critical period of the attack. All ranks were unanimous in praising his coolness and courage.' He had enlisted as a Band Boy in 1896 rising to the rank of Company Sergeant Major just before the war began. In November 1914 he was commissioned and became the officer commanding an instructional school in May 1915.

Major Albert Lewis Stewart, DSO, twice MiD, 22nd Battalion, Machine Gun Corps (Infantry) was killed in action in Glencorse Wood trying to seize ground from the Germans on 4 October 1917 aged 28 years. He was an Irish international at Rugby Union winning three caps in 1913-14, one in a defeat to Wales in 1913 and two in victories over France in 1913 and 1914. On the outbreak of war he volunteered and was commissioned into the Royal Irish Rifles in September 1914. In early 1915, while still in England, he became his Battalion's Machine-Gun Officer, and soon after arriving at the Western Front in late 1915 he was transferred to the Machine Gun Corps. He took command of his unit as a Captain in July 1916 while on the Somme. He became a Major on 1 January 1917 and was awarded the Distinguished Service Order posthumously in the New Year's Honours list in January 1919, though he was recommended for the Victoria Cross.

Private John Joseph O'Haire, MM, Medaille Militaire and Croix de Guerre (France), 1/5th (Dumfries and Galloway) King's Own Scottish Borderers died on 14 October 1918 aged 38 years. He was awarded all three medals for his role as a runner for his Battalion. He was originally buried in Geluwe Road Military Cemetery before being concentrated here after the war.

Another here is Captain Lord Richard Wellesley, MiD, No. 3 Company, 1st Grenadier Guards, killed on 29 October 1914 aged 35 years. He was son of the 4th Duke of Wellington and great grandson of the Wellington who fought Napoleon. His wife married his younger brother in 1917. He was commissioned in 1900 served in the South African Wars and became a Captain in 1910. His Battalion arrived in Belgium on 7 October 1914 and arrived at Ypres a week later. They were in an exposed position on 29 October when the Germans attacked. Their equipment failed, the fog covered the attack and rifles jammed as they had the wrong bullets. The Battalion lost all of its officers, most of whom are commemorated on the Menin Gate, and 180 men. Wellesley was posthumously Mentioned in Despatches.

You will also find Private Frank Monaghan, 2nd Northumberland Fusiliers who died of wounds on 22 February 1915 aged 23 years. He was originally buried at La Chapelle Farm near Hill 60 where he had been mortally wounded during four days of heavy fighting. He is the only man out of 50 men of the Battalion killed in the fighting who has a marked grave as they were all lost and the others are commemorated on the Menin Gate. Even Monaghan has a Special Memorial as his grave could not be identified due to the markers being destroyed by later shellfire. Though a regular in India at the start of the war, Monaghan had served for several years in the Royal Navy until dishonourably discharged in August 1911 for striking a superior.

Nearby, located on the north side of the Menin Road east of Hooge near the entrance to the Bellewaerde Theme Park, is a memorial dedicated to the officers and men of the Kings Royal Rifle Corps.

Concentrated here:
Bass Wood Cemeteries No.'s 1 & 2 - situated about 2km south-east of here on the east side of the Bassevillebeek

south of Herentage Wood. It was used from December 1917 to March 1918 and contained 48 British graves.

Koelenberg German Cemeteries – situated about 8km in an eastward direction along the Menin Road, south of the Menin Road near the village of Geluwe. They contained 163 British men, four Canadians and one Australian.

King's Own Scottish Borderers Cemetery - situated about 8km in an eastward direction along the Menin Road, 1km west of the village of Geluwe. Eighteen British men, ten of them from the 1/5th King's Own Scottish Borderers, were buried here in October 1918 after the capture of Geluwe by the 34th Division.

La Chapelle Farm – located about 3km south-west of here next to Chester Farm Cemetery, it contained the graves of seventeen British men buried in February and March 1915.

Menin Road Pill-box Cemetery – sited between Herentage Chateau and Geluveld about 1.5km away, it contained twenty British soldiers who died in October 1917.

Nieuwe Kruiseeke Cabaret Cemetery - located at the main road junction east of Geluveld and 5km from here. The cemetery was on the south-west corner of the junction where 21 British men and one Canadian were buried in October 1918.

Pill-box Cemetery - situated 450m north-east of Westhoek and about 1.5km north-east of here, it was used in October 1917 for the burial of 26 British men, 34 Australian men, two Canadian soldiers and one man of the British West Indies Regiment.

Sanctuary Wood Old British Cemetery - situated within the wood north-east of the present cemetery and less than 1km south of here, 50 British men and four Canadians were buried from 1915 to 1917.

Tower Hamlets Cemetery – located south of the Menin Road on the eastern edge of Herentage Wood by the side of a row of pill-boxes known as Tower Hamlets which were about 2km south-east of here. Thirty-six British men who died in the winter of 1917-1918 were buried there.

Westhoek Ridge Small Cemetery – located in Westhoek village about 1km north-east of here. It was said to be 'near the Area Commandant's pillbox and the A.D.S.' and was used in autumn 1917 for the burial of one British soldier and sixteen Australian servicemen.

Just to the east of the cemetery is the large Bellewaerde Pleasure Park which is open in the summer. Beyond the Park at the top of the rise is Clapham Junction. On either side of the Menin Road near the junction are Memorials to the 18th (Eastern) Division and the Gloucestershires, the 1st Battalion of which fought here in 1914 and the 2nd Battalion in 1915. Between Clapham Junction and Geluveld village there are locations such as Chateau Herentage, Dumbarton Lakes, Stirling Castle, the Tower Hamlets Ridge and Inverness Copse that became infamous during the war. In Geluveld village you can find Memorials to the 1st South Wales Borderers and 2nd Worcestershires who fought valiantly to hold the village in October 1914.

A small but excellent private café and museum are to be found opposite the cemetery. The museum, which includes some tremendous exhibits and artefacts, is housed in the former Hooge Chapel and school which had been built in the 1920's to commemorate the men who fought and died in this area. It was bought by the Smul-Ceuninck family in 1992 and the museum opened soon after. Niek and Ilse Benoot–Watteyne took over in 2009 and now the museum and café are well worth the stop and highly recommended.

UK - 5182	Aust - 513	NZ – 121
Can - 105	BWI – 2
Unnamed - 3580 (60% of total)	Area – 11981 sq mts

Special Memorials to fifteen British men, four Australians, two New Zealanders and ten Canadians known/believed to be buried among the unnamed.

Special Memorials to twelve British men buried at La Chappele Farm and two British men buried in Kruiseeke German Cemetery whose graves were destroyed.

**LOCATION**

Hooge Crater Cemetery is on the south side of the Menin Road, at the top of a rise, about 3km east of Ieper.

# HOOGSTADE BELGIAN MILITARY

**INFORMATION**

This is one of nine main cemeteries where the war dead of Belgium lie who have not been repatriated to family plots in civil cemeteries. Scattered among the Belgian war graves are twenty Commonwealth burials of the First World War. The men here died in a Belgian Military Hospital located in the 'Hospital Clep' situated about 500m to the south-east. The hospital was founded in 1869-1871 by Joseph Clep. On 29 January 1915 a hospital was moved here from the Diocesan College of Furnes and it became a Belgian Military Hospital with mainly Belgian staff in May 1916. The building remains and is now a home for the elderly.

At the end of the war the cemetery contained, with the Belgians, 972 Australian graves alongside 150 French and some British and German graves. Most non-Belgian graves were removed. The cemetery was rebuilt in 1924-1925, with the placing of the official Belgian tombstones. When the Belgian military cemetery at Reninge was cleared in 1968, 117 graves were transferred to Hoogstade. You will

**HISTORY**

The cemetery was used for the burial of British soldiers for three burials in the summer of 1915, two burials in the summer of 1917 and for fifteen men in 1918.

find a bronze plaque in the cemetery in commemoration of Colonel Physician-Ch. Willems, director of the military hospital of Hoogstade.

Buried here is Lieutenant Ronald Charles Wybrow Morgan, Royal Flying Corps and 3rd South Wales Borderers, who died of wounds received the previous day on 28 July 1917 aged 19 years. He was an only child. He was commissioned in July 1915 and attached to No. 55 Squadron, Royal Flying Corps in July 1916, gaining his pilots certificate soon after. He arrived at the Front in April 1917. He was shot down with stomach wounds, while his observer was unharmed.

UK – 20      Bel – 806

**LOCATION**
Hoogstade lies on the N8 a little over 10km north-west of Ieper and a similar distance north of Poperinge. The cemetery is 100m west of the town centre.

# HOP STORE CEMETERY

**HISTORY**
The cemetery was opened in May 1915 and remained in use until the end of the war. However, the majority of burials here date from 1915 and 1917.

**INFORMATION**
Vlamertinge was, for most of the war, at the edge of the range of German artillery. The Hop Store and its cemetery was in the 'safe' area, but remained small because of the limited space available. The site was drained by the Royal Engineers in 1917 and a moat has been created to keep the ground dry.

The large red building by which you turn to get here is the hop store which was used as a Casualty Clearing Station in the war. There are 58 men of the Royal Artillery buried here reflecting the fact that many of the men who died in the local dressing stations were from nearby artillery units, the target of German shelling. One French grave has been removed.

Buried here is Captain Aylmer Vivian Jarrett, DSO, MiD, 2nd York and Lancasters who died of wounds on 22 June 1915 aged 35 years. He was commissioned into his regiment in August 1899, promoted to Lieutenant in September 1900 and Captain in January 1908. He then served with the West African Regiment until 1911. He was Mentioned in Despatches in May 1915 and awarded the Distinguished Service Order on the day he was mortally wounded. His elder brother Major Charles Harry Brownlow Jarrett, 1st Royal Munster Fusiliers was killed in action at V Beach, Gallipoli on 25 April 1915 aged 40 years and is buried at Lancashire Landing Cemetery.

Buried here is Driver Robert Lynn, 87th Battery, Royal Field Artillery, who died on 6 August 1915 aged 30 years. Three of his brothers also died in the war. Serjeant William Edward Lynn, 1st Royal Irish Fusiliers died on 17 July 1916 aged 21 years and is buried in Auchonvillers Military Cemetery on the Somme. Private John Lynn, 1st Royal Inniskilling Fusiliers, died of wounds on 9 August 1916 aged 26 years. He is buried in Lijssenthoek Military Cemetery about 5km south-west of here. Serjeant James Lynn, 906th Company, Royal Army Service Corps died on 7 August 1920 aged 37 years and is buried in Haifa War Cemetery.

Another here whose family suffered the loss of more than one son is Gunner Sydney James Norman, 141st Heavy Battery, Royal Garrison Artillery who died on 1 July 1917 aged 27 years. His brother Serjeant James Frederick Norman, 'A' Company, 1/3rd (Royal Fusiliers) Londons died 29 May 1916 aged 23 years and is buried in St. Amand British Cemetery about 75km south of here. Rifleman William John Norman, King's Royal Rifle Corps attached 1/9th (Queen Victoria's Rifles) Londons was killed in action on 16 August 1917 aged 19 years and is commemorated on the Tyne Cot Memorial.

Another family to lose three brothers is that of Rifleman Henry Woodland Erlebach, 1/16th (Queen's Westminster Rifles) Londons who died on 24 October 1915 aged 29 years. His brother, 2nd Lieutenant Edward Eustace Erlebach, No. 45 Squadron, Royal Flying Corps was killed in action over Linselles in his Sopwith Strutter on 7 February 1917 aged 19 years and is buried in Linselles Communal Cemetery about 15km south-east of here. Another brother, 2nd Lieutenant Arthur Woodland Erlebach, No. 57 Squadron, Royal Flying Corps and General List died in a flying accident on 5 July 1917 aged 23 years and is buried in Longuenesse (St. Omer) Souvenir Cemetery.

Also of note is Private George Henry Berry, 2nd Durham Light Infantry who died on 14 October 1915. Rather more of note is his unfortunate wife. After the death of Berry, she married again, to Private Robert Herring, 2/5th West Yorkshires attached 185th Trench Mortar Battery, but he was also killed in action. He died on 24 May 1918 and is buried in Gommecourt British Cemetery No. 2 on the Somme.

Another of note is young Private Thomas Loughlin, 2nd Royal Dublin Fusiliers who died of wounds on 13 May 1915 aged 17 years. He had arrived at the Front on 3 May so saw less than ten days before being mortally wounded. He enlisted and served as Thomas Phelan to get into the army and as late as 1921 is recorded in the Medal Rolls under the name of Phelan.

Another to win the DSO buried here is Major Harold Payne Philby, DSO, twice MiD, 2nd York and Lancasters who died on 17 May 1916 aged 28 years. He was commanding the Battalion at the time of his death having taken over on the first day of May. He was commissioned into the York and Lancasters in September 1908, promoted to Lieutenant in

April 1910 and then was seconded to the West African Frontier Force from 1911 to August 1914. He returned to the 2nd York and Lancasters at the start of the war, went to France in September 1914, was promoted to Captain in November and made a Major in February 1916 taking command of his Battalion in April 1916. He was Mentioned in Despatches in September 1915 and January 1916 and also awarded the Distinguished Service Order at the same time as his first Mention in Despatches. The citation reads 'For conspicuous and consistent good service throughout the campaign, notably during the fighting at Hooge on the 9th Aug. 1915, when with the greatest coolness and energy he frequently visited all portions of the firing line under heavy shell fire, and personally supervised the despatch of reinforcement, bombs, etc.' His brother, Lieutenant Denis Duncan Philby, Royal Dublin Fusiliers attached 2nd Royal Munster Fusiliers was killed in action on 12 November 1914 aged 25 years and buried south of Clonmel Copse near what is now Sanctuary Wood. He was moved to New Irish Farm Cemetery, about 4km from here, in 1920. However, a third brother survived the war. Harry Saint John Bridger Philby, an explorer and Arabist, was the first European to cross the Rub' al-Khali, or Empty Quarter, of Arabia from east to west. He was also an author and Colonial office Intelligence Officer. His son, and nephew to Harold and Denis, was Harold 'Kim' Philby, a high ranking British Intelligence Officer who worked as a double-agent. As part of the now infamous 'Cambridge Five', Harold was believed to have been the most successful in providing secret information to the Soviet Union. He defected to the Soviet Union in 1963, and worked as an operative for the Soviet Secret Police, NKVD and KGB. He died in 1988 and is buried in Moscow, Russia.

UK - 250                Can - 1

**LOCATION**

Hop Store Cemetery is situated 70m north of the old Ieper-Poperinge road (N308) approximately 1km west of Vlamertinge and 3km west of Ieper. Access is by a private road at the west end of the Hop Store, an imposing red brick building on the north side of the N308.

## HOSPITAL FARM CEMETERY

**HISTORY**

This cemetery was in use for much of the war by the regiments fighting close to Ypres but particularly in 1915 and 1917.

**INFORMATION**

Hospital Farm, from which this cemetery gets its name, was the name given in the war to a nearby farm which was used as a Dressing Station.

Among those buried here is Private Albert Seal, 1/5th West Yorkshires killed in action on 23 July 1915 aged 17 years. He had arrived in France on 15 April 1915 so saw two months of active service. Also here is Private William H. Walton, 2nd Lancashire Fusiliers, who died of wounds on 22 June 1915 aged 16 years. He had been at the Front since 21 May so saw one month in France and Flanders.

The Belgian buried here, Marcel Top, from Oostvleteren, was aged 18 years, one of seven children in his family, when killed on 11 August 1915. Originally recorded as a French civilian, the local historians began research as this did not 'feel' correct. They discovered information in CWGC records that showed him as working at the Hospital in Poperinge, the reality was that he worked for the farm after which this cemetery is named. He was hit by a bus and killed while working nearby.

UK - 115        Belgian Civilian – 1        Unnamed – 4

Area – 1043 sq mts

**LOCATION**

Hospital Farm Cemetery is found about 6km west of Ieper and 2km north-west of Vlamertinge. The road from the Ieper-Poperinge road (N308) leads north from the centre of Vlamertinge at the church, and has CWGC signs on the corner. The cemetery, next to a field which contains a wide avenue of trees, is 150m west of the road behind the farm. There is a small path through the field and the cemetery is reached by a small bridge from the field through which you must walk to reach the graveyard. The CWGC website says 'Visitors should note that access to the site is via a field often used by livestock and is unsuitable for vehicles and wheelchairs.' The farm, and the field which is in use, do not entirely contribute to the atmosphere - just the aroma! The nearby pond, stagnant in summer, and ditch surrounding the cemetery, also detract from the area.

## HYDE PARK CORNER (ROYAL BERKS) CEMETERY

**HISTORY**

Begun by the 1/4th Royal Berkshires in April 1915, the cemetery remained in use until November 1917.

**INFORMATION**

Hyde Park Corner is the original of the two cemeteries that face each other across the main road. A junction north of Ploegsteert Wood gave the name of Hyde Park Corner. It is an attractive small cemetery dominated by the one that it faces, though both are overshadowed by Hill 63. That was to the north-west and nearby were the 'Catacombs', deep shelters capable of holding two Battalions, used from November 1916 to the end of the war.

Buried here, next to the entrance, is Rifleman Samuel McBride of the 2nd Royal Irish Rifles who was executed on 7 December 1916 at Hope Farm near Prowse Point Cemetery for desertion. He had been at the Front since December 1914 and deserted soon after being sentenced to two years imprisonment with hard labour on 25 January 1915. He was released under a suspended sentence on 3 January 1916 but went absent again in May 1916 while in the Vimy area. He was captured on 17 September near Boulogne and court-martialled on 25 November 1916.

Buried here is Lieutenant Ronald William Poulton Palmer, 1/4th Royal Berkshires, killed on 5 May 1915 aged 25 years. Originally known as Poulton he changed his name to Palmer after inheriting the Palmer (of Huntley and Palmer biscuits) fortune in 1914. His surname was never 'Poulton Palmer' but it has stuck. He was possibly better known for being England Rugby Union Captain during the 1913/14 unbeaten 'Grand Slam' season, scoring four tries against France in 1914, in the last test match prior to the outbreak of World War I. He had previously become one of only three men to score a hat-trick of tries in a Varsity match when playing for Oxford. In fact, he scored five in 1909, still the individual record for the Varsity match. On the night of 4-5 May 1915 he was leading a working party in Trench 40 (Oxford Trench), just north of a position called Anton's Farm which is a little east of here. Just after midnight, while trying to get a better view of the work, he exposed his position and was shot, becoming the first officer of the 1/4th Royal Berkshires to be killed in the war. He was buried at 6.30pm on 6 May 1915, with the Bishop of Pretoria, who was a family friend, officiating. Palmer was one of 26 England international rugby players to be killed in the war.

Buried here is Rifleman Albert Edward French, 18th (Arts and Crafts) King's Royal Rifle Corps, who died on 15 June 1916 aged 16 years. From a village near what is now Milton Keynes, he went to London to enlist in October 1915 while still 15 years of age. He claimed to be 19 years old yet all the other details he gave, such as relatives and home address were correct. He arrived in France on 2 May 1916 so served abroad for six weeks before being killed in action by machine gun fire while on a working party.

Buried here is Captain Ian Dalrymple Dewar, 5th Cameron Highlanders who died on 17 March 1916 aged 22 years. He won a 'Blue' at Oxford for Boxing and had been the Public Schools Lightweight Boxing Champion in 1911. He went to the Front in May 1915 and was wounded in August and September. He was promoted to Captain and returned to the Front as Adjutant in March 1916. A few days later, while inspecting barbed wire in front of a listening post at night, he was killed instantaneously by machine-gun fire. His father was a Liberal MP for Edinburgh South from 1899-1910, Judge of the Supreme Court in Edinburgh and a member of the distilling family. I have seen sources, notably a well-known internet information resource, that claim that Dewar died of wounds at home and is buried with his father and mother in Edinburgh.

Another buried here is Serjeant Samuel Baird, 'A' Company, 2nd Royal Irish Rifles, who died on 24 November 1916 aged 20 years. His brother, Rifleman John Cleland Baird, 14th Royal Irish Rifles, died on 17 February 1917 aged 22 years and is buried across the road in Berks Cemetery Extension.

UK - 81          Aust - 1          Can – 1
Ger - 4          Area – 758 sq mts

**LOCATION**
Hyde Park Cemetery lies on the west side of the Armentieres road, about 1km north of Ploegsteert, at the foot of Hill 63, and approximately 13km south of Ieper. The imposing Memorial opposite this cemetery is difficult to miss.

# IRISH HOUSE CEMETERY

**HISTORY**
This cemetery was opened in June 1917 for the Battle of Messines though it was a little behind the front-line on 7 June. It remained in use until September 1918 with the exception of the period from April to August 1918 when the area was in German hands.

**INFORMATION**
The cemetery gets its name from a farm that was 100m to the west, though this is not the farm that you can see today. The cemetery was begun by the 16th (Irish) Division. An attack by the 1st Gordon Highlanders, with the 2nd Royal Scots in support, was launched from here on 14 December 1914 against the German line at Petit Bois, next to the site of the present Wytschaete Military Cemetery. Their impossible task was to attack uphill across a muddy ploughed field covered with barbed wire. Even so, the 2nd Royal Scots reached the Petit Bois taking two machine-guns and 35 prisoners but losing eight officers and 157 men. Some of the Gordon Highlanders reached the German trenches but failed to hold them suffering, in the process, casualties of seventeen officers and 253 men, over 50% of their force. The Highlanders were only saved by hiding in the deep furrows of the ploughed field until they were able to return to the British trenches at night.

However, a German sniper killed eighteen men in one furrow during the day that must have seemed endless to the Highlanders. The bodies lay out in no-man's land from December 1914 until the successful attack on Messines Ridge on 7 June 1917 when they were recovered by the 11th (South Antrim Volunteers) Royal Irish Rifles. You will find 33 in a mass grave in Row A, 30 of whom are unidentified. They have a special marker as a collective burial at the end of the row. This attack was reported as a British success in the newspapers.

Only three days before, on 12 December, two other Battalions from the 3rd Division, the 1st Lincolnshires and 1/10th (Liverpool Scottish) King's (Liverpools) had been ordered to attack Petit Bois from positions near Irish House Cemetery. Four volunteers, Corporal John Williams and three Sappers from the Royal Engineers, supported by twelve men of the Lincolnshires, had been sent out at night to cut wire. While in no man's land Corporal Williams was mistaken for a dog by the Germans who threw rubbish at him, but he also found the wires of the German telephone system which he cut. The attack started prematurely while he and his men were still in no man's land armed with no more than a pair of wire cutters. Williams spent the day rescuing wounded and taking them back to dressing stations. The attack succeeded and Corporal Williams was awarded the Distinguished Conduct Medal.

Among those buried here is Lance Corporal John Scott, 6th Borders who was killed in action on 7 June 1917 aged 32 years. His family have commemorated his brother Private William Scott, 2nd Borders on the headstone. He was killed on the Somme on 30 November 1916 aged 20 years and is recorded on the Thiepval Memorial.

UK - 103  Aust - 13  Ger – 4
Unnamed - 40  Area – 569 sq mts

Special Memorial to one Australian soldier known to be buried among the unknown.

### LOCATION
Irish House Cemetery is about 7.5km south of Ieper. It lies 80m from a small side road, reached by a small path next to a farm building, that leaves the Wijtschate-Kemmel road about midway between the two villages. This isolated little cemetery lies in a valley, sombre and dark under the shelter of the trees.

## KANDAHAR FARM CEMETERY

### HISTORY
This cemetery was begun in November 1914 and used until the German Spring Offensive, when they took Wulvergem for the only time, in April 1918. The cemetery was used again when the British had retaken the village in September and October 1918.

### INFORMATION
The front-line ran close to Wulvergem just east of here until June 1917 when it was pushed to the east following the British successes during the Battle of Messines. The Germans created a small cemetery on the south side of the farm in spring 1918 but it has been removed. Many of the British buried here were from the 14th (Light) Division.

Among those buried here is Captain William Anderson Connell, DCM, 12th Australian Infantry, who died of wounds on 28 December 1917 aged 36 years. He had served in the South African Wars and re-enlisted as a Sergeant in August 1914. He was commissioned as a Lieutenant one year later and promoted to Captain in March 1916. He was awarded the Distinguished Conduct Medal in July 1915 for 'On 25th April, 1915, during operations near Gaba Tepe, for gallantly attacking an entrenched position and an enemy's machine gun.'

Also here are brothers Driver George Nixon Williamson aged 35 years and Driver Harold William Williamson aged 30 years, both 110th Howitzer Battery, 10th Brigade, Australian Field Artillery, who both died on 14 June 1917. They are buried side by side. They were killed when a German shell hit the ammunition dump called Souvenir Dump close to this cemetery. One died immediately while the other was taken to a Casualty Clearing Station in Bailleul where he died and was returned for burial here.

Sapper John Cornelius Roberts, 8th Battalion, Canadian Railway Troops died, like the Williamsons, on 14 June 1917. He was aged 44 years and had enlisted in November 1916. From Detroit, Michigan, he had served with the American army and was one of many Americans who joined the Canadian, and in some cases British army, to become involved in the war, and now lie buried in Commonwealth graves.

Pioneer Ephraim Taylor, 7th (Labour) Battalion, Royal Engineers died on 21 July 1917 aged 61 years. He had served in Egypt and the Sudan in the 1800's and in the South African Wars. The Engineers were used as emergency infantry and Ephraim was killed in action. He is the oldest recorded CWGC burial in Belgium.

However, a man aged 67 years, Lieutenant Commander Henry Thomas Gartside-Tipping, HM Yacht Sanda, Royal Naval Reserve, who was lost off the Belgian coast in 1915, is commemorated on the Nieuwpoort Memorial. He is also known for 'Tipping Plates', a form of track to assist lifeboats get across sandy beaches to launch at sea. Gartside-Tipping's wife died in strange circumstances. She worked for nearly a year at the Munitions Worker's Canteen, Woolwich, and joined the Women's Emergency Corps in January 1917 for service in France, where she was shot by a French soldier whose mind was 'disordered'. The French posthumously awarded her the Croix de Guerre and gave her a full military funeral. She was buried in Vauxbuin French National Cemetery.

UK – 218      Aust – 186      NZ – 33
Can – 6       KUG – 7         Ger - 3
Area – 2809 sq mts

Special Memorial to one Australian soldier whose grave has been lost.

### LOCATION
Kandahar Farm Cemetery lies on the east side of the road from Wulvergem to Nieuwkerke about 1km south of Wulvergem. This is approximately 10km south of Ieper.

# KEMMEL CHATEAU MILITARY CEMETERY

### HISTORY
The cemetery was begun in December 1914 and used until March 1918 when the Germans captured the village. It was used again in September and October 1918 when the area had been retaken from the Germans.

### INFORMATION
Kemmel was behind the front-lines for much of the war and many cemeteries were created nearby. The village saw bitter fighting in spring 1918 as the Germans tried to capture the Mont des Flandres. A single French Division, which had only taken over the position a week before, found itself outnumbered by three and a half German Divisions. At 2.30am on 25 April 1918 over 250 batteries of German guns opened up on Allied artillery positions in the Salient with a mixture of gas and high explosive. For the next two hours they concentrated solely on destroying the gun emplacements. After a short pause, at 5.00am the German barrage was switched to the French front line at Mont Kemmel. French soldiers who had survived the horrors of Verdun described it as the worst they had ever encountered. The Germans also used 96 aeroplanes to drop 700 bombs on Kemmel and nearby villages. By 7.30am the battle was over and Mont Kemmel (Kemmelberg) was in German hands.

The village was evacuated on 31 August 1918 when attacked by the US 27th and British 34th Divisions. While the Germans held the village it was heavily shelled. The chateau was destroyed and Kemmel Chateau Cemetery was damaged.

In the early part of the war there was a great paranoia about spies. Two locals were found moving the hands of the clock in the church and were shot by men from the Northumberland Fusiliers.

The entrance to this attractive cemetery represents the destroyed chateau, that had been owned by the Hennessy brandy family. The trees make a wide avenue to the Cross of Sacrifice. The road upon which this cemetery stands was known as Sackville Street. Kemmel Chateau was north-east of Kemmel village and the cemetery was begun on the north side of the chateau grounds.

The WW2 burials all date from the Allied withdrawal ahead of the German advance in May 1940. Also here are 66 burials in Row E of men of the Sherwood Foresters (Nottingham & Derbys) and 58 in Row N of men from Irish Regiments.

There are two men buried here who were executed in Kemmel by the British Army. Private Stanley Stewart, 2nd Royal Scots Fusiliers had been conscripted back into service having already been invalided home wounded, and out of the army, with shell shock in 1914. He deserted on 25 July 1917 and later escaped from custody before his execution on 29 August 1917 aged 21 years. At his court martial he claimed he had been in a 'lunatic asylum' for four years before the war.

Private James C. Smith of the 17th (1st Liverpool Pals) King's (Liverpools) was executed for desertion and disobedience on 5 September 1917 aged 26 years. Smith had almost lost his life on the Somme when, on 11 October 1916, a German shell buried him alive on the Transloy Ridge, with bits of his friends around him, and shrapnel created a large deep wound on his right shoulder. He was rescued and invalided to Bolton, but he never fully recovered. Nonetheless, he was sent back to the Front, but sixteen days later, he left his post without orders. On 29 December 1916, he was court-martialed and sentenced to 90 days' field punishment. On 15 July 1917 he was court-martialed for a second time for going absent without leave. He is now the subject of a play, 'Early One Morning', written by Bolton playwright Les Smith and first performed on 22 October 1998.

Buried here is Captain Capel O'Brien Butler, MC, 6th Royal Irish Regiment, who died on 7 June 1917 aged 27 years. He received the Military Cross for bravery in early 1917 and was killed on the first day of the Battle of Messines while attacking a German bunker. He was the third and last brother to die in wars for his country. One brother, Captain Charles Paget O'Brien-Butler, Royal Army Medical Corps attached 5th (Royal Irish) Lancers, died on 31 October 1914 aged 33 years. He was a well-known jockey and in 1907 he was on top of the list of winning amateur jockeys. He is buried in Bailleul Communal Cemetery about 5km south-west of here. The family had already lost Lieutenant Pierce O'Brien Butler, Army Service Corps, who died on 15 January 1902 aged 24 in the South African Wars. The eldest of the three brothers he had become an international rugby player, playing for Ireland as a full back between 1897 and 1900. Following his last International on 10 February 1900 he set sail with the Royal Dublin Fusiliers to take part in the Boer War, transferring to the Army Service Corps and being promoted to Lieutenant in November 1901. However, he fell ill with dysentery and died on 15 January 1902.

Lieutenant Colonel Guy Louis Busson Du Maurier, DSO, MiD, 3rd Royal Fusiliers, died on 9 March 1915 aged 49 years. Guy was educated at Marlborough and the Royal Military College, Sandhurst, and in 1885 became an officer in the Royal Fusiliers. He served in Burma and the South African Wars where he commanded a mounted infantry regiment earning the Distinguished Service Order in 1902. His unit were in the trenches east of Kemmel, under heavy fire when, on the night of 9 March 1915 the Battalion HQ was shelled and destroyed. Official correspondence, a machine gun, rifles and 80 sets of equipment were destroyed and du Maurier was killed. He achieved notoriety in 1909 as the author of the play 'An Englishman's Home'. He was son of the French cartoonist George du Maurier. He was brother of the actor Sir Gerald du Maurier. He was uncle to writer Angela du Maurier (1904–2002), best-seller author Daphne du Maurier (1907–1989) and painter Jeanne du Maurier. He was brother to Sylvia du Maurier who was mother to the five boys who inspired J M Barrie to write Peter Pan. His brother would interpret the role of Captain Hook in the stage production of Peter Pan. At the death of his sister Sylvia, and as requested in her will, he became co-guardian to the Llewelyn Davies boys. J M Barrie wrote to Guy's nephew, George Llewelyn Davies, to inform him of the death, but by the time Barrie received his response, George himself had been killed. He was a 21 year old 2nd Lieutenant in the 4th Rifle Brigade, was killed near to his uncle, and is buried in Voormezele Enclosure No. 3.

Lieutenant Colonel Edward MacMahon Seddon, DSO, Royal Garrison Artillery died on 24 June 1917 aged 49 years. His was awarded the Distinguished Service Order in the January 1917 New Year's Honours List. He served in Gibraltar 1896 – 97, 1903-4 and 1907-12; in Malta 1904-5; and Hong Kong from 1905-07.

Major John Angel Gibbs, DSO, 9th Welsh, died on 20 September 1917 aged 37 years. According to the History of the Welsh Regiment, by T O Marden, Gibbs shared the command of Battalion with Lieutenant-Colonel Godfrey and was in command for the Battle of the Menin Road where he was killed. He had owned a shipping Company before the war, the South Wales Steamship Company, and had married his cousin, Gladys Morel, against the initial wishes of her family. She set up a charity, the Gibbs Trust, in 1946 having already been instrumental in setting up the National Children's Home soon after WW1.

Private Albert Edward Gautier, 1st York and Lancasters, died on 9 August 1915 aged 17 years. His brother, Private Wilfred Gautier, 1st West Yorkshires, died of accidental injuries on 16 June 1921, considered on active service, and is buried in Sheffield General Cemetery. His father, Serjeant Francis Herbert Gautier, 11th Cheshires, died on 11 June 1916 aged 44 years and is buried with Wilfred.

Also of note is Private William John Styan, 4th Royal Fusiliers, died on 20 May 1916 aged 17 years. Previously in the Royal Navy he was invalided home in March 1915 and enlisted in the army in June 1915. Also here are Private John Gray McCulloch Hunter, 3rd Royal Fusiliers, died on 10 March 1915 aged 16 years. His war record shows he went to the Front on 24 February 1915 serving two weeks abroad before he was killed. Younger still is Private Reginald Wilson, 1st Devonshires, died on 3 April 1915 aged 15 years. He went to the Front on 17 February 1915, but it is worth remembering that the school-leaving age was 12 years, the army took boys at 14 years, converted to adult service at 18 and they became eligible for active service at 19 years of age.

Lieutenant Frederick Bonham Burr, 3rd Worcestershires died on 12 March 1915 aged 28 years. He played one first class cricket match for Worcestershire in 1911. His brother, Corporal Alfred Burr, MM, 1st Special Company, Royal Engineers was killed in action on 24 March 1918 and is commemorated on the Pozieres Memorial.

Captain James Patrick Roche, 47th Trench Mortar Battery, Royal Artillery died on 7 June 1917 aged 29 years. He competed in the 100 yard and 200 yard sprints at the 1908 London Olympics. He was commissioned in May 1915 and awarded the Military Cross in January 1917. He was killed with several officers when a shell exploded in their dugout.

Others of note are Serjeant Alfred Dawkins, 3rd Worcestershires, who died on 17 March 1915 aged 22 years who was a member of the winning team in the Machine Gun Challenge Cup on Salisbury Plain in September 1913; Serjeant Henry Nottridge, 267th Siege Battery, Royal Garrison Artillery, who died on 7 May 1917 aged 37 years who was an Adjutant of the Salvation Army in London; and Private Count Ove Krag-Juel-Vind-Frijs, Count of Juellinge, Lolland, Denmark, 28th Canadian Infantry, died on 15 November 1915 aged 25 years who had previously served with the Danish Life Guards and was killed by a sniper, shot through the head while repairing a trench parapet under fire.

UK – 1030          Aust - 24          NZ - 1
Can - 80  Unnamed – 4
WWII - 21 UK and 1 Fr          Area - 5506 sq mts

**LOCATION**
Kemmel Chateau Cemetery is on the northern edge of Kemmel which is about 8km south of Ieper. It is reached from the village by taking the road opposite the church in Kemmel to the cemetery about 500m north of the Kemmel-Reningelst road.

# KEMMEL CHURCHYARD

## HISTORY
The churchyard was used for the burial of British dead from October 1914 to March 1915.

## INFORMATION
For information on Kemmel in WW1 please refer to Kemmel Chateau Cemetery.

On 19 February 1917 Colonel Rowland Fielding, who was billeted in the 'Doctors House' in Kemmel, led an attack by nine officers and 190 men of the 6th Connaught Rangers towards Messines. An armistice was agreed by the Germans after the attack so that the Rangers could go into no man's land to retrieve their wounded. After all the injured had been recovered the truce was ended though one officer, who was last seen near the German lines carrying a revolver, had been taken prisoner. His price for not following 'the rules of the game'. Fielding is best known for the publication of a book after the war based on his letters home to his wife.

Commemorated by a Special Memorial is Lieutenant Percy Dale 'Toggie' Kendall 1/10th (Liverpool Scottish) Kings (Liverpools), killed in action on 25 January 1915 aged 36 years. He played rugby union as scrum half for Cambridge University, Blackheath, Birkenhead Park and England for whom he won three caps - against Scotland in 1901 and 1903 (as Captain) and Wales in 1902. He also represented the Barbarians, Cheshire on 36 occasions (Captain in 1905 v NZ) and the North of England. Percy was a pre-war Territorial with the 1/8th (Liverpool Irish) Kings (Liverpools) from 1900-06. In the 1908 reforms of the Territorial Force, the Kings ended up with five Territorial Battalions, one of which was the 1/10th (Liverpool Scottish) Kings (Liverpools). Kendall was gazetted as a 2nd Lieutenant on 14 October 1914 and went to France with the 1/10th Kings on 1 November 1914. By 27 November, they went into the front line for the first time, close to Wijtschate. The trenches were, in some places, just 40m from the German lines, so they were constantly harassed by German sniper fire. They moved back to Westouter on 30 November and remained out of the line for the remainder of 1914. On 8 January 1915, the Battalion marched to Kemmel and went into a rota of four days in and four days out of the front line. The regimental history records that little of note happened in January, but that Kendall was killed by a sniper.

2nd Lieutenant Frederick 'Freddie' Harding Turner, 1/10th Kings (Liverpools), was killed in action on 10 January 1915 aged 27 years. His grave is also commemorated by a Special Memorial. He had represented Scotland on fifteen occasions at Rugby Union and was Captain in 1913. He played in the final Rugby Test before the war began, a 16-15 victory for England against Scotland and was one of thirteen players in the match to lose their lives in the war. His record (one of several he held) for the most conversions in a Test, five v France in 1912 stood until 2007. He also played five first-class cricket matches for Oxford University. He was killed by a sniper on Sunday morning as he was walking to the end of the line held by his Platoon to check on some barbed wire entanglements. He had been in France for ten weeks. His only brother, Lieutenant William Stewart Turner, 1/10th Kings (Liverpools), was killed in action at Hooge on 16 June 1915 aged 32 years and is commemorated on the Menin Gate.

UK – 23        Unnamed - 3

Special Memorials to 15 graves destroyed by shell-fire.

## LOCATION
Kemmel Church is on the south side of the N304 in the centre of Kemmel village which is about 8km south of Ieper. The churchyard is up a flight of steps from the road. Most of the graves are found on the right from the steps though a small number are on the far side of the church from the road.

# KEMMEL No. 1 FRENCH CEMETERY, KEMMEL

## HISTORY
The history of this cemetery is unknown. It was found after the war by the French war graves service who then removed the French graves to the Ossuary on the Kemmelberg or the cemetery at Potijze. British graves were brought from the surrounding battlefield and other burial grounds in the area, including Becelaere Churchyard and Beerst German Cemetery, to add to those already here. Some German graves were also found within the cemetery.

## INFORMATION
For information on Kemmel in WW1 please refer to Kemmel Chateau Cemetery.

It is strange to think that a cemetery can be forgotten as it was behind the lines for much of the war. Local fighting during the German advance in spring 1918 when the line came just east of here was the only action here. This gives us an indication of what the fighting must have been like in 1918 and how much shelling must have gone on in the area to obliterate a burial ground.

The number of Germans in the mass grave in German Row A is not known. These are represented by a small number of headstones in two rows. Some of these burials were brought here by the Belgian war graves service.

Buried here is Corporal of Horse Arthur Rose, DCM, 1st Life Guards, killed in action on 20 November 1914 aged 27 years. Originally buried just to the east of Hill 60, Rose was moved here in 1929 being identified by his uniform and dental records. He was awarded the Distinguished Conduct Medal for twice re-entering his trench position having been blown out of it on two occasions.

| | | |
|---|---|---|
| UK – 278 | Aust – 12 | NZ – 3 |
| Can – 3 | Ger – 94 | KUG – 1 |
| Unnamed – 259 | | Area - 3923 sq mts |

### LOCATION

Kemmel No. 1 French Cemetery can be found on the south side of the road from Vierstraat to Hallebast which is south of Ieper and about 3km north of Kemmel. This is best reached from the Ieper-Kemmel road leaving it at the two unmistakeable warehouses in Vierstraat. The cemetery stands high above the road and is entered by means of a steep flight of steps. However, a side road at the west end

of the burial ground provides a rear step-free access, and parking between this and Klein-Viertsraat cemeteries. There are excellent views of the Salient from the towers of Ypres to the Kemmelberg.

## KLEIN-VIERSTRAAT BRITISH CEMETERY, KEMMEL

### HISTORY

The cemetery was begun in January 1917, used until January 1918 and then again in April 1918. After the war it was enlarged with the concentration of graves from two smaller cemeteries and from the surrounding battlefields.

### INFORMATION

This cemetery was behind the lines for most of the war, but the fighting came to this area, as indicated by the Demarcation Stone only 300m east of here, in April 1918. Hence, Klien Vierstraat was promptly closed. However, it was not lost like the cemetery next to it. This burial ground is located at the site of the Klein Vierstraat (Little Crossroads) Cabaret from which it gets its name. Of the original burials, 188 (45%) were of artillerymen. One American grave has been removed.

Plots I to III were made by medical and fighting units before the middle of January 1918. Plot IV was begun in April 1918.

Buried here is Lieutenant Colonel Ernest Slade, DSO, MC, MiD, 4th attached 8th Gloucestershires, killed on 4 May 1918 aged 29 years. He joined the Territorial Force in 1908 as a 2nd Lieutenant in the 1/4th (City of Bristol) Gloucestershires and a year later was promoted to Lieutenant. During this time he qualified at the School of Musketry. He was made a Captain in 1911 and at the outbreak of war was commanding 'C' Company. He went to France in March 1915 and the 1/4th Battalion first took over trenches in the front line, near Ploegsteert Wood, on 17 April 1915. He was promoted to the rank of Major in January 1916 and was awarded a Military Cross in the June 1916 Birthday Honours List. The Battalion fought at Ovillers in mid-July 1916 for which Slade was awarded the Distinguished Service Order 'For conspicuous gallantry during operations. He organised with great skill bombing attacks, in order to reach two companies which were isolated in a trench further to the north. On another occasion he was twice buried by shells in one night, but dug himself out and carried on as if nothing had happened'. He was also Mentioned in Despatches by Haig in November 1916. He was given command of 2/6th Gloucestershires and was promoted to Lieutenant Colonel on 12 March 1917. He led them until he became ill in November 1917 returning to the UK. In March 1918 he returned to the Front and was posted to the 8th Gloucestershires. During the Battle of the Lys in 1918 they were south of Ypres from 31 March. On 3 May 1918 the Battalion relieved the 39th Composite Division near Dikkebus and on 4 May Captain Slade was killed, probably by a shell but the details have been lost. Slade was buried near to where he died at Hallebast and in 1920, when isolated graves around the Dikkebus area were concentrated at the Klein Vierstraat British Cemetery, his remains were moved here. His brother, Corporal Frank Oscar Slade, Army Pay Corps, died on 26 October 1918 aged 28 years and is buried in Brookwood Military Cemetery.

Concentrated here:

Ferme Henri Pattyn-Vanlaeres, Poperinge - 58 British men, and one Canadian who died in May-July 1915, with one British soldier from April 1918, were buried there.

Mont Vidaigne Military Cemetery - on the west slope of the Vidaignberg near Rodeberg. It contained seventeen British men who died in July and August 1918. Seventeen French graves from April and May 1918 were moved elsewhere.

UK – 779    Aust – 8    NZ – 7
Can - 8     S Afr -1    BWI – 1
Chinese Labour Corps - 1    Unnamed - 109
Area - 3040 sq mts

**LOCATION**
Klien Vierstraat Cemetery can be found on the south side of the road from Vierstraat to Hallebast which is south of Ieper and about 3km north of Kemmel next to Kemmel No. 1 French Cemetery. This is best reached from the Ieper-Kemmel road leaving it at the two unmistakeable warehouses at Vierstraat.

## LA BELLE ALLIANCE CEMETERY

### HISTORY
This cemetery was used in February and March 1916 by the 10th and 11th King's Royal Rifle Corps for the burial of twelve men from their Battalions as well as one from the Somerset Light Infantry. It was used again in July and August 1917 mainly for the burial of men from the Sherwood Foresters or South Staffordshires.

### INFORMATION
Sited on one of the main trenches to the front, Coney Street, the cemetery was named after the farmhouse and shrine here that were both destroyed in the war and never rebuilt. The exact number buried here is unknown but eight men of the 7th South Staffordshires are thought to be buried in Row D.

Buried here is 2nd Lieutenant Percy Eric Palmer, No. 29 Squadron, Royal Flying Corps and 1st Australian Infantry, killed in action on 17 July 1917 aged 20 years. He was appointed 2nd Lieutenant (on probation) in the Special Reserve, effective 9 June 1917. He was flying a Nieuport 23 when killed. He had left Poperinge aerodrome on a patrol at 10.50am and was shot down after combat at about 12.15pm when he was attacked by a superior number of Albatros DIII scouts. This was his second sortie having joined the Squadron a few days before. In his first sortie he was forced to the ground by anti-aircraft fire.

UK – 60        Unnamed – 10
Area - 350 sq mts

### LOCATION
La Belle Alliance Cemetery lies north of Ieper and 300m north of the N38 on a road that runs parallel to the by-pass. It is reached easily from the by-pass by taking the Pilkemsweg and Zwaanhofweg (Buffs Road) which is clearly signed from the N38. The cemetery is 70m from the Zwaanhofweg at the end of a short path. The much larger Divisional Collecting Post Cemetery is almost directly opposite.

## LA BRIQUE MILITARY CEMETERY No. 1

### HISTORY
The cemetery was used from May to December 1915.

### INFORMATION
This burial ground, and its partner, the No. 2 cemetery that faces it across the road, derive their name from the brickworks that used to stand nearby. This is the smaller of the two and stands below the level of the other on the east side of the road. Notably, there is no War Stone or Cross of Sacrifice, which is less unusual than you may think for small cemeteries. However, its partner cemetery, No. 2, does not have a War Stone either, which is surprising.

On 5 June 1915 the 6th Division took over the line here from the 4th Division as the 2nd Leinsters relieved the 1st Royal Irish Fusiliers. The officers of the Leinsters claimed that they could still smell the gas that had been used two months earlier in Second Ypres.

Buried here is Drummer (or Private) Edwin George Royes, 1st Buffs (East Kents), killed in action on 2 September 1915 aged 27 years. He seemed to have joined the Royal Marine Light Infantry in 1904 but is also attested to the Buffs in 1907. His service record shows a long list of minor disciplinary offences. However, by June 1914 he has received a good conduct report and is taken back from Army Reserve, which he entered in 1910. This makes sense of his link to the Royal Marine Light Infantry in 1904 as this then fits his term of seven years service with the colours and five in reserve. He is sent to France on 7 September 1914. He was one of two men of the 1st Buffs killed holding the line at La Brique, positioned a little east of here following the halting of the German advance in Second Ypres. His brother Private Thomas Percy Royes, HMS Aboukir, Royal Marine Light Infantry, was killed in action on 22 September 1914 aged 24 years and is buried in The Hague General Cemetery. Aboukir was one of a patrol of three ancient and almost obsolete cruisers attacked and sunk by German submarine U9. Royes was among nearly 1500 men lost in the attack. Another brother, Private Frank Louis Royes, HMS Formidable, Royal Marine Light Infantry, was killed in action on 1 January 1915 aged 18 years and is commemorated on the Chatham Naval Memorial. A battleship launched in 1898, Formidable was hit by two torpedoes fired from the German submarine U24 while steaming through the Channel in a major storm. Nearly 600 men died. Consider a family that had lost three sons, the only male children I can find in the records, before the end of 1915.

UK - 91    Unnamed – 4
Area - 726 sq mts

### LOCATION
The cemeteries lie in the suburbs of north-east Ieper on the edge of a new industrial park and next to the hospital. The road north from the town side of the Menin Gate brings you to a crossroads with traffic lights. Straight over and then the first turn on the right after about 50m will bring you to the cemeteries here. Following signs to the hospital will bring you to these two cemeteries.

# LA BRIQUE MILITARY CEMETERY No. 2

### HISTORY
From February 1915 until March 1918 the irregular group of graves in Plot I was created. The cemetery was enlarged after the war with the concentration of graves.

### INFORMATION
The cemetery, and its partner the No. 1 cemetery, derive their name from the brickworks that used to stand nearby. This is the larger of the two cemeteries and stands above the level of the other on the west side of the road. The original cemetery had 383 graves laid out in irregular rows that now make up Plot I. After the war, remains were concentrated here to create Plot II and extend Plot I. One soldier was brought here from Kemmel No. 2 French Cemetery when the French graves were concentrated.

Buried here is Lance Corporal Alfred George Drake, VC, 8th Rifle Brigade, killed in action on 23 November 1915 at La Brique. He gave his life saving an officer of his Battalion, Lieutenant Henry Tryon, when they were on patrol near the German lines and came under fire. The rest of the patrol withdrew but Drake stayed with the wounded officer. They were found later, Drake's body full of bullets and the officer, still alive, beside him. The citation reads 'For most conspicuous bravery on the night of 23rd Nov., 1915, near La Brique, France. He was one of a patrol of four which was reconnoitring towards the German lines. The patrol was discovered when close to the enemy who opened heavy fire with rifles and a machine gun, wounding the Officer and one man. The latter was carried back by the last remaining man. Corporal Drake remained with his Officer and was last seen kneeling beside him and bandaging his wounds regardless of the enemy's fire. Later a rescue party crawling near the German lines found the Officer and Corporal, the former unconscious but alive and bandaged, Corporal Drake beside him dead and riddled with bullets. He had given his own life and saved his Officer.' After Tryon recovered from his wounds he returned to his unit but was killed in action at Flers-Courcelette on 15 September 1916. He is commemorated on the Thiepval Memorial.

Also here is Captain Edmond Ernest Charles Wellesley, 9th Norfolks, killed in action by a shell at 9.30pm on 30 April 1916 aged 29 years. He was the second son of the late Edmond Ernest Charles Wellesley, Captain in the Hampshire Yeomanry and son-in-law of Major John Samuels about whom it was claimed in Burke's Peerage that he had been awarded the Victoria Cross, though there is no evidence for this. Wellesley was also several generations removed in relation to the 1st Duke of Wellington, through direct line from Wellington's father. Wellesley had previously been in the Ceylon Rifles from which he resigned in 1911. He first enlisted as a Private on 22 December 1914 in the Royal Fusiliers aged 28 and was then in the Royal West Kents for most of 1915. He received a commission as a Captain in the 9th Norfolks in December 1915. He was married on 6 April 1916 returning to the Front on 13 April.

Major Bernard Maynard Lucan Brodhurst, 1/4th Gurkha Rifles, died on 27 April 1915 aged 41 years. He made one first class cricket appearance for Hampshire in 1897, the final match of the season. He had been in the Indian Army since 1892, served in the Waziristan Expedition of 1894-5 and in China in 1900. His Battalion arrived in France in November 1914 and he saw action in the main battles of early 1915. He was in temporary command of his Battalion when he was killed.

| UK – 782 | Aust – 18 | NZ – 9 |
| Can – 23 | S Afr – 7 | India – 1 |
| Unnamed – 387 | | Area - 3270 sq mts |

Special Memorials to four men known/believed to be buried among the unnamed.

### LOCATION
Directions for this cemetery are the same as for the No. 1 Cemetery finding it on the opposite side of the road.

# LA CLYTTE MILITARY CEMETERY

## HISTORY
Opened on 1 November 1914 this cemetery remained in use until April 1918. It was almost doubled in size after the war with the concentration of graves from isolated positions and small cemeteries in the local area.

## INFORMATION
The original Plots I, II and III and part of Plot IV were filled by nearly 600 graves with the concentration adding over 450. The wartime burials included 250 artillerymen and 66 engineers reflecting the nature of the activity in the rear of the Salient when the village was often used as a Brigade Headquarters. Post-war burials, completing Plot IV, and creating Plots V and VI, included 185 unnamed graves with Special Memorials to 24 men who are known to be buried among them. One of the graves, brought in from Leicester Camp Cemetery, is marked with the names of two men, one of whom is here.

Buried here is Private Leonard Mitchell, 8th York and Lancasters who was executed in the village on 19 September 1917 and buried here. He had deserted while under a suspended sentence of death for a previous desertion attempt. Mitchell had faced a court martial for self-inflicted wounds twice in early 1917. He had been awarded 42 days Field Punishment No. 1 which consisted of the convicted man being placed in restraints and attached to a fixed object, such as a gun wheel or a fence post, for up to two hours per day. He had later received a death sentence which was commuted to ten years penal servitude and later suspended four days before his brother was killed. His brother, Gunner William Henry Mitchell, 'A' Battery, 107th Brigade, Royal Field Artillery, was killed in action on 9 August 1917 aged 26 years and is buried here. Also here is Lieutenant William Knowles Tyldesley, 1/5th attached 9th Loyal North Lancashires, killed in action on 26 April 1918 aged 30 years. He played 87 first class cricket matches for Lancashire from 1908-14 as a left-handed batsman who bowled left arm medium-fast pace. He was a pre-war Territorial Corporal and was commissioned in October 1915 when he moved to the 9th Battalion. He had three brothers who all played for Lancashire, one of whom, Richard, also represented England in seven Test matches against South Africa and Australia.

Sergeant Charles Pepper, 16th Sherwood Foresters (Notts and Derbys) died on 13 September 1917 aged 42 years. As a footballer he played for Brechin and Notts County. As a cricketer he made seven first class appearances for Nottinghamshire in 1900-01. He was killed by a shell while standing outside the Battalion HQ, along with his commanding officer, Lieutenant Colonel Noel Houghton who is also buried here.

Also here is Corporal George Tocher, 1st Gordon Highlanders who died of wounds on 8 May 1915. His brother, Private James Tocher, 8th/10th Gordon Highlanders died on 31 July 1916 and is commemorated on the Thiepval Memorial. Another brother, Private John Tocher, 1st Gordon Highlanders died on 18 July 1916 and is also commemorated on the Thiepval Memorial. Private Robert Tocher, 4th Gordon Highlanders died on 15 November 1916 aged 34 years and is buried in Forceville Communal Cemetery and Extension. Peter Tocher was captured by the Germans in 1914 and spent the rest of the war in a German prisoner of war camp where he contracted tuberculosis. He returned home after the war, but died in October 1923, not officially a casualty of the war. He was buried in a pauper's grave in Trinity Cemetery in Aberdeen. Their father Peter enlisted in early 1916 but was too old for military service.

In De Klijte church there are murals dedicated to the French who died in the fighting at De Klijte and on the Scherpenberg. The church is in the village 100m south of the roundabout on the road to Loker.

| | | |
|---|---|---|
| UK – 1003 | Aust – 12 | NZ – 3 |
| Can – 51 | S Afr – 6 | BWI – 7 |
| Unnamed – 238 | | Area - 4436 sq mts |

Special Memorials to twenty-four men known to be buried among the unnamed.

## LOCATION
La Clytte Cemetery is on the south side of the N304, 100m west of the roundabout on the N375, just south of De Klijte. This is about 10km south-west of Ieper. The cemetery is deceptively large as it is positioned on the crest of a small rise with part of the burial ground hidden from the road. It has good views of the Salient from Ypres to the Monts des Flandres.

# LA LAITERIE MILITARY CEMETERY

## HISTORY
This cemetery was in use throughout most of the war having been open from November 1914 until October 1918. It was enlarged after the war with the concentration of 200 graves from the surrounding battlefields.

## INFORMATION
The cemetery was named after the dairy farm here. Much of the cemetery was developed in the same way as the regimental burial grounds common in the early part of the war. Several Plots are composed almost entirely of men from one unit. For example, Plots X, III and II are made up

of the dead of the 24th, 25th and 26th Canadian Infantry Battalions respectively while Plot VIII contains those of the 5th Northumberland Fusiliers.

On 25 April 1918, the cemetery and this area fell into German hands, but it was retaken at the beginning of September.

Buried here is Lance Corporal Daniel Hayes, 'A' Company, 9th Royal Dublin Fusiliers, killed on 31 May 1917 aged 16 years. Also here is Private Stanley Clifford Lockwood, 1st East Surreys, killed on 24 March 1915 aged 16 years. He was an only son and had been at the Front for a month when he was killed.

Another buried here is Major Adolph V. Roy, 22nd Canadian Infantry, killed in action on 6 October 1915 aged 47 years. He was the first Canadian to graduate from the Ecole Centrale de Paris, a famous engineering school, in 1892. He was a well known business man much involved in his community and had been a candidate in the local elections in Montreal campaigning to fight corruption. He joined the Canadian Expeditionary Force in November 1914. The Battalion war diary records 'Major Roy killed today. He tried to throw a live German bomb out of the trench in order to save the men around him, but it exploded while he had it in his hand. He was badly shocked and lost a lot of blood. Died before he could be gotten out of the trenches.' The 22nd Canadian Infantry was a famous francophone Battalion, mostly coming from the Quebec Province, which left Canada in May 1915.

The road was known as York Road. On it can be found, 800m to the north, the Memorial to the US 27th and 30th Divisions who fought on the Salient in 1918. These two Divisions had arrived in Belgium in May 1917. American troops were usually placed alongside either French or British Divisions from whom they would receive technical assistance and instruction. These Divisions served with the British Army throughout the remainder of the war. In the spring of 1918 Mont Kemmel (Kemmelberg) had been swiftly taken from the French, who had been there for only a few weeks, by the Germans. By 31 August 1918 the Germans had retreated from Mont Kemmel and the Americans found themselves holding the front line. The 27th Division advanced on Vierstraat and the following day both Divisions pushed on towards Voormezele. In a few days they suffered 2,100 casualties. This large white Rocheret stone monument was erected in 1929.

UK – 469    Aust – 7    Can – 196
NF – 1      Unnamed – 180   KUG – 78
Area - 5507 sq mts

Special Memorials to two soldiers who are known to be buried here but whose graves were destroyed in later fighting.

### LOCATION

La Laiterie Cemetery is on the west side of the Ieper-Kemmel road about 1km north of the Kemmel crossroads and approximately 6km south of Ieper. It is easy to miss as it is set behind a wall below the level of the road.

## LA PLUS DOUVE FARM CEMETERY

### HISTORY

Opened in April 1915 by the 48th (South Midland) Division the cemetery remained in use until May 1918 when the Germans captured the valley during their Spring Offensive.

### INFORMATION

The two sizable farms, La Plus Douve and La Petite Douve, have both been rebuilt next to each other, La Plus Douve being the nearer to this cemetery. The farm was within the British lines for most of the war and was often used as a Battalion headquarters. Hence, it was also known as Ration Farm because the Battalion transport could only get this close to the front-lines at night with rations.

It is possible to imagine the cavalry charges in the valley during the early parts of the war and also the importance of holding the ridge. In November 1914 the German Guards Cavalry Corps were ordered to take the farm. However, two Companies of the 2nd Royal Inniskilling Fusiliers managed to hold the line.

La Petite Douve was the object of a successful raid by the 7th Canadian Infantry in November 1915. It was also the approximate location at which the Germans discovered one of the mines being dug by the 171st Tunnelling Company in preparation for the Battle of Messines. The British miners knew the Germans were nearby and blew a camouflet killing the Germans. The Germans retaliated with a 6,000lb explosion, so the mine was abandoned and flooded by the River Douve.

Buried here is Captain Samuel Arnold Atkinson, 'D' Company, 2nd Battalion, 3rd New Zealand Rifle Brigade, killed in action on 5 June 1917 aged 43 years. His father, Sir Harry Albert Atkinson, KCMG, was Prime Minister of New Zealand in 1876-77, 1883-84 and 1887-91. He died in 1892 when Arnold, as he was known, was aged 17. Atkinson was a forceful advocate of conscription in New Zealand and was Secretary of the Wellington War League. He joined the army in 1915 and left New Zealand in June 1916 arriving in France in November. He was killed by a sniper while trying to rescue a fellow officer.

Also here is Private Robert Lancelot Cuthbert, 2nd King Edward's Horse, killed on 7 July 1915 aged 47 years. He was a Chartered Accountant in Scotland and a Certified Public Accountant in the USA to where he had emigrated from London in the 1890's. He was also a member of the New York Yacht Club and was a keen participant in several sports. He enlisted in the British army in London in 1914, lying about his age to get in. He was killed while scouting the area for his unit having been at the Front since May 1915. His gravestone reads 'From America he came on homeland's duty call'.

Of note buried here is Private James Jackson Mollison, 25th Australian Infantry, killed on 17 June 1916 aged 27 years. He was returning from a scouting patrol in the Messines area when he was victim to gas poisoning. He was on patrol with Private Other Beaumont Jeffreys Philpott of the same Battalion who is buried at Dranoutre Military Cemetery. They were the first Australians to die in Belgium during the war.

UK – 101    Aust – 86    NZ – 61
Can – 88    Ger – 9      Area - 3025 sq mts

**LOCATION**
La Plus Douve Cemetery lies in the valley of the River Douve about 8km south of Ieper, south-west of Messines and approximately 2km south-east of Wulvergem. It is reached by means of a well signed farm track from the Messines-Wulvergem road and is found on the edge of an attractive tree-lined avenue that leads south from the farm to Hill 63. The cemetery has good views of the valley as well as of Hill 63 and the Messines Ridge.

# LANCASHIRE COTTAGE CEMETERY

**HISTORY**
This cemetery was begun by the 1st East Lancashires, who have 84 men buried here, and the 1st Hampshires, who have 56, in November 1914. It remained in use until March 1916. A few later burials were made. The Germans created a cemetery nearby when they were here in 1918.

**INFORMATION**
Buried here is Captain George Clayhills, DSO, twice MiD, 1st East Lancashires, killed in action on 2 November 1914 aged 36 years. He was commissioned into the 4th Cheshires (Militia) in 1896 and joined the East Lancashires in 1899, served in South Africa for which he was awarded the Distinguished Service Order, was Mentioned in Despatches on two occasions and promoted to Lieutenant. He was made Captain in 1908. He went with the East Lancashires to France on 22 August 1914 and fought at Mons, on the Marne and Aisne before he was killed. Three of his great-uncles fought at Waterloo.

Also here is Private C W T Sheppard, 1/7th Sherwood Foresters (Notts and Derbys), killed on 6 March 1915 aged 21 years. He is the only man of his regiment buried here. His tale is unfortunate. During a handover of the trenches from the 1st Hampshires, some men of the Hampshires remained behind to instruct the Sherwoods, who were on their first tour in the front line, in the trenches and locality. It was during this that a Lance Corporal of the Hampshires accidently shot him. He had been in Flanders for less than a month.

You can see several farms from here, such as Hampshire Farm in the fields to the north that were important in the war. In the fields to the south is Lawrence Farm, painted by Winston Churchill when he was a Lieutenant-Colonel commanding the 6th Royal Scots Fusiliers in the winter of 1915-16. Churchill had been forced to resign from the British Government after criticism over the Gallipoli Campaign for which he was responsible. Recalled by the Prime Minister, Lloyd George, as Minister of Munitions in July 1917, he later became Prime Minister during World War II and again in the 1950's.

Approximately 1km east of the cemetery is the crossroads in Le Gheer, held by the 1st East Lancashires in November 1914 when, on the morning of 2 November, the Germans attacked killing all of the officers. Drummer Spencer John Bent took command winning the Victoria Cross by organising the men to hold the German advance.

The crossroads was estimated to be the northern limit of the famous 'Christmas Truce' of 1914, called by the British headquarters the 'fraternization episode'. There are 148 men recorded by the CWGC as having died on 25 December 1914. Take out those not on the Western Front, the one 'Alias' and you are left with 76 men killed or died of wounds on 25 December 1914. The 'Truce' was not widespread, and was only in areas which were held by the British particularly around Ploegsteert Wood and on the French border. There was no 'Truce' on French sectors. In Belgium, where most of the 'truces' took place, there were twenty men killed on Christmas Day 1914 in and around the Ypres Sector. Eight are named on the Ploegsteert Memorial, six are on the Menin Gate and five in cemeteries in and around Ploegsteert. These five are all buried within the distance one could kick a football from truce sites and it is certain that footballs were seen in no-man's land with brief matches and kickabouts. The truce is a significant story within Word War One, but it is not the only story on 25 December 1914. There are now several Memorials to the Truce and Football match, one next to Prowse Point Cemetery.

North of Le Gheer is the small hamlet of Le Pelerin on the edge of Ploegsteert Wood. Of the mines laid for the start of the Battle of Messines on 6 June 1917, two did not explode. The one at Le Pelerin finally did so in 1955 when a tree was hit by lightning, 38 years late to the month. No-one was hurt. The other mine, if it exists and there is now disagreement about that, may be in the area of, or under, the Messines-Ploegsteert road in the valley of the River Douve.

UK – 231      Aust – 23      Can – 2
Unnamed – 5      Ger - 13
Area - 2125 sq mts

Special Memorials to two men buried among the three British unnamed graves.

## LOCATION

Lancashire Cottage Cemetery lies about 1.2km east of the town square in Ploegsteert, south of Ieper, and on the south side of the old road to Warneton.

# LARCH WOOD (RAILWAY CUTTING) CEMETERY

## HISTORY

This cemetery was begun in a small plantation of larches in April 1915 and used until the German advance in April 1918. It was enlarged after the war by the concentration of 250 graves from the battlefields of the Salient and from some German cemeteries that have been removed.

## INFORMATION

This cemetery was used particularly by the 46th (North Midland) Division and the 1st Dorsets, who served in the 5th Division until 1916 and then in the 32nd Division. Unusually, it contains the grave of a Canadian Merchant Seaman. There are also Special Memorials to four British men and one Canadian buried in German cemeteries whose graves have been lost. One French and one Belgian grave have been removed. The tunnels in the wood here were used as a Battalion headquarters in 1917.

Many of the burials in Plot II Row J are men of the 1st Dorsets who were holding the line at Hill 60 on 5 July 1915 when the Germans launched a bombardment, demolishing much of the trench and killing sixteen men. The body of Private Harry Woods was found in eight pieces. His comrades ensured his remains were found and buried here with his pals.

Buried here is Lieutenant John Eden, 12th (Prince of Wales's Royal) Lancers, killed in action on 17 October 1914 aged 26 years. He was killed at the foot of the Amerikaberg nearby and buried in America Crossroads German Cemetery and moved here in November 1924. He was one of the first to be killed at Ypres when he was shot during a reconnaissance. The church at Kruiseeke was rebuilt with a financial donation from Eden's sister. His brother, who was fighting at Ploegtsteert Wood with the 21st (Yeoman Rifles) Kings Royal Rifle Corps when he heard of John's death, was later Sir Anthony Eden, the British Prime Minister. Anthony Eden married Clarisa Churchill, niece of Sir Winston Churchill, another man we know fought in Ploegsteert Wood when he was Lieutenant Colonel of the 6th Royal Scots Fusiliers. Another brother, Midshipman William Nicholas Eden, was killed at the Battle of Jutland on 31 May 1916 aged 16 years when serving on HMS Indefatigable. He is commemorated on the Plymouth Naval Memorial. At 4.02pm, HMS Indefatigable was hit by shells from SMS Von der Tann and exploded losing all but two of her 1,019 crew. Buried here is 2nd Lieutenant Arnold Septimus Guy Jarvis, 1st Northamptonshires, who died on 31 October 1914 aged 19 years. He was commissioned in January 1914 and killed when shot in the head. He lost three brothers in the war and one on active service in the aftermath of the war. Private Lewis Wyndham Jarvis, 72nd Canadian Infantry, died on 27 September 1918 aged 38 years and is buried in Quarry Wood Cemetery, Sains-Les-Marquion. He had served six years with the Cape Mounted Rifles including the South African War, and was a rancher when he enlisted on 19 March 1918 with the British Columbia Regiment. His address was given as 'US Hotel, San Francisco, California'. Sapper James Henry Jarvis, 9th Canadian Railway Troops, Canadian Engineers, died on 15 October 1918 aged 37 years and is buried in Caudry British Cemetery. He was a Labourer by trade, unmarried at the time of enlistment on 15 May 1915. Engineer Sub-Lieutenant Hugh Townley Jarvis, HMS Calgarian, Royal Naval Reserve, died on 1 March 1918 aged 28 years and is commemorated on the Portsmouth Naval Memorial. HMS Calgarian, was sunk off Rathlin Island by a torpedo from submarine U19, which was responsible for the sinking of 46 ships in total. Major Cecil Jarvis, DSO, MC, 20th Deccan Horse, died on 18 March 1919 aged 35 years. He is buried in Cairo War Memorial Cemetery. He transferred from the Middlesex Regiment to the Indian Army in May 1905 and was killed in the suppression of riots and public demonstrations seeking Egyptian independence. He was posthumously awarded the Distinguished Service Order in the Birthday Honours List in June 1919. Another brother, Lieutenant John Eustace Jarvis, fought in the war winning the Military Cross in 1917. He served with the 11th Canadian Infantry as a Private and transferred with a commission to the 2nd Northamptonshires in May 1915. He was taken prisoner in 1918. Nine members of the Jarvis family were on active service during the war. Their mother Ada Maud Jarvis died on 23 July 1919.

Also here is Rifleman Clarence Eastwood Peel, 18th King's Royal Rifle Corps, who died on 21 September 1917 and is commemorated by a Special Memorial as 'known to be buried here'. His nephew is the, in my opinion excellent, playwright Alan Bennett. Bennett has detailed his search for both the grave and the life story of his uncle in the radio monologue 'Uncle Clarence'.

There are two features close to this cemetery that played a major role in the war.

**HILL 60**. This is on the north of the road but it is on the east side of the railway. Hill 60 is preserved so that you can have access to one of the more well-known sites in the Salient. It is a strange feeling to stand on a small mound upon which so many men died and under which so many still lie, undiscovered and undisturbed.

Hill 60 was created at the end of the last century as a spoil heap dug from the railway cutting. It is not a real hill at all, and as such is a microcosm of the whole Salient being somewhere at which the Generals decided they would make their stand, of little significance at the start of the war but it was to increase in importance as time passed.

Hill 60 was captured on 10 December 1914 by the German 39th Division. Tunnelling to lay mines was begun almost immediately by the Royal Monmouth Engineers and the task was continued by the 171st Tunnelling Company. The five mines blown at 7.00pm on 17 April 1915 used approximately 10,000lbs of explosive and killed over 150 soldiers including two men of the Royal Engineers. An infantry attack by the 1st Royal West Kents, 2nd King's Own Scottish Borderers and 1/9th (Queen Victoria's Rifles) Londons then suffered few casualties. A counter-attack by the Germans at night inflicted heavy casualties forcing the British off the hill, though the next day the 2nd Duke of Wellington's and 2nd King's Own Yorkshire Light Infantry re-took the hill. The 15th Brigade relieved the 13th Brigade on 19 April, the 1st Norfolks, 1st Cheshires, 1st Bedfordshires and 1st Dorsetshires taking over the line with the 1/6th (Liverpool Rifles) King's (Liverpools) in reserve. They repulsed a German attack with the help of the 1st East Surreys.

During the attack Lieutenant (later Brigadier) George Roland Patrick Roupell, VC, CB, 1st East Surreys, won the Victoria Cross on 20 April for holding his post though wounded several times. On the same day Private (later Corporal) Edward Dwyer, VC, also 1st East Surreys, a greengrocer's son from Fulham, aged 19, found himself alone in a trench attacked by Germans but managed to single-handedly hold the position. He was wounded on 27 April and awarded the Victoria Cross which he received from King George V on 28 June 1915. The spot at which he won the Cross is now the highest point on Hill 60. In the same battle 2nd Lieutenant (later Captain) Geoffrey Harold Woolley, VC, OBE, MC, 1/9th (Queen Victoria's Rifles) Londons became the first officer of a Territorial unit to be awarded the Victoria Cross when, during 20 and 21 April, he was the only officer remaining on Hill 60. 2nd Lieutenant (later Major) Benjamin Handley Geary, VC, attached to the 1st East Surreys, was awarded the Victoria Cross during the same action for conspicuous bravery. As you may have noted this is three Victoria Cross awards for one Battalion in less than 48 hours.

Hill 60 remained in British hands while the Germans were busy with their gas attack in the north and east of the Salient but they then brought gas here on 1 May 1915. The 1st Devonshires, 1st Bedfordshires, 1st Dorsetshires and 59th Field Company, Royal Engineers, suffered heavy losses but held the hill. Another gas attack by the Germans was made on 5 May 1915 causing the 2nd Duke of Wellington's, 1st Bedfordshires and 1/6th King's (Liverpools) to fall back from the hill. The 2nd King's Own Scottish Borderers and the 2nd King's Own Yorkshire Light Infantry tried to retake the hill but suffered very heavily. Hill 60 was now in German hands. In the struggle for possession of Hill 60 the 5th Division had lost 100 officers and 3,000 men.

Between the fall of Hill 60 and the first day of the Battle of Messines on 6 June 1917 fighting here went on above and below ground. New tunnels were dug which were finished by July 1916, though the British commanders did not use them to blow mines until June 1917 and, therefore, they had to be defended and protected from German tunnellers and infantry. This task fell consecutively to 175th, 3rd Canadian and 1st Australian Tunnelling Companies.

On 6 June 1917 the mines were blown as part of the start of the Battle of Messines. 125,000lbs of explosive was used to create a crater 20m deep and 80m across killing nearly 700 men. The 11th West Yorkshires and 12th Durham Light Infantry attacked the hill taking it with ease. Those Germans who survived the explosion were too dazed to fight. It must come as no surprise that Hill 60 became known as Mount Calvary or 'the blood soaked hill of death'.

There are a number of interesting features at Hill 60 :-
1. A German/British bunker – look at the different types of concrete to see the parts of the bunker, some created by the British and some of it by the Germans.
2. Memorial to the 1/9th (Queen Victoria's Rifles) Londons.
3. Memorial to 14th (Light) Division moved here from Railway Wood in 1978.
4. Memorial to 1st Australian Tunnelling Company, this includes an account of the events here.

5. French Resistance Memorial. This commemorates Pierre Marchant and Lucien Olivier, two members of the French resistance from La Madeleine (now a suburb of Lille) who were killed here by Germans on 2 September 1944.
6. A café and restaurant.

**THE CATERPILLAR.** Named because, from the air and on maps, its shape was similar to a caterpillar. This used to be private land that could not be accessed, but it is now possible to visit the Caterpillar, and the crater blown on the first day of the Battle of Messines, in Battle Wood. Cross the bridge across the railway from Hill 60 and take the path to the left, it is clearly sign posted, and you will enter Battle Wood. There is a path of about 100m to reach the mine crater from the road. Once in the wood the crater is located on the right of the path. With Hill 60, this was a key position and can be found west of the railway and Hill 60. It seems insignificant today, but the slight rise here was enough of a feature on the landscape to be considered an important objective. Hence, many men died there.

On 6 November 1914 the line was held by the 1st Irish Guards, 2nd Grenadier Guards, 1st Royal Sussex and 1st Oxford and Bucks Light Infantry. They were losing the position when men of the 1st and 2nd Life Guards and the Royal Horse Guards arrived in support to turn the German advance by means of a cavalry charge led by General Moussy. The next day, Lord Cavan took the 4th (Guards) Brigade into action pushing the Germans to the south. In 1915 the 1/5th Leicestershires held the line when, on 23 June, the Germans blew a mine killing many men. The day was only saved by the arrival of men from the same Brigade in the form of the 1/4th Leicestershires.

For much of the winter of 1916-1917 the 47th (2nd London) Division held the trenches. On 15 February 1917 the 1/6th (London Rifles) Londons carried out one of the most successful raids on the Salient. Having staged a dummy attack the Battalion, with sappers of the 520th Royal Engineers and Australian Tunnelling Company, raided German trenches almost unopposed, capturing an officer and 117 men with five machine-guns and a large amount of valuable documents.

Concentrated here:

America Crossroads German Cemetery – located about 4km just south of east from here and named after a cafe on the Wervik-Kruiseeke road where 'Amerikastraat' crosses the main road. It contained the graves of five British men who died in October 1914.

Bruges General Cemetery, St. Michel – located nearly 40km north of here, it contained the graves of 32 British men and one Canadian Merchant seaman. One WW1 burial remains there and over 80 burials were made in WW2.

Eerneghem German Cemetery – Eerneghem is nearly 20km north of here and the cemetery was a little east of the village. Buried among the Germans was one Royal Flying Corps officer.

Ghistelles Churchyard – located about 20km north of here, there was a German aerodrome near the village. They used a Plot in the churchyard for burials which included two British men who died in July 1917.

Groenenberg German Cemetery - on the south side of Shrewsbury Forest about 1.5km north of east from here, it contained four British soldiers who died in February 1915.

Handzaeme German Cemetery - on the north side of the village which is about 15km north of here. It contained two Canadian soldiers who died in May 1915.

Ichtegem German Cemetery - a little west of the village which is about 20km north of here. It contained two unidentified Royal Air Force officers.

Kortemark German Cemetery No. 1 - a little north-west of the village which is about 15km north of here. It contained the graves of two Royal Flying Corps officers.

Leffinghe German Cemetery - on the north side of the village which is about 25km north of here. It contained the graves of one Royal Flying Corps officer killed in July 1917 and three unidentified British soldiers.

Marckhove German Cemetery – located about 15km north of here it contained ten British soldiers and airmen who died in 1918.

Oudenburg Churchyard – located close to Ostende about 25km north of here it contained two British soldiers who died in 1917.

Ten-Brielen Communal Cemetery German Extension – located about 4km south-east of here it contained six British soldiers who died in 1914.

Thourout German Cemetery No. 2 - seven British soldiers and one Canadian serviceman were buried here about 20km north of Larch Wood.

Vladslo German Cemetery - situated near the church in the centre of the village, which is about 15km north of here, and not to be confused with the current Vladso-Pratbos German Cemetery. Among the German burials it contained two Royal Flying Corps officers killed in 1917.

Warneton Sud-et-Bas German Cemetery – located about 5km south of here it contained two British unidentified soldiers who died in 1918.

Wervik Communal Cemetery and Extensions – situated on the Belgian side of the Lys about 5km south of here. It contained 62 British and six Canadian men.

Wijnendale German Cemetery – located about 20km north of here it contained two Royal Flying Corps and one Canadian Flying Corps men.

Zandvoorde German Cemetery - also known as De Voorstraat No. 49 and located about 2km south-east of here. It contained eleven British men who died in 1914.

UK – 700      Aust – 36      Can – 86  Ger - 1
BWI – 1       KUG – 33       Unnamed – 321

Area - 2736 sq mts

Special Memorials to 81 British men and one Australian known/believed to be buried among the unnamed.

Special Memorials to four British men and one Canadian whose graves in German cemeteries have been lost.

**LOCATION**

Larch Wood Cemetery lies south-east of Ieper, 150m east of the road to Comines, next to the railway line, at the end of a farm track clearly marked by CWGC signs. Situated right next to the railway, the cemetery is entered by means of a path from the road, though the tranquillity is regularly shattered by passing trains.

# LE TOUQUET RAILWAY CROSSING CEMETERY

**HISTORY**
The cemetery was in use for most of the war from October 1914 until June 1918.

**INFORMATION**
This graveyard was begun near the point where the railway used to cross the road from Ploegsteert to Le Bizet. It includes 28 graves in Rows A to E of men of the 1st Rifle Brigade who died in October and November 1914.

The 2nd Lancashire Fusiliers were in the line to the east of the cemetery during the Christmas Day Truce in 1914. A German messenger who crossed no man's land under a white flag was kept as a prisoner of war as he had seen behind the British lines and therefore could not be allowed to return.

On 10 February 1918 a trench raid was launched at Warneton by 204 men of the 3rd Australian Division which took 33 prisoners.

Buried here is Captain Penry Bruce Lendon, MVO, 3rd attached 1st King's Own (Royal Lancasters), killed in action on 21 October 1914 aged 31 years. He joined the 4th (Militia) Battalion of his regiment in 1901 from which he moved to the 3rd (Special Reserve) in 1908. He was made a member of the Victorian Order in 1905 when he carried the colours presented to the Battalion by the King. He retired in February 1914 but returned to the colours when war broke out and went to France with the 1st King's Own. He was shot through the lungs while going to the aid of a wounded man of his Battalion.

Also here is Captain Selwyn Lucas Lucas-Tooth, 3rd attached 2nd Lancashire Fusiliers, killed in action on 20 October 1914 aged 35 years. He joined the 5th [Militia] Lancashire Fusiliers in April 1904 and was promoted to Lieutenant in May 1905. In 1908, he was promoted to Captain in the 3rd Reserve Battalion. He was killed by a sniper. He was the eldest of the three sons of Baronet Sir Robert Lucas Tooth. His brother Captain Douglas Keith Lucas Lucas-Tooth, DSO, twice MiD, 9th (Queen's Royal) Lancers, was killed when hit by shell-fire on 14 September 1914 aged 33 years whilst he was seeking shelter for the horses of the regiment during the Battle of the Aisne. He is buried in Moulins New Communal Cemetery which is between Laon and Reims. He was Mentioned in Despatches for his work in the South African Wars and again for his role in the first contact with German forces in World War One while with 2nd Cavalry Brigade. He was posthumously awarded the Distinguished Service Order for commanding 'C' Squadron leading a cavalry charge at Audregnies. They were to discover that cavalry was no match for well-chosen defensive trenches, fences (later barbed wire) and machine guns with supporting artillery. The award was for getting his remaining men and horses to safety. Their father died on 19 February 1915, and their surviving brother, Archibald, inherited the baronetcy. Major Sir Archibald Leonard Lucas Lucas-Tooth, 2/1st 'B' Battery, Honourable Artillery Company attached 126th Brigade, Royal Field Artillery died of pneumonia on 12 July 1918 aged 34 years having been at the Front since June 1916. When he was killed the baronetcy expired. He is buried in Aubigny Communal Cemetery Extension near Loos.

Captain George Arthur Murray Docker, Royal Fusiliers attached 1st King's Own (Royal Lancasters) died on 17 November 1914 aged 37 years. He was in the South African Wars but contracted rheumatic fever so returned home. He was soon commissioned into the King's (Liverpools), transferred in 1901 to the Royal Fusiliers and was a Captain by 1908. He was an instructor at Sandhurst from 1907-11 and Adjutant of the 10th Middlesex from 1912-14 when he was ordered to India though this was soon changed to an order to go to France with the Lancasters. He played eleven cricket matches for the MCC from 1911-14 including a tour of the West Indies in 1913. He was excellent at many other sports including polo.

UK – 74       KUG – 21       Area - 870 sq mts
Special Memorials to three men known to be buried here.

**LOCATION**
Le Touquet Cemetery is found south of Ieper about 4km south-east of Ploegsteert. 1.4km south of the square in Ploegsteert you can find on the east side of the road, near a supermarket, a tree of CWGC signs on the corner. The road to the left and then the tree-lined avenue to the right will take you past Motor Car Corner Cemetery to a junction at which you turn left before passing Tancrez Farm Cemetery and factories. As you reach the flyover the cemetery is on the north side of the old road.

# LIJSSENTHOEK MILITARY CEMETERY

**HISTORY**
The British began to use Lijssenthoek Cemetery in June 1915 and by the time of the Armistice it had become the largest cemetery in the Salient, though that dubious honour now belongs to Tyne Cot. Some graves were concentrated here after the war.

**INFORMATION**
The area was known in the war as 'Remi Sidings' and the straight road between Poperinge and the French border

used to be the railway upon which wounded men were brought here or taken to Base Hospitals in the rear. The cemetery was begun in 1914 by the French who had a Casualty Clearing Station, the 15th Hopital d'Evacuation, at Remi Farm on the boundary of the cemetery near the road. Therefore, the earliest burials here are of French 'Poilu'.

The cemetery lay outside the range of the largest German guns for most of the war, except during the Battles of the Lys in 1918, which explains how it became so large. It served the many Casualty Clearing Stations and hospitals in the area and the fallen from many countries were buried here. Hence, there are French, German, Chinese, Indian and Algerian graves among 30 countries represented here. For example, Private Richard Van Neste, 27th Canadian Infantry, died of wounds on 10 November 1917 aged 36 years. He had emigrated from Belgium and returned with the Manitoba contingent to defend the country in which he had been born.

The first men to be buried here from the British medical units were Sylvain Avril and Adolphe Birckel buried on 6 May 1915 close to where the operating theatre was located and far from the main French Plots made in late 1914 and 1918. Approximately 350 French burials were removed after the war. Most of the hospital lay to the north-east of the cemetery with some sections on the other side of the railway (now the Poperinge-Steenvoorde road). It is worth noting that the cemetery represents a 3% death rate among those treated in the medical units here. It is also worth noting that every date of the calendar year is represented here. For example the only leap year in the war was 1916. Three burials were made on 29 February 1916. They are two Privates and a 2nd Lieutenant from the Royal Flying Corps.

From April to August 1918, the casualty clearing stations fell back before the German advance and field ambulances (including a French ambulance) took their places. While most of the cemetery was made during the war or shortly after, 24 burials were added to Plot XXXI in 1920 from isolated positions near Poperinge and seventeen added to Plot XXXII from St. Denijs Churchyard in 1981.

Despite its size I still find this one of my favourite cemeteries in the Salient. Unlike the larger Tyne Cot, which as a concentration cemetery made of burials brought together after the war with nearly 60% being unidentified, this cemetery was made next to Casualty Clearing Stations. So, almost all of the burials are identified and we can learn their stories. Consequently, there are many stories here, more than a few of which I have tried to tell.

Remi Farm still exists. In the great barn the graffiti inscribed by French and British soldiers waiting for treatment at the Casualty Clearing Stations can still be seen. There is now also a remarkably clean set of toilets, an exhibition covering the Casualty Clearing Stations and the medical process of getting men from the Front when wounded. There is a large nursery garden for the CWGC that can be seen and visited but again, ask first. In spring the flower beds are very attractive.

The earliest date of death recorded here is Captain William Arthur Mould Temple, MiD, 1st Gloucestershires, who died of wounds on 23 October 1914. He arrived in France on 14 August 1914 and was involved in the fighting at Mons, Marne, Aisne, and Ypres. He died of gunshot wounds to his right lung and shoulder received on 21 October. He died at No. 4 Casualty Clearing Station which was in the Chateau Dhondt, next to the Poperinge Old Military Cemetery. He was posthumously Mentioned in Despatches and moved here after the war. He was the son of Lieutenant Colonel William Temple who won the Victoria Cross on 20 November 1863 in New Zealand. Some of the last dates of death are members of the Labour Corps and Chinese Labour Corps who died of the flu epidemic in late 1918 and throughout 1919. However, among them are two members of the Chinese Labour Corps killed on 28 September 1919. They were shot by a local estaminet landlord as they tried to break in to his establishment.

For some time the youngest person buried here was Marcel Ramaut aged 14 years. He was one of three boys wounded in an explosion in a local ammunitions depot. They were brought here for treatment on 10 September 1915 where two of them died. They were subsequently moved and the locations are now no longer known.

One IWGC worker is also buried here. He is Thomas McGrath who had served as a Sergeant and worked as team leader for the Chinese Labour Corps. After the war he joined the Imperial War Graves Commission but died of illness at the age of 31 on St. George's Day in 1920.

Buried here is Major Frederick Harold Tubb, VC, 7th (Victoria) Australian Infantry, who died of wounds received while leading his men at Polygon Wood on 20 September 1917 when he was first shot by a sniper. Whilst being carried to the rear he was struck by British artillery shells and died here. He was awarded the Victoria Cross for his actions while still a Lieutenant at Lone Pine Trenches, Gallipoli in repulsing a German attack during which he was wounded in the head and arm. The citation reads 'For most conspicuous bravery and devotion to duty at Lone Pine trenches, in the Gallipoli Peninsula, on 9th August, 1915. In the early morning the enemy made a determined counter attack on the centre of the newly captured trench held by Lieutenant Tubb. They advanced up a sap and blew in a sandbag barricade, leaving only one foot of it standing, but Lieutenant Tubb led his men back, repulsed the enemy, and rebuilt the barricade. Supported by strong bombing parties, the enemy succeeded in twice again blowing in the barricade, but on each occasion Lieutenant Tubb, although wounded in the head and arm, held his ground with the greatest coolness and rebuilt it, and finally succeeded in maintaining his position under very heavy bomb fire.'

Lance Corporal George Alderson, AM, 10th Durham Light Infantry, died on 15 October 1915 aged 31 years at St. Jan ter Beizen. Alderson was the only soldier serving with the Durham Light Infantry to be awarded the Albert Medal First Class in Gold (only 45 were ever given). He died after having had his hand blown off. The citation reads 'On the evening of the 14th October, 1915, Alderson, with two other non-commissioned Officers, was moving some bombs into a room in a farmhouse where they were to be stored. While the bombs were being stacked, one of them fell to the floor and the percussion cap was fired. Alderson, knowing that the bomb would explode in four seconds, and that to throw it out of the window would endanger the men who were outside, picked it up and tried to reach the door. Before he could get out of the door the bomb exploded, blowing off his hand and inflicting other serious wounds, from which he shortly died. By his prompt action in picking up and carrying the bomb he probably saved the lives of the three men who were in the room with him, and by his presence of mind in not throwing it out of the window he certainly saved the lives of those standing outside. This act was the more meritorious as Alderson was fully aware of the deadly nature of the bomb and the danger to himself that his act involved.' The Albert Medal was a British medal awarded to recognise the saving of life. It has since been replaced by the George Cross.

Captain William Percival Vint, 'C' Company, 6th Battalion Machine Gun Corps, who died on 5 August 1918 aged 33 was twice recommended for the Albert Medal. He came home from Latin America, where he had worked for nine years at the Nitrate Works in Chile, to join the Army, arriving in Liverpool on 6 April 1915. Nine days later he had joined the Inns of Court Officer Training Company and just over two months after that he was discharged on his appointment to a commission. He joined the 11th Royal Irish Rifles, and was later attached to the 108th Brigade of the Machine Gun Corps, 36th Ulster Division. On 1 July 1916 he suffered shellshock during the attack by the Ulster Division near Thiepval and was soon sent home. By the end of September he was judged fit for service and was transferred to the Machine Gun Corps' training centre in Lincolnshire, where he was a bombing instructor. He was twice instrumental in saving life from bombing accidents and recommended for the Albert Medal. He returned to France gazetted as acting Captain on 28 June 1918.

Among the men from many nations buried here one was executed. Private William Baker of the 26th (Bankers) Royal Fusiliers was killed at Mizen Farm near Watou, which is about 5km north-west of here, on 14 August 1918 as the result of several desertions during the German Spring Offensive. Baker had volunteered for service but had a history of absenting himself. He was already under arrest on 22 April 1918 when he went missing again. He first tried to take the mail boat from Boulogne where he was arrested in May 1918. He escaped and tried to reach the hospital in Etaples but was arrested again on 21 June.

There are several senior officers buried here. One of the most senior to be killed in the war was Major General Malcolm Smith Mercer, CB, MiD, Commanding 3rd Canadian Division, killed in action on 3 June 1916 aged 57 years. It was highly unusual for a man of such senior rank to be killed in action. He was a barrister in Toronto and led the 3rd Canadian Division during the first two years of the war before he was killed in action at Mount Sorrel. He demonstrated courage under fire, visiting the front lines on numerous occasions at the height of battle and personally directing his forces in the face of poison gas attacks and heavy shellfire. On 2 June 1916 the 3rd Canadian Division was holding the front line between Hill 62 and Mount Sorrel. In the early morning Mercer inspected his sector. Heavy fire suddenly started as the Germans launched a major attack. Mercer was badly wounded in the leg by a bullet. Unable to be evacuated he took shelter in a trench. Early the next morning, during a fierce artillery barrage, a shrapnel shell exploded nearby killing Mercer instantly. His body was not found until 16 June 1916 when he was identified by his uniform. Mercer is the most senior Canadian officer to die in combat.

Also here are three Brigadiers. Brigadier General Hugh Gregory Fitton, CB, DSO, ADC, Order of the Medjidie 4th Class (Turkey), Khedive's Bronze Star, General Staff, Commanding 101st Brigade and late Queen's Own (Royal West Kents), died on 20 January 1916 aged 52 years. He has the unique distinction of being the only general officer to become his Division's first battle casualty. On 18 January 1916, three days after the Division completed its deployment to France, he was wounded in both thighs by a German sniper while on an instructional visit to the 16th Brigade and died two days later. He was the seventeenth British general to be killed in action or to die of wounds on the Western Front. He had served in the Sudan in 1885 for which he was awarded the Distinguished Service Order, Egypt 1885-86 and several Nile Expeditions in the 1890s. He had also served in the South African Wars 1899-1902. He was awarded the Order of the Bath (CB) in 1910.

Brigadier General Alister Fraser Gordon, CMG, DSO, MiD, General Staff Commanding 153rd Infantry Brigade late Gordon Highlanders, died on 31 July 1917 aged 45 years. He served in the Tirah Campaign in North-West India, the Ashanti Campaign of 1901, for which he was awarded the Distinguished Service Order, and also the South African War. He was wounded in the Battle of Festubert in 1915 while with the Gordon Highlanders. He was promoted to Brigadier on his return to service with the War Office when he was also made a member of the Order of St. Michael and St. George (CMG). He took command of his Brigade in May 1917. He was mortally wounded by shell-fire on 29 July while checking the trenches. His Brigade Major, Captain Hugh Henry Lean, MC, Highland Light Infantry was also killed.

Brigadier General Robert Clements Gore, CB, CMG, five times MiD, General Staff Commanding 101st Infantry Brigade late Argyll and Sutherland Highlanders, died on 13 April 1918 aged 50 years. He was given command of his Brigade in January 1916 and was killed by a shell that destroyed his headquarters.

There are sixteen Lieutenant-Colonels buried here. Between them they hold ten Distinguished Service Orders. The earliest to die was in May 1916 and the last is also the last British senior officer to die in the Salient, Lieutenant-

Colonel George Ernest Beaty-Pownall, DSO, twice MiD, 2nd Borders attached 1st King's Own Scottish Borderers. He died of wounds on 10 October 1918, aged 41 years, and is buried with some of his men who died in September and October 1918. He was awarded the Distinguished Service Order in the Birthday Honours List in June 1917. His brother Captain Thomas Trelawny Beaty-Pownall, 3rd attached 2nd Borders, died of wounds on 24 March 1917 aged 35 years. He is buried in St. Leger British Cemetery between Arras and Bapaume. They were sons of Lieutenant Colonel George Albert Beaty-Pownall. Another brother had died aged 21 years in South Africa in 1896 and yet another in 1903.

Lieutenant Colonel Douglas Swain Lewis, DSO, twice MiD, was killed in action on 10 April 1916, the second highest ranking Royal Flying Corps/Royal Air Force officer to be killed in action. He had passed out of Woolwich into the Royal Engineers in 1904, been promoted to Lieutenant in 1907 and taken his Royal Aero Club Certificate in May 1912. He went to war with No. 4 Squadron and took command of No. 3 Squadron in April 1915 before commanding No. 2 Wing. He gained the Distinguished Service Order in the New Years Honours List in December 1914 for his pioneering work in using wireless telegraphy from his aircraft. He was killed in a borrowed plane with a non-RFC observer, Captain Gale, who is buried beside him.

Lieutenant Colonel (Brevet Major) George Eric Burroughs Dobbs, Chevalier of the Legion of Honour, three times MiD, Signal Corps (Assistant Director Signals), Royal Engineers, died on 17 June 1917 aged 32 years. He was a professional soldier who joined the army in 1904 and who had been at Mons in 1914. He was a Rugby Union international who had represented England twice in 1906, against Wales and Ireland. He also played for Llanelli in the team that lost to the touring South African Springboks 16-3 in front of over 15000 supporters in 1906. He was killed when prospecting for a new cable trench when he was hit by a shell.

Another England Rugby Union international buried here is Lieutenant John Edward Raphael, 18th King's Royal Rifle Corps, who died on 11 June 1917 aged 35 years. He was born in Belgium, and died there, defending it. He had captained England during the All Blacks' first British tour in 1905. Raphael won his first Rugby Union cap in 1902 against Wales eventually winning nine caps. He also played in the 1905 and 1906 Championships as well as in Test matches against both France and New Zealand. He captained the 1910 British Lions tour to Argentina, which included their inaugural Test match. He had also made 77 first class cricket appearances from 1901-13 including for Surrey and an England XI. He gained 'Blues' for water polo and swimming as well as those from cricket and rugby while at Oxford University. He was appointed to the General Staff as ADC to General Officer Commanding (GOC), 41st Division and died of wounds received at St. Eloi on the Messines Ridge on 7 June. On a chilly autumn day in 1929 a chauffeur-driven car pulled up on the road here and out climbed an elderly lady dressed in black. The CWGC gardener paused and looked up but this lady approached him with a sense of purpose he was not used to seeing in grieving mothers and widows. What happened next is not clear, but a conversation took place. Nine months later a package arrived for the gardener. He knew what to do. He carefully carried it to this grave where he buried it. The package contained the lady's ashes – she was the mother of Jack Raphael.

Lieutenant Colonel Ronald Harcourt Sanderson, MiD, Chevalier, Legion of Honour , 148th Brigade, Royal Field Artillery, died on 17 April 1918 aged 41 years. Sanderson rowed in two victories for Cambridge in the Boat Race in 1899 and 1900. He became a member of the Leander Club and was a crew member of the Leander eight which won the gold medal for Great Britain rowing at the 1908 Summer Olympics. Sanderson joined the Royal Horse Artillery in May 1900, and served as 2nd Lieutenant in the South African War. He was promoted to Lieutenant in March 1902. Sanderson then served in the Royal Field Artillery arriving in France on 7 August 1914. He was Mentioned in Despatches and was awarded the Chevalier, Legion of Honour by France. He was killed in action on the Scherpenberg.

Among the men buried here you will find 49 Americans such as Driver Leland Wingate Fernald, 5th Brigade, Canadian Field Artillery, who died on 8 May 1916 aged 28 years. He was from Dover, New Hampshire, USA. This is not unusual as Americans fighting under Canadian, or other, flags can be found across the Western Front. Americans buried here joined the Canadian or the British Army until April 1917. As the USA was neutral, any American who joined a foreign army before then automatically lost his American citizenship and was stateless upon their deaths. In the 1920's the US Congress retroactively restored their citizenship. My research shows nine fought in the Australian Force, 53 in the British army, 194 with the Canadians, one with the New Zealand Expeditionary Force and one in the South African Brigade.

But there are three men buried here who fought with the American army. These are a Sergeant and Private from New York and a Lieutenant from Tennessee buried in the semi-circle of graves near the War Stone. They are, I believe, unique in being the only three Americans killed in WW1 and buried on the Western Front who are not in an American cemetery. However, 122 of their countrymen have been removed, either being repatriated to the USA or being moved to Flanders Fields American Cemetery. The families of these three insisted that their remains stayed where they had been originally buried.

First Lieutenant James Pigue had served in the US Marine Corps from 1904-1909 working for some time on the Panama Canal and being commissioned to Lieutenant. When the Mexican border conflict broke out in 1916, he enlisted in the First Tennessee National Guard, was quickly promoted to Second Lieutenant and while in Texas to First Lieutenant. While in Texas he married and then returned to Nashville, left the service, and again settled down to civilian life with his new wife. When America entered the war he re-enlisted but his Tennessee Guard unit was converted to artillery so he transferred to the 117th Infantry Regiment. He left for Europe on 4 May 1918, leaving behind his pregnant wife. His regiment was assigned to the British Second Army near Ypres for training. Pigue spent some time commanding British and Australian artillery units due to the shortage of experienced officers suffered by the British. But he was back with the 117th on 15 July and they entered the front-line the following day. On 18 July he was at an observation post when a sniper shot him through the heart. He was the first man from the 30th (Old Hickory) Division to be killed in action during the war. He was initially buried at Gwalia British Cemetery, but his body was moved to the 'American Plot' of Lijssenthoek Cemetery in June 1919. In 1920, the army wrote to his wife to ask if she wanted her husband's remains to be repatriated. She sent a telegram to the War Department requesting that his body not be disturbed under any circumstances. As she did not reply to any subsequent inquiries, they contacted his father. Edward Pigue travelled to Europe to see his son's final resting place for himself. In July 1921, he met with officials of the Imperial War Graves Commission, who assured him that the British government would care for the grave in perpetuity. He agreed to leave his son's remains undisturbed.

Sergeant David Beattie, 105th Infantry Regiment, 27th US Division died on 31 August 1918 aged 22 years. He was from Troy, New York and had served with the New York National Guard in the Mexican Border conflict. The unit was assigned to the 27th Division as 15th Infantry and arrived in Belgium in May 1918. Beattie was a forward artillery observer when killed at his post near Dikkebus by artillery shrapnel which hit him in the head. His family requested that his remains not be disturbed.

Private First Class Harry Arthur King, F Troop, 3rd Cavalry was born in England and emigrated to the USA in 1914. King's brother, Reginald returned to England and enlisted as a Private in a mechanical transport unit of the Army Service Corps. Another brother, Lewis, who had not gone to the USA, also enlisted eventually finding himself in the Tank Corps. Another brother George, left the USA and joined the Canadian forces so that by 1917 four of the five King brothers were in various armies. Harry arrived in France in November 1917. He was behind the front lines for most of the time, as part of a Remount unit, but as with many American troops the conditions rather than bullets or shells, ended their lives. His cause of death was officially listed as bronchial pneumonia, but in fact it was the Spanish Flu. Harry was initially buried at the Argonne American Cemetery. His mother initially requested that his remains be sent to England to be buried beside his father. However, his brother Private Reginald King, Mechanical Transport attached 25th Siege Battery, Royal Garrison Artillery had died on 17 October 1917 of shrapnel wounds to his face, left elbow and wrist, and a fractured left leg in No. 3 Canadian Casualty Clearing Station at 1.00am, and was buried here. When his mother learned of this, she changed her mind about her son Harry's burial and requested that he be buried near his brother Reggie. His remains were moved here in October 1921. King's brothers Lewis and George survived the war.

Major Henry Gorell Barnes, DSO, MiD, 19th (London) Battery, 47th Division. Royal Field Artillery, died on 16 January 1917 aged 35 years. He was the 2nd Baron Gorell who succeeded to the peerage in 1913. He joined his unit at the Front in February 1915, but he had served with them since before the war, and in March went to the Front to command the 19th Battery. He was awarded the Distinguished Service Order in November 1916 for a skilful reconnaissance under heavy fire near High Wood in September, previously having been Mentioned in Despatches. In December 1916 he returned to England on leave for a month, returning to his Division near Verbrandemolen, where he was wounded by shell-fire whilst reconnoitering a position for his Battery. He died two days later.

Also here is Captain James Ogilvie-Grant, 3rd attached 5th Cameron Highlanders, who died on 12 November 1915 aged 39 years. He was the 11th Earl of Seafield and 30th Chief of the Clan Grant. Born in New Zealand he moved to Scotland in 1906. He was commissioned a 2nd Lieutenant in the 3rd (Militia) Battalion, the Bedfordshire Regiment, on 21 June 1902. He was killed by a sniper.

Major The Honourable Sir Schomberg Kerr McDonnell, GCVO, KCB, 5th Cameron Highlanders, died on 23 November 1915 aged 54 years. He was the youngest son of the 5th Earl of Antrim and served as private secretary to Prime Minister Lord Salisbury from 1888 to 1902. He fought in the South African War and was knighted in 1902. He then headed the department responsible for managing the royal palaces. He served as Chief Intelligence Officer of the London District between 1914 and 1915. He was appointed a Companion of the Order of the Bath (CB) in 1892, for his service to the outgoing Prime Minister, and advanced to a Knight Commander (KCB) of the Order in the 1902 Coronation Honours list. He was appointed a

Commander of the Royal Victorian Order (CVO) in 1901, and promoted to Knight Grand Cross (GCVO) in the 1911 Coronation Honours list. He was wounded on 21 November 1915.

Several young men are buried here. Private Leslie Arthur Guyatt, 2nd Hampshires, died of the effects of gas poisoning on 9 August 1916 aged 16 years. He had been in Flanders since March 1916. Private Robert Edward Holt, 6th King's Own Scottish Borderers, died on 29 October 1915 aged 16 years. He arrived in France on 30 September 1915. Private John George Litherland, 2nd Durham Light Infantry, died on 22 April 1916 aged 16 years. He enlisted on 15 June 1915 stating his age as 19 years and 2 months. In reality he was only 15 when he joined up. He had been in Flanders since February 1916 when he died at No. 10 Casualty Clearing Station. Private Aungier Ernest Peacocke, 7th Northamptonshires, died on 14 March 1916 aged 16 years. He had been in Flanders since November 1915. Private Arthur Robertson, 1st Royal Scots Fusiliers was killed in action on 28 March 1916 aged 16 years. Private Wallace Wonacott, 2nd Lancashire Fusiliers, died on 12 July 1915 aged 16 years. He had been in France since 27 April 1915. Private Bernard Herbert Boseley, 1/7th Sherwood Foresters (Notts and Derbys), died on 1 August 1915 aged 16 years. He arrived in France in February 1915. Private John Daglish, 11th Highland Light Infantry, died on 27 November 1915 aged 16 years. He had been in Flanders since July 1915. Driver Charles Turner, 53rd Battery, Royal Field Artillery, died of accidental injuries on 21 September 1915 aged 16 years. He had been in Flanders since April 1915. Private Robert Cooper James Murray, 1st Australian Infantry, died of gunshot wounds to his ankles and feet in No. 3 Casualty Clearing Station on 4 October 1916 aged 16 years. He had arrived in France on 4 September 1916. His father served with the 17th Australian Infantry. Lance Corporal Herbert Austin West, 20th Australian Infantry, died of wounds in No. 2 Canadian Casualty Clearing Station on 8 October 1917 aged 16 years. He enlisted at the age of 14 years and 8 months, left Australia on 7 October 1916 and was promoted to Lance Corporal at the age of sixteen on 30 June 1917. He was wounded on 3 May 1917 when he received a shrapnel wound to his right arm but returned to the trenches one week later. He was mortally wounded by a shrapnel wound to the back and upper arm. Private Harold James Fox, 1st Canadian Infantry, died on 7 July 1916 aged 16 years. He died of gunshot wounds to the head and back in No. 3 Canadian Casualty Clearing Station. He had enlisted in November 1915 giving his date of birth as 1896. Private Alex Joseph Cameron, 2nd Canadian Railway Troops, died on 17 April 1916 aged 16 years. His attestation papers claim that he was born in 1897. Private John Leo Lightizer, 13th Canadian Infantry, died on 28 June 1916 aged 16 years. He enlisted in April 1915 while still 15 years old, giving his year of birth on his attestation papers as 1897. He died of gunshot wounds, received at Halifax Trench on Mount Sorrel, to the abdomen and chest at No. 3 Canadian Casualty Clearing Station.

Private Donald McLeod Snaddon, 1st Royal Scots Fusiliers, died on 18 January 1916 aged 15 years. Snaddon was raised by his grandmother who was to lose three of her own sons in the war as well as her grandson. He joined up in April 1915 and stated his age to be 18 though he was only 15 years old. In September 1915 he was sentenced to 21 days Field Punishment No. 2 for using obscene language. He was posted to France in November 1915. Snaddon was wounded on 14 January 1916 at Scottish Wood and was evacuated to No. 10 Casualty Clearing Station where he died of his wounds. He is one of 63 boys aged 15 years known to have been killed during the war.

Another buried here is Private John Lynn, 1st Royal Inniskilling Fusiliers, died 9 August 1916 aged 26 years. He died of the effects of gas poisoning. Three of his brothers died in the war. Serjeant William Edward Lynn, 1st Royal Irish Fusiliers who died on 17 July 1916 aged 21 years is buried at Auchonvillers Military Cemetery on the Somme. Driver Robert Lynn, 87th Battery, Royal Field Artillery, died on 6 August 1915 aged 30 years and is buried in Hop Store Cemetery near Ieper. Serjeant James Lynn, 906th Company, Royal Army Service Corps died on 7 August 1920 aged 37 years and is buried in Haifa War Cemetery.

Another to lose several brothers is 2nd Lieutenant William Keith Seabrook, 17th Australian Infantry, who died of wounds, received the day before near Polygon Wood, in No. 10 Casualty Clearing Station on 21 September 1917 aged 21 years. William carried a photo of his mother in his breast pocket which was returned to his relatives after his death. There was a bullet hole in it. His brothers Privates George Ross Seabrook, aged 25 years and Theo Leslie Seabrook aged 24 years, both 17th Australian Infantry and both killed near Polygon Wood on 20 September 1917 are also both commemorated on the Menin Gate. Their parents lost three sons in less than 48 hours.

Rifleman Roy Alfred Crichton Maitland-Addison, 1/6th (City of London Rifles) Londons died on 1 May 1917 aged 27 years. His brother, Lieutenant Alec Arthur Crichton Maitland-Addison, 1st Cheshires died on 27 October 1914 aged 28 years and is buried in Boulogne Eastern Cemetery. Another brother, Corporal Guy Robert Hurst Maitland-Addison, 188th Company, Machine Gun Corps (Infantry) died on 11 September 1917 aged 33 years and is buried in Bailleul Road East Cemetery. He was a serving officer in the Royal Marines when war broke out but was discharged for 'unsatisfactory conduct' on 27 March 1915. He gained a commission into the 17th Lancashire Fusiliers on 6 August 1915, but was again discharged from the service for signing 'rubber cheques'. He enlisted again and served with the Machine Gun Corps until his death. Their father, Major Alfred Chamberlain Maitland-Addison died in 1916.

Private Albert Waterfall, 15th Sherwood Foresters (Notts and Derbys) died on 1 August 1917 aged 20 years. His brother, Private Leonard Waterfall, 16th Sherwood Foresters (Notts and Derbys) died on 3 September 1916 aged 21 years and is buried in Knightsbridge Cemetery. Another brother, Private Alfred Waterfall, 1st Garrison Battalion, Sherwood Foresters (Notts and Derbys) died on 26 August 1917 aged 29 years and is buried in Suez War Memorial Cemetery. A fourth brother, Ernest served as a Gunner in the Royal Field Artillery and survived the war being discharged in early 1917 due to the effects of being gassed. Percy the youngest brother enlisted in 1916 (serving with a Lewis Gun Section of the Sherwood Foresters) and also survived the war.

Buried here is Sergeant Edward Alexander Keid, 9th Australian Infantry who died on 2 November 1917. His brothers are both commemorated on the Villers-Bretonneux Memorial dying on consecutive days. They are Sergeant Bennett Walter Keid, 49th Australian Infantry who died on 4 September 1916 aged 23 years and Lieutenant Leonard Keid, 49th Australian Infantry who died on 3 September 1916.

Buried here are two brothers. Captain Ross Penner Cotton, 19th Canadian Infantry attached 3rd Infantry Brigade HQ who died of wounds on 13 June 1916 aged 23 years just a few days after his brother, Lieutenant Charles Penner Cotton, Order of St. George, IVth Class (Russia), 2nd Brigade, Canadian Field Artillery who died on 2 June 1916 aged 25 years. Ross was mortally wounded by a shell while leading a bombing detachment. Charles was in command of two guns brought up to a position at Sanctuary Wood near the front line to be used in case of emergency. They were overwhelmed by a German attack from Observatory Ridge. His body was found on 25 June, buried in Maple Copse and moved here later in the war. Another brother, Henry, died as a soldier in the South African War in 1900 while a sister, Dorothy, served as a nurse during WW1.

Buried here is Private Thomas Taylor, 2nd Cameronians, killed on 15 April 1918 aged 26 years. He had survived numerous engagements and been wounded on four occasions. Private Jesse Taylor, 7th North Staffordshires, died at sea of typhoid fever on 8 November 1915 aged 26 years, was buried at sea and commemorated on the Helles Memorial. Private George Henry Taylor, 7th North Staffordshires, died on 6 April 1916 from wounds received in an attack at Kut in the Mesopotamia campaign. George was treated for his wounds, but died the next day and was hastily buried in the desert. He is commemorated on the Basra Memorial. Sergeant Arthur Taylor, 1st Cameronians, died of wounds on 17 October 1916 and is buried in Warlincourt Halte British Cemetery. He was a regular soldier who had been in from the start of the war during the retreat from Mons, First Ypres and the Somme. He was mortally wounded while the Battalion were marching between positions. Private Bertie Taylor, 10th Lancashire Fusiliers, killed on 18 October 1918 aged 18 years by a sniper and is buried in Rocquigny-Equancourt Road British Cemetery. William Taylor, 7th North Staffordshires survived the war but was crippled by injuries received fighting in Mesopotamia. He received gunshot and shrapnel wounds to his left eye and left thigh in January 1916 and was sent home.

2nd Lieutenant Ralf Hubert Robinson, MM, 10th Royal Fusiliers attached 2nd Rifle Brigade died on 23 August 1917 aged 32 years. He made four first class cricket appearances for Essex in 1912 but had a reputation as an outstanding amateur wicketkeeper. He enlisted into the Royal Fusiliers and was soon promoted gaining the Military Medal in February 1917. He was then commissioned and joined the Rifle Brigade before his death.

Lieutenant James 'Banny' William Hugh Bannerman, 2nd Otago Regiment, NZEF died on 23 December 1917 aged 30 years. He played first class cricket six times for Southland in New Zealand winning the Hawke Cup in 1911. He was a journalist and author, writing two important cricketing histories. He was commissioned in June 1917 arriving in Europe in late November and was killed a few weeks after reaching the Front.

Also of note is Staff Nurse Nellie Spindler, No. 44 Casualty Clearing Station, Queen Alexandra's Imperial Military Nursing Service, who died of wounds on 21 August 1917 aged 26 years. Her Casualty Clearing Station, which specialised in treating stomach wounds, was based at Brandhoek. This field hospital was nearer the front, because stomach wounds had to be treated as quickly as possible due to the risk of infection. It was shelled at about 10.00am during which she was mortally wounded. The enemy fire was aimed for the railway and the ammunition dump but a shell landed next to the nurse's quarters. Nellie had been resting in her tent at the time and died twenty minutes later. She was buried here with full military honours with the Last Post played over her grave. She was officially described as 'killed in action' by the War Office after only having been on the Western Front since May 1917. She is the only woman buried here and one of only two British women killed in the First World War to be buried in Belgium. The nurses who were also at Brandhoek with Spindler were all evacuated to Lijssenthoek and then to St. Omer where they continued to nurse. One of them, Sister Minnie Wood, was subsequently awarded the Military Medal for her actions that day. She was also awarded the Royal Red Cross, and the OBE [Military Division] by the King at an Investiture in December 1919.

Captain The Honourable Eric Fox Pitt Lubbock, MC, MiD, son of the 1st Baron Avebury, was killed in action on 17 March 1918, aged 23 years, as Flight Commander with No. 45 Squadron, Royal Flying Corps. He was awarded the Military Cross for 'For conspicuous gallantry and skill on October 26th, 1915, when he attacked a German Albatros machine at a height of 9,000 ft. with machine-gun fire. The hostile pilot was shot and the aeroplane was brought to the ground'. He was killed when shot down on patrol near Railway Wood at 11.15am in his Sopwith Strutter. He was attacked by two Albatros DIII's of Jasta 18. His observer Lieutenant John Thompson died but had exposed five photographic plates later salvaged from the wreckage. Another Sopwith was involved in the combat and shot down. 2nd Lieutenant Horace George Cecil Bowden and 2nd Lieutenant Douglas Baptist Stevenson did not survive. All four bodies were recovered and buried together. His wife, daughter of Lord Forster, also lost both of her brothers in the war. His brother, The Honourable Harold Fox Pitt Lubbock, Grenadier Guards, was killed by a shell on 4 April 1918 aged 29 years and is buried at Boisleux-Au-Mont Communal Cemetery near Arras.

A name of interest is that of Private Thomas Atkins, 1st Queen's (Royal West Surreys) who died on 26 September 1917 aged 35 years. Tommy Atkins (often just 'Tommy') is slang for a common soldier in the British Army, particularly in World War I. Like many 'well-known facts' in history, there is a hard held belief that the name originated with the Duke of Welklington who was inspired by the bravery of a soldier called Tommy Atkins who died in battle near him. While it may be true that the name was in common usuage after the Napoleonic wars, there is evidence that it was widly used among soldiers as early as the 1740's. Sadly, another great story goes the way of all things. However, this Tommy Atkins is one of only two that I can find who died in this war and is buried on the Western Front. The other, who has two middle names as well, is nearby at Outtersteene Communal Cemetery Extension, Bailleul. So, this Tommy Atkins from Chertsey, Surrey is the only one who carries only the name 'Tommy Atkins' buried in France and Flanders.

| UK – 7330 | Aust – 1131 | NZ – 291 |
| Can – 1053 | NF – 5 | S Afr – 29 |
| BWI – 21 | India – 3 | KUG – 3 |
| Fr - 658 | US - 3 | IWGC – 1 |
| Chinese Labour Corps – 35 | | Ger – 223 |

Special Memorials to eight men known to be buried in this cemetery

### LOCATION
Lijssenthoek Cemetery is south-west of Ieper and about 2km south of Poperinge. It is just west of the Poperinge-Steenvoorde road from which it is clearly signed. Lijssenthoek is a small hamlet to the east.

## LINDENHOEK CHALET MILITARY CEMETERY

### HISTORY
Begun in March 1915 as British units came to this part of the Salient, the cemetery remained in use until October 1917. It was enlarged after the war with the concentration of 130 graves.

### INFORMATION
A new chalet is now opposite the cemetery on the site of the old one which was destroyed in the fighting in 1918 when the Germans took the hill at great cost to both sides. The Kemmelberg was then shelled almost constantly until the Allied advance in the autumn.

The Battle Book of Ypres, by Beatrice Brice tells us that in November 1914 a Battery of the 5th Division, Royal Field Artillery was in reserve on the west side of the Kemmelberg when a Major stationed on the Lindenhoek-Wijtschate road called for their assistance. The subaltern in command of the Battery decided that the situation was so urgent that he should take his guns over the hill and down the slopes through this point of this cemetery. He helped the Division to hold the line by his actions.

Buried here is Private John Vodden, 1st Welsh, killed in action on 18 August 1915 aged 16 years. He had gone to Flanders on 29 June 1915. He lived in London before the war.

Also here is Private Cyril Charles John Kruck, 'D' Company, 4th Australian Pioneers, killed on 12 June 1917 aged 25 years. He was working with a night party when he was killed instantly by a German shell which blew his head off. He was originally buried close to where he fell at Fanny's Farm Corner about 500m north-east of Messines. He was the eldest son of a family of eleven children. Just before leaving Brisbane he rescued a drowning man and the following week stopped a bolting horse in a busy street.

| UK – 282 | Aust – 10 | NZ – 8 |
| Can – 15 | Ger – 2 | Unnamed – 67 |

Area - 1410 sq mts

Special Memorials to four Australians and two British men known/believed to be buried among the unnamed.

### LOCATION
Lindenhoek Chalet Cemetery can be found about 1km south of Kemmel, south of Ieper, on the eastern slope of the Kemmelberg. It lies 200m west of the road from Kemmel to Nieuwkerke from which it is clearly signed.

## LOCRE HOSPICE CEMETERY

### HISTORY
Begun at the start of the Battle of Messines in June 1917, the cemetery remained in use until April 1918. Four graves were brought here after the war from the garden of Loker Convent.

### INFORMATION
The Convent, or Hospice, of St. Antoine was used by field ambulances and fighting units from December 1914 to June 1917. The village was the route through which many men travelled to the front-line in the southern sectors of the Salient. Loker was in French and British hands for most

of the war. In November 1914 the 1st Grenadier Guards were sent to rest here after defending Ypres. The Battalion was by this time only a Company strong under the command of a Captain. The 2nd Scots Guards, a Captain and 69 men, joined them.

Loker was at the limit of the German advance during their Spring Offensive in 1918 though they failed to take all of the village. The village changed hands several times between 25 and 30 April 1918, when it was recaptured by the French. The British 21st, 25th and 49th (West Riding) Divisions were supporting the French in defending Loker and, though the Germans occupied part of the settlement for one day on 25 April, it was retaken by the French on 26 April. The 84th Battery, Royal Field Artillery was stationed above the village on the Rodeberg during April 1918 manned by one officer and several cooks. The guns had to be abandoned but in the evening teams of artillerymen rescued them by moving them off the hill in the direction of Loker, directly in front of the enemy lines. The Germans were too shocked by this boldness to fire upon the British soldiers. The Germans entered Loker again on 29 April but were forced out by the French on 30 April. During the course of this battle the village was completely destroyed. The hospice, or convent, was the scene of severe fighting on 20 May, but was not retaken until the first week in July. The fourteen Second World War burials date from late May 1940 and the withdrawal of the British Expeditionary Force to Dunkirk ahead of the German advance.

Buried here is Brigadier General Ronald Campbell MacLachlan, DSO, four times MiD, General Staff commanding 112th Infantry Brigade, late Rifle Brigade, killed in action on 10 August 1917 aged 45 years. He joined the Rifle Brigade in 1893, served in India and then South Africa where he was twice Mentioned in Despatches and wounded. He served in the Tibet Expedition in 1904 before being commander of the Oxford University Officer Training Corps and being awarded a Degree. He returned to fighting service when the war began, taking the 8th Rifle Brigade to Flanders in May 1915. He was wounded at Hooge, awarded the Distinguished Service Order in May 1916 and again twice Mentioned in Despatches. He was made Brigadier General in January 1917 having recovered from his wounds, but he was shot and killed by a sniper at 7.00am while visiting the forward trenches. His brother, Lieutenant Colonel Alexander Fraser Campbell MacLachlan, 12th King's Royal Rifle Corps, CMG, DSO, twice MiD, was killed in action on 22 March 1918 and is buried in Savy British Cemetery. He also served in South Africa where he was Mentioned in Despatches and awarded the Distinguished Service Order. He was in the Retreat from Mons and wounded in September 1914 before seeing service in the Salonika Campaign. He became commander of the 13th Manchesters in 1916 and was Mentioned in Despatches again before taking his last Battalion. He was awarded a Bar to his Distinguished Service Order which was converted to a Companion of the Order of St. Michael and St. George. Another brother, Major Neil Campbell MacLachlan, 1st Seaforth Highlanders was accidentally killed on the Mohmand Expedition on the North West Frontier on 24 May 1908.

There are also three Lieutenant Colonels buried here. Lieutenant Colonel Richard Chester Chester-Master, DSO & Bar, five times MiD, 13th King's Royal Rifle Corps, was killed on 30 August 1917 aged 47 years. In 1893, he joined the King's Royal Rifle Corps and became a Major in 1900. He served through the South African War, where he was twice Mentioned in Despatches. He was Commandant-General of the British South African Police in Rhodesia (Zimbabwe) from 1901 to 1905, and Resident Commissioner and Commandant-General in Southern Rhodesia from 1905 to 1908. He became Chief Constable of Gloucestershire in 1911. In March 1915, he rejoined his old Regiment and was soon in command of a Battalion. In June 1916, he was Mentioned in Despatches, again in June, 1917, and a third time in December 1917. In the Birthday Honours List of June 1917, he was awarded the Distinguished Service Order, and in August 1917 a Bar to it. The citation says: 'During operations for six days he displayed great courage and ability. His Battalion was very short of Officers, and he had no rest during that period. His splendid example and total disregard for safety inspired his men with great confidence.' He was killed by a German sniper.

Lieutenant Colonel George Monreal, Reserve attached 6th Wiltshires, was killed on 11 April 1918. He joined the Wiltshires in 1896, saw service in Africa and India, transferred to the Army Pay Department and retired in 1911. He had been with the 6th Wiltshires since 7 April 1918.

Lieutenant Colonel Walter Adams Nicholson, 104th Army Brigade, Royal Field Artillery, was killed on 4 September 1917 aged 47 years. He joined the Royal Artillery in 1888 and served in the South African Wars becoming a Major by 1904. He also served in Egypt and India retiring in 1909. He returned to service at the start of the war going to France in February 1915 but was gassed at Second Ypres and went to England to recover. He returned to France to take part in the Battles of the Somme in 1916 and was also at the Battle of Messines. Nicholson was killed by a bomb which was dropped by a German aircraft.

There are two men buried here who were executed. Private Denis Jetson Blakemore of the 8th North Staffordshires deserted from the trenches near Wijtschate on the eve of the Battle of Messines. He initially served in Ireland and then travelled with his Battalion to France in 1916. At least two of his brothers also served in the war. He was discovered hiding in a shell hole in the rear of the assembly trenches and then formed up, but later was found again to be missing. This was his second offence and the one for which he was shot at 4.30am on the Kemmelberg on 9 July 1917.

Private William Jones of the 9th Royal Welsh Fusiliers was the last deserter to escape across the Channel to the United Kingdom. Jones was a stretcher bearer in France who went missing while taking a wounded soldier to the dressing station. He absconded on 5 June 1917 and surrendered at Neath Police Station on 4 September. He may have been suffering from shell-shock when he absconded. He was shot at the same place as Private Blakemore on 25 October 1917.

Buried just outside the walls of the cemetery is Major William Hoey Kearney Redmond, MP, MiD, Legion d'Honneur, 6th Royal Irish Regiment. He was wounded at Wijtschate on 7 June 1917, and was taken to the 36th (Ulster) Division Dressing Station at Dranouter where he died aged 56 years. His body was then moved to the 16th (Irish) Division base at Loker Hospice and buried in the garden in a grave just beyond the walls of the convent. A Southern Irishmen and Nationalist MP for Wexford, he was one of the few to believe that fighting and serving in the trenches with men from the north would unite them. He believed firmly in a united Ireland. Beyond the fighting age he had persuaded his commander to let him go to the Front where he was killed. His grave is in a plot of its own beneath a Celtic Memorial Cross and can be reached by a 100m path from the cemetery entrance. Until the late 1950's the grave was maintained by a Sister from the hospice. In the 1990's the land was purchased by the Belgian State and is now maintained by the Commonwealth War Graves Commission.

| | | |
|---|---|---|
| UK – 239 | Aust – 2 | NZ – 1 |
| Can – 1 | BWI – 1 | Ger – 2 |
| Unnamed – 12 | | WW2 - 14 |

Area - 851 sq mts

Special Memorials to ten men whose graves have been destroyed by shell-fire.

**LOCATION**

Locre Hospice Cemetery lies in fields on the south-west edge of the village, which is south of Ieper. The cemetery lies in fields about 100m from the Hospice. This imposing building, still in use as School, Convent and Hospice, is hard to miss from most roads in the area of Loker, so that if you can reach the Hospice you can see the cemetery. A road from the east corner of the church in the centre of the village leads past the Hospice to a small single building on the south side of the road. A CWGC path leads from the building to the cemetery 50m from the road. It is a pleasant stroll from Loker church to the cemetery, as you walk remember that you are traversing the front-line positions of 1918 where many men died.

## LOCRE No. 10 CEMETERY

**HISTORY**

This was one of several cemeteries made in the area by the French during the German offensive in April 1918. It was taken over by the British after the war when the French graves were removed and British and German graves from the battlefields nearby were concentrated here.

**INFORMATION**

See Locre Hospice Cemetery for information on battles at Loker.

The British graves are mainly of men of the 2/14th (2nd London Scottish) Londons, 2/16th (2nd Queen's Westminsters) Londons and 2nd South Lancashires, all part of the 89th Brigade, 30th Division at the end of the war after they had been transferred from other Divisions. The 248 French graves were removed and the Germans are in a mass grave at the west end of the cemetery. Only three of the 75 German burials are identified.

Buried here is 2nd Lieutenant Charles Edward Woodroffe, 15th (Nottingham Pals) Sherwood Foresters (Notts and Derbys), killed in action on 27 July 1918 aged 30 years. He joined up with the Lancashire Hussars in September 1914 and was gazetted in 1918 with the Sherwood Foresters. He had been married for five months when killed. His father was an Alderman in Wallesey.

| | | |
|---|---|---|
| UK – 55 | Unnamed – 14 | Ger – 75 |

Special Memorials to three casualties known or believed to be buried among the unnamed

Area - 728 sq mts

**LOCATION**

Locre No. 10 Cemetery lies south of Loker, south-west of Ieper, on the south side of the Loker-Dranouter road, about 1km from Loker church.

## LOKER CHURCHYARD

**HISTORY**

The churchyard was used by the British from December 1914 until June 1917. One grave was brought in after the war from Locre French Cemetery No. 4.

**INFORMATION**

See Locre Hospice Cemetery for more information.

As was common early in the war, churchyards were used until the need for larger burial spaces was established and dedicated military cemeteries were begun. So, there are seven burials made in 1914, 38 in 1916 and 32 in 1917, with the others dating from 1915.

One feature of the churchyard is that three men buried here were executed by the British Army within a ten-day period in early 1915 and yet the churchyard was never again used for the burial of executed men. Fusiliers Andrew Evans and Joseph Byers, both of the 1st Royal Scots Fusiliers, were tried on 31 January for desertion and then executed together in a field at Six Farm near the village on 6 February 1915. They are buried side by side near the entrance to the Plot on the west side of the church. Byers was the first of Kitchener's volunteers to be executed. Byers absconded when part of a coal-collecting detail on 8 January. He was arrested ten days later on the Ieper-Poperinge road. He claimed to have been with a medical unit for a few days and was trying to find his way back to the Fusiliers. Byers pleaded guilty and did not have any representation to put forward evidence in his ten minute Court Martial. He was also unlucky in that senior officers, such as Major General Sir Horace Smith-Dorrien, wanted an example to be made as they believed discipline in the Battalion was poor. Byers was found guilty of 'attempting to desert' as you had to be absent for 28 days to be guilty of desertion. Byers lied about his age to enlist on 20 November 1914, went to France on 5 December 1914, after possibly only two weeks of basic training, (though there is a claim that he had pre-war training as a territorial) and was executed after 79 days in the army. He was probably under age and probably drunk when shot by a reluctant firing squad made up of his own comrades. It required three attempts by the squad to kill Byers. For many years it was believed Byers was aged 16 years and four months when killed. However, this now seems to have been an error as the difficulty of interpreting Census details and birth records has muddied the water showing that another Joseph Byers fitting the date of birth may have still been in Scotland. Byers gave his age as 19 years and seven months to the gendarme who arrested him. This may have been an attempt to stay in the army for if his real age was 16 he would be sent home or it may have been the truth which seems the most likely case. The CWGC record him as being 17. However, one positive aspect came from his case. After his execution, no man was allowed to plead guilty to an offence with a capital punishment and all had to be represented by counsel. Byers had two brothers, Charles and Edward. Charles was killed in action in the Dardanelles on 12 June 1915, just four months after Joseph's execution. Edward survived the war.

Evans was a 41 year old 'Regular', a reservist recalled in August 1914, and charged with 'desertion'. Along with Byers he found himself billeted in Loker for the festive season in 1914. However, by New Year's Eve, when the Battalion was ordered back to the trenches, Evans had disappeared. Fifteen days later on 15 January, Evans was arrested by a Corporal from the French Army. He pleaded not guilty to being a deserter stating that he had been drunk on Christmas Day and had gone to Bailleul. Despite not having been missing for 28 days within fifteen minutes Evans was sentenced to death for desertion.

In the next row lies Private George Ernest Collins of the 1st Lincolnshires who was executed in the village for desertion on 15 February 1915. On 27 November 1914 the 1st Lincolnshires were sent to the front line from Westouter. Collins decided to get completely drunk. The following morning, he later stated, he found himself in Paris and was unable to explain how he had got there. Following his arrest at Le Mans, he was brought back to Westouter, and charged with desertion. At his Court Martial on 7 February 1915 Collins stated that he had been sent to Le Mans to assist with horse transport but could produce nothing to prove that this was the case. Likewise, he could offer no reasonable explanation as to why, whilst everybody else was getting ready for the trenches, he went absent and got drunk. The court passed a sentence of death.

Also here is 2nd Lieutenant Robert Harold Strong, 2nd East Surreys, killed on 12 March 1915 aged 29 years. He enlisted in 1901 at the age of 15 years and rose through the ranks to become Drum-Major. He saw service in India where he won several athletics competitions and was Bandmaster running the Garrison Church music. He was commissioned in November 1914 before being sent to France and was killed by shell-fire while temporarily with the 3rd Middlesex. His brother Private Benjamin Clarence Strong, 9th East Surreys, died on 17 May 1918 aged 22 years. He is buried at Annois Communal Cemetery south of St. Quentin. He was buried by the Germans. Another brother, Private Francis William Cooper Strong, 2nd Wiltshires was killed in action on 29 July 1917 aged 29 years and is commemorated on the Menin Gate. He served as John Stewart.

Another to lose two brothers is 2nd Lieutenant Cecil Hawdon, 4th Yorkshires, who died on 27 June 1916 aged 20 years. He was killed in a raid on German lines. He joined the Battalion on 26 May 1916 and one month later was in the front line close to Kemmel. He led a patrol that found the enemy wire uncut by the artillery. They commenced cutting a passage through the wire and just before 1.30pm Hawdon and his men moved into position for a trench raid. At this point the British artillery opened up a bombardment on the enemy lines causing casualties to the raiding party and forcing it to be withdrawn. Hawdon was killed with three of his men who are now buried side by side. One brother, Chaplain 4th Class The Reverend Noel Elliot Hawdon, Army Chaplains' Department attached 45th Trench Mortar Battery, died on 16 November 1918 and is buried in Terlincthun British Cemetery. Captain Rupert Ayrton Hawdon, twice MiD, 35th Siege Battery, Royal Garrison Artillery died on 4 November 1918 aged 24 years and is buried in Ruesnes Communal Cemetery south of Valenciennes.

Also of note is Private Kenneth Powell, Honourable Artillery Company, killed on 18 February 1915 aged 29 years. He won 'blues' for Cambridge in athletics and tennis. He represented Great Britain at the 1908 London Olympics in athletics and tennis. In 1912 he again represented his country, but only in athletics at Stockholm, coming 5th in the 110m hurdles final.

There are three Memorials to French units involved in the fighting here in 1918. They were formerly on the walls of the Town Hall opposite the church but have been moved and are now on one stone at the south corner of the churchyard near the town War Memorial at the junction with the Kemmel road. The Memorials are to the 2nd Brigade of Cavalerie Legere (Light Cavalry) Francaise (17th and 18th Cavalry); 4th and 12th Regiments of French Dragoons; and the 23rd Regiment of French Infantry.

UK – 184      Can – 31      Unnamed – 2
Area - 1578 sq mts

**LOCATION**

Loker Church is in the centre of the village on the north side of the main road. Loker is south of Ieper and is reached most easily by the N375. The graves are in two Plots one on either side of the church.

## LONDON RIFLE BRIGADE CEMETERY

**HISTORY**

Begun by the 4th Division in December 1914, the cemetery remained in use until it fell into German hands in March 1918. It was used by the Germans in April and May 1918 before the British took over the burial ground again in October.

**INFORMATION**

Ploegsteert was in French and British hands for much of the war but was in German hands from 10 April to 29 September 1918.

The cemetery acquired its name when 22 men of the London Rifle Brigade were buried here in the early months of 1915. They are in what is now Plot III. A group of them are buried near to the Cross of Sacrifice.

Lieutenant-General Sir H. F. M. Wilson unveiled a tablet on the wall at the north corner of the cemetery, in June 1927. The plaque commemorates the dedication of the cemetery, on Easter Day 1915, by the Bishop of London and is in memory of the 91 officers and 1831 men of the London Rifle Brigade who fell in the war.

Buried here is 2nd Lieutenant Andrew Stevenson Thompson, MSM, MiD, No. 16 (Waikato) Company, 3rd Auckland Regiment, NZEF, killed in action on 4 August 1917 aged 23 years. He left New Zealand as a Sergeant in October 1914 probably aboard the Star of India or Waimana arriving in the Middle East later in the year. He was wounded at Gallipoli though he was also one of the last men to leave the peninsula. He went to France with the New Zealand Division and took part in the Battle of the Somme where he was wounded on 28 September 1916. He was promoted to Regimental Sergeant Major and then to 2nd Lieutenant on 26 May 1917. He was awarded the Meritorious Service Medal in January 1917. The citation reads 'For gallantry and devotion to duty. He was wounded near Flers on September 27th 1916, while endeavouring to obtain some information on the situation at a certain place, that was urgently wanted. During the whole time he has been with the Battalion he has done consistently good work.' He was also Mentioned in Despatches in December 1917 for 'On the 13th June 1917, when the situation was very obscure he boldly led his patrol into the enemy's sector under heavy fire of all calibers, obtained and sent back very useful information, established and held an important position against strong bombing attacks until reinforced, thereby ensuring the success of subsequent operations that day. He has at all times done excellent work and shown a splendid example of devotion to duty.'

UK – 263      Aust – 38      NZ – 34
Ger – 18      Unnamed – 1    Area - 1836 sq mts

**LOCATION**

London Rifle Brigade Cemetery is situated 500m south of the square in Ploegsteert, south of Ieper, on the west side of the road to Armentieres.

## LONE TREE CEMETERY

**HISTORY**

Nearly all the graves in this cemetery are of men who died on the first day of the Battle of Messines, 7 June 1917.

**INFORMATION**

This cemetery lies in what was formerly no man's land next to the German line that ran through the farm and along the edge of the Pool of Peace nearby. The Royal Irish Rifles of the 36th (Ulster) Division, who fought in this area on the first day of the Battle of Messines, have 60 men buried here.

The 36th (Ulster) Division had been rebuilt from its near annihilation on the first day of the Battle of the Somme nearly twelve months before. It now contained nine Battalions of Royal Irish Rifles who attacked in an easterly direction through the site of this cemetery making rapid progress and taking the Wijtschate-Messines road. Some of the men buried in this cemetery were killed by the fall-out of the Spanbroekmolen mine which may have exploded fifteen seconds late, or the men had left the trenches early, by which time the 8th (East Belfast) Royal Irish Rifles were already in no man's land. Significantly, the 36th Division was positioned next to the 16th (Irish) Division, the first time that men from the two branches of their religion and from north and south of Ireland had fought together.

This position had seen action before 1917. On 30 April 1916 the Germans had used gas on a front from St. Eloi to Messines. The 10th Royal Welsh Fusiliers were located here. It had limited success but inflicted great casualties.

The Spanbroekmolen mine that formed the nearby crater was placed by the 171st Tunnelling Company, Royal Engineers. It was blown at 3.10am, with eighteen others, the third largest of the charges laid by tunnellers in the build up to the battle, signalling the start of the British offensive in Flanders in 1917. All you can see from the road of the crater is a raised copse and mound of earth, but enter the gate, climb the steps and the crater blown on 7 June 1917, made by 91,000lbs of explosive, comes into view. Although the charge placed by the Royal Engineers at St. Eloi was two tonnes larger than here, that mine was by necessity deeper and the resulting crater was not as large. It was called Lone Tree Crater, later Spanbroekmolen, and was bought by Lord Wakefield for the Toc H organisation who have preserved it as a Pool of Peace. A solemn place, but pleasant in summer, the site is potentially muddy, and therefore dangerous, particularly in wet weather as the pool is 27m deep with a high rim. A path exists so that you can walk round the copse. The crater is named after the mill that had stood here for centuries until it was destroyed by the Germans during First Ypres in November 1914.

Also nearby are the Kruisstraat Craters. Like the Spanbroekmolen mine, the work to create this group of mines was commenced in 1916. Mines 1 and 2 were completed by July 1916 and No. 3 was ready at the end of August. When it became obvious that the Battle of the Somme was not going to be finished quickly the plans were put on hold. But General Plumer, in command of 2nd Army, realised that any attempt to push the Germans back from the Salient would require the taking of the Messines Ridge. For that reason he continued with his mining operations adding to those already placed. The gallery leading down past No. 1 charge to No. 3 charge was 659m making it the longest of all of those dug on the ridge. In February 1917 the Germans detonated a small counter mine called a camouflet near to the position of No. 1 mine which flooded the chamber. This necessitated the building of a new chamber called No. 4 in which a further nine tonnes of explosives was placed in April 1917. Hence, the total weight of explosives under what is now these two ponds was approximately 50 tonnes of Ammonal.

Buried here is Captain Henry Gallaugher, DSO, MiD, 'B' Company, 11th Royal Inniskilling Fusiliers, killed in action on 7 June 1917 aged 31 years. Gallaugher was commissioned into the Inniskilling Fusiliers in 1914. On the first day of the Somme, near Thiepval, all of his fellow officers were killed or wounded early. Henry noticed German snipers firing on the wounded, whereupon he shot a number of them. By the time he reached his objective only nine of his Platoon were still with him. He went into no-man's land to collect wounded men. Later he carried a wounded officer back fom the German wire to his own lines. Two nights later he formed a party to rescue men who were still screaming in despair in no-man's land. They rescued 28 men. He was recommended for a Victoria Cross but did not receive it possibly because the 36th Division had received its quota. He was awarded the Distinguished Service Order. On 7 June the 11th Inniskillings faced little or no opposition but before reaching the first objective Captain Gallaugher was wounded by a shell burst, his right arm being shattered. He continued to lead his men and with revolver in his left hand went forward to the next objective. By 5.35am his Battalion were consolidating their objectives and it was safe enough for Captain Crosbie, Royal Army Medical Corps, to move up and set up an advanced Regimental Aid Post beside Scott Farm. After seeing consolidation work was well in hand Captain Gallaugher was on his way back to the Aid Post to have his wound attended to when he was killed by another shell.

UK - 88        KUG – 6        Area - 616 sq mts

**LOCATION**

Lone Tree Cemetery is found in open fields, south of Ieper, about 2.5km south-west of Wijtschate, and approximately 600m south of the Wijtschate-Kemmel road. The side road to the cemetery is sign-posted. There is parking space at the Pool of Peace from which you can walk the short distance to the cemetery. Take care to remember to close and secure all gates as you pass through the farmer's field.

# MAPLE COPSE CEMETERY

## HISTORY
Burials in this cemetery took place mostly in 1916, but particularly during the Battle of Mount Sorrell in June.

## INFORMATION
This is one of the prettiest cemeteries on the Salient, lying below the level of the road in a quiet copse. The importance of Hill 62 becomes clear when you stand within the grounds.

Maple Copse was the name given by the British Army to a small plantation 1km east of Zillebeke, and just west of Sanctuary Wood. Its use, and use of the name, pre-dates the arrival of Canadian troops in 1916. This cemetery was associated with the Advanced Dressing Stations located in this copse close to Sanctuary Wood and Hill 62. Most of the graves were destroyed by shellfire so that, of the 256 men known to be buried here, only 26 graves could be located when the cemetery was officially created.

On 7 November 1914 the 1st Gloucestershires, 2nd Queen's (Royal West Surreys) and 1st South Staffordshires attacked from here south and east towards Armagh Wood across the road from Zillebeke. The Staffordshires were led by Captain John Franks Vallentin, who had insisted on rejoining them from hospital in Ypres and was then killed in leading the successful attack. He won the Victoria Cross and is commemorated on the Menin Gate. The Battle of Mount Sorrel took place nearby in 1916 to the east with many Canadians coming to the front line past this burial ground, or being treated in the Dressing Station that was here, though their presence is not the reason for the name. Captain The Honourable Alfred 'Fred' Thomas Shaughnessy, 'A' Company, 60th Canadian Infantry, was killed on 31 March 1916 aged 28 years and commemorated by a Special Memorial. He was the second son of the 1st Baron Shaughnessy of Montreal, Canada who had founded the Canadian Pacific Railroad, for whom Captain Shaughnessy had also worked. He had joined his Battalion in June 1915 and was killed by shellfire. His second in command in his Company was his brother in law, Captain Redmond. His son, born just after his death, Captain Alfred James (Freddie) Shaughnessy, Grenadier Guards, was the chief writer and script editor of the TV series 'Upstairs, Downstairs'. Fred was married to a descendant of President Polk of the USA. He was also related as cousin to the Grenfell family mentioned elsewhere in this book.

Also here are Privates George William Tyerman, 1812, 1/4th Yorkshires, who died of wounds on 2 March 1916 aged 23 years and Fred Tyerman, 1813, 1/4th Yorkshires, who was killed in action on 27 February 1916 aged 18 years. Note the consecutive service numbers. They are commemorated by Special Memorials side by side. Fred was acting as batman to Captain Sproxton when the officer's dugout suffered a direct hit from a shell which mortally wounded him. William was shot through the lungs a few days later and died at a dressing station. The CWGC records, and the headstones incorrectly spell, the family name as 'Tyreman'.

Another here is Private Frederick Freeman Laing, Depot Company, Royal Canadian Regiment, killed on 11 May 1916 aged 15 years. He was born on New Year's Day 1901. Frederick Laing was a Driver in the Regiment when he surrendered as a stowaway aboard the SS Caledonian on 27 Aug 1915. He was one of seven men (three of whom were Doctors) who had stowed away on board their Battalion's transport ship in Canada and had been taken on strength in mid-Atlantic in September 1915. He was transferred to 'A' Company on 13 September 1915 but returned to 'Base' Company ten days later. Laing initially went to France with his Battalion in November 1915 but rejoined it on being transferred from the 11th Reserve Battalion on 26 March 1916. His service in the field was brief. The War Diary for 11 May 1916 reads: 'No. 478051 Pte. LAING, F. Killed in Action by enemy shell at BORDER DUGOUTS. Buried I.24.c.3.9. Sheet 28 (MAPLE COPSE.)'

Nearby is the monument to the 15th Canadian Infantry which stands on the road from Zillebeke. In June 1916, during the Battle of Mount Sorrel, the Canadian 1st Division were ordered forward to support the Canadian 3rd Division who were suffering heavily from the German onslaught. A series of counter-attacks were ordered. On the night of 2 June the Division moved forward from reserve at Ouderdom, 16km away, but arrived late for their attack. The 14th and 15th Canadian Infantry pressed on in broad daylight, attacking Observatory Ridge and Maple Copse, taking significant casualties. The Germans forced the Canadians back at the cost of 250 men. Nonetheless, they contributed to holding the German attack at Mount Sorrel so that on 13 June the Canadian 1st Division recaptured all the ground that had been lost. This commemorative plaque was unveiled on 22 October 2011 by members of the 15th Battalion Memorial Project in the presence of Canadian and Belgian dignitaries.

UK – 154         Can – 154
Unnamed - 40 UK and 12 Can
Area - 4881 sq mts
Special Memorials to 230 men known to be buried here.

## LOCATION
Maple Copse Cemetery can be found east of Ieper, about 2km east of Zillebeke, and 2km south of the Menin Road. It is enclosed by a moat.

# MAPLE LEAF CEMETERY

## HISTORY
This cemetery was begun in December 1914 and used until December 1917 for British burials. Nine German graves were made here in April 1918 when this village was in German hands.

## INFORMATION
The 3rd Canadian Field Ambulance Advanced Dressing Station was stationed here from July 1915 to April 1916 when the cemetery gained its present name.
Private Albert Parry of the 2nd West Yorkshires was executed nearby for desertion and buried here on 30 August 1917. We know very little about him.

Also here is Private Harry Watson, 17751, 1st Otago Regiment, NZEF, killed in action on 6 May 1917 aged 36 years. He served as John William Black. He left New Zealand with the 15th Reinforcements, Otago Infantry Battalion, 'D' Company on 26 July 1915. John Black was one of 28 New Zealand servicemen who were court-martialled and sentenced to death during the war, though his sentence was commuted to ten years penal servitude. Black was killed during the shelling of the New Zealand position opposite Messines on the night of 6 May 1917 ten days after he had faced his court martial. After his death it was found that 'Black' was an assumed name and that he was in fact Harry Watson from Herbert, North Otago.

| UK – 80 | Aust – 4 | NZ – 43 |
| --- | --- | --- |
| Can – 39 | S Afr – 1 | Ger – 9 |

Area - 1053 sq mts

## LOCATION
Maple Leaf Cemetery lies on the French border south of Ieper and about 3km south-east of Nieuwkerke in the small hamlet of Le Romarin which is at the point of a sharp bend on the Nieuwkerke-Ploegsteert road. The cemetery is behind the cafe in Le Romarin. If you cross the border, marked by the large speed limit sign, then you have missed the turn for the cemetery. The small cemetery has pleasant views of the valley of the Lys.

# MENDINGHEM BRITISH CEMETERY

## HISTORY
The cemetery was opened in June 1916 when the 46th (1/1st Wessex) Casualty Clearing Station was located here, though the first burials did not take place until August 1916. The cemetery was then used until September 1918.

## INFORMATION
No. 46 Casualty Clearing Station at first had 200 beds but this was increased to 1,300 in preparation for the Third Battle of Ypres. After a German gas attack on 12 July 1917 the Casualty Clearing Station took more than 100 casualties for treatment over the next few days even though it was trying to clear the beds for the coming battle. Four more Casualty Clearing Stations were stationed at Proven when the cemetery gained its present name along with those known as Bandaghem and Dozinghem. The ironic name was given to the cemetery by the soldiers who were treated in the Dressing Stations here. The name humourously plays upon the Flemish language to describe the function of the Casualty Clearing Stations. One of the Casualty Clearing Stations, No. 61, was staffed by Americans from Philadelphia. Three others, No.'s 12, 46 and 64, remained in the area until 1918. You will note no unidentified burials which is typical of cemeteries associated with Casualty Clearing Stations behind the lines. Some French burials were made from May to July 1918 in an area that had been set aside for them. These have since been removed.

Buried here is Captain (temporary Lieutenant-Colonel) Bertram Best-Dunkley, VC, 2/5th Lancashire Fusiliers, who died of wounds on 5 August 1917. He was awarded the Victoria Cross for his actions on the first day of Third Ypres, 31 July 1917. In the attack his Battalion became disorganised so he went forward and rallied his men to take their objectives. The Fusiliers sustained heavy losses but his leadership helped the Battalion to succeed. In the evening he took the Battalion headquarters into battle to defeat a German counter-attack during which he was mortally wounded. The citation reads 'For most conspicuous bravery and devotion to duty when in command of his Battalion, the leading waves of which, during an attack, became disorganised by reason of rifle and machine gun fire at close range from positions which were believed to be in our hands. Lt. Col. Best-Dunkley dashed forward, rallied his leading waves, and personally led them to the assault of these positions, which, despite heavy losses, were carried. He continued to lead his Battalion until all their objectives had been gained. Had it not been for this officer's gallant and determined action it is doubtful if the left of the Brigade would have reached its objectives. Later in the day, when our position was threatened, he collected his Battalion headquarters, led them to the attack, and beat off the advancing enemy.'

There are three men buried here who were executed for desertion. Rifleman John J. Hyde, 10th King's Royal Rifle Corps had gone absent whilst his Battalion was in action during Third Ypres. This probably weighed against him for, although he did not have any previous serious crimes behind him, his superiors confirmed the death sentence. He was shot for desertion on 5 September 1917.

Private Charles Britton, 1/5th Royal Warwickshires had deserted at the start of the British Flanders Offensive in 1917 and was arrested on 16 August while his Battalion were fighting on the first day of the Battle of Langemarck. He was executed on 12 September 1917. The fact that he had gone absent just as his unit was sent to the Front would have counted against him.

Private David Gibson, 12th Royal Scots had failed to return from leave and was arrested in the United Kingdom, the last soldier to be arrested at home and sent back to France. As the Battalion was about to go into action Gibson was offered the chance of going in to battle to redeem himself. Instead he went absent again. He was arrested two days later and was executed on 24 September 1918.

Also buried here is Captain Arthur Lionel Gordon-Kidd, DSO, Silver Medal for Bravery (Montenegro), No. 19 Squadron, Royal Flying Corps and 4th Dragoon Guards (Royal Irish), died of wounds on 27 August 1917. He was wounded in a combat with the German 'ace' Werner Voss on 23 August 1917, crash-landing his aircraft at No. 23 Squadron's airfield near Dixmuide. He was awarded the Distinguished Service Order in August 1916 while still a 2nd Lieutenant. The citation says 'On one occasion he dived his machine from a height of 7,500 feet to 900 feet, and placed a bomb on the enemy's ammunition train, which set it on fire and blocked the line. A few days afterwards he performed another very hazardous undertaking well within the enemy's lines, whilst exposed the whole time to all descriptions of heavy fire.'

Another here is Company Serjeant Major James Willieson Miller, DCM, MSM, 'D' Company, 5th Cameronians (Scottish Rifles), who died of wounds on 18 April 1918 aged 23 years. He was posthumously awarded the Meritorious Service Medal on 17 June 1918 and the Distinguished Conduct Medal on 3 September 1918 'For conspicuous gallantry and devotion to duty. When the troops in front of and on the flanks of his Company had been driven in, and his platoon commanders and serjeants, except one, had become casualties, he went forward and re-oganised the position on the right, in doing which he was severely wounded. He then insisted on the stretcher bearers taking him to his Company commander, to whom he gave a clear and valuable report of the situation. He showed fine courage and determination.'

Buried here is one of three brothers killed in the war. They were from Aberdeen and all served in the Royal Engineers. Corporal Charles Copland, 401st Field Company, Royal Engineers died on 8 September 1917 aged 22 years. His elder brother, Driver George Smith Copland, 404th Field Company, Royal Engineers died on 22 March 1918 aged 24 years and is buried in Dernancourt Communal Cemetery Extension. His younger brother, Private William Smith Copland, 1/6th Black Watch (Royal Highlanders) died on 2 November 1918 aged 19 years and is buried in Abbeville Communal Cemetery Extension.

One of four brothers to die in the war is Trooper Alfred Dunne, 2nd Life Guards transferred to the Household Battalion who died on 11 October 1917 aged 17 years. Corporal Arthur Dunne, 18th (Queen Mary's Own) Hussars died on 13 May 1915 aged 21 years and is commemorated on the Menin Gate. 2nd Lieutenant Walter Edwin Dunne, 2nd Lancashire Fusiliers died on 18 October 1915 aged 35 years and is buried in Beauval Communal Cemetery. Company Serjeant Major Montague Dunne, 20th Lancashire Fusiliers died on 3 February 1918 aged 32 years and is buried in Wimereux Communal Cemetery.

Of note is Major Charles Meredith Bouverie Chapman, MC, Chevalier of the Order of Leopold and Croix de Guerre (Belgium), No. 29 Squadron, Royal Flying Corps and the Buffs (East Kents), who died on 1 October 1917 aged 25 years. He is credited with seven victories making him an 'ace'. Chapman served as a Lieutenant in the East Kents from January 1913 but was transferred to the Royal Flying Corps on 1 July 1915. He qualified as a pilot on 31 July 1915 receiving training at Shoreham before being posted to No. 22 Squadron. In April 1916 Chapman was sent to France, based eventually at Bertangles. However Chapman was transferred to 'B' Flight, No. 24 Squadron, also based at Bertangles. Chapman was successful in destroying three enemy aircraft in a short period, commencing on 22 June 1916, for which he was awarded the Military Cross. On detachment in the UK, Chapman served in a number of training units and on 1 November 1916 was promoted to Captain becoming a Flight Commander. In this capacity, he returned to France in May 1917 to join No. 29 Squadron, flying Nieuport Scouts. He died of shrapnel injuries after a German bombing raid on his Squadron's airfield at Poperinge. His brother, Lieutenant (Observer) William Wetherall Chapman, No. 22 Squadron, Royal Flying Corps and the Buffs (East Kents) was killed in action over Menin one week later on 7 October 1917 (and the day after Charles's funeral) aged 21 years and is buried under the war memorial in Neuville-en-Ferrain Communal Cemetery which is north-east of Lille.

| | | |
|---|---|---|
| UK – 2266 | Aust – 15 | NZ – 12 |
| Can – 28 | NF – 3 | S Afr – 33 |
| BWI – 26 | Ger – 52 | |
| Chinese Labour Corps – 8 | | Area - 6345 sq mts |

**LOCATION**

Mendinghem Cemetery can be found 150m west of the N308 from Poperinge to Roesbrugge, west of Ieper, approximately 8km north-west of Poperinge and on the northern outskirts of Proven. A track leads 200m from the N308 to the cemetery which is next to a private house.

# MENIN GATE MEMORIAL

## HISTORY
This Memorial was built after the war and inaugurated by Field Marshal Lord Plumer on 24 July 1927. The Imperial War Graves Commission decided that Memorials would be set up to commemorate those who had died in the Salient and who had no known graves.

## INFORMATION
I accept that this is not a cemetery in the true sense, but it is the last resting place for the names of many of the men who died on the Salient. Other Memorials are included elsewhere in this book as they are part of cemeteries, but as this is one of the most important places of remembrance on the Salient I feel that it deserves separate inclusion.

The Memorial bears the names, engraved on panels of Portland Stone, of nearly 55,000 officers and men who were killed, and have no known grave, between the start of the war and the night of 15 August 1917 when the Battle of Langemarck began. Those men of the Empire and its Dominions who were lost after that date are listed on the Tyne Cot Memorial. However, it is the only memorial for the Canadians, Australians, South Africans and members of the Indian Army who were lost in the Salient and have no identified grave.

All New Zealand men lost were to be included at a separate memorial at Tyne Cot or on Memorials at Messines Ridge and Buttes New Cemeteries. The Ploegsteert Memorial is included as part of this book having some men included on its walls who died in what I consider part of the Salient. The Menin Gate was a logical place for a Memorial as many of the men upon it would have passed through here on the way to the trenches.

During the war there was no gate on this site, the old Hangoart or Antwerp Gate having been removed in the 19th Century. There remained just two carved lions, one on either side of the road. They were given by the town to Australia in 1936 but were returned from April to November 2017 as part of the commemorations of the 100th Anniversary of the Battle of Messines and Third Ypres. They stand where the Last Post Ceremony first took place, outside of the Gate.

Above the central arches of the Menin Gate can be found a lion facing out to the front-lines, and facing the town a sarcophagus with a flag and wreath. The Gate was designed by Sir Reginald Blomfield.

Upon the memorial are words chosen by Rudyard Kipling – 'Ad Majorem Dei Gloriam - Here are recorded names of officers and men who fell in Ypres Salient, but to whom the fortune of war denied the known and honoured burial given to their comrades in death'. The latin phrase means 'To the greater glory of God'. Elsewhere you can see 'They shall receive a crown of glory that fadeth not away' and latin inscriptions 'Pro Patria' ('For Country') and 'Pro Rege' ('For King'). A French inscription 'Erigé par les nations de l'Empire Britannique en l'honneur de leurs morts ce monument est offert aux citoyens d'Ypres pour l'ornement de leur cité et en commémoration des jours où l'Armée Britannique l'a défendue contre l'envahisseur' translates as 'Erected by the nations of the British Empire in honour of their dead this monument is offered to the citizens of Ypres for the ornament of their city and in commemoration of the days where the British Army defended it against the invader'.

On either side are well kept gardens which you can reach by the steps leading from the road. It is possible to walk along the old ramparts to the Lille Gate about 800m away. The ramparts were built upon the original fortifications dating from the Twelfth Century by Vauban who was the military architect for the French King, Louis XIV. The casements beneath the ramparts were some of the safest places in Ypres during the war as not even the heaviest German guns could cause serious damage. They were almost the only thing standing in Ypres at the Armistice. The 'Wipers Times' was printed in one of the casements while others were used as bedrooms, a signal headquarters, cinema and hospital.

On the evening of the inauguration of the Gate the Last Post was sounded by buglers from the Somerset Light Infantry. In 1928, a year after the inauguration of the Menin Gate Memorial, several leading members of the community in Ypres felt they wanted to find some way to express their gratitude towards those who had died for Belgium, a country many had never heard of before they arrived to never leave. The Superintendent of the Ypres Police, Mr P Vandenbraambussche, suggested the idea of the daily sounding of the Last Post under the Menin Gate. The Last Post was a bugle call played in the British Army (and in the armies of many other lands) to mark the end of the day's labours. The 'Last Post' bugle call is used at military funerals, memorials and times of remembrance. It symbolises the 'end of the soldier's day' in so far as the dead soldier has finished his duty and can rest in peace. The privilege of playing the Last Post was given to buglers of the local volunteer Fire Brigade. The first sounding of Last Post took place on 1 July 1928 and a daily ceremony was carried on for about four months. The ceremony was reinstated in the spring of 1929 and the Last Post Committee, now Association, was established. Four silver bugles were donated to the Last Post Committee by the Brussels and Antwerp Branches of the Royal British Legion. With the exception of the period of German occupation in World War II, when the ceremony took place at Brookwood Barracks in England and the bugles were hidden, the Last Post Ceremony has taken place at 8.00pm each evening, being sounded by between one and six men of the Ypres Fire Brigade using bugles still provided by the Royal British Legion. In recent years the ceremony has grown as more people have attended, sometimes over 5000 are here, notably on weekends in the spring and summer. The road is now closed at 7.30pm by the police. The Exhortation 'They shall not grow old, as we that are left grow old: Age shall not weary them, nor the years condemn. At the going down of the sun and the morning, We will remember them', and sometimes the Kohima, are said during the ceremony. Wreaths from groups and individuals are laid, and the ceremony ends with a 'Reveille' to signal a return to 'ordinary life'. A special Last Post ceremony is held at the Menin Gate Memorial at 11.00am on 11 November. There is a ceremony held at the Ploegsteert Memorial on the first Friday of the month at 7.00pm and at the Hedd Wyn Memorial on the Langemark-Bozeinge road on the first Monday of the month at 7.00pm.

This is a very emotional ceremony and can affect young and old alike. I claim this based upon years of attending the ceremony with a wide range of companions. I have seen school children, a Company of soldiers and my parents, both ex-Royal Navy, affected by the simple ceremony. I would suggest strongly that on some evening during your visit you attend and take part in the experience.

There are eight men who won the Victoria Cross in World War I, and one other holder of the award, commemorated on the Menin Gate. Lance-Corporal Frederick 'Fred' Fisher, VC, 13th Canadian Infantry, Quebec Regiment (Royal Highlanders of Canada), died on 23 April 1915 aged 22 years. The citation reads 'On 23rd April, 1915, in the neighbourhood of St. Julien, he went forward with the machine gun, of which he was in charge, under heavy fire, and most gallantly assisted in covering the retreat of a Battery, losing four men of his gun team. Later, after obtaining four more men, he went forward again to the firing line and was himself killed while bringing his machine gun into action under very heavy fire, in order to cover the advance of supports.' According to the CWGC records Fisher was killed on 24 April 1915. There is possibly a discrepancy about the date of his death, which is given as the 23 April by the Official History of the Canadian Forces 1914-1919 and the history of the 13th Battalion. There is also a discrepancy with the date of his original action on 22 April and the date of 23 April assigned to it in the published citation in The London Gazette. According to the Official History of the Canadian Forces in The Great War 1914-1919 his action occurred on the evening of 22 April as he covered the 10th Battery before, and during, its withdrawal after the Germans launched their 'gas attack'.

Company Sergeant-Major Frederick William Hall, VC, 8th Canadian Infantry, Manitoba Regiment, killed in action on 25 April 1915 aged 28 years. The citation reads 'On 24th April, 1915, in the neighbourhood of Ypres, when a wounded man who was lying some 15 yards from the trench called for help, Company Serjeant-Major Hall endeavoured to reach him in the face of a very heavy enfilade fire which was being poured in by the enemy. The first attempt failed, and a non-commissioned officer and Private who were attempting to give assistance were both wounded. Company Serjeant-Major Hall then made a second most gallant attempt, and was in the act of lifting up the wounded man to bring him in when he fell mortally wounded in the head.' The citation underplays Hall's actions. On the night of 24-25 April, under cover of darkness he twice rescued men from the open. It was in daylight on 25 April that he tried to rescue more of his men that he was killed. He was born in Ireland and emigrated to Canada in 1910.

2nd Lieutenant Dennis George Wyldbore Hewitt, VC, 2nd Hampshires attached 14th (1st Portsmouth Pals) Hampshires, killed in action on 31 July 1917 aged 19 years. The citation reads 'For most conspicuous bravery and devotion to duty when in command of a Company in attack. When his first objective had been captured he reorganized the Company and moved forward towards his objective. While waiting for the barrage to lift, he was hit by a piece of shell, which exploded the signal lights in his haversack and set fire to his equipment and clothes. Having extinguished the flames, in spite of his wound and the severe pain he was suffering, he led forward the remains of the Company under very heavy machine gun fire, and captured and consolidated his objective. He was subsequently killed by a sniper while inspecting the consolidation and encouraging his men. This gallant officer set a magnificent example of coolness and contempt of danger to the whole Battalion, and it was due to his splendid leading that the final objective of his Battalion was gained.' He had been at the Front since September 1916.

Lieutenant Hugh McDonald McKenzie, VC, DCM, Croix de Guerre (France), 7th Company, Canadian Machine Gun Corps, killed in action on 30 October 1917 aged 30 years. The citation reads 'For most conspicuous bravery and leading when in charge of a section of four machine guns acCompanying the infantry in an attack. Seeing that all the officers and most of the non-commissioned officers of an infantry Company had become casualties, and that the men were hesitating before a nest of enemy machine guns, which were on commanding ground and causing them severe casualties, he handed over command of his guns to an N.C.O., rallied the infantry, organised an attack, and captured the strong point. Finding that the position was swept by machine-gun fire from a ' pill-box ' which dominated all the ground over which the troops were advancing, Lt. McKenzie made a reconnaissance and detailed flanking and frontal attacking parties which captured the 'pill-box', he himself being killed while leading the frontal attack. By his valour and leadership this gallant officer ensured the capture of these strong points and so saved the lives of many men and enabled the objectives to be attained.' He emigrated to Canada in 1911. He enlisted into the Princess Patricia's Canadian Light Infantry in 1914. As a Corporal, in early 1916, he received the Distinguished Conduct Medal for actions while in command of a machine-gun section. In January 1917, he was commissioned and was transferred to the Canadian Machine Gun Corps.

Captain John Franks Vallentin, VC, 1st South Staffordshires killed in action on 7 November 1914 aged 32 years. The citation reads 'For conspicuous bravery on 7th Nov., at Zillebeke. When leading the attack against the Germans under a very heavy fire he was struck down, and on rising to continue the attack was immediately killed. The capture of the enemy's trenches which followed was in a great measure due to the confidence which the men had in their Captain, arising from his many previous acts of great bravery and ability.' He was commissioned in 1899 and saw service in the South African Wars. He was wounded in fighting in late October at Geluveld and by 6 November he was hospitalised in Ypres suffering from his wounds and dysentery. He believed that he was dying and that he wanted to die with his men. So, weak and feverish he walked out of hospital and hitched a ride to Zillebeke where the Staffordshires were now located. However the Staffordshires were now a much depleted Battalion and had lost thirteen officers and 440 men in two days of fighting at Kruiseke. Vallentin now found himself as the senior officer present and leading an attack. In his severely ill state he led his men forward until killed.

Private Edward Warner, VC, 1st Bedfordshires died on 2 May 1915 aged 32 years. The citation reads 'For most conspicuous bravery near ' Hill 60 ' on 1st May, 1915. After Trench 46 had been vacated by our troops, consequent on a gas attack, Private Warner entered it single-handed in order to prevent the enemy taking possession. Reinforcements were sent to Private Warner, but could not reach him owing to the gas. He then came back and brought up more men, by which time he was completely exhausted, but the trench was held until the enemy's attack ceased. This very gallant soldier died shortly afterwards from the effects of gas poisoning.' He was mobilised from the reserves at the start of the war arriving in France on 14 August being in action almost continuously until his death. On 1 May he held the trench, sometimes almost single-handedly, against German attacks in the midst of poison gas, getting reinforcements during a lull and returning to the fight until forced to withdraw suffering from the effects of the gas. This killed him on the following day.

2nd Lieutenant Sidney Clayton Woodroffe, VC, 8th Rifle Brigade died on 30 July 1915 aged 19 years. The citation reads 'For most conspicuous bravery on 30th July, 1915, at Hooge. The enemy having broken through the centre of our front trenches, consequent on the use of burning liquids, this Officer''s position was heavily attacked with bombs from the flank and subsequently from the rear, but he managed to defend his post until all his bombs were exhausted, and then skilfully withdrew his remaining men. This very gallant Officer immediately led his party forward in a counter-attack under an intense rifle and machine gun fire, and was killed whilst in the act of cutting the wire obstacles in the open.' His brother, Lieutenant Kenneth Woodroffe, 6th Rifle Brigade attached 2nd Welsh, was a cricketer who played for Hampshire and Sussex. Kenneth was killed on 9 May 1915 aged 22 years and is commemorated on the Le Touret Memorial.

Brigadier-General Charles Fitzclarence, VC, Staff, late of the Royal Fusiliers and Irish Guards, Commanding 1st Guards Brigade and Irish Guards when killed in action on 12 November 1914 aged 49 years. He won his Victoria Cross for three different acts of bravery while a Captain in the South African Wars in 1899, the citation reads 'On the 14th October 1899, Captain Fitzclarence went with his Squadron of the Protectorate Regiment, consisting of only partially trained men, who had never been in action, to the assistance of an armoured train which had gone out from Mafeking. The enemy were in greatly superior numbers, and the Squadron was for a time surrounded, and it looked as if nothing could save them from being shot down. Captain Fitzclarence, however, by his personal coolness and courage inspired the greatest confidence in his men, and, by his bold and efficient handling of them, not only succeeded in relieving the armoured train, but inflicted a heavy defeat on the Boers, who lost 50 killed and a large number wounded. The moral effect of this blow had a very important bearing on subsequent encounters with the Boers. On the 27th October 1899, Captain Fitzclarence led his Squadron from Mafeking across the open, and made a night attack with the bayonet on one of the enemy's trenches. A hand-to-hand fight took place in the trench, while heavy fire was concentrated on it from the rear. The enemy was driven out with heavy loss. Captain Fitzclarence was the first man into the position and accounted for four of the enemy with his sword. The British lost 6 killed and 9 wounded. Captain Fitzclarence was himself slightly wounded. With reference to these two actions, Major-General Baden-Powell states that had his Officer not shown an extraordinary spirit and fearlessness the attacks would have been failures, and we should have suffered heavy loss both in men and prestige. On the 26th December 1899, during the action at Game Tree, near Mafeking, Captain Fitzclarence again distinguished himself by his coolness and courage, and was again wounded (severely through both legs).' He joined the Royal Fusiliers in 1898, transferred to Irish Guards and commanded them from 1909. He was made a Brigadier General and given command of 1st Guards Brigade in late September 1914. He had given the command to counter-attack on 31 October 1914 which stopped the German advance, notably the actions of the 2nd Worcestershires which recaptured Geluveld. He was killed leading a counter-attack near Polygon Wood. He was a grandson of the 1st Earl of Munster, an illegitimate son of William, Duke of Clarence, later King William IV and his son became 6th Earl of Munster. He is the highest-ranking officer inscribed on the Menin Gate.

Among the many names on the Memorial are those of three men who were executed but whose graves have since been lost. Corporal George H. Povey, 1st Cheshires fled from the front-line near Wulvergem on 28 January 1915 accompanied by four Privates. The Privates were imprisoned for their desertion and Corporal Povey was executed on 11 February 1915 having been found guilty of leaving his post. Driver Thomas Moore of No. 197 Company, Army Service Corps, was executed on 26 February 1916 at Busseboom, south-east of Poperinge. He had murdered Sergeant James Pick of his unit on 11 February 1916 while in camp near Busseboom. Pick is now buried in Poperinge New Military Cemetery where the largest group of executed soldiers to be buried in any cemetery on the Western Front can also be found. For Private William Scotton please refer to Suffolk Cemetery.

I am moved by the families that lost sons, fathers, brothers or other relatives in the war. To lose more than one is not a greater lost but must have had a greater impact. So, is it a surprise that we wonder at the names of families who have lost two, three, four or even five sons or brothers in the war. Space dictates the limits of what I can include here. But, there are some stories that must be told.

One family has four members on the memorial while three others have three members of their families here. Corporal William Allen, 1st South Staffordshires died on 30 October 1914 aged 26 years. Lance Corporal Thomas Allen, 2nd Sherwood Foresters (Notts and Derbys) died on 24 September 1915 aged 25 years. Private Frank Allen, 1st Northumberland Fusiliers died on 27 March 1916 aged 18 years. Private Ernest Allen, 11th Sherwood Foresters (Notts and Derbys) died on 9 April 1917. It is sad that four sons from the same family were killed in the war, but to also all be on one Memorial is remarkable.

The Racheil family have three sons here. Privates Arthur Ernest Racheil aged 21 years, Frank Albert Racheil aged 18 years and Frederick George Racheil aged 24 years, all 3rd Royal Fusiliers and all killed on 24 May 1915. They were pre-war 'regulars' who came back with the Battalion from India to become part of 28th Division.

Private John McDonnell aged 22 years and Private Patrick McDonnell aged 32 years, both died 24 May 1915. Also here is their brother Private Peter McDonnell who died on 26 April 1915 aged 42 years. They were all with the 2nd Royal Dublin Fusiliers.

Private George Henri Gray and Private George Ernest Gray and Private William Gray, all 2nd Canadian Infantry (Eastern Ontario) and all killed on 22 April 1915 are commemorated here.

Private George Aitkens aged 22 years and Private James Aitkens aged 19 years, both 16th Canadian Infantry (Manitoba) and both died 23 April 1915 aged 22 years. Also commemorated here is their brother Private John Aitkens, 'D' Company, 27th Canadian Infantry (Manitoba) died 6 April 1916 aged 29 years.

Commemorated here is a member of one of the families to lose five sons – four brothers and a half-brother. Private Frederick Smith, 20th Durham Light Infantry, was killed on 31 July 1917. Corporal George Henry Smith, 6th Durham Light Infantry was killed on 5 November 1916 aged 26 years and is commemorated on the Thiepval Memorial. His brother, Private Robert Smith, 1/6th Durham Light Infantry was killed on 19 September 1916 and is buried in Dernancourt Communal Cemetery Extension. Another brother, Private Alfred Smith, 9th Durham Light Infantry, died on 22 July 1918 and is buried in Terlincthun British Cemetery. The last sibling, a half brother John William Stout, 1/5th West Yorkshires, was killed in action on 9 October 1917 and is commemorated on the Tyne Cot Memorial.

Several families have one son here who had three brothers also lost in the war.

Corporal William Hugh Twynam, 7th Canadian Infantry died on 24 April 1915 aged 33 years. He is the second of four brothers to die in the war. Staff Sergeant John Twynam, 1st South African Mounted Rifles died on 30 November 1914, killed by lightning at Windhuk, Orange Free State and is buried in Barnea Siding Burial Ground, Bethlehem, Orange Free State, South Africa, the only CWGC grave there. 2nd Lieutenant Godfrey Twynam, 11th Borders died on 18 November 1916 in one of the last actions of the Battles of the Somme and is buried in Waggon Road Cemetery. Lieutenant Hugh Twynam, HM Submarine E36, Royal Naval Reserve died on 19 January 1917 aged 29 years and is commemorated on the Portsmouth Naval Memorial. E36 was sunk in a collision with E43 off Harwich in the North Sea with no survivors.

Private John Carroll, 7th/8th King's Own Scottish Borderers was killed attacking the Frezenberg ridge on 31 July 1917 aged 27 years. Private Joseph Carroll, MM, 2nd Duke of Wellington's died on 8 May 1918 and is buried in Lapugnoy Military Cemetery. Corporal William Carroll, 282nd Siege Battery, Royal Garrison Artillery died on 4 May 1917 aged 23 years and is buried in Bailleul Communal Cemetery Extension. Battery Quartermaster Serjeant Michael Carroll, 253rd Siege Battery, Royal Garrison Artillery, died on 27 January 1918 aged 35 years. He had seen service in the South African Wars and was a regular soldier. The family originated from Yorkshire but William and Michael had moved to the Isle of Wight and started families. Michael died at home and is buried in Totland (St. Saviour) Roman Catholic Churchyard.

Major Philip Llewellyn Howell-Price, DSO, was a bank clerk before enlisting in the 1st Australian Infantry as a Private on 14 September 1914. He was commissioned as a 2nd Lieutenant four days later and embarked for Egypt on 18 October. The Battalion landed at Gallipoli on 25 August 1915 and Philip was promoted to Lieutenant. He was Mentioned in Despatches during the Battle of Lone Pine, during which he was severely wounded. Returning after three months in hospital, he was one of the last to evacuate from Gallipoli. He was promoted to Captain on 28 January 1916 and was awarded the Distinguished Service Order for leading a raiding party near Armentieres on 27 June. He fought on the Somme in July, at Flers in November and was wounded at Bullecourt in 1917. General Birdwood soon had him appointed to the staff of the 1st ANZAC Division. He was promoted to Major on 7 June 1917 and attached to the staff of the 2nd Brigade. That month he was awarded the Military Cross. On hearing that his old Battalion was going into action he begged to be sent back to it and on 4 October he was killed in an artillery barrage at Broodseinde and is commemorated here. Buried in Heilly Station Cemetery is Lieutenant Colonel Owen Howell-Price, 3rd Australian Infantry, DSO, MC, twice MiD, killed in action on 4 November 1916. He was commissioned as a 2nd Lieutenant on 27 August 1914 and arrived in Egypt in December. During this time he was appointed Assistant Adjutant and when the Adjutant was killed on the first day at Gallipoli he succeeded him. He was promoted to Captain on 4 August 1915. During the fighting at Lone Pine he won the Military Cross and was also Mentioned in Despatches. Casualties were heavy and on 5 September he was promoted to temporary Major and assumed command of the Battalion. He was wounded on 9 September but remained on duty. The 3rd Battalion arrived in France on 28 March 1916 and Owen was promoted to Lieutenant-Colonel on 12 May. In July and August the Battalion fought at Pozières and Mouquet Farm. For his leadership he was awarded the Distinguished Service Order and Mentioned in Despatches again. On 4 November 1916, near Flers, he was shot in the head and died instantly. 2nd Lieutenant Richmond Gordon Howell-Price, MC, 1st Australian Infantry, was wounded in action on 4 May 1917 aged 20 years at Bullecourt and died later that day. Three days later it was announced that he had been awarded the Military Cross. He is buried at Vraucourt Copse Cemetery. His elder brother John ran away to sea aged 14 years and served an apprenticeship before obtaining a Master's Certificate. He joined the Royal Naval Reserve as a temporary Sub-Lieutenant on 24 March 1915 and was serving in HMS Alcantara when she met the German raider SMS Greif in the North Sea on 29 February 1916. After a fierce fight both ships were sunk, the survivors nearly freezing to death in open boats before they were rescued. For his part in the engagement John was awarded the Distinguished Service Cross. He later transferred to the submarine service and was promoted to temporary Lieutenant on 24 July 1917. He was second-in-command and navigator of the British submarine C3 which, filled with explosives, was blown up at Zeebrugge, Belgium, on the night of 22-23 April 1918. The commander of the submarine was awarded the Victoria Cross and John the Distinguished Service Order. Another brother, Frederick, was employed as a bank clerk until 17 September 1914 when he enlisted as a Driver in the 6th Company, Australian Army Service Corps. On 16 December he was promoted to 2nd Lieutenant and five days later sailed from Sydney with the 2nd Light Horse Divisional Train. He rose through the ranks in the supply service. He served during the Romani, Beersheba, Jericho Valley and Syrian operations, was promoted Major on 1 November 1917, awarded the DSO and twice Mentioned in Despatches. The family accrued one DSC, four DSO's, three MC's and were five times MiD. Three were killed. This is a considerable contribution well worth commemoration.

Private Donald Farquharson, 27th (Manitoba Regiment) Canadian Infantry, who was killed in action in a German trench mortar attack on 6 November 1917 aged 31 years is commemorated here. His brother, Private James Farquharson, 5th (Saskatchewan) Canadian Infantry, was killed on 2 March 1916 aged 26 years and is buried at RE Farm. He served as Ferguson. Another brother, Private Nathaniel Machonachie Farquharson, Royal Marine Light Infantry, HMS Indefatigable, was killed in action on 31 May 1916, one of over 1000 men killed when his ship blew up in the Battle of Jutland. A final brother, Trimmer J. Farquharson, HMS Newbury, Royal Navy Reserve, was killed in action near Dover on 15 February 1918 and is buried in Aberdeen (Allenvale) Cemetery.

Corporal Arthur Dunne, 18th (Queen Mary's Own) Hussars died on 13 May 1915 aged 21 years. Trooper Alfred Dunne, 2nd Life Guards transferred to the Household Battalion died on 11 October 1917 aged 17 years and is buried in Mendinghem Military Cemetery. 2nd Lieutenant Walter Edwin Dunne, 2nd Lancashire Fusiliers died on 18 October 1915 aged 35 years and is buried in Beauval Communal Cemetery. Company Serjeant Major Montague Dunne, 20th Lancashire Fusiliers died on 3 February 1918 aged 32 years and is buried in Wimereux Communal Cemetery.

Private James Percival Greenwood, 1st King's Own Yorkshire Light Infantry died on 8 May 1915 aged 25 years near Frezenberg in a German attack. Private John Greenwood, 1st King's (Liverpools) died a week later on 16 May 1915 aged 28 years and is commemorated on the Le Touret Memorial. Private Herbert Greenwood, 5th Northamptonshires died on 25 February 1916, killed by a sniper, and is buried in Vermelles British Cemetery. Private William Henry 'Harry' Greenwood, 3/5th Bedfordshires died on 27 June 1917 aged 23 years and is buried in Ramsey Cemetery. He was given exemption from going to the Front but died in a Military hospital and was the last son in the family.

Private Alick (Alexander) MacLeod, 1st Gordon Highlanders died on 14 December 1914. His brother, Seaman Angus MacLeod, HMS Victory (now HMS Nelson), Royal Naval

Reserve died on 24 June 1916 aged 27 years and is buried in Eye Cemetery (or Aignish Burial Ground), Isle of Lewis. Another brother, Trimmer Cook Norman MacLeod, HMS Venerable, Royal Naval Reserve died on 1 January 1919 and is commemorated on the Chatham Naval Memorial. He was attached to HM Yacht Iolaire which hit rocks and sank outside Stornoway Harbour. Another brother, Seaman William MacLeod, HM Yacht Sanda, Royal Naval Reserve died on 25 September 1915 when it was sunk by shore batteries, aged 28 years, and is also commemorated on the Chatham Naval Memorial.

One family lost four sons of whom two are commemorated here. Brothers Private John Castle, 8th Loyal North Lancashires killed on 18 July 1917 aged 32 years and Rifleman George Castle, 4th King's Royal Rifle Corps killed on 25 May 1915 aged 19 years are recorded here. Their brother, Private Fred Castle, 1st Coldstream Guards killed on 29 October 1914 aged 23 years is buried in Ypres Town Cemetery Extension. A fourth brother, too young for WW1, Gunner Oliver Castle, 336 Battery, 104 Heavy Anti-Aircraft Regiment, Royal Artillery died in WW2 on 3 April 1941 aged 34 years and is buried in Longborough (St. James) Churchyard.

Other families lost three sons. Corporal Sydney Franklin, 1st Lincolnshires died on 16 June 1915 aged 22 years. Also commemorated here is his brother, Private Vivian Franklin, 7th Queen's Own (Royal West Kents) who died on 17 July 1917 aged 19 years. Another brother, Private Oscar Franklin, 17th Middlesex died on 8 August 1916 and is commemorated on the Thiepval Memorial. They are one of many families to lose several sons with no identified grave. Private Edward Watson, 1/4th Oxford and Bucks Light Infantry died on 7 August 1917 aged 23 years. His brother, Private Hugh Watson, 11th (Prince Albert's Own) Hussars who died on 13 May 1915 is also commemorated here. Another brother, Private John Watson, 10th Lincolnshires died on 1 July 1916 aged 20 years and is commemorated on the Thiepval Memorial. Another family to lose several sons with no identified grave.

Thirty families lost a group of three brothers of whom one is commemorated here.

Private Ernest Vickers, 13th Durham Light Infantry was killed on 10 July 1917 aged 20 years. His brother Private Arnold Vickers, 7th Leicestershires died on 27 May 1918 aged 19 years and is commemorated on the Soissons Memorial. Another brother, Private Herbert Vickers, 33rd Company, Royal Army Medical Corps died on 27 November 1918 aged 29 Years and is buried in Cairo War Memorial Cemetery.

Major Wilfrid Beckett Walker, 2nd Yorkshires was killed in action on 29 October 1914 aged 38 years. His brother, Captain Oswald Bethell Walker, 15th (The King's) Hussars was killed in action on 23 August 1914 aged 39 years and is commemorated on the La Ferte-Sous-Jouarre Memorial. Another brother, Captain Roger Beverley Walker, Yorkshire Hussars Yeomanry attached 9th West Yorkshires died of wounds on 13 November 1918 aged 32 years and is buried at Terlincthun British Cemetery.

Private Arthur Walker, 8th York and Lancasters was killed in action on 9 April 1917. His brother Private Fred Walker 1/6th West Yorkshires was killed in action on 15 February 1917 and is buried in Serre Road No. 2 Cemetery. Another brother, Private Harry Walker, 10th Sherwood Foresters (Notts and Derbys) was killed in action on 6 May 1918 and is buried in Acheux British Cemetery.

Private Gavin MacMillan, 1/9th Argyll and Sutherland Highlanders was killed in action on 10 May 1915. His brother Private James MacMillan, 'C' Company, 13th Royal Scots, was killed in action on 28 March 1918 aged 32 years and is buried at Feuchy Chapel British Cemetery. Another brother, Private John Murchie MacMillan, 1st King's Own Scottish Borderers, was killed in action on 11 April 1918 and is commemorated on the Ploegsteert Memorial.

Sergeant Sydney Aubrey Kyrle Money, 1st Honourable Artillery Company was killed in action at Hooge on 16 June 1915. His brother, Captain Roy Granville Kyrle Money, 3rd attached 6th Buffs (East Kents) was killed on 9 April 1917 aged 18 years and is buried at Feuchy Chapel British Cemetery. Another brother, 2nd Lieutenant Gerald Hugh Kyrle Money, 18th Durham Light Infantry was killed in action on 27 July 1916 aged 19 years and is buried in St. Vaast Post Military Cemetery.

Lieutenant Samuel Sanford Forsyth, MiD, Royal Field Artillery died on 25 September 1915. His brother, Lieutenant-Colonel Cusack Grant Forsyth, DSO, Chevalier of the Legion of Honour, 2nd Northumberland Fusiliers attached 6th Yorkshires died on 14 September 1916 and is buried in Blighty Valley Cemetery. He was awarded the Distinguished Service Order in the January 1916 New Years Honours List. Another brother, Lieutenant and Adjutant John C. Forsyth, 23rd Brigade, Royal Field Artillery died on 22 September 1914 and is commemorated by a Special Memorial in Braine Communal Cemetery. Captain and Brevet Major Frederick Richard Gerard Forsyth, Seaforth Highlanders attached Royal Engineers, MC, twice MID survived the war while another brother had died in 1909.

Private Ernest Arthur Griffin, 3rd Royal Fusiliers died on 3 May 1915 aged 18 years. His brother, Private Archibald G Griffin, 13th Middlesex died on 26 August 1917 aged 29 years and is commemorated on the Tyne Cot Memorial. Another brother, Private Frank H Griffin, 1/8th Middlesex died on 17 September 1916 aged 19 years and is commemorated on the Thiepval Memorial. The only three sons in the family and all commemorated on memorials.

Rifleman Frederick George Collar, 2/6th (City of London Rifles) Londons died on 7 September 1917 aged 20 years and is commemorated here. Normally, a man who died after 15 August 1917 would be commemorated on the Tyne Cot Memorial. But Frederick George Collar seems to be one of the exceptions alluded to on the CWGC website, but I have been unable to find why. There are 21 other members of his Battalion commemorated on the Tyne Cot Memorial all of whom died in October and November 1917. His brother, Private Ernest Edward Collar, 7th East Surreys died at home of wounds received in action on 11 November 1915 aged 24 years and is buried in Hanwell (Kensington And Chelsea) Cemetery. Another brother, Private Frank Archibald Collar, 1st Queen's Own (Royal West Kents) died on 26 October 1917 aged 37 years and is commemorated on Tyne Cot Memorial.

Lance Corporal John Fraser, 1/9th Argyll and Sutherland Highlanders died on 10 May 1915 aged 25 years. His brother, buried in Woods Cemetery, is Private Joseph Fraser, 2nd Canadian Infantry, who died on 26 April 1916 aged 19 years. He was from the USA and one of many from that country who joined the forces of other countries to take part in the war before America joined in 1917. He enlisted in January 1915. The Germans shelled his Battalion's position, blew a mine under the line and launched an attack on 26 April 1916. Another brother, Lance Corporal George Fraser, 1st Canadian Infantry was killed on 15 June 1915 aged 25 years and is commemorated on the Vimy Memorial.

Private Thomas Dunnett, 1st Canadian Mounted Rifles died on 5 June 1916 aged 29 years. Private Daniel Dunnett, 1/5th Seaforth Highlanders died on 27 March 1916 aged 16 years and is buried in Maroeuil British Cemetery. Another brother, Private William Dunnett, 1/5th Seaforth Highlanders died on 15 June 1915 aged 19 years and is commemorated on the Le Touret Memorial.

2nd Lieutenant Geoffrey Phillip Joseph Snead-Cox, 1st Royal Welsh Fusiliers died when shot through the head on 20 October 1914 aged 19 years. His brother, 2nd Lieutenant Richard Mary Snead-Cox, 1st South Staffordshires died on 28 October 1914 and is named on the Le Touret Memorial. He was killed while leading his men in an attack near Neuve-Chapelle when shot through the heart. Another brother, Midshipman Herbert Arthur Snead-Cox, HMS Indefatigable, Royal Navy died in the Battle of Jutland on 31 May 1916 aged 16 years and is commemorated on the Plymouth Naval Memorial.

Captain Edward Wilberforce Leather, 3rd Yorkshires attached 2nd King's Own Yorkshire Light Infantry died on 18 April 1915 aged 35 years. His brother, Lieutenant Christopher Leather, 3rd attached 1st Northumberland Fusiliers died between 25 and 27 October 1914 aged 31 years and is commemorated on the Le Touret Memorial. Another brother, Major Ernest Arthur Leather, 15th attached 27th (Tyneside Irish) Northumberland Fusiliers died on 10 February 1916 and is buried in Rue-David Military Cemetery.

Captain Julian Silver Strickland Dunlop, MiD, 1st South Staffordshires died on 24 October 1914 aged 38 years. He was commissioned in 1895 and served as ADC to Sir Frederick Fryer, Lieutenant Governor of Burma. His brother, Captain Frederick Cleave Strickland Dunlop, 1st Manchesters, was killed by a sniper on 8 November 1914 aged 36 years and is buried in Royal Irish Rifles Graveyard. Another brother, 2nd Lieutenant Kenneth Strickland Dunlop, 4th attached 1st South Staffordshires was killed on 26 September 1915 aged 33 years and buried in Vermelles British Cemetery. Two other brothers served and survived the war.

Lance Serjeant Frederick Henry Mills, 2nd Royal Scots Fusiliers died on 24 October 1914 aged 25 years. A brother, Private Bertie J H Mills, 2nd Hampshires died on 23 April 1917 and is buried in Monchy British Cemetery. Another brother, Private Wilfred Hiram Mills, died at Polderhoek Chateau near Geluveld on 26 October 1917 and is commemorated on the Tyne Cot Memorial.

Corporal Edwin Paget, 2nd Wiltshires was killed on 24 October 1914 aged 27 years. A brother, 2nd Lieutenant Augustus Paget, DFC, Royal Air Force died on 30 October 1918 aged 20 years and is buried in Fontanafredda Communal Cemetery, north of Venice in Italy. He was an 'ace' with six victories and received a posthumous Distinguished Flying Cross. Another brother, Lieutenant Colin Paget, 9th Royal Warwickshires died on 1 September 1918 and is commemorated on the Basra Memorial.

Private John Thomas Boyle, 2nd Worcestershires died on 8 November 1914 aged 26 years. His brother, Sapper Robert Hamilton Boyle, 1st Signal Company, Royal Engineers died on 11 September 1914 and is buried in Aldershot Military Cemetery. Another brother, Private Alec Boyle, 4th Worcestershires died on 4 June 1915 and is commemorated on the Helles Memorial.

Private Arthur de Boynton, 45th Australian Infantry died on 10 June 1917 aged 24 years. His brother, Private Francis de Boynton, 13th Australian Infantry died on 9 August 1916 aged 20 years and is commemorated on the Villers-Bretonneux Memorial. Another brother, Corporal William de Boynton, 26th Australian Infantry died on 29 July 1916 aged 29 years and is buried in Courcelette British Cemetery.

Lance Corporal Henry Glazebrook, 2nd East Yorkshires died on 5 February 1915. His brother, Serjeant William Henry Glazebrook, 110th Battery, 24th Brigade, Royal Field Artillery died on 30 September 1916 aged 21 years and is buried in Carnoy Military Cemetery. Another brother, Leading Signalman Alfred Glazebrook, Order of St. Stanislaus (Russia), HMS Heather, Royal Navy died on Christmas Day, 25 December 1920, of 'over-eating' aged 20 years. He is buried in Cobh Old Church Cemetery.

Private David Greenhalgh, 4th King's (Liverpools) died on 27 April 1915 aged 30 years. His brother, Lance Corporal Joseph Greenhalgh, 'D' Company, 11th King's (Liverpools) died on 11 August 1916 aged 26 years and is buried in Delville Wood Cemetery. Another brother, Private John William Greenhalgh, 1st King's (Liverpools) died three days earlier on 8 August 1916 aged 29 years and is commemorated on the Thiepval Memorial.

Private Douglas Buchanan Grossart, 10th King's (Liverpools) died on 16 June 1915 aged 19 years. His brother, Private Robert Reid Grossart, 'D' Company, 1/7th King's (Liverpools) died on 16 May 1915 aged 21 years and is commemorated on the Le Touret Memorial. Another brother, 2nd Lieutenant Archibald Campbell Grossart, 10th King's (Liverpools) attached 1/5th Seaforth Highlanders died on 23 July 1918 aged 20 years and is buried in St. Imoges Churchyard south of Reims. He enlisted in 1916 and was commissioned soon after.

Private John Smith Hiddleston, No. 4 (University) Company, Princess Patricia's Canadian Light Infantry (Eastern Ontario Regiment) was killed on 2 June 1916 aged 30 years. His brother, Private James Hiddleston, 5th/6th Cameronians (Scottish Rifles) died on 22 June 1918 aged 20 years and is buried in Nine Elms British Cemetery. Another brother, Private Robert Dalziel Hiddleston, Queen's Own (Royal West Kents) posted to 2/20th Londons died on 30 August 1918 aged 30 years and is buried in H.A.C. Cemetery, Ecoust-St. Mein.

Private Clifford Leonard, 1st Argyll and Sutherland Highlanders died on 11 May 1915. His brother, Private Francis Leonard, 2nd Highland Light Infantry died on 24 November 1916 aged 18 years and is buried in the Boulogne Eastern Cemetery. Another brother, Private William Leonard, 2nd Scots Guards died a week after Clifford on 18 May 1915 and is commemorated on the Le Touret Memorial.

Lance Serjeant Richard Morrissey, 2nd Leinsters died on 21 July 1917 aged 25 years. His brother, Drummer Matthew Morrissey, also 2nd Leinsters died on 5 April 1916 aged 28 years and is buried in Ration Farm (La Plus Douve) Annexe. Another brother, Serjeant William Morrissey, 1st Base Remount Depot, Army Service Corps died on the last day of the war, 11 November 1918 aged 34 years and is buried in St. Sever Cemetery Extension, Rouen.

Lance Corporal George William Orton, 1/4th Londons (Royal Fusiliers) died on 27 April 1915 aged 25 years. His brother, Private William Frederick Orton, 1st Queen's (Royal West Surreys) died on 8 June 1916 and is commemorated on the Loos Memorial. Another brother, Private Sidney Thelwell Orton, 1/4th Londons (Royal Fusiliers) died on 3 May 1915 aged 19 years and is buried in Wimereux Communal Cemetery.

Private John Forbes Philip, 15th Canadian Infantry died on 24 April 1915 aged 24 years. His brother, Corporal Charles Forbes Philip, 2nd Kite Balloon Section, Royal Air Force died on 1 November 1918 aged 22 years and is buried in Terlincthun British Cemetery. Another brother, Lance Corporal George Philip, 6th Gordon Highlanders died on 17 June 1915 aged 21 years and is buried in Longuenesse (St. Omer) Souvenir Cemetery. Their father and two other brothers served and survived the war.

Private Sidney George Porter, 53rd Australian Infantry died on 24 September 1917 aged 24 years. A brother, Private Albert Edward Porter, 3rd Australian Infantry died between 22-27 July 1916 and is commemorated on the Villers-Bretonneux Memorial. Another brother, Private William James Porter, 13th Australian Infantry died on 22 August 1915 aged 24 years and commemorated on the Lone Pine Memorial.

Private Edward Lawrence Sprunt, MiD, 1st Honourable Artillery Company died on 16 June 1915 aged 22 years. He had twice refused a commission to be at the Front, the second time on the eve of his death when he pleaded to be able to stay with his friends. A few days more and he would have returned to England for officer training. He was killed near Hooge chateau in the afternoon when he was helping to carry a wounded comrade on a stretcher, and had got within a few metres of the dressing station when he was killed by a shell. He was posthumously Mentioned in Despatches. His brother, 2nd Lieutenant Alexander Dalzell Sprunt, 4th (Special Reserve) Bedfordshires attached 2nd South Staffordshires died on 17 March 1915 aged 24 years and is buried in Lillers Communal Cemetery. Another brother, Lieutenant Gerald Harper Sprunt, 2nd Bedfordshires died on 15 October 1919 aged 21 years and is commemorated on the Hollybrook Memorial, Southampton. He went to France in March 1918, was severely wounded in August and died of his wounds.

Private Francis William Cooper Strong (served as Stewart), 2nd Wiltshires died on 29 July 1917 aged 29 years. His brother, musician and bandsmaster, Lieutenant R H Strong, 2nd East Surreys died on 12 March 1915 aged 29 years and is buried in Loker Churchyard. Another brother, Private Benjamin Clarence Strong, 9th East Surreys died on 17 May 1918 aged 22 years and is buried in Annois Communal Cemetery.

Lance Corporal William Tomlinson, 9th York and Lancasters died on 9 June 1917 aged 32 years. His brother, Private John Robert Tomlinson, 5th Yorkshires died on 24 October 1916 aged 25 years and is commemorated on the Thiepval Memorial. Another brother, Private Thomas Bielby Tomlinson, 1/4th East Yorkshires died on 16 November 1916 aged 18 years and is also commemorated on the Thiepval Memorial.

Private Edward Webster Wood, 1st Scots Guards died on 11 November 1914 aged 34 years. His brother, Private Stanley Wood, 1st Scots Guards died on 14 October 1915 aged 21 years and is buried in St. Sever Cemetery, Rouen. Another brother, Private William Wood, 19th King's (Liverpools) died on 1 July 1916 aged 28 years and is buried in Cerisy-Gailly Military Cemetery.

In addition to the thirty families above, Private Joseph Ingate, 'B' Company, 8th South Staffordshires died on 11 February 1916 aged 28 years. A brother, Private Frederick Ingate, 11th Essex died on 20 November 1917 aged 23 years and is buried in Fifteen Ravine British Cemetery. Another brother died in WW2, Seaman Hector Ingate, HMS Rawalpindi, Royal Naval Reserve, on 23 November 1939 aged 39 years and is commemorated on the Chatham Naval Memorial. Rawalpindi was a P&O liner converted at the start of the war into an armed merchant cruiser with ten obsolete guns. She accidentally encountered two of Germany's most powerful cruisers Scharnhorst and Gneisenau north of the Faroes and was sunk in 40 minutes without causing any serious damage to the German vessels. The Captain of the Rawalpindi was father of the broadcaster Ludovic Kennedy.

While there are many families with two sons commemorated upon the Memorial, 148 that I can identify, some families have more than one son commemorated here as well as other members of the family included in CWGC records buried or commemorated somewhere else.

Brothers Privates George Ross Seabrook, aged 25 years and Theo Leslie Seabrook aged 24 years, both 17th Australian Infantry and both killed near Polygon Wood on 20 September 1917 are also both commemorated here. Their brother, 2nd Lieutenant William Keith Seabrook, 17th Australian Infantry, died of wounds, received the day before near Polygon Wood, in No. 10 Casualty Clearing Station on 21 September 1917 aged 21 years and is buried in Lijssenthoek Cemetery. William carried a photo of his mother in his breast pocket which was returned to the relatives after his death. There was a bullet hole in it. Their parents lost three sons in less than 48 hours in what was their first action.

Private Gilbert Forbes, 'B' Company, 4th Gordon Highlanders died on 25 September 1915 aged 19 years and Private Walter G Forbes, 4th Canadian Mounted Rifles (Central Ontario Regt.) killed in action on 2 June 1916 aged 23 years. Another brother also died of war wounds on service. Lance Corporal John Forbes, 12th Black Watch (Royal Highlanders) transferred to 5th Company Labour Corps and died on 10 June 1917 aged 23 years. He is buried in Aberdeen (Grove) Cemetery.

Lieutenant Walter Scott Stuart Lyon, 9th Royal Scots died on 8 May 1915 aged 28 years. He volunteered in 1914 and was sent to Belgium in February 1915. In his time at the Front he wrote several poems becoming one of the war poets. He was killed by German shelling while in dugouts in Potijze Wood. A collection of his poems was published in 1916. His brother, Lieutenant Charles James Lyon, MiD, 1st Royal Scots Fusiliers, killed on 13 November 1914 aged 24 years is also commemorated on this Memorial. Another brother, Lieutenant Alexander Patrick Francis Lyon, MiD, 1st Gordon Highlanders died on 27 August 1914 aged 26 years and is buried in Bertry Communal Cemetery. This family lost three sons in the first ten months of the war.

Additionally, there are three families of whom father and son are both recorded on the Menin Gate. Company Quartermaster Serjeant Charles Monro Devis, 2nd South African Infantry died on 20 April 1918 aged 36 years and Private John Albert Devis, 1st Wiltshires died 24 September 1915 aged 21 years. Private R J Pritchard aged 19 years and Serjeant William Pritchard aged 42 years both 3rd Monmouthshires and both died on 2 May 1915. Private James Merricks, 2nd East Surreys died on 11 February 1915 aged 18 years and Private James Merricks, 11th Queen's (Royal West Surreys) died on 7 June 1917 aged 41 years.

Naturally, the peerage and nobility, given their position within the army in 1914, are well represented here.

Lieutenant Sir Gilchrist Nevill Ogilvy, 1st Scots Guards killed on 29 October 1914 aged 22 years. He was the 11th Baronet of Inverquharity.

Captain Lord Hugh William Grosvenor, 1st Life Guards who died on 30 October 1914 aged 30 years was son of the 1st Duke of Westminster by his second marriage. He was one of the Life Guards surrounded at Zandvoorde who fought to the last man.

Captain Lord Arthur John Hamilton, 1st Irish Guards died on 6 November 1914 aged 30 years. He was son of the 2nd Duke of Abercorn and was Deputy Master of the Household of King George V from 1913. He rejoined his unit at the start of the war and was killed with many others from his Battalion.

Lieutenant Lord Ian Basil Gawen Temple Hamilton-Temple-Blackwood, 2nd Grenadier Guards died on 4 July 1917 aged 47 years. He was third son of the 1st Marquess of Dufferin and Ava and was a lawyer, spending time in South Africa, a civil servant and book illustrator, creating many of the images for works by Hilaire Belloc. He was commissioned at the start of the war joining the Intelligence Corps and went to the Front attached to the 9th Lancers. He served as a 'galloper' at the Battle of Mons and was wounded at Messines on 31 October 1914 being the only officer of the Regiment, beside Francis Grenfell, not to be captured by the Germans. While he recovered he continued with the Intelligence Corps, and was Private Secretary to the Lord Lieutenant of Ireland in 1916 until he joined the Grenadier Guards. Blackwood was killed in action in a night raid at Boezinge.

Captain Charles Edward De La Pasture, MiD, 1st Scots Guards was killed on 29 October 1914 aged 35 years. He was the eldest son of the Marquis de la Pasture who died, it is believed from shock and a broken heart, within three months. He was commissioned in 1900 joining the Scots Guards in South Africa where he saw active service. From 1907-10 he was ADC to General 'Sir' Frederick Forestier Walker at Gibraltar. He was killed near Zonnebeke and posthumously Mentioned in Despatches.

2nd Lieutenant The Honourable Francis 'Pickles' Lambton, Royal Horse Guards died on 30 October 1914 aged 43 years. He was son of the 2nd Earl of Durham. His mother died three days after his birth. He joined the regiment at the start of the war. A German shell burst on the parapet of the trench in which he and his men were waiting, about 100m from the advancing Germans. They were buried in earth, but he extricated himself, only to be shot through the head as he rose to his feet. A nephew, Lieutenant Geoffrey Lambton, 2nd Coldstream Guards was killed on 1 September 1914 aged 26 years and is buried in Guards Grave, Villers Cotterets Forest. Another nephew, Flying Officer Air Gunner John Lambton, No. 202 Squadron, Royal

Air Force Volunteer Reserve died on 11 August 1941 and is buried in Gibraltar (North Front) Cemetery.

Lieutenant The Honourable Gerald Ernest Francis Ward, MVO, 1st Life Guards died at Zandvoorde on 30 October 1914 aged 36 years. He was the son of the 1st Earl of Dudley. He played cricket for Gloucestershire, the MCC and the Household Brigade. He was commissioned into the Gloucestershires before transferring to the Life Guards and seeing service in the South African Wars. He was made a Member of the Victorian Order having served as ADC to the Lord Lieutenant of Ireland.

Captain The Honourable Archibald Rodney Hewitt, DSO, twice MiD, 2nd East Surreys died on 25 April 1915 aged 32 years. He was the second son of the 6th Viscount Lifford. He was commissioned in 1902 and by 1914 was Captain and Adjutant to the Battalion in Ireland having served in India with the 1st Battalion. He was wounded on the Marne in 1914 and was awarded the Distinguished Service Order in November 1914, one of the first set of awards of the war 'For moving out of the trenches at Le Cateau, under heavy shell fire, and bringing back men who were dribbling to the rear.' He was killed leading a counter-attack.

2nd Lieutenant The Honourable Vere Douglas Boscawen, 1st Coldstream Guards was killed on 29 October 1914 aged 24 years. He was the son of Major General Evelyn Edward Thomas Boscawen, 7th Viscount Falmouth, KCVO, CB. His brother, Major The Honourable George Edward Boscawen, DSO, 116th Battery, Royal Field Artillery died of wounds on 7 June 1918 aged 29 years and is buried in La Ville-aux-Bois British Cemetery. A nephew, Lieutenant The Honourable Evelyn Frederick Vere Boscawen, 2nd Coldstream Guards died on 20 May 1940 aged 23 years and is buried in Pecq Communal Cemetery 25km to the south-east.

Captain The Honourable Colwyn Erasmus Arnold Philipps, MiD, Royal Horse Guards died on 13 May 1915 aged 26 years. He was the eldest son of the Right Honourable the 1st Viscount St. Davids. His mother, Leonora 'Nora' Gerstenberg, was a political activist and campaigner for women's rights. A book of his poetry and prose, 'In Memoriam', was published posthumously several months after his death. He was commissioned in 1908 and served briefly with the Scots Guards returning to the Royal Horse Guards before the war. He died in a counter-attack, having entered the German line and killed several Germans before being shot at close range and killed. His brother, Captain The Honourable Roland Erasmus Philipps, MC, 9th Royal Fusiliers died on 7 July 1916 aged 26 years and is buried in Aveluy Communal Cemetery Extension.

Major The Honourable Hugh Joseph Fraser, MVO, MiD, 2nd Scots Guards died on 28 October 1914 aged 40 years. He was son of the 13th Baron Lovat. He was commissioned in 1894 and became a Major in 1907. He served in the South African Wars where he was Mentioned in Despatches. He served as Adjutant to the Lovat's Scouts from 1903-1907 and was made a Member of the Victorian Order in 1912 while he served as the ADC to the Viceroy of India from 1910-1913. His brother, the 15th Baron, is best known for being in command of a unit that relieved the men at Pegasus Bridge on D-Day. He arrived with his piper, Piper Malin, playing them in up the road to the bridge and apologised to the local commander for being late arriving one hour after the planned relief at midday.

Major The Honourable Leslie d'Henin Hamilton, MVO, MiD, 1st Coldstream Guards was killed on 29 October 1914. He was son of the 1st Baron Hamilton of Dalzell and father of the 3rd Baron. He was commissioned in 1893, served in the South African War and became a Major in 1910. He was killed near Geluveld as the Germans took his trenches.

Lieutenant The Honourable Alan George Sholto Douglas-Pennant, 1st Grenadier Guards was killed on 29 October 1914 aged 24 years. His father was the 3rd Baron Penrhyn. He received his commission in 1910, and served as ADC to the Governor of Bengal in 1914. Two of his uncles were killed in the war. Captain the Honourable George Henry Douglas-Pennant, MiD, 1st Grenadier Guards was killed at Neuve Chapelle on 11 March 1915 and is commemorated on the Le Touret Memorial, and Lieutenant the Honourable Charles D. Douglas-Pennant, 1st Coldstream Guards was killed on the same day as Alan and is buried in Perth (China Wall) Cemetery. The 1st Grenadier Guards were with 1st Coldstream Guards east of Geluveld on 29 October 1914, so the two men died within a short distance of each other.

Lieutenant William Bernard Webster Lawson, 1st Scots Guards died on 22 October 1914 aged 21 years. He was the son of Colonel The Honorable William Webster Levy-Lawson, DSO, the 3rd Baron Burnham.

Captain The Honourable Henry Lyndhurst Bruce, 3rd attached 2nd Royal Scots died on 14 December 1914 aged 33 years. He was the eldest son of the 2nd Baron Aberdare of Duffryn. He served for many years in the 3rd (Militia) Hampshires and subsequently in the Royal Scots. In 1913 and 1914 he spent several months at the Royal Scots regimental depot training recruits and instructing in musketry. He was killed near Wijtschate while leading an attack in which the first line of trenches had been taken and, as he was climbing out of the captured position to lead the assault on the second line, he fell, shot in the head.

Lieutenant The Honourable William Alfred Morton Eden, 4th King's Royal Rifle Corps died on 3 March 1915 aged 22 years. He was the eldest son of the 5th Baron Auckland. He was commissioned in 1913 and promoted a year later while serving in India. They arrived in France on 21 December 1914. He was killed in a raid to capture a German trench. The raiding party of two Companies were held up by a barricade. Eden was last seen on the German side of the barricade running at the Germans. He was the 50th heir to a peerage killed in the war to that date.

2nd Lieutenant The Honourable Simon Fraser, 3rd attached 2nd Gordon Highlanders died on 29 October 1914 aged 26 years. He was son of the 18th Baron Saltoun. He was killed, with a Lance Corporal, by a shell while waiting to move forward.

2nd Lieutenant The Honourable Gerald William 'Billy' Grenfell, 8th Rifle Brigade died on 30 July 1915 aged 25 years. He was son of the 1st Baron Desborough. His brother, Captain Julian Grenfell, DSO, Royal Dragoons was wounded on 13 May 1915, died on 26 May 1915 and is buried in Boulogne East Cemetery. His cousin, Captain Francis Octavius Grenfell, VC, is buried in Vlamertinghe Military Cemetery. The story of the Grenfell family is told in more depth there.

Lieutenant The Honourable Godfrey Evan Hugh MacDonald, 1st Scots Guards died on 2 November 1914 aged 35 years. He was the eldest surviving son of the 6th Baron MacDonald of Slate and his son became the 7th Baron. He was commissioned in 1902 and saw service in South Africa. In 1906 he was appointed to the Reserve of Officers, and rejoined his old regiment in October 1914, after it had suffered serious losses. He was killed in a trench as he was overwhelmed by Germans. A younger brother, Captain The Honourable Ronald Ian MacDonald, Legion d'Honneur, 3rd Cameron Highlanders attached as Staff, Infantry Base Depot, Cherbourg, died of pneumonia on 17 October 1918 aged 34 years and is buried in Tourlaville Communal Cemetery And Extension. His younger brother, 2nd Lieutenant The Honourable Archibald Ronald Armadale Bosville-Macdonald, 9th Lancers was killed in the South African War in 1901. His elder brother, Sub Lieutenant The Honourable Somerled Godfrey James Bosville-MacDonald, Royal Naval Volunteer Reserve died on 11 April 1913.

Captain The Honourable Lyon George H. Lyon Playfair, 69th Battery, 31st Brigade, Royal Field Artillery died on 20 April 1915 aged 26 years. He was the only son of Brigadier General George James Playfair, 2nd Baron Playfair, CVO, TD.

2nd Lieutenant The Honourable Piers St. Aubyn, 2nd King's Royal Rifle Corps died on 31 October 1914 aged 43 years. He was the fifth son of the 1st Baron Levan. He served in Thorneycroft's Horse in South Africa 1901 and was killed near Geluveld. His elder brother, Major The Honourable Edward Stuart St. Aubyn, General Staff, Staff Captain formerly King's Royal Rifle Corps was killed in the SS Persia when she sank, torpedoed by U38 near Crete, on 30 December 1915 aged 57 years and is commemorated on the Chatby Memorial.

Captain The Honourable Francis George Godfrey Willoughby, 9th Rifle Brigade died on 9 August 1915 aged 25 years. He was son of the 10th Baron Middleton. His brother, Commander Henry Ernest Digby Hugh Willoughby, HMS Indefatigable, Royal Navy was killed at the Battle of Jutland on 31 May 1916 aged 33 years and is commemorated on the Plymouth Naval Memorial.

Captain Gordon Hargreaves Brown, 1st Coldstream Guards was killed on 29 October 1914 aged 34 years. His father was a Liberal MP and made a Baronet. His son Captain Sir John Hargreaves Pigott-Brown, 2nd Coldstream Guards inherited the title but was killed in North Africa on Christmas Day 1942 and is commemorated on the Medjez-el-Bab Memorial.

Lieutenant Frederic William Joseph Miller, 2nd Grenadier Guards died on 23 October 1914 aged 22 years. He was the son of Sir William Frederic Miller, the 5th Baronet and his great uncle Lieutenant Colonel William Miller died of wounds at the Battle of Quatre Bras on 17 July 1815.

Captain Alan Arthur Fowler, 'B' Company, 2nd Cameron Highlanders died on 28 April 1915 aged 28 years. He was the youngest son of the 2nd Baronet Fowler of Braemore and his grandfather was Engineer-in-Chief on the Forth Bridge. He was killed while commanding his Company in defence of the front-line at Hill 60. His only brother and 3rd Baronet, Sir Captain & Adjutant John Edward Fowler, 2nd attached 1/4th Seaforth Highlanders was killed on 22 June 1915 aged 31 years. His remains were repatriated so that he is buried in a private cemetery, the Foich Burial Ground, on his family's estate in Scotland

Lieutenant Granville Keith Falconer Smith, 1st Coldstream Guards was killed on 29 October 1914 aged 28 years. He was the nephew of the Earl of Kintore and son-in-law of the 4th Earl of Leitrim.

Captain Charles Almeric John Cholmondeley, 2nd Borders died on 28 October 1914 aged 34 years. He was grandson of the 3rd Marquess of Cholmondeley.

Lieutenant Clement Cottrell-Dormer, 2nd Scots Guards died on 26 October 1914 aged 23 years. His brother, Lieutenant Charles Melville Cottrell-Dormer, DSO, No. 3 Company, 3rd Coldstream Guards was killed on 8 February 1915 aged 22 years and is buried in Bethune Town Cemetery. They are great grandsons of the 8th Earl of Leven and the 7th Earl of Melville and ancestors of 'Sir' Michael Mormer Lord Mayor of London in 1541 and James Dormer who served under Marlborough at Blenheim.

Captain Thomas Henry Rivers Bulkeley, CMG, MVO, 2nd Scots Guards died on 22 October 1914. He was commissioned in 1893 and gained several promotions but in 1899 he transferred to the Scots Guards returning to 2nd Lieutenant. He served in the South African Wars, was wounded in 1899 and three times Mentioned in Despatches. By December 1904 he was again a Captain and was seconded to serve as ADC to the Viceroy of India, a position he held until 1907 before moving to be ADC to Field Marshall His Royal Highness the Duke of Connaught and Strathern, Inspector General of the Forces and High Commissioner of the Mediterranean. In October 1909 he was appointed as Equerry to the Duke, who had been appointed as Governor General and Commander in Chief in Canada, a post he held until the start of the war. He was made a Member of the Royal Victorian Order in 1909 and in 1911 a Companion of the Order of St. Michael and St. George. He resigned and re-joined his Battalion in September 1914. He was killed by shellfire while leading men forward from Polygon Wood to the Menin Road.

Lieutenant Colonel William Stirling Bannatyne, MiD, 1st King's (Liverpools) died on 24 October 1914 aged 45 years He was commissioned in 1888 and took command of the Battalion in 1912 seeing service in South Africa and being Mentioned in Despatches. He was shot through the heart from a house in Westhoek which his Battalion had received orders to clear.

Lieutenant Colonel Arthur Percival Dearman Birchall, Royal Fusiliers attached 4th Canadian Infantry (Central Ontario Regiment) died on 23 April 1915 aged 38 years. While urging his men forward, carrying only a swagger stick, during the advance against Mauser Ridge on 23 April, Birchall was struck down by a hail of bullets. He was selected prior to the war for work on the Instructional Staff in Canada. His Distinguished Service Order was awarded for service at Pozieres on 23 July 1916. The citation reads 'For conspicuous gallantry and devotion to duty in action. He led forward his Company with great dash under heavy fire, entered the enemy's trenches, and, though dangerously wounded, refused any assistance till assured that the position won was firmly held.' He is recorded twice on the CWGC website, though not in the hard copy register, the website giving one entry with his full name, the other just as A P Birchall, giving different dates of death. It is claimed in some sources that these are brothers. His 'real' brother, Captain Edward Vivian Dearman Birchall, DSO, Bucks Battalion, Oxfordshire and Buckinghamshire Light Infantry died of wounds on 10 August 1916 aged 32 years and is buried in Etaples Military Cemetery.

Lieutenant Colonel Hugh Edward Richard Boxer, DSO, twice MiD, commanding 1st Lincolnshires died on 16 June 1915 aged 44 years leading his men in an advance. From a family of service in both the army and navy, Boxer was commissioned in 1892, started the war as a Major and became a Lieutenant Colonel three weeks before his death. He took part in the Nile Expedition in 1898 where he was wounded and Mentioned in Despatches, served in Malta, Egypt, India, Gibraltar and Bermuda. He was Mentioned in Despatches again in June 1915 and awarded the Distinguished Service Order at the same time.

Lieutenant Colonel Charles Slingsby Chaplin, 9th King's Royal Rifle Corps died on 30 July 1915 aged 52 years. He was commissioned in 1885, served on the Chitral Expedition and in the South African Wars, becoming a Lieutenant Colonel in 1908 and retiring in 1912. He came back to serve in August 1914 taking command of this Battalion. He was killed after a twelve hour fight, when he led his men in capturing a trench at Hooge, after which he was shot through the head in the mid-afternoon. He was buried in the chateau grounds but the grave has been lost.

Lieutenant Colonel Hugh Trevor Crispin, MiD, commanding 2nd Royal Sussex was killed on 30 October 1914 aged 46 years. He saw action in the South African Wars, during his 22 years with the Northumberland Fusiliers, and was recommended for a Victoria Cross in December 1899 but surprisingly received no award at all. He took command of the 2nd Royal Sussex in 1910, retired and returned to take command a few days before his death. He was killed with 42 of his men of which only two have identified graves.

Lieutenant Colonel Edmund Deacon, Essex Yeomanry formerly 1st (King's) Dragoon Guards died on 13 May 1915 aged 43 years. Major Deacon joined 'B' Squadron of the Essex Imperial Yeomanry in 1902, after having served with the Kings' Dragoon Guards from 1892 and as Adjutant from 1897 to 1899. He joined the Essex Yeomanry and took command in February 1909. He arrived in France in November 1914 and was involved in action when he went missing, presumably shot and killed, during an attack on a German trench.

Lieutenant Colonel Malcolm Charles Andrew Green, 2nd South Lancashires died on 17 November 1914 aged 43 years. He started the war training Kitchener's New Army on Salisbury Plain. But the senior officers of the Battalion were casualties of the attack on Hooge Chateau on 31 October so he was sent to the Front arriving four days before his death. He was commissioned in 1891 and saw service in India and the South African Wars. His grandfather commanded HMS Collingwood at the Battle of Trafalgar.

Lieutenant Colonel Archibald Walter Hay, 52nd Canadian Infantry died on 3 June 1916 aged 42 years. He was a pre-war militia soldier and took command of the Battalion in November 1914 taking it to France in February 1916. A few months later, Hay went missing while on a reconnaissance mission. Hay was a militia officer with the 8th Royal Rifles and a noted marksman. During the 1912 Governor General's prize shooting match organized by the Dominion Rifle association, Hay scored 21 consecutive bullseyes.

Lieutenant Colonel Francis Edward Bradshaw Isherwood, twice MiD, 2nd attached and commanding 1st York and Lancasters died on 9 May 1915 aged 45 years. He was commissioned in 1892 and served in the South African Wars where he was Mentioned in Despatches. He started the war as a Major in Ireland. He was again Mentioned in Despatches in February 1915 and soon after was promoted to Lieutenant-Colonel and given command of the 1st Battalion on 29 April 1915. On 8 May, having suffered losses in battles up to 7 May, and having nearly 500 reinforcements, he and his men were ordered to re-capture the trenches near Zonnebeke that they had held just days before. The attack lasted until 8.00pm but failed, the Battalion being reduced to 83 active men from 800. Isherwood was wounded in the attack and left in a trench to be taken prisoner by the Germans. He died in their hands but his grave has not been identified. There are claims that his name was originally planned to be on the Ploegsteert Memorial but his wife insisted it be recorded here where you can find it on the Addenda panel. It is surprising that this may have been considered as that would put his name on a Memorial that covers a different area. He is the father of the author, Christopher Isherwood, who is most widely known for having his book made in to the film 'Cabaret'.

Lieutenant Colonel Walter Latham Loring, twice MiD, commanding 2nd Royal Warwickshires died on 23 October 1914 aged 46 years. Commissioned in 1889, he served in Malta, India and the South African Wars, and took command of the Battalion in April 1914. In 1908 he was the first Adjutant to the Manchester University Officer Training Corps that was formed as part of the army reforms that created the Territorial Force. On 23 October his Battalion only just managed to escape a larger German force but Loring was wounded by shrapnel. He refused treatment and the next day his Battalion were sent back into action. Unable to wear a boot or bear weight on his wounded foot Loring chose to lead his men from horseback, but two were shot from under him and he was killed. He was twice subsequently Mentioned in Despatches. Within a year two brothers would be killed in the war, one on the anniversary of his death and all three brothers with no identified grave. Major Charles Buxton Loring, 37th Lancers (Baluch Horse) attached 34th Prince Albert Victor's Own Poona Horse died on 21 December 1914 aged 43 years and is commemorated on the Neuve-Chapelle Memorial. Captain William Loring, MiD, Scottish Horse died on 24 October 1915 and is commemorated on the Helles Memorial.

Lieutenant Colonel Arthur Loveband, CMG, 2nd Royal Dublin Fusiliers died on 25 May 1915. Commissioned in the early 1880's, he was Adjutant of the 3rd Battalion from 1896 until he moved to the 1st Battalion in South Africa in 1899. He returned to Ireland and started the war as a Major, but was promoted to command the 6th Battalion on 27 October 1914 and within days had been sent to the 2nd Battalion in France. He was with his Battalion in the front-line during the early gas attacks by the Germans when he was wounded in the hip at St. Juliaan. Soon back with his men, he was quick to warn them when he saw the indications that an attack was imminent. The Germans attacked at 4.30am on 25 May and the Fusiliers were soon in an isolated position but fought on until forced to pull back at the end of the day with just 22 fit men. Whilst speaking to officers outside his dugout, he was killed when a bullet struck him through the head.

Lieutenant Colonel Aylmer Richard Sancton Martin, commanding 2nd King's Own (Royal Lancasters) died on 9 May 1915 aged 44 years. He served in the South African Wars as a Captain. He was killed in a German attack near Frezenberg which reduced his unit to less than 100 men.

Lieutenant Colonel Redmond George Sylverius Moriarty, 2nd Royal Irish died on 24 May 1915. He was commissioned in 1889, seconded for service as Captain and Adjutant of the 1st Punjab Volunteer Rifle Corps in 1895 and returned as a Supernumerary Captain on half-pay on account of ill-health by 1903. He was fully active again later in the year and became a Major in 1908. He was promoted to Lieutenant Colonel in April 1915. He was elected a fellow of the Royal Geographic Society in November 1895 and used the surname of Crumpe from 1898 to 1903.

Lieutenant Colonel Frank Page, DSO & Bar, MiD, 1/1st Hertfordshires, was killed in action on 31 July 1917 aged 39 years. He had served as a Corporal in the South African Wars and, through his good service, was commissioned afterwards. In 1912 he became the youngest ever Mayor of Hertford and went to France with the Battalion in 1914. He was the Battalion's commanding officer from early in 1916 until his death. Lieutenant Colonel Page was not one to hide in the background and had several very close calls, including having his periscope shot away from his face by a sniper and his trench coat being torn from his body by shrapnel during one of the many assaults he insisted on leading from the front. Lieutenant Colonel Page was killed leading his men in the attack at St. Juliaan when the Battalion fought their way across the Steenbeek and through the village towards what is now the Canadian Memorial at Vancouver Corner. A Memorial erected in 2017 on the anniversary of the attack is now a marker of how far they progressed from a line near New Irish Farm Cemetery. The attack cost the Battalion over 500 casualties out of the 600 that attacked, most of whom have no identified grave. He was Mentioned in Despatches and awarded the Distinguished Service Order in June 1915 for services in the field. He was awarded a Bar in November 1916 'For conspicuous gallantry in action. He handled his Battalion in the attack with great courage and determination. Later he showed marked ability and judgment in consolidating his first objective, thereby repelling enemy attempts to counter-attack.'

Lieutenant Colonel Alexander Daniel Reid, DSO, MiD, Silver Medal of Italy, 7th Royal Inniskilling Fusiliers commanding 1st Royal Irish Rifles died on 31 July 1917 aged 35 years. He was a professional soldier and served with the Indian Army before migrating to Canada. He had commanded the Battalion for about three weeks before his death. He was awarded the Distinguished Service Order in the June 1917 Birthday Honours List.

Lieutenant Colonel Charles Lawson Robinson, TD, 1st Monmouthshires died on 8 May 1915 aged 45 years. He served in the South African Wars as a Major with 2nd Lancashire Fusiliers arriving as a replacement for the large number of casualties suffered by the Battalion at Spion Kop. Robinson had retired as an Honorary Colonel with the Special Reserve by the outbreak of the war, and was recalled to command the Monmouthshires. He was killed in a last desperate counter-attack by 84th Brigade to stop the German advance near Frezenberg. The determination of the attack, it is said, was such that the Germans thought it could only have been made by troops sure of speedy and strong support, not, as in fact was the case, by practically the last remaining troops between them and Ypres. The Germans dug in, and hence the Brigade's objective was achieved, though Robinson's Battalion lost all officers and almost all of their men. The few survivors, after assisting to dig trenches in the vicinity for the next two or three days, were ultimately withdrawn.

Lieutenant Colonel Alfred Ernest Shaw, 1st Canadian Mounted Rifles died on 3 June 1916 aged 35 years. Initially commissioned into the 3rd Dragoons, a militia unit, Shaw soon transferred to active duty with the Royal Northwest Mounted Police and later on with Strathcona's Horse. When the war began he raised and initially commanded the 6th Canadian Mounted Rifles, but, as the various units were being amalgamated overseas, Shaw was transferred over to the 1st Canadian Mounted Rifles. In the war diary he is listed as dying when, along with 80 other men, he tried to repulse the Germans who had taken the trenches to his right which had previously been occupied by the 4th Canadian Mounted Rifles. The 4th Canadian Mounted Rifles had lost this trench when a mine exploded under them. Shaw was last seen with Major Fred Palmer organising what remained of his Battalion to make a last stand.

Lieutenant Colonel George Hubert Shaw, VD, 4th East Yorkshires died on 24 April 1915 aged 50 years. He enlisted as a Private in 1883 and was soon commissioned becoming Honorary Lieutenant Colonel in 1904. He was killed when shot through the head by a sniper while leading two Companies into attack.

Lieutenant Colonel Ernest William Rokeby Stephenson, 3rd Middlesex died on 23 April 1915 aged 46 years. He was commissioned in 1884 and served as Adjutant from 1890-1894 taking command of the Battalion in 1912. When the war began he was in India from where the Battalion returned arriving in France in January 1915. He was killed leading his men into action, his last words being 'Die hard men, die hard' using the nickname of the regiment 'The Die-hards' which had been earned in the Peninsular Wars.

Major, Temporary Lieutenant Colonel John Murray Traill, twice MiD, 2nd Bedfordshires died on 30 October 1914 aged 49 years. He was commissioned into the Militia, joined the Bedfordshire Regiment in 1887 and served in the Isaza campaign of 1892. From 1896 to 1904 Traill served as Captain and Adjutant to the 1st (Volunteer) Battalion, Essex Regiment, becoming a Major in December 1906. He was the Battalion's second in command in South Africa in August 1914 and had been Mentioned in Despatches by the C-in-C for his handling of native uprisings in South Africa earlier that year. When the Battalion prepared for war in September 1914 the commanding officer was classed as medically unfit, so Traill took command. Traill was killed on his 49th birthday in the vicious hand to hand fighting east of Ypres, along with his second in command, and was Mentioned in Despatches for his gallantry during the battle.

Brevet Lieutenant-Colonel Charles Augustus Vivian, MiD, 15th Ludhiana Sikhs died on 27 April 1914 aged 41 years. He was commissioned in 1893 joining the Gordon Highlanders in India a year later where he served in the Chitral (1895), Malakand (1897) and Tirah Expeditions (1897-8). He became a Major in 1911 and Brevet Lieutenant-Colonel in February 1915 having arrived in France. He was wounded at the Battle of Neuve Chapelle but refused to leave the front-line for treatment until all his men were safe. He was killed leading a charge across open ground. There is a CWGC record from 1919 of his body being exhumed from a position next to Colonel Augustus 'Gussie' David Geddes just north of St. Jan and re-buried, again next to Geddes, in Ypres Reservoir Cemetery.

Major Alexander Steele, DSO, DCM, MiD, 11th Australian Infantry died on 7 October 1917 aged 29 years. He joined the Instructional Staff of the Australian Military Forces in 1910 teaching at the Royal Military College at the start of the war. He enlisted with the service number of '41'. He was soon made a Staff Sergeant-Major, placed in charge of the Machine Gun Section of the 9th Australian Infantry, and was one of the first ashore at Gallipoli on 25 April 1915. He was awarded the Distinguished Conduct Medal in the June 1915 Birthday Honours List for 'From 25th to 29th April 1915, during operations near Gaba Tepe, for distinguished conduct in manning and maintaining his machine gun, which he continued to work after the remainder of his section had been killed or wounded.' After a few days ashore he was commissioned, by February 1916 was a Captain and a Major in August in command of the 3rd Machine Gun Company. He was Mentioned in Despatches and received the Distinguished Service Order in the New Year Honours List in January 1917.

Honorary Captain De Witt Oscar Irwin, Canadian YMCA attached 10th Canadian Infantry died on 28 April 1915 aged 29 years. He was the only Canadian YMCA worker killed in combat during the war. He was unusual for a YMCA man in that he was relatively young. There was a small force of YMCA officers recruited to acCompany Canadian soldiers to Europe in order to minister to their spiritual, moral, and recreational needs. YMCA officers wore the uniform of a Canadian officer, but did not fight. Irwin was amongst the first to volunteer to go abroad yet he struggled with his role as a non-combatant. He increasingly became involved in military work, acCompanying patrols, spending more and more time in the front lines, training with the unit, and working towards a transfer into the Canadian army as an infantry officer. It was during this transitional period that Irwin was killed while leaving the trench to rescue a wounded soldier in no man's land. It was only because Irwin had initiated the process to transfer from the YMCA as a commissioned officer that he was allowed to join the attack on St. Juliaan which put him in harm's way and resulted in his death.

There are ten young men commemorated here that we know of, though there are probably more, who were aged 15 years when they died. Private Walter David Webb, 3rd Royal Fusiliers died on 26 April 1915. Private Henry Gerald Smith, 3rd Middlesex died on 24 April 1915. Private Albert Richard Ashley, 2nd East Surreys died on 27 April 1915. Private John James Averill, 1/5th North Staffordshires died on 5 August 1915. Private George Eccles Bulleid, 2nd Canadian Infantry died on 22 April 1915. Private Hector Mcdonald Cameron, 14th Canadian Infantry died on 21 April 1915. Private John I. Smith, 14th Canadian Infantry died on 7 November 1917. Private Joseph Edwards, 2nd King's Own Scottish Borderers died on 18 November 1914. Rifleman Alfred Henry Edgar Huxtable, 7th King's Royal Rifle Corps died on 6 August 1915. Private John Leonard Forsyth-Ingram, 2nd South African Infantry died at Messines Ridge on 11 April 1918.

There are a further 50 young men aged 16 years who are commemorated here. And there may be more of that age that have not been identified yet. I have include in the bibliography books that cover this topic in more detail than I have here.

Also of note with regards to age is Private George Fletcher, 1st Lincolnshires who died on 1 November 1914 and is the oldest known casualty commemorated here aged 60 years when he died. He had been in France since 22 October.

I also like the stories below from sportsmen, to politicians, those who will invent things and a few who are linked to well known individuals.

Lieutenant Colonel Edgar Roberts Mobbs, DSO, twice MiD, 7th Northamptonshires was killed on 31 July 1917 aged 37 years while attacking a machine gun post. He was an English Rugby Union international who played for, and captained, Northampton and England, playing nine times for his country and scoring England's first international try against Australia. He also played eleven matches for the Barbarians. After initially being turned down as too old to join the army, he raised his own 'sportsmans' Company of 250 sportsmen, also known as Mobbs' Own, for the Northamptonshire regiment. He was awarded the Distinguished Service Order in the January 1917 New Years Honours List having been wounded on three occasions between 1915 and the end of 1916. In 1921 the first Mobbs' Memorial Match was held between the East Midlands RFU and the Barbarians at Northampton's ground, Franklin's Gardens. The fixture continues to be played, on alternate years at Northampton and Bedford with either side facing the Army, to raise money for youth rugby in the area and the Army Benevolent Fund. The 100th anniversary of Mobb's death was marked with a match between Bedford and the Army on 28 March 2017.

Private Arthur James Wilson, 12th Royal Fusiliers died on 31 July 1917 aged 29 years. He was an international Rugby Union player who represented England in a solitary match, a victory against Ireland in 1909. He also competed in the London 1908 Olympics as part of the England Rugby Union team, made up of the Cornwall County side, which won the silver medal. Cornwall won the County Championship in the same year which was why they were chosen to represent England in the Olympics. However, the Cornish side over-indulged in the festivities of the capital and were unprepared to face Australia who beat them comprehensively. He was killed on the first day of Third Ypres in Shrewsbury Forest.

Another Rugby Union international killed on the first day of Third Ypres is Lieutenant James Young Milne-Henderson, MiD, 11th Highland Light Infantry killed on 31 July 1917 aged 26 years. He played one international for Scotland as scrum-half, a loss to England, in 1911. He was also an East of Scotland swimming champion. He was killed near Frezenberg possibly under fire from Pommern Castle and Hill 35. His brother, 2nd Lieutenant John Milne Milne-Henderson, No. 11 Squadron, Royal Flying Corps, formerly 4th Field Company, Royal Engineers was killed on 28 January 1918 aged 23 years and is commemorated on the Arras Flying Services Memorial.

2nd Lieutenant William "Billy" Purdon Geen, 9th King's Royal Rifle Corps was killed on 31 July 1915. He was a Rugby Union wing and centre, who represented Wales on three occasions from 1912-13, defeats against South Africa and England and a win over Ireland. He also played rugby for Oxford University, Newport, Monmouthshire and the Barbarians. He was last seen leading his men in hand-to-hand fighting as they advanced towards Hooge.

Captain Basil MaClear, twice MiD, 2nd Royal Dublin Fusiliers died on 24 May 1915. He was a Rugby Union international between 1905 and 1907. After being turned down by the English selectors, he was picked by Ireland and played internationally eleven times, including a match against South Africa in which he scored an 80m try, though his first match for Ireland was a victory over England. He played a record four times against the 1905 All Blacks – for Blackheath, Bedford, Munster, whom he captained, and for Ireland. He represented the Royal Military Academy Sandhurst at rugby, cricket, athletics and shooting, winning the Sword of Honour in 1900 before seeing service in the South African Wars where he was Mentioned in Despatches. He was posthumously Mentioned again in 1915. His brother, Lieutenant Colonel Percy Maclear, Royal Dublin Fusiliers commanding 2nd Nigeria Regiment, WAFF was killed on 30 August 1914 aged 38 years and is commemorated on the Lokoja Memorial in Nigeria. In 1908 Percy was awarded the Royal Humane Society's award for saving life in the River Nile at Khartoum. He was killed in a German counter-attack in northern Cameroon.

Private James 'Jimmy' Ross, 1/14th (London Scottish) Londons died on 31 October 1914 aged 34 years. He represented Scotland at Rugby Union winning five caps from 1901-03 and captained London Scottish in 1901-02 and 1904-05. He was killed in the first action by a Territorial Battalion when the London Scottish encountered the Germans at St. Eloi on the northern edge of the Messines Ridge. They suffered broken weapons, lack of ammunition and overwhelming numbers but held up the Germans long enough for the German attack to fail. His brother also played for Scotland.

Private James Simpson, 2nd Duke of Wellington's died on 11 November 1914. He was a member of the Bradford Northern Rugby League side having joined them in 1914 after returning from seven years military service in India. He never got to play as the war began. He was recalled to his Battalion and killed.

Three men who played for Oldham Rugby League side are also commemorated here. Sergeant John 'Jack' Scott, 21st Canadian Infantry died on 8 April 1917 aged 24 years. He was from the Liverpool Road in Irlam but was in Canada at the start of the war despite having a wife living near his parents. Private Adam Jardine, 10th Queen's Own (Royal West Kents) was killed on 31 July 1917. He made 67 appearance in 1903-4 and in 1907-8. Private Phillip Thomas, Yorkshire Hussars Yeomanry died on 25 May 1915 aged 31 years. He made 44 appearance from 1902-4.

Corporal Arthur Edward Ochse, 2nd South African Infantry, who died on 11 April 1918 aged 48 years was a pre-war international cricketer who, in 1888-89, played in the first two matches played by South Africa making his first-class debut in his country's first Test, which was played against England at Port Elizabeth, aged 19 years and one day. He made a total of sixteen runs in four innings for his country and played three times for Transvaal.

Lance Sergeant Leonard Cecil Leicester Sutton, 'C' Squadron, 4th Canadian Mounted Rifles was killed on 2 June 1916 aged 26 years. Whilst still at school he played cricket for Somerset, making his debut against Hampshire at Southampton in May 1909 and played for the county until 1912. He died of wounds caused by shrapnel near Zillebeke.

Captain Ronald Owen Lagden, 6th King's Royal Rifle Corps died on 3 March 1915 aged 26 years. He played 31 first-class cricket matches for Oxford University from 1910-12 and represented England at Rugby Union. He was capped once for England, in the final match of their 1911 Five Nations Championship campaign, a Calcutta Cup match against Scotland at Twickenham. Lagden, a number eight, kicked two conversions in the 13 to 8 win. His brother played cricket for Cambridge University and Surrey and was killed in an air crash in what is now Pakistan in 1944. His father had played for the MCC. He was among 300 of his Battalion killed in an attack.

Lieutenant William Stanley Yalland, 1st Gloucestershires died on 23 October 1914 aged 25 years. He was commissioned into the 3rd Leicestershires in 1910 transferring to the Gloucestershires two years later. He was made a Lieutenant in August 1914 having moved with the Battalion from Bordon Camp to France. Yalland was shot through the head and killed whilst defending his trench, along with many of his Platoon near Langemark. He was a keen sportsman playing rugby for Clifton RFC and cricket for Gloucestershire playing one match and scoring one run in the 1910 County Championship.

2nd Lieutenant Harold Edwin Hippisley, 1st Gloucestershires died on 23 October 1914. He played first-class cricket in seven matches for Somerset from 1909 to

1913. He was killed at Langemark when two Platoons held a trench against a large enemy attack, as all the officers and sixty percent of the men were killed.

2nd Lieutenant Harold Godfrey Bache, 10th Lancashire Fusiliers died on 16 February 1916 aged 26 years. He was an English cricketer playing twenty first-class matches between 1907 and 1910, seventeen for Worcestershire and three for Cambridge University. He was also a footballer, playing for Corinthians in 43 matches scoring 95 goals, and West Bromwich Albion. He also won an England Amateur cap.

Captain George Amelius Crawshay Sandeman, 3rd attached 1st Hampshires died on 26 April 1915 aged 32 years. He played cricket making six appearances for Hampshire from 1913-14 and one for the MCC in May 1914. He was killed in a surprise attack in the early misty morning near Zonnebeke.

Captain George King Molineux, 2nd Northumberland Fusiliers was killed in action on 5 May 1915 aged 28 years. He represented Oxford University four times and the Gentlemen of England twice at first class cricket in 1907-08. He had been ADC to the Viceroy of India when the war began but resigned to come back to fight. He was last seen wounded and unconscious in a trench being overrun by the Germans but could not be rescued.

Captain and Adjutant William Mackworth Parker, 8th Rifle Brigade died on 30 July 1915 aged 28 years. He made two first class cricket appearances, one for the MCC in 1913 and one for the Army against the Navy in 1914. He played for many other teams. He died in the actions related to the first use of flame throwers.

Lieutenant Edward Stone Phillips, 1st Monmouthshires died on 8 May 1915 near Frezenberg. He made ten first class cricket appearances for Cambridge University. He was also an English amateur golf champion. He was killed in an attack over open ground which destroyed the Battalion.

Captain Bernard Philip Nevile, 7th Lincolnshires died on 11 February 1916. He made six first class cricket appearances, one for Cambridge University, where he won a 'Blue' for golf but not for cricket, and five for Worcestershire in 1912-13. His brother, Lieutenant Hugh George Nevile, 2nd South Wales Borderers died on 21 August 1915 aged 36 years and is commemorated on the Helles Memorial.

Captain Hubert George Selwyn-Smith, 49th Australian Infantry died on 7 June 1917 aged 26 years. He played three first class cricket matches for Queensland from 1912-13. He enlisted and was commissioned while in Egypt. He refused a position on Staff so saw action at Pozieres in 1916 where he was wounded.

Major Eustace Frederick Rutter, MiD, 1st East Lancashires died on 13 May 1915 aged 44 years. He was commissioned in 1892 and saw service on the North West Frontier in India and in the South African Wars. He played cricket eight times for the 'Europeans' while in India. He was made a Major in December 1914 and Mentioned in Despatches.

Captain Geoffrey Charles Walter Dowling, 7th King's Royal Rifle Corps died on 30 July 1915. He was an Australian cricketer who played four matches for Sussex from 1911-1913. He was killed in the first use of flame throwers.

Major Eustace Crawley, twice MiD, 12th (Prince of Wales's Royal) Lancers died on 2 November 1914 aged 46 years. He played seventeen first class cricket matches for Cambridge University from 1887-1889. He also played for Worcestershire, the Army and the MCC. He was commissioned in 1889 serving in Africa through the 1890's for which he was Mentioned in Despatches. He served in the South African War and was Mentioned in Despatches. He served in India on Staff posts until returning to England. He was killed by a shell near Wijtschate.

Captain Hugh Montagu Butterworth, 9th Rifle Brigade killed on 25 September 1915 aged 29 years. He played three first class cricket matches in 1906, two for Oxford University gaining his 'Blue' and one for the MCC. He also achieved 'Blues' in hockey, rugby and rackets before moving with his family to New Zealand where he continued to do well at sports. He returned in 1915 and was killed after a few months. His cousin, Lieutenant George Sainton Kaye Butterworth, MC, MiD, 13th Durham Light Infantry, was killed in action on 5 August 1916 aged 31 years and is commemorated in the Thiepval Memorial. He was a renowned composer, and it is considered he may have become one of the best English composers had he lived.

Lieutenant Douglas 'Druce' Robert Brandt, 1st Rifle Brigade died on 6 July 1915. He played eight cricket matches for Oxford University from 1907-08. He was commissioned in 1911 but resigned in December 1913 only to get another commission at the start of the war. He arrived in France in May 1915 and was killed when shot through the head in a successful attack which captured the German position, one of the few casualties of the action.

Lieutenant Frederick Bisset Collins, 21st Australian Infantry died on 4 October 1917 aged 36 years. He made 36 first class cricket appearances for Victoria from 1899-1909 when he was forced to retire through injury. He enlisted into the 24th Australian Infantry and transferred to the 21st Battalion, where he received his commission, when he arrived in Belgium.

Captain Percy d'Aguilar Banks, MiD, Queen Victoria's Own Corps of Guides Infantry, (Lumsden's) Frontier Force, attached 57th Wilde's Rifles (Frontier Force) died on 26 April 1915 aged 39 years. He played first-class cricket for Somerset once in 1903 and six times in 1908. Captain Frank Miller Bingham, 5th King's Own (Royal Lancasters) died on 22 May 1915 aged 40 years. He played one first class cricket match for Derbyshire in 1896 scoring seventeen runs. He was first commissioned in the Royal Army Medical Corps in 1910 and unusually transferred soon after to be a line officer. He was killed on a reconnaissance mission after stopping to dig a man out of a collapsed trench. Captain Arnold Stearns Nesbitt, MiD, 3rd Worcestershires died on 7 November 1914 aged 35 years. He played one first class cricket match for Worcestershire in May 1914. He went straight from school to the army and was killed in a large German attack east of Ploegsteert Wood. Captain William Miles Kington, DSO, four times MiD, 1st Royal Welsh Fusiliers was killed on 20 October 1914 aged 38 years. He was commissioned in 1896 and saw action in the South African Wars where he was Mentioned in Despatches on four occasions and awarded the Distinguished Service Order. He then served with the South African Constabulary and Territorial Battalions during which he played one first class cricket match for the 'Europeans' in India which gives us a small insight into the Empire before WW1. He rejoined his regiment at the start of the war and was killed by shellfire. Another to play one match for the 'Europeans' in India, in 1899-1900, was Captain Ronald Stuart Gordon, MiD, 57th Wilde's Rifles (Frontier Force) killed in action on 31 October 1914 aged 37 years. He was commissioned in 1897 and joined the Indian Army a year later. He saw action in the Boxer Rebellion in 1900 and the North West Frontier Mohmand Expedition of 1908 for which he was Mentioned in Despatches. He was killed when shot through the head as he took a Platoon forward to cover the retreat of the rest of the Battalion. Rifleman John Thomas Gregory, 1st King's Royal Rifle Corps, died on 27 November 1914. He played one cricket match for Hampshire in 1913 and served on the staff at Trent Bridge. During the war he played cricket and football for various army units.

Captain Arthur Edward Jeune Collins, MiD, 5th Field Company, Royal Engineers died on 11 November 1914. In 1899, as a 13-year-old schoolboy, Collins scored the then highest ever recorded cricket score of 628 not out in less than seven hours during a junior school house cricket match between Clarke's House and North Town House at Clifton College. He was commissioned in 1904, served with the 2nd Sappers and Miners in India, where he had been born, and was mortally wounded when he was signaling for more men to protect the flank of his trench. His younger brother Lieutenant Herbert Collins, 24th Manchesters died of wounds on 11 February 1917 aged 27 years and is buried in Etaples Military Cemetery. His score was finally beaten in January 2016 by Pranav Dhanawade, a 15-year-old Indian boy who scored 1,009 not out from 327 balls for KC Gandhi School against Arya Gurukul School in Mumbai.

Captain Wilfred John Hutton Curwen, 6th attached 3rd Royal Fusiliers died on 9 May 1915 aged 32 years. He played in the Oxford University Football and Cricket teams gaining his 'Blue' in both sports. He also played for Surrey and the MCC at cricket. As a footballer he had 22 matches for Old Carthusians and it is claimed that in 1908 captained the English AFA v Bohemia but I can't find a record of the match or his involvement in the England amateur team. In 1900 he was commissioned into 2nd Volunteer Royal Fusiliers, retiring in 1905 and then joining the Territorial Force London Regiment. In August 1914 he was serving as ADC to the Governor-General of Australia. He returned to the Fusiliers in 1914 and was killed by heavy shellfire.

Private William Arthur Brewer, 'D' Company, 1st Wiltshires killed on 13 November 1914 aged 21 years. A pre-war footballer and territorial, he played for Chippenham Town where he was a prolific goal scorer before signing to Swindon Town in 1913. He made two first team appearances in the Swindon Southern League Championship winning team of 1913-14. He was killed by machine gun fire as he left his trench near Hooge.

Rifleman Horace Brian Brooker, 'A' Company, 1/9th (Queen Victoria's Rifles) Londons died on 21 April 1915 aged 25 years. It is believed that he represented the English AFA team three times on the continent in football but I can only find an 'A Brooker' playing for the amateur team. He was killed while helping to capture Hill 60 on 21 April 1915.

Private James Comrie, 1/7th Northumberland Fusiliers died on 9 August 1916 near Meteren. He was a Scottish professional footballer for Third Lanark (78 appearances and eighteen goals 1904-06), Reading (36 appearances and one goal 1906-07), Glossop North End (38 appearances and one goal 1907-08), Bradford City (48 appearances and three goals 1908-10), and Lincoln City (12 appearances and one goal 1910-11) finishing his career at Grantham Town and back in Scotland at Stenhousemuir. His nephew was a footballer in the English League playing for York City, Manchester City, Burnley and Crystal Palace in the 1930's.

Captain George Bertram Pollock-Hodsoll, 3rd Suffolks attached 1st Cheshires died on 9 November 1914 aged 39 years. He was a footballer who played for the Corinthians and Casuals touring with these teams both on the continent and in South Africa and captained the Army team. Of all the football clubs in the world, whether amateur or professional, Corinthians FC and Casuals FC lost more players to the war than any other. He was commissioned in 1902 and went with the Suffolks to France in October 1914 where he moved to the Cheshires. He supported the Unionist cause and National Service.

2nd Lieutenant Gerard Rupert Lawrence 'Twiggy' Anderson, MiD, 3rd attached 1st Cheshires was killed on 9 November 1914 aged 25 years. He was the Hurdling Champion of England. He won his Blue in Athletics at Oxford University and set the first official IAAF world record for 440 yard hurdles in 1910. Unfortunately for Anderson, the 400m hurdles was not on the Stockholm Olympic program in 1912, although having won the AAA 120 yard hurdles in 1910 and 1912, he was still favoured to win a medal in the high hurdles, but he fell in his semi-final. He enlisted in August 1914 and was commissioned on 16 October. He was wounded twice but stayed at the Front before the shot through the heart that killed him in a raid on German trenches near Hooge. He was Mentioned in Despatches for this action. 2nd Lieutenant Charles Reginald Fausset, 3rd attached 1st Royal Irish died on 2 May 1915 aged 36 years. He was the mile and quarter-mile athletics champion of Ireland. Lieutenant James Booker Brough Warren, 1st Borders died on 28 October 1914 aged 25 years. He was an international high hurdler.

Lieutenant Geoffrey Barron Taylor, 15th Canadian Infantry died on 24 April 1915 aged 25 years. He represented Canada in the 1908 London Olympics in the rowing eights and coxless fours winning the Bronze medal in both events. He was again in the eight for Canada at the 1912 Stockholm Olympics but did not win a medal. He joined the army in February 1915 so only saw a brief time at the Front. Lieutenant Gilchrist Stanley MacLagan, 3rd attached 1st Royal Warwickshires killed on 25 April 1915 aged 35 years. MacLagan, at cox, was one of six Old Etonians in the

Leander Olympic eight in the London 1908 Games which won the gold medal. While he was at Magdalen College, he coxed the Oxford boat for four years (1899-1902) and steered the Leander eight at Henley from 1899 to 1908, during which period he set the record of being the only man to be in the winning crew in the 'Grand Challenge Cup' six times.

Captain Ralph Chalmers, MiD, 2nd Suffolks died on 8 May 1915 aged 24 years. He competed in the Fencing individual epée event at the 1908 London Summer Olympics for Great Britain. He was son of the 1st Baron Chalmers. His brother, Lieutenant Robert Chalmers, MiD, 1/15th (Prince of Wales's Own Civil Service Rifles) Londons died from his wounds on 26 May 1915 aged 21 years and is buried in Chocques Military Cemetery.

Lieutenant Oswald Wetherald Grant, MC, 1st Canadian Infantry was killed by shellfire on 13 June 1916 aged 23 years. With his partner Lieutenant Hugh D'Alton Livingston, 116th Canadian Infantry, killed on 27 August 1918 and buried in Monchy British Cemetery, he won the Canadian Inter-Collegiate Tennis Championship in 1912.

2nd Lieutenant Clyde Bowman Pearce, 52nd Australian Infantry died on 10 June 1917 aged 29 years. He enlisted with the 10th Light Horse in May 1915 and served at Gallipoli from November, arriving on the same day as Lord Kitchener, though staying rather longer. He was commissioned in late 1916 before facing action at Bullecourt and Messines. As a Platoon officer he was leading a charge on the Germans when he was caught on wire and killed by machine-gun fire. He first came to sporting prominence in 1903, aged 15, playing off scratch in interclub golf matches and finishing 19th at the Australian Amateur Championship. From 1904 to 1910, his name was prominent in Australia's golfing circles. He reached four straight Amateur finals between 1906 and 1909, and claimed the Open/Amateur double in 1908 becoming the first Australian born winner of the Australian Golf Open.

Lieutenant William Dummer Powell Jarvis, 3rd Canadian Infantry died on 24 April 1915 aged 23 years. He was a member of the Governor General's Body Guard and was a noted yachtsman, rugby football player and amateur boxer. He was killed while retiring with his Platoon to another trench.

Lieutenant Cyril Aldin Smith, DSO, RN Division, attached HQ 6th Division, Royal Naval Volunteer Reserve died on 10 June 1916 aged 39 years. He started the war as an owner of a convoy of buses transporting troops to and from the Front. He managed to get himself a commission in the Royal Marines in September 1914 and attached to 6th Division HQ by September 1915. He experimented with bullet proof shields mounted on wheels like a small tank. The area in which he used this is near Buffs Road Cemetery, hence the road gained the name of 'Admiral's Road'. He also invented the Bangalore torpedo which was to prove vital on Omaha Beach on D-Day in WW2. He was awarded the Distinguished Service Order in April 1916 for proving the value of the shields and Bangalore Torpedo by utilising them in raids. He was reported missing in a raiding party that was surrounded by Germans on 9 June 1916.

Captain The Honourable Arthur Edward Bruce O'Neill, 2nd Life Guards was killed 6 November 1914 aged 38 years. He was a Unionist MP for Mid Antrim from January 1910 until his death and was the first Member of Parliament to be killed in the war. He was son of the 2nd Baron O'Neill of Shanes Castle, Antrim, Ireland. His son, the 3rd Baron O'Neill, Lieutenant Colonel Shane Edward Robert O'Neill was killed in the Second World War on 24 October 1944 aged 37 years with the North Irish Horse, Royal Armoured Corps and is buried in Coriano Ridge War Cemetery. Another son, Captain The Honourable Brian Arthur O'Neill, 1st Irish Guards died on 14 May 1940 and is commemorated on the Brookwood Memorial. His youngest son, Terence O'Neill (1914-90), was Prime Minister of Northern Ireland from 1963 until 1969.

Captain William Henry Dillon Bell, MiD, 1st King Edward's Horse died on 31 July 1917 aged 33 years, shot and killed by a sniper near Ferdinand Farm. The King Edward's Horse were to advance once second objectives had been achieved but dug in 150m west of the Steenbeek. Many of their horses had by this time been killed. He was a New Zealand MP, the first to go on active service in WWI and first served in the Samoa Expeditionary Force. He represented the Reform Party for Wellington Suburbs and Country from 1911 to 1914 when he gave up the seat to join the army. He was son of the first New Zealand born Prime Minister, Sir Francis Bell.

Lieutenant Francis Edward Robinson, 3rd attached 2nd South Staffordshires died on 27 October 1914 aged 19 years. He was the nephew of Sir Edward Carson the Irish Unionist Politician, barrister and judge who represented the Marquess of Queensberry in his libel case with Oscar Wilde and who defended George Archer-Shee in 1911, the case that inspired the play 'The Winslow Boy'. Ironically, Lieutenant George Archer-Shee, 3rd attached 1st South Staffordshires is commemorated on the Menin Gate as he was killed on 31 October 1914 aged 19 years. He was expelled as a naval cadet in 1908 for stealing a postal order. He was found innocent in a 1910 trial, was given £3000 in compensation, and joined the army in 1913.

Captain Walter Russell Russell, 2nd attached 1st Northamptonshires died on 23 October 1914 aged 33 years. He was the son of the late Captain Sir William Russell Russell former Minister for Defence and Colonial Secretary of New Zealand and leader of the opposition Independent Party from 1894-1901.

Captain Arthur George McCausland Burn, 2nd East Surreys attached 1st Gloucestershires was killed on 29 October 1914 aged 31 years. His great grandfather Lieutenant Colonel William Burn successfully held Delhi against Holkar in 1804-05. Lieutenant Francis Lennox Holmes, 1st South Staffordshires died on 23 October 1914 (though it may be 21 October) aged 27 years. He was killed having helped a machine gunner re-position his gun and bandaged a wounded man when he was shot in the head while taking aim at the Germans near Geluveld. His uncle served in the Crimean War and his grandfather at Waterloo.

2nd Lieutenant Arthur Oscar Hornung, 3rd attached 2nd Essex died on 6 July 1915. He was the nephew of Sir Arthur Conan Doyle, creator of Sherlock Holmes.

Lieutenant Aidan Chavasse, 17th King's (Liverpools) died on 4 July 1917 aged 26 years is the brother of the double Victoria Cross holder Noel Chavasse who is buried in Brandhoek New Military Cemetery.

UK – 40532  Aust – 6183  Can – 6928
S Afr – 560  BWI – 8  India – 412

## LOCATION

The simplest way to get to the Gate is to walk from the town square. Leave by the eastern exit diagonally opposite the Cloth Hall and tourist office and you can see the Memorial from the square.

# MENIN ROAD SOUTH MILITARY CEMETERY

### HISTORY

The cemetery was opened in January 1916 and remained in use until the summer of 1918. It was enlarged after the war with the concentration of 200 graves from the Menin Road North Cemetery and isolated locations in the battlefields nearby.

### INFORMATION

The Menin Road, one of the main routes to the front-line for the British during the war, ran from the centre of Ypres, along a route that now passes through the Menin Gate Memorial and out towards the front line to the east.

The 8th South Staffordshires and 9th East Surreys had begun this cemetery. It was always within the British lines though, during the German advance in April 1918, it came close to the front-line. By September 1918 the line south of here was just a series of posts held by the 29th Division as the trenches had been destroyed.

Buried here is 2nd Lieutenant (Acting Captain) Thomas Riversdale Colyer-Fergusson, VC, 2nd Northamptonshires killed in action on 31 July 1917. He was awarded the Victoria Cross for his actions near Bellewaerde before he was killed later in the day. In the attack by the 8th Division from Sanctuary Wood his Battalion could not keep to their plan encountering problems with the ground and the enemy wire. With a Sergeant and five men he continued the attack capturing enemy trenches and killing many Germans. Colyer-Fergusson then resisted a counter-attack capturing a German machine-gun. Later he attacked again with his Sergeant and captured a second machine-gun before being joined by his men who consolidated the position. Captain Colyer-Fergusson was killed soon after by a sniper. The citation reads 'For most conspicuous bravery, skilful leading and determination in attack. The tactical situation having developed contrary to expectation, it was not possible for his Company to adhere to the original plan of deployments, and owing to the difficulties of the ground and to enemy wire, Captain Colyer-Fergusson found himself with a Serjeant and five men only. He carried out the attack nevertheless, and succeeded in capturing the enemy trench and disposing of the garrison. His party was then threatened by a heavy counter-attack from the left front, but this attack he successfully resisted. During this operation, assisted by his Orderly only, he attacked and captured an enemy machine gun and turned it on the assailants, many of whom were killed and a large number driven into the hands of an adjoining British unit. Later, assisted only by his Serjeant, he again attacked and captured a second enemy machine gun, by which time he had been joined by other portions of his Company, and was enabled to consolidate his position. The conduct of this officer throughout forms an amazing record of dash, gallantry and skill, for which no reward can be too great, having regard to the importance of the position won. This gallant officer was shortly afterwards killed by a sniper.' His middle name is the same as the first name of one of the Grenfell family mentioned elsewhere in this book to which he is related. His eldest brother Lieutenant Max Christian Hamilton Colyer-Fergusson, Royal Army Service Corps, died on active service on 13 August 1940 aged 49 years and is buried near the family home in Andover, Hampshire.

Also here is Lance Corporal William Thomas Maddern, MM, 28th Australian Infantry, who died on 28 October 1917 aged 28 years. A former miner, he enlisted on 22 July 1915 in Kalgoordie/Boulder, Western Australia, leaving Freemantle on the HMAT Hororata on 1 October 1915 joining his Battalion in the Middle East in January 1916 and moving to France in March. He was awarded the Military Medal on 2 September 1916 for his actions during the fighting at Pozieres. There is a citation which is unusual for the Military Medal - 'When in position at POZIERES RIDGE on the night of 4th/5th August, 1916, Private MADDERN was sent back on two occasions through a heavy barrage fire with messages to Battalion Headquarters. On two later occasions he was sent back again with important messages and although badly wounded on the last occasion, he did not fail to deliver his message safely. He showed great devotion to duty under most trying conditions.' He returned to action in April 1917, was promoted to Lance Corporal on 12 April and was wounded again on 28 April being shot in the back and legs. He returned again to his unit on 20 October. He died from shrapnel wounds, received near Westhoek, on the next day, at the schoolhouse within which was the 15th Field Ambulance. It is recorded that he marched to the front-line, like many thousands of men, along the Menin Road, past this burial ground.

Buried here is Lieutenant Colonel Charles Ernest Atchison, DSO, MiD, King's Shropshire Light Infantry commanding 6th King's Own Yorkshire Light Infantry, killed on 24 August

1917 aged 42 years. He joined the Shropshire Light Infantry and served in the South African Wars, where he was slightly wounded, and was promoted to Captain at the end of the conflict. He became a Major at the start of World War One and went to France in December 1914. He was awarded the Distinguished Service Order in the June 1915 Birthday Honours List and was promoted to Lieutenant Colonel to command the Battalion on 10 July 1917. He was among 150 casualties in his Battalion on the day while holding up a German attack near Stirling Castle and Inverness Copse either side of the Menin Road just east of Hooge.

Private Arthur Hewison, 7th Lincolnshires, died on 29 November 1915 aged 21 years. He landed in France on 14 July 1915. He had been sitting in a trench, then he decided to stand up to move to keep warm when he was shot by a sniper. He was moved here from Menin Road North Cemetery and was recorded originally as H Hewison 12039 until corrected in the 1922 documentation. His brother Private William Hewison, 6th Lincolnshires died on 8 June 1917 aged 21 years and is commemorated on the Menin Gate Memorial. Another brother, Petty Officer Stoker George Hewison, HMS Laforey, Royal Navy, died on 23 March 1917 aged 27 years and is commemorated on the Chatham Naval Memorial.

Also of note is Rifleman Anthony O'Neill, 1st Royal Irish Rifles who died on 1 October 1918 aged 16 years. He was killed at Geluveld as his Battalion marched forward to engage the retreating Germans.

Buried side by side are brothers, Privates Leslie Stewart Barrington and Ronald Ethelred Barrington, both 7th Lincolnshires and both killed in action on 20 December 1915. They were together in the trench when a shell exploded nearby killing them.

Concentrated here:

Menin Road North Cemetery - on the north side of the Menin Road opposite this cemetery. It was used mainly from May 1915 to August 1916 but also in 1917 and 1918. It contained 130 British men, three Canadians and three Newfoundlanders.

| UK – 1049 | Aust – 263 | NZ – 52 |
| Can – 145 | BWI - 3 | Ger – 1 |
| KUG – 65 | Unnamed – 118 | |

Area - 6345 sq mts

Special Memorials to twenty British men and four Australians known/believed to be buried among the unnamed.

Special Memorials to 52 British men and three Newfoundlanders buried in Menin Road North Cemetery whose graves were destroyed by shell-fire.

**LOCATION**

Menin Road South Cemetery is situated in the western suburbs of Ieper, on the south side of the Menin Road 100m from the junction with the southern ring road.

# MESSINES RIDGE BRITISH CEMETERY

**HISTORY**

This cemetery was created after the war with the concentration of graves from the battlefields of Messines.

**INFORMATION**

The importance of holding the Messines Ridge is clear when you visit this cemetery, you can see how it dominates the plain below and how difficult it was to attack.

Messines saw much fighting throughout the war. On 31 October 1914 the German 26th Division attacked the village. The 9th (Queen's Royal) Lancers, 2nd Royal Inniskilling Fusiliers, and 57th (Wilde's) Rifles of the Indian Army were forced to pull back to the ridge forming a new line through the village. This was held by the 10th (Prince of Wales's Own Royal) and 11th (Prince Albert's Own) Hussars, 2nd (Queen's Bays), 4th (Royal Irish) and 5th (Princess Charlotte of Wales's) Dragoon Guards. These units were reinforced, after a new German attack, by the battle-weary and depleted 2nd King's Own Yorkshire Light Infantry and 2nd King's Own Scottish Borderers. They launched a counter-attack in which the 1/14th (London Scottish) Londons were also deployed, but the tired and outnumbered force failed. Hence, Messines fell to the Germans on 1 November 1914. As French troops failed to recapture it on 6 and 7 November 1914 the village was abandoned to the Germans until 1917.

Messines was captured by troops of the New Zealand Division on 7 June, the first day of the Battle of Messines. The Germans took the village and the ridge again during their offensive in 1918 when it fell on 10-11 April after a stubborn defence by the South African Brigade. The British over-ran Messines for the last time on 28-29 September 1918 when it was attacked by the 34th Division.

The small village of Messines (Mesen as it is now called) is officially designated a city. Messines had been reduced to less than rubble by the bombardments. Its former abbey was so badly destroyed that it was impossible to reconstruct it. The abbey and church had been founded in 1057 by the Countess Adela and she is buried in the crypt of the church. She was the daughter of the French King Robert and the wife of Baudouin V of Flanders. Their daughter, Mathilde, would become the wife of William Duke of Normandy and from 1066, Queen of England.

The church of Saint Nicolas, however was rebuilt by 1928 and is now a prominent local landmark. It has a full clarion of 61 bells, all raised by local subscription or donated and suitably inscribed with the names of the benefactors. The inspiration, and much of the hard work raising money and attention, was led by Albert Gherkiere. I remember many trips leading school groups to the crypt listening to Albert recount tales of visits by royalty and Popes to see 'his' bells. The view from the church tower was worth the climb. The village museum, and the church and crypt are an interesting stop on your travels. The crypt was used by the Germans as a headquarters and for treating wounded. One of these was Adolph Hitler who painted scenes of the battlefields during his time here. A copy of one of his paintings hangs in the museum.

A system of bunkers and tunnels bore the name of the Institution Royale, to which this ground used to belong and the Cross of Sacrifice is on the site of the Institution's windmill.

Buried here is Lance Corporal George Nathaniel Daniell, 167th Army Troops Company, Royal Engineers, killed on 20 July 1917 aged 53 years. He joined the Royal Engineers in 1884 seeing action in Egypt and the Sudan. He married and by 1901 the census shows he had five sons though he was fighting in South Africa. By 1911 he had seven sons and in 1915 rejoined the Royal Engineers at the age of 51 lying that he was 45, the upper age limit for joining the army at that time, which explains the age recorded on the CWGC website. Two of his sons joined the 2nd Grenadier Guards at the start of the war with consecutive service numbers. Private Francis George Daniell, 2nd Grenadier Guards died of wounds in a hospital in Rouen on 19 December 1917 aged 28 years, probably of wounds received at Cambrai, and is buried in St. Sever Cemetery Extension. Stanley Daniell was aged 15 years when he enlisted and was later wounded but survived the war. Three other sons also served in the army and survived the war. Cecil Henry Daniell and George Sidney Daniell were in the Royal Engineers while Edgar Douglas Daniell joined the 17th Lancers. George suffered a serious knee injury at Neuve Chapelle. The other two boys were too young to join up.

Also of note is Lance Corporal Albert Edgar Furness, 11th Lancashire Fusiliers, killed on 7 June 1917 aged 16 years.

About 800m north of the crossroads in Messines is the Memorial to the 1/14th (London Scottish) Londons. They were the first full Territorial Battalion to see action in the Salient when they were rushed to Wijtschate in London buses and were then thrown into action on the Messines Ridge north of the village during the First Battle of Ypres at the end of October 1914.

Approximately 400m south of this cemetery and west of the road to Ploegsteert is the Memorial to the men from New Zealand who fought in the battles at Messines. It lies within the New Zealand Park and was unveiled by King Albert on 1 August 1924. It is now the location of a service of remembrance on ANZAC Day, 25 April each year. The park has an obelisk, two German bunkers and a good view west from the ridge.

On the southern edge of the village, and on the west side of the road to Ploegsteert, is the 'Island of Ireland Peace Park' or 'Páirc Siochána d'Oileán na h'Éireann' with its imposing 30m high tower visible from large areas of the southern battlefield, a style of building that goes back to the Viking invasions of the 10th Century. The park also contains stones telling accounts of the Irish involvement and casualty figures. It marks the battle in which the Catholic 16th (Irish) Division and the Protestant 36th (Ulster) Division fought alongside each other in the war. However, that was at Wijtschate and the Park lies on ground attacked by the New Zealand Division. It was built by young people from all over Ireland using stone from an almshouse in Mullingar which had recently been demolished, home of the first Irish winner of the Victoria Cross in the war. It was opened by the President of the Irish Republic, Mary McAleese, on 11 November 1998 in the presence of their Majesties Queen Elizabeth II of the United Kingdom and King Albert II of Belgium.

In the village centre is the private memorial to Lance Corporal Samuel Frickleton, VC. Frickleton was serving with 3rd New Zealand Rifle Brigade on 7 June 1917 when he attacked and destroyed two German machine gun emplacements, saving the lives of many New Zealanders in his unit, for which he was awarded the Victoria Cross.

There were four German cemeteries made at Messines after the Armistice but these have been removed.

Concentrated here:

Bell Farm Cemetery - by the side of the road leading to Spanbroekmolen from opposite this cemetery. It contained 32 British men of the 25th Division who died in June 1917.

Blauwepoortebeek Cemetery – 1.6km north-east of Messines. It contained seven British graves and sixteen Australians who were buried from August to October 1917.

Bousbecques East German Cemetery - on the south side of a village in France which is about 8km east of here. It contained four British men who were buried by a German Field Hospital in November 1914.

Bristol Castle Military Cemetery - on the Messines-Wulvergem road near Wulvergem. It contained 32 British men of the 36th (Ulster) and 14th (Light) Divisions who died in September and October 1918.

Lumm Farm Cemetery - a little east of the Messines road. It contained thirteen British graves and two Australians who died from June to September 1917.

Middle Farm Cemetery - near the road to Wijtschate, 450m north of Messines. It contained fourteen British, sixteen Australian and four New Zealand graves made from July to December 1917.

Onraet Farm Cemetery 400m north of the crossroads at the turn to Somer Farm Cemetery on the road to St. Eloi. It contained 29 British men of the 36th (Ulster) Division buried in June to August 1917.

Queensland Cemetery - on the road from Messines to Warneton. It contained three British graves and 30 Australians, of whom 23 belonged to the 41st Australian Infantry, who died in June and July 1917.

River Douve Cemetery - also called Snitchel Farm, on the river bank south of Messines. It contained four British men and 24 Australians who died from June to November 1917.

UK – 986        Aust – 332        NZ – 115
Can – 1         S Afr – 56

Unnamed - 957 (65% of total)     Area - 6212 sq mts

Special Memorials to four British, ten Australian, thirteen New Zealand and one South African men known/believed to be buried among the unnamed.

Special Memorials to thirteen British men buried in other cemeteries whose graves were destroyed by shell-fire.

**Messines Ridge New Zealand Memorial**
The entrance to the burial area is guarded by the Memorial to 828 New Zealand missing of the battles in the south of the Salient. A pavilion in the cemetery is like that at Buttes New Cemetery, where there is another New Zealand Memorial. This is one of seven memorials in France and Belgium to those New Zealand soldiers who died on the Western Front and whose graves are not known. The Memorials are all in cemeteries chosen as appropriate to the fighting in which the men died. While most of the men are from New Zealand, there are also many who are natives of the United Kingdom who had emigrated to New Zealand. Similarly, there are several Australians who joined up in New Zealand. Notably, several men had been invalided out of the army and had re-joined at a later date.

Among those named on the Memorial is Private George Maurice Victor Sellars, 1st Auckland Regiment, NZEF, killed on 7 June 1917 aged 31 years. He was a Rugby Union international who played for New Zealand fifteen times, including two Test matches. He played club rugby for Ponsonby, and was first selected for Auckland in 1910, and in 1912 gained selection for the New Zealand Māori side. Sellars was selected for the All Blacks for their 1913 tour of North America where he played fourteen matches. As well, he was also in the All Blacks' side that played Australia immediately prior to their tour. Although unavailable to play for New Zealand the following year, he did represent the Māori again that season. He was killed while trying to carry a wounded man to safety.
NZ - 828
**LOCATION**
Messines Ridge Cemetery lies on the south side of the Messines-Wulvergem road 500m west of the crossroads in Messines.

# METEREN MILITARY CEMETERY

**HISTORY**
This cemetery was created by the French authorities in 1919 to concentrate graves from the battlefields and small cemeteries in the area.
**INFORMATION**
Meteren was the site of fighting at the beginning and end of the war. In 1914 the German advance was repelled by means of a bayonet charge by the 2nd Seaforth Highlanders. The Germans occupied the village in early October but their positions were captured by the 10th Brigade of the 4th Division on 13 October 1914. Lieutenant Bernard Montgomery of the 1st Royal Warwickshires was wounded twice in capturing the village during the advance by the III Corps on 13 October 1914. During a lull in the battle, Montgomery was inspecting his Platoon's defensive positions from no man's land when he was shot through the right lung by a German sniper. As he lay bleeding in no man's land, men tried to get to his aid and his Platoon Sergeant dashed out to apply first aid but he was shot in the head. This saved Montgomery's life, for the Sergeant fell on top of him protecting Montgomery. All afternoon the snipers kept firing. Montgomery was hit once more in the right knee, but the dead Sergeant caught most of the bullets. Montgomery was so badly injured that a grave was dug for him as he was not expected to survive the night. He was promoted to Captain and awarded the Distinguished Service Order. He is better known as the saviour of the 8th Army in North Africa during World War II and for his exploits in Europe following D-Day.

The next fighting that the village saw was in the German Spring Offensive in April 1918. The 33rd Division held the village until it was lost on 16 April and, though the French took the area briefly, they were forced to withdraw. It was not until 19 July that the 9th (Scottish) and 1st Australian Divisions attacked the sector with the South African Composite Battalion capturing the village.

The Communal Cemetery was created as the church and churchyard were destroyed during the Battles of the Lys in 1918. The 210 German graves that were concentrated here have been removed. There are six WW2 graves set apart on a small terrace below the rest of the graveyard.

Buried here is Colour Serjeant Philip Thornton, DCM, MiD, Medaille Militaire (France), 1st Royal Warwickshires, killed in action on 13 October 1914 aged 33 years. Thornton was a professional soldier who had served in the South African Wars and on the North West Frontier of India in 1908 and was with Montgomery for at least six years. He was very proficient in Indian languages and a skilled marksman, winning a double distinction at the Satara School of Musketry in 1912. He was awarded the Distinguished Conduct Medal for the action in which he was killed. His citation reads 'for gallant conduct in endeavouring whilst wounded and accompanied by only a few men, to capture the enemy's machine guns. In this attempt he failed owing to there being no support at hand at the moment.' It is possible, though unlikely, that Thornton had a hand in the saving of Montgomery, his Company Commander.

Concentrated here:
Berthen Churchyard - it contained thirteen British men, two Canadians and one Newfoundlander who were buried in 1916 and 1918.

Le Roukloshille Military Cemetery - south of the little hamlet on the road to Godwaersevelde. 26 British men, 38 Australians and one French soldier were buried here from April to August 1918.

Meteren Churchyard - it contained eleven British men who were buried in 1914 and 1917.

Mont des Cats British and Indian Cemeteries - on the hill south-east of the monastery. The British cemetery contained nine British men and two Canadians buried in April 1915 while the Indian burial ground contained sixteen men buried in April 1915. Another six British men, buried in the grounds of the monastery were also brought to Meteren.

| | | |
|---|---|---|
| UK – 581 | Aust – 104 | NZ – 22 |
| Can – 6 | NF – 1 | S Afr – 31 |
| India – 16 | Fr – 69 | WWII – 6 |
| Unnamed-180 | | Area - 2932 sq mts |

Special Memorials to five British men believed to be buried among the unnamed.

Special Memorial to one British soldier buried in Meteren Churchyard whose grave was destroyed by shell-fire.

Special Memorial to an Indian buried in Mont des Cats Indian Cemetery whose grave was destroyed by shell-fire.

### LOCATION
Meteren is south-west of Ieper in northern France 4km west of Bailleul. The cemetery lies in France on the west side of the Meteren-Godewaersvelde road (D18) about 300m from the town square. Meteren can be reached either through Bailleul or via the Rodeberg and Mont Noir on the N372/D318. It would be much easier to park in the town square and walk the short distance to the cemetery than park and try to turn your vehicle. The British burial ground is on the edge of the Communal Cemetery on the north-western border of Meteren. You must pass through the Town Cemetery to reach the Military one.

# MINTY FARM CEMETERY

### HISTORY
The cemetery was used from October 1917 to April 1918.

### INFORMATION
The farm from which the cemetery gets its name was used as a German blockhouse until captured during the Third Battle of Ypres, and it was then used for a British Company headquarters. It is thought that the name 'Minty Farm' originates from the period when the blockhouse was occupied by a unit from Wiltshire.

The 1/6th (Banff and Donside) Gordon Highlanders took the farm on 31 July 1917. The 51st (Highland) Division continued towards the Steenbeek and dug in about 250m short of the river during which time the Highlanders came under fire from two machine-guns across the stream. Private (later Flight-Sergeant) George Imlach Macintosh dealt with them for which he recieved the Victoria Cross.

Buried here is Lieutenant James Wilson Cordner, MC, 17th Royal Irish Rifles, killed on 16 April 1918 on the same day that he became a Lieutenant. He was from Ireland, though he had spent some time in Canada. He was training for religious orders when he enlisted in June 1915 and made a 2nd Lieutenant. Shortly after the disaster at Thiepval on 1 July 1916 he said in a service, while recruiting men for the Battalion, 'Ulster had done well but it could do better. There were still young men at home to whom the war had not yet appealed. They were still more concerned about the cut of their coats or colour of their ties' which is difficult to comprehend when the Ulster Division had already given so much. But, it is a reflection of the times, and the attitudes of many, which helps us gain an insight into the way some were thinking at the time. He went to the Front in 1917, was wounded in the summer and awarded the Military Cross at Cambrai in late 1917. The citation for his Military Cross says 'For conspicuous gallantry and devotion to duty while in charge of a wiring party. He wired 500 yards of newly captured trenches in daylight in full view of the enemy and under heavy fire. His coolness and determination were an inspiration to his men.'

Nearby is the Memorial to the 38th (Welsh) Division at the bunker at Goumier Farm which is about 100m north-west of here and shown on some wartime maps as Gournier Farm. It is on private land and not in an area over which the 38th Division fought, though part of the 15th Welsh were active here in 1917.

Between this cemetery and St. Juliaan is the Kitcheners Wood Memorial commemorating the Canadian troops who counter-attacked at Kitcheners Wood in an attempt to recapture the wood, and four British heavy guns in it, on the night of 22 April 1915 following the German gas attack.

| | | |
|---|---|---|
| UK – 192 | Ger – 1 | Unnamed – 4 |

Area - 991 sq mts

### LOCATION
Minty Farm Cemetery is found about 5km north-east of Ieper, and 2km west of St. Juliaan. It is most easily reached via the Ieper northern by-pass and the Mortelweg, known in the war as Admiral's Road, which runs north-west from the N38 at the small crossroads just west of the motorway. About 1.5km from the N38 turn north at another crossroads, where there are CWGC signs on the wall of the house on the corner. This brings you to the cemetery, which lies 30m from the road, in about 1km.

# MONT NOIR MILITARY CEMETERY

## HISTORY
Mont Noir Cemetery was begun in April 1918, during the fighting here in the German offensive, and remained in use until September. It was enlarged after the war with the concentration of British and French graves from the surrounding battlefields.

## INFORMATION
The hill was captured by the British Cavalry Corps on 13 October 1914 and remained in Allied hands until the end of the war.

The 32 French graves in the cemetery at the end of the war were of men of the 26th Dragoons or 88th Infantry Regiment who died in April and May 1918. The concentrated French graves are of men who died from March to May 1915.

Buried here is Company Serjeant Major Joseph Mitchell, DCM, 25th (Tyneside Irish) Northumberland Fusiliers, killed on 17 April 1918 aged 31 years. He was awarded the Distinguished Conduct Medal posthumously in September 1918. The citation reads 'For conspicuous gallantry and devotion to duty. Throughout heavy bombardment and repeated enemy attacks, he rendered invaluable service in organising and leading isolated and mixed parties in the absence of officers. He was responsible for the sufficient supply of ammunition from the forward dump to the firing line. He set a fine example to his men.'

Nearby is the Memorial to the 34th Division. The Germans had tried to take the Mont Noir having over-run Kemmel but were thrown back by the 34th Division who had their headquarters at the summit of the hill. Should you wish to visit the 34th Division Memorial, stay on the main road to the summit of Mont Noir passing the turn to Bailleul and Mont Noir Cemetery. At the summit the Hotel du Mont Noir has a large picnic area at the rear from which you get an impressive view of the Salient, and next to the hotel is the Memorial.

The Monts des Flandres are used by cyclists to practice hill climbing. The numbers can be substantial in summer as they can attempt three steep climbs in quick succession onto the Rodeberg, Vidaigneberg and the Zwaarteberg (Mont Noir). Between the Vidaigneberg and Zwaarteberg, in the village of Rodeberg, is a border post that I have never seen manned. There are a number of tourist attractions and several cafes and restaurants.

Concentrated here:

Wolfheok British Cemetery - 200m south-west of St. Jans-Cappel, containing 23 British men. It was used from August to September 1918, mostly by the 36th (Ulster) Division.

| | | |
|---|---|---|
| UK – 146 | Aust – 1 | NF – 2 |
| Fr – 84 | Unnamed – 15 | |
| WWII – 2 (unidentified) | | Area - 1315 sq mts |

## LOCATION
Mont Noir Cemetery is found south of Ieper on the southern edge of the village of Rodeberg. It lies in northern France on the northern slopes of the Mont Noir. It lies at the end of a dirt track leading from the D223 Mont Noir-Bailleul road and is clearly signed from Rodeberg. This cemetery is in a disused sand-pit, cut into the side of Mont Noir which stands 130m above sea level, and sunk below the level of the track by which you get to it from the main road. There is no parking or turning area at the cemetery.

# MOTOR CAR CORNER CEMETERY

## HISTORY
Begun at the start of the Battle of Messines in June 1917, the cemetery remained in use until the German advance in March 1918.

## INFORMATION
The name of the cemetery derives from the fact that this was the closest to the Front that Army vehicles were permitted. The Germans extended the cemetery in 1918 when they were in control of the area between 10 April and 29 September 1918 but their graves have been removed. There was also a light railway in the area.

Buried here are Privates Allan Holz and Ernest John Julius Holz, both 3rd Wellington Regiment, NZEF, and both killed on 13 June 1917 aged 26 and 38 years respectively. They have consecutive service numbers so enlisted together and now lie together. Sons of a German immigrant they, with their brother William, enlisted in October 1916, a year after their father's death, and arrived in France in May 1917. In the early hours of the morning, a German shell landed hitting their billets, exploding in a room in which the brothers were asleep. The blast killed Ernest and Allan, while William suffered severe wounds to his abdomen, wrist, hip and foot which ended his war. It seems the three did not see any action in the war.

UK – 36  Aust – 9  NZ – 84  KUG – 2
Ger – 1  Area - 641 sq mts

### LOCATION
Motor Car Corner Cemetery is found south of Ieper about 4km south-east of Ploegsteert. About 1.4km south of Ploegsteert square you will find on the left a tree of CWGC signs. Turn left and then right onto a tree-lined avenue leading to Motor Car Corner Cemetery on the right.

## MUD CORNER CEMETERY

### HISTORY
This cemetery was begun at the start of the Battle of Messines on 7 June 1917, when the New Zealand Division captured this site, and remained in use to December 1917.

### INFORMATION
It is easy to understand how Mud Corner got its name because in winter this low-lying spot must have been a morass of mud in which it would have been almost impossible to fight.

Buried here is Private Edward Beach, 2nd Wellington Regiment, NZEF, killed on 26 June 1917 aged 54 years. A labourer from Hamilton, he left New Zealand in November 1916 having lied, claiming to be aged 40 years, to get into the army.

Also here is Serjeant James Henry Frew, DCM, MiD, 1st Auckland Regiment, NZEF, killed in action on 26 June 1917 aged 28 years. Frew served as James Henry Francis leaving New Zealand for the Middle East on 12 April 1915. He became a Lance Corporal on 25 April 1915, a Corporal on 31 August 1915 and Temporary Sergeant on 21 October 1915 and was briefly in Gallipoli. He headed for France in April 1916 having been confirmed as Sergeant in January. He was Mentioned in Despatches in April 1916 and awarded the Distinguished Conduct Medal in June 1916. He then spent some time attached to Headquarters, NZ Division (Divisional School) from October 1916 until he rejoined his Battalion in April 1917. His brother, Private John Frew, 1st Otago Regiment, NZEF, died on 14 July 1916 and is buried in Cite Bonjean Military Cemetery.

2nd Lieutenant James Gordon Kinvig, 2nd Wellington Regiment, NZEF, died on 31 July 1917 aged 29 years. He played cricket twice for Wellington, once against the Australians and once against Hawkes Bay. He enlisted in September 1915 and was commissioned in late 1916. He was killed in an attack on La Basse Ville.

UK – 1  Aust – 31  NZ – 53
Area - 515 sq mts

### LOCATION
Mud Corner Cemetery lies at the northern edge of Ploegsteert Wood, south of Messines and about 2km north-east of Ploegsteert. It is reached most easily from the crossroads near the summit of Hill 63 on the Armentieres road. A dirt track 50m east of Prowse Point Cemetery leads to Mud Corner Cemetery in the valley below. This is the first cemetery upon entering through the official access way to Ploegsteert Wood. There is no parking here so park at Prowse Point Cemetery.

## NEW IRISH FARM CEMETERY

### HISTORY
The cemetery was opened in August 1917 once this area, which had been near the front-line, was considered to be safe. It was used until November 1917 and again in April and May 1918. After the war the cemetery was enlarged with the concentration of 4560 graves.

### INFORMATION
The cemetery is situated on what was known as Boundary Road next to the farm from which it gets its name. The crossroads at the northern corner was called Hammond's Corner. Hill Top Farm, on Buffs Road by the crossroads, was, by 1917, a series of trenches. A tree, on the edge of a trench, was turned into an observation post by hollowing it out and lining it with steel. The post was then used to guide shell-fire on to German positions. The 39th Division

attacked through the site of Hill Top Farm on the first day of Third Ypres.

At the end of the war the cemetery contained 73 burials, of which 37 were those of Artillery officers or men. These now make up the three irregular rows of Plot I on a raised area near the centre of the cemetery in front of the Stone of Remembrance.

Among those buried here is Lieutenant Charles Lindsay Claude Bowes-Lyon, 3rd attached 1st Black Watch (Royal Highlanders), who died on 23 October 1914 aged 29 years. Originally buried in the churchyard at Boezinge he is recorded as moved here in 1921. Intriguingly, there is also a CWGC record showing him as being buried in Artillery Wood British Cemetery. But that record also shows Captain Urquhart as being in Artillery Wood, which is an error as he still lies in Boezinge Churchyard. Both graves were lost for some time and discovered again after the war. Bowes-Lyon is a cousin of Queen Elizabeth II's mother and was moved here on the wishes of the family who wanted him in a British cemetery. In 1911 he went to India, and returning home in 1914, was one of the few survivors of the wreck of the 'Empress of Ireland'. He was killed attacking trenches near Pilkem. The Queen's mother lost another cousin, Lieutenant Gavin Patrick Bowes-Lyon, 3rd Grenadier Guards killed on 27 November 1917 aged 20 years and commemorated on the Cambrai Memorial, Louverval and her brother, Captain The Honourable Fergus Bowes-Lyon, 8th Black Watch (Royal Highlanders) killed on 27 September 1915 aged 26 years and buried in Quarry Cemetery, Vermelles, in the war.

Also here is Lieutenant Denis Duncan Philby, Royal Dublin Fusiliers attached 2nd Royal Munster Fusiliers who was killed in action on 12 November 1914 aged 25 years and was buried south of Clonmel Copse near what is now Sanctuary Wood. He was moved to New Irish Farm Cemetery in 1920. His brother, Major Harold Payne Philby, DSO, twice MiD, commanding 2nd York and Lancasters, was killed on 17 May 1916 aged 28 years. He is buried in Hop Store cemetery about 5km west of here. However, a third brother Harry Saint John Bridger Philby, survived the war. He was an explorer and Arabist, the first European to cross the Rub' al-Khali, or Empty Quarter, of Arabia from east to west. He was also an author and Colonial office Intelligence Officer. His son, and nephew to Harold and Denis, was Harold 'Kim' Philby, a high ranking British Intelligence Officer who worked as a double-agent for many years. As part of the now infamous 'Cambridge Five', Harold was believed to have been the most successful in providing secret information to the Soviet Union. He defected to the Soviet Union in 1963, and continued to work as an operative for the Soviet Secret Police, NKVD and KGB. He died in 1988 and is buried in Moscow.

Another of note is Private Walter Wild Speight, 13th Royal Welsh Fusiliers, formerly Army Service Corps, who died on 1 August 1917 aged 40 years. For many years he was recorded by the CWGC as being aged 61 years, making him the oldest casualty on active service in Belgium. This was corrected in 2010.

You can find the grave of Captain John Edmund Valentine Isaac, DSO, MiD, 2nd Rifle Brigade who died on 9 May 1915 aged 35 years. He was commissioned into the 5th Northumberland Fusiliers in May 1900 and soon went to fight in South Africa. He was severely wounded taking two years to recover during which time he became a Lieutenant. He was made a Captain in 1905 and moved to the Rifle Brigade in 1908 and retired in 1911 moving to Canada. He returned to the Rifle Brigade in September 1914. He was appointed ADC to Major-General Sir Thompson Capper, commanding the 7th Division, and went to Flanders on his Staff in October 1914. He fought at First Ypres, where he was badly wounded in the left arm. For his services he was Mentioned in Despatches, and awarded the Distinguished Service Order, one of the first to be gazetted in the war. With his arm still incapacitated, he returned to duty in December 1914 and joined the 2nd Rifle Brigade on 5 May 1915. Four days later he was killed, leading his men, on the Fromelles Ridge. A keen sportsman, he had represented Worcestershire and the Orange Free State in South Africa at cricket and won the Egyptian Cairo Grand National Horse Race in 1911. His brother, 2nd Lieutenant Arthur Whitmore Isaac, 5th attached 1st Worcestershires, died on 7 July 1916, when overwhelmed by Germans in Contalmaison church, aged 42 years and is commemorated on the Thiepval Memorial. Another brother, Lieutenant Herbert Crofton Isaac, 14th Regiment (West Yorkshires), died in 1896.

Lieutenant Colonel Julian Falvey Beyts, DSO, 15th Durham Light Infantry, was killed by German shelling while in the front line near Hooge with his men on 5 October 1917 aged 29 years. He was posthumously awarded the Distinguished Service Order in the New Years Honours List of January 1918. Lieutenant Colonel Arthur George Burt, 1st York and Lancasters died on 23 April 1915 aged 50 years. He was killed while his Battalion, as part of the Geddes Force, tried to halt the German advance following the use of gas the day before.

Private John Lancelot Andrews, 54th Australian Infantry, was killed in action at Polygon Wood on 26 September 1917 aged 16 years and 9 months. He had enlisted, and left Australia, in January 1917.

Concentrated here:

Admiral's Cemetery - at the junction of Admiral's and Boundary Roads, about 1km north-west of here, near No Man's Cot Cemetery. It was named after a member of the Royal Navy serving with the 6th Division. It contained nineteen British soldiers who died in 1917 and 1918.

Canopus Trench Cemetery - a little south-west of the Langemark about 2km north of here. It contained twelve British men of the 1/5th Gloucestershires who died in August 1917.

Comedy Farm Cemetery - south of Langemark near the Steenbeek about 2km north of here. It contained 29 British men who died from June to September 1915.

Crossroads Cemetery - two groups of graves at the crossroads in St. Jan about 600m south of here. They contained nineteen British men who died in June and July 1915.

Ferdinand Farm Cemetery – located about 2km north-east of here near the Steenbeek on the way to St. Juliaan. It contained fifteen British men who died from July to October 1917.

Francois Farm Cemetery – located about 2km north of here near a farm directly south of Cement House Cemetery. It contained 23 British men who died from July to October 1917.

Fusilier Farm Cemetery - on the Ypres-Pilkem road south-west of No Man's Cot Cemetery about 1km north-west of here. It contained seventeen British men of the 38th (Welsh) Division who died on 31 July 1917.

Fusilier Farm Road Cemetery, Boezinge - 400m north-west of Fusilier Farm Cemetery near Colne Valley Cemetery. It contained fourteen British men of the 38th (Welsh) Division who died from 31 July to 2 August 1917.

Glimpse Cottage Cemetery - just south of Colne Valley Cemetery. It contained eighteen British men of the 38th (Welsh) Division who died in July and August 1917.

Irish Farm Cemetery - immediately south of this cemetery. Begun by the 1st Royal Fusiliers in May 1915, it was used regularly until September 1915 and at intervals until January 1918 by which time it contained 54 British graves.

La Miterie German Cemetery – Lomme is on the western edge of Lille about 15 km south of here and La Miterie is on the north-eastern edge of Lomme. The cemetery was a little north of La Miterie. It contained eight British men who died in September 1918.

Manor Road Cemetery – located about 3.5km south of here and situated where the railway crosses the road on the south-western edge of Zillebeke. It contained nineteen British men of the 1st Royal Irish Fusiliers who died in August 1916.

Mirfield Cemetery - sited between the canal and the Ypres-Pilkem road about 1km north-west of here. It contained sixteen British men, fifteen of the 51st (Highland) Division, who died from June to August 1917.

Paratonnier's Farm Cemetery - a Belgian military cemetery, now removed, 800m south of Lizerne about 4km north-west of here. It contained the graves of thirteen British men who died from December 1917 to March 1918.

Pilkem Road Cemetery - near Colne Valley, Glimpse Farm and Fusilier Farm Road cemeteries. It contained 27 British men, eighteen of them from the 1/5th (Buchan and Formartin) Gordon Highlanders, who died in July and August 1917.

St. Jan Churchyard - 44 British men who died in 1915 were buried in the churchyard about 600m south of here.

Spree Farm Cemetery – located about 1.5km east of here and 800m south-east of St. Juliaan near Bridge House Cemetery. It contained fourteen British men and three New Zealanders who died from August to October 1917.

Vanheule Farm Cemetery - on the St. Juliaan-Ypres road just north of Seaforth Cemetery which is about 1km east of here. It contained 22 British men and one New Zealander who died from August to October 1917.

Yorkshire Cemetery, Zouave Villa - 700m west of here. It contained 24 British men, 22 of the 6th King's Own Yorkshire Light Infantry and two of the 6th East Yorkshires, who died in August 1917.

| | | |
|---|---|---|
| UK – 4272 | Aust – 65 | NZ – 23 |
| Can – 255 | NF – 3 | S Afr – 6 |
| BWI – 1 | India – 5 | Ger – 1 |
| KUG – 12 | Chinese Labour Corps – 7 | |

Unnamed - 3271 (75% of whole)

Area - 14728 sq mts

Special Memorials to 38 British men and one Canadian known/believed to be buried among the unnamed.

Special Memorials to 26 British men and four New Zealanders buried in Vanheule Farm, Francois Farm, Spree Farm and La-Miterie German cemeteries, whose graves were destroyed by shell-fire.

### LOCATION
New Irish Farm Cemetery lies 300m north of the N38 northern by-pass about 1km north of St. Jan. It is clearly signed and visible from the N38.

# NIEPPE COMMUNAL CEMETERY

### HISTORY
The Communal Cemetery was used by the British from October 1914 to November 1917 and from September to November 1918. The Germans buried one man near the entrance when he died as their prisoner in April 1918.

### INFORMATION
The 4th Division established their headquarters in Nieppe in October 1914 having pushed the Germans across the River Lys from the Mont des Flandres. A line then was established north from Armentieres to the edge of Ploegsteert Wood. Following the German attack on 21 October 1914, in which the 11th and 12th Brigades took German ground, the 4th Division extended their line north of Ploegsteert Wood.

A New Zealand Chaplain is believed to be buried under the Cross of Sacrifice though the majority of the graves are in several Plots near the middle of the cemetery, with one grave, a man who died as a German prisoner, by the entrance. The Chaplain is The Reverend James Joseph McMenamin, New Zealand Chaplains' Department attached 2nd Canterbury Regiment, NZEF, killed on 9 June 1917 aged 42 years. He had become a priest aged 28 years. When the war began, he volunteered as a Chaplain and left for Egypt in October 1914 where he served the New Zealand soldiers stationed on the Suez Canal. Chaplain

Captain McMenamin landed at Gallipoli on the first ANZAC Day, 25 April 1915. The conditions took a toll on his physical health so he returned to New Zealand in September 1915 to recover. In May 1916 he returned to Europe, and served in hospitals in England until January 1917 when he joined the 2nd Canterbury Regiment at the Front. Father McMenamin was conducting a funeral service for fallen soldiers when the enemy fired a shell into the congregation, wounding six and killing McMenamin.

UK – 43         Aust – 6         NZ – 11
S Afr – 2       Fr - 20
Area - 316 sq mts

**LOCATION**
Nieppe Communal Cemetery is situated on the northern edge of Nieppe village, 300m from the town square, and about 20km south of Ieper. It is on the eastern side of a road to Le Romarin, also signed for 'Cemetiere Bourg', that leads north from the large square in Nieppe.

## NIEUWKERKE (NEUVE-EGLISE) CHURCHYARD

**HISTORY**
The churchyard was used for British burials at various times throughout the war.

**INFORMATION**
The church was destroyed in the war but later rebuilt. The churchyard was used by field ambulances and fighting units, particularly early in the war by the 5th Division.
On 11 April 1918 the 2nd Worcestershires were east of the village but were forced back on 12 April by the German Spring Offensive. The brewery and the Town Hall opposite the church housed the 2nd Worcestershires who were having breakfast when the Germans attacked. At the end of the day the remaining 60 men of the Worcestershires broke out of the rear of the Town Hall to escape from Nieuwkerke back to the British lines west of the village. Although forced to retreat the Worcestershires had cost the enemy much in time and men. The 16th (Church Lads Brigade) King's Royal Rifle Corps came up in support but were wiped out in the battle. Corporal McBride manned a succession of machine-guns for the three days of the battle holding up the German advance. Even so, the Germans set up machine-gun posts at the crossroads on the edge of the village and behind the buildings on the south side of the square. The village was recaptured by the 36th (Ulster) Division on 2 September 1918.

This small communal cemetery holds the dead of two world wars. It saw service in the Second World War when the British Expeditionary Force was involved in the later stages of the defence of Belgium following the German invasion in May 1940, and the withdrawal to Dunkirk.
Buried here is Private Alfred Michael Mazzei, 6th (Pioneers) South wales Borderers, who died on 27 May 1917 aged 24 years. He was buried by his brother, Thomas, of the same Battalion, and the story is that the army docked Thomas's pay for using his army blanket to wrap Alfred's body in preparation for burial. Another brother, Private Louis Pelegrena Mazzei, 1st South Wales Borderers, was killed 21 on October 1914 and is commemorated on the Menin Gate. A fourth brother, Private William Mazzei, 1st South Wales Borderers and later 2nd Welsh Regiment was wounded and discharged. His only child, William John Mazzei was killed in Normandy on 21 July 1944 and is buried in Brouay War Cemetery.

UK – 76         Aust – 10        NZ – 5
Can – 1         India – 1        Fr – 4
Unnamed – 1     WWII – 10 (Also 3 Bel + 1 Fr)

**LOCATION**
Nieuwkerke Churchyard lies in the centre of the village on the edge of the large village square. Nieuwkerke is about 15km south of Ieper. The Commonwealth graves are on the left, or north, side of the church as you enter, next to the road, but three graves are set apart from the main Plot.

## NINE ELMS BRITISH CEMETERY

**HISTORY**
This cemetery was created on 16 September 1917, a consequence of Third Ypres in 1917, and used until September 1918.

**INFORMATION**
The first Plots, I to IX, contain the graves of those who died in the 3rd Australian and 44th Casualty Clearing Stations that had been moved here from Brandhoek and Lijssenthoek in September 1917 after Brandhoek had been shelled. The later Plots, X to XV, are of those who died in the German Spring Offensive and the final breakout from the Salient in 1918.

There is a German Plot containing prisoners who died from September 1917 to March 1918. There was a group of 95 American soldiers but these have been removed, as have the French graves.

The space created has been used for the burial of 22 British men who died in late May 1940. One of these is Company Sergeant-Major Cecil Tomalin Bailey, DCM, 4th Oxford and Bucks Light Infantry, who was killed on 29 May 1940, aged

44 years, and now lies among comrades with whom he may have fought twenty years before. He had served in WW1 as a Sergeant, being one of the first into Munich Trench near Beaumont-Hamel on the Somme in November 1916. He became a prisoner of war because he held the position allowing others in his party to retreat while he held up the Germans. For this act, he was awarded the Distinguished Conduct Medal. Shortly before his death he rescued a wounded man from the German advance.

A burial of note is Serjeant David Gallaher, 2nd Auckland Regiment, NZEF, who died on 4 October 1917 aged 44 years. He was the first Captain of the New Zealand All Blacks Rugby Team. Gallaher played 26 representative matches for Auckland, including the first successful Ranfurly Shield defence, and 36 matches for the All Blacks, including six tests. Gallaher's All Black career spanned from 1903 to 1906, the highlight being the captaincy of the 1905 'Originals' tour of the British Isles in which he played 26 matches including four of the six tests, one of which was the only defeat of the tour, 3-0 against Wales. Gallaher fought in the South African War serving as a Corporal in the 6th and 10th New Zealand Mounted Rifles. Although exempt from conscription due to his age, Gallaher volunteered to fight in World War I, and apparently altered his date of birth to 31 October 1876. He enlisted in July 1916, following the death of his youngest brother Douglas. He was killed in the attack on the Gravenstafel Spur when wounded by a piece of shrapnel that penetrated through his helmet, dying later that day at the 3rd Australian Casualty Clearing Station. One brother, Private Henry Fletcher Gallaher, served with the 51st Australian Infantry and was killed on 24 April 1918 at Villers-Bretonneux. He is commemorated on the Villers-Bretonneux Memorial. Company Sergeant Major Douglas Wallace Gallaher, 11th Australian Infantry, died on 3 June 1916 aged 32 years and is buried in Rue-Petillon Military Cemetery, Fleurbaix. Two other brothers also fought and survived the war. Gallaher was one of thirteen former All Black rugby internationals who were killed in the war, one in ten of those who had worn the black jersey during the previous decade. Four of them were killed within a fortnight in June 1917 when the New Zealand Division took part in the attack at Messines Ridge.

Another to lose two brothers was Private James Hiddleston, 5th/6th Cameronians (Scottish Rifles) who died on 22 June 1918 aged 20 years. A brother, Private Robert Dalziel Hiddleston, Queen's Own (Royal West Kents) posted to 2/20th (Blackheath and Woolwich) Londons died on 30 August 1918 aged 30 years and is buried in HAC Cemetery, Ecoust-St. Mein. Another brother, Private John Smith Hiddleston, No. 4 (University) Company, Princess Patricia's Canadian Light Infantry (Eastern Ontario Regiment), died on 2 June 1916 aged 30 years during the Battle of Mount Sorrel and is on the Menin Gate.

Two Battalion commanders are here. Lieutenant Colonel Alexander Tillett, DSO, MC, 2nd Devonshires, died on 3 December 1917. He received the Military Cross in the 1917 New Years Honours List and took command of the Battalion on 31 July 1917 on the death of the previous Battalion commander. He was posthumously awarded the Distinguished Service Order having been wounded at Passendale on 29 November.

Lieutenant Colonel Alec Graham Scougal, MC, 17th Royal Scots, died on 18 September 1918 aged 30 years. Early in September 1918 the 17th Royal Scots took over positions south of Ypres. The Germans shelled the area extensively and among the casualties was Scougal. He had been with the 17th through all the major battles of the war. His brother, Major Frank William Scougal, MC, 11th Cameronians (Scottish Rifles) was killed on 19 September 1918 aged 34 years and is buried in Doiran Military Cemetery in Greece.

Among the men here are some youngsters. Private Clifford Robinson Oulton, 5th Canadian Mounted Rifles, died on 1 November 1917 aged 15 years. Private Robert Routledge, Royal Canadian Regiment, died on 19 November 1917 aged 16 years. He was from Newark, New Jersey, USA, one of many to cross the border to fight in the war before America joined. Rifleman E J Lindow, 1/5th South Lancashires, died on 17 September 1917 aged 16 years.

Also buried here are two men who were executed nearby by the British Army. Private John McFarlane of the 1/4th King's (Liverpools) was shot for desertion on 22 May 1918. A pre-war Territorial soldier who had been serving on the Western Front for three years McFarlane evidently decided that he had had enough and deserted the lines.

Private Joseph Nisbet, 1st Leicestershires deserted while he was moving to the front-line, and reached Calais, while he was under a suspended sentence of death for a previous desertion attempt. He had already gained a bad reputation in the army facing several courts martial though not all with a capital offence attached. Nisbet was executed on 23 August 1918.

| | | |
|---|---|---|
| UK – 952 | Aust – 149 | NZ – 118 |
| Can – 292 | NF – 7 | S Afr – 26 |
| BWI – 2 | Bermuda – 1 | India – 1 |
| Guernsey – 8 | Ger – 37 | |
| WWII – 22 (2 unidentified) | | |

**LOCATION**

Nine Elms Cemetery can be found west of Ieper about 1km west of Poperinge. It is about 300m south of the Poperinge by-pass, on a small road leading to Hilhoek.

# NO MAN'S COT CEMETERY

**HISTORY**
This was begun at the end of July 1917 in a captured area of no man's land, and used until March 1918.

**INFORMATION**
The cemetery derived its name from a nearby farm building that was located in no man's land for much of the war before this cemetery was opened. There are 45 men buried here from the 51st (Highland) Division who attacked through the position of this cemetery of the first day of the Third Battle Ypres.

On 19 December 1915 the Germans tried to break the line that had been held for much of the previous five months by the 1/6th West Yorkshires. So much gas was released in this, the first use of phosgene, that it left crystals on the ground, but the West Yorkshires had gas masks so the line was held even though the attack caused 1069 casualties, 120 of whom died.

On 19 April 1916, the German 6th Division captured the trenches here but they were retaken by the 1st King's Shropshire Light Infantry on 21 April who found that they could only advance by lying on the mud and crawling ahead. They inflicted heavy casualties on the enemy but lost their commanding officer, eight officers and 163 men. The 1/4th Duke of Wellington's were stationed here throughout the winter of 1916-17. After one 48 hour period an officer brought back only 28 men, the rest being casualties. On 19 December 1916 the Duke of Wellingtons were ordered to withdraw from the front-line as the artillery were to fire on the nearby German lines, no man's land being very narrow at this point. As the Duke of Wellingtons withdrew the Germans launched a gas attack which decimated the Yorkshire Battalion, many of whom are buried here. A reserve Battalion of the Brigade was called up and subsequently held the line.

Buried here is Private Arthur Ewen, 10th Welsh, killed in action on 31 July 1917 aged 20 years. He enlisted into the Army Pay Corps in May 1915, and began to rise through the ranks, but due to disciplinary problems he reverted to Private, was transferred to a Training Reserve Battalion in Aldershot and joined the 10th Welsh in May 1917. He was one of six brothers who served, four of whom survived. His brother, Captain William James Ewen 3rd attached 8th Queens Own (Royal West Kents) was killed in action near Chaulnes on the 25 March 1918 while commanding 'A' Company and is commemorated on the Pozieres Memorial.

UK – 79  Area - 375 sq mts

**LOCATION**
No Man's Cot Cemetery lies north of Ieper in open fields about half way between Boezinge and St. Juliaan. It is reached most easily by taking the Pilkemsweg north from the N38 northern by-pass and following the CWGC signs. It is interesting to note the small stones marking the limit of CWGC land at the edge of the path from the road to the cemetery.

# OAK DUMP CEMETERY

**HISTORY**
This cemetery was used in July, August and September 1917 during Third Ypres.

**INFORMATION**
On 14 February 1915 the 2nd East Surreys rushed here to recapture some trenches just taken by the Germans at Triangular Wood which was just to the south of Oak Dump. The trenches on either side of the area to be recaptured were still held by British troops. Therefore, the East Surreys were ordered to advance without firing their guns. Only two officers and 25 men attended roll-call that evening.

The British front-line at the start of the Battle of Messines was 150m east of Oak Dump and the German line 200m beyond. The Germans withdrew to the Chateau in the wood on 7 June holding up the 1/7th Londons and, though the 1/6th (London Rifles) Londons arrived to help, they also failed to move the enemy. It was not until the arrival of a tank, and another artillery bombardment that the Germans withdrew. The British then turned the cellar of the Chateau into an Advanced Dressing Station.

On 26 March 1918 an observation post opposite the cemetery was destroyed during which seven men of 180th Siege Battery were killed. However, their bodies were not recovered and buried here until 1927. Of the men buried here 59 are of various Battalions of the London Regiment reflecting their contribution here. One grave, of a man who died in 1914, was brought here after the war. He is 2nd Lieutenant A. K. Nicholson, 'B' Squadron, 18th (Queen Mary's Own) Hussars, killed on 31 October 1914 aged 21 years, an only son. He is recorded as being in Voormezele Military Cemetery Extension No. 3 in 1919 and here in 1920 though he was originally buried near Hollebeke Chateau. He was born in the USA, educated at Sandhurst and commissioned in 1913. He was killed by a sniper at 6.00am while holding an advanced trench near St. Eloi.

Another man killed in 1914 is also here. Lieutenant Kenneth Croft North, MiD, 4th (Queen's Own) Hussars, was killed on 31 October 1914 aged 27 years. He was in charge of his unit's machine guns and was killed while moving them. He had been at the Front since 18 August and had been involved in several actions, including getting his guns back to his lines using a wheelbarrow, for which he was Mentioned in Despatches.

**PALLINGBEEK PARK.** The park is reached by car from the road from Zillebeke to Comines and Hollebeke, at the top of the rise 400m beyond the turn to Hill 60, on single track roads between avenues of trees leading south-west to the park. It is also possible to enter the park on foot or bicycle from many points such as at Spoilbank, Hedge Row and 1st DCLI Cemeteries or at the visitor centre near Chester Farm Cemetery. There is a cafe/restaurant, information centre and several short walks amongst the woods. Many large and important trenches, including International, Impudence and Imperial, were situated in the Park. You can find the German Third Defensive Line visible in places with the remains of bunkers, shell-holes, trenches and the old canal. Interestingly, the walk to the west, ending at Spoilbank Cemetery, will take you through the front-lines at 'The Bluff' which saw much fighting throughout the war.

UK – 109        Aust – 2        Unnamed – 5

Area - 1059 sq mts

Special Memorials to two British graves destroyed by shell-fire.

### LOCATION
Oak Dump Cemetery lies south of Ieper midway between St. Eloi and Hill 60 on the edge of the ridges here and clearly signed from the St. Eloi-Ieper road.

# OOSTTAVERNE WOOD CEMETERY

### HISTORY
This cemetery was begun on 7 June 1916, once this area had been captured on the first day of the Battle of Messines, and remained in use until September 1917. It was greatly enlarged after the war with the concentration of 1000 graves from the surrounding battlefields and from German cemeteries that had been removed.

### INFORMATION
The wood from which the cemetery gets its name was a large formal wood with avenues, walks and drives, but it was destroyed in the war and is now only a small copse.

The 'Oosttaverne Line' was one of the main objectives on the first day of the Battle of Messines. It was a line of trenches and defences that ran from the Lys to the Ypres-Comines canal and passed just east of here. Part of the defences of that line, a pill-box, can still be seen next to the cemetery. A German Trench called Obstacle Trench ran through part of the cemetery. The wood and the village were taken by the 19th (Western) and 11th (Northern) Divisions. The cemetery is situated in what had been no man's land before the Battle of Messines.

There were, in fact, two cemeteries created almost next to each other here, Oosttaverne Wood Cemetery No. 1 and Oosttaverne Wood Cemetery No. 2, now Plots I & III respectively. The first burials included two officers and a Chaplain in a group of seven men killed on 7 June 1917. What is now Plot II was begun a little later, in July 1917, as an extension to Cemetery No. 1. Most of the graves in Plot III are original burials, although fourteen men killed in 1914 have been added to Rows E & D after the war while others, who died before the cemetery was opened, have been concentrated here, mainly in Plot I but also elsewhere in the cemetery. More burials were added after the war. The cemetery was used again in WW2 during the British retreat to Dunkirk in May 1940.

An unknown number of Germans lie in Plot I. A German cemetery at the edge of the road to Wijtschate, which contained 1100 graves concentrated there after the war, was removed in the 1950's.

Buried here is Private H Tuffnell, 1st Bedfordshires who was killed in action at Hill 60 on 21 April 1915 aged 35 years. One brother Private Alfred Tufnell, 7th Bedfordshires, died on 4 November 1915 aged 33 years is buried in Dartmoor Cemetery on the Somme. Another, Private Benjamin Tuffnell, 1/5th Bedfordshires, was killed in action at Sulva Bay, Gallipoli on 15 August 1915 aged 28 years and is commemorated on the Helles Memorial. Note that the brother buried in Dartmoor Cemetery has his surname recorded with one 'f' unlike the others.

Also here is Corporal Ernest Howard Parsons, Princess Patricia's Canadian Light Infantry (Eastern Ontario Regiment), who died between 2 and 4 June 1916 aged 22 years. He was a student of Alberta University, where he played hockey and rugby, captaining the rugby team, when he enlisted in May 1915. He first joined the McGill University Company, 2nd Reinforcing Draft, hence his service number of McGill 71, before his transfer.

Another here is 2nd Lieutenant Daniel Alfred Hodges, 3rd attached 10th Queen's Own (Royal West Kents), killed on 5 May 1917 aged 25 years. He designed the two candlesticks near the fontstand in Talbot House in Poperinge. The oak candlesticks were made in the autumn of 1917 from the carved posts of an old bedstead. Each bears a small strip of shell case commemorating the Australians and Canadians who worshipped at Talbot House. The Australian candlestick was especially in memory of the Australian Engineers whose lives were sacrificed in the tunnelling operations during the Messines Offensive. Daniel Hodges was killed before the candlesticks were completed. He had rescued a wounded Sergeant, and was bringing in another wounded man, when killed.

Opposite the cemetery is the Memorial to the 19th (Western) Division, also known as the 'Butterfly' Division. It marks the site of their advance on 7 June 1917 and further actions here in 1918.

Concentrated here:

Hoogemotte Farm German Cemetery - on the Belgian side of the River Lys near Comines which is about 4km south-east of here. It contained twelve British men who died in April 1918.

Houthem-les-Ypres German Cemetery - on the west side of the village which is about 3.5km south-east of here. It contained seventeen British men who died in 1916 and 1917.

Inderster German Cemetery - on the road from Beselare to Broodseinde about 5km north-east of here, at a small crossroads 1.4km north of Beselare. It was made by the German XXVII Reserve Corps and contained 53 British men who died in October and November 1914.

Koekuit German Cemetery - on the road to Houthulst north of Langemark German Cemetery about 8km north of here. It contained eight British men who died in October 1914.

Ten Brielen Amerika German Cemetery - north of Comines about 4km south-east of here. It contained 850 Germans with six British soldiers who died in April 1917.

Three Houses German Cemetery (Hollebeke Cemetery No. 60) - near Hollebeke Chateau on the road to Kortewilde about 2km east of here. Buried among the Germans three British men and two Canadians who died in 1916.

Zwaanhoek German Cemetery - in a hamlet 400m north of Besalare which is about 5km north-east of here. It was made by the German XXVII Reserve Corps and contained six British men who died in October 1914.

UK – 923     Aust – 43     NZ – 19
Can – 133    Fr – 1        Ger - unknown no.
Unnamed - 783 (75% of total)
WW2 – 117 (5 unidentified)
Area - 4340 sq mts
Special Memorial to one British soldier buried in Three House German Cemetery whose grave has been lost.

## LOCATION
Oosttaverne Wood Cemetery is south of Ieper about 1.5km south of St. Eloi on the road signed to Rijsel (Lille). It lies on the west side of the road next to a small crossroads that has the 19th Division Memorial on the south-east corner.

# OXFORD ROAD CEMETERY

## HISTORY
Begun in August 1917 as the front-line moved east from here this burial ground remained in use until April 1918. After the war, the cemetery was greatly enlarged with the concentration of graves from isolated positions east and south-east of Ypres.

## INFORMATION
This is a deceptively large graveyard as it is in the shape of a 'Y', of which you can only see the stem from the road. The original cemetery, 134 graves in Plot I, is on the extreme left as you enter and contains the War Stone. It was named after the nearby road.

A second cemetery, Oxford Road No. 2, was begun next to No. 1 in October 1917 and used until April 1918. These were incorporated into one burial ground after the war so that the 255 graves in No. 2 cemetery now make up Plot V which is on the extreme right as you enter. The other Plots, II, III and IV, are made up of concentrated graves.

Believed to be buried here is Captain Clement Robertson, VC, 3rd Queen's (Royal West Surreys) attached 'A' Battalion, Tank Corps, killed on 4 October 1917 aged 28 years. He was involved in the British attack by 21st Division, who had been allotted four tanks, between Polygon Wood and the Menin Road. Fire from German pillboxes caused heavy casualties to the British infantry as they advanced through the muddy conditions of what had been the stream of the Polygonbeek. With the support of one of the tanks the German pillboxes were captured and the higher ground overlooking the Reutel valley was reached. The citation reads 'For most conspicuous bravery in leading his Tanks in attack under heavy shell, machine-gun and rifle fire. Capt. Robertson, knowing the risk of the Tanks missing the way, continued to lead them on foot, guiding them carefully and patiently towards their objective although he must have known that his action would almost inevitably cost him his life. This gallant officer was killed after his objective had been reached, but his skilful leading had already ensured successful action. His utter disregard of danger and devotion to duty afford an example of outstanding valour.' This was the first Victoria Cross for a member of the Tank Corps. Born in South Africa, he grew up in Ireland and then went to Egypt where he worked as an engineer on the Nile irrigation project. He enlisted at the start of the war into the 19th (2nd Public Schools) Royal Fusiliers and was commissioned in January 1915. He subsequently volunteered for tunnelling operations and joined the Royal Engineers, with whom he worked until in January 1917 when he joined the Tank Corps. He and his four brothers, who all survived the war, were keen golfers and were founder members of the Delgany Golf Club. Clement won the Captain's Prize in the first year it was played for in 1908. Private Cyril Allen, Robertson's orderly, was also on foot with Robertson and was later awarded the Distinguished Conduct Medal.

Also here is Serjeant Colin (Charlie) Blythe, 12th King's Own Yorkshire Light Infantry, died on 8 November 1917 aged 38 years. He was a professional cricketer who played for Kent County Cricket Club and England. He was a left-arm orthodox spin bowler and is regarded as one of the finest bowlers of the period between 1900 and 1914 – sometimes referred to as the Golden Age of cricket. He was named as one of Wisden's five Cricketers of the Year in 1904 and played in nineteen Test matches for England. Blythe first played for Kent in 1899, and in a stunning start, took a wicket with his very first ball in first-class cricket. He later took fifteen wickets for 99 runs in the second Test at Headingly against South Africa in the 1907 series which was not bettered in England until the extraordinary success of Jim Laker in 1956. Blythe suffered from epilepsy yet enlisted in 1914 and soon retired from first-class cricket. He was killed by shell-fire on the railway between Pommern Castle and Forest Hall near Passendale.

Another here of note is Captain Henry Ernest Sulivan, Princess Patricia's Canadian Light Infantry (Eastern Ontario Regiment), who died on 31 October 1917 aged 29 years. The Battalion war diary records that he moved to the front-line, a series of linked shell holes in front of Passendale at about 9.30pm on 30 October. He was detailed to go forward to take charge of the firing line. He was wounded, shot in the chest by a sniper, at 1.45am and was reported as dying of his wounds at 5.00am. He had joined up in 1914 and was in France by December. He was wounded by a bullet fracturing his right leg in February and not considered fit for active service again until December 1915. His jaw was fractured in February 1916 but he was back with his unit by June at which time he was promoted to Captain, though he was an Acting Major until December. He was hospitalised again from March to June 1917, the result of flu. He returned to his Battalion on 27 October after ten days leave. His brother, Captain Eugene Gilbert Sulivan, 4th attached 1st East Surreys, died on 8 May 1917 and is buried in Orchard Dump Cemetery. Another brother, 2nd Lieutenant Philip Hamilton Sulivan, 'B' Company, 2nd Royal Munster Fusiliers was killed during the Retreat from Mons on 27 August 1914 aged 20 years and is buried in Etreux British Cemetery.

Another here is 2nd Lieutenant Horace Frederick Gough, DSO, 8th North Staffordshires, who died on 21 September 1917 aged 21 years and is commemorated here by a Special Memorial. He enlisted in 1913 as a Lance Corporal in the 11th Hussars before gaining his commission in February 1917. He received the Distinguished Service Order 'For conspicuous gallantry and devotion to duty. He rallied part of a neighbouring Battalion that had lost all of its officers and had been forced back from a most important position. He personally led a counter attack, and re-took the position at the point of the bayonet, inflicting heavy casualties on the enemy. He then consolidated the captured position and remained in command until relieved. By his gallantry, individuality and resource he undoubtedly enabled the troops on his flank to regain a highly important position.'

The Memorial to the 50th (Northumbrian) Division, unveiled in September 1927, is 100m north-east of this cemetery. Further on the road towards St. Juliaan you will find the memorial is dedicated to 2nd Lieutenant Henry Anthony Birrell-Anthony and all officers and men of the 1st Monmouthshire Regiment who died in the Second Battle of Ypres in May 1915. To the east, near the motorway, are a series of bunkers known as the Cambrai Redoubt which were attacked, and taken at heavy cost, on 31 July 1917.

| | | |
|---|---|---|
| UK – 657 | Aust – 74 | NZ – 37 |
| Can 74 | NF – 9 | Guernsey – 2 |
| Unnamed – 297 | | Ger – 2 |

Area - 3706 sq mts

Special Memorials to three British men known/believed to be buried among the unnamed.

**LOCATION**

Oxford Road Cemetery can be found north-east of Ieper just east of the old road (N313) from the town, through St. Jan, to St. Juliaan. It lies on the south side of the road that used to run from St. Jan to Passendale which has been blocked by the motorway. The cemetery is well signed from the N313.

## PACKHORSE FARM SHRINE CEMETERY

**HISTORY**

This cemetery was only used from April to June 1915.

**INFORMATION**

Wulvergem was in Allied hands for much of the war. It was the scene of a German gas attack on the night of 29-30 April 1916 which was repulsed by the 3rd and 24th Divisions. The village was captured by the Germans on 14 April 1918 and reoccupied by the 30th Division on 2 September.

Packhorse Farm was the name given by the British Army to the nearby buildings. A shrine used to be just south of it at the point where the path to the cemetery now reaches the road though the shrine has been rebuilt nearer to the farm.

The 46th (North Midland) Division made two cemeteries when they were stationed here in 1915. One was at the farm, which has been removed to Lindenhoek Chalet Cemetery, and this one at the shrine. As a result, 56 of the graves here are of men of the 46th Division, of which, 27 are of the 1/5th Lincolnshires and 27 of the 1/4th Leicestershires.

Buried here are brothers Privates Ernest Arthur Proctor and James Emerson Proctor, both 1/5th Lincolnshires killed on 20 May 1915 aged 22 and 21 years respectively. They came from Scunthorpe and had both been involved with the Scouting movement before enlisting.

UK – 59        Area - 673 sq mts

### LOCATION

Packhorse Farm Shrine Cemetery lies in fields south of Ieper and about 1km south-east of Kemmel, 50m east of a local road that runs south from Lindenhoek. It is reached most easily from the crossroads in the small hamlet of Lindenhoek turning right at the fork 20m from the Ieper–Nieuwkerke road.

## PASSCHENDAELE NEW BRITISH CEMETERY

### HISTORY

This cemetery was created after the war with the concentration of graves from the battlefields of Passendale. Almost all of the burials are from the autumn of 1917 but one is identified who died in November 1914, one other who died in May 1915, one in February 1917 and fifteen in 1918.

### INFORMATION

Passendale has given its name to one of the most infamous military conflicts in history. Passendale was to be an early objective in Haig's plan to break out of the Salient, reach the Belgian coast, taking the submarine dockyards out of the war, and win the war by the end of 1917. Though the plan had failed Haig pressed on to Passendale. It took 100 days to reach Passendale from the line held on 31 July 1917, another five to take the village, and, possibly, only mounting pressure from Downing Street stopped the slaughter on the Passendale Ridge.

Each part of the advance has been given its own title in the battle nomenclature because the advance was so slow and costly. The overall campaign is dealt with in depth elsewhere in several titles in my bibliography. The battles here at Passendale took place in the worst of the weather when the army was almost drained of reserves. Hence, troops of the Dominions did much of the work in October and November 1917.

On 26 October 1917, in the valleys ranging from this cemetery north-west to Poelkapelle, the 63rd (Royal Naval) Division attacked, assisting the Canadian Corps, suffering 2481 casualties in three days. In the marsh and bottomless mud of the valleys the 63rd Division attacked and suffered counter-attack with the 1st and 2nd Royal Marine Light Infantry, and the 'Anson' and 'Hood' Battalions playing major roles in the often chaotic fighting. Though some strong points were taken and 400m gained the 188th Brigade lost fourteen officers and more than 500 men in each Battalion.

On 30 October the next stage of the attack began but as the British prepared to go 'over the top' the Germans began their morning bombardment early, decimating the 190th Brigade. A Company of 1/28th (Artists Rifles) Londons was wiped out while the 7th Royal Fusiliers, 4th Bedfordshires and 5th King's Shropshire Light Infantry also suffered greatly.

As a result a relatively new tactic, that may seem obvious to us, was employed - a night attack. The innovation, substantially different from a night raid, was used on 3 November during which the 'Drake' and 'Hood' Battalions of the 63rd Division took the ridge from here to Poelkapelle, suffering only light casualties.

Haig had decided that the Canadians should take Passendale because the Australians, New Zealanders and British had been badly depleted by the fighting of the previous four months. General Currie, commanding the Canadian Expeditionary Force, having inspected the battlefield, protested and argued against the attack predicting that it would cost approximately 16000 casualties to take the objectives - which was to prove correct. The German Jaegers that held the village were some of Germany's best Battalions and, as the roads had become the only secure ground among the muddy valleys, the Jaegers could anticipate the line of attack. The Canadians advanced in phases. In a series of attacks beginning on 26 October, 20000 men under heavy fire worked their way from shellhole to shellhole. Then on 30 October, with two British Divisions, the Canadians began the assault on Passendale village. They gained the ruined outskirts of the village during a violent rainstorm and for five days they held on, often waist-deep in mud and exposed to German shelling. On 6 November, when reinforcements arrived, 80% of the attackers were dead. The village was finally cleared of Germans by 10 November and the offensive closed on 11 November 1917.

In the fighting nearby the following Victoria Crosses were won:

1. Private (later Sergeant) Thomas Holmes, VC, 4th Canadian Mounted Rifles, captured nineteen Germans while stopping two machine guns and a pill-box on 26 October aged 19 years. He survived the war to become a pilot for the Harbour Commission and died in 1950.
2. Captain (later Major) Christopher Patrick John O'Kelly, VC, MC, 52nd Canadian Infantry, aged 21 years, captured six pill-boxes with 100 prisoners and ten machine-guns on 26 October before repelling several German counter attacks. He survived the war only to drown while prospecting in north-western Ontario.
3. Lieutenant (later Lieutenant-Colonel) Robert Shankland, VC, DCM, 43rd Canadian Infantry, on 26 October organised remnants of several units to hold exposed ground, beating off German attacks, while also reporting to HQ and leading further attacks. He remained in the military serving as a Lieutenant-Colonel in WW2.
4. Lieutenant Hugh McDonald McKenzie, VC, DCM, 7th Brigade Machine Gun Company, Canadian Machine Gun Corps, who silenced a pill-box on 30 October, was killed in the act and is commemorated on the Menin Gate. He may be buried here among the unidentified.
5. Sergeant (later Major) George Harry Mullin, VC, MM, Princess Patricia's Canadian Light Infantry, for the same action as Lieutenant MacKenzie. He survived the war.
6. Private Cecil John Kinross, VC, 49th Canadian Infantry, on 30 October advanced alone without his rifle over the open ground in broad daylight, charging a German machine gun, killing the crew of six, and destroying the gun. He enabled a further advance of 300m to be made and a highly important position to be established. He survived the war.
7. Major (later Major-General) George Randolph Pearkes, VC, PC, CC, CB, DSO, MC, CD, 5th Canadian Mounted Rifles, seized two farmhouse strong points just south of this cemetery on 30 October. He survived the war to become a politician and Governor of British Columbia.
8. Corporal (later Sergeant) Collin Fraser Barron, VC, 3rd Canadian (1st Central Ontario, Toronto) Infantry, who stopped two enemy artillery batteries on 6 November just north of this cemetery. He survived the war.
9. Private James Peter Robertson, VC, 27th (Winnipeg) Canadian Infantry, who disposed of an enemy position in the village on 6 November saving many lives in the process. He is buried in Tyne Cot Cemetery.

Passendale had seen fighting from the earliest days of the formation of the Salient. On 13 October 1914 the 7th Division, with the Household Cavalry of the 7th Cavalry Brigade who had been billeted in Passendale, advanced to Roeselare. The Life Guards and Royal Horse Guards, of the Household Cavalry, whose compliment included various ranks of the nobility, met almost no opposition before returning to their billets. They were then ordered to take Menin but the Germans had captured an officer carrying the British battle plans. Hence, they knew everything that the British intended to do and had rushed troops to Menin. Therefore, the 7th Division and Belgian troops were forced to withdraw. The cavalry occupied Passendale on 17 October handing it over to French Cavalry and Territorials on 18 October, but on 20 October 1914 the village fell to the Germans who held it until 1917.

The Germans over-ran the village during their Spring Offensive in 1918 but it was finally captured on 29 September 1918 by Belgian troops who have now erected a Monument to this event next to the cemetery. This is the last of the Albertina markers the Belgians erected to mark the passing of King Albert I. This one states 'Ein defensiv Passendale 28th September 1918', and marks the end of the last offensive here.

Buried here is Private Alexander Decoteau, 49th Canadian Infantry, killed on 30 October 1917 aged 28 years. He was a native Cree Nation Indian, born on the Red Pheasant Indian Reserve (Saskatchewan), and was an excellent sniper and athlete. He moved to Edmonton to live with his sister where its police force hired him as a constable in 1909. He was also the first 'First Nations' police officer in Canada in 1911 and the first motorcycle policeman in Canada. He became a Sergeant in 1914 and put in charge of the No. 4 Police Station. After joining the police force he began to compete nationally and won almost every race he entered including both middle and long-distance events. On Dominion Day in 1910 he won a total of four different races including the provincial championships in Lethbridge, Alberta, and one in Lloydminster, Saskatchewan, in which he set a Western Canadian record. He also entered the five mile race in Edmonton, Alberta, at the Edmonton

Exhibition and beat an Olympic Athlete. In 1912 he became the only Albertan on the Canadian team at the Olympic Games in Stockholm. He enlisted with the 202nd Edmonton Sportsmen's Battalion in 1916, but then transferred to the 49th Canadian Infantry. He was killed by a sniper.

There are several Memorials in and around Passendale. In the church there is a Memorial, in the form of three stained-glass windows, to the 66th (2nd East Lancashire) Division in the north transept. On the wall of the Town Hall, at the north end of the town square opposite the church, are five Memorials. Two tablets commemorate World War II units but the other three are to the 4th Belgian Regiment of Carabiniers, the Belgian Grenadiers and a plaque from the Western Front Association.

Near the village the Canadian Memorial is at Crest Farm, clearly signed from the town square about 400m west of the church. It had been a fortified farm on high ground on the line of the final offensive to take the village and the memorial commemorates the attack made by the 1st and 2nd Canadian Divisions on 6 November. The view from the small park is worth the visit, particularly the sight of Passendale from the direction that the Canadian troops came in the last days of the battle. Such a short distance but at what cost. This Memorial stands where Canadian soldiers encountered some of the fiercest resistance they were to meet during the war. A simple large block of Canadian granite sat on the ridge is a sombre reminder of the events that took place here.

On the Passendale-Broodseinde road south of the village, a path leads to the fields to the side of the road wher there is the Memorial to the 85th Canadian Infantry Battalion (Nova Scotia Highlanders).

UK – 1019        Aust – 292        NZ – 126
Can – 647        NF – 1            S Afr – 3
Guernsey – 4     Unnamed - 1602 (Over 75% of total)
Area - 7279 sq mts

Special Memorials to four British men and three Canadians believed to be buried among the unnamed.

### LOCATION
Passchendaele Cemetery is north-east of Ieper on the ridges about 2km north-west of Passendale. It lies 800m south-west of the Passendale-Westrozebeke road on a local road signed to St. Jan from a crossroads near a water tower.

## PERTH CEMETERY (CHINA WALL)

### HISTORY
Begun by the French in November 1914, the British took over the burial ground in June 1917 in preparation for Third Ypres and then used it as a front-line cemetery until October 1917. It was enlarged after the war with the concentration of approximately 2500 graves from the surrounding battlefields.

### INFORMATION
The 'Great Wall of China' was one of the main British communication trenches that ran just north of here to the front-line. The Perth part of the name is thought to come from the fact that the first British burials here were made by the 2nd Cameronians. For some time the cemetery was also known as 'Halfway House Cemetery'.

The original cemetery is now Plot I. A French Plot, also enlarged after the war, has been removed. Most of the Special Memorials, which are near the road close to the entrance, are grouped by cemeteries in which the graves were lost. The most recent burials, (at the time of writing) of three unidentified soldiers, were made in March 2017.

Perth Cemetery contains several men who were executed during 1915 by the British Army. Private George Ernest Roe, 2nd King's Own Yorkshire Light Infantry deserted on 20 May 1915 after fighting at Hill 60 but reported for duty at 11.00am the following day. He was executed and buried near Huts Cemetery, Dikkebus on 10 June 1915, aged 19 years, though his grave was moved here after the war. He was sent to France in November 1914. He had one other offence of absence which counted against him when he was court martialled, without representation, on 26 May. He was described as a good soldier with a character to match, but his commanding officer said he 'seemed to have lost his nerve.' George said nothing in his defence, including that his brother-in-law, Private Walter Cameron Wells, 2nd Yorkshires, had been killed on 11 March aged 35 years. He is commemorated on the Le Touret Memorial.

Private Thomas Harris, 1st Queen's Own (Royal West Kents), had joined the Army in 1913 but absconded in August 1914 shortly after the Battles of Mons and Le Cateau. He managed to evade the authorities until he was arrested in Paris by the Military police in May 1915. At his trial on 12 June he pleaded that the experience of battle had been too much for him to stand. His plea for leniency was ignored and he was executed on 21 June 1915.

Private Thomas Docherty, 2nd King's Own Scottish Borderers deserted at the same time as Private Roe and was executed on 16 July 1915. Having enlisted in June 1914 and seen action for some time, he absconded in March 1915 and remained absent for three months avoiding the Second Battle of Ypres. At his trial he claimed the effects of shellfire had caused him to desert.

On 26 July 1915 the 3rd Worcestershires executed five of its soldiers for desertion, the largest single execution by the British Army in the war. All were shot on the ramparts at Ypres but following the war, and the consolidation of smaller cemeteries the five bodies ended up in two different cemeteries. Two are here and the other three, Privates Alfred Thompson, John Robinson and Bert Hartells, are in Aeroplane Cemetery.

Corporal Frederick Ives and Private Ernest Fellows are now buried here. Fellows had served in the regiment prior to the war and as an active reservist was recalled to the colours in September 1914. Early in June 1915 the Battalion was holding a line of trenches near the Menin Road on the left to Sanctuary Wood. After four days of fighting, on 9 June 1915 the Battalion was relieved by the 2nd Royal Irish Rifles. Whilst the Battalion was resting near Poperinge Fellows went missing. He was arrested shortly afterwards and sent for court martial on 14 July 1915. At his trial he offered no evidence in his defence and was found guilty of desertion and sentenced to death.

Ives had only been in France just over a month when on 15 September 1914 he absconded during the fighting on the Marne while on remand for an earlier offence. Ives managed to avoid capture for nine months until arrested on 24 June 1915 by an officer of the Army Veterinary Corps. At the time he was wearing civilian clothes. At his court martial on 7 July Ives had claimed memory loss after concussion caused by shellfire as the reason for his absence. Consequently, the Court Martial panel recommended leniency but this failed. Ives is recorded incorrectly by the CWGC as dying on 22 July. Ives is now buried four graves away from 2nd Lieutenant Birks, VC, whose story is told below, I find it interesting, and appropriate, that men who met such different fates are honoured equally in death so close together.

Private Evan Fraser, 2nd Royal Scots was the first soldier to be executed while under a suspended sentence of death for a previous attempt to desert. Fraser absconded from his regiment at 4.00pm on 24 May 1915. He was arrested the next day at a local railway station in possession of a forged pass and was handed back to the British. Whilst in British custody he escaped, but again was caught after little more than 24 hours. Two weeks later, he escaped custody for a second time and again was arrested within a day. On 13 July he was charged with having deserted on three occasions and of conduct to the prejudice of good order in having a forged pass. He was undefended at his trial. He pleaded guilty to the forgery, but not guilty to the counts of desertion. His Battalion adjutant gave evidence, saying that Fraser was 'a continual source of annoyance', a shirker and a continual deserter. He was executed at 4.00am on 2 August 1915 aged 19 years. His grave is now marked by a Special Memorial.

Private Louis R. Phillips, 6th Somerset Light Infantry was executed on the ramparts in Ypres on 19 August 1915 and his grave was concentrated here after the war. Phillips arrived in France in April 1915 and saw action in the Salient in July, following which he went absent for four days. At his Court Martial he stated that he had been stressed by not having received any mail from home for several weeks.

Two men who won the Victoria Cross are buried here. 2nd Lieutenant Frederick Birks, VC, MM, 6th Australian Infantry, died on 21 September 1917 aged 23 years, having 'won' the Victoria Cross on the previous day. The citiation reads 'For most conspicuous bravery in attack, when, accompanied by only a Corporal, he rushed a strong point which was holding up the advance. The Corporal was wounded by a bomb, but 2nd Lt. Birks went on by himself, killed the remainder of the enemy occupying the position, and captured a machine gun. Shortly afterwards he organised a small party and attacked another strong point which was occupied by about twenty-five of the enemy, of whom many were killed and an officer and fifteen men captured. During the consolidation this officer did magnificent work in reorganising parties of other units which had been disorganised during the operations. By his wonderful coolness and personal bravery 2nd Lt. Birks kept his men in splendid spirits throughout. He was killed at his post by a shell whilst endeavouring to extricate some of his men who had been buried by a shell.' He was posted to the medical corps when he enlisted, having emigrated to Australia in 1913, and served as a stretcher-bearer at Gallipoli where he was wounded in June 1915 after being one of the first ashore on ANZAC Day 1915. In 1916 he was awarded the Military Medal for bravery at Pozieres. He was then commissioned and joined his Battalion.

Captain (Later Major) William Henry Johnston(e), VC, three times MiD, 59th Field Company, Royal Engineers, died on 8 June 1915 aged 35 years. The action for which he was awarded the Victoria Cross took place on 14 September 1914 at Missy in France. The citation reads 'At Missy, on 14th Sept., under a heavy fire all day until 7 p.m., worked with his own hand two rafts bringing back wounded and returning with ammunition; thus enabling advanced Brigade to maintain its position across the river.' After winning the Victoria Cross he was involved in tunnelling at Ypres, during which he was killed. He was commissioned in 1899 and saw service in Malta, China and at home, where he was at the Staff College in August 1914. He became a Captain in 1908 and Major four days before his death. He was Mentioned in Despatches three times between December 1914 and his death.

Commemorated here is Captain The Honourable Charles Henry Stanley Monck, 3rd Coldstream Guards, who died on 21 October 1914 aged 37 years. He was originally buried in St. Julien East German Cemetery but his grave has been lost so he has a Special Memorial here. He was the only surviving son of the 5th Viscount Monck and had faought in the South African Wars and at the Battle of Landrecies, 25-26 August 1914. He was awarded his commission in the Coldstream Guards in May 1897, becoming Lieutenant in November 1898, and Captain in November 1903.

With a similar background and killed in the same campaign is Lieutenant The Honourable Charles Douglas-Pennant, 1st Coldstream Guards, killed on 29 October 1914 aged 37 years. He was the third son of the 2nd Baron Penrhyn and had served with the Guards since 1899 seeing action in the South African Wars. He had retired to the Reserve of Officers in 1911 rejoining his Battalion at the start of the war. He was killed near Geluveld where records show that he was one of the last officers to survive as by 29 October 1914 the Battalion had lost all of its officers and only had 120 men remaining. His brother, Captain The Honourable George Henry Douglas-Pennant, MiD, 1st Grenadier Guards, was killed in action on 11 March 1915 aged 38 years and is commemorated on the Le Touret Memorial.

His nephew, Lieutenant The Honourable Alan George Sholto Douglas-Pennant, 1st Grenadier Guards, was killed in action on the same day, 29 October 1914, aged 24 years, and is commemorated on the Menin Gate. The 1st Grenadier Guards were with 1st Coldstream Guards east of Geluveld on 29 October 1914, so the two men died within a short distance of each other.

Another here is Lieutenant Colonel Victor Augustine Flower, DSO, 1/13th (Kensington) Londons, died 15 August 1917 aged 40 years. He was the youngest son of Sir William Henry Flower, the first Director of the Natural History Museum. He was a volunteer in the Artists' Rifles and in December 1895 was commissioned into the Middlesex Rifle Volunteers. In June 1898 he was promoted to Captain but resigned his commission in 1900 and left for Singapore. He joined the Malay States Volunteers and in 1914 he rejoined the Artists Rifles, soon gaining his promotion to Major. In December 1915, while in France, he took over as commanding officer of the 1/22nd (The Queen's) Londons. Shortly after he was invalided home and on his recovery was appointed to command the 1/13th (Kensington) Londons, receiving the Distinguished Service Order in the January 1917 New Years Honours List and twice being Mentioned in Despatches. He was killed at Glencourse Wood near Hooge.

Also buried here is Lieutenant Francis William Stuart Teggart, 14th Argyll and Sutherland Highlanders attached 2nd Gordon Highlanders, who died on 26 October 1917 aged 27 years. His twin brother Captain John Cameron Thomson Teggart, Royal Army Medical Corps attached 256th Brigade, Royal Field Artillery, died on 21 July 1918 and is now buried in Terlincthun British Cemetery. He was in Epernay French National Cemetery until 1964 when the 267 British graves were removed.

Buried in the cemetery, though not side by side, are brothers Privates George Allanson Hardy, died on 1 March 1916 aged 32 years and John William Hardy, died 20 December 1915 aged 41 years, both 'X' Company, 1/6th Durham Light Infantry. John was originally buried near or in Tuileries Cemetery just to the south, but was moved here with several other men in 1918.

Another pair of brothers buried here, again not side by side, are Private Edwin Archibald Imrie, 57th Australian Infantry, died on 27 October 1917 aged 29 years and originally buried near or in Tuileries Cemetery just to the south and moved here with several other men in 1918. Private Robert James Imrie, 23rd Australian Infantry, died on 4 October 1917 aged 31 years and originally buried just north of Geluveld and moved here in 1919.

Buried here is 2nd Lieutenant Samuel Franklyn Leslie Cody, No. 41 Squadron, Royal Flying Corps and General List, killed on 23 January 1917 aged 21 years. His father, Samuel Franklyn Cody (previously Cowdery) is considered to have been the first to make a powered controlled flight and landing in Britain, in 1908, and received Royal Aero Club Certificate No. 9. He was killed in an air accident in 1913. A flamboyant showman, he was often confused with Buffalo Bill Cody, whose surname he took when young. Cody arrived at the Front on October 1916. He was last seen in combat with four German planes over Passendale.

Another of note is Private John 'Jack' Warwick Huggins, 1/8th Durham Light Infantry, died on 26 April 1915 aged 28 years. He was a pre-war professional footballer with Reading and Sunderland. In the 1906-08 seasons he played for Sunderland AFC, initially as an amateur and then as a professional. He was as an outside-left in fourteen matches, and scored two goals, one against Manchester United in October 1906, and one against Sheffield United in February 1907. In 1908/09 he played professionally for Reading FC, then in the Southern League. He also played for Durham City and Wingate. In the summer he played cricket for Sunderland, Wheatley Hill and Castle Eden. He joined his Battalion at the start of the war going to France on 20 April 1915. He was reported missing in June 1915 and it was believed that he was a prisoner of war, but at the end of 1915 the Red Cross received news from the Germans that he had been mortally wounded at the Gravenstafel Ridge and buried at Wallemolen, near Roulers. He was moved here with nine others in 1924.

Concentrated here:

Beselaere German Cemetery No. 1 (246 Reserve Infantry Regiment) - situated close to the church in the village about 4km east of here. It contained 500 Germans and two British graves.

Belgian Chateau Cemetery - in the grounds of a chateau in Vlamertinge about 5km west of here. It contained twelve British men, eleven Canadians and one French soldier who died from 1914 to 1917.

Broodseinde German Cemeteries - several German cemeteries around Broodseinde, about 5km north-east of here, were concentrated into one containing 5000 German graves after the war but it, in turn, was removed in the 1950's. In addition to the Germans there were 27 British graves mainly of men who died in 1914.

Durham Cemetery - at the north end of Zillebeke 500m to the south. It contained 52 British graves, 39 from Territorial Battalions of the Durham Light Infantry, buried between December 1915 and March 1916.

Garter Point Cemetery - north of Polygon Wood on the road from Zonnebeke to Westhoek and about 33km north-east of here. It contained eight British men, nineteen Australians, one New Zealander, one German and three men 'Known Unto God' buried from September 1917 to April 1918.

Gordon House Cemetery No. 2 - sited 400m north of this cemetery. It contained 30 British men buried from 1915 to 1917.

Hans Kirchner German Cemetery – situated 1.5km south-east of Poelkapelle which is about 8km north of here. It contained four British men who died in October 1914.

Houthulst German Cemetery - at the east end of the village which is about 14km north of here. It was removed in the 1950's and contained 1000 Germans among which was buried one Royal Flying Corps officer.

Keerselaere West German Cemetery – near Vancouver Corner Canadian Memorial about 4km north of here. It contained 29 British men who died in October 1914.

Keerselaerhoek German Cemetery - 200m north-east of Tyne Cot Cemetery and about 5km north-east of here. It contained twelve British men and two Canadians who died in 1914 and 1915.

Langemarck German Cemetery No. 7 (Toten Walchden) – near the present German Cemetery which is about 6km north of here. It contained the graves of four British soldiers.

Langemarck German Cemetery No. 8 - next to the route of the old railway on the road to Houthulst and the present German cemetery. It contained 27 British men who died in October 1914.

L'Ebbe Farm Cemetery – situated 2km north-west of Poperinge which is about 8km west of here. It contained 21 British soldiers who died in 1915 and 1918.

Manneken Farm German Cemetery No. 3 – located in Houthulst Forest about 14km north of here. It contained 700 Germans and thirteen British men who died in 1917.

Manor Road Cemetery – located at the railway halt 800m south-west of Zillebeke and over 1km south of here. It contained the graves of seventeen British soldiers, mainly men of the Royal Field Artillery, who died in 1917 and 1918.

Nachtigall (or Rossignol or Vieux-Chien) German Cemetery – situated about 4km east of here 400m north of the Menin Road and 800m east of the crossroads east of Geluveld. It contained 1130 Germans and 69 British men who died from September to October 1915.

Poelcapelle German Cemetery No. 2 - 1.5km south-east of the village and about 6km north-east of here. It contained 90 British men and four Canadians who died in 1914 and 1915.

Poelcapelle German Cemetery No. 3 - 800m south of the village. It contained 23 British men and nineteen Canadians who died in 1914 and 1915.

Ration Dump Burial Ground - 300m north of here. It contained 28 British graves, mainly 1/14th (London Scottish) Londons and 1/10th (Liverpool Scottish) Kings (Liverpools), and one Canadian soldier.

Reutal German Cemetery (Kriegerfriedhof der XXVII Reserve Corps) - at the south-east corner of Polygon Wood on the Reutal-Zwaanhoek road which is about 3km north-east of here. Among the Germans, three British men, two Canadians and one New Zealander who died in 1914 to 1917 were buried here.

St. Joseph German Cemetery – situated in Hooglede about 15km north-east of here, it contained four British airmen who died in 1918.

St. Julien Communal Cemetery – located about 3.5km north of here, it contained six men of the 14th Canadian Infantry who died in April 1915.

St. Julien East German Cemetery – situated on the Langemark-Zonnebeke road about 5km north-east of here. It contained the graves of 65 British soldiers and 31 from Canada who died in October 1914 and April 1915.

Schrieboom German Cemetery - 800m east of the village that was located west of Langemark and about 6km north of here. It contained 34 British men who died in October 1914.

Transport Farm Annex – located opposite Railway Dugouts Burial Ground about 1km to the west. It contained 27 British graves, sixteen of the 1st Dorsetshires, who died from November 1914 to June 1915.

Trench Railway Cemetery - near Woods Cemetery about 1.5km to the south of here. It contained 21 British men who died in 1915 and 1916.

Treurniet German Cemetery - on the Poelkapelle-Houthulst road about 8km north of here. It contained one Canadian soldier.

Wallemolen German Cemetery - half way between Poelkapelle and Passendale south of Wallemolen hamlet and about 8km north-east of here. It contained twenty British men and fifteen Canadians who died in 1915.

Weidendreft German Cemetery - at the farm of this name located about 6km north of here. Used from October 1914 to August 1915 it contained 98 British men who died in 1914.

Westroosebeke German Cemetery No. 2 - 400m north-east of the village on the road to Hooglede and about 10km north-east of here. It contained one Royal Air Force officer killed in 1918.

UK – 2481    Aust – 147    NZ – 23
Can – 133    S Afr – 7
Unnamed - 1372 (50% of total)
Area - 8074 sq mts

Special Memorials to 26 British men and one Canadian soldier known/believed to be buried among the unnamed. Special Memorials to 91 British men, thirteen Australians, one New Zealander and three Canadians buried in other cemeteries whose graves were destroyed by shell-fire.

**LOCATION**
Perth Cemetery is found east of Ieper and lies on the eastside of the road from Zillebeke to Hellfire Corner, 700m north of Zillebeke and 750m south of Hellfire Corner.

# PLOEGSTEERT WOOD MILITARY CEMETERY

**HISTORY**
This cemetery was used from 1914 to August 1917.
**INFORMATION**
The cemetery was created by enclosing several small regimental cemeteries that lay next to each other. These dated from 1914 and 1915 and are typical of regimental burial grounds of the period.

Plots I and II were, in part, the original burials making up the 'Somerset Light Infantry Cemetery', made by the 1st Battalion in December 1914.

Plot III and parts of Plot I contains sixteen men of the 1/5th Gloucestershires, buried between April and May 1915, and twelve men of the 8th Loyal North Lancashires buried from October to December 1915. However, these plots were known as the 'Canadian Cemetery, Strand' due to the 28

Canadian graves made between June-October 1915 in Plot III, and from the trench running nearby. Plot IV, the 'Bucks Cemetery', was made by the 1/1st Buckinghamshire Battalion, Oxford and Bucks Light Infantry, in April 1915.

The wood was known to the troops as Plugstreet Wood. It is now a pleasant place in which to walk but you must keep to the paths. The land is private as signs make quite clear throughout the wood, so all paths, other than the clearly marked route, are fenced off. The track through the wood was called 'Hunter's Avenue'. It was named by the 1/5th (London Rifle Brigade) Londons when they were here in the winter of 1914-15. They also named the other tracks through the wood, for example, Strand, Charing Cross, Rotten Row, London Avenue, Fleet Street, Oxford Circus and Bunhill Row after their HQ in London. All Battalions of the London Regiment were Territorials, so had a very individual sense about themselves.

This was usually a quiet place in the war interrupted by periods of intense fighting. Soldiers have commented that in the quiet times nightingales could be heard singing in the wood as if there was no war.

Ploegsteert Wood was captured by British Cavalry in October 1914 but part of the wood fell to the Germans who were not cleared until 1917. On 20 December 1914 an attack was launched from the eastern edge of the wood near Le Gheer by the 11th Brigade of the 4th Division. The Germans were prepared for the attack because the Brigade had used telephones, into which the Germans had patched lines, to synchronize the time of the start of the attack. The result was no ground gained and 226 casualties suffered.

In early 1915 the 21st (Yeoman Rifles) King's Royal Rifle Corps arrived at the wood. They suffered their first casualty when an inexperienced officer paraded his Platoon for inspection in an area that the Germans could see. A Y.M.C.A. hut in the wood was destroyed by shell-fire in early 1916. The only remains were some coins fused together by the heat. The Germans captured the wood on 10-11 April 1918 with the British taking it back in September. While the Germans were in the wood they turned it into a fortress but, though there are still bunkers in the wood, it is not possible to visit them today. During the time that the Germans held the wood in 1918 the British destroyed it by artillery bombardment.

Among those buried here is Captain Charles Carus Maud, DSO, MiD, Egyptian Order of Medjidieh (4th Class), 1st Somerset Light Infantry, killed on 19 December 1914 aged 39 years. He joined the regiment in 1896 and saw action in the South African Wars as a Lieutenant. He continued to serve in West Africa, gained promotion to Captain and took part in the Sakoto-Burmi Operation in Nigeria in 1905 for which he was Mentioned in Despatches and received the Distinguished Service Order. He is one of 30 members of the Battalion buried here who were killed in the attack on 'The Birdcage' which was a large complex of defensive trenches and dugouts developed by the Germans into a heavily-fortified strongpoint with wire in front of the Somersets about six-feet high and six-feet deep located just to the east of Ploegsteert Wood near the hamlet of Le Pelerin. The ground they had to cross was almost impassable, covered with gaping shell-holes filled with water and slimy mud, a precursor to what was to come later in the war. The British artillery was falling short and the German machine guns began to fire as the Somersets left their trenches. The Somerset's losses included five officers killed and one taken prisoner, 27 other ranks killed, 50 wounded and 30 missing. This is also the attack in which Rifleman Barnett, buried in nearby Rifle House Cemetery, was killed aged 15 years. Most of the bodies were recovered during the 'Christmas Truce' of 1914. The regimental history records that, during the recovery of the bodies, a Saxon officer stated that Captain Maud had been the 'bravest of the brave.'

Also here is Captain Reginald Rayner Nye, MiD, 3rd Royal Scots, killed in action on 17 December 1915 aged 29 years. He wrote plays and poems, published one novel, and several short stories in 'The Bystander'. On the morning of 4 August 1914 he enlisted in the Hertfordshire Yeomanry and joined the Public Schools Battalion of The Royal Fusiliers in September. In November he was commissioned in to the Royal Scots and became a Machine Gun Instructor in December. He went to France in February 1915, being first attached to the Seaforth Highlanders and then to the 2nd Royal Scots. He was promoted to Lieutenant in April, and Captain in June. In September he was seconded to the 7th Infantry Brigade as Brigade Machine Gun Officer. He was shot through the head by a sniper while taking sights for a gun emplacement near Ploegsteert. He was posthumously Mentioned in Despatches.

Another author buried here is Lieutenant George Roworth Parr, 1st Somerset Light Infantry killed on 19 December 1914 aged 23 years. He wrote short stories, but was also an excellent linguist being a qualified German interpreter. He was killed in the attack on 'The Birdcage' in Ploegsteert Wood.

| UK – 117 | Aust – 1 | NZ – 18 |
| Can – 28 | KUG – 1 | Area - 1136 sq mts |

**LOCATION**

Ploegsteert Wood Cemetery lies in the heart of Ploegsteert Wood about 2km north-east of Ploegsteert. A dirt track 50m from Prowse Point Cemetery, which is the nearest place to park, leads to the three cemeteries in Ploegsteert Wood. The path past Mud Corner is fairly easy to follow as it is fenced on either side. There are also CWGC signs from the Armentieres road and in the wood.

# POELCAPELLE BRITISH CEMETERY

**HISTORY**
Poelcapelle Cemetery was wholly created after the war with the concentration of graves from the battlefields.

**INFORMATION**
The formal layout marks this clearly as a concentration cemetery though most of the dead here fell during the Third Battle of Ypres. Of the graves here 6231, or nearly 90%, are unnamed. The great majority of the graves date from the last five months of 1917, and in particular October, but certain plots, such as IA, VIA, VIIA, LI and LXI, contain graves of 1914 and 1915.

The village was in German hands from 1914. Poelkapelle was the site of severe fighting during the Third Battle of Ypres. On 4 October 1917 the 48th (South Midland) Division took the west part of the village with the 11th (Northern) and 14th (Light) Divisions in support. On 9 October the 11th Division, who fought their way from house to house along the main street, took the rest of the village. The 18th (Eastern) Division attacked to the east of the village on 14 October. The 8th East Surreys and 7th Buffs (East Kents) north of main road, with the 7th Queens Own (Royal West Kents) south of the road, pushed out of the village towards Westrozebeke during which the Buffs were reduced to 100 men. On 22 October the 10th Essex and 8th Norfolks attacked again reaching the area now occupied by Poelcapelle Cemetery, but this was the limit of the British advance. The village was retaken by the Germans in their advance during the spring of 1918 but was finally captured by the Belgians in September 1918.

Notably the cemetery contains the grave of a man long claimed to be the youngest soldier, at 14 years, to die on the Salient, Private John Condon, 6322, 2nd Royal Irish, who died on 24 May 1915. He was from Waterford and is buried on the far side of the cemetery from the entrance in Plot LVI, Row F. However, research has shown that the claim that he was aged 14 years when killed in action may be in error. It was long believed that John Condon was born in Waterford, Ireland in 1900 but no records can be found for a John Condon born in 1900. It seems our man was born on 16 October 1896. He enlisted as a 'Special Reservist' in October 1913 giving his age as 18, though he was 17 at the time. At the start of the war on 7 August 1914 he was mobilised to the 3rd Royal Irish, being posted to the 2nd Royal Irish in December. On 24 May 1915 he, and his best friend, now buried next to this grave which I am sure adds to the fog, Private Thomas McCarthy, aged 47 years, were killed by poison gas in action near Bellewaerde. It is also claimed that the man who enlisted in 1913 was Condon's brother, Patrick, for some unknown reason using John's identity. Another view is that this may be Rifleman Patrick Fitzsimmons, 2nd Royal Irish as the body that now lies under Condon's headstone was identified from a stamp on a boot '6322 4/R.I.R.' which was taken by the IWGC to be Regimental Number 6322 of the 4th Royal Irish. However, Condon was not, and never had been, in the 4th Royal Irish. Similarly, Fitzsimmons was not in the 4th Royal Irish at the time of his death on 16 June 1915, but he had been before transferring to the 2nd Battalion. Hence, it is argued that Fitzsimmons is here and Condon is elsewhere in an unidentified grave. Fitzsimmons body was never identified and he is commemorated on the Menin Gate. I favour this last view, as, understandably, there are many examples of mistakes made in interpreting records, but the CWGC still record the grave as that of Condon and many stick by him as the youngest to die on the Salient and even the youngest to die on the Western Front. Whatever the truth, it is a good piece of history.

Plot XVII, Row C contains seven men of the 48th Labour Company killed by an explosion on 20 October 1919 while they were working nearby. They had all been transferred to the Company from other units, mainly at the end of the war. The Company were searching the Langemark area as part of the concentration of graves at Cement House Cemetery. A detachment from the Company, in preparing the midday meal for the exhumation parties, lit a fire to boil water, and the fire exploded a buried shell killing these seven men and injuring another three.

Lieutenant Colonel Theodore Meredith Rixon, MC, 6th attached 8th King's Royal Rifle Corps, who died on 19 September 1917 aged 51 years is buried here. Records show him to have been commanding the 8th Battalion from December 1916 to February 1917 and that he was commanding the 10th Kings Royal Rifle Corps for just over a week before his death. He was awarded the Military Cross 'For conspicuous gallantry and ability in handling his command after the explosion of an enemy mine. Though badly shaken he acted with great determination, and consolidated his position under heavy fire.' This was gazetted on 25 August 1916.

Buried here is Major Roger Alvin Poore, DSO, Royal Wiltshire Yeomanry attached 2nd Royal Welsh Fusiliers, died 26 September 1917 aged 47 years. He served in South Africa where he was regarded as an excellent officer so was Mentioned in Despatches and awarded the Distinguished Service Order. In January 1915 he was appointed to command the 2/1st Royal Wiltshire Yeomanry with the rank of temporary Lieutenant-Colonel, a rank he gave up to go to the Front in February 1917. He was killed while in conversation with two other officers, when a German shell exploded amongst them. They are now buried side by side. His father, Robert, had served in the Crimean War and during the Indian Mutiny. His brother Colonel Robert

Montague Poore was a cricketer who played for the Hampshire county team.

Private Walter Malcolm, 3rd Otago Regiment, NZEF, died on 23 December 1917. He was a New Zealand cricketer who played one match for Otago.

While I have tried to include families that have lost three, four or even five sons, I have limited my writing about families that lost two sons as they are, sadly, so numerous and the book would easily be several lengths greater than it is. However, 2nd Lieutenant Ian Ferguson Duncanson, 8th Argyll and Sutherland Highlanders, died 12 October 1917 aged 21 years is unusual in that his sister died on service in the war. Nurse Una Marguerite Duncanson, Voluntary Aid Detachment, died on 31 December 1917 aged 25 years and is buried in Alexandria (Hadra) War Memorial Cemetery. She was initially an 'assistant cook and bottle washer' until she became a nurse. She travelled by train across France and Italy to Taranto where she embarked on a troopship, HMT Osmanieh, which hit a mine laid by the German submarine UC34 outside Alexandria harbour and sank taking with her Lieutenant-Commander Mason, two other officers, 21 crew, one military officer, 166 other ranks and eight nurses. The same submarine had torpedoed and sunk HMT Aragon and HMS Attack in the same area the previous day. Their brother, 2nd Lieutenant Roy Duncanson, 3rd attached 9th Duke of Wellington's, was killed on 7 July 1916 and is commemorated on the Thiepval Memorial.

Also of note, and commemorated by a Special Memorial as 'Believed to be Buried in this Cemetery', is 2nd Lieutenant Hugh Gordon Langton, 4th (Royal Fusiliers) Londons, killed in action on 26 October 1917 aged 32 years. He was a talented and well-known violinist who had studied under some of the best teachers in Europe, including Professors Secvik (Prague), Wirth (Berlin) and Auer (Russia). His headstone is unique among CWGC headstones in that it has a musical inscription. The origin of these few notes remained a mystery for a long time until a member of CWGC staff suggested that the notes are from the old American song 'After the Ball'. The final note is missing, but the line is 'Many a heart is aching' which is perhaps the family's intended meaning.

To the south-west of the village on the road to St. Juliaan and Ieper is Vancouver Corner with the tall Canadian Monument at the Keerselare crossroads. The Canadians occupied this position at the start of the first gas attack by the Germans in April 1915 and, sometimes called 'Gas Attack Corner', it marked the eastern limit of the affected area. Close by the Totenmuhle, or 'Mill of the Dead', was used as a German observation post during the war, but as it was constantly under fire from the British, the men chosen for duty here had a short lifespan.

During the German gas attack at Vancouver Corner on 24 April 1915 Captain Edward Donald Bellew of the 7th Battalion, British Columbia Regiment, Canadian Expeditionary Force, continued to fight vigourously, with any weapon that came to hand, after his unit were all killed or wounded. He was eventually captured by the Germans who court-martialed him at Staden and sentenced him to death. As the officer in charge of the execution could not carry out the order, Bellew was reprieved and when liberated awarded the Victoria Cross.

On 19, 20 and 22 August 1917 twelve, seven and eighteen tanks respectively supported the infantry in taking the pillboxes between St. Juliaan and Vancouver Corner. The success of the tanks was an encouraging event but an unusual success due to the deteriorating nature of the ground. Even so there were over 3000 casualties among the infantry.

The church in Poelkapelle was, like the rest of the village, destroyed in the war and rebuilt in the 1920's. The church bells, weighing over 16000lbs, are cast out of metal made from shell-cases collected by local inhabitants.

There were several burial grounds in the area, most of which have been removed, including, close by, Poelcapelle East German Cemetery made by the Germans, and Poelcapelle New German Cemetery made by the British.

At the roundabout in Poelkapelle is the Memorial to Georges Guynemer, the French air ace, who was killed in a 'dog-fight' over Poelkapelle on 11 September 1917. His body was not found though the Germans claimed that they had recovered it but that it was lost in a British artillery bombardment later that day. He was a member of the Escadrille des Cogognes and therefore, the flying stork, emblem of the Squadron, surmounts the monument. A tank that was disabled in the Battle of Poelcappelle in 1917 was still stuck in the mud and ruins of the village when the Guynemer Memorial was unveiled in July 1923.

Just to the north-east of the Guynemer Memorial, on the edge of the roundabout, on the side road for the shops, is the Tank Memorial. The project for a Tank Memorial for the Ypres Salient was the work of Chris Lock and his wife Milena. The land belongs in perpetuity to the Friends of the Tank Memorial Ypres Salient. The Memorial, inaugurated on 9 October 2009 and refurbished after it was damaged in a vehicle accident, commemorates the men of the Tank Corps and former Heavy Branch Machine Gun Corps who served in the Ypres Salient and who died in action or died of wounds. On 9 October 1917, the last time that tanks were deployed in action in relatively large numbers in the Ypres Salient, eight tanks attacked the village. Each was either destroyed by enemy fire or the mud. Tank D29 Damon II was finished in the mud at this crossroads.

On the road to Westrozebeke is the Memorial to Lieutenant Dewinde on the right hand side of the road who was killed on the spot in the Belgian attack on

Westrozebeke on 28 September 1918. To the right of the roundabout in Westrozebeke there is a Monument to the 1st, 2nd and 3rd Regiments of Belgian Carabiniers who took the village in September 1918.

Concentrated here:

Houthulst Forest New Military Cemetery - near the south of the forest on Houthulst-Poelkapelle road about 3km north of here. It contained several French graves and 23 British men who died in the winter of 1917-1918.

Keerselare French Cemetery - 1km west of the hamlet at Vancouver Corner 2km south-west of here. It contained two British, five Canadian and 29 French men who were buried in 1915 by the Germans.

Pilkem Road German Cemetery - next to the bridge over the Hannebeke about 3km to the west of here. It contained thirteen British men and one Canadian buried by the Germans from 1914 to 1917.

Poelkapelle Communal Cemetery – situated on the southern edge of the village about 400m from here, it contained one British soldier buried in 1915.

Poelcapelle German Cemetery No. 2 - 1km south-east of the village and just south of here. It contained 96 British and Canadian graves of men who died from 1914 to 1915.

St. Jean (Jan) Churchyard – located about 6km south-west of here, it contained 44 British men buried in 1915 but whose graves were destroyed in later fighting.

Staden French Military Cemetery – located about 6km north-east of here, it was made by the French 169th Infantry Regiment. It contained 80 French graves and one Royal Air Force officer.

Vijfwegen German Cemetery No. 1 – located just over 2km north of here, it contained three British men buried by the Germans.

| UK – 6573 | Aust – 117 | NZ – 237 |
|---|---|---|
| Can – 527 | NF – 9 | S Afr – 10 |
| Jersey – 4 | Unnamed – 6230 | |
| WWII – 1 | | Area - 22586 sq mts |

Special Memorials to eight British men and one Channel Islander known/believed to be buried among the unnamed.

Special Memorials to 24 British men and three Canadians buried by the Germans in other cemeteries but whose graves have been lost.

**LOCATION**

Poelcapelle Cemetery lies on the south side of the N313 Poelkapelle-Westrozebeke road, approximately 1km from the village and 9km north-east of Ieper.

## POLYGON WOOD CEMETERY

**HISTORY**

The cemetery was created in August 1917 and used until the German advance in April 1918. It was used again in September 1918.

**INFORMATION**

For information on the actions in this area please refer to Buttes New Cemetery.

This is an interesting small cemetery with an unusual entrance.

Buried here is Private Patrick Dunford, 2nd Otago Regiment, NZEF, died 12 December 1917, one of five brothers to join up. His brother Private Thomas Dunford, 1st Auckland Regiment, NZEF, died on 13 August 1918 and is buried in Dunedin (Anderson's Bay) Cemetery. He had a thighbone shattered at Messines in 1917 and lay immobile but conscious in a shell-hole for two days and three nights. He arrived back in New Zealand on New Year's Day, 1918.

Another brother, Trooper James Henry Dunford, 36th Reinforcements, New Zealand Mounted Rifles, died by drowning on 14 April 1918 aged 28 years and is buried in Ismailia War Memorial Cemetery.

Also here is Private John Robertson Thomson, 2nd Gordon Highlanders, died 4 October 1917 and buried in Collective Grave D 2A. His remains were discovered in 1999 in a garden in Zonnebeke and he was buried here in October 2004 with two other unidentified men. Belgian researchers were able to identify Thomson from his initials, carved on the blade of a knife, and by a badge from his Battalion.

Private George Charles Lee Wilson, 1st Canterbury Regiment, NZEF, died on 14 December 1917 aged 30 years. He made four first class cricket appearances for Canterbury from December 1913 to March 1914. This also brought him two matches representing his country against Australia.

Nearby there was a German cemetery, the Kriegerfriedhof des Reserve Infantry Regiment 248 am Polygonenwald, made in 1914-15 containing 347 German graves, but it has been removed.

Also nearby, to the west, close to the Bellewaerde theme park car parks, is the Princess Patricia's Canadian Light Infantry Memorial. Unveiled in 1985, it commemorates the Canadian Battalion which, in May 1915, suffered under heavy fire here during the Second Battle of Ypres. Only four officers and 150 soldiers escaped the battle unhurt. In the centre of the monument are flowers that may seem inappropriate. Originally the space was taken by a maple tree which wouldn't grow and had to be moved to the back of the monument.

| UK – 46 | NZ – 60 | Ger – 1 |
|---|---|---|
| Unnamed – 19 | | Area - 1780 sq mts |

Special Memorials to seventeen British men and thirteen New Zealanders known/believed to be buried among the unnamed.

**LOCATION**

Polygon Wood Cemetery is on the north-east edge of Polygon Wood which lies east of Ieper and north of the Menin Road and motorway. You can leave the Menin Road at the junction just east of the Bellewaerde Pleasure Park known in the war as Clapham Junction where a CWGC sign indicates to the left to the Princess Patricia's Canadian Light Infantry Monument.

## POND FARM CEMETERY

**HISTORY**

This cemetery was begun during the Third Battle of Ypres in July 1917 by the 3rd Rifle Brigade and 8th Buffs (East Kents). It remained in use until October 1917 and was then used again in April and September 1918.

**INFORMATION**

This area was in Allied hands for most of the war but close to the front-lines. Wulvergem fell to the Germans in April 1918 but they had tried to take it before in April 1916 when they launched an unsuccessful gas attack east of the village. The village was retaken by the 30th Division on 2 September 1918.

The cemetery lies in the grounds of the farm from which it gets its name. Of those buried here 178 were from Irish Regiments. 'Pond Farm' was in the fields about 800m east of Packhorse Farm, and on the north-west side of Pond Farm is the cemetery.

Buried here is Private William Richardson, 17th (2nd Manchester Pals) Manchesters, who died on 9 September 1917 aged 39 years. His son, Ordinary Telegraphist Clarence Richardson, HM Drifter Jeannie Murray, Royal Naval Volunteer Reserve, died on 15 February 1918 aged 18 years while on patrol in the Dover Straits when his ship was sunk killing fifteen men. The ship was one of eight vessels sunk overnight by a force of seven German destroyers. He is commemorated on the Plymouth Naval Memorial.

There is a small private museum at Pond Farm. They have a website which you use to contact the owners as viewing is by appointment only.

UK – 298       Ger – 5       Unnamed – 4

Area - 2123 sq mts

Special Memorials to three British men of the 1/7th Cheshires buried here in September 1918 but whose graves have been lost.

**LOCATION**

This is a difficult cemetery to find and access. It is behind a farm and is well hidden from the road. It lies south of Ieper about 3km south-east of Kemmel and 1km north-west of Wulvergem. It is east of the Nieuwkerke road at the small crossroads in Lindenhoek on the slopes of the Kemmelberg. Turn right and downhill at the crossroads reached in 800m. A 300m path leads through the farmer's field and farm buildings past the pond to the cemetery. The gates will open though they may seem 'sticky'. Please remember that this is private property.

## PONT-d'ACHELLES MILITARY CEMETERY

**HISTORY**

Begun in June 1917, the cemetery remained in use until the German advance during the Battles of the Lys in April 1918, but was used again in September and October.

**INFORMATION**

The village was held by the Allies from October 1914 when it was captured by the 1st Hampshires. The 1st Royal Newfoundland Regiment and 1/2nd Monmouthshires fought here, but were forced to retreat, on 11 April 1918 during the German advance as the British were pushed back along the road from Armentieres and Nieppe. This area was recaptured by the 29th Division on 29 September 1918.

When the Germans occupied the area they used the cemetery giving it the name Papot Military Cemetery. Of the graves here 33 are men of the 10th East Yorkshires.

It is believed that Stephen Grady, the son of an IWGC gardener, was in the French Resistance in WW2 and hid weapons in the cemetery at the left rear in a pit hidden from the Germans.

Buried here is Private Leigh Kilpatrick, DCM, 48th Australian Infantry, who died of wounds on 5 July 1917 aged 48 years. He proved an interesting piece of research as, while recorded by the CWGC as 'Leigh', there is almost no evidence of this man and searching the Australian records for a 'Leigh' only shows information in the nominal roll. However, searching the records using his service number the Australian records we can find a 'Robert Leigh' leaving Australia with the 16th Australian Infantry in June 1915. This also shows the recommendation for his Distinguished Conduct Medal telling us that it was at Messines Ridge for gallantry on 8 June 1917. He was recommended 'For conspicuous bravery and devotion to duty during the counter attack on Owl Trench. During the consolidation enemy snipers caused a number casualties, Private Kilpatrick crawled forward in daylight and located two snipers both of whom he killed. His work was the admiration of all who saw him.' The medal was awarded posthumously.

Also buried here is Private Ernest Worsley, 2nd Middlesex. Worsley enlisted in August 1914 and was sent to France in July 1915. After serving with the 11th Middlesex, he was transferred to the 2nd Battalion in 1916. He deserted from his Battalion while in the rear collecting rations for his unit which was in the front-line. He was arrested at Calais, a week after absconding, and executed near this cemetery on 22 October 1917.

UK – 173   Aust – 72   NZ – 48
Ger – 37   Unnamed – 7
Area - 1347 sq mts

**LOCATION**
Pont d'Achelles Cemetery is south of Ieper on the Franco-Belgian border, 150m north of the Bailleul–Armentieres road (D933), from which it is well signed. It lies in France.

## PONT-de-NIEPPE COMMUNAL CEMETERY

**HISTORY**
The cemetery was used from October 1914 until the German advance in March 1918 and again from September to November 1918.

**INFORMATION**
The village was held by the Allies from October 1914 when it was captured by the 1st Hampshires. The 6th Division used Nieppe as their Divisional Headquarters in late 1914. During the Battles of the Lys in April 1918 the 18th (1st Tyneside Pioneers) Northumberland Fusiliers held the bridge from which the village gets its name when the Germans attacked on 7 April. From Armentieres to Ploegsteert five German Divisions advanced upon five British Brigades. The pioneers held the bridge for British troops to withdraw until 11 April before blowing it as the Germans began to cross. The village was retaken by the 29th Division on 3 September 1918.

There is a large German cemetery of nearly 800 burials at the west end of the graveyard which was made when they held the village in the summer of 1918 and after the war with the concentration of German graves from the area. It includes 46 graves which were moved from the boundaries of the communal cemetery.

There is also a French Military Cemetery of 32 men killed in WW1 and WW2 next to the British Plots so that it almost seems as if the British and French dead face the German burials over a no man's land of civil graves.

There is also a grave of an IWGC (CWGC) worker killed accidentally in 1949. On the west of the Commonwealth cemetery, a group of French members of the Resistance are buried. Most of them were killed by the Nazis just before the liberation from 1-4 September 1944. This group includes eighteen civilians shot by the SS as retaliation for the actions of the Resistance. Other members of the resistance killed here in September 1944 are buried in family tombs within the cemetery. Nieppe was liberated by the British on 5 September 1944.

Buried here is Captain John Towlson Morgan, No. 70 Squadron, Royal Air Force and 1st Royal Welsh Fusiliers, previously 3/7th Middlesex, died on 29 October 1918 aged 19 years. He was made a 2nd Lieutenant in March 1915 with the Middlesex, entered Sandhurst soon after and joined the Fusiliers in April 1916. He left his airfield at 10.20am to find a crashed aircraft but stalled and crashed ten minutes later.

Also here is Major Peter Martin Connellan, twice MiD, 1st Hampshires killed in action on 20 October 1914 aged 32 years. He holds the Royal Humane Society's Medal for saving a man in his Regiment from drowning in 1909.

UK – 123   Aust – 12   Ger – 790
Fr – 32   Unnamed – 13   WW2 – 2
IWGC – 1      Area - 570 sq mts

**LOCATION**
Pont-de-Nieppe Cemetery lies south of Ieper within the village of Nieppe west of Armentieres. It can be found at the end of a road that leads north from the Bailleul-Armentieres road (D933) about 100m east of the turn to the motorway from Nieppe. The turn to the cemetery has a German War Graves Commission sign on the corner but no CWGC sign. The British graves are to the right of the entrance at the eastern end of the cemetery.

# POPERINGE COMMUNAL CEMETERY

**HISTORY**
The Communal Cemetery was used by the British from October 1914 to March 1915.

**INFORMATION**
The cemetery was used for Belgian, British and French military funerals during the period October 1914 to March 1915. Each group of British graves consists of the burials of one month, eleven of October 1914, one of November 1914, nine of December 1914 and two of March 1915 though the grave of an officer has been removed to Ypres Reservoir Cemetery. These were the first soldiers to die in Poperinge, probably in the hospital nearby. There are also the graves of six workers of the IWGC who died working in the area after the war. You can also find a group of 72 Belgian Civilian graves dating from WW2, some of whom were nursing nuns from local hospitals.

Poperinge was the main forward base in the area of the Salient. It was entered by the Germans on 4 October 1914 but when the French arrived on 15 October the Germans withdrew. The British 7th Division soon took over the town and it became a centre for hospitals, munition dumps, and entertainment in its many forms.

The area around Poperinge, due to it usually being beyond the range of German artillery, was used as a reserve area so many large hutted camps were located locally. The men would come into town to deal with any issues that could only be done when out of the line. So, pay, family and discipline matters took place in the town. The people of the town became used to meeting men from every part of the British Empire, even Chinese who were here on contract but subject to military law. However, the Chinese were kept in camps that acted almost as prisons and interaction with local people was strictly limited.

The baths in Poperinge in the war were in the Sugar Refinery which had been taken over as a delousing centre. Huge vats contained increasingly cleaner degrees of water through which the men passed while their clothes were fumigated. Even so, the men were lousy again within days. There are several interesting features in the town near the central square. The Town Hall at the east end of the Grote Markt or town square is in the Gothic style. The town hall was used for Courts Martial and the courtyard for executions. Within the Town Hall are 'execution cells' where some of the British soldiers condemned to spend their last night before death were held. There were originally four cells, which were used by the police here before the war. Two of these small rooms have been restored and an execution post erected in the courtyard.

The British army executed approximately 350 men during the war, an average of one per week. The charges upon which they were found guilty and subsequently executed were 266 for desertion, 37 for murder, eighteen for cowardice, three for mutiny, six for striking or using violence to a superior officer, five for disobedience to a lawful command, seven for quitting a post without authority, two for sleeping at their post and two for casting away their arms. Many of these had survived several previous sentences of death for desertion or other crimes. The usual pattern was to have your sentence commuted to prison with hard labour and then be sent back to the front-line, often with your original unit, to have a chance to either die in action or redeem yourself. For most who were finally executed, the temptation to abscond again was too great, and this led to the ultimate penalty. However, a few, such as Byers at Loker Churchyard, were executed for a first offence, and in some cases such as his, led to changes in the process by which Courts Martial with the possibility of capital punishment were carried out. While those executed in the war have subsequently been pardoned, and I have great sympathy for them and their families, I find it difficult to second guess, with hindsight (which some claim to be the only perfect form of vison), the judgements of the day in the circumstances that they were taken, especially in a country at war and that still had the death penalty for many crimes 'at home' in the UK. Apologising for decisions taken in the past, when we were not in the place of those who took the decisions, is a dangerous path. But, that is just my humble opinion, for what it is worth.

The execution post on display in the inner courtyard of the Town Hall is said to be that used on 8 May 1919 for Wang Ch'un Ch'ih of the 107th Chinese Labour Corps, but it is almost certainly a replica. He is buried at Poperinghe Old Military Cemetery. He was one of many Chinese here on contract to do labouring work. Even though he was not part of the army, and here on contract, he was still subject to military law. Hence, he was executed over a gambling debt. Sixteen others executed in Poperinge were buried at Poperinghe New Military Cemetery.

At the west end of the town square is an old chapel, next to which is Gassthuistraat, known in the war as Rue de L'Hopital due, unsurprisingly, to the hospital on the street. On Gassthuistraat is one of the most famous houses in Poperinge, Talbot House. In 1915, the Reverend Neville Talbot, 6th Division Chaplain, persuaded the Army to take over a house as a soldier's club, partly to provide an alternative to the less reputable establishments in the town. Talbot had his friend, Reverend Philip 'Tubby' Clayton, transferred to Poperinge to help him. They named the club after Reverend Talbot's brother, Gilbert, who was killed at Hooge in July 1915 and is buried in Sanctuary Wood Cemetery. The house provided a haven for soldiers as a club downstairs with a chapel in the attic which was open until the German Spring Offensive in 1918, and again afterwards. It was a place where everyone was welcome, where military rank did not count, and where the troops could play the piano or borrow books simply by leaving their cap as a deposit. More than half a million soldiers visited the club, which was housed in the mansion of a local hop trader who had fled the country. The interior has been largely preserved and the spirit of the place can perhaps best be experienced in the chapel, called the 'upper room', which has remained untouched since 1918. This is a great place to visit where everyone is welcome, and the coffee and tea are a treat.

The adjoining hop store, better known during the war as the Concert Hall, and the former bathhouse, or 'Slessorium', after its creator, Major Peter Slessor, were both restored in 2004. After the peaceful and quiet atmosphere of Talbot House, visitors can go to the first floor of the former hop store, the actual Concert Hall. It was this room that became the stage for many recreational activities in 1917, while current visitors are shown a film of a concert given by the performers 'The Happy Hoppers'. The ground floor has a display, small shop and toilets. This part of Talbot House, on Pottestraat, is now the entrance.

The spirit of Talbot House spawned a world-wide Christian organisation, Toc H, which is artillery signalling code for Talbot House. In 1929, Lord Wakefield, who had brought the Spanbroekmolen Mine Crater - now the Pool of Peace – for the movement, bought Talbot House for Toc H.

Opposite Talbot House was a popular shop which supplied souvenirs and material, such as methylated blocks of fuel for cookers and tobacco, that the soldiers considered essential for life in the trenches. Ironically the shop's real trade was as an undertakers. The town was a place in which officers could order their coffin. Elsewhere in Poperinge were establishments in which a man could spend some time with a young lady, no doubt for tea and scones. Officers went to a place with a blue light outside and other ranks to a location outside of which was a red light. I wish this was the origin of the phrase 'red light district' but that pre-dates the war.

Also on Gassthuistraat was 'Skindles' formerly run by Madame Beutin and her two daughters as an estaminet for officers. It was called the Cafe de la Commercedes Houblons but changed its name to Skindles at the suggestion of an officer from Maidenhead, who named it after a pub in the Berkshire town.

On Bertinstraat, next to the church, is the College Stanislas which was used as a hospital from 1915 to 1918 for civilian casualties caused by the bombing of Poperinge. The railway station on the road out of Poperinge to Ypres was the main target for the German guns as millions of troops passed through it on their way to the Front.

Buried here is Captain John Frederick Strathearn Gordon, Cameronians (Scottish Rifles) attached 1st Royal Scots Fusiliers. The son of a general, he had served in the South African War as well as seeing pre-war service in Somaliland and Nigeria. He was killed on 19 November 1914 whilst his unit was in the vicinity of Hooge.

Also here is Corporal Herbert Barrett, 2nd Worcestershires who enlisted in 1904 and had seen postings in Sri Lanka as a bandsman. His medical history show he had contracted gonorrhoea and malaria which resulted in lengthy spells in hospital, as well as a contused head wound due to 'direct violence' which sounds like a fight in barracks. Promoted to Corporal on 8 August 1914 he died of wounds on 21 October 1914.

UK – 22           IWGC - 6           Unnamed – 1
Belg Civ WW2 - 72

**LOCATION**

Poperinge Communal Cemetery, enclosed by a high red brick wall near the Old Military Cemetery, lies in Poperinge west of Ieper. It is found on the east side of the road from Reningelst to Poperinge about 700m north of the by-pass. The British graves are in two main Plots, one against the wall by the main road, and the others in the eastern part of the graveyard.

# POPERINGHE OLD MILITARY CEMETERY

**HISTORY**

The Old Military Cemetery was used from October 1914 until it was closed in May 1915, though a few burials were made after the war.

**INFORMATION**

For further information about Poperinge please refer to the Communal Cemetery.

Some of the earliest military burials were made here. The cemetery was made in a garden near the 'Kasteel D'Hondt', after a hospital was installed in this Chateau. The building is gone, but its footprint has affected the shape of the cemetery. There was a large railway siding just to the south-west of the cemetery during the war and the tracks ran across the road between the Old and New cemeteries. The lines ran off in spurs as they travelled east, passing the numerous camps that were established in the rear areas during the war.

The graves of 800 French and Belgian soldiers, as well as nearly 500 civilians, have been removed. Most of the civilians died during a typhoid epidemic in 1914. This removal has left a large area of lawn which helps to give the impression of a garden. I like this place as it feels like an English country garden.

Buried here is Captain Alexander Findlater Todd, MiD, 1st Norfolks, died of wounds on 21 April 1915 aged 41 years. He played two Rugby Union Tests for England in 1900, but four years previously he had toured South Africa with the British Isles (Lions), where he played nineteen matches, including four Tests. As did several others on that British Isles tour, he returned to South Africa a few years later to fight in the South African Wars. In 1902, he married Alice Crean and thus became the brother in law of Thomas Crean, VC, with whom he had served in South Africa. He was shot through the neck whilst in the trenches near Hill 60 on 18 April 1915, the day after returning from leave.

Also here is Serjeant Herbert Mole, 1st Queen's (Royal West Surreys), died of wounds on 27 October 1914. A few weeks later, his brother, Corporal Benjamin Mole, 1st Royal Warwickshires, died on 10 December 1914 aged 29 years and is buried in Prowse Point Military Cemetery. The youngest brother, Private Arthur Henry Mole, 1st Queen's (Royal West Surreys), died on 28 August 1916 aged 23 years. He is buried in Heilly Station Cemetery on the Somme. Two other brothers served and survived, one with the Royal Army Medical Corps and one with the Army Service Corps. But one of their sons, and nephew to the three Mole brothers killed in WW1, was killed in WW2. Flying Officer (Wireless Operator) Douglas John Mole, No. 10 Squadron, Royal Air Force Volunteer Reserve, was killed in action on 18 December 1944 aged 29 years and is buried in Taillette Communal Cemetery which is south of Charleroi.

A senior officer buried here is Lieutenant Colonel Russell Lambert Boyle, MiD, 10th Canadian Infantry who died of wounds on 25 April 1915. He was a Canadian rancher and soldier who had served in the South African Wars as a Sergeant. Boyle led the 10th Battalion in their first battle on 22 April 1915, the attack on Kitcheners' Wood to counter attack the Germans after their use of poison gas. He was hit by five machine gun bullets and died at No. 3 Casualty Clearing Station. He was posthumously Mentioned in Despatches.

Nearby is Lieutenant Colonel William Frederick Richard Hart-McHarg, MiD, 7th Canadian Infantry, died on 24 April 1915 aged 46 years. Born in Ireland of British parents and educated in Belgium, he had lived practicing law in Canada for 30 years. He also served in the Canadian Militia, enlisting as a Private and rising to Lieutenant-Colonel during which time he took part in the South African Wars. In 1913 he won a shooting competition after which he was regarded as World Champion in some quarters. He was the original commander of the 7th Canadian Infantry and was shot in the stomach while reconnoitering positions on 22 April. He was posthumously Mentioned in Despatches. It is interesting that two of the three Canadian Battalion commanders killed during Second Ypres are buried here.

Also here is Sergeant John Wilfred McKay, MiD, No. 2 Field Ambulance, Canadian Army Medical Corps who died of wounds on 26 April 1915 aged 16 years. He enlisted as a Private in late September 1914 and won rapid promotion being highly regarded for his work. He was wounded in both arms two days before his death. He was posthumously Mentioned in Despatches. His father, also Sergeant John McKay, served in the same unit.

A Chinese labourer was buried here in 1919. Coolie Wan Ch'un Ch'ih, 107th Company, Chinese Labour Corps, had murdered a fellow Chinese labourer after the war over a gambling debt. He was executed at Poperinge Town Hall on 8 May 1919. He was the last to be executed in the Salient.

UK – 397       Can – 46       Ger – 2
Chinese Labour Corps – 1
Unnamed - 22 UK and 2 Can
Area - 1555 sq mts
Special Memorials to five British men and two Canadians known/believed to be buried here.

**LOCATION**
Poperinghe Old Military Cemetery lies on the west side of the road from Reningelst to Poperinge, within the town of Poperinge, which is west of Ieper. It is about 700m north of the by-pass, from which it is clearly signed, and 500m north of the New Military Cemetery. The cemetery is set behind houses, enclosed by a high wall and set back from the road. It is entered by a walled path and through a pavilion.

# POPERINGHE NEW MILITARY CEMETERY

## HISTORY
The New Military Cemetery was opened in June 1915, as the Old Cemetery was closed when the space available was filled, and remained in use until the end of the war.

## INFORMATION
For information about the town please refer to the Communal Cemetery.

The New Cemetery is raised above the level of the road and has a good view of the spires over the town. There are a large number of French graves here.

This cemetery holds an infamous record in that it contains the largest number of men to be executed by the British Army and buried in one place. This is because most serious disciplinary matters were dealt with when Battalions were in camp away from the front-line and Poperinge was one of the most important centres for military camps in the British sector of the Western Front. Hence, there are seventeen men buried here who were executed in Poperinge for various crimes under the terms of the British Army Act. Six men who were executed are buried among the 45 men in Plot II, Row F.

- Private James H. Wilson of the 4th Canadian Infantry, deserted on 13 June 1916 during the Battle of Mount Sorrel. He was executed at 4.20am on 9 July 1916. He had served eight years with the Connaught Rangers before he emigrated to Canada. When war broke out Wilson enlisted but his conduct was poor from the start. Although Wilson was discharged as 'undesirable for military service' on 3 February 1915, he was readmitted for service on 13 March 1915, just over one month later. Before arriving in France in July 1915, Wilson had been charged at least four times with various offences including being absent without leave, kicking a NCO and using abusive language. After being in France for just over 24 hours, Wilson went absent and was found drunk. After being arrested by the military police, Wilson escaped. He was quickly recaptured and was sentenced to 70 days' Field Punishment No. 1. Wilson was later charged with disobeying a lawful command and received a punishment of 90 days' imprisonment, however this was later suspended. On 25 February 1916 Wilson again went absent until he turned himself in during May 1916.

- Private Come LaLiberte, 3rd Canadian Infantry, was executed for desertion on 4 August 1916 aged 26 years. He enlisted in June 1915 joining the 41st Canadian Infantry arriving in England in June 1915. Throughout the year he broke the rules, had received seven days' Field Punishment No. 1 and been transferred. When his new Battalion were sent to the battles at Mount Sorrel he refused and was tried for desertion. These two were among 23 Canadians executed in the war.

- Private John Bennett, 1st Hampshires deserted during a German gas attack on 8 August 1916 only six weeks after experiencing the first day of the Battle of the Somme. He was executed for cowardice on 28 August 1916 aged 19 years. Bennett had joined the 3rd Hampshires in June 1914 but was not sent to France until November 1915 when he was transferred to the 1st Hampshires. The Battalion took very heavy casualties on the Redan Ridge on 1 July 1916. On 20 July Bennett had faced a Court Martial for desertion, but was found guilty of absence without leave and sentenced to two years imprisonment with hard labour. He was sent, with his Battalion, to Ypres less than a week later and moved into the front-line on 4 August. They suffered a gas attack on 8 August during which Bennett went absent again. In the early hours of 9 August he was seen nearly 2km in the rear telling another soldier from the Battalion that he had lost his nerve and had climbed out of the trench and when he returned the Company had gone.

- Private Albert Botfield, 9th South Staffordshires, the 23rd Division Pioneers, deserted from a trenching detail near Contalmaison on the Somme on 21 September 1916 aged 28 years. He was tried for cowardice, and executed on 18 October 1916, when his Division had been posted to the Salient. He had enlisted in September 1914, went to France early in 1916 and almost immediately was sentenced to 90 days field punishment for absenting himself. He went absent twice in June while on the Somme. The unit went to Ypres in August and he went absent again for which he was tried and found guilty. Returning to the Somme in September, he was part of a group digging a trench in the open at night when a shell landed close by and he ran away. He returned to his billet when the rest of the group returned from completing the trench. The Court Martial was on 1 October. On 17 October 1916 the Division moved north to the Salient and Botfield was executed the next day.

- Private Richard Stevenson, 1/4th Loyal North Lancashires, deserted at Fricourt on the Somme on 7 September 1916 just before his Battalion fought at Guillemont suffering heavy casualties. He was captured four days later in the village of Bussy-les-Daours 15km west of Albert. His explanation was that he had left his Company to look for his brother and on his return the Battalion had gone so he had lost his head and drifted away. He was tried on 11 October, and executed for desertion on 25 October 1916 aged

23 years, when his Division had been posted to Ypres. He had been at the Front since January 1916.

- Private Bernard McGeehan, 1/8th (Liverpool Irish) King's (Liverpools) also deserted on the Somme in September 1916. He was executed for desertion at 6.16am on 2 November 1916. He landed in France in May 1915. McGeehan had joined the Battalion on its creation and had served during the early part of the Battle of the Somme when his Battalion had been involved in the assault on Guillemont village in a number of particularly bloody encounters during August, notably on 8 August when they ran into heavy wire and German machine guns so took heavy casualties. He had been ordered, along with the other men in his Battalion, to return to their trenches on 20 September 1916 to assault the village once more, but he went missing until 25 September when he turned up at Montreuil, claiming he had got lost. By 28 September the Battalion were at Brandhoek, and McGeehan was escorted to rejoin them there. He faced a Court Martial on 21 October and sentenced to death, overlooking the fact that Bernard had walked 150km attempting to find his regiment and voluntarily reported to a British army unit. He served as the focus of the play 'The Worthless Soldier' by the late playwright Sam Starrett.
- Private Reginald Thomas Tite, 13th (3rd South Downs) Royal Sussex enlisted in October 1915 arriving in France in the middle of 1916. On 1 August 1916 Tite had disobeyed a lawful command, was subsequently convicted by Court Martial and sentenced to four years penal servitude which was suspended. On 9 October Tite again refused an order and was absent on 20-21 October when his Battalion captured part of Stuff Trench on the Somme. The Court Martial was at Aveluy on 2 November 1916. He was then sent to medical units attached to 39th Division from 7 November, by which time the Division was in the Ypres area, for Pyrexia or unknown origin and bronchial catarrh. He was discharged under arrest on 22 November and was executed for cowardice at 6.53am on 25 November 1916 aged 27 years. It is claimed that Tite's brother was killed in the war, but I cannot find record of a brother in the census details. The candidate put forward, Private Joseph H Tite, 15th Queen's (Royal West Surreys) who never served in Salonika, died on 28 February 1917 aged 37 years and is buried in Salonika (Lembet Road) Military Cemetery but had different parents and never lived in London which is where Tite came from.
- Private William Henry Simmonds, 23rd (2nd Football) Middlesex, a 'Pals' Battalion, was another who had deserted on the Somme in 1916 but for whom justice was served once his Division had transferred to Belgium. He was executed for desertion on 1 December 1916 aged 23 years. His Battalion arrived on the Somme in September 1916 entering the front-line on 10 September near Delville Wood. They were in action at Flers in September and moved to Ypres in October. At some point he deserted and was tried on 19 November.
- 2nd Lieutenant Eric Sheffington Poole, 11th West Yorkshires was the first of three officers to be executed in the war. Born in Canda, he served with the Militia from 1903-05 before moving to the UK. He enlisted with the Honourable Artillery Company in 1914, was commissioned in May 1915 into the 14th West Yorkshires and moved to the 11th Battalion in May 1916. He was wounded and suffered shell shock in July 1916 returning to active service in September. He left his Platoon on 5 October as they moved to the front-line at Flers and was apprehended at Henencourt about 15km to the south-west two days later. A doctor examined him on 21 October suggesting that his mental state precluded his ability to deliberately desert but General Rawlinson insisted on a Court Martial with a charge of Desertion. Poole was tried on 24 November. After the trial he was examined again by the same doctor who saw him on 21 November. This time he declared he was of sound mind and knew he was deserting but that his mental powers were less than average. He was executed at 7.25am on 10 December 1916.
- Private James Crampton, 9th York and Lancasters, deserted in August 1916 while attached to the Royal Engineers. A reservist recalled in August 1914, he was sent to the 6th Yorkshires who went to Gallipoli in May 1915. After their arrival in France in July 1916 he was transferred to the 9th York and Lancasters with whom he was soon in the front-line on the Somme. They moved to the north in August and Crampton went absent on 16 August. He was captured in November while his unit had gone to the Somme and back to Ypres. Following Court Martial on 23 January 1917 he was executed for desertion on 4 February 1917 aged 42 years.
- Private John W. Fryer, 'D' Company, 12th (Bermondsey) East Surreys was executed on 14 June 1917 aged 23 years while under a suspended sentence of death for a previous offence. He arrived in France in May 1916. He was sentenced to death for desertion while preparing for the Battle of the Messines Ridge, though this sentence was commuted to two years imprisonment and suspended after which he was returned to his unit. He deserted again almost immediately, was caught soon after and tried after which he was executed.
- Private James S. Michael, 10th Cameronians (Scottish Rifles) was executed for desertion on 24 August 1917. He arrived in France in July 1915 and went absent in May 1916 before a trial held on 1 June 1917. There is a spread of time between conviction and execution as the Battalion, who were usually on parade to see the sentence carried out, were busy during actions in Third Ypres.
- Private Joseph Stedman, 117th Company, Machine Gun Corps, was the first member of the Corps to be executed when he was shot for desertion on 5 September 1917 aged 25 years. He deserted during the opening days of Third Ypres between 31 July and 3 August 1917 when his unit was part of the 39th Division attack on Kitchener's Wood and St. Juliaan.

His court martial was on 26 August and he was the last man of the 39th Division to be executed, the only one for desertion as the others had been for cowardice.

- Sergeant John Thomas Wall was the sixth man of the 3rd Worcestershires to be executed in the war. A 'Regular' who had enlisted in 1912, he had fought since 1914, seeing action in most major campaigns and rising through the ranks. He deserted at Hooge on the Bellewaerde Ridge in August 1917. He refused to leave a concrete bunker on 5 August and move across open ground to the front-line about 650m away, which was regarded as desertion. He put up no defence at his trial on 30 August and was executed on 6 September 1917 aged 22 years for his first offence.
- Private George Everill, 'A' Company, 1st North Staffordshires had a poor record including several desertion attempts. In March 1916 he was given a suspended year's hard labour for being insubordinate. This was swiftly followed by a ten year prison sentence, reduced to two years, for wilful defiance of which he served about nine months. In March 1917 he was given twelve months imprisonment for being absent, this being commuted to ninety days Field Punishment No. 1. That sentence had hardly expired when he was back in court for threatening an officer for which he was given three years in prison which was commuted to a further 90 days punishment. Two weeks later he defied an officer once more and the punishment was doubled. He absconded for the last time, while serving his sentence of field punishment, as his Battalion moved from Dikkebus to the front-line on 24 August 1917, but he was captured the next day. He escaped and was arrested again a few hours later. He was executed on 14 September 1917 aged 30 years.
- Private Herbert Morris, 6th British West Indies Regiment, became the only man of the Regiment to be executed on the Western Front when he was killed at 6.10am on 20 September 1917 aged 17 years. As his unit was coloured it was not supposed to be an active unit, yet he was still executed for desertion. Even being under-age was not a consideration. Morris was a volunteer involved in the supply of shells. He was charged with deserting his unit at Essex Farm on 20 August 1917 and during his Court Martial in September he was undefended. His excuse was that the Doctor 'gave me no satisfaction' when he reported unwell on Sunday 19 August. Despite the failure of his Medical Officer to appear, and testaments to his previous good behaviour, he was sentenced to be shot at dawn, partly as he had already served field punishment for a virtually identical offence that July.
- Private Frederick C. Gore, 7th Buffs (East Kents) was executed for desertion on 16 October 1917 aged 19 years. He enlisted in December 1914 and arrived in France in July 1915. Having seen action on the Somme, at Ypres and at Arras, he went absent on 10 August 1917 when the unit was sent to the front-line again. He gave himself up to the Military Police on 19 August admitting he was a deserter. At his Court Martial on 8 September 1917 his previous poor record was noted. He had been convicted in March 1916 for insubordination, in January 1917 for attempting to remove government property, in April 1917 for absence, for which he lost his Lance-Corporal's stripe, and then in July he was charged with leaving his Company without permission being found on the steps of a dugout in another trench. He was the last soldier to be executed in Poperinge, though a Chinese Labourer was executed under military law in 1919.

Two Belgian nuns are buried here, both killed by German shelling of St. Elisabeth Hospital at Poperinge on 14 July 1917, the hospital in which they treated wounded British soldiers. Sister Martha Declerq and Sister Juliana (Euphrasie Vanneste) have simple crosses in the centre of the cemetery, with the Belgian flag to mark the difference from the French graves. Sister Juliana died, aged 51 years, having looked after victims of a typhoid epidemic early in the war. She was responsible for the care and training of novice sisters in her convent, the Sacred Heart convent, where she worked with the Quakers.

Buried here is Lieutenant Edmund Joseph (Constable-) Maxwell-Stuart, 175th Tunnelling Company, Royal Engineers who was killed on 26 April 1916 aged 23 years, one of four bothers killed in the war. One brother, Lieutenant Alfred Joseph (Constable-) Maxwell-Stuart, 1st Coldstream Guards, was killed on 24 August 1918 aged 20 years and is buried in Bagneux British Cemetery. Another, 2nd Lieutenant Henry Joseph Ignatius (Constable-) Maxwell-Stuart, 3rd Coldstream Guards was killed on 9 October 1917 aged 30 years and is buried in Artillery Wood Cemetery. Lieutenant Joseph Joachim (Constable-) Maxwell-Stuart, 9th Duke of Wellington's, died on 2 March 1916 aged 19 years and is buried in Reninghelst New Military Cemetery.

The grave of Lieutenant-Colonel George Baker, 38, commanding 5th Canadian Mounted Rifles (Quebec Regiment), died on 2 June 1916 aged 38 years, who was a member of the Canadian House of Commons is here. He is the only Canadian Parliamentarian to have ever lost his life while fighting for Canada. He was the son of the Honourable George Barnard Baker KC (member of Canadian Senate). He had commanded his Battalion since January 1915 and was mortally wounded during the German attacks on Mount Sorrel.

Another senior officer here is Lieutenant Colonel Raymond Vernon Doherty-Holwell, DSO, three times MiD, Royal Engineers and Assistant Director of Army Signals, VIII Corps killed on 9 January 1917 aged 34 years. He joined the Royal Engineers in 1901 and was promoted to Lieutenant in December 1904 and Captain in 1911. He was awarded the Distinguished Service Order in the Birthday Honours Lists in June 1915 while still a Captain.

Also here is Lieutenant Colonel Sir Robert Benyon Nevill Gunter, 3rd Yorkshires, who died of wounds on 16 August 1917 aged 46 years. He was commissioned into his Battalion in 1889 becoming a Lieutenant in 1891 and Captain in 1895. He served first as a Railway Staff Officer, then as Commandant of a Remount Depot in the South African War, and in 1902 was promoted from Staff Officer to Assistant-Inspector of Remounts and Mentioned in Despatches. He was promoted to Major in 1905 and became the 2nd Baronet in 1905 before going onto the Special Reserve List as a Lieutenant Colonel in 1908. When the war began he took command of the 3rd Yorkshires, a reserve Battalion stationed in the UK and providing replacement troops for other Battalions. He was retired and on sick leave for some of the time between 1914 and April 1917 when he asked to be allowed to return to active service. He was sent to France but kept as a Base Officer in the rear for some time. He got closer to the Front when he took a room in 'Skindles' in Poperinge, but was still on administrative duties in the rear. On 4 July a shell landed in the town while Gunter was riding his horse. He was treated at 45th Field Ambulance and released to return to his club and room at Skindles. He had a dizzy spell so was taken to No. 10 Casualty Clearing Station at Remy Siding, now Lijssenthoek Cemetery where he stayed for a few days. He was discharged on 11 July but was found in bed on the morning of his death in such a state that he was considered to be having a heart attack. His stepson, 2nd Lieutenant John Oscar Pritchard-Barrett, was killed in action near Givenchy on 15 June 1915 and is commemorated on the Le Touret Memorial.

Another here is Lieutenant Colonel Herbert Stoney Smith, DSO, 1st Leicestershires, who died on 22 October 1915 aged 47 years. He was gazetted 2nd Lieutenant in the King's Own Yorkshire Light Infantry in 1888, and in 1891 was appointed to the 1st Leicestershires, then in Bermuda, later serving in Canada, South Africa, and Egypt. He became a Captain in 1908, and went to France on 8 September 1914. In October 1914, he took an active part in a desperate engagement at Rue du Bois, near Armentieres, when he personally, on a critical occasion, carried ammunition up to the firing line. He was wounded in December 1914 and went home to recover. In June 1915 he returned to the Front, was Mentioned in Despatches, and was awarded the Distinguished Service Order. He was fatally wounded by a sniper's bullet whilst inspecting the Battalion trench lines.

A young man buried here is Rifleman Alfred Robert Halford, 8th King's Royal Rifle Corps, died on 5 August 1915 aged 16 years.

Another man of note is Private George Ryan, 2nd Hampshires died on 9 August 1916 aged 22 years. His brother, Private Herbert Ryan, 2nd Hampshires died on the same day and is buried in Potijze Burial Ground Cemetery. Both were victims of a gas attack.

| | | |
|---|---|---|
| UK – 596 | Aust – 20 | NZ – 3 |
| Can – 55 | BWI – 2 | Fr – 275 |
| Chinese Labour Corps – 1 | | Ger – 1 |
| Bel – 2 | | Area - 3107 sq mts |

**LOCATION**

Poperinghe New Military Cemetery lies on the east side of the road from Reningelst to Poperinge, within the town of Poperinge, west of Ieper. It is just north of the by-pass from which it is clearly signed.

# POTIJZE BURIAL GROUND CEMETERY

**HISTORY**

The Burial Ground was used from April 1915 to October 1918 when the cemeteries at the chateau came into the front-line during the German offensive.

**INFORMATION**

Potijze was within the Allied lines during practically the whole of the war and subject to non-stop shell fire. It was from Potijze that men would enter the communication trenches that would take them east to the front line, and it was just up the road from here that an Advanced Dressing Station, set up in Potijze Chateau in April 1915 and in operation for the next two years, created the need for more than one burial ground in the vicinity.

The 2nd and 14th Durham Light Infantry have 102 men buried here, the Guards Division have 62, the 2nd Hampshires 46 and the 1st West Yorkshires 43. Although three of the four cemeteries at Potijze were begun within three days of each other at the end of April 1915 (the exception being Potijze Chateau Lawns Cemetery), Potijze Burial Ground was not used regularly until June 1915 after which it was used on a regular basis until the end of August 1916, occasionally in 1917, and just twice in 1918.

The Scots Guardsmen in Row C were killed on 30 March 1916 in the trenches at Hooge and buried in this mass grave. There were 29 Scots Guards killed on that day during a day-long German artillery barrage.

Row T contains seventeen headstones, of which the centre one bears nothing but a cross, upon which are the names of 32 men of the 2nd Hampshires killed on 9 August 1916. Row U contains the graves of as further thirteen Hampshires, some of the 1st Battalion, killed on 9 August while the Battle of the Somme was underway. All were killed by phosgene gas released by the Germans in the early hours of the morning as the two Hampshire Battalions were preparing to leave trenches just east of the village having completed ten days in the front-line. The Hampshires casualties were four officers and 109 men killed, with many more 'wounded'. At that time the British were in the process of introducing a new gas mask, the small box respirator, intended to replace the PH helmet that had been in use since the beginning of the year.

Hence, the men may have had gas masks that were ineffective against the gas, or were using the new masks and did not know fully how to make them work, which may explain how they seem to have suffered such high casualties. It is often thought that the only action in the Salient in 1916 was the Battle of Mount Sorrel involving the Canadians. But this attack by the Germans on 9 August shows that the Salient, and areas like Potijze in particular, were never truly 'quiet'.

Buried here is Rifleman Ronald Jolly, 8th King's Royal Rifle Corps, who died on 11 September 1915 aged 15 years. So is Private Donald Eric Little, 14th Durham Light Infantry, who died 19 December 1915 aged 16 years. Private Edward Yates, 2nd Sherwood Foresters (Notts and Derbys), died on 5 October 1915 aged 16 years.

The only Canadian in the cemetery, Private Arthur Duquette, 6th Canadian Railway Troops died on 1 November 1917 aged 22 years and was the final burial made in 1917.

| UK – 580 | Aust – 3 | Can – 1 |
|---|---|---|
| Ger – 2 | Unnamed – 21 | Area - 4420 sq mts |

### LOCATION
Potijze Burial Grounds Cemetery can be found east of Ieper about 200m north of the roundabout in Potijze which is at the junctions of the Ieper-Zonnebeke and St. Jan-Zillebeke roads.

## POTIJZE CHATEAU GROUNDS CEMETERY

### HISTORY
The Chateau Grounds Cemetery was used from May 1915 to September 1918. Plot II was created after the war.

### INFORMATION
This is one of three cemeteries in the grounds of the old chateau that were created in the spring of 1915. Plot II was formed after the war when graves were brought in from isolated sites and small burial grounds to the north-east. The Grounds Cemetery is separated from the Lawn Cemetery by a grass path and bank but as the two are enclosed by the same wall they are easy to confuse as being one. They are behind houses and hence seem isolated, reached by a sheltered path from the road.

The chateau, one of several known to the Army as the 'White Chateau', was within the British lines for most of the war and had an Advanced Dressing Station in the grounds. Although subject to constant shell fire Potijze Château, dating from the nineteenth century, remained mostly intact throughout the war. The chateau came close to the front-lines during the Second Battle of Ypres in 1915, when it was the headquarters for the 27th Division. The ground floor was later used as an Advanced Dressing Station while the first floor, which commanded views of the German lines, served as an observation post. For much of the war the Château was surrounded by a cluster of dug-outs and trenches and a large shed on the grounds, known to soldiers as 'Lancer Farm', which housed ammunition and trench stores. Working parties would pause here to collect tools, coils of barbed wire, duckboards, bombs and other supplies before moving up the line. Due to the fighting and heavy shelling, which also damaged the three cemeteries in its grounds, very little remains of the chateau.

Buried here is Captain Dr. George Martin Chapman, Gold Medal 'Pour Courage et Devouement' (France), Royal Army Medical Corps attached 2nd Dragoon Guards (Queen's Bays), died on 13 May 1915 aged 28 years. He gained a 'Blue' for Cambridge University for football and a 'half-blue' for boxing. He was awarded a medal for saving the life of a trawler skipper after two other soldiers had died in the attempt in freezing rough seas off Boulogne on 7 December 1914. He joined the Royal Army Medical Corps as a Lieutenant in August 1914. He was killed by shell-fire in front-line trenches east of the village while attending to the wounded. He was son of the Honourable Frederick Revans Chapman, Judge of the Supreme Court of New Zealand.

Also here is Captain Maurice Arthur De Tuyll, 10th (Prince of Wales's Own Royal) Hussars, who died on 13 May 1915 aged 26 years. He was son of Baron Carlo de Tuyll and his wife who became the Duchess of Beaufort. He had been a member of the 10th Hussars polo team, regarded as one of the best that had ever taken to the field. He was killed by shellfire having moved to occupy trenches held by the 2nd Dragoon Guards.

The French burial here is Capitaine Raoul Johnston, MiD, Liaison, Armée Britannique attached 11th Cavalry Brigade, who died on 14 May 1915 aged 45 years. He was part of a family involved in finance and banking but preferred to stay on his estates producing excellent wine. He was also a good polo player. He was killed by a bullet to the head while acCompanying the Brigade commander who was visiting the trenches for which he was Mentioned in Despatches by Foch.

| UK – 399 | Aust – 25 | NZ – 2 |
|---|---|---|
| Can – 49 | S Afr – 1 | Fr – 1 |
| Ger - 1 | KUG – 85 | Unnamed – 111 |

Area - 4003 sq mts (with the Lawn Cemetery)

Special Memorials to ten British men and ten Australians known/believed to be buried among the unnamed.

### LOCATION
The cemeteries here, east of Ieper, lie about 50m north of the road from Potijze to Zonnebeke and 200m east of the roundabout.

# POTIJZE CHATEAU LAWN CEMETERY

**HISTORY**
This cemetery was used from May to December 1915 and from July 1917 to October 1918.

**INFORMATION**
For information about this cemetery and fighting in this area please refer to the Chateau Grounds and Potijze Burial Ground Cemeteries.

At the end of the war this was a distinct and separate cemetery from the Grounds Cemetery. But concentration burials were made into the Grounds Cemetery between these two cemeteries so that, in effect, they almost became one.

Buried here is 2nd Lieutenant The Honourable Robert Henry Palmer Howard, 4th attached 2nd East Surreys, who died on 8 May 1915 aged 21 years. He was son of Baroness Strathcona and Mount Royal who succeeded to the title when her father died. It then passed to Robert's elder brother who served in WW2 as Under Secretary of State for War.

Also here is Captain Hubert De Burgh Riordan, 2nd East Surreys, killed in action on 10 May 1915 aged 27 years. He was commissioned as a 2nd Lieutenant in the 4th East Surreys in November 1905. He was promoted to Lieutenant in November 1907 and resigned his commission in November 1912 when he moved to Canada. He rejoined his former regiment as a Captain on 3 January 1915 and was sent to the 2nd Battalion on 30 April 1915 arriving with a draft of 120 men and another officer. The Battalion was ordered forward during the German attack on 8 May and spent the next 36 hours under fire moving from one position to another east of Potijze. The Battalion retired to a trench just east of Potijze Chateau and during the night of 9 May they moved position to the north of the road and spent the next day under fire. The Germans shelled the position heavily killing Captain Riordan and seventeen men.

Graves F7 to F10 are occupied by four men of No. 22 Squadron, Royal Flying Corps, who died on 21 September 1917. They left their airfield at 6.15am flying two Bristol F2B's who collided at 8.15am at 10000ft and broke up. They are Air Mechanic 1st Class H Friend, Air Mechanic 2nd Class Charles Loveland and 2nd Lieutenants A H Gilbert and Sidney MacDonald Spurway.

| UK – 191 | Aust – 4 | Can – 22 |
| S Afr – 9 | Ger – 3 | Unnamed – 29 |

Area - 4003 sq mts (with Grounds Cemetery)
Special Memorial to one British man believed to be buried here among the unnamed.

**LOCATION**
Directions for this cemetery are exactly as for the Potijze Chateau Grounds Cemetery except that this is on the left as you enter the gate.

# POTIJZE CHATEAU WOOD CEMETERY

**HISTORY**
This cemetery was used from April 1915 to June 1917 and for three burials in 1918. This is the earliest of the three 'Chateau' cemeteries.

**INFORMATION**
For information about this cemetery and fighting in this area please refer to the Chateau Grounds and Potijze Burial Ground Cemeteries.

Of the men buried here 47 are of the 2nd Hampshires, many killed in the gas attack on 9 August, and twenty men of the 1st Royal Inniskilling Fusiliers who died in the same gas attack. They lie buried close together. Among the group killed by phosgene gas are two Private Barretts. Private D Barrett, 1st Royal Inniskilling Fusiliers and Private J F Barrett, 2nd Hampshires aged 23 years. I cannot find any relationship between them except their death and their resting place.

| UK – 151 | Can – 6 | Unnamed – 6 |

Area - 799 sq mts

**LOCATION**
Directions to this cemetery are exactly the same as for the Chateau Grounds and Chateau Lawn Cemeteries. However, as you enter them you will see a gate on the far side of the path that separates the two. A path from the gate leads to this cemetery 150m away across the fields.

# PROWSE POINT MILITARY CEMETERY

## HISTORY
This cemetery was begun in November 1914, by the 2nd Royal Dublin Fusiliers and 1st Royal Warwickshires, and used until April 1918.

## INFORMATION
The cemetery is the only one on the Salient to be named after a person. Major, later Brigadier-General, Charles Bertie Prowse, DSO, 1st Somerset Light Infantry was killed on 1 July 1916, the first day of the Battle of the Somme, while commanding the 11th Infantry Brigade at Beaumont Hamel. He is buried in Louvencourt Military Cemetery.

The cemetery, and the line along the eastern edge of the wood, mark the site of the stands by the 1st Hampshires and 1st Somerset Light Infantry under Prowse in trying to hold St. Yvon in October 1914, hence the name.

Buried here is Corporal Benjamin Mole, 1st Royal Warwickshires, who died on 10 December 1914 aged 29 years. His brother Serjeant Herbert Mole, 1st Queen's (Royal West Surreys), died of wounds on 27 October 1914 and is buried in Poperinghe Old Military Cemetery. The youngest brother, Private Arthur Henry Mole, 1st Queen's (Royal West Surreys), died on 28 August 1916 aged 23 years. He is buried in Heilly Station Cemetery on the Somme. Two other brothers served and survived, one with the Royal Army Medical Corps and one with the Army Service Corps. But one of their sons, and nephew to the three Mole brothers killed in WW1, was killed in WW2. Flying Officer (Wireless Operator) Douglas John Mole, No. 10 Squadron, Royal Air Force Volunteer Reserve, was killed in action on 18 December 1944 aged 29 years and is buried in Taillette Communal Cemetery which is south of Charleroi and north-east of Reims.

Buried here is Private Wilson Davis, 10th Canadian Infantry, killed on 25 February 1915. He is the only Canadian here and the first casualty of the Battalion in combat.

Lance Serjeant Vivian Claude Kavanagh, 2nd Battalion, 3rd New Zealand Rifle Brigade died on 9 August 1917. He was a New Zealand first class cricketer who played one match for Auckland in 1912/13.

Prowse Point is where the remains of men whose bodies have been discovered in recent times in or near Ploegsteert wood have been reburied.

Among these is Private Harry Wilkinson, 2nd Lancashire Fusiliers, who died on 10 November 1914 aged 29 years. His remains were discovered in January 2000 and he was identified by his metal dog tag. He was reburied here in October 2001 on the day of the 25000th playing of the Last Post at the Menin Gate. A cross commemorating Harry Wilkinson stands by the side of the road near to where his remains were found, 86 years after he died. This cross is not too far from Prowse Point Cemetery, and is located south of the St. Yvon craters.

A similar burial was of Private Richard Lancaster, 2nd Lancashire Fusiliers, who died on the same day as Harry Wilkinson in the same action to hold the Germans in the wood. He was discovered in March 2006 with two other sets of remains who are as yet unidentified. His dog tag, number 8372, was found along with scabbard, ammunition pouches, toothbrushes, razor, fork and spoon. Until the discovery and formal identfication, Lancaster's name was recorded on the Ploegsteert Memorial to the Missing. He was reburied in July 2007 along with the two unidentified men. However, it is worth noting that the Battalion war diary records that Lancaster was hastily buried at the time with four other men close to the front line. Wilkinson was discovered close to the site of the original action in 1914. In 2006 archaeologists discovered the remains of Richard Lancaster's body only a few metres away. The remains of Privates Brown, Robinson and Sheridan, killed in action on the same night, remain to be found, though two are probably the unidentified men found with Lancaster.

Another reburial is that of Private Alan James Mather, 33rd Australian Infantry, killed on 8 June 1917. In August 2008, British archaeologists working on the Ploegsteert Project discovered the body of an Australian soldier. The soldier's rifle, haversack containing a German pickelhaube helmet trophy, badges, a corroded identification disc and other items were recovered with the body. Work over the next eighteen months led to a successful DNA match proving his identity. On 22 July 2010 he was re-interred here with full military honours.

In April 2015 six unknown British servicemen of the war were re-interred at Prowse Point Military Cemetery. The six - two from the Lancashire Fusiliers, two from the King's Own (Royal Lancasters), and two unidentified British soldiers - were reburied with full military honours.

By the Cross of Sacrifice is a small pool which was part of the front line here. The track by the cemetery is now the only official access to the cemeteries in Ploegsteert Wood.

### Christmas Truce
Next to the cemetery is a memorial to the Christmas Truce of December 1914 and further to the east is the Khaki Chums cross which also commemorates the truce. It is undeniable that a Christmas Truce took place in several locations on 25 December 1914. There is evidence in Battalion war diaries, letters home, and personal diaries of those who took part in impromptu kickabouts and even matches, and photographs of soldiers from each side stood together in no man's land. We have a record of a Chaplain performing a burial service as men took the time to recover bodies of their comrades who had been killed in 1914. The 'truces' were all on sectors held by the British. No truces took place in French sectors. In Belgium three are

recognised as having taken place. One by units in the 5th Division on the Wulvergem-Messines road and in the valley of the River Douve, one by units in the 6th Division at Frelinghien and south of the wood at Houplines and one here at St. Yvon on the edge of Ploegsteert Wood by most of the 4th Division. There were three more in France.

Part of the story is the football matches. The two memorials nearby commemorate these. Here, in Ploegsteert, known to the Tommies as 'Plugstreet', Saxon troops played the British in no-man's land. The Germans began an unofficial truce on 24 December, the day they traditionally celebrate Christmas. They decorated the parapets, sang carols and eventually a German crossed no-man's land under a white flag of truce.

In the Christmas Truce 'football match' in 1914 at Frelinghien on the French-Belgian border just north-east of Armentieres, men of the 2nd Argyll and Sutherland Highlanders played the 9th Saxon Infantry Regiment, or 133rd German Infantry Regiment. Among those at Frelinghien was Albert Schmidt, an inside right for Fussballclub 02 Schedewitz, a small town in eastern Germany. He was later killed on 20 August 1916 when his Battalion was sent from reserve to counter a night-time attack by Australian units and is buried at Villers-au-Flos German Cemetery on the Somme. On the opposing side was Sergeant James 'Jimmy' Coyle, Captain of the 2nd Argyll and Sutherland Highlanders football team and an inside left for Scottish league side Albion Rovers. He survived the war and was awarded the Military Medal.

In Belgium, where most of the 'truces' took place, there were twenty men killed on Christmas Day 1914 in and around the Ypres Sector. Eight are named on the Ploegsteert Memorial so will probably have been killed in France. But six are on the Menin Gate and five in cemeteries in and around Ploegsteert. These five are all buried within the distance one could kick a football from the truce sites.

There were 57 who died in France on Christmas Day 1914. While many of these died in hospitals near the coast or some in accidents or from 'natural' causes well behind the lines, we still have 43 killed in France in the line on Christmas Day 1914. The 2nd Grenadier Guards lost six men killed and others subsequently died of wounds. They had been heavily shelled and involved in a firefight with their German counterparts. The 2nd Coldstream Guards lost seven men killed on the same day. The 2nd Grenadiers, 2nd Coldstreams and 1/1st Hertfordshires were in the 4th (Guards) Brigade, 2nd Division at the time. Finally of note, six men serving with the Indian Army were killed in the line on Christmas Day 1914.

Of the 1/5th Cameronians (Scottish Rifles) at Frelinghien, one involved was Private Walter Sinclair Smith. Late in the afternoon of Christmas Day, while troops from opposing sides were mingling, a shot rang out from the British lines, accidentally fired by a regular from the Scottish Rifles. A German sniper returned fire, shooting Walter through the head.

So, the story of the truce and football being involved is valid. But it must be tempered and put in context to give us a wider picture. Notably, it was never repeated.

Approximately 1km to the east are the remains of two of the mines blown at start of Battle of Messines. Trench 122 and Factory Farm mines had a combined total of 60000lbs of explosive. The craters were attacked by the 3rd Australian Division led by John Monash who went on to command the Australian Corps in 1918.

UK – 165       Aust – 13      NZ – 42
Can – 1        Ger – 12       Unnamed - 6
Area - 4177 sq mts

**LOCATION**
Prowse Point Cemetery lies at the northern edge of Ploegsteert Wood, south of Messines and about 2km north-east of Ploegsteert.

## RAILWAY CHATEAU CEMETERY

**HISTORY**
The cemetery was used from November 1914 until October 1916.

**INFORMATION**
The cemetery, with the chateau as a backdrop, is set back from the road next to a private house. It was also known as 'St. Augustine Street Cabaret' and 'L.4 Post'. One French grave has been removed.

This was one of the cemeteries in which the CWGC chose to conduct their climate change trial. For eighteen months the cemetery lost its turf which was replaced with a form of hard standing looking like some of the cemeteries in much warmer areas. Thankfully, in my opinion, the CWGC put the grass back.

Buried here is Serjeant Frank Elliott, 12th (Miners) King's Own Yorkshire Light Infantry, killed on 4 September 1917. The Battalion were a Pals Battalion, raised by the West Yorkshire Coalowners Association, who became the 31st Division pioneers. Elliott enlisted in November 1917 and had been at the Front for one year and seven months without leave, seeing service on the Somme in 1916.

Between 1 July and 30 November 1917, the Battalion was attached to Fifth Army Troops for work on light railways, one of which ran alongside this cemetery. The war diary for 4 September 1917 descibes a relatively quiet day with all

four companies working on maintenance of the Front or

rear areas. The diary entry simply states '3 O.R. (Other Ranks) killed and 3 O.R. wounded.' Those three men were Frank Elliott, and two Privates, Frederick Squires of Dewsbury aged 28 years, and Frank Thackery of Sheffield aged 22 years. All three men are buried here.

UK – 105        Unnamed – 6

Area - 446 sq mts

**LOCATION**
Railway Chateau Cemetery lies in the western suburbs of Ieper about 300m north of the N308 to Poperinge, from which it is clearly signed, and 200m north of the railway.

# RAILWAY DUGOUTS BURIAL GROUND (TRANSPORT FARM)

**HISTORY**
This burial ground was used from April 1915 until 1918. It was enlarged after the war with the concentration of about 423 graves.

**INFORMATION**
This is a deceptively large, but inviting, burial ground. It is an unplanned cemetery which reflects the nature of its use in the war and the effect of the fighting. The entrance, with a large number of Special Memorials, is, I feel, particularly well designed. Burials were made in small groups, without any definite arrangement; and in the summer of 1917 a large number of graves from Third Ypres were obliterated by shell fire before they could be properly marked.

The cemetery gets its two names from the farm and from the dug-outs that were in the embankments upon which the railway runs. Many of the burials date from 1916 and 1917 when there were Advanced Dressing Stations posted in the farm.

At the end of the war, 1,705 graves were known and marked. Other graves were then brought in from the battlefields and small cemeteries in the surrounding area, while 258 burials known to have been here, mainly in the present Plots IV and VII and destroyed by artillery fire, were marked by Special Memorials.

To get here you may have passed through Shrapnel Corner at the junction of the Comines, Armentieres and Kemmel roads. It was the main route for men who were moving to the front-line as it was better sheltered than the more famous exit at Hellfire Corner.

You can see the entrance to Zillebeke Lake from here. Now there is a restaurant with a path around the lake though the soldiers only knew it as a dangerous swamp surrounded by artillery positions. The lake area was used for bathing and the area around it was used for Dressing Stations, artillery units, munitions dumps and collecting posts for Divisions stationed nearby. It was typical to use a significant feature as somewhere for units to focus their supplies and bury their dead, such as in this cemetery.

In July 1915 the railway line to Hill 60 had been ruined so that troops had to transport all supplies manually. Lieutenant Ashford, and men of the 1/6th South Staffordshires, repaired the line here so that the 'Hill 60 Express' could run again.

Buried here is Temporary 2nd Lieutenant Frederick Youens, VC, 13th Durham Light Infantry, who died on 9 July 1917. The citation for his actions on 7 July reads 'For most conspicuous bravery and devotion to duty. While out on patrol this officer was wounded and had to return to his trenches to have his wounds dressed. Shortly afterwards a report came in that the enemy were preparing to raid our trenches. 2nd Lt. Youens, regardless of his wound, immediately set out to rally the team of a Lewis gun, which had become disorganised owing to heavy shell fire. During this process an enemy's bomb fell on the Lewis gun position without exploding. 2nd Lt. Youens immediately picked it up and hurled it over the parapet. Shortly afterwards another bomb fell near the same place; again 2nd Lt. Youens picked it up with the intention of throwing it away, when it exploded in his hand, severely wounding him and also some of his men. There is little doubt that the prompt and gallant action of 2nd Lt. Youens saved several of his men's lives and that by his energy and resource the enemy's raid was completely repulsed. This gallant officer has since succumbed to his wounds'

Also here is Lieutenant Albert Niven Parker Service, 52nd Canadian Infantry, who died on 18 August 1916. He was killed by a shell in Trench 38 at Hill 60. He was brother of the Canadian poet, author and actor, Robert Service, who was nearby, working as a volunteer stretcher bearer for the Ambulance Corps of the American Red Cross having been rejected from the army, when his brother was killed.

Also of note is Lieutenant Rupert Edward Gascoyne-Cecil, 1st Bedfordshires, who died on 11 July 1915. His brother Captain John Arthur Gascoyne-Cecil, MC, 75th Brigade, Royal Field Artillery, died on 27 August 1918 aged 25 years and is buried in Bucquoy Road Cemetery. Another brother, Lieutenant Randle William Gascoyne-Cecil, Royal Horse Artillery and Royal Field Artillery, was killed on 1 December 1917 aged 28 years and is commemorated on the Cambrai Memorial. Their father was later the Bishop of Exeter. Their grandfather was Lord Salisbury, three time Prime Minister of the United Kingdom.

Two brothers commemorated here, originally buried in Valley Cottage Cemetery but whose graves have been lost, are Privates Frederick George Wild aged 27 years and Reginald Wild aged 22 years, both 43rd Canadian Infantry and both killed on 21 August 1916.

A young man buried here is Private Vernon Keith Merchant, 58th Canadian Infantry who died on 6 June 1916 aged 16 years. The inscription on his headstone reads 'The Only Child Of Aged Parents'.

A senior officer buried here is Lieutenant Colonel John Hutton Bowes-Wilson, 1st Duke of Wellington's attached 9th York and Lancasters, who died on 7 June 1916 aged 37 years. He was a professional soldier who had served in the South African Wars. His brother Captain George Hutton Bowes-Wilson, 1/4th Yorkshires was a Middlesbrough councillor and pre-war territorial soldier. He went to France in April 1915 and was soon involved in Second Ypres. He was commended for his work in late May when the Battalion came under a gas attack on the Menin Road at Hooge when he refused to go to hospital for treatment for the effects of the gas. He was killed by a German sniper on 17 June 1915 aged 38 years in Sanctuary Wood and is buried in Vlamertinghe Military Cemetery.

Another Battalion commander buried here is Lieutenant Colonel William Francis Brougham Radclyffe Dugmore, DSO, twice MiD, 1st North Staffordshires, killed on 12 June 1917 aged 48 years. He was commissioned in to the North Staffordshires in June 1894. He went to Africa where he was involved in operations against the Mazrui rebels in Unyoro in 1896-97 and in the Uganda Mutiny in 1897-98. He was employed in the Uganda Protectorate from 1899 to 1902, serving with the King's African Rifles in the East African Arab War. He was Mentioned in Despatches and received the Distinguished Service Order in 1899 for his service in Uganda. He also saw action in the South African War during which he was promoted to Captain. He was on Special Service with the Somaliland Field Force from 1902 to 1904 and was with the Liberian Development Company from 1906 to 1907 retiring in 1909. In 1914 he was Second-in-Command of the 72nd Highlanders of Canada and in August 1916 took command of the North Staffordshires.

Another of note is Lieutenant Francis 'Frank' Nathaniel Tarr, 1/4th Leicestershires, killed on 18 July 1915 aged 27 years. He represented England at Rugby Union on three occasions in 1909 losing against Australia and Wales but beating France. He played again for his country in 1913 in a victory against Scotland. He played at center for Leicester Tigers having gained three 'Blues' at Oxford University. He joined his local Territorial Force Battalion being promoted and going to France soon after the start of the war becoming the regiment's machine-gun officer. While the Germans were shelling the position, Tarr put his head out to tell some men to remain under cover when a splinter from a shell struck him in the face, killing him.

Concentrated here:

Valley Cottages Cemetery – located about 1.5km east of here east of the village on the road to Maple Copse Cemetery known during the war as 'Observatory Road'. It contained the graves of 111 British and Canadian soldiers. Many of the graves had been destroyed by shell-fire so that 73 are now represented by Special Memorials.

Transport Farm Annex - 100m south-east of here next to the road. The graves were removed to Perth Cemetery, but one officer whose grave was destroyed is commemorated here by a Special Memorial.

| | | |
|---|---|---|
| UK – 1659 | Aust – 154 | NZ – 3 |
| Can – 636 | BWI – 1 | India – 4 |
| KUG – 2 | Ger – 3 | Unnamed – 430 |

Area - 16374 sq mts

Special Memorials to 261 men known/believed to be buried among the unnamed.

Special Memorials to 30 British men and 42 Canadians buried in Valley Cottages and Transport Farm Annexe Cemeteries but whose graves were destroyed by shell-fire.

**LOCATION**

Railway Dugouts Cemetery lies south of Ieper on the west side of the road to Comines about 750m from Shrapnel Corner.

## RAMPARTS CEMETERY (LILLE GATE)

**HISTORY**

The ramparts were used for burials by the British from February 1915 to April 1918 though many of the bodies have been concentrated in other cemeteries and only one section of graves now remains.

**INFORMATION**

The cemetery is particularly beautiful with its view of the moat and is the only military cemetery within the old walls of the town. The first burials on the ramparts were made by French troops in November 1914. At the end of the war, the French graves were concentrated in St. Charles-Potijze French Military Cemetery.

The first CWGC burials now make up Rows B and C.

The Lille Gate or Rijselpoort, which used to be known as the Messines Gate, is next to the cemetery. One of the main exits from Ypres for troops moving to the Front, it was used more than the Menin Gate as this route was better sheltered from German guns. This was particularly as, after the Second Battle of Ypres in May 1915, the Menin Gate was in direct observation from the high ground around Ypres and so the Lille Gate became the main route to get to the front line. The main bastions of the gate date from 1383 though the balcony over the road and the bridge over the moat are both post-war. There are some original-style Imperial War Graves Commission direction signs on plaques in the road tunnel. During the war the ramparts were used as unit headquarters, for medical facilities and even as the base for the production of the, infamous to the Generals, newspaper, the 'Ypres Times'. The gate is where the oldest archaeological remains in Ypres have been found dating from the Roman period.

Buried here is Major George Henry Walford, MiD, Suffolk Regiment, Brigade Major, 84th Infantry Brigade, killed on 19 April 1915 aged 36 years. He won the Anson Memorial Sword and Queen Victoria's Medal at Sandhurst before joining the Suffolks in 1898. In 1903 he was with the Somaliland Field Force and was promoted to Captain in 1905 serving as Battalion Adjutant until 1909. He was appointed to the General Staff as a Brigade Major in April 1914, joining the 84th Brigade in December, becoming a Major, and moving to France in January 1915. He was with the 1st Suffolks when they took over the line at Zonnebeke on 17 April 1915. On 18 April the Germans opened a fierce bombardment and Walford was killed by shellfire while making a reconnaissance in the sector held by the 1st Welsh. He was posthumously Mentioned in Despatches.

On 31 December 1917, a working party of the New Zealand Maori (Pioneer) Battalion was shelled near Ypres and six Maoris killed on that New Year's Eve lie here. They include Private Heremia Haenga and Lance Corporal Raika Murray. Three other Maoris buried here were killed on 23 December and one on 29 December.

If you walk west along the ramparts, in the direction of the railway station, you will come to the Lion Tower which dates from 1383. There are two islands in the moat which were created as part of the town's defences and further on there is a small deer park and machine-gun post. Finally you will reach the Esplanade Gardens and Old Powder Magazine, which has a pre-Seventeenth Century base upon which the rest was built in 1818. It was one of the few buildings to survive the German artillery bombardment.

Rose Coombs, who did much to popularise Ypres and the battlefields for tourists and pilgrims through her book 'Before Endeavours Fade', had her ashes scattered in this cemetery in 1991. The path to the cemetery is named after her. Her book was the first guide book to the Western Front that I bought, and inspired me to follow in her footsteps with version one of this book. Rose, the Holts and John Giles are probably, in my mind, those who led the way in battlefield guiding for us to follow and I will ever be grateful to them for leading me to where I am now.

UK – 162        Aust – 11        NZ – 14
Can – 10        Unnamed – 10

**LOCATION**

To bring a coach here from the coach park or Cathedral involves such a tortuous route that it is not worth the effort. Walk from the Grote Markt which is no more than ten minutes away. The walk passes many interesting features that are outlined in the general information about Ieper at the start of this book. It is worth the walk.

## RATION FARM (LA PLUS DOUVE) ANNEXE

**HISTORY**

This cemetery was used from January 1915 until January 1918.

**INFORMATION**

For further information about the fighting here please refer to La Plus Douve Farm Cemetery.

The farm was in Allied hands for most of the war. It was known as 'Ration Farm' because Battalion transport could approach it at night with rations. It was used for some of the time as a Battalion HQ, but as such, it also became a depot for equipment and ammunition. Ration Farm was, like all such central points, a busy place, frequently shelled by German artillery. For example, in April 1917, German shellfire hit a store of bombs stacked next to the gate leading to the courtyard of the farmhouse, killing five New Zealand soldiers and wounding eleven. A small trench, called Plum Duff Sap, ran past the farm along which all reliefs were made. So, men were moving up the trench towards the front lines, or down the trench towards their billets in the rear. It is possible to imagine the cavalry charges in the valley during the early parts of the war and also the importance of holding the ridge.

These locations also had burial grounds as there were usually medical units, such as Regimental Aid Posts, situated in places like this. This was the first of the two cemeteries here to be used when it was begun by the 2nd Manchesters who made the first burial, Private Harold Bates, on 11 January 1917.

The last Allied burial was Private Vincent Thomas Stone, MM, 12th Australian Infantry, who was accidentally drowned on 16 January 1918 aged 21 years. He was awarded the Military Medal for his action on 15 April 1917. The citation reads 'For pluck and tenacity under heavy machine gun fire. At LAGNICOURT at dawn on 15th April when the enemy attacked in force, Pvt. Stone was in charge of a Lewis Gun. Under direction of Lieut. Roper he took up a position in rear of the sunken road and succeeded in keeping back a strong German attack against our rear, being all the time under an intense fire from two enemy machine guns. Although wounded, he continued firing until relieved by his No. 2 Gunner.' However, the final burial was the German buried here, Unteroffizier Bernhard Hedrich, buried on 24 April when the Germans briefly held this area.

Buried here is Captain Arthur Purefoy Irwin Samuels, 'C' Company, 11th (South Antrim) Royal Irish Rifles, who died of wounds at 8.00am on 24 September 1916 aged 28 years. His father was a judge, Ireland's Solicitor-General and

Attorney General, and an MP while Arthur joined the profession in 1910. In 1914 he joined the Royal Irish Rifles becoming a Captain in February 1915. He was wounded on 1 July 1916 at Thiepval and spent some time recovering from his wounds. However, he was back with his Battalion when fatally wounded by machine-gun fire at 1.00am on 24 September. His wartime diary and experiences have been published.

Buried here is Drummer Matthew Morrissey, 2nd Leinsters who died on 5 April 1916 aged 28 years. His brother, Lance Serjeant Richard Morrissey, 2nd Leinsters died on 21 July 1917 aged 25 years and is commemorated on the Menin Gate. Another brother, Serjeant William Morrissey, 1st Base Remount Depot, Army Service Corps died on the last day of the war, 11 November 1918, aged 34 years and is buried in St. Sever Cemetery Extension, Rouen.

UK – 186   Aust – 12   NZ – 4
Unnamed – 9   Ger – 1   Area - 1459 sq mts

**LOCATION**
Ration Farm Cemetery lies in the valley of the River Douve about 8km south of Ieper, south-west of Messines and about 2km south-east of Wulvergem. It is reached by means of a well signed farm track from the Messines-Wulvergem road and you will find the cemetery on the north side of the farm. A path leads to the cemetery. This is not as attractive a cemetery as its nearby partner, La Plus Douve Cemetery, but you can get good views of the valley from here as well as Hill 63 and the Messines Ridge.

## R.E. FARM CEMETERY

**HISTORY**
Begun in December 1914 by the 1st Dorsetshires, the cemetery was used until April 1916 and for some burials in 1917 though it was enlarged after the war.

**INFORMATION**
The area was taken by the Germans in November 1914 after heavy fighting and remained in their hands until June 1917. It fell to the Germans again in April 1918 after fierce fighting and was captured for the final time on 28 September 1918.

R.E. Farm was the name given by the army, its real name being the Ferme des Douze Bonniers. It was a location at which equipment stores and medical units were to be found as close as possible to the lines.

In January 1915 the 1st Dorsetshires began a second cemetery here on the other side of the farm but it was hardly used. After the war the graves in it, 23 British men and one Canadian, were concentrated into the No. 1 cemetery, along with one isolated grave from the battlefield. The three French graves have since been removed.

Buried here is Private James Farquharson, 5th (Saskatchewan) Canadian Infantry, killed on 2 March 1916 aged 26 years. He served as Ferguson. His brother, Private Donald Farquharson, 27th (Manitoba) Canadian Infantry, was killed in action in a German trench mortar attack on 6 November 1917 aged 31 years and is commemorated on the Menin Gate. Another brother, Private Nathaniel Machonachie Farquharson, Royal Marine Light Infantry, HMS Indefatigable, was killed in action on 31 May 1916, one of over 1000 men killed when his ship blew up in the Battle of Jutland. Another brother, Trimmer J. Farquharson, HMS Newbury, Royal Navy, was killed in action near Dover on 15 February 1918.

Gunner Herbert 'Nobby' Barlow Nightingale, 35th Trench Mortar Battery, Royal Garrison Artillery died on 13 January 1916 aged 28 years. A footballer who played at half-back for Charlton Athletic, he enlisted in May 1915 and was at the Front by June. He was attached to the 1st Canadian Division when he was killed by a shell just outside Messines.

UK – 132   Can – 47   Unnamed – 11
Area - 1381 sq mts

**LOCATION**
R.E. Farm Cemetery lies south of Ieper about 1km north of Wulvergem on the west side of the road from Wulvergem to Wijtschate. Only the entrance can be seen from the road, as the cemetery lies behind a farmhouse, set back from the road, and is reached by a small path.

## R.E. GRAVE, RAILWAY WOOD

**HISTORY**
The cemetery is the grave of twelve men lost from 1915 to 1917 during tunnelling operations beneath the Bellewaerde spur.

**INFORMATION**
R. E. Grave is unusual as it is a cemetery and a memorial. There are no gravestones in the small enclosure as the men are commemorated on the Cross of Sacrifice itself. The memorial is to eight Royal Engineers and four infantrymen working with them.

This is a fitting memorial to these men who are buried in tunnels many feet below the surface. The Cross of Sacrifice stands high on the spur north of the Menin Road and can be seen from some distance away. The base of the Cross of Sacrifice bears an inscription 'Beneath this spot lie the bodies of an officer, three NCO's and eight men of, or

attached to, the 177th Tunnelling Company, Royal Engineers, who were killed in action underground during the defence of Ypres between November 1915 and August 1917' and the names of the following :
- 2nd Lieutenant Charles Geoffrey Boothby, died 28 April 1916 aged 21 years
- Corporal Roland Brindley, died 28 April 1916
- Sapper Michael Carter, died 13 June 1916 aged 34 years
- Sapper George Auty Chatt, died 14 December 1915 aged 41 years
- Sapper John Henry Cotterill, died 22 July 1917 aged 37 years
- Private Thomas Edward Davies, died 25 February 1917 (17th Royal Welsh Fusiliers) aged 20 years
- Corporal Daniel Brookes Evans, died 9 April 1917 (16th Royal Welsh Fusiliers) aged 22 years
- Sapper Sidney Firth, died 9 March 1917 aged 24 years
- Private Edward Poulton, died 25 April 1917 (1/10th Kings (Liverpools)) aged 31 years
- Private Richard Roberts, died 9 April 1917 (16th Royal Welsh Fusiliers) aged 39 years
- Sapper William Spooner, died 28 April 1916 aged 46 years
- Corporal George Arthur Woolley, died 22 July 1917 aged 42 years

Of those remembered here Boothby was commissioned into the South Staffordshires on Christmas Eve 1914 and left for the Front in July 1915. He joined the Tunnelling Company in January 1916. He was killed, with two others, at about 7.45am when the Germans blew a camouflet about 10m underground. His poems and letters were published after the death of his 'fiancé' in 1990 in a book titled 'Thirty-odd Feet Under Belgium.'

The Battle of Bellewaarde was fought on 24 and 25 May 1915 as part of the Second Battle of Ypres. The British responded with unsuccessful attacks on the ridge from June to September 1915 though it was not retaken until July 1917. The ridge was given up during the German advance in April 1918 and finally re taken by the 9th (Scottish) Division on 28 September 1918.

If you continue east rather than try to turn at the dirt track you will come to the Memorial to the Princess Patricia's Canadian Light Infantry on the south side of the road. During heavy fighting, where the Princess Patricia's Canadian Light Infantry Memorial now stands, a German attack on 8 May 1915 left the regiment exposed. They were subjected to a bombardment and gas attack during which they lost all their officers. Corporal Dove lost an arm and leg using a machine-gun to defend the line but the Canadians were still forced to withdraw as was most of the British line on this day. A monument in the form of a simple circular stone seat surrounding a maple tree was erected in their honour. It bears the inscription 'Here in May 1915, The originals of Princess Patricia's Canadian Light Infantry, Commanded by the founder Major A. Hamilton-Gault, DSO, Held firm and counted not the cost'

On 16 June 1915, Battalions of the 3rd Division, the 2nd Royal Scots, 1st Royal Scots Fusiliers, 1st Wiltshires and 4th South Lancashires, attacked the spur upon which this grave stands. They were to take the German second line, after the 9th Brigade had captured the front-line here, and by 4.30am, after ten minutes of bayonet combat, they had reached their objective. The commanding officer of the 1st Lincolnshires, Major Hugh Edward Boxer, DSO, then took a party of 50 men on a raid east of here, reaching the west end of the lake about 100m away, before they were cut off. Major Boxer was wounded and sent most of his men back. He, however, never returned and was awarded the Distinguished Service Order. Despite a German counter-attack in the evening the 3rd Division had succeeded in pushing the Germans back to the Hooge Chateau grounds. The 9th Brigade took a small amount of ground but lost 143 officers and 3417 men. The 1st Lincolnshires were to spend 248 days in the Salient during 1915 losing 30 officers and 1046 men but no ground.

On 31 July 1917 the attack here by the 2nd Northamptonshires failed. During the attack Captain Colyer-Fergusson became isolated with six men but still took an enemy trench winning the Victoria Cross. He was later killed by a sniper and is buried in Menin Road South Cemetery. At the same time Lieutenant (temporary Brigadier-General and later a Major-General) Clifford Coffin, VC, CB, DSO and Bar, of the Royal Engineers won a Victoria Cross for his efforts in encouraging his men who were pinned down in shell-holes during an attack on Westhoek.

From 1-8 August 1917 the 8th South Lancashires were in action nearby in pushing the line east from Westhoek towards Zonnebeke. In doing so they gained territory in which many of the wounded of 31 July still lay. Hence, they rescued 150 men.

On the Cambridge Road leading to St. Charles, north of the Ieper-Zonnebeke road, are two private memorials on the right of the road 200m past the turn to this cemetery. Next to the road is the Memorial Cross to Captain Henry Langton Skrine, 6th Somerset Light Infantry, who was killed and buried here on 25 September 1915. The monument is also the Battalion Memorial. Close by is the Memorial to Captain Geoffrey Vaux Salvin Bowlby of the Royal Horse Guards who was killed in action on 13 May 1915. Both men are commemorated on the Menin Gate as their graves were destroyed in later fighting.

Also nearby is the Liverpool Scottish Memorial erected in July 2000. It commemorates the action at Hooge on 16 June 1915 when the Battalion lost four officers and 75 other ranks killed, eleven officers and 201 other ranks wounded and six officers and 103 other ranks reported as missing, almost all of whom were subsequently reported as killed. The stone from which the memorial was made was the keystone above the Fraser Street entrance to the Liverpool Scottish Barracks in Liverpool which was demolished in 1978. It shows the badge of the 1/10th (Liverpool Scottish) King's (Liverpools).

UK – 12          Area - 83 sq mts

**LOCATION**
R.E. Grave lies on a ridge about 500m north of the Menin Road, east of Ieper. It is reached by taking the turn north, onto what the 'Tommies' knew as Cambridge Road, from the Menin Road 200m east of Birr Crossroads Cemetery. The route from the Menin Road is clearly signed and although the roads are narrow they are passable. However, I would not advise anyone to try to take a car on the farm track that leads to the grave.

## RED FARM MILITARY CEMETERY

**HISTORY**
The cemetery was only used during the German Spring Offensive in April and May 1918.

**INFORMATION**
This is one of the smallest cemeteries on the Salient and was begun as many of the other cemeteries in the area of Vlamertinge had been filled. It was made near 'Red Farm' as a result of the number of men dying in the local Dressing Stations. The majority of the burials are artillerymen. There are no officers buried here.

Most of the casualties here date from 27 April 1918 or a few days after. About 400m north of here is Hagle Dump Cemetery and close to that was a major camp and stores depot known as Dirty Bucket Camp. It was one of the largest camps in the Salient consisting of a series of huts and tented areas and had a reputation for not being one of the best camps in the Salient. But it was beyond German artillery fire for most of the war. However, on 27 April 1918, at about 12.30pm, a large explosion was caused by a German shell striking an ammunition dump on the edge of the camp. The camp was wrecked and numerous huts set on fire by the explosion. Rescue parties at once set about recovering casualties from the debris and extinguishing the fires in face of great danger from recurring explosions from the dump. Those killed, or who subsequently died over the next few days, are buried here, in other local cemeteries such as Hagle Dump, or in cemeteries at Base Hospitals further afield in places like Boulogne.

Near to the camp were a few Belgian houses and a wooden building from which two Belgian girls served fried eggs and chips. The wooden shack had disappeared in the explosion on 27 April along with the two girls. All the houses, along with the medical units in the area, which had not been wrecked had lost their roofs. Half-way down the far side of the crater was a baby's pram. The three Belgian civilians buried in one grave in the cemetery were killed in the explosion and the headstone marks all that remained of the three individuals.

Among them is Bombardier Frederick Ludovici, 63rd Siege Battery, Royal Garrison Artillery, who died aged 23 years. He was from Sri Lanka.

UK – 46          Unnamed – 17     Bel Civilians – 3
Area - 172 sq mts

**LOCATION**
Red Farm Cemetery lies west of Ieper just north of the old road to Poperinge (N308) 500m west of the turn to the Brandhoek cemeteries.

## RENINGHELST CHURCHYARD EXTENSION

**HISTORY**
Begun in March 1915 the Churchyard and Extension were used until November 1915 when the New Military Cemetery was opened on the edge of the village.

**INFORMATION**
The Extension was used for burials from local Field Ambulances in 1915 as well as two single burials later in the war.

A large number of graves are of the 1st Dorsetshires or 2nd Duke of Wellington's made in early May 1915. They are all casualties suffered at Hill 60 in the fighting and gas attacks taking place as the British and Germans attacked each other several times to seize control of the Hill.

The Australian buried here is Chaplain 3rd Class The Reverend Michael Bergin, MC, Australian Army Chaplains

Department who died on 12 October 1917. He was an Irish Jesuit priest who had spent most of his priesthood as a missionary in the Middle East where he was when the Australians arrived in 1915. Though a civilian, he went with the 5th Light Horse Brigade to Gallipoli as a Private and acted as priest and stretcher-bearer until his official appointment as Chaplain arrived in May 1915. He remained at ANZAC sector at Gallipoli until September when he was evacuated to England with enteric fever. He returned to his unit too soon so was evacuated again. However, he went with them to France where he served through all the major campaigns in 1916 and 1917. He was killed at Passendale on 11 October 1917 when a heavy shell burst near the aid-post where he was working. He was awarded a posthumous Military Cross.

There are also two burials of men who fell during World War II. One of whom was Flight Lieutenant (Pilot) Thomas Glyn Finlayson Ritchie, No. 602 Squadron, Royal Air Force Volunteer Reserve, killed in action on 21 July 1941. A pre-war member of the RAF, he was involved in the Battle of Britain flying Spitfires with three confirmed victories until injured and out of action. On 21 July his Squadron escorted three Stirlings to attack a target at Lille. On the way in they were attacked by Me109's and Ritchie, in Spitfire IIa P8478, was shot down and killed. The other is Pilot Officer (Pilot) Kenward Ernest Knox, No. 54 Squadron, Royal Air Force Volunteer Reserve killed on 5 July 1941 aged 23 years, when his Spitfire crashed nearby.

UK - 55          Aust – 1          WWII – 2
Area - 834 sq mts

**LOCATION**
Reningelst Churchyard is in the centre of the village of Reningelst which is south-west of Ieper. The Extension is on the right side of the churchyard as you look from the road.

# RENINGHELST NEW MILITARY CEMETERY

**HISTORY**
This cemetery was opened in November 1915 when it was considered that the Churchyard and Extension were not able to cope with the number of dead from the local Dressing Stations. It remained in use until September 1918.

**INFORMATION**
The wall of the cemetery seems higher on one side because of the slope, one effect of this is that the Cross of Sacrifice is considerably raised above the level of the cemetery.

The village never fell to the Germans and always contained a number of medical units. Of the men who lie here 275 were from artillery units reflecting the nature of the activity in this area.

Buried here is Brigadier General Charles William Eric Gordon, three times MiD, 3rd Class of the Danilo Order for Valour (Montenegro), General Staff Commanding 123rd Infantry Brigade late Black Watch (Royal Highlanders) who died on 23 July 1917 aged 39 years. Brigadier-General Gordon was commissioned into the 3rd (Militia) Battalion, The Black Watch in 1897, and joined the 2nd Battalion in 1899. He served with his Regiment throughout the South African War. He then accompanied his Battalion to India, where he spent ten years, being Adjutant from 1909 to 1912. In March 1915, he went to France as Adjutant of the South Staffordshire Regiment, but in the following June he re-joined the Black Watch and was severely wounded at the Battle of Loos. In April 1916, he was appointed Lieutenant-Colonel of the 8th Black Watch and commanded it at the Battle of Longueval. In the following September he received the command of a Brigade and served at Vimy Ridge in the trenches, and at the Battle of Messines. He and his Brigade-Major were both killed by a shell when returning from the trenches near St. Eloi.

Also here is Colonel Harold Edward Street, CMG, MiD, Brevet of Honour (France), 106th Brigade, Royal Field Artillery who died on 25 August 1917 aged 41 years. He served in the South African Wars where he was Mentioned in Despatches. He was a temporary Brigadier General on the General Staff with VIII Corps in Gallipoli and with IX Corps in Egypt and France from February 1916 to his death which happened on Hill 60. He was awarded the Order of St. Michael and St. George in March 1916.

Five Lieutenant-Colonels are here. Lieutenant Colonel Francis Dawson Blandy, MC, 24th (Wessex) Field Ambulance, Royal Army Medical Corps died on 14 August 1917 aged 42 years. He qualified as a doctor in February 1900. He entered the war in June 1915. He was awarded the Military Cross 'For conspicuous gallantry and devotion to duty. He worked continuously for thirty-six hours under heavy shell fire and adverse conditions of weather, not only collecting the wounded of his own Brigade, but also those of another, who were lying in an advanced position. To do this he collected all the bearer parties that he could find, and personally led them to the spots under heavy shell fire. By his gallant conduct in going forward again and again, regardless of his personal safety, he undoubtedly saved many lives.' Blandy died as a result of wounds sustained whilst tending to injured men on the battlefield.

Lieutenant Colonel Henry Victor Mottet de la Fontaine, DSO, three times MiD, 9th East Surreys, died on 5 August 1917 aged 44 years. While observing over the parapet, de la Fontaine was shot through the head by a sniper during a German attack in the area of Klein Zillebeke, dying soon afterwards. He was commissioned into the East Surreys as a 2nd Lieutenant in February 1893, was promoted to Lieutenant two years later, to Captain in December 1901 and Major in June 1911. He served with the 2nd East Surreys in the South African Wars where he was twice Mentioned in Despatches. He was made a Lieutenant-Colonel on 19 July 1915, and given command of the 9th East Surreys the following year, being Mentioned in Despatches and awarded the Distinguished Service Order in the New Years Honours List in January 1917.

Lieutenant Colonel Henry Murray Hope-Johnstone, MC, three times MiD, 12th Royal Fusiliers, died on 31 July 1917 aged 31 years. He was commissioned into the Royal Fusiliers in May 1908. He went to France in April 1915 as a Captain, commanded the 2nd Royal Fusiliers from 1 to 22 May 1915, and was Mentioned in Despatches in August 1915, May 1916 and July 1917. He had commanded his Battalion since 11 June 1917 when he was promoted from Major but was mortally wounded as his Battalion moved up to the front-line. He was awarded the Military Cross in May 1916 while attached to the Egyptian Army. His brother Lieutenant William Gordon Tollemache Hope Johnstone, 4th Royal Fusiliers, died on 25 October 1914 aged 27 years and is commemorated on the Le Touret Memorial.

Lieutenant Colonel Arthur Graham Johnson, 33rd Division Ammunition Column, Royal Field Artillery, died on 17 September 1917 aged 55 years. He was commissioned in February 1882.

Lieutenant Colonel David Graham McNicoll, DSO, MiD, 20th (Wearside) Durham Light Infantry, died of wounds on 20 September 1917 aged 33 years. He and his brother, Captain Malcolm McNicoll, MC, joined up together as Privates in August 1914. In March 1915 he was commissioned into the East Yorkshires, while his brother was commissioned into the 2/4th Kings Own Yorkshire Light Infantry. He was Mentioned in Despatches when transferred to the Durham Light Infantry in July 1916. He was awarded the Distinguished Service Order in January 1917 in the New Years Honours List 'for courage and coolness in establishing strong points in Delville Wood on the night of 11-12 Sept 1916, and in leading his Company on the 15th successfully to the attack on Flers'. He had been in command of the Battalion for two months. His brother died of wounds received near Cambrai on 21 November 1917 and is buried in Rocquigny Equancourt Road British Cemetery. Another brother, Captain John McNicoll, MC, survived the war.

Buried here is Lieutenant Joseph Joachim (Constable-) Maxwell-Stuart, 9th Duke of Wellington's, who died on 2 March 1916 aged 19 years, one of four brothers to die in the war. Buried in Artillery Wood Cemetery is 2nd Lieutenant Henry Joseph Ignatius (Constable-) Maxwell-Stuart, 3rd Coldstream Guards who was killed on 9 October 1917 aged 30 years. Lieutenant Edmund Joseph (Constable-) Maxwell-Stuart, 175th Tunnelling Company, Royal Engineers was killed on 26 April 1916 aged 23 years and is buried in Poperinghe New Military cemetery. Lieutenant Alfred Joseph (Constable-) Maxwell-Stuart, 1st Coldstream Guards, was killed on 24 August 1918 aged 20 years and is buried in Bagneux British Cemetery.

There are three men buried here who deserted while in action but for whom justice was administered when their Battalions were in camp near Reningelst. Private Robert Loveless Barker of the 1/6th (London Rifles) Londons was charged with cowardice after his Battalion was almost wiped out during the Battle of Flers on the Somme on 15 September 1916. The interval between trial and judgement, at 36 days, was the longest any man had to wait in the war. He was serving under a suspended sentence of death. He was executed on 4 November 1916 when his unit had been transferred to the Salient.

Private Frederick Loader of the 1/22nd (The Queen's) Londons deserted when his Battalion attacked 'The Bluff' on 7 June 1916 as part of the attack on the first day of the Battle of Messines. He was serving under a suspended sentence of death. He was executed on 19 August 1917.

Private William Smith of the 3/5th Lancashire Fusiliers deserted with two others in the quagmire between the Frezenberg Ridge and Poelkapelle on 4 October 1917. They surrendered three days later but Smith was the only one to be executed when he was shot, on the site of what is now the primary school in Reningelst, on 14 November 1917.

Several reliable sources tell us of the following unhappy story. In a house on the L'Abeele road just north-west of this cemetery an event happened that serves as a good example of the danger to civilians remaining in the Salient during the war. Shrapnel fired at German aeroplanes from anti-aircraft guns in Ouderdom fell through a house. It killed a child sitting on its mother's knee, and sliced through the mother's leg. She later died in a Casualty Clearing Station at Godewaersvelde.

| | | |
|---|---|---|
| UK – 452 | Aust – 104 | NZ – 2 |
| Can – 230 | S Afr – 1 | UK Civilian – 1 |
| Chinese Labour Corps – 7 | | Ger – 2 |
| KUG – 1 | | Area - 3846 sq mts |

**LOCATION**

Reninghelst New Military Cemetery lies south-west of Ieper, about 200m north-east of the church in Reningelst, on the road from Reningelst to Poperinge. It is on the left and though there is a CWGC sign you do not see it clearly until you are at the end of the houses. The path leads beside the houses to the cemetery although it seems as if you are walking into their back gardens.

# RIDGE WOOD MILITARY CEMETERY

**HISTORY**
Begun as a regimental front-line cemetery in May 1915, the cemetery remained in use until July 1918 when the wood had come back into the front-line during the German Spring Offensive.

**INFORMATION**
The area was in British hands for almost all of the war. On 8 May 1918 the British line ran north from Ridge Wood to Scottish Wood when the Germans attacked the 98th and 19th Brigades of the 33rd Division stationed here. The 2nd Argyll and Sutherland Highlanders fought heroically but were pushed back and away from the 1st Cameronians who had suffered heavy casualties. The action of Lieutenant Liddiard, Sergeant Goode and Corporal McKirdy of the Machine Gun Corps halted the German advance so that the 5/6th Cameronians could be used in a counter-attack to retake the wood.

Ridge Wood was the name given to a wood on the western edge of the ridge that runs parallel to the Ieper-Kemmel road. The cemetery is on the western edge of the wood in a small hollow.

The first burials were made by the 2nd Royal Irish Rifles. Units that made burials here, when they occupied the front-line, included the 1/9th Durham Light Infantry, and the 18th, 19th, 20th and 21st Canadian Infantry. There were some French graves but they have been removed.

Sergeant Andrew Ross, 29th Canadian Infantry died on 6 April 1916 aged 37 years. He was a marine engineer from Edinburgh who travelled the world. While at home, he was part of a Scotland Rugby Union side on five occasion as well as gaining several other representative honours for his city.

He emigrated to Canada before the war began and had to travel from the Arctic Circle to enlist when the war began. He was killed by shellfire in his trench while attending to wounded men.

Buried here is Major Hugh Speke, 'B' Company, 10th Lancashire Fusiliers transferred from 9th Somerset Light Infantry, who died on 12 August 1915 aged 37 years. He served in the South African War with the Wiltshire Yeomanry and then became a priest working in London, Somerset and then in Canada. He returned home at the start of the war joining the 3rd Somerset Light Infantry as a Captain. He was promoted to Major and transferred to the Lancashire Fusiliers to go to the Front. On the night of 11-12 August Speke was on patrol in no-man's land near Vierstraat. They were heading back when Speke was killed by several shots to the head and body. His body was entangled in barbed wire and Company Sergeant Major J H Rogers and Sergeant E Baker waited under fire before releasing their officer and carrying him back to their lines. Both men received the Distinguished Conduct Medal.

Two young 'men' are buried here. Private Perley A Graham, 26th Canadian Infantry was killed on 6 August 1916 aged 16 years. Private Gilbert Harry Tripney, 48th Australian Infantry died on 16 October 1916 aged 16 years. He enlisted on 4 March 1916 leaving Australia a month later. He was his Battalion's rifle champion.

Also here is 2nd Lieutenant John Cyril Watmough, 2nd Northumberland Fusiliers who died on 10 July 1917 aged 26 years. His brother, Bombardier E Watmough, 'A' Battery, 315th Brigade, Royal Field Artillery was killed on 31 August 1918 aged 27 years and is buried in Achiet-le-Grand Communal Cemetery Extension. Another brother, Private Victor Watmough, 15th Royal Scots died on 22 October 1917 aged 19 years and is commemorated on the Tyne Cot Memorial.

| | | |
|---|---|---|
| UK – 258 | Aust – 44 | NZ – 3 |
| Can – 292 | Ger – 2 | KUG – 20 |
| Unnamed – 5 | | Area - 3729 sq mts |

Special Memorials to two British men whose graves have been lost

**LOCATION**
Ridge Wood Cemetery lies south of Ieper about 800m west of the road to Kemmel. It is reached by turning west at the Elzenwalle Brasserie crossroads. The road to the cemetery is left and then right at the next two junctions.

# RIFLE HOUSE CEMETERY

**HISTORY**
This cemetery was used from November 1914 until June 1916.

**INFORMATION**
For more general information about the wood please refer to Ploegsteert Wood Cemetery.

Rifle House Cemetery was named after a strong point of which no trace now exists. The earliest burials here, now Plot IV, Rows E to J, are men of the 1st Rifle Brigade who died defending a strong point which was destroyed during the war. The cemetery was in Allied hands for most of the war except from 10 April to 29 September 1918 when the Germans briefly occupied the area.

One of the most notable burials here is that of Rifleman Robert (Raphael) Barnett, 1st Rifle Brigade, who died on 19 December 1914 aged 15 years and six months. Barnett was born on 25 June 1899 in Hackney, London. His name at birth was Raphael Glitzenstein, the son of Barnett and

Esther Glitzenstein (née Bloomberg). His father was a tailor. Some time before the war there was an argument in the family and Raphael, as he was named at the time, left home. He subsequently joined the army, his service number indicates this happened in July 1914. At the time Raphael joined up the minimum age for enlistment was eighteen, so, clearly he lied about his age. He also thought it prudent, as a Jew, to change his name at the point of enlistment using his father's first name as a surname, becoming 5509 Rifleman R. Barnett, 1st Rifle Brigade. The Battalion departed for France on 19 August 1914 and Barnett joined them in Flanders on 9 October 1914 probably as a battle casualty replacement. Barnett was among three officers and 23 other ranks killed in action during an unsuccessful attack by the 11th Brigade on a position called 'The Birdcage' with the objective of keeping enemy troops from being moved as reserves to Arras where the French were attacking. A further three officers and 42 other ranks were wounded. They met heavy German machine gun and rifle fire as they tried to cross shell-holes filled with water, slimy mud and well positioned barbed wire. They also suffered casualties caused by their own artillery as they lay in no man's land. The attack failed with virtually no objectives being taken.

One of the officers killed with Rifleman Barnett and buried here is Captain The Honourable Richard George Grenville Morgan-Grenville, MiD, 1st Rifle Brigade, killed in action on 19 December 1914 aged 27 years. Grandson of the 3rd Duke of Buckingham and Chandos, son of the 11th Lady Kinloss and Master of Kinloss he was commissioned in 1910 and became a Captain at the start of the war. He was twice wounded and Mentioned in Despatches in October 1914.

Another officer from the Rifle Brigade killed in that attack and buried here is Captain The Honourable Francis Reginald 'Reg' Dennis Prittie, Legion of Honour, twice MiD, 1st Rifle Brigade, killed on 19 December 1914 aged 34 years. He was son of the 4th Baron Dunnalley and worked as Assistant Commissioner, Uganda Commission from 1910 until the start of the war.

2nd Lieutenant John Percival 'Bay' Hermon-Hodge, 1/4th Oxford and Bucks Light Infantry died on 28 May 1915 aged 24 years is buried here. He enlisted at the start of the war, was commissioned in September and arrived in France in March 1915. He was killed by a sniper, the only man in the Battalion killed that day. He was son of Sir Robert Trotter Hermon-Hodge who was Conservative MP for Accrington, South Oxfordshire and Croydon between 1886 and 1910 before he became the 1st Baron Wyfold in 1919. His brother, Captain George Guy Herman-Hodge, Royal Horse Artillery attached 165th Brigade, Royal Field Artillery was killed on 7 July 1916 aged 32 years and is buried in Gezaincourt Communal Cemetery Extension. Five other brothers fought in the war and survived. However, a nephew, Sub-Lieutenant Anthony Claude Hermon-Hodge, HMS Grove, Royal Naval Volunteer Reserve died on 12 June 1942 aged 21 years and is commemorated on the Chatham Naval Memorial.

Another son of a politician buried here is Rifleman Thomas Stapleton, 1st Rifle Brigade who died on 19 December 1915 aged 45 years in the same attack as Rifleman Barnett. His father, John Stapleton was a Liberal MP for Berwick-upon-Tweed on two occasions between 1852 and 1874.

Buried here is Private James Penton, 8th South Lancashires who died on 14 January 1916 aged 19 years. The son of a coal miner, he was an amateur boxer before the war with a promising future having won several competitions, medals and trophies. He enlisted on 2 September 1914, went to France a year later and was killed by a sniper. His two brothers survived the war though both were wounded. Another here is Captain Ernest George Dashwood, 1/4th Oxford and Bucks Light Infantry, who died on 12 May 1915 aged 35 years. Grandson of the Marquess of Hertford and son of the 6th Baronet, he served as a cadet on HMS Worcester and then worked with the P&O shipping line before taking up farming in Oxfordshire. He became a Lieutenant in the Territorial Force in 1911 and was promoted to Captain in April 1914. He was killed by a rifle grenade shortly after arriving at the Front. Five brothers served in the war, three of whom were killed. Robert and Henry survived. 2nd Lieutenant Lionel Albert Dashwood, 2nd Oxfordshire and Bucks Light Infantry, was killed in action at the Battle of Festubert on 16 May 1915 aged 27 years and is commemorated on the Le Touret Memorial. Lieutenant Wilfred James Dashwood, 1st Grenadier Guards, previously 18th (Public Schools) Royal Fusiliers died on 2 August 1917 of the wounds he received during the fighting at Pilkem Ridge during Third Ypres on 31 July aged 34 years and is buried in Dozinghem Military Cemetery.

UK – 229   Can – 1   Area - 1644 sq mts

**LOCATION**

Rifle House Cemetery lies in the heart of Ploegsteert Wood about 2km north-east of Ploegsteert. A dirt track 50m from Prowse Point Cemetery leads to the three cemeteries in Ploegsteert Wood of which this is the deepest into the wood. The path past Mud Corner is fairly easy to follow as it is fenced, and the walk is quite pleasant. CWGC signs are plentiful. Although access to the cemetery is easy, it should be noted that the wood can be very wet and boggy, and the nearest parking is at Prowse Point Cemetery which is about 1.5 km away.

# RUISSEAU FARM CEMETERY

**HISTORY**
The cemetery was begun after the Guards Division had taken the farm on 8 October 1917 and it remained in use until November 1917.

**INFORMATION**
The area around this cemetery was in German hands from April 1915 until it saw severe fighting in 1917 when the farm was taken by the Guards with French support on 8 October 1917. Incidentally, Ruisseau in French means brook or stream.

However, there was an important battle nearby in October 1914. The Germans used newly mobilised troops to attack towards the canal and southwards to Ypres on 22 October. They pushed the line held by the 1st Infantry Brigade, and in particular the 1st Black Watch, to just west and north of this cemetery but it cost them 1500 casualties. These men of the I Corps, under Sir Douglas Haig, had been thrown into action because of the French retreat from Houthulst Forest which meant that the Germans threatened to outflank the British 3rd Cavalry Division. Hence, I Corps took over the line from Zonnebeke to Bikschote until relieved by the French a few days later.

The 1st Northamptonshires were sent to assist in retaking the line from Ruisseau Farm to a crossroads on the Bikschote road known as the Kortekeer Cabaret. The Battalion took most of the trenches but could not capture the position despite an attack in which they lost five officers and over 100 men.

The 1st Loyal North Lancashires and 2nd King's Royal Rifle Corps were then sent in, reaching the Pilkem-Langemark road south-west of here early on 23 October, taking up positions on a line that ran parallel to that road south of this cemetery. But on 24 October it was decided that the trenches were too exposed and were to be abandoned. The Loyal North Lancashires were under their third commanding officer of the war, Major Aubrey John Carter, DSO, MiD. Their first, Lieutenant-Colonel Walter Reginald Lloyd, was killed on 14 September and their second, Lieutenant-Colonel Guy Cunninghame Knight, was killed during the Battle of the Marne. Major Carter was to die on 4 November 1914 and is on the Menin Gate.

Buried here is Captain Robert Coningsby Wilmot, 10th Sherwood Foresters (Notts and Derbys) who died on 29 October 1917 aged 31 years. The eldest son of a vicar he became a lawyer before enlisting at the start of the war. He joined the 16th (Public Schools) Middlesex in August 1914 and was gazetted as 2nd Lieutenant in 1915 to the Sherwood Foresters. He was wounded in France in July 1915 and was invalided home returning to France in 1916 to survive fighting on the Somme and the Battle of Arras in 1917. He was killed when a shell hit his dugout. He, and his two brothers are commemorated by a memorial window in Worcester Cathedral. Private Henry Cecil Wilmot, 8th Worcestershires, died in Lewisham Hospital from lung disease, contracted on active service, on 23 July 1917 aged 26 years and is buried in Yatton Churchyard. He returned from farming in Canada to enlist in April 1916 and went to France in December. 2nd Lieutenant Thomas Norbury Wilmot, MC, 2nd Worcestershires, died on 25 August 1916, of wounds received on the previous day near Thiepval, and is buried in Heilly Station Cemetery. He also returned from farming in Canada to join the 18th (1st Pubic Schools) Royal Fusiliers in October 1914. He was then sent to Sandhurst and commissioned into the Worcestershires in May 1915, arriving in France in June. He was Mentioned in Despatches in September 1915 and received his Military Cross in July 1916 for his part in the Auchy-les-Mines raid, north of Lens, on 1-2 July 1916 'For conspicuous gallantry. By his dash in securing and tenaciously holding a post in the enemy's position he contributed largely to the success of the operations.' He was mortally wounded when the troops which he helped to lead captured and held two lines of the German trenches.

Nearby on the Boezinge-Langemark road is the beautiful red dragon that marks the Welsh Memorial to the 38th Division's actions here on 31 July 1917 at the start of Third Ypres. On the ring road around Langemark, about 300m south east from here, is the memorial to Harry Patch, the last surviving British soldier of the war. He died in 2009.

UK – 82  Unnamed – 6
Area - 486 sq mts

**LOCATION**
Ruisseau Farm Cemetery lies about 2km west of Langemark north-east of Ieper. It is 1km north of the Langemark-Boezinge road and is reached from the crossroads, known as the Iron Cross, 400m west of Cement House Cemetery. This small cemetery is on the edge of a farmyard.

# SANCTUARY WOOD CEMETERY

## HISTORY
A cemetery was begun here in May 1915 but was severely damaged during the Battle of Mount Sorrel in June 1916. The present cemetery which was, in effect, begun in 1917, remained in use until the end of the war and was greatly enlarged after the war.

## INFORMATION
Sanctuary Wood gained its name in November 1914 when it was used to screen troops behind the front-line. Men lost from their regiments during the First Battle of Ypres gathered in the wood under the command of General Edward Stanislaus Bulfin of the 2nd Brigade who ordered that they could not be used without his permission. Hence, the word went out that this was a 'Sanctuary Wood' even though it was shelled for the first time on the night of 13-14 November 1914. The hill near the wood, and this area, is also known as Hill 62 referring to its height above sea level. A copse known as Zouave Wood immediately south of here was named after the French Colonial troops who held the position until the British came in 1914.

On 21 February 1915 the wood came into the front-line as the Germans blew three mines here. The 16th (The Queen's) Lancers held the line, and although a Lieutenant and ten men who were partially buried by the mines were captured, resolute defence by the Battalion meant that the German attack failed.

On the morning of 30 July 1915 the 126th Prussian Infantry Regiment used flame-throwers, or 'liquid fire', for the first time in war when they attacked the 8th Rifle Brigade who had only arrived on the Western Front on 18 June. The Germans bayoneted the few survivors who had already been badly burned. That afternoon the 6th Duke of Cornwall's Light Infantry, who had witnessed the German attack, retaliated on a front approximately along the length of Maple Avenue. As the Duke of Cornwall's Light Infantry started from the low ground they suffered heavy casualties but took, and held, the enemy positions until relieved.

The wood was in the centre of the Battle of Mount Sorrel in June 1916. On 2 June, when the line was held by the 3rd Canadian Division, the Germans launched a heavy bombardment upon the Canadians who had never before been in battle. The attack drove a hole 700m deep and 3000m wide in the line occupied by the British Second Army consisting of the three Divisions of the Canadian Corps and the British 20th (Light) Division. A German infantry attack followed which took much of Sanctuary Wood, Hill 62, Armagh Wood and Mount Sorrel.

The Canadian commander, General Sir Julian Byng, ordered an immediate counter-attack using four Battalions. But the attack was poorly prepared and not executed until the morning of 3 June by which time the Germans had consolidated their gains. Hence, the counter-attack was a failure. On 6 June the Germans captured more Allied trenches pushing the Canadians towards Ypres at which point Byng determined to retake the 'high ground', so careful planning and practice took place over the next week. The attack was launched at 1.30am on 13 June, in poor weather, but despite hard fighting the German Wurtembergers, who had attacked the week before, were forced back to their old trench line. This is regarded as the first planned and co-ordinated Canadian attack of the war and was a complete success. The cost was high as Canadian troops suffered 8430 casualties.

In 1917 the 18th Division attacked from here across the valley towards Hooge on the first day of the Third Battle of Ypres. The Division was meant to attack Glencorse and Polygon Woods but got lost and suffered heavy casualties. Even so, the Germans gave up all the territory in Sanctuary Wood that they had controlled since 1915.

The 56th (London) Division were in Sanctuary Wood preparing for an attack on Glencorse and Polygon Woods on 15 August 1917. The Division successfully took Glencorse Wood and some men even managed to get through the wood to see Polygon Wood a short distance away. However, they failed to achieve all of their objectives.

Sanctuary Wood was lost to the Germans in their Spring Offensive of 1918 but was retaken by the 9th (Scottish) Division on 28 September 1918.

During the war the road, Maple Avenue, or Canadalaan, from the Menin Road to Hill 62, did not exist. Beyond the cemetery is a cafe and museum at which there is a section of trenches. I have seen young pupils thigh deep in mud which has given them a good idea of what conditions were like for 'Tommies' in the front-line. The owner sells a wide range of souvenirs and refreshments.

Beyond the museum, at the end of Maple Avenue, is the Memorial to the Canadian troops who died in this part of the Salient. It is on the highest point of Observatory Ridge and gives excellent views of the battlefields. For example, Mount Sorrel can be seen to the south, Maple Copse to the east, a very good view of Ypres to the west as well as a view to the east as far as the Zandvoorde-Geluveld ridge. The memorial is about 800m north of Mount Sorrel.

Just outside the cemetery is the Memorial to 2nd Lieutenant Thomas Keith Hedley Rae of the 8th Rifle Brigade who was killed in Hooge Chateau grounds on 30 July 1915. His parents originally raised the monument in 1921 at the spot where he was believed to have died, as his body was never identified, but in 1978, Baron de Vinck, the chateau's owner, asked that the cross be moved as he could not maintain the area properly.

There were three British cemeteries in Sanctuary Wood before June 1916, containing 56, 55 and 100 graves respectively dating from the actions up to August 1915, but they were destroyed during the Battle of Mount Sorrel. The first two were on the western end of the wood, the third in a clearing further east. The traces of the only one that could be identified after the battle have formed the basis for the cemetery we see now when used by the battlefield clearance units and the IWGC as the core of the present cemetery. Sanctuary Wood Cemetery contained 137 graves at the end of the war but 88 were represented by Special Memorials as their position could not properly be identified.

The cemetery was enlarged between 1927 and 1932, making Plots II-V, as graves were brought from as far away as Nieuwpoort on the coast though most were from the Salient. Some 60% of the graves are unnamed and many are identified as buried in the cemetery but location unknown. Many graves, in all five plots, are identified in groups but not individually.

One that is identified is that of Lieutenant Gilbert Walter Lytleton Talbot, 7th Rifle Brigade after whom Talbot House in Poperinge was named. He had been President of the Oxford Union. He was commissioned in August 1914 arriving in France in May 1915. He was killed on 30 July 1915 aged 23 years during the attack that had been launched in retaliation for the first use of flame throwers. His body was recovered by his brother who went in to no-man's land at night to find him.

At the back against the wall lies the German pilot Hans Roser, who was shot down on 12 July 1915 by British pilot Lanoe Hawker, VC. The British retrieved his body from the wreckage and buried him among their own dead out of respect for his gallantry. Hawker would later win the Victoria Cross before himself being shot down by the Red Baron. Hans Roser is the only German buried here. In the register of Sanctuary Wood there is an inscription in English: 'He couldn't fly without a plane'.

Buried here are brothers Private Clarence Linnell, aged 22 years and Private Percy Linnell aged 19 years. Both were in the 1/4th Lincolnshires, both killed on 27 July 1915, originally buried on the south side of Hill 62 and moved here in 1928. They are now buried side by side as they were stood side by side when killed by the same shell.

Also here are brothers Gunner Victor Charles Eade aged 18 years and Bombardier Lawrence Eade aged 24 years, both 51st Battery, Royal Field Artillery and both killed on 20 November 1914. They are buried in the same grave.

Private James 'Peary' Pearson, 9th Royal Scots died on 22 May 1915 aged 26 years. A former pupil of George Watsons College, he played rugby and cricket for Old Watsonians, regularly leading the cricket batting averages. He represented Scotland twelve times at rugby union with a 50% win ratio. He enlisted and left for the Front on his birthday in February 1915, being killed by a sniper a few weeks later while getting water.

Also here is Lance Corporal Sam Wolstenholme, 'C' Company, 12th Manchesters, who died on 2 November 1915, aged 31 years. He was originally buried with the Linnells and moved here in 1929. He is recorded by the CWGC as an international footballer. However, the only man with that name who played for his country, England, was a prisoner of war from early in the war, survived the war and died in 1933 or 1945. He was coaching the North German Football Federation representative XI in Germany in 1914 and so was interned at the Ruhleben camp along with many other professional footballers, including England legend Steve Bloomer. He played three times for England in 1904-5 in wins over Scotland and Wales and a draw with Ireland while playing for Everton and Blackburn Rovers. Sadly, this is, I believe, not the same Sam Wolstenholme, but a lovely example of why I love researching history.

Another sportsman is Captain Frederic Marriner Aston, 6th Duke of Cornwall's Light Infantry who died on 30 July 1915 aged 48 years. He gained a 'Blue' for football at Cambridge and went on to play for Crusaders, who won the London Charity Cup, and Shrewsbury Town, who he captained to victory in the Welsh and Shropshire Cups. His Battalion arrived in France in late May 1915 and he was killed by shellfire while in Zouave Wood waiting to counter-attack after the first use of flame-throwers.

Buried here is 2nd Lieutenant Ronald Marmaduke Dawnay Harvey, 4th North Staffordshires attached 1st Bedfordshires, killed on 20 April 1915 aged 27 years. Before the war he was an actor in Australia and England with the Benson Shakespearean Company and other companies. His career faded just before the war. He was commissioned in August 1914 and killed at Hill 60 by a shell.

Concentrated here:

Beythem Communal Cemetery – now spelt Beitem, it is located about 8km north-east of here and contained one British burial made in October 1918.

Deerlyck German Cemetery – now spelt Deerlijk, it is located about 15km east of here. Four British burials were made here in October 1918 of whom two were brought to Sanctuary Wood and two taken to Dadizele.

Donegal Farm German Cemetery – located about 10km south-west of here on the road from Dranouter to Wulvergem 800m east of the village. One British unnamed officer was buried there.

Eiskellar German Cemetery - on the Menin Road near Herentage Chateau about 1km east of here. It contained one British unidentified soldier.

Flanders Field American Cemetery – located south-east of Waregem and about 25km east of here where one British Royal Air Force officer was buried.

Ingelmunster German Cemetery – located about 20km north-east of here, it contained two British Royal Flying Corps men.

Kastelhoek German Cemetery (Hollebeke Cemetery No. 61) - on the main road near Hollebeke and about 3km south of here. It contained five British men who died in January and February 1917.

Klien-ZIllebeke German Cemetery - just south of Hill 60 and about 1.5km south of here, it contained three British unidentified men.

Kortekeer German Cemetery No. 12a - north of the cabaret between Langemark and Bikschote about 7km north of here. It contained three British graves dating from 1914.

Kruiseeke German Cemetery - on the main road near the village about 3km south-east of here. Two British unnamed men were brought to Sanctuary Wood while the others were taken to Zantvoorde Military Cemetery.

L'Alouette German Cemetery - between Nieuwkerke and Hill 63 and about 12km south-west of here. It contained three British unnamed men.

Langemarck German Cemetery No. 9 - on the road to Pilkem about 6km north of here. It contained five British soldiers.

Langemarck North German Cemetery - on the road to Koekuit and Clercken where one unidentified Commonwealth soldier was buried.

Menin Communal Cemetery – located about 10km south-east of here, it contained one British grave dating from 1914.

Messines German Cemetery No. 2 - north east of the village which is about 6km south of here. It contained seven British graves dating from 1915.

Messines German Cemetery No. 3 - just east of the church. It contained one British man and one Canadian grave.

Motor Car Corner Cemetery German Extension - at the northern edge of the present Motor Car Corner Cemetery which is near Ploegsteert about 12km south of here. It contained seven British unidentified men who died in 1918.

Petit-Pont German Cemetery - near Ploegsteert and Hill 63 about 12km south of here. It contained two British unnamed officers of the Machine Gun Corps.

Rabschloss German Cemetery No. 64 – located about 6km south of here, it contained one British unnamed burial.

Reutal German Cemetery – located about 3.5km east of here, ten British unnamed graves were moved here while the others were moved to Perth Cemetery.

Slyskapelle Churchyard – located about 6km north-east of here, two British graves and one Newfoundlander were moved to Sanctuary Wood while one British burial remained there.

Terdegem Churchyard – located in France about 12km west of here, it contained four British men of the Royal Garrison Artillery and one Canadian grave. Further burials were made in the churchyard in WW2.

Three Houses German Cemetery (Hollebeke Cemetery No. 60) – located about 3km south of here, it contained one British unnamed soldier who was brought here while the others were taken to Oosttaverne Wood Cemetery.

Thourout Germen Cemetery No. 2 – located about 20km north of here, it contained two British men of the Royal Air Force who died in September 1918.

| | |
|---|---|
| UK - 1735 (1215 unnamed) | Aust - 88 (54 unnamed) |
| NZ - 18 (13 unnamed) | S Afr - 3 |
| Can - 142 (69 unnamed) | NF - 3 (2 unnamed) |
| Total unnamed - 1353 | |
| Ger – 1 | Area - 7001 sq mts |

Special Memorials to 88 men, 38 Canadian, one German and 49 British, whose graves were destroyed by shell-fire.

**LOCATION**

Sanctuary Wood Cemetery lies east of Ieper about 500m south of the Menin Road and is reached by taking Maple Avenue, which is very clearly signed from the Menin Road.

# SEAFORTH CEMETERY, CHEDDAR VILLA

**HISTORY**

This cemetery was used for only a few days in April 1915.

**INFORMATION**

This is a fascinating and unique cemetery with very good views of the Salient. All men buried here died on 25 and 26 April 1915 with the exception of two who died on 23 April and two who died on 28 April. The 2nd Seaforth Highlanders have 101 men buried here. The officers and NCO's of the Seaforths are marked on the east wall of the cemetery while the men have their headstones on the west wall, though these are markers rather than the actual graves. The farm here was known in the war as Cheddar Villa after which this cemetery was first named.

This area saw heavy fighting during the German advance in late April 1915. On 25 April the 10th Brigade counter-attacked from the site of the Oxford Road Cemetery through the position of this cemetery and Buffs Road in the early morning. The Brigade included 2nd Lieutenant Bruce Bairnsfather of the 1st Royal Warwickshires who became famous for his cartoons and postcards of characters on the Western Front. The Brigade was exceptional in that it was one of the few 'Regular' Army Brigades that was at full strength, but by the time it reached a position 1km north of Cheddar Villa 2000 men had been killed. The 1/7th Argyll and Sutherland Highlanders lost twelve officers and 425 men in this attack which took no ground.

On 8 May 1915, in another German attack at this point, the 2nd Northumberland Fusiliers held the line. In the evening a German unit appeared in the rear of the Fusiliers but they continued to fight so that when they finally withdrew only 116 men of the Battalion were alive. Eventually in 1915 the line was pushed back to the west to a line through Mousetrap Farm.

Near the cemetery is a bunker, the original Cheddar Villa, now used as a farm building. It was captured on the first day of Third Ypres by the 39th Division and turned into a Battalion headquarters by the 1/3rd Oxford and Bucks Light Infantry. On 7 August 1917 the Light Infantry began a Dressing Station here, but a shell found its way into the main entrance causing many casualties.

The name of the burial ground was changed from Cheddar Villa Cemetery in 1922. This was at the request of the commanding officer of the Seaforth Highlanders, in memory of the large number of Seaforths who were buried here but whose graves were destroyed by later shelling.

Row A, Grave 8 and Row B, Grave 1 are large graves with 75 headstones placed against the walls of the cemetery as the original graves were destroyed by shell-fire. A plaque, at the far end of the cemetery from the road, commemorates 23 officers and men of the 2nd Seaforth Highlanders who fell locally but whose graves are lost. They are officially commemorated by name on the Menin Gate. Among the men of the Seaforth Highlanders buried here is 2nd Lieutenant Granville John Henry Feilden, 2nd Seaforth Highlanders, killed in action on 25 April 1915 aged 19 years. He was commissioned from Sandhurst into his father's old Battalion on 12 August 1914 and was in France a month later. He fought throughout First Ypres and was killed instantly with his men and brother officers buried here. He was grandson of the 4th Baron Calthorpe. His father had commanded the 2nd Seaforth Highlanders with whom he was awarded the Distinguished Service Order during the South African Wars.

UK – 147          Can – 1          Unnamed – 21
Area - 1008 sq mts

Special Memorials to nineteen British graves destroyed by shell-fire.

### LOCATION
Seaforth Cemetery is north-east of Ieper and lies on the north side of the N313 north-west of the junction with the motorway and the N38 northern by-pass.

## SOLFERINO FARM CEMETERY

### HISTORY
Although the French had a Dressing Station and camp here early in the war, the cemetery was not begun until October 1917 during the Third Battle of Ypres. It remained in use until August 1918.

### INFORMATION
Solferino was the name given by the French to the farm opposite. Of the graves here 100 are men from artillery units, 21 are engineers and 24 are from Labour Battalions of the (Royal) Army Service Corps. This shows that this area was always well behind the front-lines.

Brielen was completely destroyed in the war, however, the nearby Chateau des Trois Tours was hardly touched. The chateau was the headquarters of the 1st Canadian Division in 1915 and after the war became the headquarters for the Ypres League and the Anglo-Belgian Union.

To get here you may have passed the Reigersburg Chateau in northern Ypres near the crossroads of the N8 and N38 which was used during the war, first by the Royal Field Artillery, and then as an headquarters for various units. The junction with the N8 was known as Dawson's Corner after the camp that was here in the war.

There are also five burials from WW2 made during the Allied retreat to Dunkirk in May 1940.

Buried here is Major Linwood Field, DSO, MC, 'B' Battery, 78th Brigade, Royal Field Artillery, killed in action on 26 October 1917 aged 30 years. Buried with him are Captain Paul Studholme Barker and Lieutenant Reginal Percy Chantril. Field was commander of the Battery, while Barker and Chantril were his officers. They were killed by the same shell which hit their dugout. Field was posthumously awarded the Distinguished Service Order in the New Year's Honours List in January 1918. He was awarded the Military Cross gazetted on 16 August 1917 'For conspicuous gallantry and devotion to duty. When his Battery was under heavy shell-fire he ran out into the open with utter disregard for his own life, to dig out a man who had been buried by a shell. He also removed three wounded men to a place of safety.'

UK – 293          Can – 1          NF – 1
BWI – 1           Ger – 3          Unnamed – 1
WWII - 5 UK (1 Unnamed)          Area - 1204 sq mts

### LOCATION
Solferino Farm Cemetery lies about 4km north-west of Ieper and 1km north of Brielen. The cemetery is about 600m east of the N8. The south end of the cemetery dips to a pond and gives quite a good view.

# SOMER FARM CEMETERY

## HISTORY
This cemetery was begun during the Battle of Messines in June 1917 after this area had been taken from the Germans at the start of the battle. It is named after the farm by which it stands, and remained in use until the German advance in March 1918. A number of burials were made in October 1918.

## INFORMATION
The town of Wijtschate was captured by the Germans in early November 1914. On the night of 31 October to 1 November 1914 the 1/14th (London Scottish) Londons were filling a gap in the line here. They, and the 6th (Carabiniers) Dragoon Guards, were defending Wijtschate when the Germans attacked. The rifles of the London Scots began to jam, so they suffered heavy casualties until their commanding officer issued the order to withdraw. He took the remnants of his Battalion back to Wulvergem, through the village, which fell to the Germans during the night. The London Scottish, all civilian workers in London and members of the same club, had become the first complete Territorial Battalion to fight in the war but there were only 150 of them left on the next day to tell the tale.

In 1917 the village fell to the British following the blowing of mines here on the first day of the Battle of Messines, 7 June 1917.

The village was taken by the Germans on 16 April 1918. On 25 April 1918 the 1st East Yorkshires held the line here, defending this area as part of the 64th Brigade, when the Germans attacked with a substantial superiority of numbers. The East Yorkshires were forced back across the Messines-St. Eloi road north of the village and into the woods. At the end of the day the Battalion numbered two officers and 27 men. The village was taken for the last time on 28 September 1918.

This cemetery was previously known as Somer Farm No. 1. Burials in Somer Farm No. 2 were moved to Wytschaete Military Cemetery.

Buried here is Sapper Robert Arthur, 201st Field Company, Royal Engineers, who died of wounds at No. 97 Field Ambulance on 13 October 1918 aged 39 years. His brother, Private John Stewart Arthur, 4th Brigade, Canadian Machine Gun Corps, died on 30 September 1916 aged 27 years and is buried in Contay British Cemetery. A third brother, out of seven who served, was killed in the war. I believe it to be Private William Arthur, 1st Black Watch (Royal Highlanders), who died on 21 June 1915 and is commemorated on the Le Touret Memorial.

UK – 67      Aust – 24      Area - 633 sq mts
Special Memorials to three British men and two Australians whose graves in this cemetery are lost.

## LOCATION
Somer Farm Cemetery lies west of the St. Eloi-Messines road, south of Ieper, on the north-east edge of Wijtschate. It is clearly signed from the main road, at a crossroads in Wijtschate.

# SPANBROEKMOLEN BRITISH CEMETERY

## HISTORY
The cemetery was used almost solely on the first day of the Battle of Messines, 7 June 1917.

## INFORMATION
For information about the British advance here in 1917 please refer to Lone Tree Cemetery.

This cemetery stands in a valley about 100m from the road with excellent views of Wijtschate and its position on the ridge. This gives us a good idea of the task facing the British to take the well defended village.

The cemetery is named after a windmill which stood nearby. It contains the graves of men of 36th (Ulster) Division who advanced here on 7 June 1917. All except one man buried here are from that Division and all except three died on 7 June, the others on 8 June. The cemetery was lost in later fighting and only rediscovered after the war.

On 12 March 1915 an attack by the 1st Wiltshires and 3rd Worcestershires captured a section of German trenches for two hours before they were ordered to withdraw. The attack cost casualties of twenty officers and 400 men. During the action Lieutenant (later Brigadier) Cyril Gordon Martin, VC, CBE, DSO, who led a unit of the 56th Company, Royal Engineers, won the Victoria Cross.

Near the turn from the Wijtschate-Kemmel road there are a number of craters, one of which is the Peckham Crater visited by King George V in July 1917. This indicates how safe this area was considered to have become in such a short time and how successful the British advance had been in the Battle of Messines. Peckham Farm Crater is about 150m north of here by the Wijtschate-Kemmel road. The mining to create explosions under the German line at the start of the Battle of Messines had begun many months before the battle at the direction of General Plumer, commander of 2nd Army. Nineteen were detonated though others were dug. They contributed to one of the most successful attacks of the war. The Peckham Farm mine was finished in July 1916, with a tunnel 350m long and about 20m below no-man's land. The blowing of about 87000lbs of Amatol under the German line created a crater 101m in circumference when it was detonated by the 250th Tunnelling Company, Royal Engineers at 3.10am on 7 June 1917. A second tunnel at Peckham Farm was abandoned when it flooded. A 20000lb mine is believed to be still under the nearby farm house.

Buried here is Rifleman James Edward Twaddle, 12th (Central Antrim) Royal Irish Rifles, killed in action on 7 June 1916 aged 30 years. He was born in Brooklyn, New York, USA and sailed to London to enlist where he joined the 1/5th (London Rifle Brigade) Londons before being transferred to the Irish Rifles.

UK – 58          KUG – 5          Area - 304 sq mts

Special Memorials to six graves known to have been buried in the cemetery but whose graves were lost in later fighting.

**LOCATION**
Spanbroekmolen Cemetery is south of Ieper, about 2km south-west of Wijtschate and 4km east of Kemmel. It is approximately 400m south of the Wijtschate-Kemmel road and 100m from a side road. There are CWGC signs from the main road and at the path to the cemetery which lies in the valley below the level of the road. Access is by a 200m grass path. Parking is difficult and is only possible by leaving the vehicle on the verge of a very narrow road or walking a greater distance.

# SPOILBANK CEMETERY

**HISTORY**
This cemetery was begun as the British arrived in this sector in February 1915. It was used until the German advance in March 1918 and enlarged after the war.

**INFORMATION**
For further information about 'The Bluff' please refer to 1st D.C.L.I. Cemetery.

The cemetery lies next to the old canal from Ypres to Comines, with this section known to the British as the 'Kingsway'. It is possible to walk along its route into Ypres, or, alternatively, you can take the path opposite the cemetery through Pallingbeek Park.

Spoilbank Cemetery was also known as 'Chester Farm Lower Cemetery' or 'Gordon Terrace Cemetery'. Many of the 2nd Suffolks who died on 'The Bluff' in early 1916 are buried here.

Buried here is Lieutenant Colonel Stewart Scott Binny, DSO, MiD, 10th Royal Welsh Fusiliers formerly 19th (Queen Alexandra's Own Royal) Hussars, who died on 3 March 1916 aged 44 years. He was commissioned into the Hussars in 1894 and promoted to Lieutenant four years later. He served in the South African Wars during which he was his units Adjutant and for which he was awarded the Distinguished Service Order. He became a Captain in 1903 and a Major in 1910 when he retired. He returned to duty at the start of the war and served at Deputy Director of Railway Transport in France before being promoted to Lieutenant Colonel and given command of the Fusiliers on 5 February 1916 a month before he was killed. Two other officers of the Battalion were killed with Binny when a shell hit the Battalion HQ dugout. They are Major Edward Freeman, who had been with the Royal Welsh Fusiliers for twenty years, and Captain William Thomas Lyons.

Also here is Private Robert H Reeves, 6th Duke of Cornwall's Light Infantry, killed by a grenade on 8 October 1915 aged 15 years. He had been at the Front since 3 August 1915.

Buried side by side are brothers Lieutenant John Keating and 2nd Lieutenant George Keating, both 2nd Cheshires, both died on 17 February 1915. They were regular soldiers with over twenty years of service each in the ranks, including time in India as Sergeant Major and Colour Sergeant respectively. They were commissioned in 1914. They were killed, possibly by the same machine gun, in attacks on 'The Bluff'. They were the first burials made in this cemetery.

UK – 426          Aust – 67          Can – 16
Unnamed – 125                    Area - 4160 sq mts

Special Memorials to ten British men and one Australian known/believed to be buried among the unnamed.

**LOCATION**
Spoilbank Cemetery is located south of Ieper, west of the Comines road between Zillebeke and St. Eloi. The cemetery is on the right 1.5km from the Comines road.

# St. JULIEN DRESSING STATION CEMETERY

**HISTORY**

The Dressing Station Cemetery was opened in September 1917, after the village had been captured from the Germans during the Third Battle of Ypres, and it remained in use until the German Spring Offensive in March 1918. The cemetery was doubled in size after the war with the concentration of graves from the surrounding battlefields.

**INFORMATION**

St. Juliaan, known during the war as St. Julien, saw much fighting in the war. It was an important German objective in their 1915 offensive after the British had held it since autumn 1914. In Kitchener's Wood, north-west of the village, during one hour on the night of 22 April 1915, the 10th Canadian Infantry had three commanding officers as two, Lieutenant-Colonel Russel Lambert Boyle (See Poperinghe Old Military Cemetery) and Major Joseph E McLaren, (See Vlamertinghe Military Cemetery) were killed fighting in the wood. The third, Major Ormond, decided to retreat after consultation with the commanding officer of the 16th Canadian Infantry, Lieutenant-Colonel Leckie.

The 10th Brigade were rushed to the front-line here on 24 April. Two Companies of the 3rd Canadian Infantry found themselves isolated between St. Juliaan and Kitchener's Wood, known locally as Bois des Cuisiniers, named after the area in which French troops housed their field kitchens rather than after Field Marshall Kitchener, and now just an open field. When they were finally withdrawn the 43 survivors were all wounded but had stemmed the German advance. In the action, Corporal Fisher of the 13th Canadian Infantry won the first Victoria Cross awarded to a Canadian in the war. He attacked the Germans alone with one machine-gun, and is commemorated on the Menin Gate as his body was lost.

On 25 April the 10th Brigade were sent in to a new line in front of Kitchener's Wood. The Brigade counter-attacked to within 100m of St. Juliaan Church, roughly the point of this cemetery, but they could advance no further and in some places were forced back a short distance. Many troops were buried by the Germans in the following weeks, for example, the 1st Royal Warwickshires suffered casualties of sixteen officers and over 500 men.

On 26 April the 149th (Northumberland) Brigade became the first complete Brigade of Territorials to go into action, earning much respect through their courageous advance.

They attacked along the road from Wieltje to St. Juliaan past the site of Seaforth Cemetery but achieved nothing as they had to retreat almost immediately. In this action they suffered casualties of 43 officers, including their commanding officer, Brigadier-General James Foster Riddell, buried in Tyne Cot Cemetery, and 1912 men.

The Germans used gas here on 2-3 May 1915 to force the British to retire. Hence, the 10th Brigade were withdrawn having lost 73 officers and 2346 men.

The village again saw action in 1917 when the 39th Division captured the village, which had been turned into one of the fortresses of the Langemark line, on the first day of the Third Battle of Ypres. The rain on 31 July was a problem so that the Battalions who tried to take the village suffered heavy casualties and could not hold the village though it was taken again on 3 August. In capturing the village, the 39th Division had casualties of 145 officers and 3716 men. St. Juliaan was given up to the Germans without a fight during the Battle of the Lys in 1918 when the British command had decided to 'readjust the line in the Salient'. It was taken back for the last time on 28 September 1918 when captured by the Belgians.

Many of the graves in the cemetery were destroyed by shellfire in 1918. The original cemetery of 203 graves now makes up Plots I, III and part of Plot II. Interestingly, there are ten men buried here, killed before the cemetery was begun so they were concentrated here, but there are no records of concentrations to show from where they have come. This has led some people to question if there was a small burial ground here before 1917. This is highly doubtful and would just seem to be one of those occasions when records are 'lost'.

There was a German cemetery in the village but it has been removed.

The last recorded date of death is that of Lieutenant Cecil Dutton Darlington, No. 204 Squadron, Royal Air Force who died on 15 August 1918 aged 26 years. He was shot down in the morning in his Sopwith Camel and buried by the Germans who held the village at the time.

North of the village is the Canadian Memorial known as the 'Brooding Soldier' or the 'Gas Attack Memorial' or simply 'Vancouver Corner'. Situated at what was known as Winnipeg Crossroads, it marks the line held by Canadians at the start of the German gas attack in April 1915. The 10th and 16th Canadian Infantry sustained heavy losses in filling the line lost during the gas attack and slowing rather than stopping the German attack. Their actions here were enough to allow reserves to get in place and a new line marked to which the British and Canadians could withdraw. The Memorial was unveiled in 1923 by the Duke of Connaught, with Marshal Foch, the Earl of Ypres (Sir John French) and the Canadian High Commissioner in attendance. Foch, the former Commander-in-Chief of the Allied Armies, said in tribute 'The Canadians paid heavily for their sacrifice and the corner of earth on which this Memorial of gratitude and piety rises has been bathed in their blood. They wrote here the first page in that Book of Glory which is the history of their participation in the war.' Until 1988 this plaque misleadingly read '2,000 fell and here lie buried' though no man is buried here of whom we know.

Nearby, on the road from Vancouver Corner to Zonnebeke on east side of road towards Zonnebeke near the turn to the Totenmuhle can be found the Henshaw Memorial. Private Stephen Henshaw, 1/1st Bucks Battalion, Oxford and Bucks Light Infantry died of wounds on 23 August 1917 aged 30 years. His memorial says he was wounded on 16 August 1917 and lay in the fields for six days until discovered. He died at No. 61 Casualty Clearing Station and is buried in Dozinghem Military Cemetery.

On the Zonnebeke-Langemark road, just south-east of Vancouver Corner, is a Memorial to the 1/1st Hertfordshires, unveiled in 2017, who suffered greatly in and near St. Juliaan on 31 July 1917.

UK – 290      Aust – 10      NZ – 3
Can – 14      NF – 1         S Afr – 3
KUG - 96      Unnamed – 180
Area - 1817 sq mts

Special Memorials to nine British men and two South Africans known to be buried among the unnamed.

### LOCATION
St. Julien D.S. Cemetery lies to the north-east of Ieper on the western edge of the village. It is clearly signed from the N313 as you enter the village from the direction of Ieper.

# St. QUENTIN CABARET MILITARY CEMETERY

### HISTORY
The cemetery was opened in February 1915 and used by Divisions holding this sector until the German advance in spring 1918. A further two burials, men of the South Wales Borderers, were made in September 1918.

### INFORMATION
The cabaret was an inn (the building directly opposite the cemetery) on the south side of the village of Wulvergem that was sometimes used as a Battalion headquarters or as a Regimental Aid Post.

The cemetery was begun, making what is now Plot I, Rows E and F, by the 46th (North Midland) Division. Of the graves here 80 are men of the Royal Irish Rifles of the 36th (Ulster) Division.

There are some distinct areas within the cemetery. For example, Plot II, Row C contains almost only New Zealand burials, nearly all of whom are Otago Regiment men killed on 24 March 1917. The New Zealanders set up an Advanced Dressing Station at nearby Kandahar Farm in preparation for the Battle of Messines, and sited two Regimental Aid Posts nearer the front lines, one at La Plus Douve Farm, and one here. Both were linked to Kandahar Farm ADS by a small tramway. Burials from the ADS and Aid Posts were made here.

Plot I, Row C contains mainly men of the 1st Canadian Infantry killed on 13 October 1915 by a German counter-bombardment in retaliation for a Canadian shelling of German trenches.

One man killed in 1914 is buried here. He has no concentration record, so may have been an isolated grave, or moved here at the end of the war. Private James Wilson Bremner, 'A' Company, 2nd Royal Scots was killed on 16 November 1914 aged 28 years.

Buried here is Captain John Edwin Sugden, DSO, Adjutant 10th Royal Irish Rifles, killed by a German shell on 28 September 1916 aged 38 years. He was awarded the Distinguished Service Order on 22 September 1916 for his bravery at Thiepval on 1 July 1916. He is buried in Plot I among men of the 36th (Ulster) Division who had survived the ordeal at Thiepval. The Division was moved to a 'quiet' sector here and the men were killed 'holding the line'.

Also here is Major Duncan Donald Heron Campbell, MC, MiD, Royal Garrison Artillery attached 112th Brigade, Royal Field Artillery, died on 7 June 1917 aged 33 years. From a family with a long record of military service, he arrived in France on 29 September 1915 and may have been the first man in the 25th Division to be awarded a decoration in the war. He was awarded the Military Cross in the Birthday Honours List in June 1917 'For conspicuous gallantry when directing the fire of his Battery. After his observation post had been destroyed and the infantry near him had withdrawn, he remained for four hours exposed to heavy fire, and successfully cut a wide lane in the enemy's wire'. He was Mentioned in Despatches in the New Years Honours List in January 1917. He was commissioned from Woolwich in December 1900, served in India in the Mohmand Campaign and on the North-West Frontier. He also served with the Burma Military Police as an Inspector. He was killed when he went forward with the infantry attack at Messines to reconnoitre the ridge in preparation for moving his Battery forward. He was seen carrying his wounded orderly to safety through a German barrage and in returning through it to the ridge he was killed.

Another here is Lieutenant and Quartermaster Joseph Bowyer, MC, 11th Lancashire Fusiliers, who died 9 June 1917 aged 50 years. He had been commissioned from the ranks and been Quartermaster since the Battalion had been formed in 1914. He was awarded the Military Cross in the January 1917 New Years Honours List for bravery near Le Sars on the Somme in 1916. His grandfather had been with the Lancashire Fusiliers, in a previous incarnation, in the Peninsular Wars 100 years prior to his death.

Buried here is Private Ewart Barrett, 1/6th South Staffordshires, who died on 27 May 1915 aged 16 years. A pre-war soldier as he had joined the Battalion at

Wolverhampton shortly before the outbreak of the war. He was killed by a sniper. He was the youngest 'man' in the South Staffordshires to be killed at Ypres.

Also here is Private Charles Trevyllian Constant, 1st Canadian Infantry, killed in action at 3.00pm on 3 March 1916 aged 20 years. A farmer born in England he had been sent to Canada by the Barnardo's Children's Homes in 1906. He enlisted in January 1915 and was killed by shrapnel through the heart.

UK – 316   Aust – 7   NZ – 64
Can – 68   Ger – 2    KUG – 5
Area - 4644 sq mts

**LOCATION**
St. Quentin Cabaret Cemetery lies south of Ieper about 300m south of Wulvergem and is reached via the turn opposite the church which leads into the river valley. This is a large cemetery with good views of the valley, Hill 63 and other cemeteries in the area.

# STRAND MILITARY CEMETERY

## HISTORY
The cemetery was begun in October 1914 when two burials were made from a Dressing Station located at the end of a trench, known as the 'The Strand', that led from the road into Ploegsteert Wood. The burial ground was used again from April to July 1917 but its main use was after the war when over 750 graves were concentrated here.

## INFORMATION
The British Army called this location Charing Cross, a point at the end of a trench which led into Ploegsteert Wood. Nearby was a trench called Broadway which ended at Dead Horse Corner, just north of Piccadilly Circus. The Strand was held by the Germans in the summer of 1918, when they made a few burials, though most of the men buried here in the war were from Australian units.

The wartime burials make up Plots I to VI. Plots VII to X were made after the war for men who were concentrated here mainly from the area between Wijtschate and Armentieres.

The eight Second World War burials (three of which are unidentified) all date from May 1940 and the withdrawal of the British Expeditionary force to Dunkirk ahead of the German advance.

Buried here is the first Canadian officer to die in the war at the Front. Lieutenant Duncan Peter Bell-Irving, 2nd Field Company, Canadian Engineers, was killed by shell-fire on 26 February 1915, while repairing a trench in close proximity to the Germans, while attached to a British unit. He had been in France for just a few days.

Buried here is one of five sons of Mrs Julia Souls killed in the war. The family came from Great Rissington which is found between Oxford and Cheltenham. Private Alfred Souls, 11th Cheshires, killed in action on 20 April 1918 aged 31 years (twin of Arthur William Souls), is buried here. His brothers are Lance Corporal Arthur William Souls, MM, 16th Cheshires attached 7th Queen's Own (Royal West Kents), killed in action on 25 April 1918 aged 31 years and buried in Hangard Communal Cemetery Extension; Private Albert Souls, Machine Gun Corps, killed in action on 14 March 1916 aged 20 years, and buried at Bully-Grenay Communal Cemetery; Private Frederick George Souls, 16th Cheshires, killed in action on 19 July 1916 aged 30 years, commemorated on the Thiepval Memorial; and Private Walter Davis Souls, Machine Gun Corps, died of wounds on 2 August 1916 aged 24 years, and buried in St. Sever Cemetery, Rouen.

Another of note is Captain Alfred Ernest Parker, 3rd Black Watch (Royal Highlanders) attached 2nd Seaforth Highlanders, killed on 7 November 1914 aged 34 years. His wife was Joan Isobel Margaret nee Bowes-Lyon, a cousin of the wife of King George VI. Having served in the South African War, seen time with the 10th Hussars and retired in 1912, he rejoined the Black Watch in 1912 and was killed leading an attack in Ploegsteert Wood.

Two young 'men' buried here are Private Thomas Albert Morgan, 13th Canadian Infantry, died on 5 July 1915 aged 16 years and Sapper Daniel White, 1st Tunnelling Company, Canadian Engineers who died on 26 March 1916 recorded as aged 16 years. He was killed by a German shell when it struck the shaft of the listening post that he was in with one other man. They were originally buried in the Gunner's Farm Cemetery according to the Battalion war diary. However, the evidence now shows he was actually 19 years of age when killed and used false papers to join up in December 1915 aged 18 years.

One of those buried here was one of the men who died on 25 December 1914, the date of the Christmas 'Truce(s)'. Private Jeremiah Harrington, 2nd Leinsters was originally buried on the south side of Houplines in Epinette Road Cemetery. He was a member of 'D' Company who faced Prussians unlike the other companies in the Battalion who faced Saxons. There was no truce with the Prussians and Harrington was one of two men of his Battalion killed on Christmas Day, though others were to die of wounds in the next few days.

Concentrated here:
Epinette Road Cemetery - to the south of Houplines which is about 3km south of here. It contained 24 British men who died from November 1914 to September 1915.
La Basse-Ville German Cemetery - between Ploegsteert Wood and Warneton about 4km east of here. It contained 68 British men and one South African who died as German prisoners from April to August 1918.

Le Bizet Convent Military Cemetery - near Motor Car Corner Cemetery about 2km south of here. It contained 88 British men and one Canadian who died from October 1914 to October 1916.

Nachtegaal German Cemetery No. 1 - between Merkem and Houthulst nearly 20km north of here. It contained the graves of two British Royal Flying Corps officers who died in June 1917.

Ploegsteert Wood New Cemetery - in the south-east corner of the wood near Le Gheer about 1.5km east of here. It contained nineteen British soldiers who died at Le Gheer in October 1914.

Prowse Point Lower Cemetery - between Prowse Point and Mud Corner Cemeteries about 1.5km north-east of here. It was made by the 1st Rifle Brigade and contained the graves of thirteen British soldiers who died in 1915 and 1916.

Touquet-Berthe German Cemetery - between Ploegsteert and Lancashire Cottage Cemetery less than 1km south east of here. It contained two British unidentified Royal Air Force officers who died in July 1918.

Warneton Churchyard – located about 4km east of here, it contained the grave of one British soldier buried by the Germans in December 1914.

UK – 725    Aust – 284    NZ – 87
Can – 26    S Afr – 1     Ger – 11
Unnamed – 354
WWII - 8 UK (3 unidentfied)
Area - 4562 sq mts

Special Memorials to five Australians and one New Zealander known/believed to be buried among the unnamed.

Special Memorials to twelve British men and one New Zealander whose graves in other cemeteries concentrated here have been lost in later fighting.

### LOCATION
Strand Cemetery is south of Ieper on the east side of the Armentieres road about 700m north of the square in Ploegsteert.

# SUFFOLK CEMETERY

### HISTORY
This cemetery was used in March and April 1915 by the 2nd Suffolks. It was also used in November 1917 for one burial, and again in October 1918.

### INFORMATION
Suffolk Cemetery was used by the 38th Labour Group, Royal Army Service Corps, in 1918 to bury 28 men, most of the 1/4th (Hallamshire) and 1/5th York and Lancasters who had died in the German advance of April 1918 but whose bodies had only just been recovered. At this time it was called the Cheapside Cemetery after the road here.

Buried here is Private Sergant Jessup, 2nd Suffolks who died on 24 March 1915. He is recorded in other sources as Sergeant Jessop and that he arrived at the Front on 26 January 1915. Interestingly, a man of the same name enlisted in the Royal Field Artillery in November 1913, was court-martialed in early 1914 and was discharged from the army in February 1914. Coincidentally, or possibly not, both men have recorded as next of kin being a 'C' or 'Clement' Jessup from Hadleigh in Suffolk. It would seem that the Jessup discharged in February re-enlisted in August and was forgiven his previous record.

Private William Scotton, 4th Middlesex was executed in Vierstraat and buried near this cemetery on 3 February 1915 aged 19 years. He had been convicted of desertion in December 1914 but deserted again on 23 January 1915 and surrendered to the authorities on the next day. However, his grave was lost in the war, probably when the front-line ran nearby during the German Spring Offensive in 1918. He is now commemorated on the Menin Gate. His brother, Private Albert Scotton, 1/7th King's (Liverpools) was killed on 18 September 1916 and is commemorated on the Thiepval Memorial.

UK – 47     Unnamed – 8
Area - 384 sq mts

### LOCATION
Suffolk Cemetery is located south of Ieper about 2km north of Kemmel. It is approximately 300m west of the Ieper-Kemmel road and reached from the crossroads at the two unmistakeable large warehouses in Vierstraat. At the west end of the warehouses is another CWGC sign leading to the cemetery on the west side of 'Cheapside'. The graveyard is a very small and secluded cemetery next to houses and surrounded by a high hedge, set back from the road and reached by a short path.

# TALANA FARM CEMETERY

## HISTORY
The cemetery was begun in April 1915 by French colonial troops (Zouaves) and was used by the British from June 1915 until March 1918.

## INFORMATION
Boezinge and this area was on the side of the Ieper-Ijzer canal that was in Allied hands throughout the war. From 1915 to 1917 the Germans lines were on the other side of the canal but not very far away. They were pushed back during Third Ypres.

Talana Farm was one of several features, mostly farmhouses, nearby that were named after events in the South African Wars, in this case the Battle of Talana Hill on 20 October 1899. Talana Farm was not rebuilt after the war, however, the farmhouse just to the south, known in the war as 'Hull's Farm' was. It was the location of a dressing station in the war from which men were brought here for burial. The first British burials were by the 1st Rifle Brigade and 1st Somerset Light Infantry.

There are several burials of men of the 1st East Lancashires, who died in a raid on 6 July 1915 though there are also many graves of men from the 49th (West Riding) Division who attacked from the nearby front-line at the start of the Third Battle of Ypres. The area was afterwards occupied by artillery units who buried their dead here. It is thought that there are graves in the cemetery that were destroyed in later fighting and have been lost.

The graves of 27 French and two American men have been removed. The Americans were Private Ernest Maxwell now in Flanders Field Cemetery, Waregem and Private Millard Buskirk who was repatriated to Kentucky, USA. Both were killed in late 1918. They were moved in the early 1920's.

Buried here is Lieutenant Colonel Alan Bryant, DSO, twice MiD, 1st Gloucestershires attached and commanding 9th Northumberland Fusiliers, who died on 17 October 1917 aged 48 years. He had been with the Fusiliers since 2 October. He had commanded the 17th Welsh for most of 1917 and had been on Staff since 1914. He was commissioned in 1890 and awarded the Distinguished Service Order in the New Years Honours List in January 1917 before taking command of a Battalion.

Also here is Private Norman Crowther, 1/4th Duke of Wellington's who died on 23 November 1915 aged 16 years.

You can also find 2nd Lieutenant Patrick Charles Bentley Blair, 5th attached 1st Rifle Brigade, died on 6 July 1915 aged 24 years. He played for Cambridge University RFC, winning his 'Blue' four years running, and London Scottish RFC. He was capped for Scotland in 1912-13 playing five matches losing against South Africa in 1912, losing against Wales and England in 1913 while being victorious against France and Ireland in the same season. He was in Egypt working for the Civil Service when war began and returned immediately for training with 5th Rifle Brigade from whom he was commissioned in March 1915 and transferred into the 1st Rifle Brigade at the Front in June 1915. He was killed by a German shell on the parapet of 'International Trench' on the other side of the canal close to, and north of, what is now the Yorkshire Trench preserved line.

Another sportsman is Captain Francis Bernard Roberts, 9th Rifle Brigade who died on 8 February 1916 aged 33 years. He was awarded two 'Blues' at Cambridge University, one for hockey and one for cricket. He went on to play 80 first class cricket matches for Cambridge University and Gloucestershire from 1903 to 1914. He was also a Master at Wellington College. He was killed less than eight weeks after arriving at the Front.

UK – 529        Unnamed – 14

Area - 3743 sq mts

Special Memorials to six British men whose graves have been lost.

Special Memorials to ten men whose graves are identified as a group rather than marked individually.

## LOCATION
Talana Farm Cemetery is north of Ieper in fields about 100m west of the main road from Ieper to Diksmuide and 700m south of Boezinge. There are few formal rows of graves. Hence, the disorganised nature and many single graves make the graveyard inviting.

# TANCREZ FARM MILITARY CEMETERY

## HISTORY
Begun in December 1914, the cemetery remained in use until the German Spring Offensive of March 1918.

## INFORMATION
The cemetery served a Dressing Station that was in the factory for much of the war.

This cemetery marked the point that is considered by some to be the southern limit of the Salient. It was captured by the Germans for short periods in 1914 and 1918 but was usually just behind the front-line which was about 500m east of this cemetery.

Buried here is Private Elias Ratcliffe, 11th Cheshires, died on 10 February 1917 aged 16 years. He served as G Griffiths. Nearby is Private J H Williams, 2nd South African Infantry who died on 23 May 1916 aged 16 years.

Another here is Private W Swift, 'B' Company, 2/4th Loyal North Lancashires who died on 9 June 1917 aged 28 years. His family have recorded that he was Welterweight Boxing champion of East Lancashire from 1908-1910, and had a professional career of fifteen fights. From 1908-10 he was also in the Territorials. After fighting he became a blacksmith and then enlisted in September 1914 but did not go to France until January 1917. He was killed by German shelling when his Battalion were supporting the Australians in the front-lines nearby. One brother enlisted into the same Battalion. Another had been in India with the army for ten years by 1914. Another, Major Swift, was with the 1st Loyal North Lancashires at Mons and went missing during the Battle of the Aisne. He was confirmed as killed on 14 September 1914 and is commemorated on the La Ferte-Sous-Jouarre Memorial.

Also here is 2nd Lieutenant Robert Basil Wood, 6th attached 2nd Borders who died on 12 October 1916 aged 24 years. He was killed in a night raid on German trenches near Ploegsteert Wood. Having fought his way through the German wire and bombed his way along a German trench he went back to find the rest of his men when he was mortally wounded by machine gun fire. His brother, Lieutenant Geoffrey Dayrell Wood, 7th Suffolks died on 13 October 1915 aged 24 years and is commemorated on the Loos Memorial. He played cricket for Oxford University and Suffolk. He was killed at the Hohenzollern Redoubt and was buried where he was killed. He body was lost in later fighting. Another brother, Lieutenant Colonel Richard Poingdestre Wood, MC, 2nd York and Lancasters was killed a few days before Robert Wood on 9 October 1916 aged 26 years and is commemorated on the Thiepval Memorial. He had commanded the Battalion since 25 September 1916 and was awarded the Military Cross in the New Years Honours List in January 1916. Their uncle, Lieutenant-Colonel Lewis Ironside Wood, CMG, 2nd Borders was killed in action in Festubert on 25 April 1915 and is buried in Le Touret Military Cemetery.

UK – 306         Aust – 19        NZ – 3
S Afr – 4        Ger – 2          Unnamed – 6
Area - 1872 sq mts

Special Memorial to one British soldier known to be buried here.

### LOCATION
Tancrez Farm Cemetery is found south of Ieper about 4km south-east of Ploegsteert. 1.4km south of Ploegsteert square you can find on the east side of the road, near a supermarket, a tree of CWGC signs. The road to the left and then the tree-lined avenue to the right will take you past Motor Car Corner Cemetery to a junction at which you turn left to Tancrez Farm Cemetery. This cemetery has an attractive entrance but the view is spoilt by the local factories. The Special Memorial is near the gate in the attractive and unusual entrance garden.

## THE HUTS CEMETERY

### HISTORY
The cemetery was made at the start of the Third Battle of Ypres in July 1917 and used until November 1917. This accounts for most of the burials though Plots XI and XV were added in the winter of 1917-18 before the German Spring Offensive in April 1918 almost reached this area, at which point the cemetery was closed.

### INFORMATION
In the war there was a line of huts at the roadside housing Field Ambulances from which the cemetery gets its name. The cemetery was near a series of artillery positions for much of the time that it was in use. Hence, 687 of the burials, nearly 70%, were of artillerymen who were killed by enemy shelling of their positions. On the day that the Germans achieved the limit of their advance, at Dikkebus Lake, on 8 May 1918, the line here was held by the 10th Royal Warwickshires.

As this area was usually well behind the front-lines a number of camps were located nearby. Breaches of discipline were normally matters dealt with when units were in camp in the rear. Therefore, two men are buried here, near each other in Plot XV, who were executed for their indiscipline. Private Victor Manson Spencer, 1st Otago Regiment, New Zealand Expeditionary Force, deserted for the second time in August 1917, possibly suffering from shell-shock, and was not captured until 2 January 1918 when he was found living with a French woman and her children. He was executed on 24 February 1918 at 6.40am aged 23 years. There is a possibility that the date of birth on his service record is wrong and that he was only 18 years old when he enlisted in 1915. He saw service at Gallipoli and after a month without relief in the trenches in 1916 in France he deserted and served nine months hard labour before returning to his unit. He was the last of five New Zealand soldiers executed during WW1. Private Henry Hughes of the 1/5th York and Lancasters deserted while under a suspended sentence of death for deserting in December 1917. He was the first man from the 49th Division to be executed when he was shot at 5.50am on 10 April 1918 aged 27 years. On 8 January 1918 Hughes was to join a working party in the trenches near Hussar Camp, Potijze on the north-east outskirts of Ypres but instead he deserted. Hughes was arrested on 8 February 1918 at Poperinge. He was court-martialled on 19 March.

Buried here is Lieutenant Colonel Lord Robert William Orlando Manners, CMG, DSO, MiD, King's Royal Rifle Corps commanding 10th Northumberland Fusiliers who was killed in action on 11 September 1917 aged 47 years. He was the youngest son of the 7th Duke of Rutland and half-brother to the 8th Duke. He was commissioned into the King's Royal Rifle Corps in February 1891, serving in the Isazai Expedition in 1892. During the South African Wars he saw action several times with the Natal Bearer Company for which he was Mentioned in Despatches and awarded the Distinguished Service Order. He became a Major in 1908 and retired to the Reserve of Officers in 1910 returning to service at the start of the war. Lord Manners was gazetted a Brigade Major in October 1914, and in July 1916 was given the command of 10th Northumberland Fusiliers. For his services on the Somme, August-September 1916, he was awarded the Order of St. Michael and St. George. He was killed while reconnoitring the line while his Battalion was in camp near St. Omer.

A senior officer buried here is Brigadier General Cecil Godfrey Rawling, CMG, CIE, DSO, General Staff, commanding 62nd Infantry Brigade, late Somerset Light Infantry who was killed in action on 28 October 1917 aged 47 years. He was an explorer and author whose expeditions to Tibet in 1904 and Dutch New Guinea in 1909 brought acclaim from the Royal Geographic Society and awards from the Dutch and Indian governments. He joined the Somerset Light Infantry in 1891 and served on the North-West Frontier during the Tirah Campaign in 1898. He was also the first person to reach the source of the river Brahmaputra for which he was made a Companion of the Most Eminent Order of the Indian Empire (CIE). He was made a Major upon his return from the Dutch New Guinea expedition and promoted to Lieutenant Colonel commanding the 6th Somerset Light Infantry in 1915. He was made a Brigadier General and given the 62nd Brigade in preparation for the Battle of the Somme in 1916 where his Brigade was involved in several parts of the battle suffering high casualties. He was awarded the Order of St. Michael and St. George for his services on the Somme. He was killed by German shellfire whilst chatting to friends outside the Brigade headquarters at Hooge Crater and posthumously awarded the Distinguished Service Order in the New Year's Honours List in January 1918.

Lieutenant Colonel Courtenay Talbot Saint Paul, DSO, twice MiD, 36th Battery, 45th Brigade, Royal Field Artillery, died of wounds on 31 July 1917 aged 35 years. He was awarded the Distinguished Service Order in September 1916. The citation reads 'For conspicuous gallantry and devotion to duty during the operations near Lavantie July 1916. Both on 16th and 18th July his Battery and his observing station were subjected to very heavy shell fire during wire cutting. His coolness and total disregard for danger gave complete confidence to his Battery and he accomplished his wire cutting with the greatest success. His thoroughness and devotion to duty have been most marked.' He joined the Royal Field Artillery in December 1900. His brother, Sub-Lieutenant Hugh Beresford Paul, HMS Fortune, Royal Navy was killed on 1 June 1916 aged 21 years. His ship was sunk when engaging four large German ships during the Battle of Jutland late on 31 May and in to the early hours of 1 June with the loss of 85 of her crew. He is commemorated on the Portsmouth Naval Memorial.

Colonel William Weston Hearne, DSO, five times MiD, Order of St. Maurice and St. Lazarus (Italy), Assistant Director of Medical Services (ADMS), 5th Australian Division HQ, Australian Army Medical Corps died on 17 October 1917. He served as a Surgeon Lieutenant in the South African War. On 20 August 1914 he was one of the first six doctors to enlist and sailed on 19 October on HMAT A18 Wiltshire as a Major in the 2nd Field Ambulance. He was promoted to Lieutenant Colonel in July 1915, transferred to the 3rd Field Ambulance in August and was made ADMS in 1st Australian Division at Gallipoli in September. He moved as ADMS to 5th Australian Division in November 1916, after brief periods back with Field Ambulances, and became a Colonel in June 1917. He was awarded the Distinguished Service Order in June 1917. The citation reads 'During operations near Gueudecourt on the night of 4th/5th November 1916 Lieutenant Colonel Hearne displayed great courage and resources in the collection and evacuation of the wounded. On the early morning of the 5th November he supervised the collection of wounded, during this time his party was under shell, rifle and machine gun fire, incurring some casualties. This officer collected and tended wounded in no man's land, and placed them in a deserted German dug-out, while it was impossible, owing to the fire, to bring them in during daylight. At this time he was in charge of the 2nd Field Ambulance, AAMC. Since he has been ADMS of this Division he has carried out his duties with energy and ability and has given every satisfaction.' He was promoted to Cavalier of the Order of St. Maurice and St. Lazarus (Italian) on 26 May 1917 and awarded the Medaille de la Reconnaisance Francaise. He was Mentioned in Despatches in November 1916, January, June and December 1917. He was killed by a piece of shrapnel that pierced his heart while making his way to the front-line to help at aid posts.

Also here is Major John Richmond Cowles, MC, MiD, commanding 4th Battalion, 3rd New Zealand Rifle Brigade who died on 25 November 1917 aged 31 years. He was awarded the Military Cross in September 1916. The citation reads 'For conspicuous gallantry when leading a raid on the enemy's trenches. 33 of the enemy were killed and useful identifications secured, mainly owing to his skill and resource only seven of his men were wounded.' He was Mentioned in Despatches in December 1917. The citation reads 'For conspicuous good work as Officer Commanding Brigade School. This Officer is the best instructor in the Brigade and the successful results of his work have been most marked. He is one of my most valuable Officers whose service I cannot too highly commend.' His obituary, published in December 1917, reads 'He was a member of the Samoan Advance Guard, and as a captain in the Rifle Brigade, served against the Senussi in Egypt prior to going to France. Following service at the front he was stationed at the base for instructional duties, and returned only recently to the front. Major Cowles, who was 32 years of age, was a brother of Lieutenant-Colonel J. A. Cowles, who left New Zealand early this year on his third trip abroad on active service.'

Buried here is 2nd Lieutenant Harry Thorner, AM, 90th Company, Machine Gun Corps who died on 30 December 1917. The citation for his Albert Medal reads 'Lt. Thorner was examining some Mills hand grenades in a small concrete dug-out in France prior to taking them up to his machine-gun position during an expected enemy raid. One of the grenades began to fizz when taken out of the box. There were twelve men in the dug-out at the moment and there was no possible means of disposing of the bomb. Realizing what had happened Lt. Thorner shouted to his men to clear out whilst he himself held the bomb in his hand close to his body until it exploded and killed him. By this magnificent act of courage Lt. Thorner deliberately sacrificed his own life for others. Of the twelve men who were in the dug-out all but two escaped without injury - they were slightly wounded.'

Buried here is Gunner William George Gray, MM, 'Z' (Medium) 21st Trench Mortar Battery, Royal Field Artillery, who died on 15 October 1917 aged 19 years. The citation for his Military Medal reads 'for acts of gallantry and devotion to duty under fire'. He was trying to rescue a wounded officer three months before he was killed in action. He enlisted at Horsham soon after war was declared, joining the Royal Horse Artillery as a Driver, and was later promoted to Gunner in the Royal Field Artillery.

Buried here is Acting Bombardier Thomas Finnerty, 'C' Battery, 156th Brigade, Royal Field Artillery died 20 October 1917. One brother, Gunner William Finnerty, 'C' Battery, 88th Brigade, Royal Field Artillery died on 25 July 1916 and is commemorated on the Thiepval Memorial. His other brother, Private Martin Finnerty, 6th Cheshires died on 20 August 1917 aged 24 years and is buried in Abbeville Communal Cemetery Extension.

Gunners Joseph Bird Burgess aged 25 years and Eric Burgess aged 21 years, both 14th Brigade, Australian Field Artillery and both killed on 4 October 1917 are buried side by side.

Also of note is Corporal Ernest Douglas Jenkins, Royal Army Medical Corps attached 2nd Section, 3rd Water Tank Company who died on 31 October 1917 aged 20 years. He was the youngest of seven brothers who served during the war. Corporal Wheeler Alfred Victor Boulton, 'B' Battery, 82nd Brigade, Royal Field Artillery who died on 7 August 1917 aged 24 years was one of eight brothers who served. Rifleman Harry Pond Bartlett, 9th King's Royal Rifle Corps, who died on 19 August 1917 aged 35 years was acting as Pianist and Stage Manager to the Concert Party 'The Light Blues' behind the Front when he was killed.

| | | |
|---|---|---|
| UK - 815 | Aust - 243 | NZ – 19 |
| Can - 5 | S Afr - 4 | BWI – 1 |
| India – 1 | KUG - 6 | Ger – 6 |
| Area – 4704 sq mts | | |

**LOCATION**
The Huts Cemetery is about 4km south-west of Ieper and about 500m west of Dikkebus in open fields. It is clearly signed from the village and is difficult to miss as you can see it across the fields once you leave Dikkebus heading south-west. It is best reached by a road from Dikkebus village. Enclosed by a high brick wall, which gives it the feel of an English country garden, Huts Cemetery is isolated with good views of the Monts des Flandres.

## TORONTO AVENUE CEMETERY

**HISTORY**
This cemetery was used for the burial of 78 Australians who died during the Battle of Messines from 7 to 10 June 1917.

**INFORMATION**
For further information about the fighting in Ploegsteert Wood please refer to Ploegsteert Wood Cemetery.

A secluded cemetery on the edge of the Ploegsteert Wood, this is one of three that reflect the importance of the wood and how difficult it must have been to take it. It is named after one of many trenches situated in the wood during the war. Despite the name it has no connection with Canada but is, in fact, the only all-Australian cemetery in Belgium.

Those buried here all belonged to the 9th Australian Brigade, 3rd Australian Division, many from the 36th Australian Infantry who erected a memorial here to their comrades. The 37th (Victoria) Australian Infantry also advanced here on 7 June 1917 successfully taking all their objectives. Captain Robert Cuthbert Grieve was awarded the Victoria Cross for capturing two enemy machine-gun emplacements during the action.

Buried here is Private Godfrey Hugh Wallis Allison, 33rd Australian Infantry killed in action on 9 June 1917 aged 40 years. He was killed by a shell, with four others, at about 10.00pm while consolidating captured German trenches. He was originally buried near to 'Dead Horse Corner.' He had enlisted in May 1916, left Australia in October and been wounded in the left leg on 7 May 1917, was treated by 11th Field Ambulance and re-joined his unit on 25 May.

Aust – 78       Unnamed – 2       Area - 306 sq mts

### LOCATION
Toronto Avenue Cemetery lies in the heart of Ploegsteert Wood about 2km north-east of Ploegsteert. A dirt track 50m from Prowse Point Cemetery leads to the three cemeteries in Ploegsteert Wood. The path past Mud Corner is fairly easy to follow as it is fenced and Toronto Avenue Cemetery is clearly visible from the CWGC signs at a junction of paths in the wood. There are also CWGC signs from the Armentieres road and in the wood.

## TORROKEN FARM CEMETERY No. 1

### HISTORY
This cemetery was begun by the 5th Dorsetshires in June 1917 after this part of no man's land had been captured during the Battle of Messines. The burial ground remained in use as a front-line cemetery until the German advance in April 1918.

### INFORMATION
On 1 November 1914 the line north from here defending Wijtschate was held by 400 men of the Composite Household Cavalry from the 4th Cavalry Brigade when nine Battalions of Germans attacked them. Unsurprisingly the Household Cavalry were forced to retreat through the village. The area was captured again during the Battle of Messines in June 1917. The cemetery fell to the Germans in April 1918 but was finally recaptured in September.
The cemetery was one of two made here, though there is now only one. Most of the German graves are marked by Special Memorials.

Buried here is 2nd Lieutenant Paul John Rodocanachi, No. 53 Squadron, Royal Flying Corps and General List, who died on 27 July 1917 aged 17 years. He was born in India where his father was involved in the cotton trade. While CWGC records show him as 17 years in 1917, his Aviators Certificate, gained on 25 August 1916 gives his date of birth as 7 August 1898, making him 18 years at the time and 19 when killed in action. He was flying an RE8 with 2nd Lieutenant Norman Watt as his observer when he was shot down by Leutnant Ernst Hess of Jasta 28 at 3.00pm in the Messines-Wijtschate area. Rodocanachi was killed outright, Watt was mortally wounded but managed to land the plane before dying and is buried next to him. The Rodocanachi family helped British personnel on the run in France between 1940 and 1943 during World War two. The Gestapo broke the escape line and Dr Georges Rodocanachi was deported to Buchenwald concentration camp where he died. Another member of the family had been physician to King Charles II.

UK – 70       Aust – 20       Ger – 14
Unnamed – 1                   Area - 533 sq mts

### LOCATION
Torroken Farm Cemetery is found south of Ieper, south-east of Wijtschate, about 300m east of the road to Messines. It is clearly signed from the main road and lies about 100m from the side road, behind houses in the middle of fields that are often populated by cows, hence watch where you step! Some cemeteries are entered through gardens and some through farmer's fields, but this has both garden and field. Please remember to shut and secure the gates. The path to the cemetery is securely fenced in parts.

## TRACK 'X' CEMETERY

### HISTORY
This cemetery was begun on the first day of the Third Battle of Ypres after the British had captured this area of no man's land. It remained in use until November 1917 and two further burials were made in May 1918.

### INFORMATION
The road here, Admiral's Road, was named after a Captain of the 6th Division who used to ride up and down in 1915, when it was in the front-line of battle, to encourage the troops. He used an armoured car of the Royal Navy Division for his escapades as he experimented with bullet proof shields mounted on wheels like a small tank.

On 27 April 1915 the Sirhind Brigade of the Lahore Division, Indian Army, attacked through here towards No Man's Cot and Minty Farms, the Ghurkha Battalions being followed by the 1st Highland Light Infantry and the 4th King's (Liverpools). The King's were a reserve Battalion but had been sent to France in March 1915 where they had come under the command of the Indian Army. The 1st Ghurkha Rifles reached the crossroads of Admiral's and Boundary roads 900m north of here before being pinned down in no man's land. By that time the Battalion numbered only three officers and 30 men out of a compliment of 38 officers and 1648 men. An order was made to create a Brigade out of the remaining 260 men of the 2nd Duke of Cornwall's Light

Infantry, 280 men of the 1st York and Lancasters, 400 men of the 1/5th King's (Liverpools) and 350 men of the 2nd Duke of Wellington's. The Brigade was to make a repeat attack that had decimated the Sirhind Brigade, but sense prevailed and the order was not carried out.

This part of no man's land was captured by the 39th and 48th (South Midland) Divisions on 31 July 1917. The 1/1st Hertfordshires found out on the first day of the Third Battle of Ypres just how high the cost could be in such an attack. The regiment lost its commanding officer, seven officers and 150 men dead, and almost 400 wounded or missing in the action out of 650 men who began the attack. The 1/1st Hertfordshires were wiped out in one day, a fate they were to suffer on two other occasions in the war. Most of the men lost in the attack were just that, lost, and their names are now commemorated on the Menin Gate while their remains are under headstones that say 'Known Unto God'. Three are known to be buried here.

Interestingly, there are two men of the 17th (Welbeck Rangers) Sherwood Foresters, recorded as killed on 30 July 1917 buried here. However, the cemetery was in no-man's land at the time. Further inspection of the CWGC documents shows Sergeant Christopher Harrison aged 20 years to have been killed with Private James Moody aged 22 years and several others on 6 August but Harrisons date of death to have been changed on the document to 30 July – not Moody's.

The last two burials here were made on 30 April 2004 when the bodies were found during work on the A 19 Motorway.
UK – 144          Can – 5          Unnamed – 27
Area - 719 sq mts

**LOCATION**
Track 'X' Cemetery lies north-east of Ieper about 500m north of the N38 northern by-pass. It is reached by turning from the N38, at the small crossroads just west of the end of the motorway, onto Admiral's Road, known today as Mortelweg. The cemetery is in fields 100m east of the road.

# TROIS ARBRES CEMETERY

**HISTORY**
The cemetery was used from July 1916 until the German advance in April 1918 during the Battles of the Lys, and again in October and November 1918 after the German withdrawal. It was greatly enlarged after the war with the concentration of graves from the surrounding battlefields.

**INFORMATION**
Steenwerck, to the south-west, was in British hands for most of the war but it fell to the Germans during the Battles of the Lys on 10 April 1918. The hamlet of Trois Arbres fell on 11 April, after a defence by the 34th Division, but was retaken by the British in October 1918.

As the cemetery was begun next to the 2nd Australian Casualty Clearing Station here, 50% of the graves made in the original cemetery, Plot I, are of Australians. No. 2 Australian Casualty Clearing Station was based here from 17 June 1916 until March 1918. During June 1917 the nursing staff was increased to fourteen. In July, the Sister-in-Charge wrote that they had three operating tables in use throughout the day, and usually two at night. During July and August 1917 almost 2000 operations were performed. It was on 22 July that the Casualty Clearing Station was bombed, and four nursing Sisters, Alice Ross-King, Dorothy Cawood, Mary Jane Derrer and Clare Deacon, were awarded the Military Medal.

Buried here is Major General William Holmes, CMG, DSO, VD, MiD, commanding 4th Australian Division HQ, who died on 2 July 1917 aged 55 years. In 1872 at the age of 10 years Holmes joined the 1st Infantry Regiment of the New South Wales Military Forces as a bugler and served in every enlisted rank. He was commissioned as a 2nd Lieutenant in 1886, promoted to Lieutenant in 1890, Captain in 1894 and Major in 1900. He served in the South African Wars where he was promoted to Lieutenant Colonel, Mentioned in Despatches and awarded the Distinguished Service Order. Holmes commanded the 1st Australian Infantry from 1902 to 1911. He was promoted to Colonel on 6 January 1912 and was appointed to command the 6th Infantry Brigade. When then war began Holmes commanded the force that captured New Guinea and the German held Pacific Islands. He then took the 5th Australian Brigade to Gallipoli in 1915 and was in temporary command of the 2nd Australian Division when they were the last to be evacuated from Gallipoli. He returned to his Brigade to take them to France and into action at Pozieres in 1916. He was then given command of the 4th Australian Division in January 1917 for the attacks at Bullecourt and Messines. He was made a Companion of the Order of St. Michael and St. George at the same time. He was mortally wounded by shrapnel from a German artillery shell which passed through his chest and lungs, while surveying the ground won at the Battle of Messines. He was taking the Premier of New South Wales on a tour of the Front. Holmes was the most senior Australian officer killed in action on the Western Front.

Also buried here is Private Joseph Hancock, 2nd Canterbury Regiment, NZEF, who died on 24 November 1916 aged 38 years. He served as First Steward on Shackleton's Nimrod expedition to the South Pole in 1907-09 leaving New Zealand in January 1908. He had also rescued Shackleton when he was suffering from scurvy in the 1901-03 expedition while on board the SS Morning.

There are four men buried in this cemetery who were executed for desertion during the war. Corporal George W. Latham, 2nd Lancashire Fusiliers, executed 22 January 1915 aged 23 years. He deserted in August 1914 at Le Cateau during the Retreat from Mons but was soon back among the troops treated as one of the many 'stragglers' who had become detached from his unit by accident. He soon absconded again and was captured just before Christmas. The Military Police found him living with a French woman despite being married himself. He was killed on 22 January 1915 just south-east of La Bassee about 15km south of here. His grave was moved here after the war.

Private Fortunat Auger, 14th Canadian Infantry, was executed on 26 March 1916 aged 25 years. He was one of the first to enlist and arrive in France, and was one of the first to go absent. He was the first Canadian executed in the war and this was his third offense of desertion, twice in 1915 and once in 1916. He was originally buried just south-west of Nieuwkerke about 2km north of here.

Private Peter Black, 1/7th (Fife) Black Watch, was executed on 18 September 1916. Black had been serving in France since April 1915 and had already deserted once receiving a suspended sentence of death. He deserted again in the summer of 1916 while on the Somme being absent for a month before being arrested. He was executed nearby and was one of the original burials here.

Private John King, 1st Canterbury Regiment, NZEF, was executed on 19 August 1917 aged 32 years. He was an Australian serving under an assumed name and had enlisted at the start of the war. He was legitimately absent from action on several occasions due to ill-health and accidents. He was evacuated from Gallipoli with a crushed finger and later had dysentery. He went absent in October 1916 for which he received Field Punishment. He absconded again at Christmas and was recaptured in January 1917 receiving a suspended sentence of hard labour. He deserted once more in May 1917, spent his time with Australian units, and was captured on 23 July. He was tried on 5 August and executed on 19 August 1917 which reflects the usual speed with which such matters were dealt. Had he served with the Australian Force he would not have been executed as the Australian government refused to allow their men to receive capital punishment in part due to their experience during the South African Wars.

Sergeant Laurence Frank Gatenby, 40th Australian Infantry died on 14 January 1917. Gatenby was a right handed opening batsman who played two matches for Tasmania in 1913-14. He was an original ANZAC serving at Gallipoli with the 3rd Light Horse Regiment.

On the road south to Steenwerck, on the left immediately after the bridge over the motorway, and therefore, outside the area covered by this book, there is a German Military Cemetery. This is worth a visit while you are in this area.

Concentrated here:

Douanne Cemetery - at the point where the road from Nieuwkerke reaches the Bailleul-Armentieres road about 2km north of here. It contained four British and fifteen Canadian graves of men who died from 1915-1916.

Fortrie Farm Cemetery – 1.5km west of Le Romarin and about 2km north of here. It contained 27 British soldiers who died in November and December 1914.

Linen Factory Cemetery - near Crois du Bac Military Cemetery, 4km south of here. It contained twenty British men and one Indian grave moved here, and seven Germans who were removed to Steenwerck German Military Cemetery.

| UK – 954 | Aust – 470 | NZ – 214 |
| Can – 20 | NF – 1 | S Afr – 1 |
| Guernsey – 33 | India – 1 | Unnamed – 435 |

Area - 5936 sq mts

Special Memorials to nine British soldiers and one Canadian known/believed to be buried here among the unnamed.

**LOCATION**

Trois Arbres Cemetery lies south of Ieper, in northern France, about 2km south of the Bailleul-Armentieres road (D933). It is clearly signed from the D933 and lies on the west side of the road to Steenwerck about 200m south of the railway crossing.

## TUILERIES BRITISH CEMETERY

**HISTORY**
This cemetery was only used in the early months of 1915.

**INFORMATION**
Some of the earliest British burials in the Salient were made here when 106 British soldiers were buried next to some French men in the area of the tile-works, or tuileries. However, the cemetery was then destroyed by heavy shelling and, as a result, most of the graves were lost. Just 26 could be found and marked though only ten bodies could be individually identified. The other sixteen remain unnamed, and some 80 graves were lost.

The 69 men known to have been buried here are now remembered by Special Memorials. In addition, three French soldiers who were known to have been buried here but whose graves could not be found are commemorated by a Special Memorial in the form of a French Cross near the entrance. The effect of all this is that the cemetery has a lot of open space, with the headstones of the Special Memorials around the walls, creating an unusual and interesting cemetery.

Buried here is Captain John Edward Guy Brown, 2nd attached 1st Queen's Own (Royal West Kents), who died on

Brown, Royal Navy and No. 48 Squadron, Royal Air Force, died of wounds, received three days earlier, on 6 May 1918 aged 27 years. He was mortally wounded in combat above Peronne, but landed his plane saving the life of his observer. He is buried in Heath Cemetery, Harbonnieres.

Also here is Lieutenant Haldane Day Stokes, MVO, 2nd King's Own (Royal Lancasters), who died on 17 February 1915 aged 29 years. He became a Member of the Victorian Order, 5th Class when he carried the colours when they were presented by the King in 1905 to the regiment's Militia Battalions. He then transferred to the regular army and was serving in India when the war began having been promoted to Lieutenant in 1910. He was killed in action near Zillebeke.

22 February 1915 aged 22 years. He joined the army in 1911 and went to India with 2nd Queen's Own (Royal West Kents). He became a specialist in Indian languages with the aim of joining the Indian Army where the chances of promotion were often better than in British regiments. He was sent back to Europe and was at the Front by late 1914. He was working as a reconnaissance and bombing officer as well as being a Company commander when he was killed. His brother, 2nd Lieutenant Alexander Claud Garden

UK – 26    Unnamed – 16    KUG – 11
Area - 1875 sq mts

Special Memorials to 69 British men and three French soldiers known to be buried here but whose graves were destroyed by shell-fire.

**LOCATION**

Tuileries Cemetery is east of Ieper on the west side of the road from Zillebeke to Hellfire Corner, about 500m north of Zillebeke church. It is set back from the road behind the houses and is reached by a short path.

# TYNE COT CEMETERY

**HISTORY**

This cemetery was opened two days after the German line here had been captured during the Battle of Broodseinde. It was next to an Advanced Dressing Station established in a captured pill-box and used until the German Spring Offensive in March 1918. It was greatly enlarged after the war with the concentration of 11500 graves.

**INFORMATION**

This is a breath-taking cemetery, on a hill, at one of the highest points of the Salient. The position of the Cross of Sacrifice, on a pill-box with the backdrop of the Memorial, is stunning and stands out against the ridge from a very great distance. In fact, it is sometimes best seen for the first time from across the valleys towards Langemark.

Passendale and this area were in German hands from 1914. The area was most well known as the site of action in late 1917 during the Third Battle of Ypres as the front was pushed towards Passendale. This location was a strong point in the German line captured by the 2nd Australian Division on 4 October 1917. Several pill-boxes remain preserved within the cemetery. The 34th Australian Infantry reached the blockhouses here before being stopped.

The blockhouse now used as the base for the Cross of Sacrifice was the Advanced Dressing Station here in 1917 and 1918 around which the original cemetery grew. The 11th Canadian Field Ambulance had three squads of eight men working in each pill-box as it took six or more men to carry one stretcher in the mud. You can make out that original burial ground as the irregular group of 343 graves between the Cross and the terrace. The graves were made by the 50th (Northumberland) and 33rd Divisions. The belief had been long held that the 50th Division named the Advanced Dressing Station, and consequently the cemetery, after the main river in the north-east and a 'cot' being their local dialect for a small building, once the ridge had been captured. However, trench maps pre-dating the attack by the Australians on the Broodseinde Ridge show 'Tyne Cott' marked at this location. This place had already been named, probably by men of the Northumberland Fusiliers in trenches nearby, before the attack in 1917. They had given the name to a barn which stood near the level crossing on the Passendale-Broodseinde road about 300m east of here. The barn, which had become the centre of five or six German blockhouses, was captured by the 3rd Australian Division on 4 October 1917. So, the story of naming the cemetery after the attack is a myth. Sadly, not the only myth about Tyne Cot (and other locations) that crept its way into the first version of this book and that I hope I have now rectified. One of the joys of studying history is learning new things every day.

This cemetery is still in use for the burial of remains found in the Salient during work today. Three unidentified South

Africans buried in July 2013 lie near the north-west bunker. It is also a very busy cemetery, by the nature of it being the largest in the world, receiving over 300,000 visitors each year. Time visits in the relatively early morning or late in the afternoon for a more tranquil experience. There are toilets, at a cost, and a visitor, or interpretive, centre.

The inscription on the blockhouse upon which stands the Cross of Sacrifice reads 'This was the Tyne Cot Blockhouse captured by the 3rd Australian Division 4 October 1917'. It read 2nd Division until corrected in the 1990's.

If you stand at the Cross of Sacrifice and look back towards the entrance, scan the area beyond and you will see some of the ground fought over on 4 October 1917, known as the Abraham Heights. The obelisk that you may see in the distance is the Memorial to the New Zealand Division who fought in the Battle of Broodseinde.

Although the Germans attempted to retake this vital position they failed. Tyne Cot was consolidated by the ANZAC's in one of the most important successes of the war because the Germans no longer held the heights around Ypres. It fell quickly in 1918 during the German advance and was cleared again in September by the Belgian Army.

It is now the largest Commonwealth war cemetery in the world in terms of burials. Notably, about 70% of the burials are unidentified as they were first buried somewhere else and all means of identification perished in the mud of Belgium. At the suggestion of King George V, who visited the cemetery in 1922, the Cross of Sacrifice was placed on the original large pill-box. He also suggested that the lower part of the base of the memorial should have steps for people to use it as a viewing platform, in the way steps and stands had been created for him. He expected the higher part of the Memorial, where the stones are too high to be steps, to be treated as that – a Memorial respected for its purpose. The cemetery was formally opened on 19 June 1927.

There are three men buried here who have been awarded the Victoria Cross. Captain Clarence Smith Jeffries, VC, 34th (New South Wales) Australian Infantry, died on 12 October 1917 aged 23 years. He enlisted in 1912 and was commissioned in August 1914, arriving at the Western Front in November 1916 becoming a Captain just after the Battle of Messines. On 12 October, commanding 'B' Company, in rain and appalling conditions, his Battalion set off from the west side of the cemetery heading east. He captured over 60 prisoners and silenced two machine gun positions. In attacking a third he was wounded when the machine gunner realised Jefferies, with about ten men, was coming from behind the German. He wounded Jefferies in the stomach, usually a mortal wound. His body was briefly lost until discovered in September 1920 and identified by his Captain's pips, and initials C S J upon the groundsheet in which he had been buried. This is another example for which I have to hang my head in shame. In the first version of this book I claimed that Jefferies attacked the blockhouses in this cemetery and was killed where he is now buried. In fact he was killed and buried at Augustus Wood, about 400m north-east from where he is now buried, being moved here in 1920. The citation for his Victoria Cross reads 'For most conspicuous bravery in attack, when his Company was held up by enemy machine-gun fire from concrete emplacements. Organising a party, he rushed one emplacement, capturing four machine guns and thirty-five prisoners. He then led his Company forward under extremely heavy enemy artillery barrage and enfilade machine-gun fire to the objective. Later, he again organised a successful attack on a machine-gun emplacement, capturing two machine guns and thirty more prisoners. This gallant officer was killed during the attack, but it was entirely due to his bravery and initiative that the centre of the attack was not held up for a lengthy period. His example had a most inspiring influence.'

Company Sergeant Major Lewis McGee, VC, 40th (Tasmania) Australian Infantry, died on 12 October 1917 aged 29 years. He enlisted on 1 March 1916 and arrived at the Front on 9 December 1916, five days after being promoted to Corporal. He became a Sergeant on 12 January 1917. He was one of 248 members of the 40th Australian Infantry to become casualties on the Broodseinde Ridge. This at a time when all Australian Battalions were suffering from lack of manpower as Australia did not introduce conscription so the supply of volunteers fell later in the war. He was awarded the Victoria Cross for attacking a pill-box just north of this cemetery on 4 October at the start of the Battle of Broodseinde. The German machine-gun had held up his men and they were taking heavy casualties. He rushed forward to enable his Battalion to achieve its objectives which they had done within three hours of jumping off from their start point at 6.00am in Dab Trench which ran along what is now the access road to the cemetery on its west side. The citation reads 'For most conspicuous bravery when in the advance to the final objective, Sjt. McGee led his platoon with great dash and bravery, though strongly opposed, and under heavy shell fire. His platoon was suffering severely and the advance of the Company was stopped by machine gun fire from a "Pill-box" post. Single-handed Sjt. McGee rushed the post armed only with a revolver. He shot some of the crew and captured the rest, and thus enabled the advance to proceed. He reorganised the remnants of his platoon and was foremost in the remainder of the advance, and during consolidation of the position he did splendid work. This Non-commissioned Officer's coolness and bravery were conspicuous and contributed largely to the success of the Company's operations.' He did not know he had been awarded the Victoria Cross. On 12 October he was again here having been promoted to Company Sergeant Major that morning. Again his men ran into trouble at a pill-box and again McGee rushed forward. He was hit in the head and died instantly. He was originally buried about 1km north of here near the spot where he was killed.

Private James Peter Robertson, VC, 27th, 2nd Manitoba (Winnipeg) Canadian Infantry, died on 6 November 1917, aged 35 years. He enlisted in June 1915. The citation reads 'For most conspicuous bravery and outstanding devotion to duty in attack. When his platoon was held up by uncut wire and a machine gun causing many casualties, Pte. Robertson dashed to an opening on the flank, rushed the machine gun and, after a desperate struggle with the crew, killed four and then turned the gun on the remainder, who, overcome by the fierceness of his onslaught, were running towards their own lines. His gallant work enabled the platoon to advance. He inflicted many more casualties among the enemy, and then carrying the captured machine gun, he led his platoon to the final objective. He there selected an excellent position and got the gun into action, firing on the retreating enemy who by this time were quite demoralised by the fire brought to bear on them. During the consolidation Pte. Robertson's most determined use of the machine gun kept down the fire of the enemy snipers; his courage and his coolness cheered his comrades and inspired them to the finest efforts. Later, when two of our snipers were badly wounded in front of our trench, he went out and carried one of them in under very severe fire. He was killed just as he returned with the second man.' He was originally buried north of Passendale village.

A good friend has told me the story of his great-uncle, 2nd Lieutenant Herbert Albert Edwin Milnes, 'A' Company, 3rd Auckland Regiment, NZEF who was killed on the Abraham Heights on 4 October 1917 aged 42 years. His tale serves as a good example of the attitude of the men who fought in the war. Milnes had been forced to leave England for health reasons in 1905 becoming Principal of the Auckland Training College and education lecturer at Auckland University College from 1906-1916. Before his arrival in New Zealand in 1905, Milnes had worked as a house tutor at Borough Road College, now part of Brunel University of which, therefore, Herbert and I are both alumni. His family had made considerable financial sacrifices to be able to send Milnes to New Zealand to escape the English winters, but in March 1916 Herbert enlisted and was soon commissioned. It is ironic that 'love of his country of birth and his hatred of injustice and oppression of the weak' brought him back to Europe into the worst conditions that man can imagine. He was killed by an explosion whilst sitting in a shell-hole during an attack on Otto Farm. He was first buried in the shell-hole, though his body was unmarked. It is said of him that, as Principal of his college, he was a worthy exponent of the college motto 'Totis Viribus'.

Buried here is Brigadier General James Foster Riddell, General Staff commanding 149th (1/1st Northumberland) Infantry Brigade, late 2/5th Northumberland Fusiliers, who died on 26 April 1915 aged 52 years. He was commissioned as an officer in the Northumberland Fusiliers in 1881, and served in campaigns in Africa between 1888 and 1902. In August 1914 he was appointed to command the 149th Infantry Brigade, which was made up of the Territorial Battalions of the Northumberland Fusiliers. Initially the Brigade was tasked with guarding the north-east coast but after the regular army had suffered heavy losses in the opening battles of the war the Territorials were sent to war 21 April 1915 and were put in reserve near Ypres. Following the gas attack on 22 April 149th Brigade were rushed to the Front in commandeered London buses and on 26 April they were ordered to counter-attack alongside the Lahore Division, from the village of St. Juliaan. As the Northumberland Fusiliers pushed forward they were exposed to very heavy machine gun and artillery fire. Although this prevented them from pushing the Germans back it helped to re-establish the line. The cost was high, with over 2000 casualties. Brigadier General Riddell was one, hit in the head by a sniper as he conferred with his officers. He was originally buried with three unidentified men near Railway Wood north of the Menin Road and his remains concentrated here.

Also here is Lieutenant Colonel Stephen Hamilton Dix, MC, Leinster Regiment commanding 12/13th Northumberland Fusiliers, who died on 4 October 1917 aged 39 years. The 12th and 13th Northumberland Fusiliers amalgamated on 8 August 1917. He had commanded the 13th Battalion since June 1917. He was shot, with his four Company commanders, attacking the area near the Polderhoek Chateau close to Becelare. He was originally buried between Polygon Wood and Becelare.

Another here is Captain Vivian Hugh Nicholas Wadham, MiD, No. 15 Squadron, Royal Flying Corps and 1st Hampshires, who died on 17 January 1916 aged 24 years. He was one of the first pilots with the Royal Flying Corps to arrive in France at the start of the war when he was one of the 34 pilots who flew from Salisbury Plain to France on 12 August 1914 while with No. 3 Squadron. On 22 August 1914, Wadham, and his observer Captain L E O Charlton, while on reconnaissance which was almost all the Royal Flying Corps was expected to do early in the war, made the crucial observation of the First German Army's approach towards the flank of the British Expeditionary Force threatening its destruction. This information allowed Field Marshal French to realign his front and save his army around Mons, fighting the Battle of Mons the following day. It could be said that Wadham and Charlton's work prevented the defeat of the BEF during the first weeks of the war. Wadham joined No. 15 Squadron in May 1915. On 17 January 1916 he took off in his BE2c at 7.35am on a reconnaissance flight with Sergeant Nigel Vincent Piper as his observer. Their aircraft was brought down near Passendale. Wadham was killed in the forced landing, and

Piper was made a prisoner of war. Wadham was originally buried by the Germans just south of Oostnieuwkerke about 8km north of here.

There are many men here from families who experienced more than one loss in the war. I have covered just some of them below. Private John Nicholas Crowley, 34th Australian Infantry, died on 12 October 1917 aged 52 years. He was killed by shellfire near Passendale. As a newspaper editor before the war, he was giving a speech to encourage men to join up when he realised he could not ask others to do what he would not do himself. He lied about his age as he was too old so enlisted on 16 November 1916 claiming to be 44 years of age and left Sydney nine days later. His son, Private Reginald Baden Crowley, 34th Australian Infantry, died between 4 and 5 April 1918 aged 18 years, being shot with a revolver at close range by a German officer while attacking at Hangard Wood, and is commemorated on the Villers-Bretonneux Memorial. His brother, Private Matthew Nicholas Crowley, 13th Australian Infantry, died on 6 May 1915 aged 37 years and is commemorated on the Lone Pine Memorial. He was wounded at Dead Man's Ridge, Gallipoli, on 2 May 1915, was evacuated on the Hospital Ship Gascon and died of his wounds at sea. Crowley had two other sons serving during the war who both survived.

One of the original burials here is Private William Neill, 21st Canadian Infantry who died between 3 and 4 November 1917 aged 33 years. He enlisted into the 168th Battalion in January 1916, his brother James enlisting in the same Battalion one month later. He arrived in England in November 1916 and joined the 21st Battalion in March 1917. They took over the line at Crest Farm near Passendale on 3 November and then faced several attacks by the Germans over the next 24 hours. During one of these, Neill was killed and then buried in Tyne Cot Cemetery. His brother, Private James Vance Neill, of the same Battalion, was killed in action during the attack at Hill 70 and was buried in the Aix-Noulette Communal Cemetery. Their younger brother, who had not emigrated to Canada from Scotland, Private Andrew Cloakie Neill, MM, 'C' Company, 12th Royal Scots was killed on 25 April 1918 aged 27 years and is on the Tyne Cot Memorial.

Private Samuel Spilsbury, 1/6th Cheshires was killed on 31 July 1917 aged 22 years. His brother, Lance-Corporal William Spilsbury of the same Battalion was killed on the same day aged 19 years. They were mobilised together in August 1914, served together and were both originally reported missing. By January 1918, Samuel's body had been found and he is buried here while William is commemorated on the Menin Gate. Samuel is one of a very few men of the 1/6th Cheshires 118 casualties to have a known grave.

2nd Lieutenant Arthur Conway Young, 4th attached 7th/8th Royal Irish Fusiliers was killed on 16 August 1917 aged 26 years. His epitaph, one of few that question the war to be found on the Western Front, says 'Sacrificed to the fallacy that war can end war'. He was born in Japan where his father was the owner of 'The Japan Chronicle', an influential English language newspaper. He returned to England to join the army in 1915 though being a pacifist like his father and two brothers, both of whom also served, Douglas George as a Captain in the Royal Flying Corps and Corporal Eric Andrew as a despatch rider. The inscription was chosen by his uncle, George Young, who held unusual views for that time.

There is a collective grave in Plot XXVII, Row H for Bombardier Herbert Johnson, Gunner L C Withams, MM, Gunner Ernest Halliwell and Bombardier R Clifton, 'D' Battery, 232nd Brigade, Royal Field Artillery, killed in action on 12 October 1917. Their remains were found in a sandbag and they are commemorated as believed to be here together. The CWGC concentration sheet simply says 'bones in a bag'.

Buried here is Regimental Serjeant Major Charles Frederick Jagger, MC, 1/4th East Yorkshires who died on 13 December 1917. He was awarded the Military Cross in the New Years Honours List in January 1917. It is unusual for a non-officer to be awarded the Cross rather than the Military Medal but it did happen for some senior non-commissioned officers. He went to the Front in June 1915 as a Sergeant.

Private John Asquith Atkinson Nelson, 11th Cheshires died on 12 August 1917 aged 28 years. He played one cricket match for Lancashire, a victory in 1913.

Buried here is Lance Corporal Richard Verhaeghe, MM, 5th Canadian Mounted Rifles, killed between 30 and 31 October 1917 aged 39 years. He had emigrated to Canada from his birthplace in Ostende, Belgium. He enlisted in August 1915. He was awarded the Military Medal for bravery at Regina Trench on the Somme on 1-2 October 1916 when he rescued several men. He was was killed in a gas attack or during a trench raid only 50km from his birthplace and is the only Belgian buried here.

Among those buried here who, like Verhaeghe, was not a member of the Commonwealth, but like many others, mainly American, joined the Canadian forces, is Pioneer Dominick Naplava, 107th Canadian Pioneers killed on 12 November 1917 aged 25 years. He was born in Zadovice, Moravia, in what was then the Austro Hungarian Empire and is now part of the Czech Republic near the Slovakian border before migrating to the USA. He travelled from Texas to Canada and enlisted when the war began. He was killed in action at Kansas Cross near Wieltje and was buried in the Levi Cottage Cemetery one of the eight Canadians buried there. However, his grave was destroyed by shellfire and he is commemorated at Tyne Cot by a Special Memorial next to the wall by the main entrance. In 2014 his headstone was replaced and the original given to the Military History Museum of the Czech Republic. It may be the only CWGC headstone to have been gifted on permanent loan to a non Commonwealth nation.

The Memorial to the 7th Division, one of the first to be erected on the Salient, in commemoration of their actions here on the ridge in 1914 and 1917, is to the south of the roundabout at Broodseinde through which you may have passed to reach the cemetery from Zonnebeke. The hill from Zonnebeke to Broodseinde was known as 'Devil's Hill'. A number of German and British cemeteries were made by the Germans on either side of the road during the war but they have been removed.

Near the Broodseinde-Passendale road, but north of the roundabout, is a monument honouring the 85th (Nova Scotia Highlanders) Canadian Infantry upon which is inscribed 'in memory of the gallant comrades who gave their lives in the operation before Passchendaele at Decline Copse and Vienna Cottage October 28th to 31st 1917' and the names of those killed.

Concentrated here:

Iberian South Cemetery and Iberian Trench Cemetery - 1000m south-east of Bridge House Cemetery and 1000m west of Dochy Farm Cemetery at a farm known to the Army as Iberian Farm, which is about 2.5km east of here. They contained 30 British men who died in August to September 1917 and March 1918.

Kink Corner Cemetery - at the Potsdam Reboubt about 3km south-west of here. It contained fourteen British men, nine Canadians and nine Australians who died from September to November 1917.

Levi Cottage Cemetery - near the Zonnebeke-Langemark road about 1km west of here. It contained ten British men, eight Canadians and three Australians who died from September to November 1917.

Oostnieuwkerke German Cemetery – located about 8km north-east of here, it contained two British men.

Staden German Cemetery - just south-west of the village about 8km north of here. It contained fourteen British men and ten Canadians who died from 1915 to 1917.

Vladslo-Praatbos German Military Cemetery - the present German cemetery, located about 10km north-west of here near Diksmuide, contained six officers of the Royal Flying Corps and Royal Air Force who died in 1917 and 1918.

Waterloo Farm Cemetery - on the road to Passendale 500m north-east of the Gravenstafel Memorial and 500m north of here. It contained seven British men, ten Canadians and two New Zealanders who died in 1917 and 1918.

Zonnebeke British Cemetery No. 2 - on the road to Broodseinde known as Devil's Hill about 600m south of here. It contained 38 British men buried by the Germans in one of four cemeteries they made for British soldiers who died in their hands. Of those, eighteen were of the 2nd Buffs (East Kents), twenty of the 3rd Royal Fusiliers and all died in April 1915.

| | | |
|---|---|---|
| UK – 8961 | Aust – 1368 | NZ – 520 |
| Can – 1011 | NF – 14 | S Afr – 90 |
| BWI - 2 | Guernsey – 6 | Ger – 4 |

Unnamed - 8373 (70% of total)
Area - 35103 sq mts

Special Memorials to 38 British, 27 Canadian, fifteen Australian soldiers and a New Zealander believed/known to be buried among the unnamed.

Special Memorials to sixteen British and four Canadian men buried in other cemeteries but whose graves have been lost.

**Tyne Cot Memorial to the Missing**

The Memorial at the north-east end of the cemetery is one of three on the Salient, as covered by this book, built to commemorate the men of Britain and the Dominions whose bodies were lost and have no known grave. The Tyne Cot Memorial, opened in June 1927, bears the names of all 34949 British soldiers and one Newfoundlander who were lost in Belgian Flanders from 15 August 1917 to the end of the war. The Monument is a semi-circular wall with three apses. The central apse is one of seven Memorials to the men of New Zealand whose graves are lost on the Western Front. This one commemorates 1179 who died nearby in October 1917. You can also find New Zealand Memorials covered in this book at the Buttes Cemetery and Messines Ridge Cemetery. One caveat is that there are addendum panels so the numbers change occasionally.

Three men commemorated on the Memorial were awarded the Victoria Cross. Lieutenant-Colonel Philip Eric Bent, VC, DSO, twice MiD, 9th Leicestershires was killed on 1 October 1917 aged 26 years. He joined the Royal Navy as a cadet in 1909 but left a year later. When the war began he enlisted as a Private in 'A' Company, 15th (1st Edinburgh) Royal Scots but was soon commissioned as a 2nd Lieutenant in the 7th Leicestershires. He was promoted to Lieutenant in June 1915 and joined the 9th Leicestershires a month later going to France with them in August. He became a Captain in July 1916, Major a month later becoming the second in command. In September he took command of the Battalion and became a Lieutenant-Colonel which was made permanent in February 1917. He saw action on the Somme in 1916, had been twice wounded in action and twice Mentioned in Despatches in June 1916 and May 1917. He was awarded the Distinguished Service Order in the 1917 Birthday Honours List. He was awarded the Victoria Cross for his actions at Polygon Wood on 1 October 1917. The citation reads 'For most conspicuous bravery, when during a heavy hostile attack, the right of his own command and the Battalion on his right were forced back. The situation was critical owing to the confusion caused by the attack and the intense artillery fire. Lt. Col. Bent personally collected a platoon that was in reserve, and together with men from other companies and various regimental details, he organised and led them forward to the counter-attack, after issuing orders to other officers as to the further defence of the line. The counter-attack was successful and the enemy were checked. The coolness and magnificent example shown to all ranks by Lt.-Col. Bent resulted in the securing of a portion of the line which was of essential importance for subsequent operations. This very gallant officer was killed whilst leading a charge which he inspired with the call of 'Come on the Tigers.'

Corporal William Clamp, VC, 6th Yorkshires, died on 9 October 1917 aged 26 years. He had eight brothers and nine sisters. On 22 January 1914, he joined the 1/6th Cameronians (Scottish Rifles), a Territorial Army unit. In August 1914 he was called up and saw fighting with the 1/6th Cameronians at Festubert in 1915. He was twice seriously wounded and when he came out of hospital the second time, in January 1917, he was transferred to the 6th Yorkshires. He was awarded the Victoria Cross for his actions near Poelkapelle on 1 October 1917. The citation reads 'For most conspicuous bravery when an advance was being checked by intense machine-gun fire from concrete blockhouses and by snipers in ruined buildings. Corporal Clamp dashed forward with two men and attempted to rush the largest blockhouse. His first attempt failed owing to the two men with him being knocked out, but he at once collected some bombs, and calling upon two men to follow him, again dashed forward. He was first to reach the blockhouse and hurled in bombs, killing many of the occupants. He then entered and brought out a machine-gun and about twenty prisoners, whom he brought back under heavy fire from neighbouring snipers. This non-commissioned officer then again went forward encouraging and cheering the men, and succeeded in rushing several snipers' posts. He continued to display the greatest heroism until he was killed by a sniper. His magnificent courage and self-sacrifice was of the greatest value and relieved what was undoubtedly a very critical situation.'

Lance-Corporal Ernest Seaman, MM, VC, 2nd Royal Inniskilling Fusiliers, died on 29 September 1918 aged 25 years. He emigrated to Canada in 1912 but returned to England in December 1915. However, classified as unfit for active front line service he ended up as a baker in the Army Service Corps. It was not until 1917, when men were needed for the infantry, that he was re-classified and was allowed to join a front-line unit. He was promoted to Lance Corporal about two weeks before his death. The citation for the award of the Victoria Cross relating to his actions on 29 September 1918 at Terhand reads 'For most conspicuous bravery and devotion to duty. When the right flank of his Company was held up by a nest of enemy machine guns, he, with great courage and initiative, rushed forward under heavy fire with his Lewis gun and engaged the position single-handed, capturing two machine guns and twelve prisoners and killing one officer and two men. Later in the day he again rushed another enemy machine-gun position, capturing the gun under heavy fire. He was killed immediately after. His courage and dash were beyond all praise, and it was entirely due to the very gallant conduct of Lce. Cpl. Seaman that his Company was enabled to push forward to its objective and capture many prisoners.' It is possible that he did not receive the Military Medal as it was 'upgraded' to a Victoria Cross.

There are twelve Lieutenant Colonels commemorated on the memorial. One, Bent, has been covered above and one Moorhouse, below in the section on those on the Memorial who had relatives killed in the war.

Lieutenant Colonel Harold George Fairfax Longhurst, 6th Royal Berkshires died on 12 October 1917. Formerly of the Kings Royal Rifle Corps he had become a Captain in November 1914 and Major in May 1917. He had commanded the Battalion since August and was killed leading an attack at Poelkapelle which had commenced in pouring rain at 1.00am.

Lieutenant Colonel Hugh Thomas Kay Robinson, DSO & two Bars, 12th attached 13th Royal Sussex died on 26 April 1918. He had commanded the Battalion since 7 June 1917. He was awarded the Distinguished Service Order in the Birthday Honours List in June 1917 while a Captain and just before promotion to command the 13th Royal Sussex. The Bar to the DSO was awarded in December 1917 for 'For conspicuous gallantry and devotion to duty when in command of his Battalion during three days' operations. In the assembly of his troops, in launching them for the attack, in the attack itself, and in holding the position, he displayed high qualities of leadership and courage'. The second Bar was awarded on 18 September 1918 'For conspicuous gallantry and devotion to duty while commanding a composite Battalion. He handled his Battalion in such a way as to prevent the enemy entering a gap in the line, and so turning the right flank of the Division. Later, when in command of another Battalion, he, by skilful leadership and courageous example, caused the enemy's advance to be checked at a critical moment with heavy loss.'

Lieutenant Colonel Neville Reay Daniell, DSO, Duke of Cornwall's Light Infantry commanding 9th King's Own Yorkshire Light Infantry, died on 4 October 1917 aged 28 years. He was awarded the Distinguished Service Order posthumously in the New Years Honours List in January 1918.

Lieutenant Colonel George Koberwein Fulton, DSO, 9th Cheshires formerly 6th Wiltshires died on 14 April 1918 aged 34 years. He had commanded the Battalion since December 1917. While at Oxford University he had been cox of the Brasenose College eight. He had survived the German attack in March 1918 near Cambrai escaping with three officers and a handful of men. Fulton was again engaged with his Battalion at Nieuwkerke in desperate fighting until he was killed during a personal reconnaissance. He was posthumously awarded the Distinguished Service Order for his leadership.

Lieutenant Colonel James Hugh Coles, DSO, 1st East Yorkshires, was killed on 24 April 1918 near Wijtschate leading his men of whom he had been in command since 8 April. He was posthumously awarded the Distinguished Service Order for his actions in March 1918 while still a Captain 'For conspicuous gallantry and devotion while commanding his Battalion during several days of severe fighting. By his remarkable coolness and courage in face if the most difficult circumstances, he was enabled to extricate his Battalion on at least two occasions when practically surrounded. His fine qualities of leadership and devotions to duty greatly inspired those around him'.

Lieutenant Colonel Alfred Winter-Evans, DSO, DCM, twice MiD, 3rd New Zealand Rifle Brigade, NZEF, died on 12 October 1917. He is commemorated in the New Zealand Apse. He served in the ranks in the South African Wars where he gained both the Distinguished Conduct Medal and a commission. He became Major and Officer Commanding 'C' Company, 4th New Zealand Rifle Brigade in February 1916 and Lieutenant Colonel of 3rd New Zealand Rifle Brigade in November 1916. He was awarded the Distinguished Service Order in August 1917 for his actions at Messines in June 1917 'For conspicuous gallantry and devotion to duty. During an attack and the subsequent consolidation of the captured position he showed the greatest coolness and energy, inspiring all ranks by his magnificent personal example and never sparing himself to make the operation of his Battalion the success which it was. His work at all times has been of the same high standard.' He had gone ahead to encourage his troops forward, but moving from shell-hole to shell-hole, he drew upon himself machine gun fire by which he was mortally wounded. He and Lieutenant Colonel George Augustus King, DSO & Bar, 1st Canterbury Infantry, NZEF, were the highest ranking New Zealand officers to die on 12 October 1917 when 845 men were killed in just four hours which was their worst day of war. King is buried in Ypres Reservoir Cemetery.

Lieutenant Colonel Duncan Hamilton Blunt, DSO, twice MiD, 1st Devonshires, was killed on 3 October 1917 aged 39 years. He was commissioned in to the Devonshires as a 2nd Lieutenant in January 1899, served in the South African Wars, was promoted to Captain in 1903, Major in 1915 and temporary Lieutenant Colonel in March 1916 when he took command of his Battalion. He was awarded the Distinguished Service Order in November 1916 'For conspicuous gallantry in action. He led his Battalion with great dash in the attack and capture of a wood, and established his position in a captured enemy trench beyond. He thus greatly facilitated the further advance'. In 1896 he won the Public Schools Fencing Championship.

Lieutenant Colonel William Allsop Wistance, 5th South Staffordshires, DSO, MC, died on 25 April 1918. He had commanded the Battalion since January 1917 and was awarded the Military Cross in the Birthday Honours List in June 1916 and the Distinguished Service Order in December 1917.

Lieutenant Colonel Arthur Gordon Cade, DSO, MC & Bar, three times MiD, 2nd Middlesex attached and commanding 1st Wiltshires, was killed on 26 April 1918 aged 26 years. The Distinguished Service Order was awarded in January 1918 'For conspicuous gallantry and devotion to duty when in command of his Battalion. Hearing that the left flank of his Battalion was held up, he at once went forward with as many men and machine guns as he could collect, and throughout the whole day under intense hostile fire, reorganised his Battalion, with the uppermost disregard of personal safety in full view of the enemy. He strengthened the exposed flank and held on in the face of determined counterattacks. His courage and coolness were beyond all praise and it was solely due to his personal efforts that he kept his Battalion in good morale throughout the day'. The Military Cross was awarded on 23 June 1915. The Bar was awarded on 21 December 1916 'For conspicuous gallantry in action. He led his Company with great courage and determination, destroying an enemy machine gun and killing the team. He maintained his position for five days under very trying circumstances.' He was promoted to Lieutenant Colonel to take charge of the Wiltshires and had been in command of the Battalion for four days when killed.

Lieutenant Colonel Robert Arthur Hudson, DSO, 1/8th West Yorkshires died on 9 October 1917 aged 37 years. He commanded the 1/6th West Yorkshires from July to October 1916 and then took command of the 1/8th Battalion from December 1916. He was awarded the Distinguished Service Order in the January 1916 New Years Honours List.

There are many men on the Memorial who lost a brother or other relative. There are also many who lost more than one brother. I have not been able to include them all, but here are a sample as I do not claim to have completed a definitive full list.

One example, notable because two brothers are commemorated on the Memorial, is Private Joseph Lockley, 2/8th Royal Warwickshires killed on 4 October 1917 aged 26 years and commemorated here with his brother Sapper William Lockley, 134th Army Transport Company, Royal Engineers who died a few weeks later on 26 October 1917 aged 27 years. Another brother, Serjeant T Lockley, DCM, 1/5th Cheshires died on 28 December 1915 aged 23 years and is buried in Suzanne Communal Cemetery Extension. He posthumously won the Distinguished Conduct Medal for attacking a machine gun position and making gaps in the German wire under fire.

Captain Harold Cecil Round, DSO, MC, MiD, 6th attached 9th Rifle Brigade, was killed in action on 24 August 1917 aged 21 years. He was awarded the Distinguished Service Order as a 2nd Lieutenant near Cherisy on 3-4 May 1917. The citation says 'When our troops were forced to withdraw he collected a few men and made a strong-point within 70 yards of the enemy trench. This position he held for two days without supplies of any kind. He was finally able to get a valuable report through before being ordered to withdraw.' One brother, an original burial in Serre Road Cemetery No. 2, is Captain James Murray Round, MC, 13th Essex, killed on 13 November 1916 aged 22 years. Another brother, Lieutenant Auriol Francis Hay Round, 2nd Essex, died of tetanus in hospital in London on 5 September 1914, while convalescing from wounds received at Le Cateau on 26 August, aged 22 years. He is buried in Witham (All Saints) Churchyard near the family home. He was a County cricketer for Essex.

Private John Tame, 2nd Royal Berkshires was killed in action on 19 August 1917. His two brothers, Lance Corporal Alfred Tame and Corporal William George Tame, both 2nd Royal Berkshires and both died on 9 May 1915 are commemorated on the Ploegsteert Memorial a few kilometres to the south.

Another is Rifleman William John Norman, King's Royal Rifle Corps attached 1/9th (Queen Victoria's Rifles) Londons, was killed in action on 16 August 1917 aged 19 years at Langemark. His brother, Serjeant James Frederick Norman, 'A' Company, 1/3rd Londons (Royal Fusiliers), was killed in action on 29 May 1916 aged 22 years and is buried in St. Amand British Cemetery. Another brother, Gunner Sydney James Norman, 141st Heavy Battery, Royal Garrison Artillery, was killed on 1 July 1917 aged 27 years and buried at Hop Store Cemetery.

Private Victor Watmough, 15th Royal Scots died on 22 October 1917 aged 19 years. Buried in Ridge Wood Cemetery is 2nd Lieutenant John Cyril Watmough, 2nd Northumberland Fusiliers who died on 10 July 1917 aged 26 years. Bombardier E Watmough, 'A' Battery, 315th Brigade, Royal Field Artillery was killed on 31 August 1918 aged 27 years and is buried in Achiet-le-Grand Communal Cemetery Extension.

Remembered here is Lance Corporal John McAulay Munn, 7th Cameron Highlanders who died 20 August 1917 aged 32 years. He lost four brothers in the war. Pioneer Andrew Brown McAulay Munn, 33rd Divisional Signal Company, Royal Engineers died on 16 September 1915 aged 21 years and buried in Cite Bonjean Military Cemetery. Private Walter Munn, 1st King's Own Scottish Borderers, died on 3 January 1916 aged 25 years and is commemorated on the Helles Memorial. Private Daniel Munn, 1st Highland Light Infantry, died on 30 October 1918 aged 34 years and is buried in the Baghdad (North Gate) War Cemetery. Lance Corporal James Munn, 8th Black Watch (Royal Highlanders) formerly Royal Garrison Artillery, was killed in action on 15 July 1916 aged 26 years and is commemorated on the Thiepval Memorial. Strangely the brothers died in age order, the youngest first, eldest last.

Also commemorated here are twin brothers Private Adolphus Gallienne, 1st Royal Guernsey Light Infantry killed on 23 March 1918 aged 24 years and Private Archibald Gallienne, 1st Royal Guernsey Light Infantry killed on 21 March 1918 aged 24 years. A third brother, Private Thomas John Gallienne, 1st Royal Guernsey Light Infantry was killed in the Battle of Cambrai on 30 November 1917 and is commemorated on the Cambrai Memorial at Louverval.

Private Charles Sowden, 1st Devonshires died on 4 October 1917 aged 24 years. Nearby on the Memorial is his brother, Private Ernest Albert Sowden, 10th Royal Warwickshires who died on 19 April 1918 aged 24 years. Another brother, Company Serjeant Major Frederick Arthur Sowden, Machine Gun Corps (Infantry) died at home of his wounds on 31 January 1920 aged 28 years and is buried in Washford Pyne (St. Peter) Churchyard. Two other brothers served and survived the war.

Another family lost three sons one of whom is commemorated here. Lance Corporal Arthur Wrench, MM, 10th Cheshires, was killed on 26 April 1918 aged 23 years. His brother, Private Fred Wrench, 1/6th Cheshires, died on 6 June 1918 aged 20 years and is commemorated on the Soissons Memorial. Another brother, Private John Charles Wrench, 2nd Royal Welsh Fusiliers, died on 11 June 1917 aged 34 years and is buried in Mont Huon Military Cemetery, Le Treport.

Lance Corporal Ernest Matthews, 30th Machine Gun Corps (Infantry) died on 10 May 1918 aged 28 years. His brother, Private Leonard Matthews, 1/1st Hertfordshire Yeomanry died on 5 September 1917 aged 24 years and is buried in Baghdad (North Gate) War Cemetery. Another brother, Private Alfred Edmund Matthews, also 1/1st Hertfordshire Yeomanry, died on 24 July 1917 aged 36 years and is buried in Amara War Cemetery.

Private Bertram Rushen, 10th Queen's (Royal West Surreys) died on 20 September 1917 aged 19 years and is commemorated here. Private Stanley Rushen, 11th Tank Corps died on 25 August 1918 aged 20 years and is commemorated on the Vis-en-Artois Memorial. Private Joseph Rushen, 7th Queen's (Royal West Surreys) died on 1 July 1916 aged 20 years and is commemorated on the Thiepval Memorial. This is a family with no grave at which to mourn three relatives.

Private James Dugan, 2nd Hampshires died on 21 August 1917 aged 43 years. His brother, Private Wesley Dugan, 15th Hampshires died on 15 September 1916 and is commemorated on the Thiepval Memorial. Private Edwin Dugan, 2nd Hampshires died on 19 April 1918 and is commemorated on the Ploegsteert Memorial. Once again a family to lose several members and have no grave to visit.

Private Albert Pickup, 20th (Tyneside Scottish) Northumberland Fusiliers died on 16 October 1917 aged 39 years. Private Ernest Pickup, 10th Cameronians (Scottish Rifles) died on 17 October 1916 aged 21 years and is commemorated on the Thiepval Memorial. Private Robert Pickup, 10th King's Own Yorkshire Light Infantry, died on 1 July 1916 and is also on the Thiepval Memorial.

Private Frank Hunsley, 4th Londons (Royal Fusiliers) died on 26 September 1917 aged 26 years. His brother, Private Robert Hunsley, 1/4th Northumberland Fusiliers died on 15 September 1916 aged 29 years and is commemorated on the Thiepval Memorial. Private Thomas Hunsley, 2nd East Yorkshires died on 16 November 1916 aged 30 years and is commemorated on the Doiran Memorial in Greece. Another family with no grave at which to mourn.

Private Harry Adcock, 9th King's Own Yorkshire Light Infantry died on 26 April 1918 aged 19 years and is commemorated here. His brother, Private Walter Sydney Adcock, 12th Duke of Wellington's died on 23 October 1916 aged 22 years and is commemorated on the Thiepval Memorial. Another brother, Private Percy Adcock, 2/4th York and Lancasters died on 3 May 1917 aged 25 years and is commemorated on the Arras Memorial. Three brothers with no identified graves.

Private Archibald G Griffin, 13th Middlesex died on 26 August 1917 aged 29 years and is commemorated here. His brother, Private Frank H Griffin, 1/8th Middlesex died on 17 September 1916 aged 19 years and is commemorated on the Thiepval Memorial. Another brother Private Ernest Arthur Griffin, 3rd Royal Fusiliers died on 3 May 1915 aged 18 years and is on the Menin Gate. The only three sons in the family and all commemorated on memorials.

Private Charles Edward Squires, 4th Worcestershires died on 9 October 1917 while attacking along the line of the old railway north-east of Langemark. His brother Rifleman Albert Thomas Squires, 1/8th Hampshires died on 19 April 1917 and is commemorated on the Jerusalem Memorial. Another brother, Lance Corporal Harry Reeves Squires, MM, 2nd Hampshires died on 24 August 1917 aged 29 years and is buried in Dozinghem Military Cemetery.

Private Charles Richard Russell, 2/4th Queen's (Royal West Surreys) died on 8 October 1918 aged 20 years. His brother, Rifleman William R Russell, 2nd King's Royal Rifle Corps died on 10 July 1917 aged 27 years and is commemorated on the Nieuport Memorial. Another brother, Private A E Russell, 1/1st Londons (Royal Fusiliers) died on 14 January 1917 and is buried in Laventie Military Cemetery, La Gorgue. Three other brothers served and survived the war.

Private Cyril Kisby, 14th Royal Warwickshires died on 24 October 1917 aged 34 years. His brother, Private Arthur Walling Kisby, 'B' Company, 2nd South Staffordshires died on 13 November 1916 and is buried in Serre Road Cemetery No. 1 Cemetery. Another brother, Private Clarence Wilfred Kisby, 1/4th Lincolnshires died on 3 July 1916 and is buried in Doullens Communal Cemetery Extension No. 1.

Private Alfred Victor Gardner, 2/4th East Lancashires died on 10 October 1917 aged 30 years. One brother, Private James Gardner, 49th Training Reserve died at home on 2 November 1917 aged 26 years and is buried in Lancaster Cemetery, Lancashire. Another brother, Lance Corporal Reginald Gardner, 8th King's Own (Royal Lancasters) died on 9 April 1917 aged 20 years and is commemorated on the Arras Memorial.

Private Frank Archibald Collar, 1st Queen's Own (Royal West Kents) died on 26 October 1917 aged 37 years and is commemorated here. His brother, Private Ernest Edward Collar, 7th East Surreys died at home of wounds received in action on 11 November 1915, aged 24 years and is buried in Hanwell (Kensington And Chelsea) Cemetery. Another brother, Rifleman Frederick George Collar, 2/6th (City of London Rifles) Londons died on 7 September 1917 aged 20 years and is commemorated on the Menin Gate. Normally, a man who died after 15 August 1917 would be commemorated on the Tyne Cot Memorial. But Frederick George Collar seems to be one of the exceptions alluded to on the CWGC website. However, I have been unable to find out why he is not commemorated here. There are 21 other members of his Battalion who died in October and November 1917 commemorated on the Tyne Cot Memorial.

Private George Alfred Busby, 5th Oxford and Bucks Light Infantry died on 19 August 1917 aged 19 years. His brother, Private William Albert Busby, 2/6th Gloucestershires died on 26 September 1917 aged 21 years and is buried in Sunken Road Cemetery, Fampoux. Another brother, Frederick Busby, 10th Entrenching Battalion, late 7th Wiltshires died between 24 and 25 April 1917 aged 24 years and is buried in Doiran Military Cemetery in Greece.

Rifleman Percival Buckle, 1/8th West Yorkshires died on 9 October 1917 aged 27 years. His brother, Lance Corporal Leonard Buckle, 1/5th West Yorkshires died on 3 September 1916 aged 23 years and is buried in Connaught Cemetery, Thiepval. Another brother, Lance Corporal Tom Buckle, 'B' Company, 16th King's Royal Rifle Corps died on 29 October 1918 aged 22 years and is buried in Awoingt British Cemetery.

And don't forget the Neills covered above. One commemorated here, one buried in Tyne Cot Cemetery and one buried in Aix-Noulette Communal Cemetery.

Others relatives commemorated here include father and son Lieutenant Colonel Harry Moorhouse, DSO, TD, Chevalier de Legion D'Honneur, and Captain Ronald Wilkinson Moorhouse, MC, both 1/4th Kings Own Yorkshire Light Infantry both killed on 9 October 1917 near Bellevue on the Ravebeke. The Battalion had been supporting the 1/5th Kings Own Yorkshire Light Infantry when Ronald was mortally wounded. He was carried to his father's headquarters, not far behind the front line. As soon as Harry saw how seriously injured his son was, he insisted on setting out to find a doctor to tend his wounds. Several people tried to detain him and go in his place, but his concern for Ronald was so great that he set out himself. He was shot by sniper fire and died in the arms of one of his men. Ronald died within the hour. This is possibly the only example of a father and son dying together at Passendale. Ronald's Military Cross was awarded in June 1917 for leading a raiding party. Harry's Distinguished Service Order was awarded in the June 1916 Birthday's Honours List.

Also commemorated here are brothers Rifleman Walter James Castro aged 31 years and Rifleman William Frederick Castro aged 35 years, both 9th King's Royal Rifle Corps and both killed on 23 August 1917. They had consecutive service numbers so joined up together and died together. They died in operations on the Westhoek Ridge near the Menin Road west of Geluveld when killed by the same shell.

Another pair of brothers here are Lance Corporal Dennis Alfred O'Donoghue aged 24 years and Lance Corporal Reginald Charles O'Donoghue aged 22 years, both 'A' Company, 1/28th (Artists' Rifles) Londons, and both died on 30 October 1917. They had consecutive service numbers so joined up together. Both were teachers.

More brothers commemorated here are Private Archie Callaway, 1/6th Royal Warwickshires who died on 17 August 1917 aged 27 years and Private Frederick Callaway, 8th Somerset Light Infantry who died on 4 October 1917 aged 32 years.

Another pair of brothers here are Private John McAvoy, 8th Northumberland Fusiliers who died on 16 August 1917 aged 44 years and Private Thomas McAvoy, 2nd Royal Munster Fusiliers who died on 10 November 1917 aged 34 years.

Some young men are remembered here. Private Patrick Joseph Murray, 11th Royal Sussex died on 24 September 1917 aged 16 years. Private Jesse Haynes, 6th King's Shropshire Light Infantry died on 16 August 1917 aged 16 years. Rifleman Philip Henry Thomas, 1st Royal Irish Rifles died on 29 April 1918 aged 16 years.

Remembered here is Company Serjeant Major The Honourable Jacob John Astley, 2/5th Sherwood Foresters (Notts and Derbys), who died on 26 September 1917 aged 32 years. He was son of the 20th Baron Hastings and had earlier been a Lieutenant in the 16th Lancers.

Commemorated here is 2nd Lieutenant The Honourable Denis Sydney Buxton, 2nd Coldstream Guards who died on 9 October 1917 aged 19 years. He was son of the 1st Viscount Buxton later Earl Buxton who was a Liberal MP until he became Governor of South Africa in 1914 when he was made a peer. Denis was the eldest surviving son so with his death the title became extinct.

Also here is Lieutenant Gordon Williams, RVM, 'F' Company, 1/28th (Artists' Rifles) Londons who died on 30 October 1917 aged 26 years. He was awarded the Royal Victorian Medal while a Sergeant in the Battalion and is recorded in the Battalion history as being a Captain.

Commemorated here is Captain Arnold Edwin Bare, MVO, Territorial Force Efficiency Medal, 'B' Company, 1/28th (Artists' Rifles) Londons, who died on 30 October 1917 aged 36 years. He joined his Battalion, a territorial force unit, in 1897. In August 1916 he commanded a Guard of Honour to the King and was made a Member of the Victorian Order. His son, Captain Jack Stormont Bare, Artist's Rifles attached Royal Welch Fusiliers and No. 2, Commando, Royal Navy, died on 4 February 1944 aged 29 years during a raid on the island of Hvar in Yugoslavia and is buried in Belgrade War Cemetery.

Private David 'Dai' Westacott, 2/6th Gloucestershires died on 28 August 1917. He was a former Welsh Rugby Union international, playing one international, a defeat to Ireland in 1906. He was part of the Cardiff team that beat the touring Australia side in 1908. Westacott was part of a British advance on German positions at Springfield Farm on 27 August 1917. After taking the bunker positions around the farm, Westacott was killed in action the following day. Springfield Farm was on the road between Zonnebeke and Langemark midway between the two and just north of what is now the Canadian Memorial at Vancouver Corner.

Lieutenant Allan Ivo Steel, 2nd Coldstream Guards was killed on 8 October 1917 aged 25 years. As a right-handed batsman and a right-arm slow bowler, he represented MCC and Middlesex in two first-class matches in 1912. His brother Lieutenant John 'Jack' Haythorne Steel, Royal Navy was washed overboard, in heavy seas, and drowned on 18 April 1918, aged 28 years, on route to take command of HMS Munster. His is commemorated on the Portsmouth Memorial. Their father, Alan Gibson Steel, played in the first ever cricket Test Match in England at The Oval in 1880, and then in the famous Test which England narrowly lost in 1882 after which the Ashes were created. He then toured Australia winning the Ashes for the first time. He also scored the first Test century at Lords as well as being President of the MCC for some time.

2nd Lieutenant Eric Balfour 'Bill' Lundie, 3rd Coldstream Guards died on 12 September 1917. He was a right-arm fast bowler who played one Test for South Africa against England at Port Elizabeth in February 1914 when he bowled 46 overs into a strong wind, taking 4 for 106 but finding himself on the losing side. He enlisted with the South African Service Corps before gaining his commission. He was killed by a shell when his Battalion were being relieved by the 2nd Irish Guards.

2nd Lieutenant William Ward Odell, 9th Sherwood Foresters (Notts & Derbys) died on 4 October 1917 aged 36 years. He made 193 first class cricket appearances from 1901 to August 1914 taking 737 wickets, the first of which was W G Grace, and scoring 14416 runs. He represented Leicestershire, several different versions of the 'Gentleman' and a W G Grace side. He enlisted in 1914 before he was commissioned and was awarded the Military Cross just a few weeks before he was killed.

Rifleman Thomas James Bryden, 4th Battalion, 3rd New Zealand Rifle Brigade was killed on 12 October 1917 aged 40 years. He was a New Zealand cricketer who played two matches for Otago between 1912 and 1914. Lieutenant Richard Angwin Rail, 3rd Coldstream Guards died on 9 October 1917 aged 29 years. He played one first-class cricket match for Western Province in South Africa. Lance Corporal Donald Lacy Priestley, 1/28th (Artists' Rifles) Londons was killed on 30 October 1917 aged 30 years. He played cricket seven times for Gloucestershire from 1909-10. His brother, Lieutenant Stanley Noel Priestley, 8th Gloucestershires died on 23 July 1916 and is commemorated on the Thiepval Memorial. Another brother had been on two expeditions to the Antarctic before the war.

Lieutenant Duncan MacKinnon, 1st Scots Guards died on 9 October 1917 aged 30 years. He was a rower in the Magdalen College, Oxford University Coxless Four who won two cups at the Henley Regatta in 1907. The team was chosen to represent Great Britain at the 1908 summer Olympics in London where they won the Gold medal. He went on to win three Oxford-Cambridge Boat Races. At the start of the war he returned from the family business in India and was commissioned into the Royal North Devon Hussars before transferring to the Scots Guards.

2nd Lieutenant Harry Crank, 1/2nd attached 17th Lancashire Fusiliers died on 22 October 1917 aged 28 years. He enlisted in December 1915 into the 22nd Lancashire Fusiliers, a training Battalion where he became a Sergeant soon after enlisting. He remained with training units until the end of 1916. He was commissioned in May 1917. He represented Great Britain at Diving in the 1908 Olympics.

Gunner Robert 'Bob' Torrance, 'A' Battery, 162nd Brigade, Royal Field Artillery died on 24 April 1918 aged 30 years. A professional footballer as a central defender for Bradford City he was 'Man of the Match' in the 1911 FA Cup Final Replay against Newcastle United which Bradford won. Bought for £5.00 in 1907 he made his debut, against Everton, in 1908. He was killed by German shellfire as they moved the Battery. Though the memorial opened in July 1927, Robert's name wasn't added, along with 90 others at the time, until 1930 on the addenda panel.

Private Henry Phillips, 12th Gloucestershires died on 2 October 1917 aged 30 years. He played for Bristol Rovers from 1908 making 63 appearances in the Southern League scoring twice.

Bombardier Albert Milton, 'B' Battery, 64th Brigade, Royal Field Artillery died on 11 October 1917 aged 31 years. He was an English footballer who played for Barnsley and

Sunderland as a full back. Though Milton played for Sunderland from 1908 to 1914, he never won a League Championship, as in the 1912–13 season he was injured and missed the majority of matches, as well as the 1913 FA Cup Final defeat to Aston Villa.

Corporal Thomas Owen Jones, 9th Welsh died on 20 September 1917 aged 30 years. Before the war he played Rugby League (Northern Code) for Oldham making 46 appearances.

UK – 34949      NZ - 1179

### LOCATION
Tyne Cot Cemetery is north-east of Ieper about 3km south-west of Passendale. It lies approximately 300m from the Becelare-Passendale road (N303). Once on the side road you will see the clearly marked right turn to reach the parking area. You can then chose your entrances – past the visitor centre to the front, or through the rear entrance/exit by the toilets.

## UNDERHILL FARM CEMETERY

### HISTORY
This cemetery was opened in June 1917 during the Battle of Messines and remained in use until January 1918.

### INFORMATION
The cemetery lies in the shadow of Hill 63, one of the most prominent features of the southern part of the Salient. Hill 63 was also known as the Rossignol Heights upon which are the remains of the Chateau de la Hutte and the Rosenberg Chateau from which burial plots were removed to Berks Cemetery Extension. The hill was defended by the 19th (Queen Alexandra's Own Royal) Hussars and 1st Dorsetshires in 1914, and in 1918 by the 25th Division. The cemetery was used in the spring of 1918 when it was briefly in German hands and it was known as the 'Military Cemetery at the Foot of Nightingale Hill'.

Much of the Bois de la Hutte stands on Hill 63 beneath which were constructed, initially by Australian tunnellers beginning in August 1916, tunnels large enough to accommodate two Battalions in relative comfort. Similarly, near to the cemetery is Red Lodge, the site of the second dressing station and also used as a Battalion HQ. There are many other structures still to be found in the wood.

Buried here is Lance Corporal Reginald 'Reg' Taylor, 1st Wellington Regiment, NZEF, killed on 20 June 1917 aged 28 years. He was a Rugby Union international who played two tests for New Zealand All Blacks against Australia in September 1913 having shown his class with the Taranaki team. He played in one defeat and one victory in a '2nd Team' as another 'All Black' side was touring the USA. He enlisted and served in Gallipoli and on the Somme as well as surviving the first day of the Battle of Messines. He was killed in one of the follow up actions on the Messines Ridge. Also here is Corporal Francis Horward Vercoe, DCM & Bar, 145th Siege Battery, Royal Garrison Artillery who was killed on 4 June 1917 aged 28 years. He won the Distinguished Conduct Medal in 1915 'for conspicuous gallantry and devotion to duty near Ypres on 29 December 1915, when, under heavy fire of high explosives and gas shells, he left his dug-out and went about 200 yards through a dense cloud of gas to a farm where another Battery was billeted and rendered first aid to several wounded men. While he was doing this a bursting shell blew him across the room in which he was working, but he coolly picked himself up and returned to his work.' A couple of months later he received a Bar for rescuing a seriously injured officer despite being wounded himself. The citation reads 'For conspicuous gallantry. He went out with his Officer under heavy shell fire and assisted in rescuing the Drivers of a wagon which had been hit by a shell. Drivers and horses being wounded. He and his Officer were then wounded by a shell, the latter very severely. Gunner Vercoe, wounded as he was, carried him back under heavy fire and refused to have his own wounds attended to till he had assisted to dress those of his Officer.' He was killed by a shell whilst off duty and sitting reading outside his dugout.

UK – 103         Aust – 47        NZ – 39
Can – 1          Unnamed – 8      KUG – 1

Area - 1690 sq mts

Special Memorials to two British men and three Australians whose graves here were destroyed in later fighting and lost.

### LOCATION
Underhill Farm Cemetery is found south of Ieper, 1km west of the Armentieres road, and about 2km north-west of Ploegsteert. The turn from the N365 is at the foot of Hill 63 though the CWGC sign is only visible from the Ploegsteert direction.

## VLAMERTINGHE MILITARY CEMETERY

### HISTORY
The cemetery was begun by the French in 1914. A small number of British men were buried here in 1914, but this did not became an official British cemetery until 1915. It was then used until June 1917 when, as the available space had been filled, the New Military Cemetery was opened to the south of the village.

**INFORMATION**

The village, at the limit of the range of German guns, was destroyed by artillery during the war, so that only the church tower was left by 1918. Vlamertinge was held by the Germans briefly from 7 to 10 October 1914, after that it became an important Allied centre for hospitals, camps and munition dumps.

The cemetery, named when the village was spelt with an 'h', lies above the level of the road, and a notable feature is the way men of the same unit are buried together. Many of the 55th (West Lancashire) Division are buried here as the Battalions in that Division made every effort to get their dead from the front-line to this cemetery for burial. There are four graves of men who died in World War II who were killed in the Allied retreat to Dunkirk in May 1940. The French graves have been removed.

The gates to the cemetery were donated by Lord Redesdale in memory of his son, Major The Honourable Clement Bertram Ogilvy Freeman-Mitford, DSO, 'A' Squadron, 10th (Prince of Wales's) Hussars, killed in action on 13 May 1915, who lies in this cemetery. Clement Freeman-Mitford entered the Army in 1899. He served with the 10th Hussars during the South African War and later became Regimental Adjutant from 1904-1907. In 1912 Clement was promoted to Major. At the beginning of the war he was put in command of 'A' Company and was badly wounded at Zandvoorde on 21 October 1914. He was awarded a Distinguished Service Order in February 1915 for services in connection with operations in the field. He was killed during the Second Battle of Ypres in temporary command of his regiment during the retirement on 13 May 1915.

Buried here is Captain Francis Octavius Grenfell, VC, 9th (Queen's Royal) Lancers, killed in action on 24 May 1915 aged 35 years. He was awarded the Victoria Cross for his actions on 24 August 1914 at Audregnies for saving the guns of the 119th Battery, Royal Field Artillery near Doubon and for bravery against infantry on the same day. The very brief citation, gazetted on 16 November 1914 reads 'For gallantry in action against un-broken Infantry at Andregnies, Belgium, on 24th August, 1914, and for gallant conduct in assisting to save the guns of 119th Battery, Royal Field Artillery, near Doubon the same day.' Grenfell was commissioned in the King's Royal Rifle Corps in May 1901 but transferred to the 9th (Queen's Royal) Lancers on 4 August 1914. They moved to France on 16 August, Grenfell commanding 'B' Squadron. On 22 August 1914 patrols of the 9th Lancers and the 4th Dragoon Guards sighted German patrols east of Mons and on 24 August the Retreat from Mons began. The 2nd Cavalry Brigade was ordered to charge the flank of the advancing German Army but 'B' Squadron had to take shelter from German artillery behind a railway embankment. South of the embankment was 119th Battery, Royal Field Artillery which was under fire from three German batteries. Grenfell offered his services and was then hit in the leg and hand by shrapnel. Major Alexander, commanding 119th Battery, asked if Grenfell could find an exit for the guns, which he did riding out through the German shell-fire. Captain Grenfell called for volunteers and all of his Squadron ran forward, although it appeared they would be killed, to turn the guns and push them out by which time the German infantry was within 500m. By the evening he was overcome by his wounds and was transferred to England. He returned at the start of October to see action at Ypres where he was again wounded being sent for treatment in Dublin. Once more he joined his regiment, in April 1915, in Ypres. The unit went to the front line on 12 May moving to Vlamertinge on 14 May having lost 82 casualties. They were in the front line at Hooge on 23 May when, in the night, four German Divisions launched a heavy assault using gas. Forty men survived to return to Vlamertinge bringing with them the body of Grenfell who had been shot through the back. He was initially buried in Vlamertinge Churchyard. At the same time buried nearby was Acting Sergeant Joseph William Hussey of whom it was said at the graveside 'How happy old Hussey would have been to know that he died with Francis.' The burial ground did not become an official cemetery until 1915 and Sergeant Hussey was re-interred in Hop Store Cemetery. Grenfell's twin brother, Captain Riversdale Nonus Grenfell, Royal Buckinghamshire Hussars attached 9th (Queen's Royal) Lancers was killed in action on 14 September 1914 aged 34 years and is buried in Vendresse Churchyard. He was a banker, unlike Julian who was a professional soldier. Riversdale trained with the Yeomanry and transferred to be with his brother when the war began. An older brother, Lieutenant Robert Septimus Grenfell, 21st (Empress of India's) Lancers, was killed in a cavalry charge during the Battle of Omdurman in 1898. Francis was cousin of poet Captain Julian Grenfell, DSO, Royal Dragoons who was wounded on 13 May 1915 near where Francis was killed. Julian died on 26 May 1915 and is buried in Boulogne East Cemetery. Julian's younger brother Gerald William (Billy) Grenfell, another cousin of Francis Grenfell, was killed in action on 30 July 1915 within 2km of where Julian had been wounded. A cousin, Lieutenant Claude George Grenfell of Thorneycroft's Mounted Infantry, was killed at Spion Kop during the South African War.

Buried here are two men who were executed during the war by the British Army. Driver Alexander Lamb, 21st Battery, 2nd Brigade, Royal Field Artillery deserted on 19 October 1914, soon after arriving in France, and on the train taking him to the Front. He was not captured until 19 June 1915 in Calais where he had been living with a woman and had civilian clothing in his possession. An unusually long time passed before his trial but he was executed in the village soon after the trial held on 2 October 1915.

Private Albert Rickman, 1st Royal Dublin Fusiliers deserted on 2 July 1916 after taking part in the first day of the Battle of the Somme. He had served with his Battalion in Gallipoli from April 1915 until January 1916. He then went with the Battalion to France in March 1916. On 1 July 1916 the Fusiliers advanced at 8.00am in the second wave attacking on Hawthorn Ridge near Beaumont-Hamel. Casualties were eleven officers and 300 other ranks. On 2 July the survivors held the British front line near Auchonvillers, gathering up the dead and wounded. Rickman was caught on 20 July 1916 but not tried until September when his Battalion had moved to the Salient. He was executed nearby at 6.00am on 15 September 1916 aged 27 years.

Captain Guy Bonham-Carter, MiD, 19th (Queen Alexandra's Own Royal) Hussars attached Queen's Own Oxfordshire Hussars, who died of wounds on 15 May 1915 aged 30 years is buried here. He was commissioned to the 19th Hussars in 1905. From 1910 to 1911 he served with the Mounted Infantry in West Africa and in 1913 was appointed Adjutant to the Queen's Own Oxfordshire Hussars. He went to France with them in September 1914 and served through the earlier battles of the war, being mentioned in Lord French's Despatch of 31 May 1915. The Battle of Frezenberg is considered to have ended by midnight on 13 May 1915 and was a qualified success for the Germans since they had been able to make some of their closest gains to the town of Ypres in the war. He was wounded by a sniper in a support trench near Ypres during the night of 14-15 May and died shortly afterwards. He is related to a General, an Air Commodore, Admirals, several MP's and peers as well as the actress, Helena Bonham-Carter.

Lieutenant Colonel Eustace Robert Ambrose Shearman, 10th (Prince of Wales's Own Royal) Hussars, died on 13 May 1915 aged 39 years. Shearman received his commission in September 1895. He was promoted to Captain in 1901 and Major in 1905. Shearman saw service during the South Africa War and accompanied his regiment to the Western Front on outbreak of war in 1914. With the Royal Horse Guards and the Essex Yeomanry, the 10th Hussars formed the 9th Cavalry Brigade in the 3rd Cavalry Division with Shearman commanding the 10th Hussars. He was another to die on the Frezenberg Ridge. Shearman's Adjutant, Captain Gerald Charles Stewart, 10th (Prince of Wales's Own Royal) Hussars, died on 13 May 1915 aged 28 years alongside him and is buried here.

Buried here is Major Joseph McLaren, MiD, 10th Canadian Infantry, who died on 23 April 1915. In Kitchener's Wood, north-west of St. Juliaan, during one hour on the night of 22 April 1915, the 10th Canadian Infantry had three commanding officers as two, Lieutenant-Colonel Russell Lambert Boyle and McLaren, were killed in the fighting in the wood. The third, Major Ormond, decided to retreat after consultation with the commanding officer of the 16th Canadian Infantry, Lieutenant-Colonel Leckie.

Captain William Gerald Forester Renton, MiD, 1st (King's) Dragoon Guards, was killed in action on 2 June 1915. Ironically, he had a decoration from the Austrian Emperor, holding the Order of the Knights Cross of Franz Joseph awarded in 1906 when he was Adjutant of the unit. The Honorary Colonel-in-Chief of the regiment was the Emperor of Austria, an appointment granted by Queen Victoria in 1896. He was killed by German machine gun fire as he walked in front of the trenches during a heavy German bombardment.

2nd Lieutenant Harold 'Hal' Parry, 17th King's Royal Rifle Corps, died on 6 May 1917 aged 20 years. Parry was educated at Queen Mary's Grammar School, Walsall winning the Queen's Prize for History at his school and an Open History Scholarship at Exeter College, Oxford. Shortly before his 19th birthday he wrote to his mother that he was going to try to join the army. In January 1916, he was commissioned as a 2nd Lieutenant in The King's Own Yorkshire Light Infantry, before transferring to the 17th King's Royal Rifle Corps. He served on the Somme and moved with the Battalion to the Salient in November 1916. He was killed by shellfire in May 1917 on the Yser canal sector. Before the war he was a prolific poet, which he continued during the war. A book of his letters and poems titled 'In Memoriam: Harold Parry' was published posthumously.

Private Noel Finucane, 1/10th (Liverpool Scottish) King's (Liverpools), died on 4 January 1917 aged 26 years. Finucane survived the sinking of the Lusitania on 7 May 1915. Carrying over 1900 passengers and crew on route to Britain from New York the Cunard liner was torpedoed by the German submarine U-20 off the west coast of Ireland at Kinsale. Over 120 US citizens were amongst the 1198 men, women and children who lost their lives. This fact had a part in the USA joining the war. Finucane went on to serve in the SS Aquitania helping in the evacuation of Gallipoli before joining his Battalion. He was killed by machine-gunners whilst helping to repair a position known as Durham Trench.

Gunner Douglas Morgan, 168th Siege Battery, Royal Garrison Artillery died on 31 December 1916 aged 26 years. He was a Scottish professional football left back who played in the Football League for Hull City making 52 appearances between 1913-15.

Captain/Flight Commander John William Washington Nason, No. 46 Squadron, Royal Flying Corps and 14th Royal Sussex died on 26 December 1916 aged 27 years. He was a first class cricketer and good at several sports such as football and golf. He debuted aged 17 years, scored more than 1600 runs in 57 matches for Sussex (1906-10), , and Gloucestershire (1913-14) before the war, when he was commissioned as a Captain in the Royal Sussex. He also played for Cambridge University (1909-10) for whom he won a 'Blue', and the Gentleman of the South in a 1907 victory over the 'Players of the South', both regarded as first class cricket teams. Nason's Squadron flew reconnaissance missions in French-built Nieuport 12 biplanes, spotting and photographing hostile positions in support of 38th Division artillery. Nason and his observer Lieutenant Claud A Felix-Brown, also buried here, were killed over Railway Wood on Boxing Day near Hooge by a fighter of Jagdstaffel 8.

Private James Duffy, 16th Canadian Infantry died on 23 May 1915 aged 25 years. Born in Scotland he had set the Scottish record for five miles before emigrating to Canada. He ran in the marathon at the 1912 Stockholm Olympics coming fifth, the best result by a Canadian athlete in the marathon to date. He enlisted at the start of the war and was among the first Canadians to see action. He was killed by shrapnel in a night-time counter attack by the Canadians at Kitcheners Wood near St. Juliaan.

| | | |
|---|---|---|
| UK – 1113 | Aust – 4 | Can – 52 |
| NF – 2 | S Afr – 2 | India – 3 |
| Ger – 3 | KUG – 1 | WWII – 4 |

Area - 6875 sq mts

## LOCATION
Vlamertinghe Military Cemetery is 5km west of Ieper in the village of Vlamertinge. The cemetery is on the right of a side road 50m north of Vlamertinge church and the N308 on the way to Hospital Farm.

# VLAMERTINGHE NEW MILITARY CEMETERY

### HISTORY
This cemetery was opened on 1 June 1917 in preparation for Third Ypres as the Military Cemetery in Vlamertinge had been filled. It remained in use until the end of the war though most of the burials were made by the end of 1917.

### INFORMATION
The cemetery is on two levels with the Cross of Sacrifice, War Stone and pavilion raised above the level of the graves. Although the cemetery continued in use until October 1918, most of the burials are from July to December 1917. Of the men here, 884 were from artillery units, reflecting the distance from the front-line and the activity in this area, and one was a member of the YMCA.

Buried here is Acting Company Serjeant Major John Kendrick Skinner, VC, DCM, Croix de Guerre (France), 1st King's Own Scottish Borderers killed in action on 17 March 1918 aged 35 years. John Skinner won his Victoria Cross on 16 August 1917 during the Third Battle of Ypres. As his battalion was advancing it came under fire from three blockhouses near Langemark. Skinner and his commanding officer, Captain Currie, crawled forward and silenced three machine-guns and two trench mortars. Then Skinner continued to the blockhouses as Currie gave covering fire, bombing two of them into surrender, and capturing 60 prisoners, so that Captain Currie could order the Company forward in a successful, but costly, attack. The citation reads 'For most conspicuous bravery and good leading. Whilst his Company was attacking, machine gun fire opened on the left flank, delaying the advance. Although CSM Skinner was wounded in the head, he collected six men, and with great courage and determination worked round the left flank of three blockhouses from which the machine gun fire was coming, and succeeded in bombing and taking the first blockhouse single-handed; then, leading his six men towards the other two blockhouses, he skilfully cleared them, taking sixty prisoners, three machine guns, and two trench mortars. The dash and gallantry displayed by this warrant officer enabled the objective to be reached and consolidated.' Skinner received his Victoria Cross from King George V and took fourteen days leave, but when he tried to return to his Battalion he was posted to the reserve in Edinburgh. Risking a Court Martial, Skinner used his travel warrant to get back to his unit. He had a bet with Quarter-Master Sergeant-Major Victor Ross as to which of them would be wounded for the ninth time first. Skinner won the bet, though he did not live to collect the money, because he was shot between the eyes on 17 March 1918, while trying to rescue a comrade. A wounded man missing from patrol the night before was crying out in no man's land, and Skinner went over the top to bring him in. Ironically, records show that in his seventeen year military career since he had joined the Army in 1900 at the age of 16, Skinner had already been wounded nine times, three in the South African War and six times from 1914 to 1917. At his funeral on 19 March six holders of the Victoria Cross of the 29th Division, (a Division often used to do the toughest fighting and hence, more than usually endowed with live holders of the Victoria Cross), carried his coffin in a ceremony unique in military history. He was probably the only soldier to be carried to his resting place on the Western Front upon a gun carriage drawn by a team of horses with full military honours. Sergeant W H Grimaldston, 1st King's Own Scottish Borderers won a Victoria Cross in the same action as Skinner.

Among those buried here is Private Edward Delargy, 1/8th Royal Scots, executed on 6 September 1917 aged 19 years for desertion. He had already served a sentence of 112 days given in July 1916 for failing to join his unit. The Battalion was the Pioneer Battalion in 51st (Highland) Division to which he was posted in January 1917. They were working near Arras in January and February. Delargy spent some time in a Medical Unit in February and then absented himself remaining absent until 6 August when he was arrested 15km from Arras.

Buried here is Captain Oscar Eugene Gallie, DSO, MC, 'A' Battery, 156th Brigade, Royal Field Artillery who died on 7 December 1917 aged 28 years. He first served as a Gunner with 'D' Battery, New Zealand Field Artillery in Samoa from August 1914 to March 1915. He then went to England and obtained a commission in the Royal Field Artillery. The citation for his Military Cross, awarded posthumously but for an act while he was still a 2nd Lieutenant, says: 'For conspicuous gallantry and devotion to duty. During hostile shelling of his Battery position, an ammunition dump in a building was set on fire. This officer rushed in on his own initiative and displayed the greatest gallantry in stifling the flames. As some of the ammunition had already exploded, and the remainder might have done so at any moment, his pluck and devotion to duty cannot be too highly praised.' His Distinguished Service Order was awarded in November 1917 just before his death. The citation reads 'His Battery was very heavily shelled while in action, four guns were destroyed, and ammunition dumps were set on fire. He set the Battery a splendid example by walking up and down in the open, encouraging the remaining detachments and putting out fires. Later, the Battery was again heavily shelled when firing in reply to an SOS signal, and he again behaved with the utmost gallantry, encouraging the men, putting out fires and keeping the guns firing. He set a magnificent example of courage and devotion to duty throughout the operations.' His younger brother, Lieutenant Victor James Gallie, also in the Royal Field Artillery was also awarded the DSO, and also received the French Croix de Guerre. He died in 1929 of wounds received during the war.

There are several families who have men buried here who lost two sons or brothers. But two families lost three sons in the war. Gunner Allan Adie, 8th Brigade, Canadian Field Artillery died on 20 November 1917 aged 21 years. He enlisted in July 1916 and was killed instantly by a fragment from a German shell, during the afternoon, whilst beside his gun. His brother Lieutenant John McClelland Adie, 1st Canadian Motor Machine Gun Brigade died of wounds on 3 November 1918, aged 35 years and is buried in Auberchicourt British Cemetery. He had enlisted as a Trooper in the 12th Canadian Mounted Rifles in June 1915 before he was commissioned in 1918. Another brother, Private Archibald William Adie, 18th Canadian Infantry, died on 10 April 1918, aged 26 years and is buried in Etaples Military Cemetery. He enlisted in April 1917 and died at No. 6 British Red Cross Hospital. A fourth brother, Captain Robert Adie, spent much of the war in England training machine gunners having been wounded in 1916. A cousin, also from St Catherines, Ontario was killed. Lieutenant Harry Morton Ellis Adie, No. 8 Squadron, Royal Flying Corps died in an accident when flying as observer on 1 May 1916, aged 29 years. He enlisted in October 1914 into the 19th Canadian Infantry, and transferred to Royal Flying Corps in February 1916

Private Charles Walter King, 35th Royal Fusiliers, 104th Company, Labour Corps, died on 12 August 1917 aged 22 years. His mother, Charlotte Bibby King, is reported to have pulled chunks of her hair out on receiving the news of his death. His brother, Private Edward King, 2nd Essex, died of wounds on 9 October 1917 aged 36 years and is buried nearby in Dozinghem Military Cemetery. A third brother, Private Thomas Robert King, 7th Queen's (Royal West Surreys) died on 20 November 1916 aged 27 years and is buried in Albert Communal Cemetery Extension.

Two brothers are buried side by side. Shoeing Smith Sidney George Smith and his brother, Gunner Albert Edward Smith, both 2/1st (Warwick) Battery, Royal Horse Artillery died on 20 July 1917. Albert was aged 25 years while Sidney was aged 30 years. Their service numbers are almost consecutive. They were killed, with several others from their unit who are also buried here, by a German shell that fell on them while they were sleeping in a barn. The brothers were found sat up against the wall without a mark on them. They had been at the Front since 21 June 1917.

Gunner Edwin 'Eddie' Gladstone Latheron, 73rd Battery, 5th Brigade, Royal Field Artillery died on 14 October 1917. He was a footballer who played as an inside forward for Blackburn Rovers, helping them to win the Football League title in 1912 and 1914. He also made two appearances for England in 1913 and 1914. He scored in a 4-3 victory over Wales in 1913 but was in the side that lost 3-0 to Ireland in 1914. He was killed by German counter-Battery fire when a shell burst near their dugout and the splinters, passing through the opening, killed him and another Gunner.

Another of note is German pilot Leutnant Erich Reicher, Jasta 6 killed in action on 24 June 1917 while attacking No. 9 Kite Balloon Section. He was killed by defending fire rather than in combat with another plane. He had been with his unit only a short time but had already gained some experience of bringing down balloons.

| UK – 1610 | Aust – 44 | NZ – 1 |
| Can – 154 | S Afr – 3 | Guernsey – 1 |
| Ger – 7 | Unnamed - 12 | |

**LOCATION**
Vlamertinghe New Military Cemetery lies on the southern edge of Vlamertinge west of Ieper. It is 500m south of the dual carriageway Ieper-Poperinge road behind housing on the east side of the Vlamertinge-Reningelst road. A CWGC sign indicates the path from the road to the cemetery set back from the road. When I visited the New Military Cemetery for the first time I had to persuade myself that I was not entering private property. Trust your instincts and you will see the cemetery once you are behind the houses.

# VOORMEZEELE ENCLOSURES No.'s 1 AND 2

**HISTORY**
This cemetery was used from March 1915 until April 1918, when the village fell to the Germans, and again after the German withdrawal.

**INFORMATION**
The village was in British hands for most of the war though it fell to the Germans on 26-27 April. It was attacked by the US 30th Division on 31 August 1918 and fully taken back in September.

The enclosures were originally regimental burial grounds typical of those made early in the war. No.'s 1 and 2 are now treated as one cemetery and bounded by the same wall but it is possible to distinguish between the two. There were four cemeteries in the village though one has been concentrated.

Enclosure No. 1 is the larger and further from the road and is now Plot I. It was begun in March 1915 by the 28th Division and remained in use until the end of the war, though it was used by the Germans when they held the village in the summer of 1918. One grave was brought into Row F after the war from a position in the village.

Enclosure No. 2, now Plot II, was used from March 1915 to April 1917. Enclosure No. 4, formerly sited a short distance to the south and concentrated here after the war, was used by the French in December 1914 and by the 4th Rifle Brigade from January to November 1915. It contained 42 British men and two Germans brought here after the war while the graves of 33 French soldiers were moved elsewhere.

Among those buried here is Gunner Michael Joseph Cahill, 4th Brigade, Australian Field Artillery, killed on 1 September 1917 aged 38 years. The men in his Battery were sitting near a dugout in the trench outside the cookhouse eating their dinner, to which they had arrived late, when a shell exploded nearby killing Cahill as shrapnel passed through his head.

Also here is Gunner Albert Victor Greenslade, 146th Heavy Battery, Royal Garrison Artillery killed on 31 July 1917 aged 21 years. Prior to the war he was a salesman and enlisted on 5 June 1916. He arrived in France on 26 September 1916 with the 110th Heavy Battery, Royal Garrison Artillery with whom he was twice wounded. He was transferred to the 146th Heavy Battery on 19 June 1917 and was killed by shellfire six weeks later.

UK – 520    Aust – 17    NZ – 2
Can – 53    Ger – 6    Unnamed – 40
Area - 2644 sq mts

Special Memorials to nineteen British men and one German soldier whose graves here were destroyed by shell-fire.

Special Memorials to two British men buried in Enclosure No. 4 whose graves were destroyed and lost.

### LOCATION
The Voormezeele Enclosures are in the village of Voormezele south of Ieper. These are on the south side of the road into the village 700m east of the large crossroads on the N375.

## VOORMEZEELE ENCLOSURE No. 3

### HISTORY
This cemetery was begun by the Princess Patricia's Canadian Light Infantry in February 1915 when the Canadians were part of the 27th Division, and remained in use until April 1918. The cemetery was used again in October 1918 and after the war for the concentration of over 1200 graves.

### INFORMATION
This is now the largest of the three Enclosures that remain in Voormezele, a fourth has been removed, though its position on the edge of the village next to modern housing creates a strange atmosphere. The original graves are in Plot III. The other Plots from I to IX were made by individual regiments as their burial grounds. Plots XIII to XVI are the graves concentrated here after the war. The concentrated graves include many of the 15th (Carabiniers) Hampshires who captured this village in September 1918. Several French graves were removed after the war.

Buried here is 2nd Lieutenant George Llewelyn Davies, 6th King's Royal Rifle Corps attached 4th Rifle Brigade who died of a shot to the head on 15 March 1915 aged 21 years. He was Barrie's step-son and the inspiration for Sir J M Barrie's 'Peter Pan'. With his four brothers, he was one of Barrie's 'Lost Boys'. In the 1904 play 'Peter Pan, or The Boy Who Wouldn't Grow Up', Peter Pan is roughly 10, the same age that Davies was when Barrie began writing the play in 1903. Barrie became the boys' guardian after the death of their father in 1907 and mother in 1910. George's uncle, Guy du Maurier, is buried in Kemmel Chateau Military Cemetery and I have written in depth about the family in the section on that cemetery. Barrie's nephew, Lieutenant William Cowan Ogilvy Barrie, 5th Black Watch (Royal Highlanders) was killed in action on 14 October 1916 aged 34 years and is commemorated on the Thiepval Memorial.

Also here is Company Serjeant Major George Warren, DCM & Bar, MiD, 15th (Hampshire Yeomanry) Hampshires, who died on 4 September 1918 aged 30 years. The Distinguished Conduct Medal was awarded on 22 October 1917 'For conspicuous gallantry and devotion to duty (at 'Tower Hamlets', Passchendaele). When his Company was ordered to return and hold the (battle) line, he dashed forward in the face of heavy machine gun fire and aircraft attack and regained the position. Later he returned to the position, after it had been evacuated, under intense machine gun fire, to find some of his men who were still sniping. Throughout he showed tremendous courage.' The Bar was awarded on 3 September 1918, the day before he died, and was also 'for conspicuous gallantry and devotion to duty (at Gommecourt, near Albert) when in charge of a fighting patrol. In spite of heavy rifle and machine gun fire, he sent back valuable information, which greatly assisted in the re-taking of a village. He also rendered valuable work when in charge of a ration party, when the enemy launched their second counter attack. His indifference to personal danger was magnificent.' He was killed in an attack at Kemmel.

Two successive commanders of the same Battalion are buried here. Lieutenant Colonel Francis Douglas Farquhar, DSO, three times MiD, Legion of Honour, Princess Patricia's Canadian Light Infantry (Eastern Ontario Regiment), died on 21 March 1915 aged 40 years. He was son of a Baronet and spoke French, Somali and Chinese. He joined the Coldstream Guards in 1896 and had seen action in the South Africa War, China in 1901 and Somaliland from 1903-1904 becoming a Lieutenant Colonel in 1913. He was Mentioned in Despatches and awarded the Distinguished Service Order for his services in South Africa. He was Military Secretary to Canada's Governor General, His Royal Highness, The Duke of Connaught, when he was asked to command the Battalion from its formation in August 1914. He took them through mobilisation, training and to the Front. Farquhar was mortally wounded and died at 2.30am during a tour at the front near St. Eloi while supervising wire-laying. He was Mentioned in Despatches on 14 April 1915 and 22 June 1915. The province of British Columbia honoured him by naming Mount Farquhar after him.

Major, Temporary Lieutenant-Colonel, Herbert Cecil Buller, DSO, MiD, Rifle Brigade attached and commanding Princess Patricia's Canadian Light Infantry (Eastern Ontario Regiment), died on 2 June 1916 aged 34 years. He was killed in Sanctuary Wood during the actions in the Battle of Mount Sorrell while leading 'the remaining two platoons of No 3 Company, men from Battalion headquarters and the few remnants of No 1 Company to fight their way to the front along the communication trenches and join up with the two hard-pressed platoons defending them. He was shot dead directing the advance.' He became Captain and Adjutant, having been moved from the Rifle Brigade, with whom he had joined the army in 1900, in August 1914. He was made Lieutenant-Colonel on the death of Farquhar in March 1915 until wounded near Ypres on 4 May 1915 when he lost an eye hit by shrapnel. He took command again in December 1915 until his death. Like Farquhar he was on staff with the Governor General when the war began and worked with Farquhar until Farquhar's death.

He was Mentioned in Despatches and awarded the Distinguished Service Order in the Birthday Honours List in June 1915. Many members of his family served their country. His father, Admiral Sir Alexander Buller, served in the Crimean War and commanded the China Station in the late 1890's. His brother died as a result of wounds received in the war while another served in the Royal Navy becoming an Admiral and commanding the Royal Yacht. His nephew died on active service in WW2.

Also here is Private William Dulgarians Crombie, 10th Queen's Own (Royal West Kents), who died on 9 November 1916 aged 16 years. I have seen several spellings of his middle name in army records.

Concentrated here:

Eikhof Farm Cemetery - south of Oak Dump Cemetery and east of St. Eloi about 1km east of here. It contained nineteen British men who died in June 1917.

Elzenwalle Chateau Cemetery – located about 1km south-west of here in the grounds of the chateau north of the Elzenwalle Brasserie Cemetery. It contained 30 British men, mainly of the 1st Wiltshires and Honourable Artillery Company, who died from February to June 1915.

Haringhebeek Cemetery - 600m east of La Laiterie Cemetery on the bank of the stream which is about 3km south of here. It contained thirteen British soldiers who died on 7 June 1917.

Pheasant Wood Cemetery - on the 'Dammstrasse' and south-east of St. Eloi about 1.5km south-east of here. It contained thirteen British men who died in July and August 1917.

Vijverhoek Brasserie Cemetery - at the northern edge of Dikkebus Lake near the main road about 1km west of here. It contained sixteen British men, one Canadian and one New Zealander who died in April, May and October 1918.

| UK – 1481 | Aust – 8 | NZ – 2 |
| --- | --- | --- |
| Can – 100 | S Afr – 1 | KUG – 1 |
| Unnamed – 608 | | Area - 5772 sq mts |

Special Memorials to twelve British men and three Australians known/believed to be buried here among the unnamed.

Special Memorials to five British men buried in Pheasant Wood Cemetery whose graves have been destroyed in later fighting and lost.

**LOCATION**

Directions are the same as those for the No. 1 & 2 Enclosures but No. 3 is on the north side of the road 50m west of the others.

# WATOU CHURCHYARD

**HISTORY**

This churchyard was used occasionally from April 1915 until April 1918. There are five burials made in 1915, two in 1916, four in 1917 and one in 1918.

**INFORMATION**

Watou was always well behind the front-line and was, therefore, used as a centre for camps. Many theatrical shows were performed in the village for soldiers in reserve. This was also an area in which there were camps for Belgian refugees. Among those refugees were the monks of the Trappist Mont des Cats Monastery who moved here to their sister religious institution, St. Bernadus, which had opened in 1904 as an annex for monks from the Mont des Cats. Both are renowned breweries.

Buried here is Serjeant Albert John Clayton, No. 20 Squadron, Royal Flying Corps and 1st King's Royal Rifle Corps who was an observer. He died of his wounds received when shot in the chest by ground fire during an attack on the German Rumbeke airfield two days before his death on 26 April 1917 aged 33 years. He enlisted in January 1904 into the Kings Royal Rifle Corps, moving into Reserve in 1907 and being recalled in December 1914. In 1915 he became a Lance Corporal in April, a Corporal in August and Sergeant in December. He was wounded twice in July 1916 and returned to his Battalion before joining the Royal Flying Corps in March 1917 where he spent most of the month training as an aerial gunner and observer joining his Squadron one month before he was mortally wounded.

Also here is 2nd Lieutenant Robert Edgar Paul Priest, 276th Brigade, Royal Field Artillery who died on 15 August 1917 aged 22 years. He had gone to France in April 1915 as a Bombardier before he was commissioned. The Register of Soldiers Effects says his wounds were self-inflicted.

Private Philip Dougherty, 11th King's (Liverpools) died in a training accident during bombing instruction on 15 November 1915 aged 38 years. He had enlisted in August 1914.

UK – 11         Can – 1
Bel – 25 (including 2 from WW2)

### LOCATION
Watou Churchyard is in the centre of the village that can be found 20km west of Ieper and about 8km west of Poperinge. It is 500m east of the French-Belgian border which is also one of the boundaries of the area covered by this book. The churchyard is located centrally in the village on the Watouplein. The graves are on the northern side of the church in two small Plots.

# WELSH CEMETERY (CAESAR'S NOSE)

### HISTORY
This cemetery was begun during the Third Battle of Ypres in July 1917 by the 38th (Welsh) Division and remained in use until November 1917.

### INFORMATION
For most of the war, the east side of the village of Boezinge directly faced the German front line. Located some distance from the road in the middle of fields, this is an isolated little cemetery positioned on the German front-line of 31 July 1917 at a point known as Caesar's Nose. It was named after a small German Salient that looked, on maps, like a nose. Though many of the burials are of the 38th (Welsh) Division, other units are also represented in the cemetery.

On 26 April 1915 the Lahore Division of the Indian Army pushed the Germans back from Colne Valley to the north and east of here as far as No Man's Cot. All the Battalions of the Lahore Division suffered heavy casualties. Serving in the Division were the 1st Manchesters, who by the end of the attack found most companies were being commanded by Sergeants. The attack cost 1943 men, the 47th Sikhs numbered two officers and 92 men, while the 40th Pathans had lost 30 officers and 300 men.

The 1st Welsh Guards of the 38th Division made a preliminary attack through here on 29 July 1917. The Division also took a large area from the Germans on 31 July 1917. During the attack Sergeant Robert James Bye gained the Victoria Cross by capturing two pill-boxes and accounting for 70 Germans.

Buried in Plot II, Row A are eight men of 'D' Battery, 92nd Brigade, Royal Field Artillery killed on 29 September 1917. All held the rank of Driver.

Also here is Captain Percy Lloyd Humphreys, 15th Welsh killed in action on 31 July 1917 aged 35 years. He had been a bank manager before the war but felt it was right to enlist which he did in 1914. He was soon commissioned and became a Captain before completing training with the Battalion. He saw service on the Somme, including at Mametz Wood. His unit were not in the first wave on 31 July but were to go over the top 20 minutes later. He was looking over the parapet from his trench when a shell landed nearby killing him instantly.

The Memorial to the Welsh Division is close by at Goumier Farm. See Minty Farm Cemetery for directions.

Also nearby is the Yorkshire Trench, a British dugout and trenches from 1917 excavated between the summer of 1998 and April 2000. The restored section of trench is only 57m in length, whereas the original was a system of many hundreds of metres. This restoration is a compromise between authenticity based on archaeological research such as the trenches at Passendale Museum in Zonnebeke or the German reconstructed trenches at Bayernwald, how long is it supposed to last, safety as many schoolchildren from across the world now visit the site, costs and aesthetics.

UK – 68  Unnamed – 6  Area - 395 sq mts

**LOCATION**
Welsh Cemetery lies in fields about 3km north of Ieper and about 2km south-east of Boezinge. It is reached most easily via Boezinge and the French Memorial on the Boezinge-Langemark road. Turn south past the entrance to Dragoon Camp Cemetery and then left at the crossroads reaching the path to the cemetery on the south side of the road in 400m.

## WESTHOF FARM CEMETERY

**HISTORY**
The cemetery was begun in May 1917 and remained in use until the German advance during the Battles of the Lys in April 1918.

**INFORMATION**
The cemetery was named after the farm that stood on the road here known as Waterloo Road, which served as Divisional headquarters for the New Zealand Division in May and June 1917. It also housed a Main Dressing Station in late 1917 until 1918.

There are 45 graves of men from artillery units. The Germans used the cemetery briefly in the summer of 1918 from the time they captured the area in April until it was retaken by the 36th (Ulster) Division in September 1918.

A soldier buried here was executed for desertion nearby when his unit had been withdrawn from the front-line. Rifleman Thomas Donovan, 16th (Church Lads Brigade) King's Royal Rifle Corps already had a poor service record when he absconded for the fourth time on 22 August 1917. He was captured on 1 September 1917, tried on 17 October and executed on 31 October 1917.

Also here is Gunner Cedric Wyndham, MM, 5th Divisional Trench Mortar Battery, Australian Field Artillery who died on 12 December 1917. He worked on the family farm until he enlisted in July 1915 with the 12th Light Horse. He soon transferred to the 6th Australian Infantry and served briefly at Gallipoli before becoming ill spending time in hospital in England. He returned to Egypt in February 1916 where he transferred to the 5th Divisional Field Artillery, where he served first as a Driver and then as a Gunner with the 5th Division's Trench Mortar Brigade. On 24 July 1917, Wyndham's unit was providing support to a party carrying out a trench raid when a German Howitzer made a direct hit on one of the gun pits. Under continuing heavy fire, Wyndham and two others quickly dismounted the mortar and moved it to another pit, and once again began firing for which Wyndham received the Military Medal. He was wounded a few days later but was soon back in the action. He was killed near Hollebeke.

UK – 73  Aust – 43  NZ – 14
Can – 1  Ger – 5
Area - 536 sq mts

Special Memorials to four British men and two New Zealanders whose graves here were destroyed by shell-fire.

**LOCATION**
Westhof Farm Cemetery is south of Ieper and about 2km south-west of Nieuwkerke. It is reached from the road south of Nieuwkerke by turning west at a junction, with a CWGC sign on the corner, in the hamlet of Le Maloy. The cemetery is on the south side of the road and is hidden by a house. This is an isolated little graveyard on the edge of the ridge, partly above the level of the road. The entrance is up a flight of steps but the effect of the slope is that some of the cemetery is at road level.

## WESTOUTER CHURCHYARD AND EXTENSION

**HISTORY**
The Churchyard and its Extension were used occasionally from November 1914 to September 1918.

**INFORMATION**
The two parts of this burial ground are almost indistinguishable, the only difference being that the two Plots are separated by a few yards. The Churchyard, containing twelve British graves and four Canadians, makes up Plot I and the Extension is Plot II. The burials in the churchyard date from 1915 and one from 1914.

Westouter is a pretty village with a green, sports area, church and several good cafe-bars. It lies on the edge of the Monts des Flandres, and it is clear to see how they dominated the battlefield.

After the First Battle of Ypres the 3rd Division came to camps in the village. Divisional headquarters was at Mont Noir Chateau with the day-time command post on the eastern slope of the Scherpenberg. It was always behind Allied lines though came within 3km of the front-line during Fourth Ypres (Battle of the Lys).

Buried here are brothers Private Charles Fredrick Robinson, 594th Motor Transport Company, Army Service Corps and Gunner James Alfred Robinson, 12th Battery, 35th Brigade, Royal Field Artillery who both died on 16

September 1917 and are buried in the same grave. Another brother, Private William Charles Robinson, 7th Duke of Cornwall's Light Infantry died on 24 August 1918 and is buried in London Cemetery and Extension on the Somme.

Also buried here is Lieutenant Colonel Alexander George Stuart, MiD, 40th Pathans, attached HQ as GSO1, 50th Division and late 2nd Royal Scots who died on 4 June 1916 aged 43 years. According to his Medal Index Card he was attached to Staff to be in charge of liaison with the press. He joined the Royal Scots in 1893, was commissioned to Captain in 1900, transferred to the Indian Army in 1904 and was promoted again to Captain in 1912. He held Staff appointments in India, and was Mentioned in Despatches. He was killed while carrying out a reconnaissance.

| | | |
|---|---|---|
| UK – 76 | Aust – 1 | NZ – 1 |
| India – 1 | Can – 19 | Ger – 3 |
| Unnamed – 1 | Bel – 2 | Area - 446 sq mts |

### LOCATION
Westouter Churchyard and Extension is found in the centre of the village which is 12km south-west of Ieper and 5km south of Poperinge. It can be found at the junction of the N315 and N398. Plot I is closer to the church while Plot II has been extended by the addition of Belgian civil graves.

# WESTOUTRE BRITISH CEMETERY

### HISTORY
This cemetery was begun in October 1917 and used until the German advance in April 1918 when this village came close to the front-line. It was used again from August to October 1918 and was enlarged after the war with the concentration of graves from the surrounding battlefields.

### INFORMATION
The cemetery, spelt in the French form still in use just after the war, was used by the French when they were defending the Monts des Flandres from April to August 1918 but their 72 graves have been removed. Approximately 50 British graves were concentrated here in their place.

The four WW2 burials all date from May 1940 and the retreat to Dunkirk. There is also one French WW2 burial.

Commemorated here by a Special Memorial is Major Eric Stuart Dougall, VC, MC, 'A' Battery, 88th Brigade, Royal Field Artillery, killed in action on 14 April 1918 aged 32 years four days after the act for which he was awarded the Victoria Cross. When the infantry had been pushed back to the line of artillery on the Kemmelberg, Acting Captain Dougall, unable to withdraw his guns, took command and formed a new infantry line just in front of the guns. He inspired and encouraged the troops who held the German advance for twelve hours but was ordered to withdraw at night when out of ammunition. Dougall was killed four days later while directing the fire of his Battery. His grave was destroyed in later fighting and is marked by a Special Memorial. The citation for his Victoria Cross reads 'For most conspicuous bravery and skilful leadership in the field when in command of his Battery. Capt. Dougall maintained his guns in action from early morning throughout a heavy concentration of gas and high-explosive shell. Finding that he could not clear the crest owing to the withdrawal of our line, Captain Dougall ran his guns on to the top of the ridge to fire over open sights. By this time our infantry had been pressed back in line with the guns. Captain Dougall at once assumed command of the situation, rallied and organised the infantry, supplied them with Lewis guns, and armed as many gunners as he could spare with rifles. With these he formed a line in front of his Battery which during this period was harassing the advancing enemy with a rapid rate of fire. Although exposed to both rifle and machine gun fire this officer fearlessly walked about as though on parade, calmly giving orders and encouraging everybody. He inspired the infantry with his assurance that "So long as you stick to your trenches I will keep my guns here". This line was maintained throughout the day, thereby delaying the enemy's advance for over twelve hours. In the evening, having expended all ammunition, the Battery received orders to withdraw. This was done by man-handling the guns over a distance of about 800 yards of shell-cratered country, an almost impossible feat considering the ground and the intense machine gun fire. Owing to Captain Dougall's personality and skilful leadership throughout this trying day there is no doubt that a serious breach in our line was averted. This gallant officer was killed four days later whilst directing the fire of his Battery.' Soon after the war began, being unable to return from India where he was working, he joined the Bombay Light Horse, and it was not till the end of 1915 that he arrived in England applying for a commission before moving to France in July 1916 taking part in the Battles of the Somme. In May 1917, he was promoted to Acting Captain as second in command of his

Battery. He was awarded the Military Cross for his actions on 7 June 1916 during the Battle of Messines. The citation reads 'For conspicuous gallantry and devotion to duty as Group Intelligence Officer and F.O.O. He took up a succession of observation posts in advanced and exposed positions, from which he successfully maintained communication with Headquarters. He was slightly wounded, but remained at duty and has frequently performed work requiring initiative under heavy fire with great coolness and gallantry.' He was involved in the retreat from the German assault in March 1918 and then moved north to Ypres, being promoted to Acting Major on 4 April. He was still officially a Lieutenant, though shown as Acting Captain in his citation, but was acting as a Major when he was killed.

There are three holders of the Meritorious Service Medal buried here which is unusual. The eligibility for this medal is open to Warrant Officers and non-commissioned officers above the rank of Corporal, or equivalent, who are of irreproachable character with at least twenty years of service and already hold the Long Service and Good Conduct Medal. This was difficult to achieve during the war so to find three such characters buried in one cemetery is in itself unusual. However, during 1916–1919, army NCOs could be awarded the medal immediately for meritorious service in the field which explains the comparative youth of the holders buried here who have not completed twenty years' service. They are Serjeant F M Ralph, MSM, North Riding Heavy Battery, Royal Garrison Artillery killed on 25 April 1918 aged 30 years; Quartermaster Serjeant Horace Harrington, MSM, Royal Army Medical Corps attached Assistant Director Medical Services, 5th Division died on 10 November 1917; and Company Quartermaster Serjeant Percy John Dix Farmer, MSM, 9th Norfolks died on 17 April 1918 aged 31 years.

Two cemeteries have been concentrated in Westoutre Military Cemetery. They are the Bikschote German Cemetery also known as 'Friedhof XI', which contained dead from 1914 and 1915, and the Kemmel French Cemetery No. 2 which was near the No. 1 Cemetery that we can still visit today.

On route to Westouter it is possible to drive onto the Scherpenberg. Turn from the N375 approximately 1km south of De Klijte as the road reaches a crest. This is onto a very small road that rises rapidly onto the Scherpenberg, there are hardly any passing places. However, there are some excellent views of the battlefields below the Scherpenberg as you can see to the Kemmelberg and beyond. Dug-outs still exist in the hill that were used in the war particularly during the German advance in 1918 when they were halted here by the French with limited help from British units.

UK – 162        NZ – 3         Can – 5
Chinese Labour Corps – 3      Unnamed – 52
WWII - 4 UK and 1 Fr          KUG - 2
Area - 1350 sq mts

Special Memorials to five British men known/believed to be buried among the unnamed.

**LOCATION**
Westoutre Military Cemetery lies about 200m north of the village green in Westouter which is south-west of Ieper. The cemetery is on the east side of the Westouter-Reningelst road. The cemetery is entered by means of a few steps and stands among the new housing on the northern edge of the village.

## WHITE HOUSE CEMETERY

### HISTORY
Begun in March 1915, by units holding the front-line nearby, the cemetery remained in use until April 1918. Over 700 graves were concentrated here after the war into what are now Plots III and IV as well as filling the other Plots.

### INFORMATION
The cemetery was near the site of forward dressing stations situated within cellars in 1915 in the village.

Among those buried here there are four men who were executed during the war and whose graves were concentrated here after the war. Private Herbert Henry Chase, 2nd Lancashire Fusiliers absconded during a German gas attack at Mousetrap Farm near Buffs Road Cemetery on 23 May 1915. This was his second offence of desertion. Chase was executed for cowardice at St. Sixtus Monastery, near Dozinghem Cemetery north of Poperinge, and buried nearby on 12 June 1915 aged 21 years while his unit were in camp near to Proven. It was stated that he had 'misbehaved before the enemy in such a manner as to show cowardice'. He had already faced a court martial in December 1914 for desertion in August 1914 for which he had been given a sentence of three years in prison commuted to a suspended sentence of two years hard labour. He was released from military prison in Rouen on 6 May 1915 just seventeen days before he deserted again. His remains were moved here in July 1919.

Private William J. Turpie, 2nd East Surreys deserted while his Battalion was moving from Vlamertinge to the front-line near Zonnebeke on 16 April 1915. He was one of the few deserters to reach England but was arrested two days after his arrival. Turpie was executed and buried near Dikkebus on 1 July 1915 aged 24 years. He was brought here in 1921.

Privates Alfred E. Eveleigh and Robert W. Gawler, both of the 1st Buffs (East Kents), had each previously deserted. Though joining at different times they had served together on the Western Front but by the end of 1915 both had convictions for desertion. Eveleigh enlisted in the Buffs late in 1905 at the age of 17. He joined his Battalion with a draft of 21 other men on 28 January 1906. Five months later he was awarded a 2nd Class Certificate of Education. On 27 September 1906 he embarked for South Africa. Gawler had enlisted a number of years after Eveleigh. Gawler had earlier in the war received a sentence of three months' imprisonment with hard labour, but had remained with the Battalion when his sentence was commuted to Field Punishment No. 1. Gawler was not deterred, and deserted twice more before being court martialled on 10 February 1916. At his trial he was undefended, but when the proceedings were reviewed, Brigadier-General C L Nicholson recommended that his death sentence be commuted on the grounds of Gawler's medical and family history. Three days after this trial, Eveleigh was also sentenced to death. They were executed together at 7.00am on 24 February 1916 at Burgomaster Farm, south-west of Poperinge, and buried nearby. Gawler was aged 20 at the time of his death and Eveleigh 27 years. They were moved here in July 1919 and are buried side by side.

Another man buried here with links to the Buffs is Brigadier General Julian Hasler, twice MiD, General Staff commanding 11th Infantry Brigade formerly the Buffs (East Kents), killed on 26 April 1915 aged 46 years. He attended Sandhurst Military Academy before joining the Buffs in 1888 as a 2nd Lieutenant, and being the recipient of regular promotions he became Lieutenant Colonel in 1910. He served extensively in Africa and on the North West Frontier in India, raising Hasler's Australian Scouts in the South African War where he was severely wounded. He went to the Front at the beginning of the war in command of his Battalion, and was wounded in October 1914. He returned to France in December, and at the end of February 1915 was promoted to Brigadier General and appointed to command the 11th Infantry Brigade. He had been twice Mentioned in Despatches. He was killed in action by a German shell on 26 April 1915 according to the CWGC, but a day later, according to other sources, when his Brigade took over the front line from Berlin Wood to Fortuin. General Bulfin, GOC 28th Division, commented 'I saw poor Julian Hasler on the 27 April, the place was being heavily shelled - I sent him up Grogan and Le Preu, my GSO2 and 3, to help him, and some signallers, but all the lines were constantly cut so I ordered him to get out as soon as it was dark. He was killed about 9 pm that night - he could have got out at 6 pm but delayed.' His brother, 2nd Lieutenant Algernon Hasler, 2nd Grenadier Guards was mortally wounded at Lesboeufs and died on 18 September 1916. He is buried in Heilly Station Cemetery.

Buried here is Private Robert Morrow, VC, 1st Royal Irish Fusiliers who died of wounds received at St. Juliaan on 26 April 1915 aged 24 years. The citation for his Victoria Cross reads 'For most conspicuous bravery near Messines on 12th April, 1915, when he rescued and carried successively to places of comparative safety, several men who had been buried in the debris of trenches wrecked by shell fire. Private Morrow carried out this gallant work on his own initiative and under very heavy fire from the enemy.' He joined the Battalion in 1911 and had previously done several actions which could have seen him killed such as crossing open ground under fire to get water. He was mortally wounded when again trying to rescue wounded men from his Battalion.

Three men holding the rank of Lieutenant Colonel are buried here. Lieutenant Colonel William 'Bill' Edward Green, DFC, TD, commanding 5th Northamptonshires died on 23 May 1940 aged 41 years. He began his military career as a World War I flying ace. He was credited with nine aerial victories while flying the Airco DH4, making him one of the few World War I aces who were bomber pilots. Green was commissioned a 2nd Lieutenant in August 1917. He completed training and was posted to No. 57 Squadron in September 1917 and scored his first victory in January 1918. His Distinguished Flying Cross was gazetted after the war in December 1918. The citation reads 'A skilful, courageous pilot and a brilliant leader, conspicuous for his sound judgment. No difficulties daunt him, and he has never failed to carry out any task that he may have been set. He sets a splendid example to the whole Squadron.' After the war he resigned his commission and then joined the Northamptonshires in the Territorial Force. He eventually became the Colonel of the Battalion and took them to France in WW2 where he was killed in the retreat to Dunkirk.

Lieutenant Colonel Henry William Ernest Hitchins, twice MiD, 1st Manchesters, was killed on 26 April 1915 aged 49 years. After Sandhurst he was commissioned as a 2nd Lieutenant to the 1st Manchesters in August 1886. He was promoted to Captain in May 1895. In 1906, by now a Major, Hitchins was posted to India. On the outbreak of war in 1914 he was temporarily in command of his Battalion which left India with the Lahore Division at the end of August. On 20 December 1914, during the fight for Givenchy, the Manchesters were was in action for 30 successive hours, and earned the name of 'The Gallant Manchesters'. He was Mentioned in Despatches for his actions at the capture of Givenchy on 20 December 1914 when he was wounded in the thigh. Recovering from injury Hitchins returned to command his Battalion on 1 April 1915. He was killed when shot through the heart and Mentioned in Despatches again.

Lieutenant Colonel Francis Alexander Umfreville Pickering, DSO, 2nd Dragoons (Royal Scots Greys) commanding 9th Rifle Brigade was killed on 23 December 1917. He was wounded in the South African War, had served on the Western Front in 1914, in Gallipoli in 1915, and as a Staff Officer in 1916 but volunteered to go back to the Front in 1917. On the night of 22/23 December 1917, a single shell landed near the dressing station at Waterloo Farm near Gravenstafel. Pickering had just arrived to check on his wounded men before leaving the front-line. He was struck by shrapnel along with his adjutant, Captain Joseph Buckley, and both men were killed. They are buried beside each other. He was awarded the Distinguished Service Order in the January 1917 New Years Honours List.

Also here are Private Harry Wharton, 7th King's Own Yorkshire Light Infantry, killed on 26 June 1916 and Private

Arthur Ernest Williams, 8th Canadian Infantry killed on 25 April 1915 both aged 16 years when they died.

Concentrated here:

Basseville Farm German Cemetery - situated just over 5km south-east of here on the Zandvoorde-Zillebeke road at the foot of Zandvoorde hill. It contained five British men killed in November 1914.

Bavaria House Cemetery – located about 1.5km east of here at the Advanced Dressing Station on the Zonnebeke road just east of Verlorenhoek. It contained seventeen British men, four Australians, three New Zealanders, four Canadians and one man of the British West Indies Regiment, who died from September to November 1917.

Bedford House Enclosure No. 1 - situated on the Ypres-St. Eloi road about 1km south of the town. It contained fourteen British men who died in 1915 and 1917.

Cottage Garden Cemetery - in St. Jan close to the church about 300m east of here. It contained 44 British men and one Canadian who died in 1914 and 1915.

Green Hunter Cemetery - close to the Den Groenen Jaeger Cabaret estaminet at a crossroads on the Vlamertinge-Voormezele road which is about 3.5km south-west of here. It contained twenty British men who died in 1915 and 1918.

Hengebarte Cemetery – 1.5km north of Dikkebus and about 4km south-west of here. It contained ten Royal Air Force men and fifteen Australians who died from 1915 to 1917.

North Bank Cemetery - also known as the Lankhof, this cemetery was situated about 400m south of Bedford House near the canal and about 2.5km south of here. It contained eleven Canadians killed in April and May 1916 but the cemetery was completely destroyed.

Wilde Wood Cemetery - north of the railway in Zonnebeke and about 3.5km east of here. It contained seventeen British men who died from July to September 1917.

| UK – 991 | Aust – 45 | NZ – 25 |
| Can – 85 | S Afr – 5 | Bermuda – 1 |
| BWI – 1 | India - 1 | Unnamed – 322 |

WWII - 9 (8 UK and 1 Bel)

Area - 4902 sq mts

Special Memorials to fifteen British men and one Canadian known to be buried here.

Special Memorials to twelve British men, eleven Canadians and five Australians buried elsewhere but whose graves were destroyed by shell-fire.

**LOCATION**

White House Cemetery is in the northern suburbs of Ieper on the north side of the road to St. Jan, called the Brugseweg or N313. This is about 1km west of the centre of St. Jan.

# WIELTJE FARM CEMETERY

**HISTORY**

This cemetery was used from July to October 1917 during Third Ypres.

**INFORMATION**

The cemetery is set back from the road in fields that were just behind British front-lines for much of the war. The farm from which it gets its name was destroyed in the war and never rebuilt.

There used to be another farm about 300m south of Wieltje Farm Cemetery called Prowse Farm, named after Major Charles Bertie Prowse, DSO, who led the 1st Somerset Light Infantry into action here during the German offensive in 1915 before being promoted to Brigadier-General in command of 11th Brigade.

Buried here is 2nd Corporal (Lance Corporal) Archie Forrest, 'P' Special Company, Royal Engineers who was killed on 26 August 1917 aged 20 years. The Special Companies of the Royal Engineers worked with gas. His Company were moving cylinders overnight from Poperinge for use in the front-line. He was hit by machine gun fire a little past midnight at St. Jan, on his way back to safety, and died of his wounds the same day.

Also here is Company Serjeant Major Arthur Henry Godfrey, DCM, 419th Field Company, Royal Engineers killed on 31 July 1917 aged 37 years. The citation for his Distinguished Conduct Medal, awarded in March 1916, reads 'For conspicuous gallantry and devotion to duty on several occasions, notably on a night when he assisted wounded men into cover at great personal risk. Also in the same place, when after being buried in his dug-out, he assisted others who had also been buried, and carried wounded men into safety under heavy shell fire.' He was at the time a Sergeant-Instructor in the 1/1st West Lancashire Field Company, Royal Engineers which was re-designated the 419th Company in January 1917. He had served in the army as a pre-war regular soldier and arrived in France on New Year's Eve 1914.

| UK – 113 | NZ – 1 | Can – 1 |
| Ger – 1 | Unnamed – 10 | |

Area - 480 sq mts

Special Memorials to twenty British men whose graves were destroyed in later fighting and have been lost.

**LOCATION**

Wieltje Farm Cemetery lies in fields about 2km north-east of Ieper between the N38 northern by-pass and the old road to St. Juliaan, the Brugseweg (N313). It is reached by a path from the N313 that is clearly marked by a CWGC sign.

# WOODS CEMETERY

## HISTORY
The cemetery was begun in April 1915 and remained in use until September 1917.

## INFORMATION
For further information about the fighting at 'The Bluff' please refer to 1st DCLI Cemetery.

The cemetery was begun by the 1st Dorsetshires and 1st East Surreys next to a wood in an area known as 'The Ravine'. The irregular shape of the cemetery is due to the conditions in which burials were made under fire at the times when the front line was just beyond the wood.

Many of the graves are men of the 2nd, 3rd and 10th Canadian Infantry or the London Regiment. The number of burials in Plot I, Row B is unknown but is thought to be six. Buried here is Private Joseph Fraser, 2nd Canadian Infantry, who died on 26 April 1916 aged 19 years. He was from the USA and one of many from that country who joined the forces of other countries to take part in the war before America joined in 1917. He enlisted in January 1915. The Germans shelled his Battalion's position, blew a mine under the line and launched an attack on 26 April 1916. His brother, Lance Corporal John Fraser, 1/9th Argyll and Sutherland Highlanders died on 10 May 1915 aged 25 years and is commemorated on the Menin Gate. Another brother, Lance Corporal George Fraser, 1st Canadian Infantry was killed on 15 June 1915 aged 25 years and is commemorated on the Vimy Memorial.

Also buried here is Serjeant Bugler Sydney Harvey Moxon, 1/15th (Prince of Wales' Own Civil Service Rifles) Londons, killed 25 October 1916 aged 38 years. He was a King's Trumpeter, an elite group of musicians who were obliged to perform at His Majesty's special request. He had also been a member of the Royal Society of Musicians since 1909 and had played with the London Symphony Orchestra since 1907. He and the LSO travelled to America in 1912 on the very first tour by a European orchestra. He came from a family of jewellers and was the only boy not to follow the family trade. He enlisted in September 1914, went to the Front in March 1915 and was killed while carrying a wounded man to safety.

The three cemeteries here are in Pallingbeke Park with benches, long grassed avenues and public artwork. They reflect the very social nature of the Belgian nation, where Saturdays and Sundays are still days for friends to gather and take part in a social activity organised by Trade Unions, the Church, Scouting movement or private groups making the weekend 'special', which is something I admire.

UK – 212  Aust – 3  Can – 111
KUG – 32  Area - 3181 sq mts

## LOCATION
Woods Cemetery is about 5km south of Ieper lying in fields halfway between the Comines and Warneton roads south-west of Zillebeke near Hill 60. There is a turn from the Comines road to several cemeteries about 200m south of the turn to Zillebeke. Near Chester Farm Cemetery is a left turn, at CWGC signs, on to a narrow road leading to the three cemeteries on 'The Bluff' that you can see in the fields to the south of the road. This is the nearest to the road of the three cemeteries associated with 'The Bluff'. Therefore, it is the most accessible of the group.

# WULVERGEM CHURCHYARD

## HISTORY
The churchyard was used from November 1914 to April 1915.

## INFORMATION
The village was close to the front-line in 1914 but was in Allied hands for most of the war. By February 1915 only two houses were still standing in the village. The Germans launched an unsuccessful gas attack here on 30 April 1916 when the line nearby was held by the 2nd Leinsters. Wulvergem fell to the Germans on 14 April 1918 during the Battles of the Lys but was retaken by the 30th Division on 2 September. The church was destroyed in the war and later rebuilt being completed in 1925 but a large number of the graves were lost.

Buried here is Squadron Serjeant Major Harry William Baker, 11th (Prince Albert's Own) Hussars who died on 30 October 1914 aged 36 years. A Regular with nearly 20 years' service, it was discovered, after his death, that Baker was a German. In 1915, his wife had to apply for a certificate to show she was British having married a German, which legally made her a German. She only discovered that she had married a German when she read in the paper that a Mrs Leibold had been prosecuted for not registering under the Aliens Restriction Order. The report went on that Mrs Leibold's son had been killed with the 11th Hussars while serving under the name of Baker.

Baker had come from Germany when he was less than three years old but had never been naturalised and, therefore, quite unknown to himself, had remained a German national. He was killed by shellfire while pointing out the location of enemy guns.

UK – 33          Unnamed – 1          KUG – 5

Special Memorials to 23 men whose graves were destroyed by shell-fire.

### LOCATION
Wulvergem Churchyard is in the centre of the village which is about 8km south of Ieper and can be reached either through Messines or Kemmel.

## WULVERGHEM-LINDENHOEK ROAD MILITARY CEMETERY

### HISTORY
The cemetery was begun in December 1914 and remained in use until June 1917. It was used again from September to October 1918 and was enlarged after the war with the concentration of graves from the surrounding battlefields.

### INFORMATION
See Wulvergem Churchyard for information about the battles here.

The burial ground begun by the 5th Division next to the Dressing Station here was first known as 'Wulverghem Dressing Station Cemetery'. By the time of the end of the war it contained 162 graves that now form Plot I. The other graves, in Plots II to V, were concentrated here after the war. Many of the men brought here were killed during the German Spring Offensive at Kemmel and during the break-out from the Salient.

Buried here are brothers Privates Thomas Day Hamblyn and William Charles Hamblyn, both 1st Wellington Regiment, NZEF with consecutive service numbers, and both killed in action on 8 June 1917. William was originally buried just south of the road from Wulvergem to Messines about midway between the two villages. Thomas was originally buried about 100m west of William.

Also here is Private Harry Sherman Pope, 3rd Canadian Infantry who died on 8 January 1916 aged 15 years. He enlisted in June 1915 while still only 14 years of age. The Battalion war diary states that he was 'shot and killed while working on C.T. (communication trench)....'.

Another buried here is Corporal George Cockshoot, MM, 2nd South Lancashires killed on 25 September 1918 aged 25 years. He was posted to the Front in July 1916 and was wounded for the first time in August 1916. He was wounded twice more as well as being buried by the results of shellfire. He was promoted to Corporal in April 1918 and was awarded the Military Medal for bravery on 27 June 1918. He was shot and killed by a sniper.

Concentrated here:

Auckland Cemetery - just east of the village on the road to Messines and on the north bank of the Douve. It contained twelve New Zealanders who died on the first day of the Battle of Messines, 7 June 1917.

Cornwall Cemetery - 140m west of Auckland Cemetery. It contained 21 British men, twenty of the 1st Duke of Cornwall's Light Infantry who died from December 1914 to January 1915. Two of those buried in this cemetery are now represented by Special Memorials as their graves were lost.

Frenchman's Farm – 1.5km north of Wulvergem. It contained 29 British men in several groups of graves, and one French 'Poilu', removed elsewhere, who died in 1914 to 1915. Five of those buried in this cemetery are now represented by Special Memorials as their graves were lost.

Nieuwkerke North Cemetery - situated in the river valley on the road to Lindenhoek. It contained twenty British men, sixteen of the 1st Royal Irish Fusiliers who died on 2 and 3 September 1918.

Nieuwkerke Railway Halt Cemetery - on the south side of the village. It contained fourteen British men, seven of the 1/9th (Queen Victoria's Rifles) Londons who died on 5 January 1915.

UK – 843         Aust – 35        NZ – 69
Can – 54         S Afr – 9        Unnamed – 352

Area - 4017 sq mts

Special Memorials to two British men known/believed to be buried among the unnamed.

Special Memorials to seven British men buried in cemeteries concentrated here but whose graves were destroyed by shell-fire and lost.

### LOCATION
Wulverghem-Lindenhoek Road Cemetery can be found about 700m west of Wulvergem and 8km south of Ieper. It is on the south side of the road from Wulvergem to the N331 Nieuwkerke-Kemmel road.

# WYTSCHAETE MILITARY CEMETERY

## HISTORY
This cemetery was made after the war with the concentration of graves from other cemeteries and isolated positions on the battlefield around Wijtschate.

## INFORMATION
The village, known to then troops as 'Whitesheet' was held by the French and British at the start of the war until the Germans attacked, and captured Wijtschate, on 1 November 1914. This was despite a defence by several Allied regiments to the east of the village. On 2 November 1914 troops from the reserve grouped to the west of this cemetery and attacked with the aim of driving the Germans from Wijtschate. This force included the 12th (Prince of Wales's Royal) Lancers, 800 men of the 1st Lincolnshires, 350 men of the 1st Northumberland Fusiliers from Kemmel, the 3rd (King's Own) Hussars, the 20th Hussars and a detachment of the French 32nd Division. In the early light of day the Lincolnshires and Fusiliers moved forward towards the village aiding the 1/14th (London Scottish) Londons in pushing the enemy across the Messines Road south of the village and reaching the area where you can now find Torroken Farm Cemetery. While the Germans were thus occupied the 12th Lancers and 20th Hussars attacked north of the village almost clearing it by 10.00am. However, German troops over-ran Wijtschate again and remained in the village until 1917.

The village was captured comparatively easily by the 16th (Irish) Division on the first day of the Battle of Messines, 7 June 1917. Wijtschate fell to the Germans during their Spring Offensive in 1918 on 16 April but was finally retaken on 28 September 1918.

Buried here is Captain William Lancelot Young, MC, 45th Australian Infantry killed on 7 June 1916 aged 26 years. He enlisted in February 1915 and sailed from Sydney to Egypt as a Quartermaster Sergeant in August 1915. He served at Gallipoli from October 1915 until the evacuation when he was deployed to garrison work on the Suez Canal. He received his commission in Egypt in February 1916 and was made a Captain. He was awarded the Military Cross in October 1916 after leading four raids at Ypres. The citation reads 'For conspicuous gallantry in action. He organised and led a raid against the enemy trenches with great courage and skill. He has previously done fine work.'

Next to the cemetery can be found the Memorial to the 16th (Irish) Division. It was unveiled on 22 August 1926 to commemorate the capture of Wijtschate by the Division. There are more recent memorials to the Division to be found in the local area such as that at the Maedelstade Farm complex and crater. There are also small memorials to the 36th (Ulster) Division.

The area of Maedelstade Farm was part of the German line before the Battle of Messines. The 250th Tunnelling Company, Royal Engineers created the mine that ran beneath the farm as well as other mines beneath Hollandsheschuur Farm and Peckham Crater. The mine at Maedelstade contained 94,000lbs of explosive at the end of a tunnel nearly 500m long. It made a crater 65m wide. This with seventeen others destroyed the German defences and allowed a great success in capturing the ridge on 7 June 1917. Slightly north of Maedelstade Crater are the Petit Bois Craters made by the same tunnelling Company but only using 30,000lbs of explosive. The Germans had blown two counter-mines in June 1916 destroying 250m of tunnel. The explosion trapped twelve Sappers, eleven of whom suffocated while one, an experienced miner, survived. Unlike most other tunnels in the war, this was partly made by the same type of tunnelling machine as was being used to create the railways and underground tunnels across the United Kingdom. The machine was abandoned and remains in its tunnel as it was being choked by the clay soil and only cut a total of 60m of tunnel.

Concentrated here:

Rest and Be Thankful Farm – 1.5km north of Kemmel and 2km north-west of here. It contained 23 British men, including thirteen of the 2nd Suffolks, who died in 1915.

RE (Beaver) Farm - near Kemmel on the road to Godezonne Farm Cemetery and just over 1.5km north-west of here. It contained eighteen British men and four Canadian Royal Engineers who died from 1915 to 1917.

Cemetery Near Rossignol Estaminet - 300m north of the Kemmel crossroads on main road and about 2.5km west of here. It contained eighteen British men, eleven of the 1st Wiltshires, who died from January to April 1915.

Gordon Cemetery - between the American Monument and La Laiterie Cemetery just over 1.5km west of here. It contained nineteen British soldiers, including fifteen from the Gordon Highlanders, who died from January to May 1915.

Somer Farm No. 2 - next to the present Somer Farm Cemetery on the east side of Wijtschate. It contained thirteen British men buried by the IX Corps in June 1917.

| | | |
|---|---|---|
| UK – 511 | Aust – 31 | NZ – 7 |
| Can – 19 | S Afr – 11 | KUG – 423 |
| Ger – 1 | Unnamed – 673 (67%) | |

Area - 3267 sq mts

Special Memorials to sixteen British men known/believed to be buried here among the unnamed.

Special Memorials to nine British men buried in other cemeteries concentrated here, four British men buried at Rossignol Estaminet, three British men buried at R.E. (Beaver) Farm and two British men buried at Rest And Be

Thankful Cemeteries, whose graves were destroyed in fighting and have been lost.

**LOCATION**
Wytschaete Military Cemetery lies on the western edge of Wijtschate village, south of Ieper, on the north side of the road to Kemmel. It is 300m from the town square.

# YPRES RESERVOIR CEMETERY

**HISTORY**
Opened in October 1915 the cemetery remained in use until shortly after the war when it contained about 1100 graves. It was doubled in size after the war with the concentration of 1500 graves.

**INFORMATION**
There were three cemeteries made in this area near the old western gate of Ypres, two of which were concentrated here in the third, known during the war as the 'Cemetery North of the Prison' and then 'Ypres Reservoir North Cemetery' before it gained its present name. It was used for the burial of men who died near or in Ypres, many at the ADS stationed here. It was given its name after the war so that relatives did not think their men had died in prison. The area used to be known as the 'Plien d'Amour', the 'Plain of Love'. This was an area of common ground situated between the inner and outer fortified walls of the town. It was widely used as a place of recreation by the townspeople as well as for animals to graze. It is now occupied by a school and sports area. Due to the location near the Plein the cemetery was sometimes colloquially known as 'Love's Place Cemetery'.

There are graves of officers and men of the 6th Duke of Cornwall's Light Infantry who were killed in the vaults of the Cathedral, which was often used by troops billeted in or passing through Ypres, when it was shelled on 12 August 1915. At 6.15am the Germans began to shell the area but the men in the cloisters, thinking they were safe, did not move. The German guns got their range, directed by the pilot of a German aeroplane who had spotted an observation post in the Cathedral tower, so the first direct hit brought down most of the west end and buried several men. The enemy continued to fire for five hours. Many of the men who went to rescue their comrades were themselves buried and when the warning was conveyed to Battalion HQ Major Barnett and the adjutant Lieutenant Blagrove ran over to the cloisters to try to get the men out but were also instantly killed. The survivors were rescued by men of the 11th King's (Liverpools), the 14th (Light) Division Pioneers, but the dead were not recovered until after the war.

Among those buried here are three men who were executed in Ypres Prison for desertion during the war. Private Thomas Lionel Moles, 54th (2nd Central Ontario) Canadian Infantry, originated from Somerset and had previously served in the British Army. He enlisted in July 1915 and already had a poor record when he was tried for desertion on 4 October 1917. He was executed on 22 October 1917 aged 28 years.

Private Ernest Lawrence, 2nd Devonshires deserted on 5 May 1917 having taken the chance whilst on a ration run. He reached Rouen before he gave himself up. He was taken back to his regiment and sent back up to the front line but he deserted again on 8 May, was recaptured again in Rouen but this time with false documents, escaped and took up work repairing aircraft for the RFC, before he was captured in August once more. Lawrence was executed on 22 November 1917.

Private Charles F. McColl, 1/4th East Yorkshires served well from 1914 until wounded by a shell at Neuve Chapelle in September 1916 and invalided home with heart failure to recover. He was sent back to the Front with the 1/4th East Yorkshires and deserted almost immediately. He was sentenced to ten years imprisonment which was suspended so he went back to the Front. He then deserted again on 28 October 1917 near Houthulst Forest and made his way to Calais. He was caught four days later, brought to trial and was executed on 28 December 1917. He was held in a military prison at Brandhoek, then on the eve of his execution brought to the prison at Ypres. As dawn approached he was manacled and blindfolded with a reversed gas mask, taken out and strapped to a chair to be executed.

Buried here is Brigadier General Francis Aylmer Maxwell, VC, CSI, DSO & Bar, MiD, General Staff, commanding 27th Infantry Brigade, 9th (Scottish) Division late 18th King George's Own Bengal Lancers, killed in action on 21 September 1917 aged 46 years. The citation for his Victoria Cross, won at Korn Spruit on 21 March 1900 during the South African Wars when he was a Lieutenant in the Indian Staff Corps attached to Roberts's Light Horse, reads 'Lieutenant Maxwell was one of three Officers not belonging to "Q" Battery, Royal Horse Artillery, specially mentioned by Lord Roberts as having shown the greatest gallantry, and disregard of danger, in carrying out the self-imposed duty of saving the guns of that Battery during the affair at Korn Spruit on 31st March 1900. This Officer went out on five different occasions and assisted to bring in two guns and three limbers, one of which he, Captian Humphreys, and some Gunners, dragged in by hand. He also went out with Captain Humphreys and Lieutenant Stirling to try to get the last gun in, and remained there till the attempt was abandoned. During a previous Campaign (the Chitral Expedition of 1895) Lieutenant Maxwell displayed gallantry in the removal of the body of Lieutenant-Colonel F D Battye, Corps of Guides, under fire, for which, though recommended, he received no reward.' In 1910 he was ADC to Lord Kitchener who was at that time Commander in Chief in India. He was awarded the Distinguished Service Order for his services during the Tirah Campaign in 1897-8. He was awarded a Bar to the DSO in November 1916 for leading his Battalion under fire. He was created a Companion of the Order of the Star of India in 1911.

Also buried here is Brigadier General Arthur Cecil Lowe, CMG, DSO, Royal Field Artillery, Commander Royal Artillery (CRA) of 66th Division, formerly Honourable Artillery Company who died on 24 November 1917 aged 49 years. He served in the South African Wars for which he was awarded the Distinguished Service Order. He became Commander Royal Artillery (CRA) in the 66th Division in August 1917.

Another here is Colonel Augustus 'Gussie' David Geddes, MiD, 2nd Buffs (East Kents) who died on 28 April 1915 aged 48 years. He was killed by a shell during Second Ypres while he was in command of the 'Geddes Detachment' as it became known which was formed by 23 April 1915. This force included his own regiment, the Buffs, and three others, given the task of filling a gap in the line to prevent the Canadians being outflanked. They played a fluid role without a defined line of command for several days in the gas and confusion of Second Ypres. Geddes had spent the night before his death at 13th Brigade Headquarters at St. Jan and was about to leave for Potijze to re-join his regiment when he realised he had lost his map. He asked Brigadier General O'Gowan for another and whilst the General was out of the room to find a map for him a shell landed in the room. Colonel Geddes was killed and his two staff officers, Major H C M Makgill and Lieutenant J Nicholls, were seriously wounded. He was posthumously Mentioned in Despatches in May 1915. He joined the Buffs in 1887 and served in the South African War where he was severely wounded. After he recovered he was a staff officer to the Base Commandant (DAAG) in South Africa until 1902. He held other staff posts and was fluent enough in Russian to act as an interpreter. He took command of his Battalion in 1911. He had two brothers who were also senior officers, Brigadier-General John Gordon Geddes and Lieutenant-Colonel George Hessing Geddes.

There are ten men holding the rank of Lieutenant Colonel buried here. Lieutenant Colonel John Wyndham Maxwell, DSO, MC, 7th Rifle Brigade attached 8th King's Royal Rifle Corps died on 4 December 1917 aged 36 years. He joined the army in September 1914 as a Lieutenant in 7th Rifle Brigade. He was made a Captain in 1915 and was attached to the Royal Berkshires in 1916. Back with his own Battalion he became a Major in 1916 and became commanding officer of the 8th King's Royal Rifle Corps in 1917. He died of wounds received at Passendale when he was hit by shellfire. He was awarded the Military Cross in 1916 and a posthumous Distinguished Service Order in the 1918 New Year's Honours List.

Lieutenant Colonel Edward Robert Burne, DSO, six times MiD, 15th Brigade, Royal Field Artillery died on 1 October 1918 aged 42 years. He served in the South African Wars where he was Mentioned in Despatches. He was Mentioned in Despatches a further five times in WW1. He was awarded the Distinguished Service Order in the 1916 New Year's Honours List.

Lieutenant Colonel Everard Ferguson Calthrop, MiD, 38th Brigade, Royal Field Artillery died on 19 December 1915 aged 39 years. He served in the South African Wars where he was Mentioned in Despatches. He was the Military Attaché in Tokyo from 1914-1915 where he wrote a translation of 'Art of War' by Sun Tzu, though he also served in Japan from 1904-08 and 1910-14. He was given permission to return to Europe arriving in France in September 1915 shortly before he was killed.

Lieutenant Colonel George Augustus King, DSO & Bar, five times MiD, Croix de Guerre (France), 1st Canterbury Regiment, NZEF, died on 12 October 1917 aged 32 years. He joined the New Zealand forces in 1910 and served in Gallipoli for which he was awarded the Distinguished Service Order. He was given command of the New Zealand Pioneer Battalion in February 1916 after recovering from wounds received at Gallipoli. This Battalion under his command was so respected that it gained the nickname 'diggers' after which all ANZAC units became known. He was killed during an artillery barrage on his Battalion headquarters and awarded a posthumous Bar to his DSO. The French Croix de Guerre was awarded because the New Zealand Pioneers were temporarily attached to the French in 1917. He and Lieutenant Colonel Alfred Winter-Evans, DSO, DCM, twice MiD, 3rd New Zealand Rifle Brigade, NZEF, were the highest ranking New Zealand officers to die on 12 October 1917 when 845 men were killed in just four hours which was their worst day of war for New Zealand. Māori soldiers of the New Zealand Pioneer Battalion performed a waiata tangi, normally reserved for high-ranking chiefs, during his funeral.

Lieutenant Colonel Richard Percy Lewis, MiD, Devonshire Regiment attached 1/10th Manchesters died on 7 September 1917. He played first class cricket in 36 matches for Oxford University, the MCC and Middlesex from 1894-1907. He was involved in the South African Wars being commissioned into the Devonshires in 1901. In 1904, he was appointed to the Central Africa Battalion of the King's African Rifles and took part in the Nandi Expedition of 1905-1906, being Mentioned in Despatches. In 1908, he was appointed to the Egyptian Army, and was in Egypt as an intelligence officer for some time after war broke out. He took command of the Manchesters in early 1917. He died of wounds after he was hit by a splinter from a shell during a heavy bombardment near the villages of Frezenberg and Westhoek. He was also a member of Surrey Cricket Club.

Lieutenant Colonel John McDonnell, 5th Leinsters attached 1st Royal Inniskilling Fusiliers died on 29 September 1918 aged 40 years. In 1897 he joined the 5th (Militia) Battalion of the Leinster Regiment and served with them during the South African War. In August 1914, he was called up and for the greater part of the war served on the staff at Queenstown in Ireland. After some months in command of his old Battalion, he was sent in August 1918 to join the 1st Royal Inniskilling Fusiliers in France. His son, Lieutenant

Robert Edward McDonnell, 8th King's Royal Irish Hussars, Royal Armoured Corps (Desert Rats) died of wounds on 16 February 1941 and is buried in Benghazi War Cemetery.

Lieutenant Colonel Athelstan Moore, DSO, twice MiD, 1st Royal Dublin Fusiliers died on 14 October 1918 aged 38 years. He joined the Fusiliers in 1899 and served with them in the South African Wars where he was Mentioned in Despatches and awarded the Distinguished Service Order. He was seconded to the West African Field Force in December 1902, and saw active service in 1903 in the Kano-Sokoto Campaign, Northern Nigeria, in Southern Nigeria from 1903-6 including the Bende-Onitsha Hinterland Expedition for which he was again Mentioned in Despatches. Having been promoted to Captain in 1908 he went to New Zealand in 1911 when he was appointed Instructor in Infantry Duties of the Otago Military District moving on to be Brigade Major of the Otago Infantry. He commanded the 2nd Otago Regiment on the Suez Canal in 1914-15, landing in Gallipoli in April 1915. In November of the same year he was severely wounded. He rejoined the Otago Regiment in France in May 1916, and was transferred to command the 2nd Royal Munster Fusiliers in August 1916 fighting with them on the Somme until the end of 1916 when he was wounded again. He commanded the Dublin Fusiliers from April 1917. He died of wounds received at Dadizeele.

Lieutenant Colonel Audley Charles Pratt, DSO, three times MiD, 11th Royal Inniskilling Fusiliers died on 16 August 1917 aged 43 years. He was commissioned to the 1st Royal Scots in 1895, and was promoted Lieutenant in 1896, and Captain in 1902. He served with his Battalion in the South African War, where he was Mentioned in Despatches. He retired in 1913. In August 1914 he re-joined the army as second-in-command of the 9th Royal Irish Fusiliers and in August 1916 he was given command of the 11th Royal Inniskilling Fusiliers. He recieved the Distinguished Service Order in the 1917 New Year's Honours List and was twice Mentioned in Despatches during the war. He was killed by a shell outside his dug-out on the morning that he was on his way up to Battalion Headquarters before an attack.

Lieutenant Colonel St. Barbe Russell Sladen, TD, 5th commanding 1st Queen's (Royal West Surreys) died on 12 March 1918 aged 45 years. A pre-war Territorial soldier he was a Major by August 1914. He began the war in command of civilians building a defensive line around London. He was desperate to get back to his Battalion, who had volunteered for overseas service, and were being sent to India. He made it back in time to leave in late October 1914 arriving in December 1914. He returned to England in October 1915 to take up the command of the 2/5th Queens in expectation of serving overseas with it but by 1917 he discovered it was about to be demobilised. He applied for another position and was attached to the 1st Queens in France. Sladen was on the point of accepting an offer from the commanding officer of 1/5th Queens, still out in India, to resign his command letting Sladen take over, when a training ground accident to the commanding officer of 1st Queens saw Sladen appointed to command. He was one of a few Territorials to command a 'Regular' Battalion. On 8 March 1918 he took temporary command of 19th Infantry Brigade while the Brigadier was on leave and, while on a tour of inspection of the front line, was killed by a shell near Passendale.

Lieutenant Colonel Norman McDonald Teacher, DSO, four times MiD, 1st Royal Scots Fusiliers died on 26 September 1917 aged 39 years. He was commissioned in 1898, served in the South African Wars and was a Captain by 1904. He became a Major in 1915 and a Lieutenant Colonel in April 1917 when he took command of the Battalion. He was awarded the Distinguished Service Order in the 1916 New Year's Honours List. His son, Lieutenant Commander Norman Joseph McDonald Teacher, DSO, HMCS Quebec, Royal Navy was killed in WW2 on 28 February 1943 when he was the commanding officer of Combined Operations Pilotage Party (COPP) 3 which was lost on a reconnaissance operation of the southwest coast of Sicily in preparation for the invasion, and is commemorated on the Portsmouth Naval Memorial.

A further highly decorated senior officer is Major Fred Davenport, DSO, MC, MiD, 'A' Battery, 295th Brigade, Royal Field Artillery who died on 25 September 1917 aged 44 years. He was posthumously awarded the Distinguished Service Order in January 1918. The citation reads 'For conspicuous gallantry and devotion to duty. Under an intensely concentrated and accurate hostile bombardment of his Battery position he superintended the withdrawal of his men to their dug-outs, but on his way back was buried by a shell which destroyed the mess in which he had been compelled to take refuge. The instant he was extricated he reorganised his Battery and answered two S.O.S. calls before taking part in an offensive barrage. He conducted the latter with complete success under very difficult conditions, the original orders having been destroyed. It was entirely due to his gallantry and invariable cheerfulness under fire that the fire of his Battery was available during the whole of this critical and important period.' His Military Cross is gazetted at the same time for the extraction of a burning ammunition dump in a gun pit at Ronssoy Wood in August 1917. The citation reads 'For conspicuous gallantry and devotion to duty. During an intense hostile bombardment of his Battery position, he returned with volunteers after his detachment had been withdrawn, and extinguished a burning gun pit containing over 100 rounds of ammunition, setting a splendid example of fearlessness and presence of mind.' A Sergeant and two Gunners were awarded a Military Medal while two other officers also received the Military Cross. In the same month Davenport was also Mentioned in Despatches in 35th Divisional Orders. He was killed 'by a direct hit by an 8 inch mortar on 'A' Battery Mess.'

Buried side by side are brothers, Major James Leadbitter Knott, DSO, 10th West Yorkshires killed on 1 July 1916 on the Somme aged 33 years and Captain Henry Basil Knott, 9th Northumberland Fusiliers killed on 7 September 1915 aged 24 years. They were sons of Sir James Knott who owned the Prince shipping line, among the largest lines in the world at the time. After their death, he sold the Prince line and created a trust for charity work. He also commemorated his sons through his provision of the bell tower at the Church of St. George in Ypres. As I write, 100 years later, the church is raising money to install bells in the tower. He tried to have the boys repatriated but as he was not allowed to do this. For him, the next best thing was to have them together, though they died in different battles, which he achieved after the war. James' Battalion was almost wiped out in 1 July 1916 on the Somme at Fricourt, losing over 700 casualties including all senior officers.

Also here are brothers Private John Thomas Dixon, 1st Lancashire Fusiliers killed on 9 October 19018 aged 27 and Serjeant William Dixon, 12th Durham Light Infantry killed on 20 September 1917 aged 26 years. John was killed in hand to hand fighting near Geluveld. William was killed by shrapnel while supplying the line near Sanctuary Wood.

Private Gavin Gordon Bulkeley Gavin and Lance Corporal James Tinnock Bulkeley Gavin, both 26th Australian Infantry and both killed on 4 October 1917, are buried a few graves apart in the same row. Both arrived in France in May 1917 but their first time in the front-line was 2 October and they were both mortally wounded in the attack on the Broodseinde Ridge. Gordon was originally buried at Tyne Cot but moved here at the request of his parents in 1922.

Also buried together are Privates Sydney Styles and William Styles, 1st Grenadier Guards both killed on 20 March 1916. They had arrived in France on 1 May 1915 and saw their first action at Festubert in June. Another brother Private Henry A Styles, 2nd Middlesex, was killed in action on 18 May 1916 and is buried in Aveluy Communal Cemetery.

Private Albert Isherwood, 12th Manchesters who died on 17 December 1915 aged 21 years lost two brothers in the war. Private John Isherwood, 20th Manchesters died on 1 February 1917 aged 27 years and is buried in Etaples Military Cemetery. Private Peter Isherwood, 20th Royal Fusiliers died on 18 December 1916 aged 30 years and is commemorated on the Thiepval Memorial.

Buried here is Captain Eric Waterlow, MC, DFC, MiD, No. 25 Squadron, Royal Air Force died on 16 July 1918. He enlisted into the 10th Canadian Mounted Rifles in December 1914 and was commissioned into the Royal Flying Corps in May 1917. He died when he was pilot of a photographic mission to Tournai in a DH4 that left the airfield at 1.20pm accompanied by Lieutenant James Matthew Mackie as photographer. They encountered Sergeant Piechulck from the German Jagdstaffel 56 and were shot down near Pilkem at 2.40pm. He was awarded the Military Cross in June 1918. The citation reads 'For conspicuous gallantry and devotion to duty. He carried out two long range reconnaissances, flying at a very low altitude, and brought back most valuable information. During one of these flights he was attacked by a hostile scout, which he destroyed. He has carried out four exceptionally long flights, during each of which he took a great number of photographs. He has always undertaken himself the longest and most arduous operations given to his flight, and by his skill, gallantry and determination has on each occasion completed his task with the greatest success.' He was posthumously awarded the Distinguished Flying Cross in September 1918. The citation read 'This officer has carried out thirty-three bombing raids and over forty solo photographic and long-distance reconnaissances far over the enemy lines. In one flight he took no less than 108 photographs. In these services he has proved himself an exceptionally skilful and resolute pilot; his railway reconnaissances have been markedly successful.' Mackie is commemorated on the Arras Flying Services Memorial.

Another of note is Pioneer Arthur Edwin Wood, 123rd Canadian Pioneers who died on 21 October 1917 aged 33 years. Wood was a world amateur and professional track and cross country champion who held many world titles. To train and improve, on leaving work, he would race against his family's homing pigeons to see if he could beat them home. As a member of the Essex Beagles he was chosen to represent England in the amateur International Cross Country Championships of 1908, 1909 & 1910. In the latter two years he won becoming international and what was then considered 'world' champion. In late 1910 he took the major step of leaving Waltham Abbey and travelling to the USA to seek his fortune as a professional runner where he beat America's best. He became Ten and Fifteen Mile World Champion, and in May 1912, during the world 15 mile championship, he broke three world lap time records and became world champion. He retired from professional running in 1915 and moved to Ontario where he became a farmer. He was called to war service with Tom Longboat and other athletes in March 1916, joining the 180th (Sportsmen) Canadian Infantry and moving to the Pioneers in February 1917. He died as one of twenty soldiers of 'C' Company killed by a high explosive shell that hit their Platoon as they marched towards Ypres.

Captain Lewis Robertson, 1st Cameron Highlanders died on 3 November 1914 aged 31 years. He was commissioned in 1902 and played rugby while stationed with his regiment in the United Kingdom. He played for several sides including London Scottish and captained the Army. He represented Scotland nine times between 1908 and 1913. He was wounded on 2 November but returned to the line where he was mortally wounded.

Young soldiers buried here include Private Herbert Alfred Dancer, 6th King's Own Yorkshire Light Infantry who died on 20 September 1915 aged 16 years. He is commemorated by a Special Memorial as he was first buried in Ypres Reservoir Middle Cemetery but his grave has been lost. He had arrived in France on 21 May 1915 and saw action at Hooge when flame throwers were first used. Private Patrick Finn, also 6th King's Own Yorkshire Light Infantry, also died on 20 September 1915 aged 16 years, was also buried in Ypres Reservoir Middle Cemetery and moved here after the war. He joined the Battalion as a draft on 20 June 1915 and died in the same action as Dancer.

Concentrated here:

Ypres Reservoir South Cemetery - situated between the prison and the reservoir. It was also called 'Broadley's Cemetery' and 'Prison Cemetery No. 1'. The cemetery contained eighteen British men buried between October 1914 and October 1915.

Ypres Reservoir Middle Cemetery - just north of the 'South' cemetery. It was also called 'Prison Cemetery No. 2' and 'Middle Prison Cemetery'. The graveyard contained 107 British men, 41 of the 6th King's Own Yorkshire Light Infantry, and one Belgian who were buried in August and September 1915.

Infantry Barracks Cemetery - also known as 'The Esplanade'. It contained fourteen British men, ten of the 6th Siege Battery, Royal Garrison Artillery, buried from April 1915 to July 1916.

| UK – 2255 | Aust – 143 | NZ – 28 |
| Can – 151 | NF – 4 | S Afr – 12 |
| BWI – 6 | Guernsey – 2 | India – 1 |
| Ger – 1 | KUG – 10 | Unnamed – 1035 |

Area - 11924 sq mts

Special Memorials to two British men known/believed to be buried among the unnamed.

Special Memorials to ten British men buried in cemeteries concentrated here, two British men buried at the Infantry Barracks and eight British men buried in Ypres Reservoir Middle Cemeteries, whose graves were destroyed by shell-fire.

**LOCATION**

Ypres Reservoir Cemetery is in the north of the town not far from the Grote Markt. The easiest route by car is via the Elverdingsesstraat and a turn at the prison There are a number of other routes through the town to the cemetery but it is easy to get lost. However, it is worth trying to walk through the back streets of Ieper to the cemetery as a good way to take in the atmosphere of the town. The cemetery is on the south side of the Maarschalk Plumerlaan, named after Field Marshal, Viscount Plumer, architect of the successful Battle of Messines. This cemetery provides an excellent view of the spires of the town.

# YPRES TOWN CEMETERY

**HISTORY**

This burial ground was used by the British Army from October 1914 until May 1915 and again for one burial in 1918.

**INFORMATION**

The Town Cemetery is a large graveyard that is still in use and there are British burials in many locations. There is a small group in the south corner against the Menin Road but the largest group is to the left of the main path.

The British section is interesting in the way that the chaotic nature of a communal graveyard has had the same effect on the usually organised layout of a CWGC cemetery. There are a large number of IWGC and CWGC burials and also a small Belgian Military Cemetery. The sites are also used by the Commonwealth War Graves Commission for its own permanent staff and their families, with alternative designs of headstones slightly set apart.

The earliest burial was that of Lieutenant Philip John Egerton, 1st Borders who died on 17 October 1914. The last and only burial in 1918 was that of Private Ralph Kinsay, 1/5th York and Lancasters who died on 6 June 1918.

One of the most notable graves is that of Lieutenant Prince Maurice Victor Donald of Battenberg, KCVO, MiD, 1st King's Royal Rifle Corps, killed in action at the Broodseinde Ridge on 27 October 1914. He was the youngest grandchild of Queen Victoria. His cousins fought on the German side. The Battenbergs were hereditary enemies of the Hohenzollerns and had been treated by Bismarck and Kaiser William II very badly. His nephew was known to us, once the family anglicised its name during the war, as Earl Mountbatten. His father was Prince Henry of Battenberg, son of Prince Alexander of Hesse. His mother was Princess Beatrice, youngest child of Queen Victoria. His eldest sister became Queen of Spain from 1906 to 1932. He was mortally wounded by shrapnel and died before his men could take him to safety.

Lieutenant Colonel Charles Bernard Morland, twice MiD, 2nd Welsh was killed on 31 October 1914 aged 47 years. He was commissioned into the Welsh Regiment in February 1887 and saw service in the South African War as a Captain and Adjutant of his Battalion, becoming a Major at the end of the war. He was promoted to Lieutenant Colonel in March 1914 and appointed commanding officer of the 2nd Welsh. The Battalion was at Bordon on the outbreak of the war and arrived in France on 13 August. Following the Retreat from Mons and the subsequent actions along the Aisne, Morland was Mentioned in Despatches before First Ypres. On 31 October his Battalion were almost destroyed by German shellfire. In the early afternoon, Morland was standing in a trench, with officers of several Battalions also depleted of men, discussing how Geluveld could be retaken when a shrapnel shell burst in front killing an officer and mortally wounding Morland. At the same time an order had been sent to make Morland temporary commander of 3rd Brigade which arrived after he had been taken back to a Dressing Station in Ypres where he died.

Captain The Honourable Arthur Annesley, 10th (Prince of Wales's Own Royal) Hussars was killed on 16 November 1914 aged 34 years. He was the eldest son of the 11th Viscount Valentia and 1st Baron Annesley. He was an excellent polo player, winning many championships in India. He joined the 10th Hussars in April 1900 serving in the South African Wars becoming a Captain in 1907. He served as ADC to Major General the Honourable Julian Byng in Egypt from 1912-14. He was killed in action by a sniper a month after arriving in Belgium.

Captain The Honourable Andrew Edward Somerset Mulholland, 1st Irish Guards, died on 1 November 1914 aged 32 years. He was son of the 2nd Baron Dunleath who was MP for North Londonderry from 1885-1895. He joined the Guards in 1906 and became a Captain in 1913. His Battalion were in action from August 1914 and had spent two weeks at Ypres, in and out of action, before he was killed. At about 2.00pm he was hit by a bullet while rallying his men in Polygon Wood, and died at 9.00pm.

Major The Honourable William George Sidney Cadogan, MVO, MiD, Cross of Honour of the Order of the Crown (Kingdom of Württemberg), 10th (Prince of Wales's Own Royal) Hussars and General Staff was killed on 12 November 1914 aged 35 years. He was son of the 5th Earl Cadogan. He played a single match of first-class cricket, for the 'Europeans' team in the 1904 Bombay Presidency Match, in which he scored no runs during a comprehensive defeat. He joined the Hussars in 1899 and saw action in the South African Wars. In March 1906, he was made Honorary ADC to George, Prince of Wales (later King George V), and made a Member of the Victorian Order. He was also an equerry to the Prince of Wales (later Edward VIII) from 1912-14 having been promoted to Major. He went with the Hussars to France in October 1914 and was killed when shot in the groin.

Major Lord Charles George Francis Mercer-Nairne Petty-Fitzmaurice, MVO, Legion of Honour (France), Order of Military Merit (Spain), Order of the Crown (Prussia), Order of the Iron Crown Class II (Austria), 1st (Royal) Dragoons attached Staff, 6th Cavalry Brigade was killed on 30 October 1914 aged 40 years. He was son of the 5th Marquess of Lansdowne. He was made a Member of the Victorian Order in 1911. He joined the 1st King's Dragoon Guards in 1895, and served as an aide-de-camp to Field Marshall Roberts during the South African Wars remaining with Roberts until 1904. From 1909 he was an equerry to the Prince of Wales and King George V until he was killed in action. Mercer-Nairne was positioned within the Chateau Hollebeke holding back the Germans when killed.

Major Arundell Neave, MiD, Chevalier of the Legion of Honour (France), 16th (The Queen's) Lancers was killed on 21 February 1915 aged 39 years. He was one of five officers of the Lancers killed, with four buried here side by side, in an attack by the Germans at Shrewsbury Forest that began at 6.00am. A cousin, Airey Neave, MP, would be murdered in the car park of the House of Commons by the Irish National Liberation Army in 1979. A Conservative, Airey Neave was the first British officer to escape from Colditz Castle in WW2.

Another from the Lancers killed in the attack is Captain Edward Radcliffe Nash, MiD, 16th (The Queen's) Lancers killed on 21 February 1915 aged 26 years. He was an excellent sportsmen in athletics and riding representing Great Britain at the Stockholm 1912 Olympics in Equestrian events. His brother, Captain Llewellyn Charles Nash, 2nd King's Royal Rifle Corps was killed a few months later on 28 September 1915 aged 29 years and is buried in Lapugnoy Military Cemetery.

Honorary Lieutenant and Quartermaster Edmund Wilkinson, DCM, MiD, Long Service and Good Conduct Medal, 1st Loyal North Lancashires died on 31 October 1914 aged 43 years. He joined his regiment in 1888 when he was 15 years of age and saw action in the South African Wars for which he was awarded the Distinguished Conduct Medal, by which time he was the Battalion's Colour Sergeant. He rose through the ranks and was commissioned in June 1912 and sailed to France on 12 August 1914. He was killed near Geluveld in an action that saw the Battalion reduced to one officer and 35 men, for which he was subsequently Mentioned in Despatches.

Lieutenant George Garth Marshall, 11th (Prince Albert's Own) Hussars was killed on 4 November 1914 aged 29 years. He joined the Hussars in 1907 and became ADC to Lieutenant-General Sir E H Allenby, commanding the Cavalry Corps just before the war. He was killed by shellfire while carrying a despatch from Allenby to Haig, the commander of I Corps. He was great-grandson of the 4th Earl of Aberdeen.

Captain Arthur Craven 'Kid' Charrington, 1st (Royal) Dragoons was killed on 20 October 1914 aged 32 years. He was an amateur jockey who once, at the Simla Race Meeting, rode thirteen winners and one second out of fifteen mounts. He was also a good polo player.

Captain Frederick Alexander Charles Liebert, North Somerset Yeomanry formerly 3rd Dragoon Guards (Prince of Wales' Own) was killed on 17 November 1914 aged 32 years. He was born in Bruges, a few kilometers north of Ypres, and joined the army for a short period before becoming a 'Territorial' with the North Somerset Yeomanry in December 1905. He was made a Captain at the start of the war and his unit went to France on 26 October arriving in the Salient on 12 November. He was killed a few days later in the first action his Battalion faced. He was killed in a front-line trench as he turned to call up more men when a piece of shrapnel hit him in the back of the head.

Also of note here is Pierre Vandemnbraambussche, OBE who died on 6 April 1936 and is buried in the civilian section. He was Commissioner of Police in Ypres in the 1920's and became a key founder of the Last Post Committee responsible for the nightly ceremony at the Menin Gate. He is near the wall by the Menin Road.

UK – 144   India – 1   IWGC – 49
Bel – 23   Unnamed - 9

**LOCATION**

Access to Ypres Town Cemetery is very much like that to other cemeteries in the town. It is far easier to walk than it is to bring a vehicle. Walk to the Menin Gate from the Grote Markt and continue up the hill. The Town Cemetery is behind high walls on the right of the Roselare and Zonnebeke road 200m beyond the traffic lights. One wall backs onto the Menin Road not far from the Menin Gate but there is no entrance from this side.

# YPRES TOWN CEMETERY EXTENSION

## HISTORY
Begun a few days after the first British burial in the Town Cemetery in October 1914, the Extension remained in use until February 1915. It was used again in 1918, after the war for the concentration of widely scattered graves, and also in World War II.

## INFORMATION
The extension was enlarged after the war when 367 graves were brought in from small cemeteries and isolated positions east and north of Ypres. The Extension is also used by the CWGC for its own staff and their families, with alternative designs of headstones.

One notable grave is that of Lieutenant Lord Charles Sackville Pelham Worsley, 'C' Squadron, Royal Horse Guards killed while taking part in the defence of Zandvoorde on 30 October 1914, aged 22 years. He was son of the 4th Earl of Yarborough and related by marriage to Haig. His body was buried by the Germans when every man of the unit was killed defending their position. He was transferred here by the British after the war in 1921, the original grave site having been identified by the Germans during the war when a map of his burial location was passed on via diplomatic channels to the British, which enabled them to relocate his grave in December 1918. The Memorial to the Household Cavalry at Zandvoorde stands on the spot where his body was found.

There were 43 World War II burials made in the Extension when Ypres fell after heavy fighting in 1940. The Allied Commanders had tried to make their stand at Ypres, as had been done in World War I. But Hitler's army was stronger than the Kaiser's had been, and the British and French were weaker, so the attempt failed. During and after the fighting of May 1940, three civilian hospitals in the town, Hopital de Notre Dame, the Clinique des Soeurs Noires and the Red Cross Hospital in St. Aloisius School, D'Hondstraat, cared for the wounded, and those who died were buried in the Town Cemetery Extension. Others buried on the battlefield were later brought in.

Buried here is Colonel Frederic Walter Kerr, DSO, twice MiD, 1st Gordon Highlanders attached as GSO1 of 1st Division HQ Staff, General Staff killed on 31 October 1914 aged 47 years. He is one of several officers killed when a German shell hit the 1st Division HQ at Hooge Chateau which was the headquarters for various units including, at times, Sir John French and Douglas Haig before French was removed and Haig promoted. He joined the Highlanders in 1886 and was involved in the storming of the Malakand Pass in the Chitral Expedition in 1895 for which he was awarded the Distinguished Service Order. He served in the South African Wars and was Mentioned in Despatches being Mentioned again posthumously. On 31 October 1914, during the First Battle of Ypres, the Staffs of the 1st and 2nd Divisions were in conference in Hooge Chateau when shells fell on the meeting. The first shell landed in the garden and drew the officers to the window. The second shell landed in front of the widow. The 2nd Division commander, Monro, had moved to another room, but the 1st Division commander, Lieutenant-General Lomax, was severely wounded and returned home where he died of his wounds on 10 April 1915. Only one officer was unhurt and most were killed. Major George Paley, Rifle Brigade, GSO2 1st Division HQ Staff, aged 42 years; Lieutenant Colonel Arthur Jex Blake Percival, DSO, Cross of the Legion of Honour, Northumberland Fusiliers attached to 2nd Division Staff, General Staff aged 43 years; Captain Francis Maxwell Chevenix Trench, MiD, Royal Field Artillery attached as Brigade Major Royal Artillery, 2nd Division Staff, aged 36 years and Captain Rupert Ommanney, Royal Engineers attached as GSO3 2nd Division Staff aged 36 years are all buried here.

Another here is Captain Alfred Squire Taylor, Royal Army Medical Corps attached 10th/11th Highland Light Infantry who died on 31 July 1917 aged 29 years. He was a Rugby Union international playing four times at centre for Ireland. Having served in Mesopotamia, on the Somme and at Arras, he was killed near Frezenberg on the first day of Third Ypres while tending to the wounded. Lieutenant James Young Milne-Henderson, MiD, a Scottish International in the 10th/11th Highland Light Infantry, was killed in action on the same day and is commemorated on the Menin Gate.

Private Fred Castle, 1st Coldstream Guards was killed on 29 October 1914 aged 23 years. His brother, Private John Castle, 8th Loyal North Lancashires was killed on 18 July 1917 aged 32 years and is commemorated on the Menin Gate. Another brother, Rifleman George Castle, 4th King's Royal Rifle Corps was killed on 25 May 1915 aged 19 years and is also commemorated on the Menin Gate. A fourth brother, too young for WW1, Gunner Oliver Castle, 336 Battery, 104 Heavy Anti-Aircraft Regiment, Royal Artillery died in WW2 on 3 April 1941 aged 34 years and is buried in Longborough (St. James) Churchyard.

Among those buried here killed in WW2 is Sergeant Karel Pavlik, No. 313 (Czech) Squadron, Royal Air Force Volunteer Reserve killed on 5 May 1942. He rests alongside fellow pilots who were killed above and around Ypres during a dogfight, when five Spitfires were downed during the disastrous Operation Circus 157 mission. Circus 157 was the code-name for an Allied bombing attack on Lille by six Bostons covered by 24 Spitfires which failed due to the cloud level over the target. The bombers and their Spitfire escort turned for home. At about 3.30pm the group was intercepted and a dog-fight between the Spitfires and 21 German FW 190s took place. The other pilots who were shot down were Czechoslovak Squadron Leader Frantisek Fajtl who survived and escaped; Belgian Flight Lieutenant Baudovin Marie Ghislain De Hemptinne, No. 122 (RAF) Squadron, Royal Air Force Volunteer Reserve, now buried in the Brussels Town Cemetery Belgian Airmen's Field of Honour having been moved there from this cemetery after the war; Canadian Sergeant Pilot Rolland Albert Joffre Ribout, No. 122 (RAF) Squadron, Royal Canadian Air Force aged 31 years and Flight Sergeant Stacey Douglas Jones, No. 122 (RAF) Squadron, Royal Air Force Volunteer Reserve both buried here. Several other pilots only just managed to return home due to severe battle damage. No German aircraft were later confirmed as being lost that day. Pavlik crashed on the slope of the Kemmelberg (Mont Kemmel) and his plane was recovered, with his body still in the pilot's seat, in May 1945, when he was laid to rest with his comrades. Ribout fell to his death in Nieuwkerke because his parachute did not work. Engine-problems caused Jones to crash near Poperinge. Hemptinne was injured and although he managed to land his plane near Dranouter he died shortly afterwards. There is a memorial erected for Pavlik near the Kemmelberg, one to Ribout at Ploegsteert and one for de Hemptinne on the village square of Dranouter.

Concentrated here:

Dragoon Camp - 300m south of Potijze and about 750m east of here. It contained 24 British men, including twenty of the 11th Argyll and Sutherland Highlanders, who died in June and July 1917.

La Premiere Borne - on the south side of Menin Road near this cemetery. It contained twenty British graves.

Ypres Benedictine Convent Grounds - it contained ten British men buried from July to September 1915. Four were moved here and six to the Reservoir Cemetery.

| UK – 597 | Aust – 13 | Can – 15 |
|---|---|---|
| S Afr – 1 | India – 1 | Ger – 2 |
| Unnamed – 141 | | IWGC – 22 |

WWII - 42 UK and 1 Canadian (13 unidentified)

Special Memorials to sixteen British men believed to be buried here among the unnamed.

**LOCATION**

Directions are as for the Town Cemetery but the Extension is at the west end of the Communal area and has its own entrance from the road. This is much smaller than the main burial ground and is separated from it by a wall and hedge. It is set back from the road behind houses.

# ZANTVOORDE BRITISH CEMETERY

**HISTORY**

The cemetery was created after the war with the concentration of graves from the surrounding battlefields.

**INFORMATION**

On the morning of 26 October 1914 the trenches of the 1st South Staffordshires and 2nd Borders, in the fields that you can see between Kruiseeke and Zandvoorde, were destroyed by shell-fire. The Borders were overwhelmed and the Germans outflanked the 2nd Scots Guards and 1st Grenadier Guards so that when Lord Dalrymple of the Scots eventually surrendered it was with only five surviving men. On 29 October 1914 the ridge running north from here towards the Menin Road was thinly held by the 2nd Royal Scots Fusiliers and 1st Royal Welsh Fusiliers who had been in action since 19 October. Throughout the day the Germans attacked believing the line to be strongly defended, but a combination of valiant defence and German incompetence - shells landing in the midst of their own machine-gun sections - meant that the line held until the evening when the surviving officers decided it was time to fall back from a position that was now almost surrounded. Only 120 wounded men reached the new British line closer to Ypres, and of the Welsh Fusiliers only 86 returned.

On the 30 October approximately 350 men of the 1st and 2nd Life Guards held the front-line on the slopes of Zandvoorde hill. It was bombarded for over an hour with heavy guns and then taken by the 39th German Division and three attached Battalions. In the German attack that took place a Squadron of each Life Guards regiment became isolated as the message to withdraw had not reached Captain Lord Hugh Williams Grosvenor commanding his Squadron of the 1st Life Guards. Hence, his men gave up no wounded and no prisoners, every man dying at his post. Lord Grosvenor was related by marriage to General Haig, then commanding I Corps, who heard of the loss of Zandvoorde while at his headquarters a few miles away.

The British bodies were buried by the Germans. That of Lord Worsley was buried by Leutnant von Neubert of the 1st Bavarian Jaeger Regiment who made a map of the exact site of the burial and sent it via the War Office in Berlin to Worsley's home. After the war Worsley's body was recovered and buried in Ypres Town Cemetery Extension. Lord Worsley should not have been in the line at all as his regiment, the Royal Horse Guards, had been relieved by the Life Guards. Lord Worsley and a machine-gun section had remained behind. The situation was made worse for these cavalrymen because they were dismounted, an undignified position for the premiere cavalry troops of the British Empire.

The line from Zandvoorde to Geluveld, held by the 1st Queen's (Royal West Surreys), 2nd King's Royal Rifle Corps, 1st Loyal North Lancashires and 1st Royal Welsh Fusiliers, was attacked by thirteen German Battalions who followed a heavy bombardment with an attack which broke through between the Queen's and King's Royal Rifle Corps. The Queen's lost their commanding officer so another officer was sent to headquarters for orders, but when he returned and searched for his Battalion he could not find them. They had lost 624 men. As the line was forced back, the 1st Loyal North Lancashires, who were ordered to cover the retreat, lost 400 men.

The battle continued for two weeks but even the German Kaiser, Wilhelm II, had come to realise that Ypres would not fall easily. On 2 November he withdrew from his forward headquarters at Kortrijk having become frustrated at the inability to head his victorious army through Ypres as he had demanded on 31 October. It was at this time that the proud survivors of First Ypres heard the Kaiser had called them a 'contemptible little army' and happily took on the nickname the 'Old Contemptibles'.

The village could not be retaken and remained in German hands until 28 September 1918.

The cemetery contains the bodies of many men who fell in this area in 1914 but because of the nature of the fighting, and the fact that they were buried by Germans, the identity of the soldier buried in each grave was often lost. Hence, most of the graves concentrated into this cemetery after the war are unnamed.

Buried here is Captain James Anson Otho Brooke, VC, 2nd Gordon Highlanders killed on 29 October 1914 aged 30 years. The action for which he was awarded the Victoria Cross was that he, while still a Lieutenant as he was promoted to Captain posthumously, led the attacks on Geluveld under heavy fire, recapturing lost trenches, and preventing the enemy from breaking the line when no reserves were available. He was killed later in the day. The citation reads 'For conspicuous bravery and great ability near Gheluvelt on the 29th October, in leading two attacks on the German trenches under heavy rifle and machine-gun fire, regaining a lost trench at a very critical moment. He was killed on that day. By his marked coolness and promptitude on this occasion Lieutenant Brooke prevented the enemy from breaking through our line, at a time when a general counter-attack could not have been organised.' This was the same action in which Major Stucley (below) was killed. Brooke had been awarded the Sword of Honour at Sandhurst. He was originally buried near the crossroads, now a roundabout, east of Geluveld on the Menin Road.

Serjeant Louis McGuffie, VC, 1/5th King's Own Scottish Borderers was killed on 4 October 1918 aged 24 years. The action for which he was awarded the Victoria Cross happened a few days before his death. The citation reads 'For most conspicuous bravery and resourceful leadership under heavy fire near Wytschaete on 28th September, 1918. During the advance to Piccadilly Farm, he, single-handed, entered several enemy dugouts and took many prisoners, and during subsequent operations dealt similarly with dugout after dugout, forcing one officer and twenty-five other ranks to surrender. During the consolidation of the first objective he pursued and brought back several of the enemy who were slipping away, and he was also instrumental in rescuing some British soldiers who were being led off as prisoners. Later in the day, when in command of a platoon, he led it with the utmost dash and resource, capturing many prisoners. This very gallant soldier was subsequently killed by a shell.' The advance began at 5.30am under cover of a smoke barrage but they had to make several attempts during the day to take and hold their objectives. All officers were killed or wounded so McGuffie had to take charge of a Platoon and was at the front of several attacks on bunkers and machine gun positions. He was originally buried about 2km east of here.

Major Humphrey St. Leger Stucley, MiD, King's Company, 1st Grenadier Guards was killed on 29 October 1914 aged 37 years. Stucley was second in command of the Battalion who had been in Belgium since 7 October and by 29 October thinly, having lost many men, held the line south of the Menin Road between Zandvoord and Geluveld. He was bringing his Company to the front-line where they were desperately needed, but they had to advance under heavy machine-gun fire and suffered terrible casualties. Stucley ignored all cover and dashed forward at the head of the King's Company determined to save the situation. In the hail of bullets he fell shot through the head. Losses in the Battalion were very heavy so that only four officers and 100 men retired that night to Hooge and the Germans had little idea of how few men stood between them and victory at Ypres in 1914. He was the son of the late 'Sir' George Stucley, 1st Baronet and had served in Egypt in 1898 and in the South African War. He was originally buried near Brooke. His son, Major Lewis Robert Carew Stucley, Grenadier Guards, Brigade Major, 201st Guards Brigade was killed in action on 16 September 1943 aged 32 years and is buried in Bone War Cemetery in Algeria.

Major (Brevet Lieutenant-Colonel) Henry William Crichton, DSO, MVO, twice MiD, Legion of Honour, Royal Horse Guards was killed on 31 October 1914 aged 42 years. He was Viscount Crichton, son of the 4th Earl of Erne. He fought in the South African Wars where he was Mentioned in Despatches and awarded the Distinguished Service Order. He was ADC to the Duke of Cornwall (later King George V) on his Colonial tour in 1901 and became his equerry when he became Prince of Wales between 1901 and 1909 and then Extra Equerry between 1909 and 1914. He was made a Member of the Royal Victorian Order in 1906 and was decorated with the award of the Legion of Honour (4th Class). By 30 October the unit were fighting as infantry in trenches to the east of the village. The Germans launched an overwhelming attack forcing the Horse Guards to withdraw but Crichton was one of the two Squadrons cut off and destroyed. For his actions he was again Mentioned in Despatches. He was originally buried in Wervik Communal Cemetery.

Lieutenant Colonel Beauchamp Tyndall Pell, DSO, twice MiD, 1st Queen's (Royal West Surreys) died of wounds on 4 November 1914 aged 48 years. He joined the army in 1887, served on the North-West Frontier in India from 1897-98 where he was Mentioned in Despatches, and was posted to China in 1900 for which he was awarded the Distinguished Service Order and again Mentioned in Despatches. He then saw action in the South African Wars.

He served on Staff until he took command of the 1st Queens in September 1914. On 31 October his Battalion were overwhelmed by the German attacks, many being killed as they retreated into Geluveld which had already been captured by the Germans. Only two officers and twelve other ranks succeeded in escaping. Pell was wounded and his men tried to carry him back on a stretcher. They were captured and Pell taken to the 15th German Army Hospital where he did not survive an operation so they buried him in Wervik Communal Cemetery. His brother, Major Albert Julian Pell, 9th Suffolks died of a cerebral hemorrhage on 28 August 1916 aged 52 years having served as Divisional Musketry Officer, Northern Area, Western Command and on Staff for much of the war until his death.

Private Thomas Reilly, 2nd Gordon Highlanders was killed on 18 June 1915 aged 16 years.

Also of note is Follower Sher Sing, Followers Central Depot, 34th Division who died on 2 October 1918. Like most other Hindu soldiers killed in the war he was, by the traditions of his religion, cremated as soon as possible after his death. His original grave marker, a cross, was placed about 6km south-west of here near the Ypres-Comines canal. But like all Hindu soldiers in the war they now have a grave marker even though there are, or should be, no remains present. However, mistakes were made at the time reflecting the lack of cultural awareness in the early part of the century.

The Memorial to the Household Brigade, 200m from the town square on the road to Comines is set back from the road and reached by a small path from the road. Unveiled by Earl Haig in May 1924, it stands on the spot that Lord Worsley's body was found in 1914 as the land had been purchased by Worsley's mother.

Concentrated here:

Kruiseeke German Cemetery - at the north end of Kruiseke about 4km south of here. It contained 138 British men most of whom died in October and November 1914.

Wervik German Cemetery - on the north side of the road to Comines about 4km south-east of here. It contained two British men and one Canadian.

UK – 1525     Aust – 2     Can – 22
India – 1     WW2 - 1
Unnamed - 1135 (70% of total)
Area - 4766 sq mts

Special Memorial to a British soldier known/believed to be buried among the unnamed.

Special Memorials to 32 British men buried in German cemeteries but whose graves are lost.

**LOCATION**

Zantvoorde Cemetery lies on the eastern edge of the village of Zandvoorde on the north side of the road to Kruiseeke. This is about 6km south-east of Ieper and is reached most easily via Geluveld. An interesting return route to Ieper is via Zillebeke, which brings you by the south side of Shrewsbury Forest across the battlefield of 1914 on an uncomfortable cobbled road that the 'Tommies' must have experienced. You should pass Battle Wood and just to the east of Hill 60 before descending into Zillebeke. You can see the importance of holding the high ground and the ridges towards the north and west from here.

# ZILLEBEKE CHURCHYARD

**HISTORY**

The churchyard was mainly used in 1914 but a few burials were made later in the war, two in 1915 and six in 1916.

**INFORMATION**

Zillebeke was in the front-line for much of the war and its buildings were destroyed by the fighting. This area became the scene of heavy fighting when, in October 1914, the Irish Guards held the village. From 1914 the positions around the lake were taken over by artillery. The 10th Siege Battery, Royal Garrison Artillery, were stationed here and lost over twenty men in two weeks.

From the beginning of 1915 the Cavalry Corps held the village until the 18th (Eastern) Division relieved them in July. On 28 March 1915 a raid on trenches east of the village captured a German officer who warned of the gas attack that we now know as the start of the Second Battle of Ypres. However, his story seemed so improbable that it was ignored at the time. Zillebeke fell to the Germans in April 1918 but was retaken in September.

In the early days of the war, whilst the front line was still mobile, specific cemeteries for soldiers were comparatively rare and the dead were often buried in local churchyards or municipal burial grounds near where they were killed. Hence, typical of that period, some of the earliest burials in the Salient were made in this churchyard, including fourteen from the Foot Guards or Household Cavalry. Many early war casualties lie here, including several members of the aristocratic pre-war regulars.

There are some unusual headstones, breaking the 'equality in death' principle the Commission was founded under, that seem to be made by families and not the CWGC. In some respects this can be called an 'Aristocrats' Cemetery'. The six burials of 1916 are the Canadians buried here. A number of French graves have been removed.

One of my favourite tombstones is that of Lieutenant-Colonel Gordon Chesney Wilson, MVO, twice MiD, Legion d'Honneur, Royal Horse Guards, killed in action on 6 November 1914 aged 49 years. Carved upon the headstone are the words 'Life is a city of crooked streets, death is the market place where all men meet'. He was commissioned in 1888 and became a Lieutenant Colonel in 1911 taking command of the regiment. He served in the South African War, where one of his brothers died, as ADC to Major General Robert Baden-Powell, founder of the Scouting movement. He was made a Member of the Victorian Order at the end of the war. He was also one of two Eton boys who disarmed Roderick MacLean when he tried to assassinate Queen Victoria in 1882. The Royal Horse Guards landed at Zeebrugge on 7 October 1914 and had fought several actions before arriving at Ypres on 16 October. Wilson was killed near Zandvoorde whilst leading his Regiment in the attack to retrieve the situation when 1st Irish Guards and 2nd Grenadier Guards had been exposed by the retirement of French troops. He was married to Lady Sarah Isabella Augusta Spencer-Churchill, youngest daughter of the 7th Duke of Marlborough and aunt to Winston Churchill. His brother, Captain Herbert Haydon Wilson, DSO, twice MiD, Royal Horse Guards was killed on 11 April 1917 aged 42 years and is buried in the Faubourg d'Amiens Cemetery, Arras. In the London 1908 Olympics Herbert was a member of the British polo team Roehampton, which won the gold medal.

There are two private grave markers. 2nd Lieutenant Baron Alexis George de Gunzburg, 11th (Prince Albert's Own) Hussars attached Royal Horse Guards died on 6 November 1914 aged 27 years. Born in Russia and living in Paris, he was a naturalised subject of the United Kingdom in August 1914 so that he could serve in the British Army for whom he had offered himself as an intelligence officer. He was killed working as an interpreter while carrying a message, while crossing an open field having had no military training, for Lord Kavanagh, the Brigade Commander to Lieutenant-Colonel Gordon Chesney Wilson.

The other is for Lieutenant John Henry Gordon Lee Steere, 3rd Grenadier Guards who was killed on 17 November 1914 aged 19 years. He arrived at the Front on 3 November with the 2nd Grenadier Guards, though officially still with the 3rd Battalion who did not go abroad until August 1915. He had taken over command of his Company after the death of Captain Symes-Thompson, also buried here. After trying to find the sniper responsible, he himself was shot through the head.

Killed in the same action is Captain Cholmeley Symes-Thompson, 2nd Grenadier Guards who died on 17 November 1914 aged 33 years. He was commissioned in 1899, became a Captain in 1910 and moved from the 1st to the 2nd Battalion in August 1914, many men moving in the other direction to bring both Battalions up to strength. The Germans launched a heavy bombardment on the morning of 17 November, one of the last dates of action in First Ypres, followed by an infantry attack in the afternoon. An early casualty was Captain Cholmely Symes-Thompson commanding No. 1 Company shot by a sniper.

Lieutenant The Right Honourable Henry Bligh Fortesque Parnell, 5th Baron Congleton, MiD, 2nd Grenadier Guards died on 10 November 1914 aged 24 years. He was commissioned in 1911 while still at Oxford University and joined his Battalion on the Aisne in September 1914. He was Mentioned in Despatches for the skilful handling of his Platoon on 6 November 1914 when his Platoon had stopped a group of Germans getting through the gap which he had been able to hold between the Royal Sussex and the Cavalry. He was killed when shot through the heart when leading No. 3 Company. He had two brothers, John Brooke Molesworth Parnell, a Lieutenant in the Royal Navy, who succeeded him as 6th Baron. The other was Lieutenant The Honourable William Alastair Darmer Parnell, MC, No. 4 Company, 2nd Grenadier Guards who joined the Guards in 1915 and was killed on 25 September 1916 aged 22 years at Lesboeufs on the Somme and is buried in Guards' Cemetery, Lesboeufs.

Major Lord Bernard Charles Gordon-Lennox, MiD, 2nd Company, 2nd Grenadier Guards was killed on 10 November 1914 aged 36 years. He was the third son of the 7th Duke of Richmond and Gordon. He served in the South African Wars and in China. He appeared in a single first-class cricket match for Middlesex in a victory against Gloucestershire in the 1903 County Championship. He was killed by German shellfire and was Mentioned in Despatches in January 1915. He had two sons, one of whom, Lieutenant-General George Charles Gordon-Lennox, DSO, MiD, served in WW2 winning a Distinguished Service Order. Bernard's grandson was also a Major General. The other is Rear-Admiral Sir Alexander Henry Charles Gordon-Lennox, KCVO, CB, DSO who served in WW2 and the Malayan Emergency. The 8th Duke and Brigadier-General Lord Esmé Gordon-Lennox were his elder brothers. His wife was killed in 1944 when a German V1 'doodlebug' hit the Guards Chapel in London.

Major Robert Edward Rising, DSO, MiD, 1st Gloucestershires was killed on 7 November 1914 aged 43 years. He was commissioned in 1892 and, after India, served in the South African Wars. He was awarded the Distinguished Service Order for his actions in command of three Platoons at Langemark on 23 October 1914. The citation reads 'he went up with supports and conspicuously controlled the defence of the Battalion's trenches against a determined attack by the enemy.' His was among the first Distinguished Service Orders to be awarded when gazetted on 9 November 1914 and he was later Mentioned in Despatches. He was killed, by now second in command of the Battalion as a Captain (he was promoted posthumously), as they moved forward in two lines to occupy German trenches that they had incorrectly been informed had already been captured. They came under heavy fire and many men had to lie in the open all day before they could find their way back to their trenches. His headstone bears the inscription 'Dulce et decorum est Pro patria mori.'

Lieutenant The Honourable William Reginald Wyndham, Lincolnshire Yeomanry attached 1st Life Guards, was killed on 6 November 1914 aged 38 years and is commemorated here by a Special Memorial. He was commissioned in 1896 in the 17th (Duke of Cambridge's Own) Lancers. He did not go with the regiment to South Africa and in 1903 he was badly injured in a riding accident. With the Regiment being under orders to serve in India, he resigned his commission later gaining a commission in the Lincolnshire Yeomanry. He joined the Life Guards on 8 October 1914 seeing his first action on 27 October. He was killed as his unit moved forward to support the 4th (Guards) Brigade his body being recovered that night. He was the third son of the 2nd Baron Leconfield.

Lieutenant Colonel Arthur De Courcy Scott, 1st Cheshires was killed on 5 May 1915 aged 49 years, one of only two officers buried here who did not die in 1914. He was commissioned in 1885, saw active service in the Burma operations of 1887-89 and then in India before taking part in the South African Wars with the 2nd Cheshires. Back in India he became a Major in 1907 and moved to France in January 1915. He transferred, and was promoted, to command the 1st Cheshires on 1 May 1915 as they suffered such high casualties. He led them for the first time in action between the railway and Hill 60 where he was killed a few days later. His father was a Major General in the Royal Engineers who saw action in the Crimean War at the Siege of Sebastopol.

Those buried here in 1916 are all Canadians, some of whom were killed in the battles nearby on Mount Sorrell, Hill 62 and other ridges. Two were killed outside the churchyard on 7 June 1916 when a shell burst among No. 5 Platoon at 11.45am as they were marching past towards the front-line. They are Private John Carron Sime and Private William John Croft, 'B' Company, 24th (Victoria Rifles) Canadian Infantry. It would seem there were enough remains of some men to carry them for burial elsewhere, but two had to be buried almost where they were killed.

The church has been rebuilt over the remains of the original which was destroyed during the war. In the church there is a stained glass window installed as a memorial to 2nd Lieutenant Harold Avenal Blight St. George, 1st Life Guards who was killed in action on 15 November 1915.

The village is at the east end of Zillebeke Lake, which was created in the Medieval period to provide fish for Ypres. The lake can be reached by a path from opposite the church to the eastern point of the lake, known as Hellblast Corner.

UK – 22        Can – 10
Unnamed – 6 (2 UK and 4 Can)
Area - 743 sq mts
Special Memorials to two British men whose graves here have been destroyed by shell-fire.

**LOCATION**
Zillebeke Churchyard is in the centre of the village which is east of Ieper and reached through either Shrapnel or Hellfire Corners.

# MISCELLANEOUS CEMETERIES
## Ten or Fewer WW1 CWGC Burials

**BAS-WARNETON (NEERWAASTEN) COMMUNAL CEMETERY** – the village is about 8km just west of south from Ieper. It lies between the N58 and the French border. The cemetery is on the southern edge of the village on the banks of the River Lys close to the canal. The casualties here are all men killed within a few days in the withdrawal to Dunkirk in May 1940. Among those here is Lieutenant Giles Bill Clutterbuck, 1st Oxford and Bucks Light Infantry, killed on 27 May 1940. His cousin, Lieutenant Peter Clutterbuck, 1st East Yorkshires, was killed in action on 20 October 1914 and is commemorated on the nearby Ploegsteert Memorial. Both men killed years apart in the early actions of two wars and commemorated less than 5km apart.

**BOEZINGE CHURCHYARD** - Boezinge churchyard is in the centre of the village which lies just west of the main road from Ieper to Diksmuide. All the British graves are on the far side of the church from the road. In 1914 two British officers were buried here but one grave was moved. The churchyard was also used in May 1940. The church, St. Michael's, was rebuilt after the war and now contains four 17th Century tapestries that depict the life of St. Franciscus Xaverius (1506-52), one of the earliest missionaries to China and India. There is also a plaque to the French 87th Territorial Infantry who suffered so greatly nearby during the first gas attack in 1915. They have another Memorial on the other side of the canal. There is a Belgian 'Demarcation' Stone in centre of the village. It is one of a series along the front line in Belgium and France that mark the limit of the German advance or more accurately the line of departure from which the Allies had launched their victorious offensive against the German Army in the summer of 1918. The stones were the idea of renowned sculptor Paul Moreau-Vauthier, who fought for France during the war. The proposal was for 240 stones, 28 in Belgium and 212 in France. The first was unveiled at Chateau-Thierry on 11 November 1921. While the idea was initially very popular support fell away so that only 118 stones were put in place over seven years from 1921 to 1927; 22 in Belgium (sixteen funded by the Touring Club de Belgique and six by the Ypres League) and 96 in France (funded by the Touring Club de France). Two more were added in 1929 and 1930 but 24 were destroyed in WW2. Behind the hedge is a German blockhouse. The remaining WW1 burial is that of Captain Edward Frederick Maltby Urquhart, 1st Black Watch (Royal Highlanders), killed in action on 23 October 1914 aged 37 years. He had passed out from Sandhurst into his regiment in 1897, being promoted to Lieutenant in 1899 and Captain in 1902. He served in the South African Wars, then with the Egyptian army from 1902, in Ireland from 1906 and was in India in 1912. He had been in action commanding 'A' Company for just four weeks before his death at Koortekeer Cabaret, located about 1.5km north of Pilkem, fighting off repeated German attacks. The other WW1 burial made, and now moved to New Irish Farm on the wishes of his family who wanted him in a 'British' cemetery, is Lieutenant Charles Lindsay Claude Bowes-Lyon, 3rd attached 1st Black Watch (Royal Highlanders) killed, with Captain Urquhart, on 23 October 1914 aged 29 years. He was a cousin of the Queen's Mother and lost a brother in the war. Both graves were lost in later shelling and rediscovered after the war, though for a period they were commemorated in Artillery Wood Cemetery. There are also fourteen soldiers who died during World War II buried in the churchyard just a little apart from Captain Urquhart. They are men of the British Expeditionary Force which was involved in the later stages of the defence of Belgium following the German invasion in May 1940. They were just a few of many casualties suffered in covering the withdrawal to Dunkirk.

**COMINES (KOMEN) COMMUNAL CEMETERY** - the village is about 8km south-west from Ieper. It lies between the N58 and the French border. The cemetery is on the western edge of the village and near the old Ieper-Comines canal. During the Second World War, the British Expeditionary Force was involved in the later stages of the defence of Belgium following the German invasion in May 1940, and suffered many casualties in covering the withdrawal to Dunkirk. The Commonwealth plot in Comines Communal Cemetery, which is close to the entrance, was created by the municipality when scattered graves were brought in from the local area. All were killed in the heavy fighting which occurred in the area at the end of May 1940. The cemetery contains 100 Second World War burials, five of them unidentified. Among those here is 2nd Lieutenant Paul Cooke, 1st Oxford and Bucks Light Infantry, killed in action on 28 May 1940 aged 23 years. He had represented Oxford University at Rugby Union, gaining a 'Blue'. He went on to represent England twice facing Wales and Ireland in early 1939 in the last Five Nations series before the war. In 1956 building works forced the closure of the German Extension to this cemetery and the remains of 4283 German soldiers were moved. Despite these changes, the memorial erected in their honour still stands in Comines Cemetery.

**GELUVELD COMMUNAL CEMETERY** – Geluveld is about 8km east of Ieper on the Menin Road and high on the ridge that the Germans were so desperately attacking in First

Ypres in late 1914. The cemetery is north of the Menin Road in the heart of the village near the main square and next to the church. It was used for the burial of one man during the retreat to Dunkirk in 1940. He is Trooper Geoffrey Hugh Rudkin, 12th Royal Lancers, Royal Armoured Corps, killed on 28 May 1940 aged 20 years. In the village is the monument that commemorates the part played by the 2nd Worcestershires in the successful counter-attack on 31 October 1914 to retake the village. Also here is the South Wales Borderers Memorial, located at the site of the 1914 windmill, that commemorates the part played by the South Wales Borderers in the fight to hold Geluveld village during the First Battle of Ypres in October and November 1914.

**HOOGSTADE CHURCHYARD** - Hoogstade is a little over 10km north-west of Ieper and a similar distance north of Poperinge. It lies on the N8. The church is set back from the N8 behind houses on the east side. There are twelve British World War II graves dating from May 1940 in the northern corner of the churchyard. All died on 29 May except one. He is Lieutenant Francis Victor Beaufort, 5th Royal Inniskilling Dragoon Guards, Royal Armoured Corps, killed on 27 May 1940 aged 23 years.

**HOUTHULST CHURCHYARD** – Houthulst is about 15km north of Ieper. In the village churchyard, which is about 100m west of the main crossroads in town, seven British men who died in World War II are buried. There are three soldiers from May 1940 and four airmen of 1941. Enter the churchyard by the main entrance and as you reach the main door turn left and follow the narrow path. The seven war graves are on the right hand side of the path about 15m from the church. The airmen were the crew of a Handley Page Hampden from RAF Scampton in Lincolnshire which crashed at Houthulst, while taking part in a night raid on Cologne. In Klerken nearby, in W Coppensplein, is a memorial to Belgium's leading fighter ace after whom the road is named. During 1918 he specialised in attacking balloons. He was credited with 37 confirmed victories and six probables though he did not have his first success until April 1918. He and 39 other Belgians learned to fly on their own expense in Britain in 1915 where he qualified in December. His last mission in October 1918 went badly and he lost his leg. For his wartime service he was knighted, becoming Willy Omer Francois Jean Coppens de Houthulst. He was decorated by Belgium, France, Portugal, Italy, Poland, Serbia and Britain, who awarded him a Distinguished Service Order and the Military Cross, Between the two World Wars Coppens was Belgian air attaché to four nations. In September 1928, despite his disability, he set a parachute jump record, which stood for four years, by leaping from over 6000m. He retired to Switzerland in 1940, organising resistance work and marrying. In the late 1960s he returned to Belgium and lived his last five years with fellow Belgian ace Jan Olieslagers's only daughter until his death in 1986.

**LA CRECHE COMMUNAL CEMETERY** - La Creche Cemetery is found 600m south of the Bailleul-Armentieres road (D933) in France about 12km south of Ieper. On the north side of the village and clearly signed from the D933, it is on the east side of the Rue du Cemetiere. For most of the war La Creche was behind the front-line. It was in German hands only during the Battles of the Lys in 1918. There are three British soldiers who died in 1915 buried here. They are on the left hand side of the cemetery as you enter, one near the gate and two further away. Buried here is 2nd Lieutenant Hugh Henry O'Sullivan, 1/6th North Staffordshires, killed in action on 10 June 1915 aged 27 years, when struck by a bullet while working with a machine gun team. He had been at the Front since March after being commissioned into the Battalion in February 1914. Before the war he worked as a chemist with his father having gained a BSc degree from London University and an MSc from Birmingham University. His brother, 2nd Lieutenant Fergus N. O'Sullivan, No. 22 Squadron, Royal Flying Corps and 1/6th North Staffordshires (formerly Machine Gun Corps) was killed in action on 23 April 1917 aged 20 years. He and Lieutenant Eric Arthur Barltrop were killed when their FE2b broke up in mid-air following a collision with a DH2 of No. 24 Squadron flown by 2nd Lieutenant M A White near Le Verguier, All are buried in Jeancourt Communal Cemetery Extension. The others here are two men of the 1st Royal Warwickshires, Private Allen Yapp and Private Joseph Fitzgerald, who died on 8 February 1915. They were part of a group of men from the Battalion, who having been at the Front since August 1914, left their billets to have a look around and try to buy some food locally. They were returning to their billets along the railway in the evening when a light engine came and accidentally killed Yapp and Fitzgerald. The Battalion war diary records the day as quiet with men washing at the nearby Pont de Nieppe. No casualties are recorded.

**METEREN (MONT-DES-CATS) COMMUNAL CEMETERY**- situated on one of the three 'Mountains' of Flanders. This 'mountain' is clearly visible to the north of Meteren as it has a large television mast on the top. It is about 2.5km north of the town, which is in the north of France between Hazebrouck and Bailleul about 15km south-west of Ieper. The Communal Cemetery is at the base of the mast and the Commonwealth war graves plot is opposite the main gate. There is one Plot of 24 graves dating from WW2 of which seven are unidentified. Five men of the 1/5th Queens Royal West Surreys who died on 28 and 29 May 1940 are here. They arrived in France on 2 April 1940 and played a role in the fighting retreat to Dunkirk.

*Meteren (Mont-Des-Cats) Communal*

**METEREN COMMUNAL** – Meteren is in the north of France between Hazebrouck and Bailleul about 15km south-west of Ieper. The cemetery is just north of the crossroads in the centre of town on the D18. In it, close to, but outside, the western boundary wall of Meteren Military Cemetery, which is accessed through the Communal Cemetery, is a small group of six British graves of men killed in WW2, of which only two can be identified. They are hidden behind trees near the Cross of Sacrifice in the Military Cemetery.

**NOORDSCHOTE CHURCHYARD** – The village is about 10km north of Ieper and the church is in the village centre on the left hand side of the road from Reninge. There are fourteen British World War II graves, three unidentified, on the north side of the church. They were all killed in the retreat to Dunkirk in May 1940. Most are men of 1st Suffolks and 2nd East Yorkshires who died on 28-31 May 1940. 29 May was the day that Ypres fell and the Germans crossed the canal to the north after an artillery duel. It was the day known as the beginning of the 'break for the coast'. Many men were cut-off so attempted to break through the Germans to re-join their main forces which resulted in a few last ditch stands.

**OOSTVLETEREN CHURCHYARD** - in the centre of the village, 10km north-west of Ieper, the church is 400m east of the N8 on the road to Reninge. There are five Belgian grave made in World War II and 39 French graves dating from 1914-1918 in the north-west corner with seventeen British World War II graves, ten men who died in May 1940 and seven airmen who died on 11 May 1944. One is unidentified. The airmen were in one aeroplane, a Lancaster bomber from RAF Skellingthorpe, that crashed returning from a raid by 85 Lancasters and 4 Mosquitoes on Lille. Nine aircraft where shot down, two in Belgium. There are a Pilot, Flight Engineer, Navigator, Air Bomber, Wireless Operator/Gunner and two Air Gunners.

**PLOEGSTEERT CHURCHYARD** - Ploegsteert Churchyard is at the south-west corner of the town square in Ploegsteert which is on the main road south from Ieper to Armentieres about 15km south of Ieper. The churchyard was used for the burials of Allied forces from October 1914 to February 1915. There are six graves of men of the 1st Hampshires near the church on the south side of the churchyard. They brought their officers here for burial while the enlisted men are in Lancashire Cottage Cemetery. Buried here is Captain Eric John Wester Dolphin, killed in action on 7 November 1914. He led a trench raid which, when completed, led to the apparent surrender of German troops. When he went forward to accept their surrender, they shot him. The other British soldier buried here is 2nd Lieutenant Richard John Lumley of the 11th (Prince Albert's Own) Hussars who was killed in action on 17 October 1914. Two Canadians were buried here on 26 February 1915, one of whom was Lieutenant Herbert Beaumont Boggs, the first casualty suffered by the 7th Canadian Infantry. In the town square on the Marie you will find a plaque honouring Winston Churchill who served nearby in early 1916 as the commanding officer of the 6th Royal Scots Fusiliers after he resigned from the government on 12 November 1915 for his role in pushing forward the Gallipoli campaign. Haig felt Churchill, who was determined to be given a senior command, needed experience before taking a greater role, so rather than give Churchill command of a Brigade, he was placed at Battalion level.

**POLLINKHOVE CHURCHYARD** - the church is in the centre of the village which is about 18km north-west of Ieper. There are eight British World War II graves in the north-east part of the church, men killed in the retreat to Dunkirk in late May 1940. Among them is 2nd Lieutenant Kenneth Dening Dudley, 659 General Construction Company, Royal Engineers, killed in a bombing attack near Hoogstade on 24 May 1940 aged 27 years. He was a structural engineer who had qualified from Imperial College, London.

*Pollinkhove Churchyard*

**PROVEN CHURCHYARD** – the village is about 5km north-west of Poperinge on the road to the French border and Dunkirk. This is about 17km north west of Ieper. The churchyard is on the east side of the road set back behind houses. The five British men buried here were killed in the retreat to Dunkirk in the last week of May 1940. There is also one Belgian military casualty, Jeroom Caestecker, killed on 11 September 1917 aged 20 years. Buried here is 2nd Lieutenant Robert David Hutton-Squire, 53 (The Worcestershire Yeomanry) Anti-Tank Regiment, killed in action on 30 May 1940 aged 31 years. His uncle Major Robert Henry Edmund Hutton-Squire, DSO, Royal Garrison Artillery attached 85th Battery, 11th Brigade, Royal Field Artillery, was killed in action on 8 April 1917 aged 39 years and is buried in Barlin Communal Cemetery Extension.

**RENINGELST CHURCHYARD** - Reningelst Churchyard is in the centre of the village which is about 5km south-west of Ieper. There are three headstones in the Churchyard in the far right corner (east) as you look from the road, close to the Extension. They are two British graves and one Special Memorial to a British soldier whose grave was destroyed by shell-fire and lost. The village was in Allied hands throughout the war. Lieutenant Charles Geoffrey Butcher, 1st Dorsetshires, was killed on 2 May 1915 aged 23 years and was a casualty of a gas attack at Hill 60 on 1 May. He was lost with 52 of his men while another six officers and 200 men had to receive treatment for the effects of gas. Only one man was wounded by a bullet.

**ST. JAN-TER-BIEZEN COMMUNAL CEMETERY** – the village is located about 14km east of Ieper between Poperinge and the French border. The cemetery is on the south side of the village just south of the church but on the other side of the street and set back from the road about 100m east of Kapellestraat. It was used for one burial, that of Private Alfred Smith, 1/5th Gloucestershires, who died on 30 April 1918. One point of interest is that the 1/5th Gloucestershires were in Italy in April 1918. So, it would seem he was detached from his Battalion, possibly having recovered from injury, and then been rushed back to Flanders due the desperate need for men in 1918. But, he was not yet recorded as attached to another unit, though his medal index card suggests he may have been with the 8th Gloucestershires when he died.

**STADEN COMMUNAL CEMETERY** – the village is at the extreme north-east corner of the area covered by this book. It is about 20km from Ieper. The cemetery is on the north side of the village centre reached from the town square by taking the Bruggestraat towards Kortemark and then the first road north called De Carninstaraat which can also be found from the N38 from the town square towards Dixmuide where it is the first road east once you leave the village centre. The single grave is located along the main path, then take the fourth path on the left and the first right to reach Plot IV. Buried here is Flight Lieutenant (Pilot) Peter James Nankivell, No. 609 (West Riding) Squadron, Royal Air Force Volunteer Reserve, who died on 7 February 1943 aged 23 years. He was killed at about 2.30pm when his Hawker Typhoon crashed after a dogfight with a German Fokker Wulf 190 above the Kortemark-Ieper railway having left RAF Manston in Kent earlier that Sunday. While at Biggin Hill, his Squadron acquired a goat, soon named William, which became their official mascot. The goat was awarded an honorary Distinguished Service Order and Flying Cross, and the rank of Air Commodore.

**VOORMEZELE CHURCHYARD** –the village is 2km south of Ieper. The churchyard is south-east of the CWGC Enclosures. In the churchyard there is a Special Memorial to a British officer who was buried there but whose grave was destroyed by shell-fire. Lieutenant Robinson Edwin Winwood, 'D' Squadron, 5th (Royal Irish) Lancers, killed in action on 25 October 1914 aged 26 years. A professional soldier, he had been a Lieutenant since August.

**WARNETON (WAASTEN) COMMUNAL CEMETERY** – the village is located about 10km south of Ieper on the river that forms the boundary between Belgium and France and one of the boundaries of the area covered by this book. The cemetery is between the N58 and the village on the northern edge of the village on the south side of a small road called 'Chemin Vert'. There are 21 men buried here who were killed in the retreat to Dunkirk in May 1940. Three are unidentified. There are no officers and two members of the Royal Air Force share a grave. Their Squadron undertook reconnaissance missions from Crecy-en-Ponthieu in Bristol Blenheims before being forced to retreat. Not much is known about how they died in those chaotic days but their Squadron had already withdrawn to the UK when they died.

**WESTVLETEREN BELGIAN MILITARY CEMETERY** - as to the churchyard in the village, and then follow the road round by the church towards Poperinge and in 100m you will see, if you look carefully, a small road on the left at which is a small blue and white sign bearing the words 'Militaire Begraafplaats'. The cemetery is at the end of a dead-end lane 100m from the road next to a car park. There are 1208 graves here including 33 unidentified burials. The French army began the cemetery in 1914. The St. Sixtus Abbey was a refugee centre during the war and the local area served as camps for many British men. Hence, many medical units were also stationed here including a Military Hospital in the girls' school. The Belgians took the cemetery from the French in June 1916. It was enlarged after the war, including 123 graves from Reninge Military Cemetery moved here in 1968, and the French graves were removed. One British burial is Gunner I Kennedy, Royal Garrison Artillery, who died on 26 June 1916.

**WOESTEN CHURCHYARD** - this is in the centre of the village, which is 7km north-west of Ieper, on the east side of the N8 and town square. There are 282 French graves in the north-east corner dating from 1914-1918, and on the south side there are nine World War II British graves made in May 1940 during the retreat to Dunkirk. One is unidentified. Six are men of the 2nd Royal Ulster Rifles killed in covering the retreat to Dunkirk.

**ZANDVOORDE CHURCHYARD** - See Zantvoorde British Cemetery for the history of the fighting in and near the village. Zantvoorde Churchyard is in the centre of the village which is about 6km south-east of Ieper and is reached most easily via Geluveld. The churchyard contains four men of the 10th (Prince of Wales's Own Royal) Hussars, who died on 26 October 1914, buried on the north side of the church. Among them is Captain Sir Frank Stanley Day Rose, aged 37 years. He was the 2nd Baronet, son of a Liberal MP who died in 1913 after taking his first flight in an aeroplane, and was killed by shellfire. He had two brothers killed in the South African Wars in which he also served. Also here is Lieutenant Christopher Randolph Turnor, aged 28 years. He was the grandson of the 9th Earl of Galloway and great grandson of the 6th Duke of Beaufort. He was commissioned in 1908 serving in India and South Africa until the war began arriving at the Front on 8 October. He was killed while trying to find the enemy using his field glasses. After the war Turnor's parents paid for a stained glass window in his memory in the Church.

**ZUIDSCHOTE CHURCHYARD** – the village is about 4km north of Ieper and the churchyard is in the centre of the village on the west side of the road north to Lo-Reninge. There are five WW1 graves of French soldiers here, all unidentified. By the end of November 1914 the majority of the population fled the heavy German shelling, as it had caused some civilian casualties, and the village became a ruin. Any civil life was impossible during and after the gas attack on 22 April 1915. This became a zone for military activities only as the village was transformed with a maze of trenches and other fortifications. From 1915 it became a small railhead for an important supply line that had become seven lines by 1918. There are 76 graves of British soldiers killed in the retreat to Dunkirk in May 1940, mostly in the last week of the month, of which fourteen are unidentified. Almost all are men of the Lincolnshires, Royal Berkshires or Suffolks. Among those buried here is Captain James Anthony Hamilton Cartland, 2nd Lincolnshires killed in action on 29 May 1940 aged 27 years. He joined the Lincolnshires in 1933 and from 1936-38 was ADC to Lieutenant-General Sir George Weir when he was GOC in Chief in Egypt. His brother, Major John Ronald Hamilton Cartland, 53 (The Worcestershire Yeomanry) Anti-Tank Regiment, Royal Artillery was killed in action one day later on 30 May 1940 aged 33 years and is buried in Hotton War Cemetery, Belgium near the Luxembourg, Dutch and German borders. He was moved there after the war from Watou Temporary Burial Ground about 10km west of here. He was MP for Kings Norton from 1935. Their father, Major James Bertram Falkner Cartland, 1st Worcestershires was killed on 27 May 1918 by shellfire aged 42 years and is commemorated on the Soissons Memorial. Their sister was the prolific author, notably of romantic fiction, Barbara Cartland.

Zuidschote was in the French and Belgian sector of the front which begins at Boezinge and, therefore, the nearby Memorials are to French and Belgian units or individuals. However, the journey through this northern section of the Salient gives a different perspective on the battles at Ypres. Importantly, the area is a 'dynamic' environment – so things change.

I will deal with each Memorial in turn giving directions from the junction, at Lizerne, north of Boezinge, on the N369 road to Diksmuide where you turn left to Zuidschote. It is possible to visit all of these Memorials in one morning.

Belgian Carabiniers, 1915 - just north of the Lizerne crossroads west of the N369. The Memorial is a plaque 2m above the ground between the windows on the wall of the house which is next to a brick tower.

Cross Of Reconciliation To The First Victims Of Gas, 1915 - a tall narrow cross made of aluminium on the north side of the N369 just north-east of the turn for Zuidschote. It is a French Memorial which replaced the original one erected in memory of those, especially the 418th French Infantry Regiment, killed and affected by the gas attack in April 1915. The first Cross was destroyed in 1942 by the German Trophy Company who did not like the reference on the inscription calling Germans 'barbarians'. The present Memorial was designed by Paul Tourneau and inaugurated in 1961 on the base of the original.

Belgian Grenadiers, 1915 - 400m west of the N369 on the side road by the Cross of Reconcilliation. The monument, an obelisk, is also the monument to the enthronement of King Leopold III in 1934.

3rd/23rd Belgian Infantry, 1915 - this small monument is 100m beyond the Cross of Reconciliation on the road to Diksmuide, on the right just before the hotel and bridge over the canal.

Gebroeders Van Raemdonck (d. 26-3-17), 6th/24th Belgian Infantry - next to the footpath on the north-east bank of the Ypres-Ijzer canal about 300m north of the N369.

The next group of Memorials is near Merkem. Continue on the N369 for 3.2km to a left turn to Merkem.

3rd Belgian Division, 1918 - this is on the left of the main N369 200m before the turn to Merkem. It takes the form of a plaque on a stone and marks the area from which this Division advanced in the final breakout from the Salient in 1918.

9th Belgian Infantry, 1918; 11th Belgian Infantry, April 1918; and 13th Belgian Infantry, 1918. The Memorial plaques to these three regiments that fought in the defence of Merkem during the German Spring Offensive, can be found on the ground floor wall between the windows at the south-east corner of Merkem Town Hall.

19th Belgian Infantry, April 1918 - beyond the Town Hall as the road bears right before the church. The Memorial is an obelisk, situated in front of the wood on the left hand side of the road, to a regiment that was also involved in the defence of Merkem in 1918.

1st Zouaves, 1914 - north-west of Merkem next to the canal bridge is a cafe at Driegrachten. The Memorial to the Zouaves who died in 1914 but have no known grave is on the wall of the cafe. There is a demarcation stone 100m beyond as the Germans just crossed the canal here in 1918 during their Spring Offensive. The Belgians also fought here when an attack was repulsed on 5 April 1915.

Adjutant Armand Van Eecke (d. 9-9-18), 3rd Belgian Infantry - situated on the west side of the N369 500m beyond the crossroads with the Houthulst road. This small Memorial is surrounded by a hedge between houses opposite a field and is very easy to miss.

Adjutant Taymans (d. 18-11-17), 19th Belgian Infantry - just before the crossroads described above, there is a small right turn next to the cement/stone store and shop. In 300m on this very poor road there is a farm on the left and the monument is in the farmyard.

# Non-British Cemeteries - Belgian

## HOUTHULST FOREST BELGIAN MILITARY CEMETERY

**HISTORY**
This is a concentration cemetery created after the war.

**INFORMATION**
This is a large Belgian Military Cemetery, one of nine to which Belgian soldiers who were not repatriated to family plots have been concentrated for burial. It is peaceful, beautiful and well worth a visit. The cemetery takes the form of a six-pointed star, with paths that reinforce the star shape making an overall hexagon. A central path leads to a flagpole with the Belgian flag. In 1923 the State bought this plot of land and grouped together here those Belgian casualties that had not been buried in their native villages. Most of the men buried here died in the September breakout from the Salient.

In the topmost point of the star you will find the graves of Italian prisoners of war who had been used by the Germans as labourers in Roeselare and Izegem. Most of those who died fell victim to illness or disease. Their remains were later transferred to Houthulst, where they now lay along the forest's edge.

The forest, which Napoleon called 'the key to the Low Countries', though it is much smaller than in his day, fell to the Germans on 21 October 1914 and remained in their hands, during which time they installed artillery capable of shelling Ypres, until Third Ypres in 1917. The forest was one of the key routes to the North Sea ports, and as a result, there was heavy fighting here. The forest and village did not fall until 28 September 1918 when the Belgians took this area during the breakout from the Salient.

It is possible to find trenches in parts of the wood. Although it is possible to walk in the forest there are areas fenced off to the public that you must not try to enter. They are used by the Belgian Army Disposal Service who deal with the unexploded munitions that appear from the mud of the Salient every year. It is estimated that in an average year the Disposal unit will have to remove thousands of unexploded shells, including gas shells, that they detonate twice a day during the summer. Some men have lost their lives clearing the mess left by earlier armies, for example, on 7 May 1986, four men were killed in one accident.

Among those here is Lieutenant Victor Charles Joseph Callemayn, 10th Regiment of the line, killed on 29 April 1918. He was a minor pre-war poet who enlisted on the day of the German invasion in 1914. He was wounded but recovered to fight on and was subsequently commissioned. He later won the Knight's Cross of the Order of Leopold for bravery.

There are a number of French graves here and three Memorials in the forest and village. These are to the 1st, 7th and 13th Belgian Artillery, 1914-1918; 3rd/23rd Belgian Infantry for their actions here on 28 September 1918; and the 4th/24th Belgian Artillery, 1914-1918. There is also an Albertina marker stone outside the cemetery.

Bel – 1723 (493 unidentified)   Fr – 146
    Italian – 81

**LOCATION**
Houthulst Forest Belgian Cemetery is about 15km north-east of Ieper on the east side of the road from Poelkapelle to Houthulst (N301).

**POELKAPELLE COMMUNAL** – the village is 9km north-east of Ieper. The Communal cemetery lies on the southern edge of the village. It is reached by taking the road south from the roundabout and Guynemer Memorial for 100m and then turn east on Kwellestraat following this until you find the cemetery on the north side of the road after about 250m. It contains four Belgian Military graves.

**ZONNEBEKE COMMUNAL** – the village is about 6km north-east of Ieper. The communal cemetery is on the north side of the road that leads up the hill, known as Devil's Hill in the war as it featured four German cemeteries, to the roundabout at which you turn north towards Passendale and Tyne Cot Cemetery. So, it lies upon a well-worn path though few will know it is here. It contains the graves of fourteen Belgian soldiers, eleven killed in WW1 and three in WW2. There is also a military burial from 1830.

# Non-British Cemeteries - French

## MONT KEMMEL (OSSUARY)

**HISTORY**
The Ossuary was created after the war with the concentration of unidentified graves from the battlefields.

**INFORMATION**
Situated on the edge of the Kemmelberg the ossuary, created in the 1922 and redeveloped in 1924 and 1932, when many of the unidentified dead in St. Charles de Potyze French Military Cemetery were moved here, overlooks an area in which many French soldiers died in 1914 and 1918 particularly in defending the Mont. It was further renovated in 1961-62 and 1986-1989. There are over 5000 unknown 'Poilu' buried beneath the obelisk as well as a small number of identified men whose names are inscribed on a plaque. The 57 identified are listed alphabetically by name on the front of the obelisk in the centre of the cemetery. On the other side is a plaque which gives the total number. There are 50000 French soldiers buried in Belgium of whom 38000 are unidentified. Most identified remains have been repatriated to France.

There are good information boards outside of the ossuary. The hill was the objective of one of Ludendorff's attacks in April 1918. A push by the Germans on 17 April and 19 April were both thrown back. The French then took over the hill, though the 9th (Scottish) Division stayed in support. The Germans attacked again on 25 April, at which point the 12th Royal Scots were almost cut off and the hill fell to the Germans. The British 25th Division tried to win it back on 26 April but failed due to the weak situation of the French. Hence, the Kemmelberg (Mont Kemmel) stayed in German hands until taken by the US 27th and 30th Divisions and British 34th Division in September.

On route you may pass the Cafe Belvedere as you climb to the summit of the hill. The tower was used by Sir Douglas Haig and other commanding officers as a vantage point over the Salient. It was rebuilt on the site of the original café, which was destroyed in 1918, when the French were pushed off the Kemmelberg

On the summit of the Kemmelberg (159m) a site has been chosen for a Memorial to the French who died in Belgium during the war, the Mémorial aux Soldats Français 1914-1918, especially those who fell defending the hill between 15 and 30 April 1918. It was unveiled in 1932 by Marshal Petain, who had masterminded the defence of Verdun in 1916 and went on to be the Leader of Vichy France in World War II, for which he was sentenced to death. The column is 18m high with a winged Nike, the goddess of victory, on the front. It used to have a 'Poilu's' helmet carved on top but it was not replaced after being struck by lightning.

Fr – 5294        KUG – 5237        Area - 2050 sq mts

**LOCATION**
The Kemmelberg is about 8km south of Ieper, 1km south of Kemmel, and is clearly signed from the centre of the village. The climb is very steep, on a cobbled road passing the Cafe Belvedere, to the summit. At this point the road bears right and downhill for 100m to the Ossuary but I recommend parking at the Monument and walking the short distance to the Ossuary.

## St. CHARLES-POTIJZE FRENCH MILITARY CEMETERY

**HISTORY**
Although the burial ground was begun during the war most of the graves in this cemetery were concentrated here after the war.

**INFORMATION**
The cemetery was created early in the war when French troops who were holding the line set up an aid post in a school that once stood here, burying their dead in a nearby garden. After the French handed over this section to the British in 1915, the cemetery was unused. But, being so close to the front line, was shelled throughout much of that time. After the war it was redeveloped or expanded in 1920, 1922 and 1925-29 to concentrate the burials from

many small and isolated locations throughout Belgium. This is the only French Military Cemetery in Belgium.

It is almost impossible to miss this large cemetery. There are 3548 graves of which 2983 are in individual graves. The other 'Poilu' are unidentified or are buried in a mass grave. Poilu literally means 'the hairy ones', and has become the nickname for a French soldier.

Some men buried here were killed in the first gas attack on 22 April 1915. They were from the 87th Division who held the northern sector of line.

Sculptures within the cemetery are of a Breton Calvaire Monument by Jean Freour, based on the Crucifixion; a Mourning Mother and a Memorial to the 17th Infantry Regiment. The men concentrated here came from many cemeteries including those at L'Abeele, Dikkebus, Geluveld, Hooge, Kemmel, Langemark, Loker, Passendale, Ploegsteert, Poelkapelle, Poperinge, St. Juliaan, Voormezele, Westouter, Wijtschate, Ypres, Zandvoorde, Zillebeke and Zonnebeke.

The cemetery still accepts burials and around the mass grave to the rear are a number of rows of more recent arrivals. For example, four unidentified French soldiers were buried here in April 2006.

French – 3600            Unnamed – 762
WW2 – 2 (Unidentified)
KUG – 609 in an ossuary

Area - 29,900 sq mts
**LOCATION**
Potijze French Cemetery lies on the south side of the Zonnebeke road, east of Ieper, and about 900m east of Potijze.

**WESTVLETEREN CHURCHYARD** - the church is in the village about 14km north-west of Ypres, on the south side of the N321, 2km west of the N8. There are 189 French World War I graves at the eastern end of the church.

# Non-British Cemeteries - German

# LANGEMARK GERMAN MILITARY CEMETERY

**HISTORY**

The origins of this cemetery are a small group of German graves made in 1915. It was then used later in the war. However, it was completely redesigned and enlarged after the war when bodies were concentrated here in the 1920's and again in the 1950's.

**INFORMATION**

German soldiers have said of Ypres that it was 'The worst of the hell of Verdun plus the horror of the Somme'.

At the end of the war some 670 German War Cemeteries existed in West Flanders. Between the wars the German War Graves Service (Volksbund Deutsche Kriegsgräberfürsorge or VDK) undertook to care for the 128 German War Cemeteries which remained in existence after many had been concentrated following the war. At the end of the war there were 859 graves here, 627 Germans and others that were French, British and Belgian soldiers. From the mid 1920s this cemetery was named 'Langemarck-Nord' to distinguish it from the sixteen other German burial grounds in the area. In 1930 it was renamed 'German Military Cemetery Number 123' and gained its current name when formally opened on 10 July 1932 with over 10000 graves. In June 1940 Hitler made a visit to the cemetery as he was stationed in Langemark in 1914.

In 1954, a War Cemeteries Agreement between Belgium and the new state of West Germany superseded the agreement of 1925. It was agreed there would be three German collecting cemeteries for First World War dead in Flanders: Langemark, Menin and Vladslo with another nearby at Hooglede. Partly this was due to management as it was easier to care for fewer cemeteries than the 68 in West Flanders that existed by 1945. It is also partly, I believe, as a consequence of the second invasion of Belgium by Germans in a generation and the desire to see less of a German presence in Belgium at that time. The Volksbund charity, from that point, took responsibility for the extension and maintenance of the cemeteries which remained after 1954-6 when the other German Cemeteries were concentrated or remains were repatriated to Germany. In the whole of Belgium there are thirteen German military cemeteries.

Besides the existing 10000 graves, a new plot was made with 9000 graves as well as the mass grave. Many identified remains were buried in single graves while the unknown, and other, partly identified, and those believed to be here, remains, were placed in a mass grave. Single graves in the cemetery are so close together that up to forty men are marked on each gravestone. The final concentrations were made in 1970-72, though 40 were added when the cemetery was re-designed in October 2015. Remains were removed here from cemeteries that included those in Langemark-Kerselaere, four in Moorslede, two in Passendale, five in Poelkapelle, two in Staden, one in Westrosebeke, two in Zillebeke and one in Zonnebeke-Polygon. The Volksbund today cares for the cemeteries and provides much the same service as the CWGC, though without government funding, for those who wish to find the graves of relatives who fell in the war.

It is entered, having used the path via the introductory area from the car and coach park, through a building made of red stone brought from the Vosges. Inside the building there are two Chapels of Remembrance, one contains a map of German War Cemeteries in Belgium, while the other contains, carved on oak tablets, the names of 6313 soldiers killed in battle who were buried in the original cemetery.

There have been redevelopments in the cemetery, completed in October 2015, so that a wall with visitor information is the first thing you see as you pass through the entrance building. This is part of the original design. Walk to the left and you will soon see the mass grave, the Kameraden Grab (Comrades Grave), which contains the remains of 24917 German soldiers, surrounded by a series of bronze blocks bearing the 16940 names of men known to be in the grave. 366 graves were moved to make room for this. The coats of arms of eight Belgian provinces lie in front of the grave.

The blocks also name Lieutenant Wolfgang Kühne, who died on 6 August 1915. In fact, Kühne is in the civil cemetery at Wervik. People of other nationalities are here including Danes serving in the German army as Northern Schleswig, now part of Denmark, belonged to Prussia at the time; Poles as part of Poland that was in Germany until 1918; a Belgian citizen; Russian and Italian prisoners of war that were put to work behind the Front as well as Austrians that belonged to a unit attached to the Germans. There are also several nurses (Hilferinnen) in this mass grave.

At the wall or entrance end of the Kameraden Grab can be seen a set of four bronze mourning soldiers, the work of Professor Emile Krieger, erected here in 1958 where they are now and moved to the perimeter wall opposite the mass grave in the early 1980's. They have been moved back as part of the redevelopment, putting the cemetery back to its original configuration after the WW2 extension. The design is based on a widely used photo taken in 1918 of a set of mourning soldiers at a grave of their comrades.

The cemetery is in two distinct sections. You enter the Alter (Older) Friedhof, the original burial ground planted with oaks and, as such, always cool. I have known many people comment on the temperature difference at all times of the year. Within this part of the cemetery 10143 men are buried, 3836 of whom are unnamed.

To the right from the entrance building, at the north end of the cemetery, is the more open Einbettungs Friedhof Nord (Embedding Cemetery North) in which lie 9475 men. It includes three bunkers and a series of tank traps that formed part of the Langemark line. Upon the tank traps are Memorials to many of the German units who fought here.

One of the main German attacks upon the village, on 23 October 1914, was by students from Hiedelberg and Munich who went into battle singing and linking arms. It is believed they were singing the first stanza of what later, in 1919, became the national anthem 'Deutschland, Deutschland über alles'. The students formed Reserve Corps No.'s 22 to 27, in which 75% of the men were under military age, and most of the officers were cadets or from the retired list. They had received less than six weeks training when they were thrown into the battle, so the German Command was severely criticized for the use of volunteers such as these in war. It has even been claimed that the students were unarmed when they moved forward. However, they were not alone in the attack as only fifteen percent of the German soldiers involved in the Battle of Langemarck were students. The others were inexperienced German infantry who suffered severe casualties when they made a frontal attack on, and were stopped by, experienced French and British infantry. General Haig's first involvement in the war was here, on the same day, as commander of the I Corps. Many of the students now lie in this cemetery in what was originally known as the 'Studentenfriedhof'. It is important to remember that in all probability this was part of the 'Langemark myth' that began in the 1920's but was seized upon by the Nazis in the 1930's as an example of the sacrifice for the Motherland by the youth. After the Second World War, the Langemark myth vanished. Whether it is just a myth or based on truth is now part of the fog of war.

Though the village fell briefly to the Germans, it was retaken by the French on 4 December 1914. The village was over-run again by the Germans during their gas attack in 1915. This was despite the fact that the British knew the attack was coming because on 14 April 1915 a prisoner from the 234th Reserve Regiment, XXVI Corps, who had been taken near Langemark, revealed the German plans.

The cylinders used for the German gas attack were stored just north of the present cemetery in 1915. On 24 April the German line was 100m north of the cemetery facing French Zouaves, colonial troops, who were positioned 100m south of the cemetery when the gas was released from the point where the Houthulst road crosses the St. Jansbeek. Four thousand containers released 168 tons of chlorine gas in ten minutes.

Langemark was not retaken until the Third Battle of Ypres in 1917 when it was captured at great cost by the 20th (Light) Division. On 4 October 1917 an attack was launched from here against Hill 19 and Eagle Trench which was north of the village, across the road to Poelkapelle, and part of a huge German defensive line. The 2nd Seaforth Highlanders, 3/10th Middlesex and 1st Royal Warwickshires succeeded in taking the hill so that the 2nd East Lancashires and 1st Royal Dublin Fusiliers could form a new line east of Langemark during the night. During the German Spring Offensive, in early April 1918, the Germans again occupied Langemark, but on 28 September 1918 it was finally taken by the Belgians.

Buried here in the Kameraden Grab are two British soldiers. They were brought here when the concentrations into the mass grave took place and are now among the Germans with whom they had originally been buried. Private Albert Carlill, 1/4th Loyal North Lancashires, died on 4 November 1918 aged 19 years. He died as a German prisoner and was buried in Louvain Communal Cemetery near or among German graves because his grave later could not be located and was believed lost. He was given a Special Memorial in Cement House Cemetery until 2004 when he was discovered to be here.

Private Leonard Harry Lockley, 4th Seaforth Highlanders, died on 30 October 1918. He was from Portsmouth and was formerly in the Royal Inniskilling Fusiliers. He died as a German prisoner and was at first buried in Jemappes Communal Cemetery where he had a Special Memorial for many years.

They are commemorated here by a small plaque on the last of the Kameraden Grab blocks and you will find them in the St. Julien ADS hard copy CWGC register, pasted onto the last page. It is also worth considering that, as several British graves buried by Germans in 'their', or civil, cemeteries could not be identified at the time of concentration in the 1950's, there may be other Allied soldiers in the Kameraden Grab.

Buried here in the Kameraden Grab is Leutnant Werner Voss, Jasta 10, one if Germany's greatest fighter aces. He was awarded the 'Blue Max' in March 1917 having been credited with 22 victories. He had been in the cavalry, served on Eastern and Western Fronts and commanded several Jastas, never quite finding his niche. By September 1917 the strain was beginning to show on Voss. On 23 September, after dining with his two brothers, he took off becoming involved in a dogfight with RFC Squadrons that included Captain

James McCudden, VC, DSO & Bar, MC & Bar, MM. He was buried by the British where he crashed and subsequently moved to the Kameraden Grab.

Also here in the Kameraden Grab is Leutnant Erwin Bohme, Jasta 2. On 28 October 1916 he collided in mid-air with Oswald Boelke, another of Germany's great aces of the war, while they both attacked a DH2 of No. 24 Squadron, Royal Flying Corps. Boelke, who had 40 confirmed victories, was killed in the crash. Bohme survived until 29 November 1917 when he was shot down over Zonnebeke. He was buried next to Tyne Cot Cemetery until his remains were concentrated here in 1955. Two of his brothers were killed in the war, one being buried in Vladslo German Cemetery. He was a holder of the German 'Blue Max'.

Brothers Bruno and Martin Loets from the small village of Reepsholt in Ostfriesland, Germany were both volunteers of No. 10 Kompanie, 234th Reserve Infanterie Regiment who died near Wallemolen on 10 November 1914. Martin is buried here in the Kameraden Grab while Bruno rests in Menin German Cemetery.

On the south-west edge of the village, and on the north side of the road to Boezinge, is a memorial commemorating the 60th and 61st Brigades of the 20th Division which engaged the Germans on 16 August 16 1917.

Just north of the cemetery are two small Memorials. They are on the road running next to the St. Jansbeek which is north of the cemetery. The Memorial to the 34th Division Royal Artillery and Royal Engineers is on the right in front of a bunker used as an Advanced Dressing Station in September 1918. It was also used as a headquarters for the 34th Division Artillery, 152nd and 160th Brigade Field Artillery and the Divisional Ammunition Column. When the stream had to be crossed in 1917 it took the Artillery and Engineers eight to ten hours to get an 18 pounder artillery piece across. The other Memorial, to Adjutant Andre Malliavin and Brigadier Emilien Girault of the French 2nd African Hunters who both died on 9 October 1917, is in a field on the other side of the stream.

There is now a Memorial, inaugurated on 11 November 2016, to the WW1 Blacksmiths. It is next to the car/coach park at the north end of the cemetery. A steel sheet, standing 7m high, bears the image of a single Flanders poppy to commemorate the role of blacksmiths and farriers in the war.

Ger – 44535              Unnamed – 11813

Area - 2676 sq mts

**LOCATION**

Langemark German Cemetery lies on the northern edge of Langemark about 5km north-east of Ieper. It is on the west side of the road from Langemark to Madonna and Houthulst and is clearly marked from the centre of the village. There is a car and coach parking area at the north end of the cemetery, with a path, through an introductory area, leading to the main entrance. Beware of walking on what looks like a lovely alternative path, avoiding the trees, as this is a cycle path and the cyclists take no prisoners.

**PONT-DE-NIEPPE GERMAN CEMETERY** - lies south of Ieper within the village of Nieppe west of Armentieres. It can be found at the end of a road that leads north from the Bailleul-Armentieres road (D933) about 100m east of the turn to the motorway from Nieppe. There is a large German cemetery of nearly 800 burials at the west end of the graveyard which was made when they held the village in the summer of 1918 and after the war with the concentration of German graves from the area. It includes 46 graves which were moved from within the boundaries of the communal cemetery.

# COMMONWEALTH WAR GRAVES COMMISSION

During the first months of the War in 1914 the dead were buried by their comrades, or by local inhabitants, in communal cemeteries, and burial returns were made by chaplains or serving officers. The Royal Engineers were involved in fighting so they could not perform the task as they had done in the South African Wars.

General Fowke, Engineering Adviser to the British Expeditionary Force, was happy to hand over the task of marking and registration of graves to Fabian Ware. He had volunteered his ambulance unit for the job at the end of October 1914 before Lord Kitchener, Minister of War, sanctioned the development. The unit was officially appointed by Sir John French, Commander-in-Chief, in February 1915 and was given the title of Graves Registration Commission. It was still a civilian group, manned by the Red Cross but became a military unit in October 1915 with Army officers in charge of Graves Registration Units (GRU's).

The Commission's task was the systematic marking and registration of all graves in France and Flanders. To achieve this the British zone of warfare was divided into seven areas in which all known graves were located with an appropriate religious marker, and photographs taken of every grave. Late in 1915 the French Government donated land for cemeteries to Britain and the Dominions. At the same time the British Government set up a national committee to make provision for the care of all graves in France and Flanders.

The committee, called the Commission of Graves Registration and Enquiries, headed by the Prince of Wales, was to arrange for the care of the graves, acquire land and provide a service for the relatives of the dead. It set up units in each sector to care for thirty-three cemeteries and 49,413 graves then identified. In May 1916 the Commission suggested that identity disks should be made of metal and that each man have two to replace the leather disks used previously.

Usually up to 1916 the dead were buried where they fell or in scattered graves in the rear. However, it became normal for trenches to be pre-dug before battles in preparation for the dead, a system that eased the job of identification and continued until the end of the War.

The Commission received a Royal Charter on 21 May 1917 and its membership represented all the countries of the Empire and Dominions who were taking part in the War and had dead buried on the battlefields. In 1919 the Commission announced that, despite many families wanting the remains of the dead to be repatriated, the bodies would remain where they fell and would not be returned to Britain. The main reason for this was the expense, though the care lavished on the cemeteries over the century has outstripped the cost of removal to Britain, and the effect has been a much more effective memorial to the fallen of the Great War.

The Imperial (now Commonwealth) War Graves Commission took over from the Empire War Office in 1921. The cost of its work is shared by those countries who have dead in Commission Cemeteries and in proportion to the number of dead from each country.

The main objective of the Commission at the end of the War, in caring for what French lamented as the 'Silent Army' of the dead, was to commemorate each individual equally. Thus, all men received the same tribute in the form of a headstone or as a line on a Memorial such as the Menin Gate. Each headstone is 2ft 8ins in height and 1ft 3ins wide, upon which is carved the badge of the regiment or unit, rank, name, date of death and age with an appropriate religious symbol. At the foot of the stone relatives were allowed to have a small inscription at their own expense. Exceptions to this design are for the few men who were awarded the Victoria Cross or the headstones that bear an inscription such as 'Known (or Believed) to be buried in this Cemetery' when the exact place of burial is lost. For bodies that could not be identified the headstone bears the simple, but effective, words, chosen by Rudyard Kipling, 'Known unto God'.

Each cemetery has a character of its own though a number of features, particularly the Cross of Sacrifice set upon an octagonal base and bearing a crusaders sword of bronze, are common to all. The larger cemeteries also have the War Stone, a plinth that looks like an altar and bears the words 'Their Name Liveth for Evermore', chosen by Rudyard Kipling, from the Book of Ecclesiastes. Most headstones are set in rows or narrow borders planted with a variety of flowers and shrubs.

The developmental work of the Commission was completed in 1938 with the unveiling of the Australian National Memorial in France. The area of the front had been divided into squares, each searched six times for bodies, between 1921 and 1928 nearly 30,000 corpses, of which only 25% could be identified, were re-buried. Even today when remains are still being found and interred in the War Cemeteries, there are still over 500,000 missing on the Western Front.

A visitor information center was opened in Ypres on 10 May 2017, some distance from the original office, on the town side of the Menin Gate at 33 Menenstraat. It will provide a range of services which is a great support for visitors to the Salient. It is open from Wednesdays to Sundays from 2.30pm to 9pm.

The work of the Commission is protected by international agreements. It is a shame that the registers of each cemetery cannot be equally well protected. A record for each cemetery is held at the offices of the Commission in Ypres and at Beaurains, France, but there used to be a relevant copy stored in most cemeteries. Found in small repositories usually near the entrance, too many have been removed for the Commission to afford constantly replacing them. My finding three registers to be missing in one day is part of the inspiration for this book.

I cannot thank the officers of the Commission enough for their help in compiling this book. Their advice, information and immense efforts over the years has eased my work and research on innumerable occasions.

# YPRES – IEPER

During the First Battle of Ypres in October and November 1914 the German Kaiser demanded of his troops that they "Take Ypres or die". They died as Ypres did not fall. It remained in Allied hands, a symbol of defiance to the German Army who tried to capture the town in a series of monumental battles. Even so, many men from Britain, Ireland, Canada, New Zealand, Australia, South Africa, the Indian subcontinent, the USA, Belgium, France, the Caribbean and elsewhere will forever defend the town of Ypres and the Salient as they died and are buried here. A possibly apocryphal story is of a Scottish soldier fighting in the Salient in 1917 who said 'Ypres, well may they call it Ypres'. The Scottish Gaelic word for sacrifice is 'iobairt' which when pronounced sounds very like 'Ypres'. Even in Irish Gaelic the word 'íobair' for sacrifice is very similar to Ypres when pronounced.

Ypres was first settled in 962 AD though there is some archaeological evidence of an earlier Roman settlement at the site of the Lille Gate. The town became one of the main textile trading centres in Flanders and Europe during the Middle Ages, centre of a population of over 200,000. As Ypres became less important as a commercial centre it grew more strategically important and was regularly besieged, particularly in the years 1383, 1584, 1689-92, 1713, 1744 and 1792-4. Ypres became a pawn of the European powers, coming under the dominance of the Spanish, Austrians, French and Dutch.

The fortifications were begun by the Spanish before 1670, but following the Peace of Nijmegen, when Ypres was ceded to the French, the walls were made stronger notably with a citadel at the Antwerp of Hangoart (Menin) Gate, the most ornate of the four gates of Ypres. The defences, partially dismantled during the French rule which lasted from 1744-92, were rebuilt under the Austrians in the next year and taken down again by the French in 1794. The Antwerp Gate was re-named the Napoleon Gate in 1804 and the defences rebuilt, just before the Battle of Waterloo in 1815, by the British. From 1815-38 Belgium and Holland were one country and the defences were built up against the French, at which time the Menin Gate acquired its name. In 1838 Belgium achieved its independence and Ypres began to dismantle its defences once more, including the Menin Gate, for the building of railways and general growth of the town. As a result, when the Great War began in August 1914, only the Lille Gate was still standing.

The 3rd Cavalry Division of the German IV Cavalry Corps entered Ypres on 13 October 1914 but they retreated when the British Expeditionary Force arrived the next day. The civilians did not leave Ypres until the bombardment during the Second Battle of Ypres in 1915. The town nearly fell during the German Spring Offensive in 1918 when the Germans reached its outskirts. The Salient was broken in September and October 1918.

## FEATURES

GROTE MARKT. One of the grandest market squares in Flanders. If you are lucky there will be one of the numerous fairs held when you visit but it is important to remember that the weekly market is in the square on Saturday mornings, therefore no parking areas are available at that time.

CLOTH HALL. The original Cloth Hall was built over a period of 45 (1260-1304) years, though the Nieuwkerke at the east end was not added until 1609. The only surviving section of the pre-1914 hall is now beneath the Belfry around the 'Donkerspoort' where you can see the coats of arms.

Externally the building appears to be as it was prior to 1914, when it was destroyed by German shelling, particularly by incendiary devices which were specifically aimed at damaging the ancient town. There are now modern offices in the building, including the main Tourist Office on the ground floor where the staff are always willing to help with any enquiry. You will find the Flemish people generally open and friendly, I am always impressed by their linguistic ability. The first time that I visited the Tourist Office the young lady helping me was doing so in English, while holding a conversation with another man in Flemish and answering a telephone call in French - I felt very inadequate with my limited schoolboy French.

On the first floor is the 1914-1918 Ypres Salient War Museum, known as 'In Flanders Fields'. Its entrance is well signed from the main square on the southern side of the Cloth Hall. There is a separate entrance and exit, the exit taking you through the café and small book and souvenir shop. Both exit and entrance have free public toilets.

On the outside walls of the Cloth Hall are several plaques and Memorials. The number is growing but includes:

- Earl Baldwin IX and Queen Margaret of Champagne.
- King Albert and Queen Elizabeth.
- Our Lady of Thuyne.
- The Sacred Heart.
- The French killed during 1914-18 on the Salient.
- Polish Memorial - recently returned to the Cloth Hall after it had been removed in order that an additional three fallen Polish soldiers from General Maczek's 1st Polish Armoured Division, whose names had previously been omitted, could be finally be included alongside their fallen comrades. These omissions only came to light during research by a local historian for a book.
- Victims of Chemical Weapons Memorial

St. MARTIN'S CATHEDRAL. Situated north of the Cloth Hall. The original church was built in 1073 and the cathedral in the thirteenth century. It was destroyed in the war and later rebuilt in the original Gothic style. A spire which had been part of the original blueprint, but had not been built, was also added. Within the Cathedral a number of features include Memorial Windows to King Albert, the RAF, the BEF, the 5th (Princess Charlotte of Wales's) Dragoon Guards, Memorial plaques to the British Commonwealth dead and the French dead on the Salient as well as the graves of several personalities from the history of Ypres.

Behind the cathedral are the cloisters containing original fragments of the cathedral destroyed in the war and a Memorial to the men of Munster who fell in the war. Just outside the south exit of the Cathedral are some original pre-war cobblestones. The road in front of the Cathedral is the Vandenpereboomplein which was formerly a canal to the Cloth Hall for transporting wool and materials. It is the location from which the annual 'Poppy Parade' departs to the Menin Gate on 11 November each year.

St. GEORGE'S MEMORIAL CHURCH. Located on the corner of the Vandenpereboomplein and Elverdingsestraat. Designed by Sir Reginald Blomfield, who designed many of the cemeteries on the Salient including Tyne Cot, it was built after Field Marshal Lord French had the idea of a church for the large numbers of British still living and working in Flanders, especially building the cemeteries and memorials for the IWGC, as well as for pilgrims to the Salient. Sir John French led the original BEF and was Commander-in-Chief of the British Army until December 1915. He was made the First Earl of Ypres in 1921. The foundation stone was laid by Field Marshal Lord Plumer on 24 July 1927 and a service of dedication led by the Lord Bishop of Fulham on 24 March 1929. Plumer led the V Corps at Ypres from January-May 1915 and was then commander of the Second Army until the end of the war. He planned and led the British victory at the Battle of Messines in June 1917 for which he was highly regarded. Known to the troops as 'Daddy' or 'Plum' he was made a Field Marshal in 1919 and Viscount, the 1st Baron Plumer of Messines, in 1929. There was also an Eton Memorial School, for the children of workers of the IWGC and other officials, near the church, that existed to 1948. In the church each chair and kneeler is an individual memorial and there are many Regimental plaques, banners and a bust of Lord French. The aim, as this book is completed in 2017, is for a public appeal to raise money to provide bells for the church.

BELGIAN MEMORIAL. Found near the Cloth Hall across the road at the west end of the hall. Next to it is a memorial to the 13th Belgian Artillery and the Town WW2 Memorial.

RIJSELSTRAAT. This is the road to the Lille Gate that I have recommended for a walk to Ramparts Cemetery. There are a number of interesting buildings, for example, at No. 38 the Belle Alms House or Belle Godhuis has some of the original sixteenth century building remaining. Founded in 1279 and rebuilt in 1616, there is a plaque to Master Jan Yperman, the 'father' of Flemish surgery who worked here from 1304-29. No. 70, the old Post Office, is a replica of a fourteenth century house that was possibly owned by the Knights' Templar. The St. John's Alms House was founded in 1277 and is now an art gallery. St. Peter's Church, near the Lille Gate, was built in the twelfth century in the Romanesque style and was rebuilt after the war.

SALVATION CORNER. Found at the Ypres end of the N369 road to Dixmuide. It gained this name because of the Salvation Army hut that was situated on the corner here throughout the war. Nearby, at the town end of the Ypres-Ijzer canal, is a bend known to the British as TATTENHAM CORNER, one of many similarly named junctions on the Western Front.

There are many excellent hotels, B&B's and restaurants, in town and around the Salient. It would be invidious of me to highlight any particular one, though this is a trap into which I have fallen fully and thunderously in the past. Each brings a different 'something' to offer and your choice should very much be based upon what you prefer. For me, any restaurant that serves a good Flemish Stew is a target. I have my favourites, who are all run by lovely people who will make every endeavour to have your experience of the town be memorable. I also have my favourite chocolate and souvenir shops, particular chocolate, notably one near the corner of the square that makes my management of school parties that I am leading around the Salient significantly easier.

Having said that, I am going to single out one. The Hotel Regina is named not for its accommodation or food, though both are excellent, and it is run by great staff and management. I single out the Hotel Regina for its role in WW2. It was known as the 'House of the Broken Wings' for its role as the start point of an escape route where Allied aircrew, who had been shot down and were evading German capture, were hidden and protected before they began their journey back to England. Much of this dangerous work was carried out by local resistance members and patriotic citizens. By conclusion of the war many were dead, mostly due to betrayals by informers. In 2011 a local historian, Chris Lock, and his wife Milena Kolarikova, working with the town's Royal Entente organisation, erected a remembrance plaque on the outside wall of the hotel commemorating the Belgian citizens who helped the resistance activities in the hotel during WW2.

There are other places of interest in Ypres that you may consider worth visiting. I do not claim this to be a definitive list, merely some of the more relevant features for someone interested in the Ypres Salient and the Great War.

# THE YPRES SALIENT

## THE START OF THE SALIENT

The Salient began life as part of the first, and short-lived stage of the war, the 'War of Movement', that culminated in the 'Race to the Sea'. The Germans who had seen their meticulous, and seemingly invincible, Schlieffen Plan, fail because of the resilience of the Belgians, the unexpected arrival of the British Expeditionary Force, and to some extent the indecisiveness of their own leaders. They decided that it was now vital to take the Channel Ports as a means of defeating the Allies.

During this early period from 3 October 1914, and before the arrival of the British 7th Division, the only troops at Ypres were the Yeomanry of the Queen's Own Oxfordshire Hussars who were the first Territorials in Flanders. They were present because of the intervention of Winston Churchill, then First Lord of the Admiralty, who had ordered in September, that when the Royal Marines were sent to hold the northern sector, particularly Dunkirk, a unit of cavalry must go with them. Although there were no cavalry units to spare from the fighting Churchill knew of a Yeomanry regiment that could do the job. These just happened to be Yeomanry with whom his family had a long relationship and within which some of his family were serving - a quick way for them to get to the war. Hence, for some time the Hussars were the only troops between the German Army and the Channel ports.

The Germans managed to enter Ypres and a few local villages before being forced back to the ridges around Ypres by the arrival of the British 7th Division. French, Commander-in-Chief of the B.E.F., hurled his forces at the Germans in an heroic action forming a line from La Bassee to just north of Ypres. Then from mid-October to mid-November the struggle raged to take Ypres which became known as the First Battle of Ypres.

## FIRST BATTLE OF YPRES

| | |
|---|---|
| Battle of Messines | 12 October - 2 November |
| Battle of Armentieres | 13 October - 2 November |
| Battles of Ypres, 1914 | 19 October -22 November |
| Battle of Langemarck | 21 October - 24 October |
| Battle of Gheluvelt | 29 October - 31 October |
| Battle of Nonne Bosschen | 11 November |

The two sides that faced each other in this daily series of battles were unevenly matched as the B.E.F. was outnumbered, poorly equipped and poorly positioned. The battles of late 1914 saw a change in the nature of warfare from mobile infantry, with some use of cavalry charges, to full scale trench warfare where defence was the best form of attrition. Although the Belgians had dug three lines of trenches at Liege before the war, trench warfare was not at first the usual form of fighting. Fortunately for the B.E.F. and the Allies the defenders at Ypres in 1914 were the forces of the 'Entente'.

Possibly the most important action of the First Battle of Ypres was at Geluveld. From 29-31 October the Germans attacked the British Battalions trying valiantly to hold the village and the line north and south of the Menin Road. Even so, the line broke temporarily and it seemed as if the road to Ypres was open.

On 31 October, north of the Menin Road, the 1st Scots Guards, 2nd Welsh and 1st South Wales Borderers were fighting in Geluveld chateau grounds, and though the Welsh had only eighteen working rifles the line to Polygon Wood was just holding. General Fitzclarence, VC, commanding the 1st Brigade, called for reinforcements so three companies of the 2nd Worcestershires were sent from Polygon Wood. The 357 men of the Worcestershires charged with the Scots Guards and South Wales Borderers, taking the Germans by surprise to save the day and halt the Kaiser's march on Ypres.

The Germans tried again on 11 November as the Prussian Guard were ordered to break through and take Ypres. They broke the first line but were stopped by men of 16th, 22nd and 51st Batteries, Royal Field Artillery and the 5th Field Company, Royal Engineers - cooks, drivers and the like. The guns and rifle fire seemed like a strong new line to the Prussians amongst whom the shells caused havoc, so they fell back into Nonne Boschen (Nun's Wood). The 2nd Oxford and Bucks Light Infantry then counter-attacked south through the wood driving the Prussian Guard before them either into Glencorse Wood, where they were attacked by 1st Cameron Highlanders, or east towards Polygon Wood where the 5th Field Company awaited them.

During the night Battalions of the Territorials were rushed up to the front-line to fill the gaps. They were proud to claim Nonne Boschen as their first battle honour of the war, though the fight was really over by the time of their arrival. Even so, they were greatly welcomed by the remnants of the B.E.F.

The German Kaiser also seemed to realise that the first attempt to take Ypres had failed. He had ordered his strongest and most famous regiments to take Ypres and break the British Army on 11 November. Over 17500 Germans in twelve Divisions had attacked on a nine mile front against less than 8000 British troops and failed to overcome them.

During the First Battle of Ypres the original B.E.F. ceased to exist, for example, General Capper, commanding the 7th Division, once described himself as a divisional commanding officer without a command. His Division had lost 732 officers and 9493 men in eighteen days since it had come to the Front. In the 100 days from 4 August to the end of the First Battle of Ypres the British Army had lost more officers than it had in all the wars involving British troops during the previous 100 years. British casualties in 1914 numbered 90,000, or 90% of original size of the B.E.F., of which 30% lay in the soil of Belgium. German casualties in the same period were 134315. Average Battalion size was one officer and 30 men out of 30 officers and 1000 men, and of the 84 British Battalions at Ypres on 1 November 1914, eighteen had less than 100 men, 31 less than 200 men, 26 less than 300 men and only nine had greater than 300 men.

By the end of the First Battle of Ypres many British regiments had almost ceased to exist, but the German

Army and the ambitions of its leaders, who could not believe that such a 'thin line' had held at Ypres, had been severely blunted. The town itself was to die during subsequent actions but in 1914 a cause had been born. The 'Contemptible Little Army', as the German Kaiser, Wilhelm II, had called the B.E.F. in his Order of the Day on 19 August 1914, was no more, and those who could call themselves 'Old Contemptibles' had much of which to be proud.

## SECOND BATTLE OF YPRES

| | |
|---|---|
| Battles of Ypres, 1915 | 22 April - 25 May |
| Battle of Gravenstafel | 22 April - 23 April |
| Battle of St. Julien | 24 April - 4 May |
| Battle of Frezenberg | 8 May - 13 May |
| Battle of Bellewaarde | 24 May - 25 May |

The British were glad to use the quiet of the winter to recuperate, though some may find the word 'quiet' a strange choice. For example, in December 1914 the 3rd Division suffered casualties of 33 officers and 717 men. The defence of Ypres in 1914 had established a political significance for the town that greatly outweighed its strategic and military importance. However, the British Army, always officially titled the B.E.F., had held it once and were determined to continue to hold Ypres.

The fighting in 1915 again saw the British strategically in the poorer position. The Germans introduced a new element of war, gas, used, for the first time, on 22 April 1915, in the north of the Salient against French troops. There was a time when Ypres was open to the Germans, but the actions of Canadian troops in closing and holding the line in the north-east of the Salient is well known. Less well known is the contribution of British troops, notably the 'Geddes Detachment'.

In the attack on 24 April 1915 Frezenberg was defended by 122nd Heavy Battery, 37th Howitzer Battery, a section of the 6th Battery of the Canadian Field Artillery and a Company of the 8th Middlesex. These were soon supplemented by sections from the 356th and 367th Batteries of the 28th Division Royal Field Artillery. This then was the complete extent of the British defences from Zonnebeke to Potijze but these Batteries temporarily halted the German attack.

Another German advance was attempted again at Frezenberg on 8 May. A new British line had been formed but the defenders had been greatly depleted in numbers over the previous weeks. The 1/3rd Monmouthshires numbered four officers and 130 men; the 2nd King's Own four officers and 94 men; the 1st King's Own Yorkshire Light Infantry five officers and 201 men. From 23 April to 8 May the 83rd Brigade had lost 128 officers and 4379 men. It is thought that the Brigade's defence at Frezenberg, in holding the Germans and ignoring orders to retire, was probably the turning point in British fortunes during the Second Battle of Ypres.

The Germans then spent the next month trying to defeat the defenders of Ypres. Action took place mostly in the north and east of the Salient, and although the line contracted substantially during the month, the town did not fall. However, it was during this battle that the civilians were evacuated from Ypres as a result of what the Germans called a 'hate shoot' on the town on 24 April. In holding Ypres the British suffered 60000 casualties. The 10th Brigade lost 73 officers and 2,346 men, almost ceasing to exist; the 149th Brigade 42 officers and 1192 men, or 75 % of their total. German losses were 34933. These were shocking figures at the time though small by the scale of what was to follow.

During 1916 the main action was elsewhere on the Somme and at Verdun. Even so there were some battles at Ypres, notably that of Mount Sorrel.

As a result of the disasters of 1916 General Haig, Commander-in-Chief since 1915, and the Chief of the Imperial General Staff, Robertson, needed a new plan leading to a victory. Douglas Haig had become Commander-in-Chief of the British Army on 18 December 1915 and was later made a Knight and Field Marshal. He had begun the war as commander of the I Corps and achieved some notable victories though these are mostly masked by the horrors of trench warfare and his policy of attrition. Haig decided to capture the ridges around Ypres and push through to the Belgian coast, hence, stopping the U-boat threat to the British convoys. Although this plan met with opposition from the Prime Minister, David Lloyd George, Haig gained enough support for the plan to be implemented. Even so, Haig decided on a preliminary event in the south of the Salient before implementing the main event in the north.

## THIRD BATTLE OF YPRES

| | |
|---|---|
| Battle of Messines | 7 June - 14 June |

The preliminary action in the south, known as the Battle of Mesen, had the aim of taking the Messines-Wijtschate Ridge on 7 June 1917. Extremely thorough preparation was undertaken involving the development of a cohesive plan, extensive training and the placing of massive mines under the German lines. The objective was the Oosttaverne Line occupied by General Sixt von Armin's Fourth Army and General Otto von Below's Sixth Army.

The German position, in a small salient south of Ypres, relied mainly on the physical advantages of holding the ridge. The British ranged round it on a nine mile front from the north at Hill 60 to south of Wijtschate 100000 troops in the 41st, 47th (London), 23rd, 36th (Ulster), 16th (Irish) and 19th (Western) Divisions with the II ANZAC Corps made up of the 3rd Australian, New Zealand and British 25th Divisions in the extreme south near Messines.

After an artillery bombardment using 3,258,000 (144,000 tons) shells from 2250 guns, nineteen mines were blown at 3.10am on 7 June, using 933,200lbs of ammonal, destroying the German front-line in the largest single explosion up to that date. The mines were the idea of J. Norton-Griffiths MP who developed the initial plan in May 1915 though it was not accepted until 1916. By the end of 1916, fifteen mines were in place and by 7 June 1917 another six were ready, though one had been discovered, one damaged and two abandoned. They were set at Hill 60 and under the nearby hill called 'The Caterpillar' by the 1st Australian Tunnelling Company; St. Eloi by the 1st Canadian Tunnelling Company; Hollandscheschuur Farm, Petit Bois, Maedelstede Farm and Peckham by the 250th Tunnelling

Company; Spanbroekmolen, Kruistraat and Ontario Farm by the 171st Tunnelling Company; and Trench 127 and Factory Farm by the 3rd Canadian Tunnelling Company.

The attack was a complete success. Most enemy positions were over-run with ease, some Battalions lost as few as ten men, though the 47th Division encountered stiff resistance at St. Eloi on the Dammstrasse and there was heavy fighting at Ravine Wood, Battle Wood and Hill 60. Allied casualties were light, vindicating the careful planning and caution of Plumer, and some 6400 German prisoners were taken.

| | |
|---|---|
| Battles of Ypres, 1917 | 31 July - 10 November |
| Battle of Pilckem Ridge | 31 July - 2 August |
| Battle of Langemarck | 16 August - 18 August |
| Battle of the Menin Road | 20 September - 25 September |
| Battle of Polygon Wood | 26 September - 3 October |
| Battle of Broodseinde | 4 October |
| Battle of Poelcappelle | 9 October |
| Battle of Passchendaele I | 12 October |
| Battle of Passchendaele II | 26 October - 10 November |

Six weeks later, after a bombardment from 16 to 31 July using 4.3 million shells from 3091 guns, including 100000 rounds of gas shells, the Third Battle of Ypres began. The basic plan was an attack by General Gough's relatively new, and untested, Fifth Army consisting of ten Divisions, east of Ypres on a seven mile front, with the French on its left, and five Divisions of Plumer's Second Army on the right, with seventeen Divisions in reserve. Hubert de la Poer Gough, known as 'Goughie', was in command of the 3rd Cavalry Division when the war started. On 26 May 1915, at the age of 45, he became the youngest Army Commander when he took over the Fifth Army, but was recalled to England after the German attack on the Somme in 1918. The Battle of Pilckem Ridge did not have the preparation and planning of Messines. The German defences, deploying fifteen front-line Divisions, were significantly better developed than in the south.

The battle opened, in rain, on 31 July at 3.50am, at the beginning of what was to become, at times, one of the wettest August to November periods on record. The first day saw most objectives taken, Pilkem fell to the 38th (Welsh) Division, the Steenbeek to the 51st (Highland) Division, Frezenberg to the 15th (Scottish) Division and Pomern Castle to the 55th (West Lancashire) Division, though at great cost, notably for the 8th and 30th Divisions on the Menin Road at Hooge, before the rain halted any effective further action. On the first day of the attack 15000 casualties were incurred (31850 by 2 August), twelve Victoria Crosses won, and twelve villages captured in a penetration of 2 to 3kms.

This pattern, of heavy casualties suffered in taking increasingly limited objectives, was repeated through the late summer and autumn. The offensive developed in three phases - 31 July to 2 August by Gough's Fifth Army; 20 September, 26 September and 4 October by Plumer's Second Army; and 26 October to 11 November by the Canadian Corps. These battles were some of the clearest examples of the advantage in the Great War of defence. Why did Haig persist when his original plan had failed? Did he believe in ultimate success? Was there any real alternative to such infantry attacks? Was he forced to continue because he had to show some success - the taking of Passendale - for such cost? Certainly when 270000 casualties were incurred in the advance something had to be seen to be achieved.

Passendale was captured in early November by the Canadians with the British 63rd (Royal Naval) Division and Territorials in support. The Germans had been pushed off a small part of the ridge around Ypres but at a considerable sacrifice. As a Sergeant from Scotland wrote in a letter home "Ypres; well may they call it Ypres", for this had a sad meaning at his home in Argyllshire as Ypres is Gaelic for 'sacrifice'. That the British Army did not suffer a mutiny like the French can only tell us much about the British character.

**FOURTH BATTLE OF YPRES**

| | |
|---|---|
| Battles of the Lys | 9 April - 29 April |
| Battle of Estaires | 9 April - 11 April |
| Battle of Messines, 1918 | 10 April - 11 April |
| Battle of Hazebrouck | 12 April - 15 April |
| Battle of Bailleul | 13 April - 15 April |
| Battle of Kemmel I | 17 April - 19 April |
| Battle of Bethune | 18 April |
| Battle of Kemmel II | 25 April - 26 April |
| Battle of Scherpenberg | 29 April |

This battle was Germany's 'Great Gamble', a spring offensive to win the war using troops released from Russia before the 'Doughboys' arrived from the USA. Having started on the Somme in March, the offensive came to the Salient in April 1918, along the valley of the Lys when the Allied front-line was pushed back to the outskirts of Ypres accentuating the Salient. The Germans used 49 Divisions in the attack against troops who had previously been involved in the battles on the Somme and had been transferred north to recuperate.

In early April the Germans pushed the line that was south of Ypres from a position east of Armentieres and Ploegsteert Wood back to the Monts des Flandres and west of Bailleul. The Battle of the Scherpenberg began at 5.40am as thirteen German Divisions attacked on a ten mile front. The British commanders, Plumer and Haig, contemplated withdrawing to a new line at St. Omer abandoning Ypres but on 30 April the German Commander, General Ludendorff, halted Operation Georgette, as the Battles of the Lys were then known to the German High Command. He planned a number of diversionary attacks to the south to draw the French troops away from Ypres before recommencing the attack.

All the ground taken by the British at such great cost only six months before was given up in a 'planned withdrawal' to shorten the line and concentrate troop dispositions to turn the tide. Fresh troops, French support and some desperate last ditch stands such as those by the 12th Royal Scots, 6th King's Own Scottish Borderers, 26th Brigade and advances by the 39th Division (Composite) Brigade played an important part in holding the Germans.

However, the most important element of the failure was that the British naval blockade was finally having an effect on Germany and their 'Gamble' failed through lack of resources. This was fortunate for the Allies because only 48 British Divisions were considered to be prepared for battle.

## THE FINAL BREAKOUT

Battle of Ypres, 1918    28 September - 2 October
Battle of Courtrai       14 October - 19 October

The final breakout from the Salient came in September 1918 using the same plan as that used in 1917, a series of staged advances. But the Germans did not have the strength of 1917 to face the Allied Flanders Army Group, under King Albert of Belgium, composed of thirteen Belgian, ten British and six French Divisions. Therefore, the advance and breakout were completed in two stages. The first, on a 23 mile front, saw the edge of the Salient reached.

The attack began on 28 September 1918. By midday Geluveld, the Wijtschate-Messines Ridge and Zandvoorde had been taken, and in the afternoon Beselare fell to the 11th and 12th Royal Scots. By 30 September 1918 the Menin-Roeselare road had been crossed. However, although the British Second Army had advanced up to six miles, casualties numbered 4500 Belgian and 4695 British, and lines of communication were being stretched due to the unexpectedly speedy advance, so a period of consolidation was undertaken.

As a result, key objectives such as the towns of Roeselare and Menin had not been taken, though 11000 prisoners, 300 artillery pieces and 600 machine-guns had been captured.

Finally the British troops pushed on in the Battle of Courtrai, unwilling to wait for a French and Belgian breakthrough to their north. The British Second Army of sixteen Divisions, supported by the Royal Air Force who dropped over 40 tons of bombs, and a Franco-Belgian force began the attack at 5.30am against the German Fourth Army composed of sixteen Divisions. An eighteen mile advance took 12000 prisoners and 550 artillery pieces, and with the fall of Ledegem the Salient was decreed to have been broken. By the day of the Armistice the British Army was 51 miles from the Salient.

# FIRST BATTLE OF YPRES (OCTOBER - NOVEMBER 1914)

**1st CAVALRY DIVISION** : Major-General H de B de Lisle
- Battle of Messines 12 Oct - 2 Nov (Cavalry Corps)

**1st Cavalry Brigade** : Brigadier-General C J Briggs
2nd (Queen's Bays) Dragoon Guards
5th (Princess Charlotte of Wales's) Dragoon Guards
11th (Prince Albert's Own) Hussars
**2nd Cavalry Brigade** : Brigadier-General R L Mullens
4th (Royal Irish) Dragoon Guards
9th (Queen's Royal) Lancers
18th (Queen Mary's Own) Hussars
1st Queen's Own Oxfordshire Hussars

**2nd CAVALRY DIVISION** : Major-General H de la P Gough
- Battle of Messines 12 Oct - 2 Nov (Cavalry Corps)
- Battle of Armentieres 13 - 17 Oct (Cavalry Corps)
- Battle of Gheluvelt 30 - 31 Oct (I Corps)

**3rd Cavalry Brigade** : Brigadier-General J Vaughan
4th (Queen's Own) Hussars
5th (Royal Irish) Lancers
16th (The Queen's) Lancers
**4th Cavalry Brigade** : Brigadier-General Hon. C E Bingham
3rd (King's Own) Hussars
6th (Carabiniers) Dragoon Guards
Composite Battalion of the Household Cavalry
**5th Cavalry Brigade** : Brigadier-General Sir P W Chetwode, Bt
2nd Dragoons (Royal Scots Greys)
12th (Prince of Wales's Royal) Lancers
20th Hussars

**3rd CAVALRY DIVISION** : Major-General Hon. J H G Byng
- Battle of Langemarck 21 - 24 Oct (IV Corps)
- Battle of Gheluvelt 29 - 31 Oct (I Corps)
- Battle of Nonne Bosschen 11 Nov (I Corps)

**6th Cavalry Brigade** : Brigadier-General E Makins to 7 Nov (Sick); Lieutenant Colonel O B B Smith-Bingham to 9 Nov; Brigadier-General D G M Campbell
1st (Royal) Dragoons
3rd (Prince of Wales's) Dragoon Guards (from 4 Nov)
10th (Prince of Wales's Own Royal) Hussars
**7th Cavalry Brigade** : Brigadier-General C T Kavanagh
1st Life Guards
2nd Life Guards
Royal Horse Guards

**1st DIVISION** : Major-General S H Lomax to 31 Oct (wounded); Major-General H J S Landon
- Battle of Langemarck 21 - 24 Oct (I Corps)
- Battle of Gheluvelt 29 - 31 Oct (I Corps)
- Battle of Nonne Bosschen 11 Nov (I Corps)

**1st (Guards) Brigade** : Brigadier-General C Fitzclarence, VC
1st Coldstream Guards
1st Scots Guards
1st Black Watch
1st Cameron Highlanders
1/14th (London Scottish) Londons (from 7 Nov)
**2nd Brigade** : Brigadier-General E S Bulfin to 1 Nov (wounded); Colonel C Cunliffe-Owen
2nd Royal Sussex
1st Loyal North Lancashires
1st Northhamptons
2nd King's Royal Rifle Corps
**3rd Brigade** : Brigadier-General H J S Landon to 31 Oct; Colonel A C Lovett
1st Queen's (Royal West Surreys) (to 9 Nov)
1st Gloucesters
1st South Wales Borderers
2nd Welsh
2nd Royal Munster Fusiliers (from 9 Nov)

**2nd DIVISION** : Major-General C C Monro
- Battle of Langemarck 21 - 24 Oct (I Corps)
- Battle of Gheluvelt 29 - 31 Oct (I Corps)
- Battle of Nonne Bosschen 11 Nov (I Corps)

**4th (Guards) Brigade** : Brigadier-General F R Earl of Cavan
2nd Grenadier Guards
1st Irish Guards
2nd Coldstream Guards
3rd Coldstream Guards
**5th Brigade** : Colonel C B Westmacott
2nd Worcesters
2nd Oxford & Bucks Light Infantry
2nd Highland Light Infantry
2nd Connaught Rangers
**6th Brigade** : Brigadier-General R Fanshawe
1st King's (Liverpool)
2nd South Staffordshires
1st Royal Berkshires
1st King's Royal Rifle Corps

**3rd DIVISION** : Major-General F D V Wing
- Battle of Messines 31 Oct - 2 Nov (Cavalry Corps)
- Battle of Nonne Bosschen 11 Nov (I Corps)

**7th Brigade** : Brigadier-General F W N McCraken
3rd Worcesters
2nd South Lancashires
1st Wiltshires
2nd Royal Irish Rifles
**8th Brigade** : Brigadier-General W H Bowes
2nd Royal Scots
2nd Suffolks
4th Middlesex
1st Gordon Highlanders
1st Honourable Artillery Company (from 9 Nov)
**9th Brigade** : Brigadier-General F C Shaw
1st Northumberland Fusiliers
4th Royal Fusiliers
1st Lincolns
1st Royal Scots Fusiliers

**4th DIVISION** : Major-General H F M Wilson
- Battle of Armentieres 13 Oct - 2 Nov (III Corps)
- Battle of Messines 21 - 31 Oct  (2nd Essex on 21 Oct, 2nd Royal Inniskilling Fusiliers on 30-31 Oct)

**10th Brigade** : Brigadier-General J A L Haldane
1st Royal Warwickshires
2nd Seaforth Highlanders
1st Royal Irish Fusiliers
2nd Royal Dublin Fusiliers
**11th Brigade** : Brigadier-General A G Hunter-Weston
1st Somerset Light Infantry
1st East Lancashires
1st Hampshires
1st Rifle Brigade
**12th Brigade** : Brigadier-General F G Anley
1st King's Own
2nd Lancashire Fusiliers
2nd Royal Inniskilling Fusiliers
2nd Essex

**5th DIVISION** : Major-General T L N Morland
- Battle of Messines 31 Oct - 2 Nov (2nd King's Own Scottish Borderers & 2nd King's Own Yorkshire Light Infantry in Cavalry Corps)
- Battle of Armentieres 1 - 2 Nov (1st Dorsets in III Corps)
- Battle of Nonne Bosschen 11 Nov (2nd King's Own Scottish Borderers, 2nd Duke of Wellington's, 1st Bedfords, 1st Cheshires in III Cps)

**13th Brigade** : Colonel A Martyn to 7 Nov (Wounded); Lieutenant Colonel W M Withycombe
2nd King's Own Scottish Borderers
2nd King's Own Yorkshire Light Infantry
2nd Duke of Wellington's
1st Royal West Kents
**14th Brigade** : Brigadier-General F S Maude
1st Devonshires
2nd Duke of Cornwall's Light Infantry
1st East Surreys
2nd Manchesters
**15th Brigade** : Brigadier-General Count Gleichen
1st Norfolks
1st Bedfordshires
1st Cheshires
1st Dorsets

**6th DIVISION** : Major-General J L Keir
- Battle of Armentieres 13 Oct - 2 Nov (III Corps)

**16th Brigade** : Brigadier-General E C Ingouville-Williams
1st Buffs
1st King's Shropshire Light Infantry
2nd York & Lancasters
1st Leicesters
**17th Brigade** : Brigadier-General W R B Doran
1st Royal Fusiliers
1st North Staffordshires
2nd Leinsters
3rd Rifle Brigade
**18th Brigade** : Brigadier-General W N Congreve, VC
1st West Yorkshires
1st East Yorkshires
2nd Sherwood Foresters
2nd Durham Light Infantry
**19th Brigade** : Brigadier-General Hon. F Gordon
2nd Royal Welsh Fusiliers
2nd Argyll & Sutherland Highlanders
1st Middlesex
1st Cameronians

**7th DIVISION** : Major-General T Capper
- Battle of Langemarck 21 - 24 Oct (IV Corps)
- Battle of Gheluvelt 29 - 31 Oct (I Corps)

**20th Brigade** : Brigadier-General H Ruggle-Brise
1st Grenadier Guards
2nd Scots Guards
2nd Border
2nd Gordon Highlanders
**21st Brigade** : Brigadier-General H E Watts
2nd Bedfordshires
2nd Yorkshires
2nd Royal Scots Fusiliers
2nd Wiltshires
**22nd Brigade** : Brigadier-General S T B Lawford
2nd Queen's (Royal West Surreys)
2nd Royal Warwickshires
1st Royal Welsh Fusiliers
1st South Staffordshires

# SECOND BATTLE OF YPRES (APRIL - MAY 1915)

**1ST CAVALRY DIVISION** : Major-General H de B de Lisle
- Battle of Frezenberg 9 - 13 May (Cavalry Corps, Second Army)
- Battle of Bellewaarde 24 May (Cavalry Corps, Second Army)

**1st Cavalry Brigade** :Lieutenant Colonel T T Pitman to 15 May; Brigadier-General E Makins
2nd (Queen's Bays) Dragoon Guards
5th (Princess Charlotte of Wales's) Dragoon Guards
11th (Prince Albert's Own) Hussars
**2nd Cavalry Brigade** : Brigadier-General R L Mullens
4th (Royal Irish) Dragoon Guards
18th (Queen Mary's Own) Hussars
9th (Queen's Royal) Lancers
**9th Cavalry Brigade** : Brigadier-General W H Greenly
15th (The King's) Hussars
19th (Queen Alexandra's Own Royal) Hussars

**2ND CAVALRY DIVISION** : Major-General C T Kavanagh
- Battle of St Julien 26 Apr - 3 May (Plumers Force, Second Army)
- Battle of Bellewaarde 24 - 25 May (V Corps, Second Army)

**3rd Cavalry Brigade** : Brigadier-General J Vaughan
4th (Queen's Own) Hussars
5th (Royal Irish) Lancers
16th (The Queen's) Lancers
**4th Cavalry Brigade** : Brigadier-General Hon C E Bingham
Household Cavalry
3rd (King's Own) Hussars
6th (Carabiniers) Dragoon Guards
**5th Cavalry Brigade** : Brigadier-General Sir P W Chetwode, Bt
2nd Dragoons (Royal Scots Greys)
12th (Prince of Wales's Royal) Lancers
20th Hussars

**3RD CAVALRY DIVISION** : Major-General C J Briggs
- Battle of Frezenberg 11 - 13 May (Cavalry Corps, Second Army)

**6th Cavalry Brigade**: Brigadier-General D G M Campbell
3rd (Prince of Wales's) Dragoon Guards
1st (Royal) Dragoons
1st North Somerset Yeomanry
**7th Cavalry Brigade** : Brigadier-General A A Kennedy
1st Life Guards
2nd Life Guards
1st Leicester Yeomanry
**8th Cavalry Brigade** : Brigadier-General C B Bulkeley-Johnson
Royal Horse Guards
10th (Prince of Wales's Own Royal) Hussars
1st Essex Yeomanry

**4TH DIVISION** : Major-General H F M Wilson
- Battle of St Julien 25 Apr - 4 May (V Corps, Second Army)
- Battle of Frezenberg 8 - 13 May (V Corps, Second Army
- Battle of Bellewaarde 24 - 25 May (V Corps, Second Army)

**10th Brigade** : Brigadier-General C P A Hull
1st Royal Warwickshires
2nd Seaforth Highlanders
1/7th Argyll & Sutherland Highlanders
1st Royal Irish Fusiliers
2nd Royal Dublin Fusiliers
**11th Brigade** : Brigadier-General J A Hasler, killed in action 27 April; Lieutenant Colonel F R Hicks to 29 April ; Brigadier-General C B Prowse, DSO
1st Somerset Light Infantry
1st East Lancashires
1/5th (London Rifle Brigade) Londons
1st Hampshires
1st Rifle Brigade
**12th Brigade** : Brigadier-General F G Anley
1st King's Own
2nd Lancashire Fusiliers
1/5th South Lancashires
2nd Royal Irish
2nd Essex
1/2nd Monmouths

**5TH DIVISION** : Major-General T L N Morland
- Battles of Ypres 23 Apr - 1 May (V Corps, Second Army)
- Battle of Gravenstafel Ridge 23 April (13th Brigade only)
- Battle of St Julien 24 April - 1 May (13th Brigade only)

**13th Brigade** : Brigadier-General R Wanless O'Gowan
2nd King's Own Scottish Borderers
2nd Duke of Wellington's
1/9th (Queen Victoria's Rifles) Londons
1st Royal West Kents
2nd King's Own Yorkshire Light Infantry
**14th Brigade** : Brigadier-General G H Thesiger
1st Devonshires
1st East Surreys
2nd Manchesters
1st Duke of Cornwall's Light Infantry
1/5th (Earl of Chester's) Cheshires
**15th Brigade** : Brigadier-General E Northey
1st Norfolks
1st Bedfordshires
1/6th (Liverpool Rifles) King's (Liverpool)
1st Cheshires
1st Dorsets

**27th DIVISION** : Major-General T Snow
- Battle of Gravenstafel Ridge 22 - 23 April (V Corps, Second Army)
- Battle of St Julien 24 April - 4 May (V Corps, Second Army)
- Battle of Frezenberg 8 - 13 May (V Corps, Second Army)
- Battle of Bellewaarde 24 -25 May (V Corps, Second Army)

**80th Brigade**: Brigadier-General W E B Smith
2nd King's Shropshire Light Infantry
4th Rifle Brigade
3rd King's Royal Rifle Corps
4th King's Royal Rifle Corps
Princess Patricia's Canadian Light Infantry
**81st Brigade** : Brigadier-General H L Croker
1st Royal Scots
1/9th (Highlanders) Royal Scots
2nd Cameron Highlanders
2nd Gloucesters
1st Argyll & Sutherland Highlanders
1/9th (Dumbartonshire) Argyll & Sutherland Highlanders
**82nd Brigade** : Brigadier-General J R Longley
1st Royal Irish
2nd Duke of Cornwall's Light Infantry
2nd Royal Inniskilling Fusiliers
1st Leinsters
1/1st Cambridgeshires

**28th DIVISION** : Major-General E S Bulfin
- Battle of Gravenstafel Ridge 22 - 23 April (V Corps, Second Army)
- Battle of St Julien 24 Apr - 4 May (II Corps, Second Army)
- Battle of Frezenberg 8 - 13 May (II Corps, Second Army)
- Battle of Bellewaarde 24 -25 May (II Corps, Second Army)

**83rd Brigade** : Brigadier-General R C Boyle to 13 May (sick); Lieutenant Colonel T O Marden; Brigadier-General H S L Ravenshaw
1st King's Own Yorkshire Light Infantry
1/5th King's Own
2nd East Yorkshires
2nd King's Own
1st York & Lancasters
1/3rd Monmouths
**84th Brigade** : Brigadier-General L J Bols
2nd Northumberland Fusiliers
1/1st Monmouths
1/12th (Rangers) Londons (to 20 May)
2nd Cheshires
1st Suffolks
1st Welsh
**85th Brigade** : Brigadier-General A J Chapman to 18 May; Brigadier-General C E Pereira
2nd Buffs
3rd Royal Fusiliers
1/8th Middlesex
2nd East Surreys
3rd Middlesex

**50th (NORTHUMBRIAN) DIVISION** : Major-General Sir W F L Lindsay
- Battle of St Julien 24 Apr - 3 May (V Corps until 28 April then Plumers Force, Second Army)
- Battle of Frezenberg 11 - 13 May (V Corps, Second Army)
- Battle of Bellewaarde 24 - 25 May (149th Brigade only)

**149th (Northumberland) Brigade** : Brigadier-General J F Riddell, killed in action, 26 Apr; Lieutenant Colonel A J Forster, 26 Apr; Lieutenant Colonel A H Coles to 27 Apr; Brigadier-General G P T Feilding
1/4th Northumberland Fusiliers
1/5th Northumberland Fusiliers
1/6th Northumberland Fusiliers
1/7th Northumberland Fusiliers
**150th (York & Durham) Brigade** : Brigadier-General J. E. Bush
1/4th East Yorkshires
1/5th Durham Light Infantry
1/4th Yorkshires
1/5th Yorkshires
**151st (Durham Light Infantry) Brigade** : Brigadier-General H. Martin
1/6th Durham Light Infantry
1/7th Durham Light Infantry
1/8th Durham Light Infantry
1/9th Durham Light Infantry

**3RD (LAHORE) INDIAN DIVISION** : Major-General Sir H D'Urban Keary
- Battle of St. Julien 24 April – 4 May (V Corps, Second Army)

**7th (Ferozepore) Brigade** : Major-General R G Egerton
1st Connaught Rangers
57th Wilde's Rifles
1/4th Londons
129th Duke of Connaught's Own Baluchis
9th Bhopal Infantry
**8th (Jullundur) Brigade** : Brigadier-General E P Strickland
1st Manchesters
59th Scinde Rifles
40th Pathans
47th Sikhs
1/4th Suffolks
**9th (Sirhind) Brigade** : Brigadier-General W G Walker
1st Highland Light Infantry
125th Napier's Rifles
15th Ludhiana Sikhs
1/1st King George's Own Gurkha Rifles
1/4th Gurkha Rifles
4th Kings (Liverpool)

**1st CANADIAN DIVISION** : Lt-Gen E A H Alderson
- Battle of Gravenstafel 22-23 April (V Corps, Second Army)
- Battle of St Julien 24 April - 4 May (V Corps, Second Army)

**1st Canadian Brigade** : Brigadier-General M S Mercer
1st (Western Ontario) Canadian Infantry
2nd (Eastern Ontario) Canadian Infantry
3rd (Toronto) Canadian Infantry
4th Central Ontario) Canadian Infantry
**2nd Canadian Brigade** : Brigadier-General A W Currie
5th (Western Cavalry) Canadian Infantry
7th (1st British Columbia) Canadian Infantry
8th (90th Rifles) Canadian Infantry
10th (Canadians) Canadian Infantry
**3rd Canadian Brigade** : Brigadier-General R E W Turner
13th (Royal Highlanders) Canadian Infantry
14th (Royal Montreal) Canadian Infantry
15th (48th Highlanders) Canadian Infantry
16th (Canadian Scottish) Canadian Infantry

# THIRD BATTLES OF YPRES (JUNE-NOVEMBER 1917)

**GUARDS DIVISION** : Major General G P T Feilding
- Battle of Pilckem Ridge 31 July - 2 Aug (XIV Corps, Fifth Army)
- Battle of Poelcappelle 9 Oct (XIV Corps, Fifth Army)
- First Battle of Passchendaele 12 Oct (XIV Corps, Fifth Army)

**1st Guards Brigade** : Brigadier General G D Jeffreys to 22 September; Brigadier General C R Champion de Crespigny
2nd Grenadier Guards
1st Irish Guards
2nd Coldstream Guards
3rd Coldstream Guards
**2nd Guards Brigade** : Brigadier General J Ponsonby to 22 August; Brigadier General B N Sergison-Brooke
3rd Grenadier Guards
1st Scots Guards
1st Coldstream Guards
2nd Irish Guards
**3rd Guards Brigade** : Brigadier General Lord H C Seymour
1st Grenadier Guards
4th Grenadier Guards
2nd Scots Guards
1st Welsh Guards
Pioneers : 4th Coldstream Guards

**1st DIVISION** : Major General E P Strickland
- Battle of Passchendaele II 5 - 10 Nov (II Corps, Second Army)

**1st Brigade** : Brigadier General C J C Grant
1st Black Watch
10th Gloucesters
1st Cameron Highlanders
8th Royal Berkshires
**2nd Brigade** : Brigadier General G C Kemp
2nd Royal Sussex
1st Northamptons
1st Loyal North Lancashires
2nd King's Royal Rifle Corps
**3rd Brigade** : Brigadier General R C A McCalmont
1st South Wales Borderers
2nd Welsh
1st Gloucesters
2nd Royal Munster Fusiliers
Pioneers : 6th Welsh

**3rd DIVISION** : Major General C J Deverell
- Battle of the Menin Road 22 - 25 Sept (V Corps, Fifth Army)
- Battle of Polygon Wood 26 - 30 Sept (V Corps, Fifth Army to 28 Sept II A.N.Z.A.C. Corps, Second Army)

**8th Brigade** : Brigadier General H G Holmes
2nd Royal Scots
7th King's Shropshire Light Infantry
1st Royal Scots Fusiliers
8th East Yorkshires
**9th Brigade** : Brigadier General H C Potter
1st Northumberland Fusiliers
13th King's (Liverpool)
4th Royal Fusiliers
12th West Yorkshires
**76th Brigade** : Brigadier General C L Porter
2nd Suffolks
8th King's Own
1st Gordon Highlanders
10th Royal Welsh Fusiliers
Pioneers : 20th (British Empire League) King's Royal Rifle Corps

**5th DIVISION** : Major General R B Stephens
- Battle of Polygon Wood 1 - 3 Oct (X Corps, Second Army)
- Battle of Broodseinde 4 Oct (X Corps, Second Army)
- Battle of Poekapelle 9 Oct (X Corps, Second Army)
- Second Battle of Passchendaele 26 Oct - 10 Nov (X Corps, Second Army)

**13th Brigade** : Brigadier General L O W Jones
2nd King's Own Scottish Borderers
14th (1st Birmingham Pals) Royal Warwickshires
15th (2nd Birmingham Pals) Royal Warwickshires
1st Royal West Kents
**15th Brigade** : Brigadier General M N Turner
1st Norfolks
1st Cheshires
1st Bedfordshires
16th (3rd Birmingham Pals) Royal Warwickshires
**95th Brigade** : Brigadier General Lord E C Gordon-Lennox
1st Devonshires
1st Duke of Cornwall's Light Infantry
1st East Surreys
12th (Bristol Pals) Gloucesters
Pioneers : 1/6th (Renfrewshire) Argyll & Sutherland Highlanders

**4th DIVISION** : Major General T G Matheson
- Battle of Polygon Wood 28 Sept - 3 Oct (XIV Corps, Fifth Army)
- Battle of Broodseinde 4 Oct (XIV Corps, Fifth Army)
- Battle of Poelcappelle 9 Oct (XIV Corps, Fifth Army)
- Second Battle of Passchendaele I 12 Oct (XIV Corps, Fifth Army)

**10th Brigade** : Brigadier General A G Pritchard
Household Battalion
2nd Seaforth Highlanders
1st Royal Warwickshires
3/10th Middlesex
**11th Brigade** : Brigadier General R A Berners
1st Somerset Light Infantry
1st Manchesters
1st East Lancashires
1st Rifle Brigade
**12th Brigade** : Brigadier General A Carton de Wiart, VC
1st King's Own
2nd Duke of Wellington's
2nd Lancashire Fusiliers
2nd Essex
Pioneers : 21st (Wool Textile Pioneers) West Yorkshires

**7th DIVISION** : Major General T Capper
- Battle of Polygon Wood 1 - 3 Oct (X Corps, Second Army)
- Battle of Broodseinde 4 Oct (X Corps, Second Army)
- Battle of Poelcappelle 9 Oct (X Corps, Second Army)
- Second Battle of Passchendaele 26 - 29 Oct (X Corps, Second Army)

**20th Brigade** : Brigadier General H C R Green
2nd Border
2nd Gordon Highlanders
8th Devonshires
9th Devonshires
**22nd Brigade** : Brigadier General J Steele
2/1st Honourable Artillery Company
20th (5th Manchester Pals) Manchesters
1st Royal Welsh Fusiliers
2nd Royal Warwickshires
**91st Brigade** : Brigadier General R T Pelly
21st (6th Manchester Pals) Manchesters
22nd (7th Manchester Pals) Manchesters
2nd Queen's (Royal West Surrey)
1st South Staffordshires
Pioneers : 24th (Oldham Pals) Manchesters

**8th DIVISION** : Major General W C G Heneker
- Battle of Pilckem Ridge 31 July - 1 Aug (II Corps, Fifth Army)
- Battle of Langemarck 16 - 18 Aug (II Corps, Fifth Army)

**23rd Brigade** : Brigadier General G W St G Grogan, VC
2nd Devonshires
2nd Cameronians
2nd West Yorkshires
2nd Middlesex
**24th Brigade** : Brigadier General H W Cobham
1st Worcesters
1st Sherwood Foresters
2nd East Lancashires
2nd Northamptons
**25th Brigade** : Brigadier General C Coffin, VC
2nd Lincolns
1st Royal Irish Rifles
2nd Royal Berkshires
2nd Rifle Brigade
Pioneers : 22nd (3rd County of Durham Pals) Durham Light Infantry

**11th (NORTHERN) DIVISION** : Major General H R Davies
- Battle of Messines 9 - 14 June (IX Corps, Second Army)
- Battle of Langemarck 16 - 18 Aug (XVIII Corps, Fifth Army)
- Battle of Polygon Wood 26 Sept - 3 Oct (XVIII Corps, Fifth Army)
- Battle of Broodseinde 4 Oct (XVIII Corps, Fifth Army)
- Battle of Poelcappelle 9 Oct (XVIII Corps, Fifth Army)

**32nd Brigade** : Brigadier General T H F Price
9th West Yorkshires
8th Duke of Wellington's
6th Yorkshires
6th York & Lancasters
**33rd Brigade** : Brigadier General A C Daly to 15 Sept; Brigadier General F G Spring
6th Lincolns
7th South Staffordshires
6th Border
9th Sherwood Foresters
**34th Brigade** : Brigadier General S H Pedley to 22 Aug; Brigadier General B G Clay
8th Northumberland Fusiliers
5th Dorsets
9th Lancashire Fusiliers
11th Manchesters
Pioneers : 6th East Yorkshires

**9th (SCOTTISH) DIVISION** : Major General H T Lukin
- Battle of the Menin Road 20 - 23 Sept (V Corps, Fifth Army)
- First Battle of Passchendaele 12 Oct (XVIII Corps, Fifth Army)

**26th Brigade** : Brigadier General J Kennedy
8th Black Watch
10th Argyll & Sutherland Highlanders
7th Seaforth Highlanders
5th Cameron Highlanders
**27th Brigade** : Brigadier General F A Maxwell, VC, killed in action 21 Sept; Lieutenant Colonel H D N McLean to 23 Sept; Brigadier General W D Croft
11th Royal Scots
12th Royal Scots
6th King's Own Scottish Borderers
9th Cameronians
**South African Brigade** : Brigadier General F S Dawson
1st South African Infantry
2nd South African Infantry
3rd South African Infantry
4th South African Infantry
Pioneers : 9th Seaforth Highlanders

**14th (LIGHT) DIVISION** : Major General V A Couper
- Battle of Langemarck 18 Aug (II Corps, Fifth Army)
- First Battle of Passchendaele 12 Oct (X Corps, Second Army)

**41st Brigade** : Brigadier General P C B Skinner
7th King's Royal Rifle Corps
8th King's Royal Rifle Corps
7th Rifle Brigade
8th Rifle Brigade
**42nd Brigade** : Brigadier General G N B Forster
5th Oxford & Bucks Light Infantry
5th King's Shropshire Light Infantry
9th Rifle Brigade
9th King's Royal Rifle Corps
**43rd Brigade** : Brigadier General P R Wood to 1 Sept; Brigadier General R S Tempest
6th Duke of Cornwall's Light Infantry
6th King's Own Yorkshire Light Infantry
6th Somerset Light Infantry
10th Durham Light Infantry
Pioneers : 11th King's (Liverpool)

**15th (SCOTTISH) DIVISION** : Major General H F Thuillier
- Battle of Pilckem Ridge 31 July - 2 Aug (XIX Corps, Fifth Army)
- Battle of Langemarck 17 - 18 Aug (46th Brigade only)

**44th Brigade** : Brigadier General F J Marshall
9th Black Watch
8/10th Gordon Highlanders
8th Seaforth Highlanders
7th Cameron Highlanders
**45th Brigade** : Brigadier General W H L Allgood
13th Royal Scots
11th Argyll & Sutherland Highlanders
6/7th Royal Scots Fusiliers
6th Cameron Highlanders
**46th Brigade** : Lieutenant Colonel K J Buchanan to 2 Aug; Brigadier General D R Sladen
7/8th King's Own Scottish Borderers
10/11th Highland Light Infantry
10th Cameronians
12th Highland Light Infantry
       Pioneers : 9th Gordon Highlanders

**17th (NORTHERN) DIVISION** : Major General P R Robertson
- First Battle of Passchendaele 12 Oct (XIV Corps, Fifth Army)
- Second Battle of Passchendaele 8 - 10 Nov (XIX Corps, Fifth Army)

**50th Brigade** : Brigadier General C Yatman
10th West Yorkshires
7th Yorkshires
7th East Yorkshires
6th Dorsets
**51st Brigade** : Brigadier General C E Bond to 14 Oct (sick); Lieutenant Colonel F E Metcalfe
7th Lincolns
10th Sherwood Foresters
8th South Staffordshires
7th (Westmorland & Cumberland Yeomanry) Borders
**52nd Brigade** : Brigadier General A J F Eden
9th (Northumberland Hussars Yeomanry) Northumberland Fusiliers
12th (Duke of Lancaster's Own Yeomanry) Manchesters
3/4th Royal West Kents
10th Lancashire Fusiliers
9th Duke of Wellington's
Pioneers : 7th York & Lancasters

**16th (IRISH) DIVISION** : Major General W B Hickie
- Battle of Messines 7 - 9 June (IX Corps, Second Army)
- Battle of Pilckem Ridge 31 July - 2 Aug (Reserve, XIX Corps, Fifth Army)
- Battle of Langemarck 16 - 18 Aug (XIX Corps, Fifth Army)

**47th Brigade** : Brigadier General G E Pereira
6th Royal Irish
7th Leinsters
6th Connaught Rangers
1st Royal Munster Fusiliers
**48th Brigade** : Brigadier General F W Ramsey
7th Royal Irish Rifles
2nd Royal Dublin Fusiliers
8th Royal Dublin Fusiliers
9th Royal Dublin Fusiliers
10th Royal Dublin Fusiliers
**49th Brigade** : Brigadier General P Leveson-Gower
2nd Royal Irish
7/8th Royal Irish Fusiliers
7th Royal Inniskilling Fusiliers
8th Royal Inniskilling Fusiliers
Pioneers : 11th Hampshires

**18th (EASTERN) DIVISION** : Major General R P Lee
- Battle of Pilckem Ridge 31 July (II Corps, Fifth Army)
- Battle of Langemarck 16 - 17 Aug (53rd Brigade with 56th Division)
- First Battle of Passchendaele 12 Oct (XVIII Corps, Fifth Army)
- Second Battle of Passchendaele 5 - 10 Nov (XIX Corps, Fifth Army)

**53rd Brigade** : Brigadier General H W Higginson
8th Norfolks
10th Essex
8th Suffolks
6th Royal Berkshires
**54th Brigade** : Brigadier General C Cunliffe-Owen to 22 Oct; Brigadier General L W de V Sadleir-Jackson
11th Royal Fusiliers
6th Northamptons
7th Bedfordshires
12th Middlesex
**55th Brigade** : Brigadier General B D Price
7th Queen's (Royal West Surreys)
8th East Surreys
7th Buffs
7th Royal West Kents
Pioneers : 8th Royal Sussex

**20th (LIGHT) DIVISION** : Major General W Douglas-Smith
- Battle of Langemarck 16 - 18 Aug (XIV Corps, Fifth Army)
- Battle of the Menin Road 20 - 25 Sept (XIV Corps, Fifth Army)
- Battle of Polygon Wood 26 - 28 Sept (XIV Corps, Fifth Army)

**59th Brigade** : Brigadier General R C Browne-Clayton to 26 Aug; Brigadier General H H G Hyslop
10th King's Royal Rifle Corps
11th King's Royal Rifle Corps
10th Rifle Brigade
11th Rifle Brigade
**60th Brigade** : Brigadier General Hon. L J P Butler
6th Oxford & Bucks Light Infantry
6th King's Shropshire Light Infantry
12th Rifle Brigade
12th King's Royal Rifle Corps
**61st Brigade** : Brigadier General W E Banbury
7th King's Own Yorkshire Light Infantry
7th Duke of Cornwall's Light Infantry
12th King's (Liverpool)
7th Somerset Light Infantry
Pioneers : 11th Durham Light Infantry

**21st DIVISION** : Major General D G M Campbell
- Battle of Polygon Wood 29 Sept - 3 Oct (X Corps, Second Army)
- Battle of Broodseinde 4 Oct (X Corps, Second Army)
- Second Battle of Passchendaele 26 Oct - 10 Nov (X Corps, Second Army)

**62nd Brigade** : Brigadier General C G Rawling, killed in action 28 Oct; Captain G M Sharpe to 1 Nov; Brigadier General G H Gater
12th Northumberland Fusiliers
13th Northumberland Fusiliers
3/4th Queen's (Royal West Surreys)
1st Lincolns
10th Yorkshires
**64th Brigade** : Brigadier General H R Headlam
1st East Yorkshires
9th King's Own Yorkshire Light Infantry
15th Durham Light Infantry
10th (Shropshire & Cheshire Yeomanry) King's Own Yorkshire Light Infantry
**110th Brigade** : Brigadier General Lord Leach
6th Leicesters
7th Leicesters
8th Leicesters
9th Leicesters
Pioneers : 14th Northumberland Fusiliers

**23rd DIVISION** : Major General J M Babington
- Battle of Messines 7 - 14 June (X Corps, Second Army)
- Battle of the Menin Road 20 - 24 Sept (X Corps, Second Army)
- Battle of Polygon Wood 28 Sept - 2 Oct (X Corps, Second Army)
- First Battle of Passchendaele 12 Oct (X Corps, Second Army)

**68th Brigade** : Brigadier General G N Colvile to 27 Sept; Lieutenant Colonel M. G H Barker
10th Northumberland Fusiliers
11th Northumberland Fusiliers
12th Durham Light Infantry
13th Durham Light Infantry
**69th Brigade** : Brigadier General T S Lambert
11th West Yorkshires
10th Duke of Wellington's
8th Yorkshires
9th Yorkshires
**70th Brigade** : Brigadier General H Gordon
11th Sherwood Foresters
8th Kings Own Yorkshire Light Infantry
8th York & Lancasters
9th York & Lancasters
Pioneers : 9th South Staffordshires

**24th DIVISION** : Major General L J Bols
- Battle of Messines 7 - 14 June (X Corps, Second Army)
- Battle Pilkem Ridge 31 July - 2 Aug (II Corps, Fifth Army)
- Battle of Langemarck 16 - 18 Aug (II Corps, Fifth Army)

**17th Brigade** : Brigadier General P V P Stone
8th Buffs
3rd Rifle Brigade
1st Royal Fusiliers
12th Royal Fusiliers
**72nd Brigade** : Brigadier General W F Sweny
8th Queen's (Royal West Surrey)
8th Royal West Kents
9th East Surreys
1st North Staffordshires
**73rd Brigade** : Brigadier General W J Dugan
9th Royal Sussex
13th Middlesex
7th Northamptons
2nd Leinsters
Pioneers : 12th Sherwood Foresters

**25th DIVISION** : Major General E G T Bainbridge
- Battle of Messines 7 - 14 June (II A.N.Z.A.C. Corps, Second Army)
- Battle of Pilckem Ridge 31 July - 2 Aug (II Corps, Fifth Army)

**7th Brigade** : Brigadier General C C Onslow
10th Cheshires
8th Loyal North Lancashires
3rd Worcesters
1st Wiltshires
**74th Brigade** : Brigadier General H K Bethell
11th Lancashire Fusiliers
9th Loyal North Lancashires
13th Cheshires
2nd Royal Irish Rifles
**75th Brigade** : Brigadier General H B D Baird
11th Cheshires
2nd South Lancashires
8th Border
8th South Lancashires
Pioneers : 6th South Wales Borderers

**29th DIVISION** : Major General H de B de Lisle
- Battle of Langemarck 16 - 18 Aug (XIV Corps, Fifth Army)
- Battle of Broodseinde 4 Oct (XIV Corps, Fifth Army)
- Battle of Poelcappelle 9 Oct (XIV Corps, Fifth Army)

**86th Brigade** : Lieutenant Colonel H Nelson to 24 Aug; Brigadier General G R H Cheape
2nd Royal Fusiliers
16th (Public Schools) Middlesex
1st Lancashire Fusiliers
1st Royal Dublin Fusiliers
Royal Guernsey Light Infantry (from 2 Oct)
**87th Brigade** : Brigadier General C H Lucas
2nd South Wales Borderers
1st Royal Inniskilling Fusiliers
1st King's Own Scottish Borderers
1st Border
**88th Brigade** : Brigadier General D E Cayley to 1 Oct; Brigadier General H Nelson
4th Worcesters
1st Essex
2nd Hampshires
1st Royal Newfoundlanders
Pioneers : 1/2nd Monmouths

**30th DIVISION** : Major General W de L Williams
- Battle of Pilckem Ridge 31 July - 2 Aug (II Corps, Fifth Army)

**21st Brigade** : Brigadier General G D Goodman
18th (2nd Liverpool Pals) King's (Liverpool)
19th (4th Manchester Pals) Manchesters
2nd Yorkshires
2nd Wiltshires
**89th Brigade** : Brigadier General W W Norman
17th (1st Liverpool Pals) King's (Liverpool)
19th (3rd Liverpool Pals) King's (Liverpool)
20th (4th Liverpool Pals) King's
2nd Bedfordshires
**90th Brigade** : Brigadier General J H Lloyd
16th (1st Manchester Pals) Manchesters
17th (2nd Manchester Pals) Manchesters
2nd Royal Scots Fusiliers
18th (3rd (Clerks & Warehousemen) Pals) Manchesters
Pioneers : 11th (St Helens Pals) South Lancashires

**33rd DIVISION** : Major General P R Wood
- Battle of the Menin Road 24 - 25 Sept (X Corps, Second Army)
- Battle of Polygon Wood 26 - 27 Sept (X Corps, Second Army)

**19th Brigade** : Brigadier General C R G Mayne
20th (3rd Public Schools) Royal Fusiliers
1st Cameronians
2nd Royal Welsh Fusiliers
5/6th Cameronians
**98th Brigade** : Brigadier General J D Heriot-Maitland
4th King's (Liverpool)
2nd Argyll & Sutherland Highlanders
1/4th Suffolks
1st Middlesex
**100th Brigade** : Brigadier General A W F Baird
1st Queen's (Royal West Surrey)
16th (Church Lads Brigade) King's Royal Rifle Corps
2nd Worcesters
1/9th (Glasgow Highland) Highland Light Infantry
Pioneers : 18th (1st Public Works) Middlesex

**34th DIVISION** : Major General C L Nicholson
- Battles of Ypres 13 - 23 Oct (XIV Corps, Fifth Army)

**101st Brigade** : Brigadier General R C Gore
15th (1st City of Edinburgh) Royal Scots
16th (2nd City of Edinburgh) Royal Scots
10th (Grimsby Chums) Lincolns
11th (Cambridge) Suffolks
**102nd Brigade** : Brigadier General N A Thomson
20th (1st Tyneside Scots) Northumberland Fusiliers
21st (2nd Tyneside Scots) Northumberland Fusiliers
22nd (3rd Tyneside Scots) Northumberland Fusiliers
23rd (4th Tyneside Scots) Northumberland Fusiliers
**103rd Brigade** : Brigadier General H E Trevor to 21 Oct (gassed); Lieutenant Colonel E M Moulton-Barrett
24th (1st Tyneside Irish) Northumberland Fusiliers
25th (2nd Tyneside Irish) Northumberland Fusiliers
26th (3rd Tyneside Irish) Northumberland Fusiliers
27th (4th Tyneside Irish) Northumberland Fusiliers
Pioneers : 18th (1st Tyneside Pioneers) Northumberland Fusiliers

**35th DIVISION** : Major General G Franks
- Second Battle of Passchendaele 26 Oct - 4 Nov (XIV Corps, Fifth Army to 30 Oct XIX Corps, Fifth Army)

**104th Brigade** : Brigadier General J W Sandilands
17th (1st South-East Lancashire Pals) Lancashire Fusiliers
18th (2nd South-East Lancashire Pals) Lancashire Fusiliers
20th (4th Salford Pals) Lancashire Fusiliers
23rd (8th Manchester Pals) Manchesters
**105th Brigade** : Brigadier General A H Marindin
15th (1st Birkenhead Pals) Cheshires
16th (2nd Birkenhead Pals) Cheshires
14th (West of England) Gloucesters
15th (Nottingham Pals) Sherwood Foresters
**106th Brigade** : Brigadier General J H W Pollard
17th (Earl of Roseberry) Royal Scots
18th (4th Glasgow Pals) Highland Light Infantry
17th (2nd Leeds Pals) West Yorkshires
19th (2nd County of Durham Pals) Durham Light Infantry
Pioneers : 19th (2nd Tyneside Pioneers) Northumberland Fusiliers

**36th (ULSTER) DIVISION** : Major General O S W Nugent
- Battle of Messines 7 - 9 June (IX Corps, Second Army)
- Battle of Langemarck 16 - 17 Aug (XIX Corps, Fifth Army)

**107th Brigade** : Brigadier General W M Withycombe
8th (East Belfast Volunteers) Royal Irish Rifles
9th (West Belfast Volunteers) Royal Irish Rifles
10th (South Belfast Volunteers) Royal Irish Rifles
15th (North Belfast Volunteers) Royal Irish Rifles
**108th Brigade** : Brigadier General C R J Griffith
11th (South Antrim Volunteers) Royal Irish Rifles
12th (Central Antrim Volunteers) Royal Irish Rifles
13th (1st County Down Volunteers) Royal Irish Rifles
9th (County Armagh, Monaghan & Cavan) Royal Irish Fusiliers
**109th Brigade** : Brigadier General A Ricardo
9th (County Tyrone Volunteers) Royal Inniskilling Fusiliers
10th (County Derry Volunteers) Royal Inniskilling Fusiliers
11th (Donegal & Fermanagh Volunteerss) Royal Inniskilling Fusiliers
14th (Belfast Young Citizens) Royal Irish Rifles
Pioneers : 16th (2nd County Down Volunteers) Royal Irish Rifles

**37th DIVISION** : Major General H Bruce-Williams
- Battle of Pilckem Ridge 31 July - 2 Aug (IX Corps, Second Army)
- Battle of the Menin Road 22 - 25 Sept (112th Brigade with 39th Division, 22 -23 Sept and 19th Division, 23 -25 Sept)
- Battle of Polygon Wood 27 Sept - 3 Oct (IX Corps, Second Army)
- Battle of Broodseinde 4 Oct (IX Corps, Second Army)
- Battle of Poelcappelle 9 Oct (IX Corps, Second Army)
- First Battle of Passchendaele 12 Oct (IX Corps, Second Army)

**63rd Brigade** : Brigadier General E L Challenor
8th Lincolns
4th Middlesex
8th Somerset Light Infantry
10th York & Lancasters
**111th Brigade** : Brigadier General C W Compton
10th (Stock Exchange) Royal Fusiliers
13th Royal Fusiliers
13th King's Royal Rifle Corps
12th Rifle Brigade
**112th Brigade** : Brigadier General R C Maclachlan, killed in action 11 Aug; Lieutenant Colonel R C Chester-Master to 16 Aug; Brigadier General A E Irvine
11th Royal Warwickshires
8th East Lancashires
6th Bedfordshires
10th Loyal North Lancashires
Pioneers : 9th North Staffordshires

**38th (WELSH) DIVISION** : Major General C G Blackader
- Battle of Pilckem Ridge 31 July - 2 Aug (XIV Corps, Fifth Army)

**113th Brigade** : Brigadier General L A E Price-Davies, VC
13th (1st North Wales Pals) Royal Welsh Fusiliers
14th (Caernarvon & Anglesey Pals) Royal Welsh Fusiliers
15th (1st London Welsh) Royal Welsh Fusiliers
16th Royal Welsh Fusiliers
**114th Brigade** : Brigadier General T O Marden
10th (1st Rhondda Pals) Welsh
13th (2nd Rhondda Pals) Welsh
14th (Swansea Pals) Welsh
15th (Carmarthenshire Pals) Welsh
**115th Brigade** : Brigadier General G Gwyn-Thomas
16th (Cardiff City Pals) Welsh
17th (Landudno Pals) Royal Welsh Fusiliers
10th (1st Gwent - Colliers & Ironworkers - Pals) South Wales Borderers
11th (2nd Gwent Pals) South Wales Borderers
Pioneers : 19th (Glamorgan Pioneers) Welsh

**39th DIVISION** : Major General G J Cuthbert to 20 Aug; Major General E Feetham
- Battle of Pilckem Ridge 31 July - 2 Aug (XVIII Corps, Fifth Army)
- Battle of Langemarck 16 - 18 Aug (X Corps, Second Army)
- Battle of the Menin Road 20 - 25 Sept (X Corps, Second Army)
- Battle of Polygon Wood 26 - 27 Sept (X Corps, Second Army)
- Second Battle of Passchendaele 29 Oct - 10 Nov (X Corps, Second Army)

**116 Brigade** : Brigadier General M L Hornby
11th (1st South Downs) Royal Sussex
12th (2nd South Downs) Royal Sussex
13th (3rd South Downs) Royal Sussex
14th (1st Portsmouth Pals) Hampshires
**117th Brigade** : Brigadier General G A Armytage
16th (St Pancras) Rifle Brigade
17th (British Empire League) King's Royal Rifle Corps
16th (Chatsworth Rifles) Sherwood Foresters
17th (Welbeck Rangers) Sherwood Foresters
**118th Brigade** : Brigadier General E H C P Bellingham
1/6th Cheshires
1/1st Cambridgeshires
4/5th Black Watch
1/1st Hertfordshires
Pioneers : 13th (Forest of Dean) Gloucesters

**41st DIVISION** : Major General S T B Lawford
- Battle of Messines 7 - 14 June (X Corps, Second Army)
- Battle of Pilckem Ridge 31 July - 2 Aug (X Corps, Second Army)
- Battle of the Menin Road 20 - 22 Sept (X Corps, Second Army)

**122nd Brigade** : Brigadier General F W Towsey
12th (Bermondsey) East Surreys
11th (Lewisham) Royal West Kents
15th (2nd Portsmouth Pals) Hampshires
18th (Arts & Craftsmen) King's Royal Rifle Corps
**123rd Brigade** : Brigadier General C W E Gordon, killed in action 24 July; Brigadier General W F Clemson to 3 Aug; Brigadier General E Pearce-Serocold
10th (Kent County) Royal West Kents
20th (Wearside) Durham Light Infantry
11th (Lambeth) Queen's (Royal West Surreys)
23rd (2nd Football) Middlesex
**124th Brigade** : Brigadier General W F Clemson to 24 July; Lieutenant Colonel W C Clark to 2 Aug; Brigadier General W F Clemson
10th (Battersea) Queen's (Royal West Surreys)
21st (Yeoman Rifles) King's Royal Rifle Corps
26th (Bankers) Royal Fusiliers
32nd (East Ham) Royal Fusiliers
Pioneers : 19th (2nd Public Works) Middlesex

**47th (2nd LONDON) DIVISION** : Major General Sir G F Gorringe
- Battle of Pilckem Ridge 31 July - 2 Aug (In Reserve, X Corps, Second Army)

**140th (4th London) Brigade** : Brigadier General H B P L Kennedy
1/6th (London Rifles) Londons
1/7th Londons
1/8th (Post Office Rifles) Londons
1/15th (Civil Service Rifles) Londons
**141st (5th London) Brigade** : Brigadier General R McDouall
1/17th (Poplar & Stepney) Londons
1/18th (London Irish Rifles) Londons
1/19th (St. Pancras) Londons
1/20th (Blackheath & Woolwich) Londons
**142nd (6th London) Brigade** : Brigadier General V T Bailey
1/21st (Surrey Rifles) Londons
1/22nd (The Queen's) Londons
1/23rd Londons
1/24th (The Queen's) Londons
Pioneers : 4th Royal Welsh Fusiliers

**48th (SOUTH MIDLAND) DIVISION** : Major General R Fanshawe
- Battle of Langemarck 16 - 18 Aug (XVIII Corps, Fifth Army)
- Battle of Polygon Wood 28 Sept - 3 Oct (XVIII Corps, Fifth Army)
- Battle of Broodseinde 4 Oct (XVIII Corps, Fifth Army)
- Battle of Poelcappelle 9 Oct (XVIII Corps, Fifth Army)

**143rd (Warwickshire) Brigade** : Brigadier General G C Sladen
1/5th Royal Warwickshires
1/6th Royal Warwickshires
1/7th Royal Warwickshires
1/8th Royal Warwickshires
**144th (Gloucester & Worcester) Brigade** : Brigadier General H R Done
1/4th (City of Bristol) Gloucesters
1/6th Gloucesters
1/7th Worcesters
1/8th Worcesters
**145th (South Midland) Brigade** : Brigadier General D M Watt
1/4th Oxford & Bucks Light Infantry
1/1st (Bucks) Oxford & Bucks Light Infantry
1/5th Gloucesters
1/4th Royal Berkshires
Pioneers : 1/5th (Cinque Ports) Royal Sussex

**49th (WEST RIDING) DIVISION** : Major General E M Perceval
- Battle of Poelcappelle 9 Oct (II A.N.Z.A.C. Corps, Second Army)

**146th (1st West Riding) Brigade** : Brigadier General M D Goring-Jones
1/5th West Yorkshires
1/6th West Yorkshires
1/7th (Leeds Rifles) West Yorkshires
1/8th (Leeds Rifles) West Yorkshires
**147th (2nd West Riding) Brigade** : Brigadier General C G Lewes
1/4th Duke of Wellington's
1/5th Duke of Wellington's
1/6th Duke of Wellington's
1/7th Duke of Wellington's
**148th (3rd West Riding) Brigade** : Brigadier General R L Adlercron
1/4th King's Own Yorkshire Light Infantry
1/5th King's Own Yorkshire Light Infantry
1/4th (Hallamshire) York & Lancasters
1/5th York & Lancasters
Pioneers : 19th (3rd Salford Pals) Lancashire Fusiliers

**50th (NORTHUMBRIAN) DIVISION** : Major General P S Wilkinson
- Second Battle of Passchendaele 26 Oct - 9 Nov (XIV Corps to 29 Oct XIX Corps, Fifth Army)

**149th (Northumberland) Brigade** : Brigadier General E P A Riddell
1/4th Northumberland Fusiliers
1/5th Northumberland Fusiliers
1/6th Northumberland Fusiliers
1/7th Northumberland Fusiliers
**150th (York & Durham) Brigade** : Brigadier General B G Price
1/4th East Yorkshires
1/5th Durham Light Infantry
1/4th Yorkshires
1/5th Yorkshires
**151st (Durham Light Infantry) Brigade** : Brigadier General C T Martin
1/5th (West Cumberland) Border
1/6th Durham Light Infantry
1/8th Durham Light Infantry
1/9th Durham Light Infantry
Pioneers : 1/7th Durham Light Infantry

**51st (HIGHLAND) DIVISION** : Major General G M Harper
- Battle of Pilckem Ridge 31 July - 2 Aug (XVIII Corps, Fifth Army)
- Battle of the Menin Road 20 - 24 Sept (XVIII Corps, Fifth Army)

**152nd (1st Highland) Brigade** : Brigadier General H P Burn
1/5th (Sutherland & Caithness) Seaforth Highlanders
1/6th (Morayshire) Seaforth Highlanders
1/6th (Banff & Donside) Gordon Highlanders
1/8th (Argyllshire) Argyll & Sutherland Highlanders
**153rd (2nd Highland) Brigade** : Lieutenant Colonel H G Hyslop to 2 Aug; Brigadier General A T Beckwith
1/6th (Perthshire) Black Watch
1/7th (Fife) Black Watch
1/5th (Buchan & Formartin) Gordon Highlanders
1/7th (Deeside Highland) Gordon Highlanders
**154th (3rd Highland) Brigade** : Brigadier General J G H Hamilton
1/9th (Highlanders) Royal Scots
1/4th Gordon Highlanders
1/4th (Ross-shire) Seaforth Highlanders
1/7th Argyll & Sutherland Highlanders
Pioneers : 1/8th Royal Scots

**55th (WEST LANCASHIRE) DIVISION** : Major General H S Jeudwine
- Battle of Pilckem Ridge 31 July - 2 Aug (XIX Corps, Fifth Army)
- Battle of the Menin Road 20 - 23 Sept (V Corps, Fifth Army)

**164th (North Lancashire) Brigade** : Brigadier General C I Stockwell
1/4th King's Own
2/5th Lancashire Fusiliers
1/8th (Liverpool Irish) King's (Liverpool)
1/4th Loyal North Lancashires
**165th (Liverpool) Brigade** : Brigadier General L B Boyd-Moss
1/5th King's (Liverpool)
1/6th (Liverpool Rifles) King's (Liverpool)
1/7th King's (Liverpool)
1/9th King's (Liverpool)
**166th (South Lancashire) Brigade** : Brigadier General F G Lewis
1/10th (Liverpool Scottish) King's (Liverpool)
1/5th South Lancashires
1/5th King's Own
1/5th Loyal North Lancashires
Pioneers : 1/4th South Lancashires

**57th (2nd WEST LANCASHIRE) DIVISION** : Major General R W R Barnes
- Second Battle of Passchendaele 26 Oct - 7 Nov (XIV Corps to 29 Oct XIX Corps, Fifth Army)

**170th (2nd/1st North Lancashire) Brigade** : Brigadier General F G Guggisberg
2/5th King's Own
2/4th Loyal North Lancashires
2/5th Loyal North Lancashires
4/5th Loyal North Lancashires

**171st (2nd/1st Liverpool) Brigade** : Brigadier General H N Bray
2/5th King's (Liverpool)
2/6th King's (Liverpool)
2/7th King's (Liverpool)
2/8th King's (Liverpool)

**172nd (2nd/1st South Lancashire) Brigade** : Brigadier General G C B Paynter
2/9th King's (Liverpool)
2/10th King's (Liverpool)
2/4th South Lancashires
2/5th South Lancashires

**58th (2/1st LONDON) DIVISION** : Major General H D Fanshawe to 6 Oct; Major General A B E Cator
- Battle of the Menin Road 20 - 25 Sept (XVIII Corps, Fifth Army)
- Battle of Polygon Wood 26 - 27 Sept (XVIII Corps, Fifth Army)
- Second Battle of Passchendaele 26 Oct - 10 Nov (XVIII Corps, Fifth Army to 2 Nov II Corps, Second Army)

**173rd (3rd/1st London) Brigade** : Lieutenant Colonel W R H Dann to 3 Oct; Brigadier General R B Worgan
2/1st Londons
2/2nd Londons
2/3rd Londons
2/4th Londons

**174th (2nd/2nd London) Brigade** : Brigadier General C G Higgins
2/5th Londons
2/6th Londons
2/7th Londons
2/8th Londons

**175th (2nd/3rd London) Brigade** : Brigadier General H C Jackson
2/9th Londons
2/10th Londons
2/11th Londons
2/12th Londons

**59th (2nd NORTH MIDLAND) DIVISION** : Major General C F Romer
- Battle of the Menin Road 23 - 25 Sept (V Corps, Fifth Army)
- Battle of Polygon Wood 26 - 30 Sept (V Corps, Fifth Army to 28 Sept II A.N.Z.A.C. Corps, Second Army)

**176th (2nd/1st Staffordshire) Brigade** : Brigadier General T G Cope
2/5th South Staffordshires
2/6th South Staffordshires
2/5th North Staffordshires
2/6th North Staffordshires

**177th (2nd/1st Lincoln & Leicester) Brigade** : Brigadier General C H L James
2/4th Lincolns
2/5th Lincolns
2/4th Leicesters
2/5th Leicesters

**178th (2nd/1st Notts & Derby) Brigade** : Brigadier General T W Stansfeld
2/5th Sherwood Foresters
2/6th Sherwood Foresters
2/7th Sherwood Foresters
2/8th Sherwood Foresters

**61st (2nd SOUTH MIDLAND) DIVISION** : Major General C J MacKenzie
- Battle of Langemarck 18 Aug (XIX Corps, Fifth Army)

**182nd (2nd/1st Warwickshires) Brigade** : Brigadier General Hon. C J Sackville-West
2/5th Royal Warwickshires
2/6th Royal Warwickshires
2/7th Royal Warwickshires
2/8th Royal Warwickshires

**183rd (2nd/1st Gloucester & Worcester) Brigade** : Brigadier General A H Spooner
2/4th Gloucesters
2/6th Gloucesters
2/7th Worcesters
2/8th Worcesters

**184th (2nd/1st South Midland) Brigade** : Brigadier General Hon. R White
2/4th Oxford & Bucks Light Infantry
2/1st Buckinghamshire (Oxford & Bucks) Light Infantry
2/5th Gloucesters
2/4th Royal Berkshires

**63rd (ROYAL NAVAL) DIVISION** : Brigadier General C E Lawrie
- Second Battle of Passchendaele 26 Oct - 5 Nov (XVIII Corps, Fifth Army)

**188th (1st Royal Naval) Brigade** : Brigadier General R E S Prentice
Howe
Anson
1st Royal Marines Light Infantry
2nd Royal Marines Light Infantry

**189th (2nd Royal Naval) Brigade** : Brigadier General L F Philips
Drake
Nelson
Hawke
Hood

**190th (Royal Marine) Brigade** : Brigadier General A R H Hutchinson
7th Royal Fusiliers
10th Royal Dublin Fusiliers
1/4th King's Shropshire Light Infantry
4th Bedfordshires
1/28th (Artist Rifles) Londons
Pioneers : 14th (Severn Valley Pioneers) Worcesters

**66th (2nd EAST LANCASHIRE) DIVISION** : Major General Hon. H A Lawrence
- Battle of Poelcappelle 9 Oct (II A.N.Z.A.C. Corps, Second Army)

**197th (2nd/1st Lancashire Fusiliers) Brigade** : Brigadier General O C Borrett
3/5th Lancashire Fusiliers
2/6th Lancashire Fusiliers
2/7th Lancashire Fusiliers
2/8th Lancashire Fusiliers

**198th (2nd/1st East Lancashire) Brigade** : Brigadier General A J Hunter
2/4th East Lancashires
2/5th East Lancashires
2/9th Manchesters
2/10th Manchesters

**199th (2nd/1st Manchester) Brigade** : Brigadier General J O Travers
2/5th Manchesters
2/6th Manchesters
2/7th Manchesters
2/8th Manchesters
Pioneers : 10th (Cornwall Pioneers) Duke of Cornwall's Light Infantry

**1st AUSTRALIAN DIVISION** : Major General H B Walker
- Battle of the Menin Road 20-25 Sept (I ANZAC Corps, Second Army)
- Battle of Polygon Wood 26 Sept – 3 Oct (I ANZAC Corps, Second Army)
- Battle of Broodseinde 4 Oct (I ANZAC Corps, Second Army)
- Battle of Poelcappelle 9 Oct (I ANZAC Corps, Second Army)
- Second Battle of Passchendaele 26 Oct – 10 Nov (I ANZAC Corps, Second Army)

**1st (New South Wales) Brigade** : Brigadier-General W R Lesslie
1st Battalion
2nd Battalion
3rd Battalion
4th Battalion

**2nd (Victoria) Brigade** : Brigadier-General J Heane
5th Battalion
6th Battalion
7th Battalion
8th Battalion

**3rd Brigade** : Brigadier-General H G Bennett
9th (Queensland) Battalion
10th (South Australia) Battalion
11th (West Australia) Battalion
12th (Tasmania, S and W Australia) Battalion
Pioneers : 1st Australian Pioneer Battalion

**2nd AUSTRALIAN DIVISION** : Major General N M Smythe
- Battle of the Menin Road 20-25 Sept (I ANZAC Corps, Second Army)
- Battle of Polygon Wood 26 Sept – 3 Oct (I ANZAC Corps, Second Army)
- Battle of Broodseinde 4 Oct (I ANZAC Corps, Second Army)
- Battle of Poelcappelle 9 Oct (I ANZAC Corps, Second Army)
- Second Battle of Passchendaele 26 Oct – 10 Nov (I ANZAC Corps, Second Army)

**5th (New South Wales) Brigade** : Brigadier General R Smith
17th Battalion
18th Battalion
19th Battalion
20th Battalion

**6th (Victoria) Brigade** : Brigadier-General J Paton
21st Battalion
22nd Battalion
23rd Battalion
24th Battalion

**7th Brigade** : Brigadier-General E A Wisdom
25th (Queensland) Battalion
26th (Queensland & Tasmania) Battalion
27th (South Australia) Battalion
28th (West Australia) Battalion
Pioneers : 2nd Australian Pioneer Battalion

**3rd AUSTRALIAN DIVISION** : Major General J Monash
- Battle of Messines 7-14 June (II ANZAC Corps, Second Army)
- Battle of Polygon Wood 26 Sept – 3 Oct (II ANZAC Corps, Second Army)
- Battle of Broodseinde 4 Oct (II ANZAC Corps, Second Army)
- First Battle of Passchendaele 12 Oct (II ANZAC Corps, Second Army)

**9th (New South Wales) Australian Brigade** : Brigadier General C Rosenthal
33rd Battalion
34th Battalion
35th Battalion
36th Battalion
**10th Australian Brigade** : Brigadier General W R McNicholl
37th (Victoria) Battalion
38th (Victoria) Battalion
39th (Victoria) Battalion
40th (Tasmania) Battalion
**11th Australian Brigade** : Brigadier General J H Cannan
41st (Queensland) Battalion
42nd (Queensland) Battalion
43rd (South Australia) Battalion
44th (Western Australia) Battalion
Pioneers : 3rd Australian Pioneer Battalion

**5th AUSTRALIAN DIVISION** : Major General J J T Hobbs
- Battle of Polygon Wood 26 Sept – 3 Oct (II ANZAC Corps, Second Army)
- Battle of Broodseinde 4 Oct (II ANZAC Corps, Second Army)
- First Battle of Passchendaele 12 Oct (II ANZAC Corps, Second Army)

**8th Brigade** : Brigadier-General E Tivey
29th (Victoria)Battalion
30th (New South Wales)Battalion
31st (Queensland & Victoria) Battalion
32nd (Western Australia & South Australia)Battalion
**14th (New South Wales) Brigade** : Brigadier-General C J Hobkirk
53rd Battalion
54th Battalion

55th Battalion
56th Battalion
**15th (Victoria) Brigade** : Brigadier-General H E Elliott
57th (New South Wales)Battalion
58th Battalion
59th Battalion
60th Battalion
Pioneers : 5th Australian Pioneer Battalion

**4th AUSTRALIAN DIVISION** : Major General E G Sinclair-MacLaglan
- Battle of Messines 7-14 June (II ANZAC Corps, Second Army)
- Battle of Polygon Wood 26 Sept – 3 Oct (II ANZAC Corps, Second Army)
- Battle of Broodseinde 4 Oct (II ANZAC Corps, Second Army)
- First Battle of Passchendaele 12 Oct (II ANZAC Corps, Second Army)

**4th Brigade** : Brigadier-General C H Brand
13th (New South Wales) Battalion
14th (Victoria) Battalion
15th (Queensland & Tasmania) Battalion
16th (South & West Australia) Battalion
**12th Brigade** : Brigadier-General J C Robertson
45th (New South Wales) Battalion
46th (Victoria) Battalion
47th (Queensland & Tasmania) Battalion
48th (South & West Australia) Battalion
**13th Brigade** : Brigadier-General T W Glasgow
49th (Queensland) Battalion
50th (South Australia & Tasmania) Battalion
51st (West Australia) Battalion
52nd (West & South Australia, Tasmania) Battalion
Pioneers : 4th Australian Pioneer Battalion

**NEW ZEALAND DIVISION** : Major-General A. H. Russell
- Battle of Messines 7-14 June (II ANZAC Corps, Second Army)
- Battle of Polygon Wood 26 Sept – 3 Oct (II ANZAC Corps, Second Army)
- Battle of Broodseinde 4 Oct (II ANZAC Corps, Second Army)
- First Battle of Passchendaele 12 Oct (II ANZAC Corps, Second Army)

**1st New Zealand Brigade** : Brigadier-General C H J Brown, Killed 8 June; Brigadier General C W Melvill
1st Auckland Battalion
2nd Auckland Battalion
1st Wellington Battalion
2nd Wellington Battalion
**2nd New Zealand Brigade** : Brigadier-General W G Braithwaite
1st Otago Battalion
2nd Otago Battalion
1st Canterbury Battalion
2nd Canterbury Battalion
**3rd New Zealand (Rifles) Brigade** : Brigadier-General H T Fulton; Brigadier General F E Johnston, killed 7 June; Brigadier General R Young, wounded 9 August; Lieutenant Colonel A E Stewart
1st Battalion, NZ Rifle Brigade
2nd Battalion, NZ Rifle Brigade
3rd Battalion, NZ Rifle Brigade
4th Battalion, NZ Rifle Brigade
**4th New Zealand Brigade** : Brigadier-General H E Hart
3rd Wellington
3rd Canterbury
3rd Auckland
3rd Otago
Pioneers : New Zealand Pioneer Battalion

**1st CANADIAN DIVISION** : Major General A C MacDonnell
- Second Battle of Passchendaele 26 Oct – 10 Nov (Canadian Corps, Second Army)

**1st Brigade** : Brigadier-General W A Griesbach
1st Battalion (Ontario)
2nd Battalion (East Ontario)
3rd Battalion (Toronto)
4th Battalion
**2nd Brigade** : Brigadier-General F O W Loomis
5th Battalion (Western Cavalry)
7th Battalion (1st British Columbia)
8th Battalion (90th Rifles)
10th Battalion
**3rd Brigade** : Brigadier-General G S Tuxford
13th Battalion (Royal Highlanders)
14th Battalion (Royal Montreal)
15th Battalion (48th Highlanders)
16th Battalion (Canadian Scottish)
Pioneers : 1st Canadian Pioneer Battalion

**3rd CANADIAN DIVISION** : Major-General L J Lipsett
- Second Battle of Passchendaele 26 Oct – 10 Nov (Canadian Corps, Second Army)

**7th Brigade** : Brigadier-General H M Dyer
Princess Patricia's Canadian Light Infantry
Royal Canadian Regiment
42nd (Royal Highlanders) Battalion
49th (Edmonton) Battalion
**8th Brigade** : Brigadier-General J H Elmsley
1st Battalion, Canadian Mounted Rifles
2nd Battalion, Canadian Mounted Rifles
4th Battalion, Canadian Mounted Rifles
5th Battalion, Canadian Mounted Rifles
**9th Brigade** : Brigadier-General F W Hill
43rd (Cameron Highlanders) Battalion
52nd (North Ontario) Battalion
58th (Central Ontario) Battalion
60th (Victoria Rifles) Battalion
Pioneers : 3rd Canadian Pioneer Battalion

**2nd CANADIAN DIVISION** : Major General H E Burstall
- Second Battle of Passchendaele 26 Oct – 10 Nov (Canadian Corps, Second Army)

**4th Brigade** : Brigadier General R Rennie
18th (West Ontario) Battalion
19th (Central Ontario) Battalion
20th (Central Ontario) Battalion
21st (Eastern Ontario) Battalion
**5th Brigade** : Brigadier-General J M Ross
22nd (Canadien-Français) Battalion
24th (Victoria Rifles) Battalion
25th (Nova Scotia Rifles) Battalion
26th (New Brunswick) Battalion
**6th Brigade** : Brigadier-General H D B Ketchen
27th (City of Winnipeg) Battalion
28th (North West) Battalion
29th (Vancouver) Battalion
31st (Alberta) Battalion
Pioneers : 2nd Canadian Pioneer Battalion

**4th CANADIAN DIVISION :** Major-General D Watson
- Second Battle of Passchendaele 26 Oct – 10 Nov (Canadian Corps, Second Army)

**10th Brigade** : Brigadier-General E Hilliam
44th Battalion
46th (South Saskatchewan) Battalion
47th (British Columbia) Battalion
50th (Calgary) Battalion
**11th Brigade** : Brigadier-General V W Odlum
54th (Kootenay) Battalion
75th (Mississauga) Battalion
87th (Canadian Grenadier Guards) Battalion
102nd (Central Ontario) Battalion
**12th Brigade** : Brigadier-General J H MacBrien
38th (Ottawa) Battalion
72nd (Seaforth Highlanders) Battalion
78th (Winnipeg Grenadiers) Battalion
85th (Nova Scotia Highlanders) Battalion
Pioneers : 67th Canadian Pioneer Battalion

# BATTLES OF THE LYS FOURTH YPRES APRIL 1918)

**2nd CAVALRY DIVISION** : Brigadier-General T T Pitman
- Battle of Hazebrouck 14 - 15 April (Cavalry Corps, Second Army)

**3rd Cavalry Brigade** : Brigadier-General J A Bell-Smyth
4th (Queen's Own) Hussars
5th (Royal Irish) Lancers
16th (The Queen's) Lancers
**4th Cavalry Brigade** : Brigadier-General C H Rankin
3rd (King's Own) Hussars
6th (Carabiniers) Dragoon Guards
1st Queen's Own Oxfordshire Hussars
**5th Cavalry Brigade** : Brigadier-General N W Haig
2nd Dragoons (Royal Scots Greys)
12th (Prince of Wales's Royal)Lancers
20th Hussars

**1st DIVISION** : Major-General E P Strickland
- Battle of Estaires 9 - 11 Apr (I Corps, First Army)
- Battle of Hazebrouck 15 Apr (3rd Brigade with 55th Division, XI Corps, First Army)
- Battle of Bethune 18-19 Apr (I Corps, First Army)

**1st Brigade** : Brigadier-General W B Thornton
1st Black Watch
1st Cameron Highlanders
1st Loyal North Lancashires
**2nd Brigade** : Brigadier-General G C Kelly
2nd Royal Sussex
2nd King's Royal Rifle Corps
1st Northamptons
**3rd Brigade** : Brigadier-General H H S Morant
1st South Wales Borderers
2nd Welsh
1st Gloucesters
Pioneers : 6th Welsh

**3rd DIVISION** : Major-General C J Deverell
- Battle of Estaires 9 - 11 Apr (I Corps, First Army)
- Battle of Hazebrouck 12 - 15 Apr (I Corps, First Army)
- Battle of Bethune 18 Apr (I Corps, First Army)

**8th Brigade** : Brigadier-General L A E Price-Davies, VC, to 12 Apr; Brigadier-General B. D. Fisher
2nd Royal Scots
1st Royal Scots Fusiliers
7th King's Shropshire Light Infantry
**9th Brigade** : Brigadier-General H C Potter
1st Northumberland Fusiliers
13th King's (Liverpool)
4th Royal Fusiliers
**76th Brigade** : Brigadier-General C L Porter
2nd Suffolks
8th King's Own
1st Gordon Highlanders
Pioneers : 20th (British Empire League) King's Royal Rifle Corps

**4th DIVISION** : Major-General T G Matheson
- Battle of Hazebrouck 13 - 15 Apr (I Corps, First Army)
- Battle of Bethune 18 Apr (I Corps, First Army)

**10th Brigade** : Brigadier-General H W Green to 16 Apr; Brigadier-General J Greene
1st Royal Warwickshires
2nd Seaforth Highlanders
2nd Duke of Wellington's
**11th Brigade** : Brigadier-General T S H Wade
1st Somerset Light Infantry
1st Rifle Brigade
1st Hampshires
**12th Brigade** : Brigadier-General E A Fagan
1st King's Own
2nd Essex
2nd Lancashire Fusiliers
Pioneers : 21st (Wool Textile Pioneers) West Yorkshires

**5th DIVISION** : Major-General R B Stephens
- Battle of Hazebrouck 12 - 15 Apr (XI Corps, First Army)

**13th Brigade** : Brigadier-General L O W Jones
2nd King's Own Scottish Borderers
1st Royal West Kents
14th (1st Birmingham Pals) Royal Warwickshires
15th (2nd Birmingham Pals) Royal Warwickshires
**15th Brigade** : Brigadier-General R D F Oldman
1st Norfolks
1st Cheshires
1st Bedfordshires
16th (3rd Birmingham Pals) Royal Warwickshires
**95th Brigade** : Brigadier-General Lord E C Gordon-Lennox
1st Devonshires
1st Duke of Cornwall's Light Infantry
1st East Surreys
12th (Bristol Pals) Gloucesters
Pioneers : 1/6th (Renfrewshire) Argyll & Sutherland Highlanders

**6th DIVISION** : Major-General T O Marden
- Battle of Bailleul 13 - 15 Apr (71st Brigade with 49th Divisions, IX Corps, Second Army)
- First Battle of Kemmel 17 - 19 Apr (71st Brigade with 49th Division)
- Second Battle of Kemmel 25 - 26 Apr (XXII Corps, Second Army)
- Battle of Scherpenberg 29 Apr (XXII Corps, Second Army)

**16th Brigade** : Brigadier-General H A Walker
1st Buffs
2nd York & Lancasters
1st King's Shropshire Light Infantry
**18th Brigade** : Brigadier-General G S G Craufurd
1st West Yorkshires
11th Essex
2nd Durham Light Infantry
**71st Brigade** : Brigadier-General P W Brown
1st Leicesters
9th Norfolks
2nd Sherwood Foresters
Pioneers : 11th (City of Leicester Pals) Leicesters

**9th (SCOTTISH) DIVISION** : Major-General H H Tudor
- Battle of Messines 10 - 11 Apr (IX Corps, Second Army)
- Battle of Bailleul 13 - 15 Apr (XXII Corps, Second Army)
- First Battle of Kemmel 17 - 19 Apr (XXII Corps, Second Army)
- Second Battle of Kemmel 25 - 26 Apr (XXII Corps, Second Army)
- Battle of Scherpenberg 29 Apr ( South African Brigade with 49th Division)

**26th Brigade** : Brigadier-General J Kennedy
8th Black Watch
5th Cameron Highlanders
7th Seaforth Highlanders
**27th Brigade** : Brigadier-General W D Croft
11th Royal Scots
12th Royal Scots
6th King's Own Scottish Borderers
**South African Brigade** : Brigadier-General W E C Tanner
1st South African Infantry
2nd South African Infantry
4th South African Infantry
9th Cameronians (from 23 April)
2nd Royal Scots Fusiliers (from 26 April)
Pioneers : 9th Seaforth Highlanders

**21st DIVISION** : Major-General D G M Campbell
- Battle of Messines 10 - 11 Apr (62nd Brigade with 9th Division, IX Corps, Second Army)
- Battle of Bailleul 13 - 15 Apr (62nd Brigade with 9th Division)
- First Battle of Kemmel 17 - 19 Apr (XXII Corps, Second Army)
- Second Battle of Kemmel 25 - 26 Apr (XXII Corps, Second Army)
- Battle of Scherpenberg 29 Apr (XXII Corps, Second Army)

**62nd Brigade** : Brigadier-General G H Gates
1st Lincolns
2nd Lincolns
12/13th Northumberland Fusiliers
**64th Brigade** : Brigadier-General H R Headlam
1st East Yorkshires
15th Durham Light Infantry
1st King's Own Yorkshire Light Infantry
**110th Brigade** : Brigadier-General H R Cumming
6th Leicesters
7th Leicesters
8th Leicesters
Pioneers: 14th Northumberland Fusiliers
*Served with 21st Division:*
*39th Composite Brigade, from 10 April to 1 May*
*146th Brigade, 49th (West Riding) Division, from 10 to 19 April*
*21st Brigade, 30th Division, from 20 April to 2 May*
*89th Brigade, 30th Division, from 25 April to 2 May*
*58th Brigade, 19th (Western) Division, from 28 to 30 April*

**19th (WESTERN) DIVISION** : Major-General G D Jeffreys
- Battle of Messines 10 - 11 Apr (IX Corps, Second Army)
- Battle of Bailleul 13 - 15 Apr (IX Corps, Second Army)
- First Battle of Kemmel 17 - 18 Apr (IX Corps, Second Army)

**56th Brigade** : Brigadier-General R M Meath
9th Cheshires
8th North Staffordshires
1/4th King's Shropshire Light Infantry
**57th Brigade** : Brigadier-General T A Cubitt
10th Royal Warwickshires
10th Worcesters
8th Gloucesters
**58th Brigade** : Brigadier-General A E Glasgow
9th Royal Welsh Fusiliers
6th (Wiltshire Yeomanry) Wiltshires
9th Welsh
Pioneers : 5th South Wales Borderers

**25th DIVISION** : Major-General E G T Bainbridge
- Battle of Estaires 9 - 11 Apr (74th Brigade only, XV Corps, First Army)
- Battle of Messines 10 - 11 Apr (less 74th Brigade, IX Corps, Second Army)
- Battle of Bailleul 13 - 15 Apr (IX Corps, Second Army)
- First Battle of Kemmel 17 - 19 Apr (IX Corps, Second Army)
- Second Battle of Kemmel 25 -26 Apr (XXII Corps, Second Army)
- Battle of Scherpenberg 29 Apr (XXII Corps, Second Army)

**7th Brigade** : Brigadier-General C J Griffin
10th Cheshires
1st Wiltshires
4th South Staffordshires
**74th Brigade** : Brigadier-General H M Craigie-Halkett
11th Lancashire Fusiliers
9th Loyal North Lancashires
3rd Worcesters
**75th Brigade** : Brigadier-General C C Hannay
11th Cheshires
2nd South Lancashires
8th Border
Pioneers : 6th South Wales Borderers

**29th DIVISION** : Major-General D E Cayley
- Battle of Estaires 10 - 11 Apr (less 88th Brigade, XV Corps, First Army)
- Battle of Messines 10 - 11 Apr (88th Brigade with 25th Division on 10 April and 34th Division on 11 April, IX Corps, Second Army)
- Battle of Hazebrouck 12 - 13 Apr (less 88th Brigade, XV Corps, Second Army)
- Battle of Bailleul 13 - 14 Apr (88th Brigade with 34th Division, IX Corps, Second Army)

**86th Brigade** : Brigadier-General G R H Cheape
2nd Royal Fusiliers
1st Lancashire Fusiliers
Royal Guernsey Light Infantry
**87th Brigade** : Brigadier-General G H N Jackson
2nd South Wales Borderers
1st Border
1st King's Own Scottish Borderers
**88th Brigade** : Brigadier-General B C Freyberg, VC
4th Worcesters
2nd Hampshires
1st Royal Newfoundlanders
Pioneers : 1/2nd Monmouths


**30th DIVISION** : Major-General W de L Williams
- First Battle of Kemmel 17 - 19 Apr (89th Brigade only, IX Corps, Second Army)
- Second Battle of Kemmel 25 - 26 Apr (89th & 21st (Composite) Brigades, XXII Corps, Second Army)
- Battle of Scherpenberg 29 Apr (89th & 21st (Composite) Brigades, XXII Corps, Second Army)

**21st (Composite) Brigade** (with 21st Division from 19 Apr): Brigadier-General G D Goodman
2nd Bedfordshires
16th (1st Manchester Pals) Manchesters
17th (2nd Manchester Pals) Manchesters (2 Companies)
2nd Wiltshires (2 Companies)
2nd Yorkshires
**89th Brigade** : Brigadier-General R A M Currie
17th (1st Liverpool Pals) King's (Liverpool)
18th (Lancashire Hussars) King's (Liverpool)
19th (3rd Liverpool Pals) King's (Liverpool)
Pioneers : 11th (St Helens Pioneers) South Lancashires


**31st DIVISION** : Major-General R J Bridgford
- Battle of Estaires 11 Apr (XV Corps, First Army)
- Battle of Hazebrouck 12 - 14 Apr (XV Corps, Second Army)

**4th (Guards) Brigade** : Brigadier-General Hon. L J P Butler
4th Grenadier Guards
2nd Irish Guards
3rd Coldstream Guards
**92nd Brigade** : Brigadier-General O de L Williams
10th (Hull Commercials) East Yorkshires
11th (Hull Tradesmen) East Yorkshires
11th (Accrington Pals) East Lancashires
**93rd Brigade** : Brigadier-General S C Taylor
15th (1st Leeds Pals) West Yorkshires
18th (1st County of Durham Pals) Durham Light Infantry
13th (1st Barnsley Pals) York & Lancasters
Pioneers : 12th (Halifax (Miners) Pals) King's Own Yorkshire Light Infantry


**33rd DIVISION** : Major-General R J Pinney
- Battle of Messines 11 Apr (100th Brigade in Reserve to 25th Division, IX Corps, Second Army)
- Battle of Hazebrouck 12 - 15 Apr (IX Corps, Second Army)
- Battle of Bailleul 13 - 15 Apr (100th Brigade only with 25th Division)
- First Battle of Kemmel 17 - 19 Apr ( IX Corps, Second Army)

**19th Brigade** : Brigadier-General C R G Mayne
1st Queen's (Royal West Surrey)
1st Cameronians
5/6th Cameronians
**98th Brigade** : Brigadier-General J D Heriot-Maitland
4th King's (Liverpool)
2nd Argyll & Sutherland Highlanders
1st Middlesex
**100th Brigade** : Brigadier-General A W F Baird
2nd Worcesters
1/9th (Glasgow Highland)Highland Light Infantry
16th (Church Lads Brigade) King's Royal Rifle Corps
Pioneers : 18th (1st Public Works) Middlesex


**34th DIVISION** : Major-General C L Nicholson
- Battle of Estaires 9 - 11 Apr (XV Corps, First Army)
- Battle of Bailleul 12 - 15 Apr (IX Corps, First Army)
- First Battle of Kemmel 17 - 19 Apr (IX Corps, First Army)

**101st Brigade** : Brigadier-General R C Gore, killed in action 14 Apr; Lieutenant-Colonel A Stephenson
15th (1st City of Edinburgh) Royal Scots
16th (2nd City of Edinburgh) Royal Scots
11th (Cambridge) Suffolk
**102nd Brigade** : Brigadier-General N A Thomson
22nd (3rd Tyneside Scots) Northumberland Fusiliers
23rd (4th Tyneside Scots) Northumberland Fusiliers
25th (2nd Tyneside Irish) Northumberland Fusiliers
**103rd Brigade** : Brigadier-General J G Chaplin
10th (Grimsby Chums) Lincolns
1st East Lancashires
9th (Northumberland Hussars) Northumberland Fusiliers
Pioneers : 18th (1st Tyneside Pioneers) Northumberland Fusiliers


**36th (ULSTER) DIVISION** : Major-General O S W Nugent
- Battle of Messines 10 - 11 Apr (108th Brigade only with 19th Division, IX Corps, Second Army)
- Battle of Bailleul 13 - 15 Apr (108th Brigade only with 19th Division)
- First Battle of Kemmel 17 - 18 Apr (108th Brigade only with 19th Division)

**108th Brigade** : Brigadier-General C R J Griffith
12th (Central Antrim Volunteers) Royal Irish Rifles
9th (North Irish Horse) Royal Irish Fusiliers
1st Royal Irish Fusiliers

**39th DIVISION** : Major-General C A Blacklock
- First Battle of Kemmel 17 - 19 Apr (39th Division Composite Brigade, XXII Corps, Second Army)
- Second Battle of Kemmel 25 - 26 Apr (39th Division Composite Brigade)
- Battle of Scherpenberg 29 Apr (39th Division Composite Brigade)

**39th Division Composite Brigade** : Major-General C A Blacklock
No. 1 Btn - 11th (1st South Down) Royal Sussex & 1/1st Hertfordshires
No. 2 Btn - 13th (Forest of Dean Pals) Gloucesters & 13th (3rd South Down) Royal Sussex
No. 3 Btn - 117th Brigade - 16th (Chatsworth Rifles) Sherwood Foresters, 17th (British Empire League) King's Royal Rifle Corps, 16th (St. Pancras) Rifle Brigade
No. 4 Btn - 118th Brigade - 1/6th Cheshires, 4/5th Black Watch, 1/1st Cambridgeshires

**40th DIVISION** : Major-General J Ponsonby
    Battle of Estaires 9 - 11 Apr (XV Corps, First Army)
    Battle of Hazebrouck 12 - 13 Apr (XV Corps, Second Army)

**119th Brigade** : Brigadier-General F P Crozier
13th (Wandsworth) East Surreys
21st (Islington) Middlesex
18th (2nd Glamorgan Pals) Welsh
**120th Brigade** : Brigadier-General C J Hobkirk
10/11th Highland Light Infantry
14th Argyll & Sutherland Highlanders
2nd Royal Scots Fusiliers
14th Highland Light Infantry
**121st Brigade** : Brigadier-General J Campbell
12th (East Anglian) Suffolks
20th (Shoreditch) Middlesex
13th Yorkshires
Pioneers : 12th (Teeside Pioneers) Yorkshires

**41st DIVISION** : Major-General S T B Lawford
- Battles of the Lys 9 - 29 Apr (VIII Corps to 13 Apr then II Corps, Second Army)

**122nd Brigade** : Brigadier-General F W Towsey
12th (Bermondsey) East Surreys
15th (Carabiniers) Hampshires
15th King's Royal Rifle Corps
**123rd Brigade** : Brigadier-General E Pearce-Serocold
11th (Lambeth) Queens (Royal West Surrey)
23rd (2nd Football) Middlesex
10th (Kent County) Royal West Kents
**124th Brigade** : Brigadier-General W F Clemson
10th (Battersea) Queens (Royal West Surrey)
20th (Wearside) Durham Light Infantry
26th (Bankers) Royal Fusiliers
    Pioneers : 19th (2nd Public Works) Middlesex

**49th (WEST RIDING) DIVISION** : Major-General N J G Cameron
- Battle of Estaires 10 - 11 Apr (147th Brigade only, XV Corps, First Army)
- Battle of Messines 10 - 11 Apr (148th Brigade only, IX Corps, Second Army)
- Battle of Bailleul 13 - 15 Apr (IX Corps, Second Army)
- First Battle of Kemmel 17 - 19 Apr (IX Corps, Second Army; 146th Brigade with XXII Corps)
- Second Battle of Kemmel 25 - 26 Apr (XXII Corps, Second Army)
- Battle of Scherpenberg 29 Apr (XXII Corps, Second Army)

**146th (1st West Riding) Brigade** : Brigadier-General G A P Rennie
1/5th West Yorkshires
1/6th West Yorkshires
1/7th (Leeds Rifles) West Yorkshires
**147th (2nd West Riding) Brigade** : Brigadier-General C G Lewes
1/4th Duke of Wellington's
1/6th Duke of Wellington's
1/7th Duke of Wellington's
**148th (3rd West Riding) Brigade** : Brigadier-General L F Green-Wilkinson
1/4th (Hallamshire) York & Lancasters
1/5th York & Lancasters
1/4th King's Own Yorkshire Light Infantry
Pioneers : 19th (3rd Salford Pals) Lancashire Fusiliers

**50th (NORTHUMBRIAN) DIVISION** : Major-General H C Jackson
- Battle of Estaires 9 - 11 Apr (XV Corps, First Army)
- Battle of Hazebrouck 12 Apr (XV Corps, First Army)

**149th (Northumberland) Brigade** : Brigadier-General E P A Riddell
1/4th Northumberland Fusiliers
1/5th Northumberland Fusiliers
1/6th Northumberland Fusiliers
**150th (York & Durham) Brigade** : Brigadier-General H C Rees
1/4th Yorkshires
1/5th Yorkshires
1/4th East Yorkshires
**151st (Durham Light Infantry) Brigade** : Brigadier-General H Martin
1/5th Durham Light Infantry
1/6th Durham Light Infantry
1/8th Durham Light Infantry
Pioneers : 1/7th Durham Light Infantry

**51st (HIGHLAND) DIVISION** : Major-General G T C Carter-Campbell
- Battle of Estaires 9 - 11 Apr (XI Corps, First Army)
- Battle of Hazebrouck 12 - 15 Apr (XI Corps, First Army)

**152nd (1st Highland) Brigade** : Brigadier-General J K Dick-Cunyngham to 12 Apr (captured); Major A A Duff to 15 Apr; Lieutenant-Colonel J M Scott
1/5th (Sutherland & Caithness) Seaforth Highlanders
1/6th (Morayshire) Seaforth Highlanders
1/6th (Banff & Donside) Gordon Highlanders

**153rd (2nd Highland) Brigade** : Brigadier-General A T Beckwith to 11 Apr (wounded); Lieutenant-Colonel L M Dyson to 13 Apr; Major W H Newson on 13 Apr; Lieutenant-Colonel J M Scott to 15 Apr; Brigadier-General W Green
1/6th (Perthshire) Black Watch
1/7th (Fife) Black Watch
1/7th (Deeside Highland) Gordon Highlanders

**154th (3rd Highland) Brigade** : Brigadier-General K G Buchanan
1/4th (Ross Highland) Seaforth Highlanders
1/7th Argyll & Sutherland Highlanders
1/4th Gordon Highlanders
Pioneers : 1/8th Royal Scots

**55th (WEST LANCASHIRE) DIVISION** : Major-General H S Jeudwine
- Battle of Estaires 9 - 11 Apr (XI Corps, First Army)
- Battle of Hazebrouck 12 - 15 Apr (I Corps, First Army)

**164th (North Lancashire) Brigade** : Brigadier-General C I Stockwell
1/4th King's Own
1/4th Loyal North Lancashires
2/5th Lancashire Fusiliers

**165th (Liverpool) Brigade** : Brigadier-General L B Boyd-Moss
1/5th King's (Liverpool)
1/6th (Leeds Rifles) King's (Liverpool)
1/7th King's (Liverpool)

**166th (South Lancashire) Brigade** : Brigadier-General R J Kentish
1/5th King's Own
1/5th South Lancashires
1/10th (Liverpool Scottish) King's (Liverpool)
Pioneers : 1/4th South Lancashires

**59th (2nd NORTH MIDLAND) DIVISION** : Major-General C F Romer
- Battle of Bailleul 14 - 15 Apr (IX Corps, Second Army)
- First Battle of Kemmel 17 - 18 Apr (IX Corps, Second Army)

**176th (2nd/1st Staffordshire) Brigade** : Brigadier-General T G Cope
5th North Staffordshires
2/6th North Staffordshires
2/6th South Staffordshires

**177th (2nd/1st Lincoln & Leicester) Brigade** : Brigadier-General C H L James
4th Lincolns
2/5th Lincolns
2/4th Leicesters

**178th (2nd/1st Nottingham & Derby) Brigade** : Brigadier-General T W Stansfeld
2/5th Sherwood Foresters
2/6th Sherwood Foresters
7th Sherwood Foresters
Pioneers : 6/7th Royal Scots Fusiliers

**61st (2nd SOUTH MIDLAND) DIVISION** : Major-General C J MacKenzie
- Battle of Estaires 11 Apr (XI Corps, First Army)
- Battle of Hazebrouck 12 - 15 Apr (XI Corps, First Army)
- Battle of Bethune 18 Apr (XI Corps, First Army)

**182nd (2nd/1st Warwickshire) Brigade** : Brigadier-General W K Evans
2/6th Royal Warwickshires
2/7th Royal Warwickshires
2/8th Royal Warwickshires

**183rd (2nd/1st Gloucester & Worcester) Brigade** : Brigadier-General A H Spooner
1/9th (Highlanders) Royal Scots
1/5th (Buchan & Formartin) Gordon Highlanders
1/8th (Argyllshire) Argyll & Sutherland Highlanders

**184th (2nd/1st South Midland) Brigade** : Brigadier-General A W Pagan
2/5th Gloucesters
2/4th Royal Berkshires
2/4th Oxford & Bucks Light Infantry
Pioneers : 1/5th Duke of Cornwall's Light Infantry

**1st AUSTRALIAN DIVISION** : Major General H B Walker
- Battle of Hazebrouck 12 - 15 Apr (XV Corps, First Army)
- Defence of the Nieppe Forest

**1st (New South Wales) Brigade** : Brigadier-General W R Lesslie
1st Battalion
2nd Battalion
3rd Battalion
4th Battalion

**2nd (Victoria) Brigade** : Brigadier-General J Heane
5th Battalion
6th Battalion
7th Battalion
8th Battalion

**3rd Brigade** : Brigadier-General H G Bennett
9th (Queensland) Battalion
10th (South Australia) Battalion
11th (West Australia) Battalion
12th (Tasmania, S and W Australia) Battalion
Pioneers : 1st Australian Pioneer Battalion

# THE FINAL ADVANCE IN FLANDERS (SEPTEMBER-OCTOBER 1918)

**9th (SCOTTISH) DIVISION** : Major-General H H Tudor
- Battle of Ypres 28 Sept - 2 Oct (II Corps, Second Army)
- Battle of Courtrai 14 - 19 Oct (II Corps, Second Army)

**26th Brigade** : Brigadier-General Hon. A G A Hore-Ruthven, VC
8th Black Watch
5th Cameron Highlanders
7th Seaforth Highlanders
**27th Brigade** : Brigadier-General W D Croft
11th Royal Scots
6th King's Own Scottish Borderers
12th Royal Scots
**28th Brigade** : Brigadier-General J L Jack
2nd Royal Scots Fusiliers
9th Cameronians
1st Royal Newfoundlanders
Pioneers : 9th Seaforth Highlanders

**14th (LIGHT) DIVISION** : Major-General P C B Skinner
- Battle of Ypres 28 Sept - 2 Oct (XIX Corps, Second Army)
- Battle of Courtrai 14 - 19 Oct (XV Corps, Second Army)

**41st Brigade** : Brigadier-General W F Sweny
18th York & Lancasters
29th Durham Light Infantry
33rd (Rifle Brigade) Londons
**42nd Brigade** : Brigadier-General H T Dobbin
6th (Wiltshire Yeomanry) Wiltshires
14th Argyll & Sutherland Highlanders
16th (1st Manchester Pals) Manchesters
**43rd Brigade** : Brigadier-General G E Pereira
12th (East Anglian) Suffolks
10th Highland Light Infantry
20th (Shoreditch) Middlesex
Pioneers : 15th Loyal North Lancashires

**29th DIVISION** : Major-General D E Cayley
- Battle of Ypres 28 Sept - 2 Oct (II Corps, Second Army)
- Battle of courtrai 14 - 19 Oct (II Corps, Second Army)

**86th Brigade** : Brigadier-General G R H Cheape
2nd Royal Fusiliers
1st Lancashire Fusiliers
1st Royal Dublin Fusiliers
**87th Brigade** : Brigadier-General G H N Jackson
1st South Wales Borderers
1st Border
1st King's Own Scottish Borderers
**88th Brigade** : Brigadier-General B C Freyberg, VC
4th Worcesters
2nd Hampshires
2nd Leinsters
Pioneers : 1/2nd Monmouths

**30th DIVISION** : Major-General W de L Williams
- Battle of Ypres 28 Sept - 2 Oct (X Corps, Second Army)
- Battle of Courtrai 14 - 19 Oct (X Corps, Second Army)

**21st Brigade** : Brigadier-General G D Goodman
7th (South Irish Horse) Royal Irish
1/6th Cheshires
2/23rd Londons
**89th Brigade** : Brigadier-General R A M Currie
2nd South Lancashires
7/8th Royal Inniskilling Fusiliers
2/17th Londons
**90th Brigade** : Brigadier-General G A Stevens
2/14th Londons
2/15th Londons
2/16th Londons
Pioneers : 6th South Wales Borderers

**31st DIVISION** : Major-General J Campbell
- Battle of Ypres 28 Sept - 2 Oct (XV Corps, Second Army)

**92nd Brigade** : Brigadier-General O de L Williams
10th (Hull Commercials) East Yorkshires
11th (Hull Tradesmen) East Yorkshires
11th (Accrington Pals) East Lancashires
**93rd Brigade** : Brigadier-General S C Taylor
15th (1st Leeds Pals) West Yorkshires
13th (1st Barnsley Pals) York & Lancasters
18th (1st County of Durham Pals) Durham Light Infantry
**94th (Yeomanry) Brigade** : Brigadier-General A Symons
12th (Norfolk Yeomanry) Norfolks
12th (Ayr & Lanark Yeomanry) Royal Scots Fusiliers
24th (Denbigh Yeomanry) Royal Welsh Fusiliers
Pioneers : 12th (Halifax (Miners) Pals) King's Own Yorkshire Light Infantry

**34th DIVISION** : Major-General C L Nicholson
- Battle of Ypres 28 - 29 Sept (X Corps, Second Army)
- Battle of Courtrai 14 - 19 Oct (X Corps, Second Army)

**101st Brigade** : Brigadier-General W J Woodcock
2/4th Queen's (Royal West Surrey)
1/4th Royal Sussex
2nd Loyal North Lancashires
**102nd Brigade** : Brigadier-General E Hilliam
1/4th Cheshires
1/7th Cheshires
1/1st Herefordshires
**103rd Brigade** : Brigadier-General R I Rawson
1/5th King's Own Scottish Borderers
1/5th Argyll & Sutherland Highlanders
1/8th Cameronians
Pioneers : 2/4th Somerset Light Infantry

**35th DIVISION** : Major-General A H Marindin
- Battle of Ypres 28 Sept - 2 Oct (XIX Corps, Second Army)
- Battle of Courtrai 14 - 19 Oct (XIX Corps, Second Army)

**104th Brigade** : Brigadier-General J W Sandilands
17th (1st South East Lancashire Pals) Lancashire Fusiliers
18th (2nd South East Lancashire Pals) Lancashire Fusiliers
19th (2nd County of Durham Pals) Durham Light Infantry
**105th Brigade** : Brigadier-General A. J. Turner
15th (1st Birkenhead Pals) Cheshires
15th (Nottingham Pals) Sherwood Foresters
4th North Staffordshires
**106th Brigade** : Brigadier-General J. H. W. Pollard
17th (Earl of Roseberry) Royal Scots
18th (Glasgow Yeomanry) Highland Light Infantry
12th Highland Light Infantry
Pioneers : 19th (2nd Tyneside Pioneers) Northumberland Fusiliers

**36th (ULSTER) DIVISION** : Major-General C Coffin, VC
- Battle of Ypres 28 Sept - 2 Oct (II Corps, Second Army)
- Battle of Courtrai 14 - 19 Oct (II Corps, Second Army)

**107th Brigade** : Brigadier-General H J Brock
1st Royal Irish Rifles
2nd Royal Irish Rifles
15th (North Belfast Volunteers) Royal Irish Rifles
**108th Brigade** : Brigadier-General E Vaughan
12th (Central Antrim Volunteers) Royal Irish Rifles
1st Royal Irish Fusiliers
9th (North Irish Horse) Royal Irish Fusiliers
**109th Brigade** : Brigadier-General W F Hessey
1st Royal Inniskilling Fusiliers
2nd Royal Inniskilling Fusiliers
9th (County Tyrone Volunteers) Royal Inniskilling Fusiliers
Pioneers : 16th (2nd County Down Volunteers) Royal Irish Rifles

**40th DIVISION** : Major-General Sir W E Peyton
- Battle of Ypres 28 Sept - 2 Oct (XV Corps, Second Army)

**119th Brigade** : Brigadier-General F P Crozier
13th Royal Inniskilling Fusiliers
13th East Lancashires
12th North Staffordshires
**120th Brigade** : Brigadier-General C J Hobkirk
10th King's Own Scottish Borderers
15th King's Own Yorkshire Light Infantry
11th Cameron Highlanders
**121st Brigade** : Brigadier-General G C Stubbs
8th Royal Irish
23rd Lancashire Fusiliers
23rd Cheshires
Pioneers : 17th Worcesters

**41st DIVISION** : Major-General S T B Lawford
- Battle of Ypres 28 Sept - 2 Oct (XIX Corps, Second Army)
- Battle of Courtrai 14 - 19 Oct (XIX Corps, Second Army)

**122nd Brigade** : Brigadier-General S V P Weston
12th (Bermondsey) East Surreys
15th (Carabiniers) Hampshires
15th King's Royal Rifle Corps
**123rd Brigade** : Brigadier-General M Kemp-Welch
11th (Lambeth) Queen's (Royal West Surrey)
23rd (2nd Football) Middlesex
11th (Lewisham) Royal West Kents
**124th Brigade** : Brigadier-General R L Adlercron
10th (Battersea) Queen's (Royal West Surrey)
26th (Bankers) Royal Fusiliers
20th (Wearside) Durham Light Infantry
Pioneers : 19th (2nd Public Works) Middlesex

| | UK | Aust | NZ | Can | NF | SAfr | RGLI | BWI | India | Chi | Fr | Bel | Ger | Other | Un-named | KUG | SM | WWII | TOTAL |
|---|---|---|---|---|---|---|---|---|---|---|---|---|---|---|---|---|---|---|---|
| Abeele Aerodrome Military | 104 | | | | | | | | | | | | | | | | | | 104 |
| Aeroplane | 831 | 208 | 17 | 47 | 1 | 1 | | | | | | | | | 637 | 1 | 8 | | 1114 |
| Artillery Wood | 1255 | 5 | 2 | 30 | 10 | 1 | | | | | | | | | 506 | 4 | 12 | | 1319 |
| Bailleul Communal | 585 | | | 21 | | | | | 4 | | 132 | 2 | 8 | | 10 | | 17 | | 769 |
| Bailleul Communal Extension | 3453 | 398 | 252 | 290 | 1 | 1 | 1 | 1 | 5 | 31 | 2 | | 154 | | 181 | 1 | 11 | 17 | 4617 |
| Bard Cottage | 1619 | | | 9 | 6 | 2 | | 3 | | | | | 4 | | 39 | | 3 | | 1646 |
| Bas-Warneton (Neerwaasten) Communal | | | | | | | | | | | | | | | | | | 47 | 47 |
| Bedford House | 4422 | 249 | 36 | 390 | | 21 | 3 | 6 | 21 | | | | 2 | 2 | 2513 | 501 | 50 | 69 | 5772 |
| Belgian Battery Corner | 430 | 125 | 8 | 7 | | | | | 2 | | | | | | 8 | 1 | 2 | | 575 |
| Berks Cemetery Extension | 467 | 180 | 80 | 146 | | 1 | | | | | | | 4 | | | 3 | | | 880 |
| Bertenacre Military | 109 | | | 2 | | | | | | | | | | | | | 1 | 32 | 144 |
| Bethleem Farm East | 1 | 43 | | | | | | | | | | | | | | | 1 | | 45 |
| Bethleem Farm West | 24 | 114 | 26 | | | | | | | | | | | | 8 | | 1 | 1 | 166 |
| Beveren-Ijzer Churchyard | 17 | | | | | | | | | | | 6 | | | 2 | | 3 | 8 | 34 |
| Birr Crossroads | 660 | 143 | 12 | 15 | 1 | 1 | | 1 | | | | 1 | | | 333 | | 27 | | 861 |
| Blauwepoort Farm | 82 | | | | | | | | | | | | | | | 7 | | | 89 |
| Bleuet Farm | 437 | | | 1 | 1 | 3 | | | | | | | 1 | | | | | 9 | 452 |
| Boezinge Churchyard | 1 | | | | | | | | | | | | | | | | | 14 | 15 |
| Brandhoek Military | 600 | 4 | | 63 | | | | 2 | | | | | 2 | | 4 | | | | 671 |
| Brandhoek New Military | 512 | 11 | | 6 | | | | | 1 | | | | 28 | | | | | | 558 |
| Brandhoek New Military No. 3 | 850 | 46 | 18 | 54 | | 5 | | 1 | | 1 | | | | | 1 | | | | 975 |
| Bridge House | 45 | | | | | | | | | | | | | | 4 | | | | 45 |
| Buffs Road | 265 | 13 | | 10 | | | | | | | | | | | 86 | | 10 | | 299 |
| Bus House | 192 | 10 | 1 | 2 | | 1 | | 1 | | | 2 | | | | 12 | | 2 | 79 | 289 |
| Buttes New British, Polygon Wood | 1297 | 564 | 162 | 50 | | | | | | | | | | | 1677 | 30 | 35 | | 2138 |
| Cabin Hill | 42 | 25 | | | | | | | | | | | | | | | | | 67 |
| Calvaire (Essex) Military | 218 | | | | | | | | | | | | | | | | | | 218 |
| Canada Farm | 879 | | | 5 | 4 | | | 19 | | | | | | | | | | | 907 |
| Cement House | 3472 | 19 | 10 | 58 | 14 | 1 | 5 | | 1 | | 1 | | 1 | | 2425 | 1 | 11 | 22 | 3615 |
| Chester Farm | 306 | 21 | | 87 | | | | | | | | | 4 | | 7 | | 6 | | 424 |
| Colne Valley | 47 | | | | | | | | | | | | | | 4 | | | | 47 |
| Comines (Komen) Communal | | | | | | | | | | | | | | | | | | 100 | 100 |
| Croonaert Chapel | 74 | | | | | | | | | 1 | | | | | 7 | | | | 75 |
| Derry House No. 2 | 126 | 37 | | | | | | | | | | | | | | | | | 163 |
| Dickebusch Old Military | 43 | | | 3 | | | | | | | | | 1 | | 3 | | | 10 | 57 |

| | UK | Aust | NZ | Can | NF | SAfr | RGLI | BWI | India | Chi | Fr | Bel | Ger | Other | Un-named | KUG | SM | WWII | TOTAL |
|---|---|---|---|---|---|---|---|---|---|---|---|---|---|---|---|---|---|---|---|
| Dickebusch New Military | 529 | 11 | 84 | | | | | | | | | | | | 8 | | | | 624 |
| Dickebusch New Military Extension | 520 | 24 | | 2 | 1 | | | | | | | | 1 | | 5 | | | | 548 |
| Divisional | 188 | | 65 | 26 | | | | | | | | | | 1 | | 1 | | | 281 |
| Divisional Collecting Post | 86 | | | | | | | | | | | | | | | | | | 89 |
| Divisional Collecting Post Extension | 493 | 102 | 5 | 73 | 2 | 1 | | | | | | | | | 511 | | 2 | | 676 |
| Dochy Farm New British | 523 | 304 | 98 | 82 | 1 | 17 | | | | | | | | | 958 | 412 | 2 | 73 | 1439 |
| Dozinghem Military | 3021 | 6 | 14 | 61 | 19 | 15 | | 34 | | 3 | | | 65 | | 1 | 1 | | | 3312 |
| Dragon Camp | 66 | | | | | | | | | | | | | | 10 | | | | 66 |
| Dranouter Churchyard | 79 | | | | | | | | | | | | | | 2 | | | | 79 |
| Dranoutre Military | 422 | 16 | 1 | 19 | | | | | | | | | 1 | 1 | 3 | | | | 463 |
| Duhallow ADS | 1442 | 13 | 6 | 26 | 12 | 3 | | 2 | 2 | | | 1 | 54 | | 231 | 40 | | 1 | 1564 |
| Elzenwalle Brasserie | 106 | | | 41 | | | | 2 | | | | | | | 5 | | | | 149 |
| Essex Farm | 1088 | | 9 | | | | | | | | | | 5 | | 102 | 83 | 19 | | 1185 |
| Ferme-Olivier | 409 | | | | | | | | | | | | 3 | | | | | | 412 |
| First DCL, The Bluff | 76 | | | | | | | | | | | | | | 13 | | | | 76 |
| Geluveld Communal | | | | | | | | | | | | | | | 1 | | | 1 | 1 |
| Godewaersvelde British | 988 | 65 | 2 | 5 | | 2 | | | 3 | | | | 19 | | | | | | 1084 |
| Godezonne Farm | 74 | 1 | | 1 | | 3 | | | | | | | | | 44 | | | | 79 |
| Grootebeek British | 99 | 1 | 1 | | | 1 | | | 7 | | | | 1 | 1 | 1 | 2 | 2 | | 113 |
| Gunners' Farm Military | 163 | 2 | 1 | | | 9 | | | | | | | 4 | | | | | | 179 |
| Gwalia | 435 | 2 | 5 | 5 | | 1 | | | | | | | 3 | | | | | | 469 |
| Hagle Dump | 397 | 26 | | 14 | | | | 14 | | | | | 2 | | 139 | 5 | | | 439 |
| Haringhe (Bandaghem) Military | 732 | 2 | 11 | 1 | 5 | 7 | | 4 | 4 | | 1 | | 39 | 1 | | 2 | 5 | | 817 |
| Hedge Row Trench | 94 | | | 2 | | | | | | | | | | | 2 | | | | 98 |
| Hooge Crater | 5182 | 513 | 121 | 105 | | | | 2 | | | | | | | 3580 | 45 | 96 | | 5923 |
| Hoogstade Belgian Military | 20 | | | | | | | | | | | 806 | | | | | | | 826 |
| Hoogstade Churchyard | | | | | | | | | | | | | | | | | | 12 | 12 |
| Hop Store | 250 | | | 1 | | | | | | | | | | | | | | | 251 |
| Hospital Farm | 115 | | | | | | | | | | 1 | | | | 4 | | | | 116 |
| Houthulst Belgian | | | | | | | | | | | 146 | 1723 | | 81 | | | | | 1950 |
| Houthulst Churchyard | | | | | | | | | | | | | | | | | | 7 | 7 |
| Hyde Park Corner (Royal Berks) | 81 | 1 | | 1 | | | | | | | | | 4 | | | | | | 87 |
| Irish House | 103 | 13 | | | | | | | | | | | 4 | | 40 | 1 | | | 121 |
| Kandahar Farm | 211 | 186 | 33 | 6 | | | | | | | | | 3 | | | 7 | 1 | | 447 |

| | UK | Aust | NZ | Can | NF | SAfr | RGLI | BWI | India | Chi | Fr | Bel | Ger | Other | Un-named | KUG | SM | WWII | TOTAL |
|---|---|---|---|---|---|---|---|---|---|---|---|---|---|---|---|---|---|---|---|
| Kemmel Chateau Military | 1030 | 24 | 1 | 80 | | | | | | | | | | | 4 | | | 22 | 1157 |
| Kemmel Churchyard | 23 | | | | | | | | | | | | | | | | 15 | | 23 |
| Kemmel No. 1 French | 278 | 12 | 3 | 3 | | | | | | | | | 94 | | 3 | 1 | | | 391 |
| Klien-Vierstraat British | 779 | 8 | 7 | 8 | | 1 | | 1 | | | | | | | 109 | | | | 805 |
| La Belle Alliance | 60 | | | | | | | | | | | | | | 10 | | | | 60 |
| La Brique Military No. 1 | 91 | | | | | | | | | | | | | | 4 | | | | 91 |
| La Brique Military No. 2 | 782 | 18 | 9 | 23 | | 7 | | | 1 | | | | | | 387 | | 4 | | 844 |
| La Clytte Military | 1003 | 12 | 3 | 51 | | 6 | | 7 | | | | | | | 238 | | 24 | | 1082 |
| La Creche Communal | 3 | | | | | | | | | | | | | | | | | | 3 |
| La Laiterie Military | 469 | 7 | | 196 | 1 | | | | | | | | | | 180 | 78 | 2 | | 753 |
| La Plus Douve Farm | 101 | 86 | 61 | 88 | | | | | | | | | 9 | | | | | | 345 |
| Lancashire Cottage | 231 | 23 | | 2 | | | | | | | | | 13 | | 5 | | 2 | | 271 |
| Langemark German Military | | | | | | | | | | | | | 44535 | | 11813 | | | | 44535 |
| Larch Wood (Railway Cutting) | 700 | 36 | | 86 | | | | 1 | | | | | 1 | | 321 | 33 | 87 | | 857 |
| Le Touquet Railway Crossing | 74 | | | | | | | | | | | | | | 21 | | 3 | | 74 |
| Lijssenthoek Military | 7330 | 1131 | 291 | 1053 | 5 | 29 | | 21 | 3 | 35 | 658 | | 223 | 4 | 24 | 3 | 8 | | 10794 |
| Lindenhoek Chalet Military | 282 | 10 | 8 | 15 | | | | | | | | | 2 | | 67 | | 6 | | 317 |
| Locre Hospice | 239 | 2 | 1 | 1 | | | | 1 | | | | | 2 | | 12 | | 10 | 14 | 260 |
| Locre No. 10 | 55 | | | | | | | | | | | | 75 | | 14 | | 3 | | 133 |
| Loker Churchyard | 184 | | | 31 | | | | | | | | | | | 2 | | | | 215 |
| London Rifle Brigade | 263 | 38 | 34 | | | | | | | | | | 18 | | 1 | | | | 353 |
| Lone Tree | 82 | | | | | | | | | | | | | | | 6 | | | 88 |
| Maple Copse | 154 | | | 154 | | | | | | | | | | | 52 | | 230 | | 308 |
| Maple Leaf | 80 | 4 | 43 | 39 | | 1 | | | | | | | 9 | | | | | | 176 |
| Mendinghem Military | 2266 | 15 | 12 | 28 | 3 | 33 | | 26 | | 8 | | | 52 | | | | | | 2443 |
| Menin Road South Military | 1049 | 263 | 52 | 145 | | | | 3 | | | | | 1 | | 118 | 65 | 79 | | 1657 |
| Messines Ridge | 986 | 332 | 115 | 1 | | 56 | | | | | | | | | 957 | | 41 | | 1531 |
| Meteren (Mont-des-Cats) Communal | | | | | | | | | | | | | | | | | | 24 | 24 |
| Meteren Communal | | | | | | | | | | | | | | | | | | 6 | 6 |
| Meteren Military | 581 | 104 | 22 | 6 | 1 | 31 | | | 16 | | 69 | | | | 180 | | 7 | 6 | 843 |
| Minty Farm | 192 | | | | | | | | | | | | 1 | | 4 | | | | 193 |
| Mont Kemmel French | | | | | | | | | | | 5294 | | | | 5237 | | | | 5294 |
| Mont Noir Military | 146 | 1 | | | 2 | | | | | | 84 | | | | 15 | | | 2 | 235 |
| Motor Car Corner | 36 | 9 | 84 | | | | | | | | | | 1 | | | 2 | | | 132 |
| Mud Corner | 1 | 31 | 53 | | | | | | | | | | | | | | | | 85 |
| New Irish Farm | 4272 | 65 | 23 | 255 | 3 | 6 | | 1 | 5 | 7 | | | 1 | | 3271 | 12 | 69 | | 4719 |

| | UK | Aust | NZ | Can | NF | SAfr | RGLI | BWI | India | Chi | Fr | Bel | Ger | Other | Un-named | KUG | SM | WWII | TOTAL |
|---|---|---|---|---|---|---|---|---|---|---|---|---|---|---|---|---|---|---|---|
| Nieppe Communal | 43 | 6 | 11 | | | 2 | | | | | 20 | | | | | | | | 82 |
| Nieuwkerke Neuve-Eglise) Churchyard | 76 | 10 | 5 | 1 | | | | | 1 | | 5 | 3 | | | 1 | | | 10 | 111 |
| Nine Elms British | 952 | 149 | 118 | 292 | 7 | 26 | 8 | 2 | 1 | | 37 | | | 1 | | | | 22 | 1615 |
| No Man's Cot | 79 | | | | | | | | | | | | | | | | | | 79 |
| Noordschote Churchyard | | | | | | | | | | | | | | | | | | 14 | 14 |
| Oak Dump | 109 | 2 | | | | | | | | | | | | | | | 2 | | 113 |
| Oostvleteren Churchyard | | | | | | | | | | | | | | | 5 | | | 17 | 57 |
| Oosttaverne Wood | 923 | 43 | 19 | 133 | | | | | | 1 | | | 25 | | 783 | | 1 | | 1145 |
| Oxford Road | 657 | 74 | 37 | 74 | 9 | | 2 | | | 39 | | | 2 | | 297 | | 3 | | 858 |
| Packhorse Farm Shrine | 59 | | | | | | | | | | | | | | | | | | 59 |
| Passchendaele New | 1019 | 292 | 126 | 647 | 1 | 3 | 4 | | | | | | | | 1602 | | 7 | | 2099 |
| Perth (China Wall) | 2481 | 147 | 23 | 133 | | 7 | | | | | | | | | 1372 | | 135 | | 2791 |
| Ploegsteert Churchyard | 7 | | | 2 | | | | | | | | | | | | | | | 9 |
| Ploegsteert Wood Military | 117 | 1 | 18 | 28 | | | | | | | | | | 1 | | | | | 165 |
| Poelcapelle British | 6573 | 117 | 237 | 527 | 9 | 10 | | | | | | 4 | | | 6230 | | 36 | 1 | 7478 |
| Poelkapelle Communal | | | | | | | | | | | | 4 | | | | | | 8 | 8 |
| Pollinkhove Churchyard | | | | | | | | | | | | | | | | | | 4 | 4 |
| Polygon Wood | 46 | | 60 | | | | | | | | | | 1 | | 19 | | 30 | | 107 |
| Pond Farm | 298 | | | | | | | | | | | | 5 | | 4 | | 3 | | 306 |
| Pont-d'Achelles Military | 173 | 72 | 48 | | | | | | | | | | 37 | | 7 | | | | 330 |
| Pont-de-Nieppe Communal | 123 | 12 | | | | | | | | | 32 | | 790 | 1 | 12 | 2 | | | 960 |
| Poperinge Communal | 22 | | | | | | | | | | | | | 78 | 1 | | | | 100 |
| Poperinghe New Military | 596 | 20 | 3 | 55 | | | | | | 1 | 275 | 1 | 1 | | 24 | | 7 | | 953 |
| Poperinghe Old Military | 397 | | | 46 | | | | | 1 | | | | 2 | | | 85 | | | 453 |
| Potijze Burial Ground | 580 | 3 | | 1 | | | | | | | | | 2 | | 21 | | | | 586 |
| Potijze Chateau Grounds | 399 | 25 | 2 | 49 | | 1 | | | | | | | 1 | | 111 | 20 | | | 478 |
| Potijze Chateau Lawn | 191 | 4 | | 22 | | 9 | | | | | | | 3 | | 29 | 1 | | | 230 |
| Potijze Chateau Wood | 151 | | | 6 | | | | | | | | | | | 6 | | | | 157 |
| Proven Churchyard | | | | | | | | | | | | 1 | | | 6 | | | 5 | 6 |
| Prowse Point Military | 165 | 13 | 42 | 1 | | | | | | | | 12 | | | | | | | 233 |
| Railway Chateau | 105 | | | | | | | | | | | | | | | | | | 105 |
| Railway Dugouts Burial Ground (Transport Farm) | 1659 | 154 | 3 | 636 | | 1 | 4 | | | | | | 3 | | 430 | 2 | 333 | | 2462 |
| Ramparts, Lille Gate | 162 | 11 | 14 | 10 | | | | | | | | | | | 10 | | | | 197 |
| Ration Farm (La Plus Douve) | 186 | 12 | 4 | | | | | | | | | | 1 | | 9 | | | | 203 |
| R.E. Farm | 132 | | | 47 | | | | | | | | | | | 11 | | | | 179 |

270

| | UK | Aust | NZ | Can | NF | SAfr | RGLI | BWI | India | Chi | Fr | Bel | Ger | Other | Un-named | KUG | SM | WWII | TOTAL |
|---|---|---|---|---|---|---|---|---|---|---|---|---|---|---|---|---|---|---|---|
| R.E. Grave, Railway Wood | 12 | | | | | | | | | | | | | | | | | | 12 |
| Red Farm Military | 46 | | | | | | | | | | | 3 | | | 17 | | | | 49 |
| Reningelst Churchyard | 2 | | | | | | | | | | | | | | | | 1 | | 3 |
| Reninghelst Churchyard Extension | 55 | 1 | | | | | | | | | | | | | | | | 2 | 58 |
| Reninghelst New Military | 453 | 104 | 2 | 230 | | 1 | | | | 7 | | | 2 | | | 1 | | | 800 |
| Ridge Wood Military | 258 | 44 | 3 | 292 | | | | | | | | | 2 | | 5 | 20 | 2 | | 621 |
| Rifle House | 229 | | | 1 | | | | | | | | | | | | | | | 230 |
| Ruisseau Farm | 82 | | | | | | | | | | | | | | | | | | 82 |
| Sanctuary Wood | 1735 | 88 | 18 | 142 | 3 | 3 | | | | | | | 1 | | 1353 | | 88 | | 1990 |
| Seaforth, Cheddar Villa | 147 | | | 1 | | | | | | | | | | | 21 | | 19 | | 148 |
| Solferino Farm | 293 | | | 1 | 1 | | | 1 | | | | | 3 | | 1 | | | 5 | 304 |
| Somer Farm | 67 | 24 | | | | | | | | | | | | | | | 5 | | 91 |
| Spanbroekmolen British | 58 | | | | | | | | | | | | | | | 5 | 6 | | 58 |
| Spoilbank | 426 | 67 | | 16 | | | | | | | | | | | 125 | | 11 | | 520 |
| St Charles French | | | | | | | | | | | 3600 | | | | 764 | 609 | | | 4209 |
| St Jan-ter-Biezen Communal | 1 | | | | | | | | | | | | | | | | | | 1 |
| St Julien Dressing Station | 290 | 10 | 3 | 14 | 1 | 3 | | | | | | | | | 180 | 96 | 11 | | 428 |
| St Quentin Cabaret Military | 316 | 7 | 64 | 68 | | 4 | | 1 | 1 | | | | 2 | | 5 | 5 | | | 462 |
| Staden Communal | | | | | | | | | | | | | | | | | | 1 | 1 |
| Strand Military | 725 | 284 | 87 | 26 | | 1 | | | | | | | 11 | | 354 | | 19 | 8 | 1161 |
| Suffolk | 47 | | | | | | | | | | | | | | 8 | | | | 47 |
| Talana Farm | 529 | | | | | | | | | | | | | | 14 | | 16 | | 529 |
| Tancrez Farm | 306 | 19 | 3 | | | 4 | | | | | | | 2 | | 6 | | 1 | | 335 |
| The Huts | 815 | 243 | 19 | 5 | | 4 | 6 | 2 | | | | | 6 | | | 6 | | | 1100 |
| Toronto Avenue | | 78 | | | | | | | | | | | | | 2 | | | | 78 |
| Torreken Farm No. 1 | 70 | 20 | | | | | | | | | | | 14 | | 1 | | | | 104 |
| Track 'X' | 144 | | | 5 | | | | | | | | | | | 27 | | | | 149 |
| Trois Arbres | 954 | 470 | 214 | 20 | 1 | 1 | 33 | | 1 | | | | | | 435 | | 10 | | 1704 |
| Tuileries British | 26 | 19 | | | | | | | | | 3 | | | | 16 | 11 | 69 | | 98 |
| Tyne Cot | 8961 | 1368 | 520 | 1011 | 14 | 90 | 6 | | | | | | 4 | | 8373 | | 101 | | 11976 |
| Underhill Farm | 103 | 47 | 39 | 1 | | | | | | | | | | | 8 | 1 | 5 | | 190 |
| Vlamertinghe Military | 1113 | 4 | | 52 | 2 | 2 | | | 3 | | | | 3 | | | 1 | | 4 | 1184 |
| Vlamertinghe New Military | 1610 | 44 | 1 | 154 | | 3 | 1 | | | | | | 7 | | 12 | | | | 1820 |
| Voormezeele Enclosures No.'s 1 & 2 | 520 | 17 | 2 | 53 | | | | | | | | | 5 | | 40 | | 21 | | 597 |
| Voormezeele Enclosure No. 3 | 1481 | 8 | 2 | 100 | | 1 | | | | | | | | | 608 | 1 | 20 | | 1612 |

| | UK | Aust | NZ | Can | NF | SAfr | RGLI | BWI | India | Chi | Fr | Bel | Ger | Other | Un-named | KUG | SM | WWII | TOTAL |
|---|---|---|---|---|---|---|---|---|---|---|---|---|---|---|---|---|---|---|---|
| Voormezele Churchyard | 1 | | | | | | | | | | | | | | | | 1 | | 1 |
| Warneton (Waasten) Communal | | | | | | | | | | | | | | | | | | 21 | 21 |
| Watou Churchyard | 11 | | | | | | | | | | | 25 | | | | | | | 37 |
| Welsh (Caesar's Nose) | 68 | | | | | | | | | | | | | | | | | | 68 |
| Westhof Farm | 73 | 43 | 14 | 1 | | | | | | | | | 5 | | | | | | 136 |
| Westoutre Churchyard & Extension | 76 | 1 | 1 | 19 | | | | | 1 | | | | | | | | | | 103 |
| Westoutre British | 162 | | 3 | 5 | | | | | | 3 | | 2 | | | 52 | 2 | 5 | 5 | 180 |
| Westvleteren Belgian | 1 | | | | | | | | | | | | 3 | | 1 | | | | 1209 |
| Westvleteren Churchyard | | | | | | | | | | | | 1208 | | | | | | | 1209 |
| White House | 991 | 45 | 25 | 85 | | 5 | | 1 | 1 | | 199 | | 1 | 1 | 322 | 44 | 9 | | 1163 |
| Wieltje Farm | 113 | 1 | 1 | 1 | | | | | | | | | 1 | | 10 | | 20 | | 116 |
| Woesten Churchyard | 212 | 3 | | 111 | | | | | | | 282 | | | | | 32 | 9 | 9 | 291 |
| Woods | | | | | | | | | | | | | | | | | | | 326 |
| Wulvergem Churchyard | 33 | | | | | | | | | | | | | 1 | 1 | 5 | 23 | | 38 |
| Wulverghem-Lindenhoek Road Military | 843 | 35 | 69 | 54 | | 9 | | | | | | | | | 352 | 9 | 9 | | 1010 |
| Wytschaete Military | 511 | 31 | 7 | 19 | | 11 | | | | | | | 1 | | 673 | 423 | 25 | | 1003 |
| Ypres Reservoir | 2255 | 143 | 28 | 151 | 4 | 12 | 2 | 6 | 1 | | | | 1 | | 1035 | 10 | 12 | | 2613 |
| Ypres Town | 144 | | | | | | | | | | | 23 | | 49 | 9 | | | | 217 |
| Ypres Town Extension | 597 | 13 | | 15 | | 1 | | | 1 | | | | 2 | 22 | 141 | | 16 | 43 | 672 |
| Zandvoorde Churchyard | 4 | | | | | | | | | | | | | | | | | | 4 |
| Zantvoorde British | 1525 | 2 | | 22 | | | | | 1 | | | | | | 1135 | | 33 | 1 | 1584 |
| Zillebeke Churchyard | 22 | | | 10 | | | | | | | | | | | 6 | | 2 | | 32 |
| Zonnebeke Churchyard | | | | | | | | | | | | 14 | | | | | | | 14 |
| Zuidschote Churchyard | | | | | | | | | | | 5 | | | | | | | 76 | 81 |
| TOTAL | 113275 | 10063 | 3704 | 9521 | 145 | 475 | 65 | 169 | 87 | 107 | 10854 | 38223 | 46451 | 247 | 64543 | 2578 | 2177 | 846 | 202977 |

**MEMORIALS**

| | UK | Aust | NZ | Can | NF | SAfr | RGLI | BWI | India | Chi | Fr | Bel | Ger | Other | Un-named | KUG | SM | WWII | TOTAL |
|---|---|---|---|---|---|---|---|---|---|---|---|---|---|---|---|---|---|---|---|
| Ypres (Menin Gate) | 40532 | 6183 | | 6928 | 560 | | | 8 | 412 | | | | | | | | | | 54623 |
| Tyne Cot | 34949 | | 1179 | | | | | | | | | | | | | | | | 36128 |
| Ploegsteert | 11366 | | | | 13 | | | | | | | | | | | | | | 11379 |
| Buttes NZ | | | 378 | | | | | | | | | | | | | | | | 378 |
| Messines Ridge NZ | | | 828 | | | | | | | | | | | | | | | | 828 |
| TOTAL | 86847 | 6183 | 2385 | 6928 | 573 | 0 | 0 | 8 | 412 | 0 | 0 | 0 | 0 | 0 | 0 | 0 | 0 | 0 | 103336 |

# VICTORIA CROSS HOLDERS BURIED IN CEMETERIES OR COMMEMORATED ON MEMORIALS INCLUDED IN THIS BOOK

Ackroyd, H, MC, temporary Captain, RAMC attached 6th Royal Berkshires. Killed in action 11 August 1917, buried in Birr Crossroads Cemetery.

Barratt, T, Private, 7th South Staffordshires. Killed in action 27 July 1917, buried in Essex Farm Cemetery.

Bent, P E, DSO, temporary Lieutenant-Colonel, 9th Leicestershires. Killed in action 1 October 1917, commemorated on Tyne Cot Memorial.

Birks, F, MM, 2nd Lieutenant, 6th (Victoria) Australian Infantry. Killed in action 21 September 1917, buried in Perth Cemetery (China Wall).

Brooke, J A O, Lieutenant (posthumously Captain), 2nd Gordon Highlanders. Killed in action 29 October 1914, buried in Zantvoorde British Cemetery.

Bugden, P J, Private, 31st (Queensland and Victoria) Australian Infantry. Killed in action 28 September 1917, buried in Hooge Crater Cemetery.

Chavasse, N G, VC & Bar, MC, Captain, Royal Army Medical Corps attached 1/10th (Liverpool Scottish) King's (Liverpools). Died of wounds 4 August 1917, buried in Brandhoek New Military Cemetery.

Clamp, W, Corporal, 6th Yorkshires. Killed in action 9 October 1917, commemorated on Tyne Cot Memorial.

Colyer-Fergusson, T R, 2nd Lieutenant (acting Captain), 2nd Northamptonshires. Killed in action 31 July 1917, buried in Menin Road South Military Cemetery.

Davies, J L, Corporal, 13th (1st North Wales Pals) Royal Welsh Fusiliers. Killed in action 31 July 1917, buried in Canada Farm Cemetery.

Dougall, E S, MC, acting Captain, 88th Brigade, Royal Field Artillery. Killed in action 14 April 1918, buried in Westoutre British Cemetery.

Drake, A G, Corporal, 8th Rifle Brigade. Killed in action 23 November 1915, buried in La Brique Military Cemetery No. 2.

Best-Dunkley, B, Captain (temporary Lieutenant-Colonel), commanding 2/5th Lancashire Fusiliers. Died of wounds 5 August 1917, buried in Mendinghem Military Cemetery.

Fisher, F, Lance-Corporal, 13th (Quebec Regiment, Royal Highlanders of Canada), Canadian Infantry. Killed in action 24 April 1915, commemorated on Menin Gate Memorial.

Fitzclarence, C, Brigadier-General, commanding 1st Brigade, 1st Division, late of the Royal Fusiliers and Irish Guards. Killed in action 12 November 1914, commemorated on Menin Gate Memorial. (Won when he was a Captain)

Grenfell, F O, Captain, 9th (Queen's Royal) Lancers. Killed in action 24 May 1915, buried in Vlamertinghe Military Cemetery.

Hackett, W, Sapper, 254th Tunnelling Company, Royal Engineers. Killed in action 27 June 1916, commemorated on Ploegsteert Memorial.

Hall, F W, Company Sergeant-Major, 8th (Manitoba Regiment) Canadian Infantry. Killed in action 25 April 1915, commemorated on Menin Gate Memorial.

Hallowes, R P, MC, temporary 2nd Lieutenant, 4th Middlesex. Killed in action 30 September 1915, buried in Bedford House Cemetery.

Hewitt, D G W, 2nd Lieutenant, 2nd Hampshires attached 14th (1st Portsmouth Pals) Hampshires. Killed in action 31 July 1917, commemorated on Menin Gate Memorial.

Jeffries, C S, Captain, 34th (New South Wales) Australian Infantry. Killed in action 12 October 1917, buried in Tyne Cot Cemetery.

Johnston(e), W H, Major, 59th Field Company, Royal Engineers. Killed in action 8 June 1915, Buried in Perth Cemetery (China Wall). (Won when he was a Captain)

Lynn, J, DCM, Order of St. George, 4th Class (Russia), Private, 2nd Lancashire Fusiliers. Died of wounds 2 May 1915, buried in Grootebeek British Cemetery.

McGee, L, Sergeant, 40th (Tasmania) Australian Infantry. Killed in action 13 October 1917, buried in Tyne Cot Cemetery.

McGuffie, L, acting Sergeant, 1/5th King's Own Scottish Borderers. Killed in action 4 October 1918, buried in Zantvoorde British Cemetery.

McKenzie, H, DCM, Lieutenant, 7th Company, Canadian Machine Gun Corps. Killed in action 30 October 1917, commemorated on Menin Gate Memorial.

Mackenzie, J, Private, 2nd Scots Guards. Killed in action 19 December 1914, commemorated on Ploegsteert Memorial.

Maxwell, F A, CSI, DSO and Bar, Brigadier-General, Indian Staff Corps, attached Robert's Light Horse, commanding 27th Brigade, 9th (Scottish) Division. Killed in action 21 September 1917, buried in Ypres Reservoir Cemetery. (Won when he was a Lieutenant)

Morrow, R, Private, 1st Royal Irish Fusiliers. Killed in action 26 April 1915, buried in White House Cemetery.

Mottershead, T, DCM, Sergeant, Royal Flying Corps. Died of wounds, 12 January 1917. Buried in Bailleul Communal Cemetery Extension.

Pryce, T T, MC and Bar, acting Captain, 4th Grenadier Guards, Special Reserve. Killed in action 13 April 1918, commemorated on Ploegsteert Memorial.

Robertson, C, acting Captain, 3rd Queen's (Royal West Surreys), Special Reserve, attached Tank Corps. Killed in action 4 October 1917, buried in Oxford Road Cemetery.

Robertson, J P, Private, 27th (2nd Manitoba, Winnipeg Regiment) Canadian Infantry. Killed in action 6 November 1917, buried in Tyne Cot Cemetery.

Seaman, E, MM, Lance-Corporal, 2nd Royal Inniskilling Fusiliers. Killed in action 29 September 1918, commemorated on Tyne Cot Memorial.

Skinner, J, DCM, acting Company Sergeant-Major, 1st King's Own Scottish Borderers. Killed in action 17 March 1918, buried in Vlamertinghe New Military Cemetery.

Tubb, F H, Lieutenant (later Major), 7th (Victoria) Australian Infantry. Killed in action 20 September 1917, buried in Lijssenthoek Military Cemetery.

Vallentin, J F, Captain, 1st South Staffordshires. Killed in action 7 November 1917, commemorated on Menin Gate Memorial.

Warner, E, Private, 1st Bedfordshires. Killed in action 2 May 1915, commemorated on Menin Gate Memorial.

Woodroffe, S C, 2nd Lieutenant, 8th attached 2nd Rifle Brigade. Killed in action 30 July 1915, commemorated on Menin Gate Memorial.

Youens, F, temporary 2nd Lieutenant, 13th Durham Light Infantry. Died of Wounds on 9 July 1917, buried in Railway Dugouts Burial Ground (Transport Farm).

# Terms and Abbreviations

ADS. - Advanced Dressing Station
AIF - Australian Imperial Force
ANZAC - Australian and New Zealand Army Corps
Aust - Australia
BEF - British Expeditionary Force
Bel - Belgian/Belgium
Bt - Baronet
Btn - Battalion
BWI - British West Indies Regiment
Can – Canada
CB – Companion of the Order of the Bath
CCS – Casualty Clearing Station
CMG –Companion of the Order of St. Michael and St. George
CWGC - Commonwealth War Graves Commission
DCLI - Duke of Cornwall's Light Infantry
DCM - Distinguished Conduct Medal
DFC – Distinguished Flying Cross
DS - Dressing Station
DSO - Distinguished Service Order
Fr - France/French
Ger - Germany
HAC - Honourable Artillery Company
Hon - Honourable
IWGC - Imperial War Graves Commission

KCVO - Knight Commander of the Victoria Order
KUG - Known Unto God
MC - Military Cross
MM - Military Medal
NA - New Army
No. - Number
NCO - Non-Commissioned Officer
NF - Newfoundland
NZ - New Zealand
NZEF – New Zealand Expeditionary Force
OBE - Order of the British Empire
RAF – Royal Air Force
RAMC - Royal Army Medical Corps
RE - Royal Engineers
RFC – Royal Flying Corps
S Afr - South Africa
SM - Special Memorial
sq mts - square metres
TF - Territorial Force
UK - United Kingdom (British)
US - United States of America
VC - Victoria Cross
WWII - World War Two
YMCA - Young Men's Christian Association

**Regiments**

The Argyll and Sutherland Highlanders (Princess Louises's)
The Black Watch (Royal Highlanders)
The Buffs (East Kent Regiment)
The Queen's Own Cameron Highlanders
The Cameronians (Scottish Rifles)
The Duke of Wellington's Regiment (West Riding)
The King's Regiment (Liverpool)
The King's Own Royal (Lancaster) Regiment
The Middlesex Regiment (Duke of Cambridge's Own)
The North Staffordshire Regiment (Prince of Wales's)
The Queen's Royal Regiment (West Surreys)
The Rifle Brigade (The Prince Consort's Own)
The Royal Berkshire Regiment (Princess Charlotte of Wales's)
The Royal Fusiliers (City of London Regiment)
The Royal Irish Fusiliers (Princess Victoria's)
The Royal Scots (Lothian Regiment)
The Queen's Own (Royal West Kent Regiment)
The Seaforth Highlanders (Ross-shire Buffs, The Duke of Albany's)
The Sherwood Foresters (Nottinghamshire and Derbyshire Regiment)
The Somerset Light Infantry (Prince Albert's)
The South Lancashire Regiment (Prince of Wales's Volunteers)
The West Yorkshire Regiment (Prince of Wales's Own)
The Wiltshire Regiment (Duke of Edinburgh's)
The Yorkshire Regiment (Alexandra, Princess of Wales's Own)
For names by which Pals Battalions referred to themselves eg 1st Salford Pals, please refer to the Orders of Battle

**Divisions**

| | |
|---|---|
| Guards Division | 46th (North Midland) Division |
| 9th (Scottish) Division | 47th (1/2nd London) Division |
| 10th (Irish) Division | 48th (South Midland) Division |
| 11th (Northern) Division | 49th (West Riding) Division |
| 12th (Eastern) Division | 50th (Northumbrian) Division |
| 13th (Western) Division | 51st (Highland) Division |
| 14th (Light) Division | 52nd (Lowland) Division |
| 15th (Scottish) Division | 53rd (Welsh) Division |
| 16th (Irish) Division | 54th (East Anglian) Division |
| 17th (Northern) Division | 55th (West Lancashire) Division |
| 18th (Eastern) Division | 56th (1/1st London) Division |
| 19th (Western) Division | 57th (2nd West Lancashire) Division |
| 20th (Light) Division | 58th (2/1st London) Division |
| 36th (Ulster) Division | 59th (2nd North Midland) Division |
| 38th (Welsh) Division | 60th (2/2nd London) Division |
| 42nd (East Lancashire) Division | 61st (2nd South Midland) Division |
| 43rd (Wessex) Division | 62nd (2nd West Riding) Division |
| 44th (Home Counties) Division | 63rd (Royal Naval) Division |
| 45th (2nd Wessex) Division | 66th (2nd East Lancashire) Division |
| | 74th (Yeomanry) Division |

# BIBLIOGRAPHY

**REFERENCE**

*The Order of Battle of Divisions, Parts 1, 2A, 2B, 3A & 3B*; Major A. F. Becke (H.M.S.O.)
*Official History of the Great War in France and Belgium*; Brig-Gen. James E. Edmunds (H.M.S.O.)
*Commonwealth War Graves Commission Registers*
*Officers Died in the Great War 1914 - 1919* (J. B. Hayward and Son)
*Soldiers Died in the Great War 1914 - 1919* (J. B. Hayward and Son)
*British Regiments 1914-1918*; Brig-Gen. E. A. James, O.B.E. (Samson Books)
*A Record of the Battles and Engagements of the Brotish Armies in France and Flanders, 1914-1918;* Captain E. A James (London Stamp Exchange)
*The VC and DSO, Volume II and III*; Sir O'Moore Creagh, VC, GCB, GCSI and E M Humphris (Standard Art Book Company)
*Register of the VC* (This England)
*British Battalions on the Somme*; Ray Westlake (Pen and Sword)
*De Ruvigny's Roll of Honour 1914-18* (Naval and Military Press)

**FURTHER READING**

*Symbol of Courage, A History of the Victoria Cross*; Max Arthur (Sidgwick and Jackson)
*My Bit, A Lancashire Fusilier at War 1914 - 1918*; George Ashurst (Crowood Press)
*For the Sake of Example*, Anthony Babington (Leo Cooper)
*Sir Douglas Haig's Despatches*; J H Boraston (J M Dent & Sons)
*An Illustrated Companion to the First World War*; Anthony Bruce (Michael Joseph)
*The Battle Book of Ypres; A reference to Military Operations in the Ypres Salient 1914 - 18*; Beatrix Brice (Spa Books)
The *Imperial War Museum Book of the First World War*; Malcolm Brown (Sidgwick and Jackson Ltd.)
*An Illustrated Companion to the First World War*; Anthony Bruce (Michael Joseph)
*Wipers: The First Battle of Ypres*; T. Carew (Hamish Hamilton)
*Armegeddon Road, A V.C.'s Diary 1914 -1916*, Billy Congreve, V.C. (William Kimber & Co)
*Before Endeavours Fade, A Guide to the Battlefields of the First World War*; Rose Coombs, M.B.E. (After the Battle Publications)
*Machine Gunner 1914-1918, Personal Experiences of the Machine Gun Corps*; edited by C. E. Crutchley (Bailey Brothers and Swinfen Ltd.)
*Bloody Red Tabs*; Frank Davies and Graham Maddocks (Leo Cooper)
*Silent Cities in Flanders Fields;* Wayne Evans, Pierre Vandervelden & Luc Corremans (Lannoo)
*Death of an Army: The First Battle of Ypres*; A. Farrar-Hockley (Barker)
*In Continuing and Grateful Memory : From Ypres to Zillebeke*; Paul Foster (Minutecircle Services)
*In Continuing and Grateful Memory : The Ploegsteert Sector;* Paul Foster (Minutecircle Services)
*In Continuing and Grateful Memory : The Menin Gate Volume I, II & III*; Paul Foster (Minutecircle Services)
*Flanders Then and Now*; John Giles (After the Battle Publications)
*Ypres, 1917: a personal account*; N. Gladden (Kimber)
*Chronical of the First World War, Volumes 1 and 2*; Randal Gray and Christopher Argyle (Facts on File Ltd)
*The Greater Game*; Clive Harris and Julian Whippy (Pen and Sword)
*The Sky Their Battlefield*; Trevor Henshaw (Grub Street)
*Stand To! A Diary of the Trenches 1915-1918*; Captain F. C. Hitchcock, M.C. (Gliddon Books)
*Major And Mrs Holt's Battlefield Guide To Ypres;* Toni and Valmai Holt; (Pen and Sword)
*Passchendaele in Perspective;* Peter H Liddle (Pen & Sword)
*The Soldier's War 1914-18*; Peter H. Liddle (Blandford Press)
*1914*; Lyn Macdonald (Michael Joseph)
*1914-1918: Voices and Images of the Great War*; Lyn Macdonald (Penguin)
*Roses of No Mans Land*; Lyn Macdonald (Michael Joseph)
*They Called it Passchendaele*; Lyn Macdonald (Michael Joseph)
*Final Wicket, Test & First Class Cricketers Killed in the Great War;* Nigel McCrery (Pen & Sword)
*Into Touch, Rugby Internationals Killed in the Great War;* Nigel McCrery (Pen & Sword)
*The Extinguished Flame, Olympians Killed in the Great War;* Nigel McCrery (Pen & Sword)
*Gas! The Battle for Ypres 1915*; James L. McWilliams and R. James Steel (Vanwell)
*Poor Bloody Infantry, A Subaltern on the Western Front 1916-1917*; Bernard Martin (John Murray)
*The Third Ypres, Passchendaele, The Day by Day Account*; Chris McCarthy ((Arms and Armour Press)
*Walking with the ANZACs*; Mat McLachlan (Hachette)
*The Great War Generals on the Western Front*; Robin Neillands (Robinson)
*Battleground Europe : Airmen & Airfield Ypres;* Mike O'Connor (Pen & Sword)
*The Immortal Salient: an historical record and complete guide for pilgrims to Ypres*; Sir William Pulteney and Beatrix Brice (Ypres League)

*Murderous Tommies*; Julian Putkowski and Mark Dunning (Pen and Sword)
*Shot at Dawn, Executions in World War One by Authority of the British Army Act*; Julian Putkowski and Julian Sykes (Wharncliffe Publishing)
*Battleground Europe : Walking the Salient;* Paul Reed (Leo Cooper, Pen and Sword)
*Forgotten Victory*; Gary Sheffield (Review)
*The German Army at Passchendaele;* Jack Sheldon (Pen & Sword)
*World War One, The Western Front*; Peter Simkins (Colour Library Books)
*The Old Contemtibles*; Keith Simpson (George Allen and Unwin)
*The Fields of Death, Battle Scenes of the First World War*; Peter Slowe and Richard Woods (Robert Hale)
*Passchendaele, The Sacrificial Land;* Nigel Steel and Peter Hart (Cassell & Co)
*Het Verwoeste Gewest (The Devastated Region);* Herman Stynen (Marc Van de Wiele)
*History of World War One*; A. J. P. Taylor (Macdonald & Co.)
*Boy Soldiers of the Great War*; Richard van Emden (Bloomsbury)
*Famous 1914-1918*; Richard van Emden and Victor Puik (Pen and Sword)
*Passchendaele: The Story Behind the Tragic Victory of 1917*; P. Warner (Sidgwick and Jackson Ltd.)
*Honour Satisfied, A Dorset Rifleman at War 1916-1918*; Second Lieutenant Frank Warren (Crowood Press)
*Death's Men, Soldiers of the Great War*; Denis Winter (Penguin)
*The Experience of World War One*, J. M. Winter (Macmillan)
*Ypres and the battles of Ypres: An Illustrated History and Guide*; Michelin Tyre Co., Ltd.
*The Wipers Times;* (Conway)
*The Pilgrim's Guide to the Ypres Salient;* (Herbert Reiach for Talbot House)

**ADDITIONAL SOURCES**
*Stand To!* The Journal of the Western Front Association
CD – N&M Press - War Diaries of the Battalions
County Record Offices
The Army Records Centre, Hayes, Middlesex
The National Army Museum
The Imperial War Museum
The Regimental Museum of the Royal Corps of Transport
The Rifle Brigade (Royal Green Jackets) Museum
The Hertfordshire Yeomanry and Artillery Museum
The Army Museums Ogilby Trust
In Flanders Fields
The families of Herbert Milnes, Ernest Sinfield, Harold Sinfield, Archibald Sinfield and Sidney Sinfield.
Websites –
www.inmemories.com by Pierre Vandervelden
battlefields1418.50megs.com by Paul Reed
www.ww1wargraves.co.uk
www.webmatters.net by Simon Godly
silentwitness.freeservers.com
www.greatwar.co.uk by Joanna Legg (née Parker), Graham Parker and David Legg
www.1914-1918.net by Chris Baker

**ACKNOWLEDGMENTS**
Commonwealth War Graves Commission
In Flanders Fields Cloth Hall Museum, Ieper
Ieper Tourist Office
Gerald Gliddon
Richard Pearson
Guild of Battlefield Guides and all members of the Guild, particularly those who have helped, even when they did not know they were helping, with this book and with many other things. But I want to single out Mike Peters for his support of the past few years
Friends and colleagues on the battlefields, whether it be hoetliers, restaurateurs or guides etc. Thank you all

# Index
## Military Units

Australian Imperial Force (AIF)
Australian Corps, 157; II ANZAC Corps, 240
Divisions
ANZAC, 9; 1st ANZAC, 106; 1st, 123, 181; 2nd, 184, 186, 187; 3rd 22, 86, 157, 182, 186, 187, 240; 4th 184; 5th 33, 34, 52, 181
Brigades
1st, 30; 2nd, 106; 5th, 184; 9th, 182
Cavalry
5th Light Horse Brigade, 164; 3rd Light Horse, 185; 10th Light Horse, 119; 12th Light Horse, 204; Hasler's Australian Scouts 207; 2nd Light Horse Divisional Train, 106
Artillery
4th Brigade, Australian Field Artillery, 22, 201; 14th Brigade, Australian Field Artillery, 182; 110th Howitzer Battery, 10th Brigade, Australian Field Artillery, 73; 5th Divisional Trench Mortar Battery, Australian Field Artillery, 204; 4th Battery, 2nd Brigade, Australian Field Artillery, 30; 36th Australian Heavy Artillery, 59
Engineers
Australian Tunnelling Company, 85; 1st Australian Tunnelling Company, 84; 4th Australian Pioneers, 93
Infantry
1st, 78, 91, 105, 106, 184; 3rd, 4, 106, 109; 4th, 33; 6th, 138, 204; 7th, (Victoria), 87; 8th, 14, 48, 67; 9th, 92, 115; 11th, 115, 130; 12th, 73, 160; 13th, 108, 109, 189; 16th, 146; 17th, 16, 91, 110; 18th, 50; 19th, 16; 20th, 91; 21st, 117; 23rd, 139; 25th, 53, 82; 26th, 22, 108, 166, 215; 28th, 120; 31st (Queensland and Victoria), 34, 67; 33rd, 22, 156, 182; 34th (New South Wales), 34, 186, 187, 189; 36th, 182; 37th (Victoria), 182; 40th (Tasmania), 185, 187; 41st, 122, 150; 42nd, 22; 45th, 47, 108, 211; 46th, 14; 47th, 42; 48th, 19, 146, 166; 49th, 34, 92, 117; 50th, 38; 51st, 34, 130; 52nd, 119; 53rd, 15, 109; 54th, 127; 56th, 33; 57th, 139; 59th, 35

Australian Army Medical Corps 181; 1st Australian Casualty Clearing Station, 7; No. 2 Australian Casualty Clearing Station 184; 3rd Australian Casualty Clearing Station, 28, 129; 32nd Australian Casualty Clearing Stations, 28; 44th Australian Casualty Clearing Stations, 28; 2nd Australian Field Ambulance, 14
3rd Machine Gun Company, AIF, 1
6th Company, Australian Army Service Corps, 106;
Australian Army Chaplains Department, 163
Australian Young Men's Christian Association 52

British Army
Armies
Allied Flanders Army Group, 242; Second Army, 98, 174, 238, 241, 242; Fifth Army, 157, 241
Egyptian Army, 165, 213, 224
Corps
Cavalry Corps, 217, 221
I Corps, 168, 217, 219, 234, 240; III Corps, 123; IX Corps, 164; VIII Corps, 152, 164

Divisions
1st, 66, 218; 2nd, 47, 66, 157, 218; 3rd, 66, 73, 134, 162, 204, 240; 4th, 30, 32, 37, 49, 78, 123, 128, 141, 157; 5th, 83, 84, 129, 157, 206, 210; 6th, 3, 27, 78, 119, 127, 146, 147, 157, 183; 7th, 47, 66, 127, 136, 147, 190, 239; 8th, 16, 66, 67, 120, 241; 9th (Scottish), 33, 61, 67, 123, 162, 169, 212, 231; 11th (Northern), 35, 42, 132, 142; 14th (Light), 22, 27, 57, 73, 84, 122, 142, 212; 15th (Scottish), 4, 241; 16th (Irish), 4, 29, 41, 72, 95, 98, 122, 211, 240; 17th, 37; 18th (Eastern), 67, 69, 142, 169, 221; 19th (Western), 41, 132, 133, 240; 20th (Light), 39, 59, 169, 234, 235; 21st, 94; 23rd, 150, 240; 24th, 52, 134; 25th, 8, 9, 94, 122, 176, 196, 231, 240; 27th, 154, 201; 28th, 105, 200, 207; 29th, 6, 7, 49, 67, 120, 199; 30th, 67, 95, 135, 145, 241; 31st, 7, 47, 157; 32nd, 83; 33rd, 42, 123, 166, 186; 34th, 7, 69, 74, 125, 184, 221, 231, 235; 35th, 214; 36th (Ulster), 21, 41, 88, 98, 122, 124, 125, 129, 173, 176, 204, 211, 240; 37th, 42; 38th (Welsh), 51, 57, 58, 124, 128, 168, 203, 241; 39th (Composite), 12, 77, 241; 39th, 53, 126, 151, 152, 171, 175, 184; 41st, 89, 240; 46th (North Midland), 83, 135, 176; 47th (2nd London), 13, 85, 240, 241; 48th (South Midland), 46, 81, 142, 184; 49th (West Riding), 12, 40, 57, 58, 63, 94, 179, 181; 50th (Northumberland), 134, 186, 205; 51st (Highland), 39, 57, 124, 128, 131, 199, 241; 55th (West Lancashire), 4, 197, 241; 56th (London), 169; 58th (2/1st London), 46, 53; 59th (North Midland), 7, 30; 63rd (Royal Naval), 49, 119, 135, 183, 241; 66th (2nd East Lancashire), 137, 213; 1st Cavalry, 51; 3rd Cavalry, 168, 198, 241; Guards, 5, 6, 36, 58, 153, 168
Brigades
1st Brigade, 168, 239; 2nd Brigade, 169; 3rd Brigade, 92, 216; 6th Infantry Brigade, 184; 7th Infantry Brigade, 141; 8th Brigade, 67; 9th Brigade, 162; 10th Infantry Brigade, 18, 123, 171, 175; 11th Infantry Brigade, 128, 141, 156, 167, 207, 208; 12th Brigade, 128; 13th Brigade, 84, 213; 15th Brigade, 84; 16th Brigade, 3, 88; 18th Brigade, 3; 19th Infantry Brigade, 6, 166, 214; 20th Brigade, 26; 22nd Brigade, 47; 26th Brigade, 241; 27th Infantry Brigade, 212; 60th Brigade, 37, 235; 61st Brigades, 37, 23; 62nd Infantry Brigade, 181; 64th Brigade, 173, 217; 72nd Brigade, 52; 82nd Brigade, 53; 83rd Brigade, 240; 84th Brigade, 30, 114, 160; 89th Brigade, 95; 90th Brigade, 67; 98th Brigade, 166; 101st Infantry Brigade, 88; 112th Infantry Brigade, 94; 123rd Infantry Brigade, 164; 147th (West Riding) Brigade, 7; 149th (1/1st Northumberland) Infantry Brigade, 188, 175, 240; 153rd Infantry Brigade, 88; 188th Brigade, 135; 189th Royal Naval Brigade, 3; 190th Brigade, 135; 1st Cavalry Brigade, 4; 2nd Cavalry Brigade, 86, 197; 4th Cavalry Brigade, 183; 6th Cavalry Brigades, 4; 7th Cavalry Brigades, 4, 136; 8th Cavalry Brigade, 4; 9th Cavalry Brigade, 198; 11th Cavalry Brigade, 154; 1st Guards Brigade, 104; 3rd Guards Brigade, 26; 4th (Guards) Brigade, 7, 45, 85, 157, 222

279

Cavalry
Household Brigade, 221; Household Cavalry, 136, 221; Composite Household Cavalry, 183; Household Battalion, 101, 106; Royal Dragoons, 197; Dragoons, 111; Royal Horse Guards, 4, 14, 20, 85, 110, 111, 136, 162, 198, 218, 219, 220, 221, 222; Life Guards, 136; 1st (King's) Dragoon Guards, 113, 198, 217; 1st (Royal) Dragoons, 10, 217; 2nd (Queen's Bays) Dragoon Guards, 4, 121, 154; 2nd Dragoons (Royal Scots Greys), 14, 207; 1st Life Guards, 8, 77, 85, 110, 111, 219, 222, 223; 2nd Life Guards, 38, 85, 101, 106, 119, 219; 3rd (King's Own) Hussars, 211; 3rd Dragoon Guards (Prince of Wales' Own), 217; 4th (Queen's Own) Hussars, 132; 4th Dragoon Guards (Royal Irish), 101, 121, 197; 5th (Royal Irish) Lancers, 7, 75, 227; 5th (Princess Charlotte of Wales's) Dragoon Guards, 22, 121, 237; 6th (Carabiniers) Dragoon Guards, 173; 6th (Inniskilling) Dragoons, 49; 9th (Queen's Royal) Lancers, 35, 86, 110, 112, 121, 197; 10th (Prince of Wales's Own Royal) Hussars, 4, 121, 154, 177, 197, 198, 217, 228; 11th (Prince Albert's Own) Hussars, 15, 107, 121, 210, 217, 222, 226; 12th (Prince of Wales's Royal) Lancers, 83, 117, 211; 15th (The King's) Hussars, 107; 16th (The Queen's) Lancers, 169, 217; 17th (Duke of Cambridge's Own) Lancers, 11, 122, 222; 18th (Queen Mary's Own) Hussars, 65, 101, 106, 132; 19th (Alexandra, Princess of Wales's Own) Hussars, 15; 19th (Queen Alexandra's Own Royal) Hussars, 8, 27, 132, 174, 196, 198; 20th Hussars, 211; 1st King Edward's Horse, 119; 2nd King Edward's Horse, 82; Essex Imperial Yeomanry, 113; Essex Yeomanry, 4, 113, 198; Glasgow (Queen's Own Royal) Yeomanry, 15; 1/1st Hertfordshire Yeomanry, 141, 193; Imperial Yeomanry, 15; Lanarkshire (Queen's Own Royal Glasgow) Imperial Yeomanry, 15; Lancashire Hussars, 95; Leicestershire Yeomanry, 45; Lincolnshire Yeomanry, 222; North Somerset Yeomanry, 217; Northumberland Hussars Yeomanry, 33; Queen's Own Oxfordshire Hussars, 198, 239; Royal Buckinghamshire Hussars, 197; Royal North Devon Hussars, 195; Royal Wiltshire Yeomanry, 142, 166; 2/1st Royal Wiltshire Yeomanry, 142; Scottish Horse 113; Yorkshire Hussars Yeomanry, 107, 116; Corps of Guides, 213

Royal Navy, 25, 49, 50, 52, 75, 83, 108, 112, 121, 127, 161, 181, 186, 190, 195, 202, 222

Royal Naval Volunteer Reserve, 19, 49, 112, 119, 145; Royal Naval Reserve, 74, 83, 105, 106, 107, 109; Anson Battalion, 135; Drake Battalion, 49, 135; Hood Battalion, 135; Royal Marines, 91, 119, 239; Royal Marine Light Infantry, 78, 79, 106, 161; 1st Royal Marine Light Infantry, 135; 2nd Royal Marine Light Infantry, 135; Fourth Cruiser Squadron, 16; West Indies Squadron, 16; HM Drifter Jeannie Murray, 145; HM Submarine C3, 106; HM Submarine E36, 105; HM Yacht Iolaire, 107; HM Yacht Sanda, 74, 107; HMCS Quebec, Royal Navy (WW2), 214; HMS Aboukir, 79; HMS Alcantara 106; HMS Calgarian, 83; HMS Defence, 50; HMS Formidable, 79; HMS Fortune, 181; HMS Grove, Royal Naval Volunteer Reserve (WW2), 167; HMS Heather, 108; HMS Indefatigable, 83, 106, 108, 112, 161; HMS Laforey, 121; HMS Laurentic, 19; HMS Monmouth, 16; HMS Munster, 195; HMS Narborough, 25; HMS Newbury, 106; HMS Newbury, 161; HMS Rawalpindi, 109; HMS Venerable, 107; HMS Victory (now HMS Nelson), 106; Royal Naval Air Service, 38

Royal Engineers, 5, 7, 10, 12, 17, 18, 27, 39, 49, 52, 59, 62, 73, 84, 89, 98, 101, 107, 122, 151, 152, 161, 162, 208, 218, 223, 235, 236

36th (Ulster) Division, 52; 38th Division, 49; 1/1st West Lancashire Field Company, 208; 4th Field Company, 116; 5th Field Company, 118, 239; 12th Field Company, 27; 15th Field Company, 16; 56th Field Company, 7, 173; 57th Field Company, 58; 59th Field Company, 19, 30, 51, 84, 138; 61st Field Company, 27; 79th Field Company, 67; 83rd Field Company, 37; 101st Field Company, 60; 154th Field Company, 60; 201st Field Company, 173; 401st Field Company, 101; 404th Field Company, 101; 419th Field Company, 208; 520th Field Company, 85; 171st Tunnelling Company, 81, 84, 98, 241; 175th Tunnelling Company, 6, 66, 84, 152, 165; 177th Tunnelling Company, 162; 250th Tunnelling Company, 41, 174, 211, 240; 253rd Tunnelling Company, 26; Signal Corps, 89; 1st Signal Company, 108, 141, 156, 179, 208; 23rd Division Signal Company, 14; 33rd Divisional Signal Company, 193; 6th Army Tramway Company, 12; 12th Light Railway Operating Company, 64, 65; 21st Light Railway Operating Company, 64; 29th Light Railway Operating Company, 64, 65; 61st Broad Gauge Workshop Company, 65; 474th Field Survey Company, 31; Royal Monmouth Engineers, 84; 1st Special Company, 75; 'P' Special Company, 208; 2nd Section, 3rd Water Tank Company, 182; 7th (Labour) Battalion, 73; 167th Army Troops Company, 122; 134th Army Transport Company, 192; Inland Water Transport Unit, 11

Royal Artillery, 36, 49, 50, 52, 54, 58, 70, 94, 235

'C' Battery, 2nd City of Edinburgh Brigade, 44; Honourable Artillery Company, 12, 18, 23, 27, 41, 54, 97, 151, 213, 202; 1st Honourable Artillery Company, 107, 109; 2/1st 'B' Battery, Honourable Artillery Company, 86; 12th Citizen Batter 52; 45th Trench Mortar Battery, 96; 47th Trench Mortar Battery, 75; 74th Trench Mortar Battery, 11; 111th Trench Mortar Battery, 19; 185th Trench Mortar Battery, 70

Royal Field Artillery, 12, 51, 38, 89, 91, 107, 140, 158, 178, 181, 182, 199, 200, 213, 218

5th Division, 93, 204; 28th Division, 240; 15th Brigade, 213; 38th Brigade, 213; 46th Brigade, 10; 51st Brigade, 65; 52nd Brigade, 44; 58th Brigade, 46; 75th Brigade, 158; 94th Brigade, 60; 104th Brigade, 94; 106th Brigade, 164; 112th Brigade, 176; 126th Brigade, 86; 148th Brigade, 89; 152nd Brigade, 235; 160th Brigade, 235; 165th Brigade, 167; 232nd Brigade, 29; 23rd Brigade, 107; 240th (1st South Midland) Brigade, 38; 256th Brigade, 139; 276th Brigade, 203; 280th Brigade, 67; 296th Brigade, 50; 'A' Battery, 59th Brigade, 50; 'A' Battery, 88th Brigade, 205; 'A' Battery, 107th Brigade, 80; 'A' Battery, 156th Brigade, 199; 'A' Battery, 162nd Brigade 195; 'A' Battery, 295th Brigade, 214; 'A' Battery, 315th Brigade, 166, 193; 'B' Battery, 122nd Brigade, 59; 'B' Battery, 291st Brigade, 13; 'B' Battery, 64th Brigade, 195; 'B' Battery, 78th

Brigade, 172; 'B' Battery, 82nd Brigade, 182; 'B' Battery, 291st (London) Brigade, 12; 'C' Battery, 47th Brigade, 10; 'C' Battery, 52nd Brigade, 25; 'C' Battery, 63rd Brigade, 45; 'C' Battery, 88th Brigade, 182; 'C' Battery, 156th Brigade, 182; 'C' Battery, 173rd Brigade, 52; 'C' Battery, 290th Brigade, 31; 'D' Battery, 52nd Brigade, 45; 'D' Battery, 92nd Brigade, 203; 'D' Battery, 232nd Brigade, 189; 'Z' (Medium) 21st Trench Mortar Battery, 182; 6th Battery, 40th Brigade, 27; 12th Battery, 35th Brigade, 204; 14th Battery, 4th Brigade, 19; 15th Battery, 10; 16th Battery, 239; 19th (London) Battery, 47th Division, 90; 21st Battery, 2nd Brigade, 197; 22nd Battery, 239; 37th Battery, 43; 36th Battery, 45th Brigade, 181; 51st Battery, 170, 239; 53rd Battery, 91; 69th Battery, 31st Brigade, 112; 73rd Battery, 5th Brigade, 200; 84th Battery, 11th Brigade, 26, 94; 85th Battery, 11th Brigade, 227; 87th Battery, 70, 91; 110th Battery, 24th Brigade, 19, 57, 59, 108; 116th Battery, 111; 119th Battery, 197; 356th Battery, 240; 367th Battery, 240; 1st (Welsh) Howitzer Brigade, 53rd (Welsh) Division, 58; 122nd Heavy Battery, 37th Howitzer Battery, 240; 126th Howitzer Battery 65; V/38th Trench Mortar Battery, 12; 33rd Division Ammunition Column, 165; 34th Divisional Ammunition Column, 235

Royal Horse Artillery 10, 49, 65, 158, 182

15th (Warwick) Brigade, 50; 'J' Battery, 35; 2/1st (Warwick) Battery, 200; Q Battery, 212

Royal Garrison Artillery 19, 75, 171, 176, 193, 227, 228

2nd Siege Battery, 26; 6th Siege Battery, 216; 35th Siege Battery, 96; 10th Siege Battery, 221; 63rd Siege Battery, 163; 145th Siege Battery, 196; 168th Siege Battery, 198; 180th Siege Battery, 132; 230th Siege Battery, 24; 253rd Siege Battery, 11, 105; 254th Siege Battery, 13; 267th Siege Battery, 75; 282nd Siege Battery, 10, 105; 299th Siege Battery, 59; 16th Heavy Artillery Group, 10, 27; 110th Heavy Battery, 201; 131st Heavy Battery, 12; 136th Heavy Brigade, 37; 141st Heavy Battery, 70, 193; 146th Heavy Battery, 201; North Riding Heavy Battery, 206; 35th Trench Mortar Battery, 161; 20th Trench Mortar Battery, Trench Howitzer School, 44; Mechanical Transport attached 25th Siege Battery, 90; Royal Garrison Artillery (Transport), 39

(Royal) Army Service Corps, 7, 20, 75, 90, 127, 149, 156, 172, 191

No. 197 Company, 105; 906th Company, 70, 91; 10th Entrenching Battalion, 194; 1st Base Remount Depot, 109, 161; 26th Horse Transport Company, 60; 594th Motor Transport Company, 32, 204; Labour Corps 62, 87; 38th Labour Group, 178; 8th Labour Battalion, 15; 9th Labour Battalion, 15; 5th Company, 110; 13th Company, 53; 48th Company, 142; 104th Company, 50, 200; 1002nd Russian Company, 15; X Corps Heavy Artillery, 32

Infantry

Argyll and Sutherland Highlanders 88, 139; 1st, 109; 2nd, 12, 157, 166; 4th, 27; 1/7th, 171; 1/8th, 12, 143; 1/9th (Dumbartonshire), 19, 26, 31, 107, 108, 209; 11th, 47, 219

Bedfordshires, 1st, 84, 104, 132, 158, 170; 2nd, 115; 4th (Special Reserve), 109, 135; 1/5th, 132; 3/5th, 106; 7th, 132; 8th, 52

Black Watch (Royal Highlanders) 127, 164; 1st, 33, 34, 127, 168, 173, 224; 3rd, 127, 177, 224; 5th, 23, 201; 1/6th, 101; 1/7th (Fife), 185; 8th, 23, 164, 193; 9th, 47; 12th, 110

Borders, 1st, 7, 21, 37, 118, 216; 2nd, 21, 73, 89, 112, 180, 219; 3rd, 89; 1/5th, 46, 52; 6th, 73, 180; 8th, 11; 11th, 105

Buffs (East Kents) 8, 101, 207; 1st, 3, 78, 207; 2nd, 190, 213; 3rd, 107; 6th, 35, 107; 7th, 142, 152; 8th, 40, 145

Queen's Own Cameron Highlanders, 33; 1st, 34, 215, 239; 2nd, 44, 112; 3rd, 90, 112; 5th, 63, 72, 90; 6th, 29, 47; 7th, 26, 48, 193

Cameronians (Scottish Rifles), 1st, 92, 166; 2nd, 92, 137; 1/5th, 101, 157; 5th/6th, 109, 130, 166; 6th, 191; 10th, 151, 193; 11th, 130

Cheshires, 11; 1st, 11, 84, 91, 105, 118, 223; 2nd, 11, 30, 174, 223; 3rd, 118; 4th, 11; 1/5th, 192; 1/6th, 182, 189, 193; 1/7th, 11; 9th, 41, 191; 10th, 193; 11th, 9, 75, 177, 179, 189; 13th, 11; 16th, 11, 177

Chinese Labour Corps, 11, 87; 107th Company, 147, 149

Coldstream Guards 62, 202; 1st, 6, 27, 36, 37, 57, 107, 111, 112, 138, 139, 152, 165, 218; 2nd, 6, 36, 50, 110, 112, 157, 195; 3rd, 6, 19, 30, 57, 112, 138, 152, 165

Connaught Rangers, 16; 6th, 76

Devonshires, 7, 213; 1st, 5, 75, 84, 192, 193; 2nd, 16, 130, 212; 3rd, 11; 1st, 83, 84, 140, 161, 163, 196, 209, 227; 5th, 183

Duke of Cornwall's Light Infantry, 191; 1st, 5, 37, 57, 60, 210; 2nd, 183; 6th, 169, 170, 174, 212; 7th, 205

Duke of Wellington's, 12, 40, 45, 46; 1st, 159; 2nd, 11, 12, 46, 84, 105, 116, 163, 184; 3rd, 143; 1/4th, 40, 131, 179; 2/7th, 45; 8th, 19, 42; 9th, 6, 143, 152, 165; 12th, 193

Durham Light Infantry, 88, 139, 165; 2nd 67, 68, 70, 91, 153; 1/6th 18, 105, 139; 1/8th, 139; 1/9th, 105, 166; 10th, 11, 88; 11th, 59; 12th, 84, 215; 13th, 107, 117, 158; 14th, 153, 154; 15th, 127; 18th, 107; 20th (Wearside), 165, 105

East Lancashires, 1st, 82, 117, 179; 2nd, 19, 234; 2/4th, 194

East Surreys, 165; 1st, 15, 20, 21, 81, 84, 111, 134, 209; 2nd, 15, 96, 109, 110, 111, 115, 119, 131, 155, 165, 206; 4th, 134, 155; 7th, 108, 194; 8th, 26, 142; 9th, 96, 109, 120, 165; 12th (Bermondsey), 151

East Yorkshires, 1st, 20, 173, 191, 224; 2nd, 40, 108, 193; 1/4th, 109, 114, 189, 212; 6th, 128; 7th, 13; 8th, 32; 10th, 145; 13th, 19

Essex Regiment, 38; 2nd, 17, 35, 38, 50, 55, 119, 192, 200; 3rd, 119; 4th, 31; 9th, 19, 35, 36, 61; 10th, 142; 11th, 109; 13th, 192

Gloucestershires, 63; 1st, 69, 87, 99, 116, 119, 179, 222; 2nd, 15, 69; 1/4th (City of Bristol), 77; 1/5th, 127, 140, 227; 6th, 18; 2/6th, 77, 194, 195; 8th, 77, 195, 227; 12th, 195

Gordon Highlanders, 33, 88, 115, 139, 211; 1st, 27, 57, 67, 72, 80, 106, 110, 218; 2nd, 111, 144, 220, 221; 3rd, 111; 1/4th, 57, 80, 110; 1/5th (Buchan and Formartin),

128; 1/6th (Banff and Donside), 109, 124; 7th, 27; 8th/10th, 47, 80

Grenadier Guards, 93, 99; 1st, 6, 49, 68, 94, 111, 138, 139, 167, 215, 219, 220; 2nd, 6, 33, 85, 110, 112, 122, 157, 207, 222; 3rd, 127, 222; 4th, 18

Hampshires, 1st, 82, 117, 145, 146, 150, 153, 188, 226; 2nd, 19, 49, 91, 103, 108, 153, 155, 193, 194; 3rd, 117, 150; 1/8th, 49, 54, 194; 11th, 29; 14th (1st Portsmouth Pals), 54, 103; 15th (Carabiniers or Hampshire Yeomanry), 19, 27, 193, 201

Hertfordshires, 1/1st, 54, 114, 157, 176, 184

Highland Light Infantry, 88; 1st, 183, 193; 2nd, 33, 109; 10th/11th, 218; 11th, 91, 116; 12th, 16, 47

Irish Guards, 104, 221; 1st, 33, 38, 49, 56, 110, 217, 222; 2nd, 36, 49, 195

King's (Liverpools), 86; 1st, 106, 108, 112; 3rd, 12; 1/4th, 12, 62, 108, 130, 183; 1/5th, 184; 1/6th (Liverpool Rifles), 84; 1/7th, 108, 178; 1/8th (Liverpool Irish), 76, 151; 1/10th (Liverpool Scottish), 28, 29, 73, 76, 108, 140, 162, 163, 198; 11th, 28, 108, 203, 212; 17th (1st Liverpool Pals), 28, 74, 120; 18th (2nd Liverpool Pals), 42; 19th, 109; 49th Training Reserve, 194

King's Own (Royal Lancasters), 156; 1st, 86; 2nd, 33, 114, 186, 240; 3rd, 86; 5th, 117; 8th, 57, 194

King's Own Scottish Borderers, 1st, 19, 25, 89, 107, 193, 199; 2nd, 25, 84, 115, 121, 137; 1/5th (Dumfries and Galloway), 68, 69, 220; 6th, 91, 241; 7th/8th, 11, 47, 105

King's Own Yorkshire Light Infantry, 153, 198; 1st, 33, 106, 240; 2nd, 84, 108, 121, 137; 1/4th, 63, 194; 2/4th, 165; 1/5th, 30, 194; 6th, 120, 128, 215, 216; 7th, 49, 207; 8th, 19; 9th, 191, 193; 10th, 193; 12th (Miners), 19, 134, 157

King's Royal Rifle Corps, 3, 40, 64, 69, 70, 94, 112, 181, 191, 203, 213; 1st, 118, 202, 216; 2nd, 112, 168, 194, 217, 219, 220; 3rd, 32; 4th, 32, 107, 111, 218; 6th, 116, 142, 201; 7th, 67, 115, 117; 8th, 142, 153, 154, 213; 9th, 58, 113, 116, 182, 194; 10th, 78, 101, 142; 11th, 3, 78; 12th, 94; 13th, 94; 16th (Church Lads Brigade), 129, 194, 204; 17th (British Empire League), 50, 198; 18th (Arts and Crafts), 72, 84, 89; 21st (Yeoman Rifles), 17, 83, 141

King's Shropshire Light Infantry, 120; 1st, 131; 2nd, 32; 5th, 13, 135; 6th, 194

Lancashire Fusiliers, 10, 59, 156, 166; 1st, 215; 2nd, 31, 61, 71, 86, 91, 101, 106, 114, 156, 185, 206; 1/2nd, 195; 3rd, 86; 2/5th, 100; 3/5th, 165; 9th, 62; 10th, 57, 92, 117, 166; 11th, 61, 122, 176; 15th (1st Salford Pals), 54; 17th, 68, 91, 195; 20th, 101, 106; 22nd, 195

Leicestershires, 1st 21, 130, 153; 3rd, 116; 1/4th, 85, 135, 159; 1/5th, 51, 85; 7th, 107, 190; 9th, 190

Leinsters, 1st, 23, 32; 2nd, 17, 21, 27, 78, 109, 161, 177, 209; 5th, 213

Lincolnshires, 1st, 73, 96, 107, 113, 115, 162, 211; 2nd, 19, 20; 1/4th, 51, 170, 194; 1/5th, 135; 2/5th, 10; 6th, 121; 7th, 117, 121; 10th, 107

London Regiment, 141, 209; London Rifle Brigade, 66, 97; 1/5th (London Rifle Brigade), 141, 174; 1/6th (City of London Rifles), 85, 91, 131, 165; 2/6th (2nd City of London Rifles), 26, 107, 194; 1/7th, 131; 1/8th (Post Office Rifles), 16; 1/9th (Queen Victoria's Rifles), 70, 84, 118, 192, 210; 1/12th (Rangers), 30; 1/13th (Kensington), 20, 139; 1/14th (London Scottish), 32, 116, 121, 122, 140, 173, 211; 2/14th (2nd London Scottish), 42, 95; 1/15th (Prince of Wales's Own Civil Service Rifles), 50, 119, 209; 1/16th (Queen's Westminster Rifles), 40, 42, 70; 2/16th (2nd Queen's Westminsters), 95; 1/18th (London Irish Rifles), 19, 39; 1/19th (St. Pancras), 56; 2/20th (Blackheath and Woolwich), 109, 130; 1/21st (First Surrey Rifles), 66; 1/22nd (The Queen's), 139, 165; Artists Rifles, 139; 1/28th (Artists Rifles), 14, 20, 38, 50, 135, 194, 195

Loyal North Lancashires, 38, 45, 54; 1st, 168, 180, 217, 220; 1/4th, 150, 234; 2/4th, 180; 1/5th, 38, 80; 8th, 107, 140, 218; 9th, 61, 80

Machine Gun Corps, 91, 166, 171, 177, 193, 225; 108th Brigade, 88; 6th Battalion, 88; 14th Battalion, 12; 22nd Battalion, 68; 52nd Battalion, 6; 19th Company, 42; 25th Company, 20; 30th Company, 193; 46th Company, 47; 50th Company, 46; 63rd Company, 63; 90th Company, 182; 113th Company, 58; 117th Company, 151; 118th Company, 63; 143rd Company, 63; 149th Company, 24; 188th Company, 91; 248th Company, 42

Manchester Regiment, 57; 1st, 8, 203, 207; 2nd, 39, 40, 57; 1/10th, 213; 12th, 170, 215; 13th, 94; 17th (2nd Manchester Pals), 145; 20th, 19, 33, 34, 215; 21st, 33; 24th, 118

Middlesex Regiment, 83; 2nd, 146, 192, 215; 3rd, 96, 114, 115; 4th, 13, 14, 27, 37, 60, 67, 178; 5th, 27; 3/7th, 146; 1/8th, 107, 193, 240; 10th, 86; 3/10th, 234; 11th, 35, 146; 12th, 65; 13th, 107, 193; 16th, 37; 17th, 107; 21st (Islington), 19, 57; 23rd (2nd Football), 151

Monmouthshires, 1/1st, 30, 31, 114, 117, 134; 1/2nd, 35, 145; 1/3rd, 33, 58, 110, 240

Norfolk Regiment, 38; 1st, 25, 38, 84, 149; 8th, 142; 9th, 79, 206

North Staffordshires, 9, 10; 1st, 4, 32, 152, 159; 4th, 170; 1/5th, 115; 1/6th, 225; 7th, 92; 8th, 94, 134

Northamptonshires, 1st 33, 83, 119, 168; 2nd, 20, 84, 119, 120, 162; 3rd, 20; 5th, 106; 6th, 65; 7th, 91, 115

Northumberland Fusiliers, 18, 45, 74, 113, 186; 1st, 45, 105, 108, 211; 2nd, 68, 107, 117, 166, 171, 193; 1/4th, 108, 193; 1/5th, 11, 81, 127; 2/5th, 188; 1/6th, 14; 1/7th, 118; 8th, 194; 9th, 24, 179, 214; 10th, 45, 181; 12/13th, 188; 15th, 108; 18th (1st Tyneside Pioneers), 146; 20th (Tyneside Scottish), 193; 25th (Tyneside Irish), 125; 27th (Tyneside Irish), 108

Oxford and Bucks Light Infantry, 1st, 85; 2nd, 33, 49, 60, 167, 239; 1/1st Buckinghamshire Battalion, 113, 141, 176; 1/3rd, 171; 1/4th, 49, 60, 107, 167; 5th, 194

Queen's (Royal West Surreys), 1st, 93, 109, 149, 156, 214, 219, 220; 2nd, 99; 3rd, 133; 2/4th, 194; 1/5th, 214; 2/5th, 214; 7th, 26, 50, 193, 200; 10th (Battersea), 21, 63, 193; 11th (Lambeth), 35, 61, 64, 110; 15th, 151

Queen's Own (Royal West Kents), 79, 88, 109, 130; 1st, 12, 84, 108, 137, 185, 194; 2nd, 185, 186; 3rd, 131, 133; 7th, 12, 107, 142, 177; 8th, 131; 10th (Kent County), 35, 36, 61, 63, 64, 116, 133, 202

Rifle Brigade, 10, 37, 40, 57, 94, 127, 202, 218; 1st, 8, 20, 86, 117, 166, 167, 178, 179; 2nd, 4, 8, 20, 92, 127; 3rd, 8, 145; 4th, 8, 32, 75, 201; 5th, 179; 6th, 104, 192; 7th,

170, 213; 8th, 56, 67, 79, 94, 104, 111, 117, 169; 9th, 112, 117, 179, 192, 207; 10th, 37; 11th, 37; 12th, 37, 56; 16th (St. Pancras), 19, 57

Royal Berkshires, 213; 1st, 45; 2nd, 20, 192; 3rd, 45; 1/4th, 71, 72; 6th, 24, 67, 191

Royal Dublin Fusiliers, 7, 71, 75, 127; 1st, 113, 198, 214, 234; 2nd, 31, 70, 105, 113, 116, 156; 9th, 81

Royal Fusiliers, 29, 75, 79, 86, 104, 112, 141, 165; 1/1st (Royal Fusiliers) Londons, 21, 128, 194; 1/2nd (Royal Fusiliers) Londons, 15, 20, 21, 165; 1/3rd (Royal Fusiliers) Londons 62, 70, 75, 105, 107, 115, 118, 190, 193, 194; 2/3rd Royal Fusiliers, 62; 1/4th (Royal Fusiliers) Londons, 9, 15, 18, 32, 75, 109, 143, 165, 193; 6th, 118; 7th, 135; 9th, 35, 111; 10th, 19, 36, 92; 12th, 116, 165; 18th (1st Pubic Schools), 49, 167, 168; 19th (2nd Public Schools), 134; 20th, 215; 22nd (Kensington), 27; 23rd (1st Sportsmen's), 36; 25th (Frontiersmen), 19; 26th (Bankers), 88; 35th, 200

Royal Guernsey Light Infantry, 1st, 193

Royal Inniskilling Fusiliers, 1st, 5, 6, 30, 53, 59, 70, 91, 155, 213; 2nd, 20; 2nd, 10, 22, 53, 81, 121, 191; 5th, 6; 7th, 21, 114; 8th, 29; 11th, 98, 214

Royal Irish, 8, 21; 1st, 8, 118; 2nd, 8, 21, 114, 142; 3rd, 8, 118, 142; 4th, 142; 6th, 7, 74, 95

Royal Irish Fusiliers, 10, 53; 1st, 46, 70, 78, 91, 128, 207, 210; 2nd, 27; 4th, 30, 189; 5th, 37; 7th/8th, 55, 189; 9th, 21, 30

Royal Irish Rifles, 42, 97, 98, 161, 176; 1st, 43, 114, 121, 194; 2nd, 17, 43, 72, 138, 166; 8th (East Belfast), 98; 10th, 176; 11th (South Antrim Volunteers), 73, 88, 160; 12th (Central Antrim), 174; 14th, 17, 72; 17th, 124

Royal Munster Fusiliers, 1st, 70; 2nd, 7, 8, 71, 127, 134, 194, 214

1st Royal Newfoundland Regiment, 54, 145; 1st Royal Scots, 214; 2nd, 60, 72, 111, 138, 141, 162, 176, 205; 3rd, 141; 5th, 19; 1/8th, 50, 199; 1/9th (Highlanders), 27, 57, 110, 170; 11th, 242; 12th, 101, 189, 231, 241, 242; 13th, 19, 47, 107; 15th (1st Edinburgh), 166, 190, 193; 17th, 130

Royal Scots Fusiliers, 1st, 7, 44, 91, 96, 110, 148, 162, 214; 2nd, 74, 108, 219; 6th, 82, 83; 6th/7th, 47

Royal Sussex, 36; 1st, 85; 2nd, 113; 9th, 29; 11th (1st South Downs), 31, 55, 194; 12th (2nd South Downs), 31, 191; 13th (3rd South Downs), 31, 151, 191; 14th, 198

Royal Warwickshires, 10; 1st, 118, 123, 149, 156, 171, 175, 225, 234; 2nd, 17, 20, 33, 113; 3rd, 118; 1/5th, 101; 1/6th, 194; 2/8th, 192; 9th, 108; 10th, 35, 180, 193; 11th, 42, 53, 56; 14th, 194

Royal Welsh Fusiliers, 51, 54; 1st, 68, 108, 117, 146, 219, 220; 2nd, 142, 193; 9th, 95; 10th, 98, 174; 13th (1st North Wales Pals), 36, 51, 127; 15th (London Welsh), 5, 51; 16th, 162; 17th, 162

Scots Guards, 26, 33; 1st, 20, 60, 109, 110, 111, 112, 195, 239; 2nd, 18, 20, 31, 60, 94, 109, 111, 112, 219; 3rd, 60

Seaforth Highlanders, 62, 107, 141; 1st, 94; 2nd, 112, 123, 171, 172, 177, 234; 1/4th, 112, 234; 1/5th, 108; 1/6th (Morayshire), 62

Sherwood Foresters (Nottingham & Derbys), 63, 74, 78, 91; 2nd, 19, 30, 105, 154; 3rd, 31; 2/5th, 195; 1/7th, 82, 91; 8th, 32; 2/8th, 31; 9th, 195; 10th, 107, 168; 11th, 105; 15th (Nottingham Pals), 39, 95; 15th Sherwood Foresters) 91; 16th (Chatsworth Rifles), 30, 80, 91; 17th (Welbeck Rangers), 184; 1st Garrison Battalion, 91

Somerset Light Infantry, 78, 181; 3rd, 166; 6th, 138, 162, 181; 8th, 194; 9th, 166

South Lancashires, 2nd, 9, 95, 113, 210; 4th, 162; 1/5th, 130; 8th, 162, 167

South Staffordshires, 78, 162, 164; 1st, 99, 104, 105, 108, 119, 219; 2nd, 109, 119, 194; 3rd, 119; 4th, 108; 5th, 192; 1/6th, 158, 176; 7th, 56, 78; 8th, 109, 120; 9th, 150

South Wales Borderers, 176, 225; 1st, 50, 69, 129, 239; 2nd, 50, 117; 3rd, 50, 70; 6th (Pioneers), 129

Suffolks, 1st, 30, 160; 2nd, 57, 119, 174, 178, 211; 3rd, 118; 7th, 35, 61, 180; 8th, 67; 9th, 221; 12th, 19

Tank Corps, 90, 134; 'A' Battalion, Tank Corps, 133; 1st Tank Battalion 33; 11th Tank Corps 193

Welsh 216; 1st, 93; 2nd, 104, 129, 216, 239; 9th, 75, 196; 10th, 131; 13th (2nd Rhondda Pals), 58; 15th, 124, 203; 17th, 179

Welsh Guards, 1st, 203

West Yorkshires, 1st, 75, 153; 2nd, 19, 100; 1/5th, 71, 105, 194; 2/5th, 70; 1/6th, 107, 131, 192; 1/8th, 192, 194; 9th, 107; 10th, 42, 214; 11th, 84, 151; 12th, 32; 14th, 151

Wiltshires, 1st, 41, 43, 110, 118, 162, 173, 192, 202, 211; 2nd, 33, 52, 96, 108, 109; 6th, 94, 191; 7th, 194

Worcestershires, 1st, 127, 228; 2nd, 33, 69, 108, 129, 148, 168, 225, 239; 3rd, 4, 5, 46, 75, 117, 137, 152, 173; 4th, 49, 108, 194; 5th, 127; 1/7th, 35, 36, 52; 1/8th, 35, 168

York and Lancasters, 18; 1st, 40, 75, 113, 127, 184; 2nd, 70, 71, 113, 127, 180; 3rd, 6, 46; 1/4th (Hallamshire), 54, 63, 178; 2/4th, 193; 1/5th, 178, 181, 216; 7th, 57; 8th, 80, 107; 9th, 109, 151, 159; 13th, 19

Yorkshires, 2nd, 24, 107, 137; 3rd, 108, 152, 153; 4th, 96; 5th, 109; 6th, 107, 151, 191; 7th, 14

Royal Flying Corps, 3, 38, 70, 85, 87, 89, 101, 139, 170, 178, 188, 190, 200, 203, 212, 215, 234; No. 2 Wing, 89; No. 1 Squadron, 11; No. 3 Squadron, 89, 188; No. 4 Squadron, 89; No. 6 Squadron, 3; No. 7 Squadron, 38; No. 8 Squadron, 200; No. 11 Squadron, 116; No. 15 Squadron, 188; No. 19 Squadron, 101; No. 20 Squadron, 9, 202; No. 22 Squadron, 101, 155, 225; No. 23 Squadron, 101; No. 24 Squadron, 3, 101, 225, 235; No. 25 Squadron, 9, 215; No. 29 Squadron, 78, 101; No. 41 Squadron, 139; No. 45 Squadron, 70, 92; No. 46 Squadron, 198; No. 53 Squadron, 183; No. 55 Squadron, 70; No. 57 Squadron, 70, 207; No. 66 Squadron, 27; Army School of Ballooning, 52; No. 4 Kite Balloon Section, 19, 30; No. 9 Kite Balloon Section, 200; 20th Balloon Company, 27

Royal Air Force, 3, 27, 38, 39, 50, 85, 89, 108, 140, 144, 170, 171, 178, 190, 208, 228, 237; No. 48 Squadron, 186; No. 70 Squadron, 146; No. 204 Squadron, 38, 175; 2nd Kite Balloon Section, 109

Royal Army Medical Corps, 3, 7, 24, 28, 29, 42, 58, 60, 63, 67, 75, 98, 117, 139, 149, 154, 156, 182, 206, 218; No. 2 General Hospital, 28; No. 2 Casualty Clearing Station, 7; No. 3 Casualty Clearing Station, 7, 91, 149; No. 4 Casualty Clearing Station, 87; No. 8 Casualty Clearing Station, 7; No. 10 Casualty Clearing Station, 91, 110, 153; No. 11 Casualty Clearing Station, 7, 53, 59, 60; No. 12 Casualty Clearing Station, 100; No. 32 Casualty Clearing Station, 28; No. 33 Casualty Clearing Station, 37; No. 36 Casualty Clearing Station, 53, 64; No. 37 Casualty Clearing Station, 59; No. 41 Casualty Clearing Station, 59; No. 44 Casualty Clearing Station, 53, 92, 129; No. 46 (1/1st Wessex) Casualty Clearing Station 100; No. 47 Casualty Clearing Stations, 48; No. 48 Casualty Clearing Station, 48; No. 53 Casualty Clearing Station, 7; No. 58 Casualty Clearing Station, 60; No. 61 Casualty Clearing Station, 48, 100, 176; No. 62 Casualty Clearing Station, 64; No. 63 Casualty Clearing Station, 64; No. 64 Casualty Clearing Station, 100; 1/1st West Riding Field Ambulance, 63; 3rd East Lancashire Field Ambulance 3; 3rd Field Ambulance, 181; 4th Field Ambulance, 19; 5th Field Ambulance, 28; 9th Field Ambulance, 58; 11th Field Ambulance, 58, 183; 15th Field Ambulance, 120; 16th Field Ambulance, 58; 16th Special Reserve Field Ambulance, 3; 24th (Wessex) Field Ambulance, 164; 33 Field Ambulance, No. 18 Corps Main Dressing Station, 13; 45th Field Ambulance, 153; 62nd Field Ambulance, 58; No. 97 Field Ambulance, 173; 112th Field Ambulance, 29; 113th Field Ambulance, 29; 129th Field Ambulance, 58; 130th Field Ambulance, 58; 33rd Company, 107; 36th (Ulster) Division Dressing Station, 95; 19th London Sanitary Section, 4; No. 6 British Red Cross Hospital, 200; Territorial Nursing Force, 60; Queen Alexandra's Imperial Military Nursing Service, 92

Other

'Old Contemptibles', 220; 'Geddes Detachment', 127, 213, 240; 1st Volunteer Battalion, The Queen's Own (Royal West Kents), 62; 1st (Volunteer) Battalion, Essex Regiment, 115; 2nd Volunteer Royal Fusiliers, 118; 3rd (Militia) Battalion, the Bedfordshire Regiment, 90; 3rd (Militia) Battalion, The Black Watch, 164; 5th [Militia] Lancashire Fusiliers, 86; 5th (Militia) Leinster Regiment, 213; 20th Middlesex (Artists) Volunteer Rifle Corps, 14; Middlesex Rifle Volunteers, 139; British West Indies Regiment, 15, 69, 208; 6th British West Indies Regiment, 152; West African Frontier Force, 70, 71, 214; 2nd Nigeria Regiment, 116; King's African Rifles, 159, 213; 41st Divisional Reception Camp, 64; Army Chaplains Department, 28, 46, 49, 96; Army Cyclist Corps, 62; 9th Divisional Company, Army Cyclist Corps, 61; 3rd Cyclist Company, 3rd Infantry Division, 43; Army Pay Corps, 20, 77, 94; Army Veterinary Corps, 138; Inns of Court Officer Training Company, 88; Intelligence Corps, 110; Manchester University Officer Training Corps, 113; Graves Registration Units (GRU's), 236; Natal Artillery, (S African Wars), 52; Natal Mounted Rifles, (S Afrrcan Wars), 52; Durban Garrison Artillery (S African Wars), 52; Voluntary Aid Detachment, 143; Women's Emergency Corps, 74

Canadian Expeditionary Force (CEF)
Canadian Forces, 50, 90
Canadian Expeditionary Force, 81
Canadian Corps, 136, 169, 241
Divisions
1st, 40, 99, 137, 172; 2nd, 137; 3rd, 88, 99, 169
Cavalry
Canadian 3rd Dragoons, 114
Canadian Mounted Rifles, 200; 1st Canadian Mounted Rifles, 108, 114; 4th Canadian Mounted Rifles (Central Ontario Regt.), 110, 114, 116, 136; 5th Canadian Mounted Rifles (Quebec Regiment), 130, 136, 152, 189; 6th Canadian Mounted Rifles, 114; 10th Canadian Mounted Rifles, 215; Strathcona's Horse, 114
Artillery
2nd Brigade, Canadian Field Artillery, 92; 5th Brigade, Canadian Field Artillery, 89; 8th Brigade, Canadian Field Artillery, 200; D/21 Battery, Canadian Field Artillery, 48; 23rd Battery, 2nd Brigade, Canadian Field Artillery, 60; 6th Battery, Canadian Field Artillery, 240
Canadian Royal Engineers, 30, 211; 2nd Field Company, Canadian Engineers, 30, 177; 1st Canadian Tunnelling Company, Canadian Engineers, 177, 240; 3rd Canadian Tunnelling Company, 84, 241; 107th Canadian Pioneers, 189; 123rd Canadian Pioneers, 215; 2nd Canadian Railway Troops, 91; 6th Canadian Railway Troops, 154; 8th Battalion, Canadian Railway Troops, 73; 9th Canadian Railway Troops, Canadian Engineers, 83
Infantry
1st , 91, 108, 119, 176, 177, 209; 2nd (Eastern Ontario Regt.), 105, 108, 115, 209; 3rd Canadian (1st Central Ontario, Toronto) Infantry, 14, 119, 136, 150, 175, 209, 210; 4th (Central Ontario Regiment), 112, 150; 5th (Saskatchewan), 4, 106, 161; 7th (British Columbia), 14, 44, 81, 105, 143, 149, 226; 8th, Manitoba Regiment, 103, 208; 10th, 115, 149, 156, 198, 209; 11th, 83; 13th, Quebec Regiment (Royal Highlanders of Canada), 91, 103, 175, 177; 14th, 99, 115, 185; 15th, 99, 109, 118; 16th, (Manitoba Regiment) 105, 175, 198; 18th, 166, 200; 19th, 92, 166, 200; 20th, 166; 21st , 14, 116, 166, 189; 22nd (Quebec), 55, 81; 24th (Victoria Rifles), 44, 223; 24th, 81; 25th , 81; 26th, 81; 27th (City of Winnipeg, Manitoba Regiment), 87, 105, 106, 136, 161, 188; 28th, 75; 29th , 166; 31st (Alberta), 30; 41st; 42nd, 60; 43rd, 136, 158; 47th, 44; 49th, 136, 137; 52nd, 113, 136, 158; 54th (2nd Central Ontario), 212; 58th, 159; 60th, 99; 72nd, 83; 72nd Highlanders of Canada, 159; 85th (Nova Scotia Highlanders), 137, 190; 116th, 119; 180th (Sportsmen), 215; British Columbia Regiment, 83; Princess Patricia's Canadian Light Infantry (Eastern Ontario Regiment), 32, 34, 43, 63, 104, 109, 130, 133, 134, 136, 144, 162, 201, 202; Royal Canadian Regiment, 130; 11th Canadian Reserve Battalion, 99
Canadian Medical Corps, 56; 1st Canadian Casualty Clearing Station, 7; No. 2 Canadian Casualty Clearing Station, 91; No. 3 Canadian Casualty Clearing Station, 90, 91; No. 2 Field Ambulance, Canadian Army Medical Corps, 149; 3rd Canadian Field Ambulance Advanced

Dressing Station, 100; 11th Canadian Field Ambulance, 186

Canadian Machine Gun Corps, 104; 1st Canadian Motor Machine Gun Brigade, 200; 4th Brigade, Canadian Machine Gun Corps, 173; 7th Brigade Machine Gun Company, Canadian Machine Gun Corps, 136; 7th Company, Canadian Machine Gun Corps, 103; Canadian Flying Corps, 85; Depot Company, Royal Canadian Regiment, 99; Canadian YMCA, 115

Indian Army, 8, 29, 31, 83, 118, 157, 183, 203, 205
Lahore Division, 31, 183, 203, 207
Sirhind Brigade, 31, 183, 184
Bombay Light Horse, 205
20th Deccan Horse, 83
9th Hodson's Horse, 29
18th King George's Own Bengal Lancers, 212
37th Lancers (Baluch Horse), 113
34th Prince Albert Victor's Own Poona Horse, 113
Queen Victoria's Own Corps of Guides Infantry, (Lumsden's) Frontier Force, 117
57th (Wilde's) Rifles, Indian Army, 22, 61, 117, 118, 121
1st Ghurkha Rifles, 183
1/4th Gurkha Rifles, 79
15th Ludhiana Sikhs, 115
40th Pathans, 8, 203, 205
1st Punjab Volunteer Rifle Corps, 114
1st Battalion, 23rd Sikh Pioneers, 28
47th Sikhs, 203
4th Madras Pioneers, 58
2nd Sappers and Miners, Indian Army, 118

New Zealand Expeditionary Force (NZEF)
New Zealand Division, 9, 97, 121, 122, 126, 130, 187, 204, 240,
Brigades
New Zealand, 10; 1st New Zealand, 9, 10; 4th New Zealand, 47
New Zealand Mounted Rifles, 144; 6th New Zealand Mounted Rifles, 130; 10th New Zealand Mounted Rifles, 130; Wellington Mounted Rifles, 45
New Zealand Field Artillery, 45; 12th Battery, New Zealand Field Artillery, 46; 'D' Battery, New Zealand Field Artillery, 199; 4th (Howitzer) Battery, New Zealand Field Artillery, 45; 5th Battery, New Zealand Field Artillery, 46
Infantry
1st Auckland, 123, 126, 144; 2nd Auckland, 9, 130; 3rd Auckland, 97, 188; 1st Canterbury, 144, 185, 192, 213; 2nd Canterbury, 128, 129, 185; Otago Infantry, 176, 214; 1st Otago, 11, 45, 100, 126, 180; 2nd Otago, 92, 144, 214; 3rd Otago, 143; 1st Wellington, 196, 210; 2nd Wellington, 126; 3rd Wellington, 125; 2nd Battalion, 3rd New Zealand Rifle Brigade, 81, 156; 3rd New Zealand (Rifle) Brigade, 9, 10, 122, 192, 213; 4th Battalion, 3rd New Zealand Rifle Brigade 181, 195; 4th New Zealand Rifle Brigade 192
4th NZ Infantry Brigade Reserve Camp 10
New Zealand Base Depot for convalescing New Zealand soldiers 9
New Zealand Chaplains' Department 128

New Zealand Maori (Pioneer) Battalion 160
New Zealand Pioneer Battalion 213
New Zealand Training Unit 45

South African Army, 34
South African Brigade, 121
1st South African Mounted Rifles, 105
2nd South African Infantry, 110, 115, 116, 179; 4th South African Infantry, 20; South African Composite Battalion, 123
South African Constabulary, 28, 94
South African Service Corps, 195

WW2
8th Army, 123; 1st Polish Armoured Division, 237; 201st Guards Brigade, 220; 1st Irish Guards, 119; 1st Oxford and Bucks Light Infantry, 224; 1st Suffolks, 226; 1st The Queen's Royal Regiment (West Surrey), 21; 2nd East Yorkshires, 226; 2nd Lincolnshires, 228; 2nd Royal Scots Fusiliers, 32; 2nd Royal Ulster Rifles, 228; 2nd Coldstream Guards, 111; 4th Oxford and Bucks Light Infantry,, 129; 5th (Cinque Ports) Royal Sussex Regiment (WW2)., 21; 5th Battalion, 13th Frontier Force Rifles, 49; 5th Northamptonshires, 207; 1/5th Queens Royal West Surreys, 225; 10th Lancashire Fusiliers, 11; Artist's Rifles, 195; Oxfordshire and Bucks Light Infantry, 10; Royal Berkshires, 228; Royal Warwickshire Regiment, 49; Royal Welch Fusiliers, 195; Suffolks, 228; Royal Armoured Corps, 11, 119; 5th Royal Inniskilling Dragoon Guards, Royal Armoured Corps, 225; 12th Royal Lancers, Royal Armoured Corps, 225; 8th King's Royal Irish Hussars, Royal Armoured Corps (Desert Rats), 214; 51 Medium Regiment, Royal Artillery, 59; 53 (The Worcestershire Yeomanry) Anti-Tank Regiment, Royal Artillery, 227, 228; 336 Battery, 104 Heavy Anti-Aircraft Regiment, Royal Artillery, 107, 218; 659 General Construction Company, Royal Engineers, 226; Royal Army Ordnance Corps, 20; Royal Army Service Corps, 120; Royal Air Force Volunteer Reserve, 54; No. 10 Squadron, Royal Air Force Volunteer Reserve, 149, 156; No. 122 (RAF) Squadron, Royal Air Force Volunteer Reserve, 219; No. 202 Squadron, Royal Air Force Volunteer Reserve, 110; No. 313 (Czech) Squadron, Royal Air Force Volunteer Reserve, 218; No. 54 Squadron, Royal Air Force Volunteer Reserve, 164; No. 602 Squadron, Royal Air Force Volunteer Reserve,, 164; No. 609 (West Riding) Squadron, Royal Air Force Volunteer Reserve, 227; No. 617 Squadron, (The Dambusters), 54; Royal Canadian Air Force, 219; No. 2, Commando, Royal Navy, 195; No. 8 Commando, 20

French
Army, 13; 32nd Division, 60, 211; 45th Division (Les Joyeux), 6; 87th Division, 232; 87th Territorial Infantry Division (Les Peperes), 6; 154th Division, 51; 2nd rigade of Cavalerie Legere (Light Cavalry) Francaise (17th and 18th Cavalry), 97; 4th Regiment of Dragoons, 97; 12th Regiment of Dragoons, 97; 26th Dragoons, 125;  Regiment of Chasseurs Alpins (Mountain Hunters), 25; 1st Groupe Regiment

d'Artillerie Provisoire (97, 98 and 99 Batteries), 16; 17th Infantry Regiment, 232; 23rd Regiment of Infantry, 97; 88th Infantry Regiment, 125; 169th Infantry Regiment, 144; 418th Infantry Regiment, 229; 1st Battalion of Light Infantry, 41; 2nd African Hunters, 235; 1st Zouaves, 229; Colonials (Zouaves), 179, 234; 87th Territorial Infantry, 224; Escadrille des Cogognes, 143; 15th Hopital d'Evacuation, 87

Belgian
Army, 24, 39, 187; 3rd Division, 229; 1st Artillery, 230; 4th/24th Artillery, 230; 6th/24th Infantry, 229; 7th Artillery, 230; 13th Artillery, 230, 238; Grenadiers, 137; Carabiniers, 229; 1st Carabiniers, 144; 2nd Carabiniers, 144; 3rd Carabiniers, 144; 4th Carabiniers, 137; 3rd Infantry, 229; 3rd/23rd Infantry, 229, 230; 9th Infantry, 229; 10th Regiment, 230; 11th Infantry, 229; 13th Infantry, 229; 19th Infantry, 229

German
Fourth Army, 240, 242; Sixth Army, 240; IV Cavalry Corps, 237; XXVI Corps, 234; Guards Cavalry Corps, 81; Reserve Corps No. 22, 234; Reserve Corps No. 23, 234; Reserve Corps No. 24, 234; Reserve Corps No. 25, 234; Reserve Corps No. 26, 234; Reserve Corps No. 27, 234; XXVII Reserve Corps, 133; 6th Division, 131; 26th Division, 121; 39th Division, 84, 219; 3rd Bavarian Cavalry Division, 7; 3rd Cavalry Division, 237; 3rd Cavalry Brigade, 7; Leib-Dragoner-Regiment Nr 24, 7; Prussian Guards, 33, 239; 126th Prussian Infantry Regiment, 169; 133rd Infantry Regiment, 157; 185th Infantry Regiment, 50; 234th Reserve Infanterie Regiment, 235; 234th Reserve Regiment, 234; 1st Bavarian Jaeger Regiment, 219; 9th Saxon Infantry Regiment, 157; 16th Bavarian Reserve Infantry Regiment, 41; Jagdstaffel 8, 198; Jagdstaffel 56, 215; Jasta 2, 235; Jasta 6, 200; Jasta 10, 234; Jasta 18, 92; Jasta 27, 59; Jasta 28, 183; 15th Army Hospital, 221

US
27th Division 3, 74, 81, 231; 30th (Old Hickory) 81, 90, 200, 231; 3rd Cavalry 90; Marine Corps 90; First Tennessee National Guard Regiment, 90; 105th Infantry Regiment, 27th Division, 90; 117th Infantry Regiment, 90

Battles and Campaigns
Aisne, 10, 82, 87, 180, 216, 222
Arras, 6, 10, 48, 168
Aubers Ridge, 20
Bailleul, 7, 241
Broodseinde Ridge, 16, 47, 48, 106, 186, 187, 215, 216, 241
Second Bullecourt, 16
Coronel, 16
Festubert, 88, 167
Flers-Coucelette, 9, 79
Fromelles, 15
German South-West Africa, 52
Hill 60, 15, 25, 45, 46, 83, 84, 104, 112, 118, 132, 149, 158, 163, 164, 170, 227, 240, 241
Hooge, 14
3rd Krithia, 9
Landrecies, 137
Le Cateau, 137
Longueval, 164
Loos, 10, 19, 20, 27, 29, 33, 49, 56, 164
Marne, 10, 32, 82, 87, 111, 138, 168
Messines, 5, 9, 16, 17, 22, 32, 35, 36, 40, 41, 43, 59, 62, 66, 72, 73, 75, 81, 83, 84, 85, 93, 94, 97, 98, 102, 121, 125, 126, 131, 132, 157, 164, 165, 173, 174, 176, 182, 183, 185, 187, 196, 206, 210, 211, 216, 238, 239, 240
Mount Sorrell, 99, 202, 223
Retreat from Mons, 10, 36, 38, 52, 58, 65, 82, 87, 89, 92, 94, 110, 134, 137, 180, 185, 188, 197, 216
Polygon Wood, 12, 15, 30, 33, 87, 91, 104, 110, 127, 241
Somme, 9, 10, 19, 38, 60, 94, 97, 98, 105, 150, 151, 153, 156, 181, 198, 205, 241
Vimy Ridge, 16, 164
First Ypres, 10, 32, 33, 66, 92, 98, 122, 127, 169, 172, 204, 216, 218, 220, 222, 224, 225, 237, 239
Second Ypres, 44, 47, 52, 53, 63, 78, 79, 94, 134, 137, 144, 149, 154, 159, 162, 197, 213, 221, 237, 240
Third Ypres, 4, 5, 10, 12, 16, 26, 28, 32, 33, 36, 37, 40, 42, 45, 46, 47, 48, 51, 53, 57, 58, 59, 62, 64, 65, 66, 100, 101, Fourth Ypres/Lys, 3, 7, 21, 33, 61, 63, 77, 87, 123, 145, 146, 175, 184, 204, 209, 225, 241
102, 116, 124, 127, 129, 131, 137, 142, 145, 151, 158, 167, 168, 169, 171, 172, 175, 179, 180, 183, 184, 186, 199, 203, 208, 218, 230, 240, 241
Ashanti Campaign, 88Blenheim, 112
Boxer Rebellion, 118
Crimean War, 119, 142, 202, 223
East African Arab War, 159
Indian Mutiny (First War of Independence), 142
Malakand Expedition, 115
Nandi Expedition, 213
Omdurman, 197
Peninsular Wars, 114, 170
Quatre Bras, 112
South African Wars, 7, 8, 10, 11, 12, 16, 18, 20, 26, 27, 36, 37, 38, 43, 44, 45, 47, 49, 52, 56, 58, 63, 68, 73, 74, 75, 82, 83, 86, 88, 89, 90, 92, 94, 104, 105, 111, 112, 113, 114, 116, 117, 121, 123, 130, 138, 141, 148, 149, 152, 159, 164, 165, 166, 172, 174, 177, 179, 181, 184, 185, 192, 197, 199, 207, 212, 213, 214, 216, 217, 218, 220, 222, 223, 224, 228, 236
Tirah Campaign, 8, 30, 58, 63, 88, 115, 181, 213
Trafalgar, 113
Uganda Mutiny, 159
Waterloo, 92, 119
Waziristan Expedition, 79

# Other

**Decorations**

VC, 3, 9, 13, 14, 17, 18, 24, 28, 29, 31, 32, 33, 36, 49, 55, 56, 61, 67, 68, 79, 82, 84, 87, 98, 99, 100, 103, 104, 106, 111, 113, 120, 122, 124, 133, 134, 136, 138, 143, 149, 158, 162, 170, 173, 175, 182, 187, 188, 190, 191, 197, 199, 203, 205, 207, 212, 220, 235, 236, 239, 241,

DSO, 3, 6, 9, 10, 12, 15, 16, 18, 26, 28, 29, 30, 33, 37, 38, 44, 45, 46, 49, 51, 56, 58, 62, 64, 65, 68, 70, 71, 75, 77, 82, 83, 86, 88, 89, 90, 94, 98, 101, 106, 107, 111, 112, 113, 114, 115, 117, 119, 121, 123, 127, 130, 134, 139, 141, 142, 152, 153, 159, 162, 165, 172, 174, 176, 179, 181, 184, 190, 191, 192, 194, 197, 202, 207, 213, 214, 218, 220, 222, 225, 227

MC, 3, 4, 7, 12, 13, 14, 18, 21, 24, 27, 28, 30, 36, 38, 42, 47, 48, 49, 53, 54, 57, 62, 63, 64, 65, 67, 74, 77, 83, 92, 101, 106, 124, 130, 142, 164, 165, 168, 172, 176, 180, 181, 189, 192, 194, 195, 199, 206, 211, 213, 214, 215, 225, 235

DCM, 4, 9, 13, 14, 16, 25, 26, 31, 35, 36, 44, 54, 55, 56, 61, 62, 63, 64, 65, 73, 77, 101, 104, 115, 123, 125, 126, 129, 130, 134, 136, 146, 166, 192, 196, 199, 201, 208, 213, 217

MM, 10, 14, 16, 19, 35, 44, 46, 48, 49, 54, 65, 92, 120, 138, 157, 160, 182, 184, 189, 191, 204, 210, 214

MSM, 63, 97, 101, 206

DFC, 3, 38, 54, 108, 207, 215

DFM, 54

DSC, 106

AM, 52, 64, 65, 88, 182

Edward Medal, 52

GC, 52, 88

KCB, 8, 44, 90

CB, 9, 10, 26, 49, 84, 88, 111, 136, 162, 222

KCMG, 82

CMG, 10, 20, 30, 88, 94, 112, 113, 164, 180, 181, 184, 213

KCVO, 111, 216, 222

CVO, 91, 112

GCVO, 90, 91

MVO, 43, 58, 86, 111, 112, 186, 195, 217, 220, 221

KCIE, 49

CIE, 181

Indian OM, 61

CBE, 173

OBE, 3, 92, 217

VD, 58, 114, 184

**Memorials**

Arras, 24, 36, 193, 215; Arras Flying Services, 19, 30, 116, 215; Brookwood, 20, 119; Buttes New Zealand Missing, 34, 123; Cairo War, 83; Cambrai, 127, 158, 193; Chatby, 112; Doiran, 193; Helles, 19, 92, 108, 113, 117, 132, 193; Hollybrook, Southampton, 109; Ismailia War, 144; Jerusalem, 49, 194; La Ferte-Sous-Jarre, 37, 107, 180; Le Touret, 8, 12, 20, 50, 57, 104, 106, 108, 109, 111, 137, 138, 153, 165, 167, 173; Lokoja, Nigeria, 116; Lone Pine, Gallipoli, 109, 189; Loos, 26, 29, 109, 180; Medjez-el-Bab, 112; Menin Gate, 11, 14, 19, 21, 28, 33, 64, 68, 76, 79, 82, 91, 96, 99, 101, 102, 103, 105, 110, 119, 120, 121, 129, 130, 136, 139, 142, 156, 157, 159, 161, 162, 168, 172, 175, 178, 184, 189, 194, 209, 217, 218, 236, 237; Messines New Zealand Missing, 123; Munster, 237; Neuve Chapelle, 113; Nieuwpoort, 74, 194; Ploegsteert, 17, 30, 31, 57, 72, 82, 156, 157, 192, 193, 224; Port Said War, 50; Pozieres, 42, 46, 75, 131; Rangoon, 11, 21; Soissons, 107, 193, 228; Thiepval, 11, 18, 19, 52, 60, 73, 79, 80, 105, 107, 108, 109, 117, 127, 143, 177, 178, 180, 182, 193, 194, 195, 201, 215; Tower Hill, 27; Tyne Cot, 16, 19, 20, 49, 54, 70, 102, 105, 107, 108, 166, 189, 190, 194; Tyne Cot New Zealand Missing, 190; Villers-Brettoneux Australian Missing, 14, 19, 22, 92, 108, 109, 130, 189; Vimy Ridge, 108, 209; Vis-en-Artois, 193; Chatham Naval, 79, 107, 109, 121, 167; Portsmouth Naval, 83, 105, 181, 195, 214; Plymouth Naval, 26, 50, 83, 108, 112, 145; 7th Division, 190; 14th (Light) Division, 84; 16th (Irish) Division, 211; 18th (Eastern) Division, 69; 19th (Western/Butterfly) Division, 133; 20th (Light) Division, 39; 25th Division, 8; 34th Division, 125; 34th Division RE & RA, 235; 36th (Ulster) Division, 211; 38th (Welsh) Division, 124, 203; 49th (West Riding) Division, 57; 50th (Northumbrian) Division, 134; 66th (2nd East Lancashire) Division, 137; 5th Australian Division, 34; 60th & 61st Brigades, 235; Gloucestershires, 69; Hertfordshires, 114, 176; Household Cavalry Brigade, 218, 221; Kings Royal Rifle Corps, 68; Liverpool Scottish, 162, 163; 1/9th (Queen Vistoria's Rifles) London, 84; 1/14th (London Scottish) Londons, 122; 1st Monmouthshires, 134; 1st South Wales Borderers, 69, 225; Tank, Poelkapelle, 143; 2nd Worcestershires, 69, 225; 36th Australian Infantry, 182; 1st Australian Tunnelling Company, 84; Princess Patricia's Canadian Light Infantry, 144, 162; D/21 Battery Canadian Field Artillery, 48; 15th Canadian Infantry, 99; 85th Canadian Infantry, 137; Canadian Crest Farm, 137; Canadian, Hill 62, 169; Vancouver Corner, 114, 139, 175, 195; New Zealand Gravenstafel, 48, 190; New Zealand, Messines, 122; Irish Peace Park, 122; Scottish, St Jan, 5, 48; Welsh Park, Pilkem, 5, 39, 168; Tunnellers, 18; Black Watch Corner, 33, 34; Football/Christmas Truce, 83, 156; Kitcheners Wood, 124; Western Front Association, 137; Gas Victims, 229; Blacksmiths, 235; Coppensplein, 225; Frickleton, VC, 122; Harry Patch, 168; Ledwidge, 5; MacRae, 56; French Mont Kemmel, 231; French 32nd Infantry Division, 60; French 87th Territorial Infantry Division, 6, 41, 51, 204, 224; French 45th Territorial Infantry Division, 6, 41, 51, 204; French 2nd Brigade of Light Cavalry, 97; French 4th and 12th Regiments of Dragoons, 97; French 17th Infantry, 232; French 23rd Infantry, 97; French 418th Infantry, 229; French 1st Battalion of Light Infantry, 41; 1st Zouaves, 230; French 2nd African Hunters, 235; Guynemer, 143, 230; French Resistance, 85, Suez War, 91, Basra, 92, 108; 3rd Belgian Division, 229; Belgian Grenadiers, 137, 229; Belgian 4th Carabiniers, 137, 229; 3rd Belgian Infantry, 230; 3/23rd Belgian Infantry, 229; 6/24th Belgian Infantry, 229; 9th Belgian Infantry, 229; 11th Belgian Infantry, 229; 13th Belgian Infantry, 229; 19th

Belgian Infantry, 230; 1st Belgian Artillery, 230; 4/24th Belgian Artillery, 230, ; 7th Belgian Artillery, 230, ; 13th Belgian Artillery, 230, ; Belgian Langemark, 39; US 27th Division, 81; US 30th Division, 81; Private; Bowlby, 14, 162; Brodie, 34; Lasnier, 41; Redmond, 95; Hedd Wynn, 103; Birrell-Anthony, 134; Dewinde, 143; Skrine, 162; Rae, 169; Henshaw, 176; Pavlik, 219; Blight St. George, 223; Taymans, 230;

Educational Institutions
Alberta University, 131; Auckland University, 188; Birmingham University, 225; Brunel University, 188; Cambridge University, 6, 11, 26, 57, 59, 76, 116, 117, 154, 179, 198; Edinburgh University, 27; Eton College, 20, 118, 222, 238; Glasgow University, 27; Harvard University, 6; Hipperholme Grammar, 40; Lancing College, 40; London University, 51, 225, 226; Manchester University, 113; Marlborough College, 75; McGill University, 131; Oxford University, 65, 76, 89, 94, 116, 117, 118, 159, 180, 191, 195, 213, 222, 224; Rugby School, 65; St Andrews University, 23; Trinity College, Dublin University, 11, 21; Wellington College, 65, 179

People (Selected)
King Charles II, 183; King William IV, 105; Queen Victoria, 7, 198, 216, 222; King Edward VII, 4; King George V, 110, 217, 220; King George VI, 177; King Edward VIII, 217; Queen Elizabeth II, 122, 127, 224; King Albert II of Belgium, 122; Kaiser Wilhelm II of Germany, 10, 216, 220; Prince Arthur, Duke of Connaught and Strathearn, 43, 112, 175, 202; Field Marshal Sir John French, 8, 66, 175, 188, 198, 218, 238, 239; Field Marshal Sir General Gough, 241; Field Marshal Earl Haig, 6, 56, 66, 77, 135, 168, 217, 218, 219, 221, 226, 231, 234, 240, 241; Field Marshal Earl Kitchener, 119, 175, 213; Field Marshal Bernard Montgomery, 123; Field Marshal Viscount Plumer, 98, 174, 216, 238, 241; Marshal Foch, 154, 175; Marshal Petain, 231; General Ludendorff, 241; 2nd Duke of Abercorn, 110; 6th Duke of Beaufort, 228; 3rd Duke of Buckingham and Chandos, 167; Duke of Marlborough, 1st 112, 7th, 222, Duke of Richmond & Lennox, 7th & 8th, 222; Duke of Rutland, 7th & 8th 181; Duke of Wellington, 1st, 68, 79, 4th, 68; 1st Duke of Westminster, 110; Earl Mountbatten, 216; Marquess of Queensberry, 119; Anthony Eden PM, 83; David Lloyd George PM, 82, 240; Lord Salisbury PM, 90, 158; Robert Baden Powell, 222; Bruce Bairnsfather, 171; J M Barrie, 75, 201; Hilaire Belloc, 110; Alan Bennett, 84; Bismarck, 216; Edmund Blunden, 55; Helena Bonham Carter, 198; Barbara Cartland, 228; Winston Churchill, 82, 83, 222, 226, 239; Buffalo Bill Cody, 139; Samuel Cody, 52, 139; Sir Arthur Conan Doyle, 119; Daphne du Maurier, 75; W G Grace, 195; Lanoe Hawker VC, 3, 170; Christopher Isherwood, 113; Ludovic Kennedy, 110; Alice Keppel, 4; Jim Laker, 134; Edward Ledwidge, 6; John MacRae, 56, 57; James McCudden VC, 235; Napoleon, 68; Kim Philby, 71, 127; Sir John Redmond, 6; Paul Revere, 50; Ernest Shackleton, 185; Oscar Wilde, 119; Hedd Wynn, 5;

Sports
Athletics, 13, 24, 96, 97, 116, 118, 136, 137, 161, 198, 215, 217; Boxing, 27, 72, 154, 180; Diving, 195; Fencing, 119, 192; Football, 48, 80, 83, 117, 118, 139, 154, 157, 161, 170, 195, 198, 200; Golf, 12, 36, 117, 119, 134, 198; Hockey, 117, 133, 179; Olympics, 11, 13, 20, 24, 27, 28, 50, 75, 89, 97, 116, 118, 119, 137, 195, 198, 217, 222; Polo, 86; Rackets, 117; Rowing, 20, 50, 89, 118; Rugby Union, 7, 11, 21, 33, 36, 59, 68, 72, 75, 76, 89, 115, 116, 117, 119, 123, 130, 133, 149, 159, 170, 195, 196, 215, 218, 224; Rugby League, 116, 196; Swimming, 89, 116; Shooting, 20, 65, 113, 116, 149; Tennis, 97, 119; Water Polo, 89;

Misc
Anglo-Belgian Union, 172; Buchenwald Concentration camp, 183; Cambridge Five, 71, 127; Colditz Castle, 217; D-Day, 111, 119, 123; Gneisenau, 109; NKVD & KGB, 71, 127; Omaha Beach, 119; Pegasus Bridge, 111; Peter Pan, 75, 201; Punch Magazine, 56; Royal British Legion, 56; Scharnhorst, 109; Talbot House/Toc H, 98, 133, 170; The Winslow Boy, 119; Ypres League, 172

Lightning Source UK Ltd.
Milton Keynes UK
UKHW050615231022
410953UK00003B/4